This Dog'll Really Hunt

Hunt

**An Informative and Entertaining
Texas Dictionary**

Wallace O. Chariton

This Dog'll Really Hunt

An Informative and Entertaining Texas Dictionary

Wallace O. Chariton

Republic of Texas Press

Library of Congress Cataloging-in-Publication Data

Chariton, Wallace O.
  This dog'll really hunt : an informative and entertaining Texas
  dictionary / Wallace O. Chariton.
      p.   cm.
  ISBN 1-55622-653-5
  1. English language—Dialects—Texas—Glossaries, vocabularies,
  etc. 2. English language—Texas—Slang—Dictionaries.   3. Popular
  culture—Texas—Dictionaries.   4. Americanisms—Texas—Dictionaries.
  I. Title.
  PE3101.T4C48   1998
  427'.9764—dc21   98-48971
                                                        CIP

Republic of Texas Press is an imprint of Wordware Publishing, Inc.
No part of this book may be reproduced in any form or by
any means without permission in writing from
Wordware Publishing, Inc.

Printed in the United States of America

ISBN 1-55622-653-5
10 9 8 7 6 5 4 3 2 1
9903

All inquiries for volume purchases of this book should be addressed to Wordware
Publishing, Inc., at 2320 Los Rios Boulevard, Plano, Texas 75074. Telephone
inquiries may be made by calling:

(972) 423-0090

dog'll \dog-ul\ Of rural origin from Texas and the deep South. It is actually a contraction for the phrase "dog will." Thus the phrase "this dog'll really hunt" translates into "this dog will really hunt," which means it will work real well.

Introduction

Ten years ago when *This Dog'll Hunt* first appeared in print it turned out to be the beginning of the story and not the end. The preface to that original edition concluded with, "Till we meet again, keep the fireflies out of the buttermilk and your wagon between the ditches." Well, here we are again. To those who enjoyed the original *This Dog'll Hunt*, I hope your buttermilk is firefly-free and your wagon is still on the road. If this is your first experience with the book, find a soft place to sit, kick off your boots, prop your feet, open a can of your favorite beverage, and get ready to be entertained. And if you're not careful, you might just learn a thing or two. That's the plan anyway.

The original version was the result of a thirty-year collection of Texas words and sayings. Even though the book was published, I continued to collect anything related to the language, and I was aided in that cause by a lot of nice folks who responded to my request to share their sayings that were not in the book. Incredibly, I still get cards and letters and I appreciate all of them. When I had received enough new sayings for another book, *That Cat Won't Flush* appeared in print. Still the letters kept coming, and my collection kept growing.

A funny thing happened, however, that alarms me no end. While I got letters, I began to notice that I was picking up fewer and fewer sayings from everyday conversations. It seems clear that the language of Texas is changing at a frightening pace. Every day, it seems to me, we are losing a little more of our heritage. Every now and then I stop and ponder what Texas might be like when our heritage is completely gone. The images I conjure up are unsettling, and, frankly, I hope I'm not around when that day comes because it is going to sad indeed.

The good news is I am still around and still determined to do my part to preserve at least one little part of Texas heritage, namely the language. This is my latest and most ambitious effort toward that end.

The genesis for this book actually came from my mother. She often told me that of all the books I have written, she liked *This Dog'll Hunt* the best. I suspect the reason was that she grew up loving the Texas language, and when she read my words I know a lot of wonderful memories would come to mind. Although the book was her favorite, it was also the only one of my works that she criticized. On a couple of occasions she held up the book and commented, "It should have been a lot bigger!" At first I was disappointed, but the more I researched and the more material I collected, I realized she was correct; the first version was way too small.

About five years ago I began assembling material for a new, greatly expanded edition and this is the fruit of that labor. Actually, this book is a combination of several parts. I started with the material from *This Dog'll Hunt* and trimmed out a little fat and some material that I don't know why I included in the first place. Next, I siphoned off the very best of *That Cat Won't Flush*. Those two books, edited down and updated where necessary, formed the skeleton for the new edition. From there I actually drew on advice I had received over the years.

One very nice lady from Houston, Texas wrote and suggested I include more information on Texas towns, especially on how to properly pronounce the names. "I'm tired of all the Yankees mispronouncing the names of places in Texas," she wrote. I agreed and I've included a pronunciation guide for the names of Texas towns, at least most of the ones that folks tend to get wrong.

A young man from Austin suggested I include more dictionary-type entries for the terms that are occasionally encountered in Texas. Again, I agreed and have included a "whole passel" of words complete with the Texas-style definition. These words include farm and ranch terms, cowboy words, and a lot more.

The most difficult request I got was from a young man at Texas A&M University. He sent me a copy of words unique to the Corps of Cadets. "If you are going to write a dictionary on Texas," he wrote, "how can you leave out the Aggies since they are as much a part of Texas as anything else." Since my allegiance is to Texas Tech and the University of Texas, my first reaction was that I could ignore the Aggies if I darn well wanted to. Upon further review I realized the young man was correct. The Aggie language ought to be preserved. Not only that, it occurred to me that if I would publish the words, then students at other universities could know what in the world those Aggies are talking about. All such entries are identified with the notation (Aggie) or with Texas A&M. To balance the ledger, I couldn't resist taking a couple of shots at the Aggies; but to the Corps members who carry swords, I would remind them it is all in fun. Really! As a public service, I did have the book printed very slowly so the Aggies wouldn't have any trouble reading it. One thing, though, the list supplied by the Aggie was obviously copied from a published book, which was not identified, and efforts to locate a copy failed. Since some of the words and phrases were most strange, I asked an Aggie friend to look over the list to be sure someone wasn't playing an Aggie joke on me. Although the friend wasn't in the corps, he is of the opinion the material is accurate and I decided to accept his word. I am supremely confident, however, that if any of the entries are wrong, or if words were omitted, I will hear from the Aggies. I only hope the postman doesn't get a hernia delivering the letters.

The final piece of the puzzle was to mix in the vast amount of new sayings and special words that I collected over the years. I was amazed when I realized just how much material I had accumulated, and I offer my sincere thanks to all who contributed material.

This book is the result of all of the above. Like my other volumes, it is a labor of love. This work is much more comprehensive and, I believe, a lot better. I hope you will enjoy the material and use it. If everybody in Texas would make it a point to use one new saying a day, we might, in some small way, stem the tide of language homogenization that seems inevitable. My only regret is that my mother didn't live to see this book. I would have liked to have seen her face when I gave her a copy. I believe she would have liked it and it might, just might, have been comprehensive enough to suit her. Who knows, maybe heaven has a reading room. I hope so.

I also believe I have achieved my purpose of recording and preserving much of the language of Texas. On the other hand, I suspect there is much more work to be done; so who knows, perhaps yet another edition will some day come creeping off the printing presses. If you would care to submit material that somehow escaped my net, or comment on the material that I did catch, I can be reached at P.O. Box 941551, Plano, Texas 75074 or by e-mail at ReblTexn@aol.com. Hope to hear from you soon.

Sincerely,
Wallace O. Chariton

Dedication

This book is lovingly dedicated to the memory of Helen Owen Chariton, one of the finest ladies to ever leave footprints in Texas. She brought me into this world and taught me to love Texas, for which I shall be forever grateful. If Heaven has a Texas corner, I'll bet the farm she's in it right now looking for a loophole that would allow her to come back to the Lone Star State that she loved so much. I wish she could find that loophole because I miss her more than I ever could have imagined.

A

A: 1. used to strengthen verbs and add color to the language as in "It was a hailin' and a lightin', and how in the hell could I putt." 2. of, as in "time a day"

A lot: forty-leven dozen, as in "Bubba has tried to get Betty Lou to go out with him forty-leven dozen times but she's stood her ground so far." [In practice, forty-leven dozen is used to mean any large amount. In fact, forty-leven dozen is 4,011 dozen, or 48,132.]

Abandoned [abayun-dun'd]: left high and dry

Abandoned as: 1. last year's bird nest 2. a dry well 3. an Arkansas still when a Treasury agent comes calling [Somehow those ol' moonshine boys just always seem to know when trouble is on the way.]

Aberdeen (Collingsworth County): pronounced ABB'r-dean; named for Scotland's Earl of Aberdeen who once owned the Rocking Chair Ranch that was headquartered at Aberdeen

Abide: tolerate

Abilene (Taylor County): pronounced Abb-a-lean [Named for Abilene, Kansas; the founders intended the Texas version to be an even more important cattle shipping point than its namesake. To distinguish the Texas town from its Kansas counterpart, some people refer it as Abilene on the Cat Claw because Cat Claw Creek runs nearby.]

Ability: know how

Ability, natural: 1. took to that like a duck takes to water (or a jackrabbit takes to runnin') 2. learned how to do that while he was still in the oven (womb)

Ability without control: 1. has plenty of go but he don't know when to say whoa 2. got the speed but lacks control

Able: 1. still got some snap in his garters 2. still has a rustle in her dress 3. got what it takes to get what there is to be got *See also Capable*

Able at one time: used to could

Able but unwilling: puts his lamp under a bushel basket. Like a lot of country sayings, this one has its roots in the Bible (fifth chapter of Matthew). It means that someone hides a lamp under a basket instead of putting it on top of the basket so all can share.

About: 'bout or near 'bout, as in "It's near 'bout four miles to town."

About now: most anytime now

About time: high time, as in "It's high time we painted the barn."

About to: 1. fixin' to, as in "He's fixin' to mow the lawn." [Fixin' to generally means someone is about to do something as soon as he gets good and ready to do it. Thus, "I'm fixin' to pay off my mortgage" means I'm about to do just that as soon as I raise the money.] 2. getting ready to commence to begin

About to cry: puddlin' up

About to die: 1. circling the drain 2. quit buying bananas 3. at the hinge creak of death 4. keep the battery charged on the hearse

About to fall apart: 1. shacklin 2. held together by nuthin' more than a spider's web 3. barely held together 4. the spit and balin' wire are comin' loose

About to leave: getting' ready to git

Above reproach: 1. clean as cat fur 2. couldn't touch him with a ten-foot pole

Abra (Collingsworth County): pronounced A-bra, not Ab-ra

Absconded: slipped the bridle

Absentminded: 1. could hide his own Easter eggs 2. could lose a new bar of soap inside a wash rag 3. could lose his keys in his vest pocket 4. scratched his watch and wound his hair

Absolute: pure-d

Absolutely: 1. bet your boots 2. sure as shooting 3. dead certain fact 4. darn tootin' 5. you ain't just whistling "Dixie" 6. that's the stomp down truth 7. cross my heart and hope to die and go to hell the next minute 8. pure out 9. right as rain *See Certain; Fact*

Absolutely (guaranteed)**:** 1. Would a ten-foot chicken lay a big egg? 2. Would a two-ton hog make a lot of bacon? *See also Believe me; Yes*

Absquatulated: *See Disappeared suddenly*

Abundance: 1. lashin's and lavin's 2. more than you could shake a stick at in a whole week

Acala (Hudspeth County)**:** pronounced Ah-CALL-ah, not Ac-a-la; named for the long-staple Mexican cotton that was grown in the area

Accept: 1. what can't be cured must be endured 2. bite the bullet [This is a reference to the days before anesthetics when Old West doctors offered patients a bullet to bite while being operated on.] 3. hump up and take it like an old bull in a blue norther 4. stand your watch

Accept it: 1. gotta grab a root and growl 2. somebody has to have the hard seat 3. cinch up your belt and go get dirty 4. let the hide go with the hair

Accept responsibility: 1. better to pass gas and bear the blame than to not pass gas and bear the pain 2. if your dog trees it, you gotta eat it 3. gotta take your medicine no matter how bitter the taste

Accept the inevitable: Texan T. Boone Pickens said: "I hate to fail but when it's time to take a bath, I get in the tub." *See also Inevitable*

Accept your fate: 1. bloom where you're planted 2. gotta play the cards you're dealt 3. gotta wear the underwear you got, dirty or not

Acceptable: 1. tolerable 2. that dog'll hunt 3. that'll do for me and any old gal I'd go out with 4. like a dead horse, I won't kick at that 5. suits me to a fare-thee-well 6. can sit still for that 7. can live with that 8. that'll drill (oil patch) 9. close enough for government work [This refers to the general belief that when you are working for the government, any government, close is considered acceptable.] 10. have stacked my wood on worse 11. up to snuff *See also Agree*

Acceptable, barely: 1. beats a poke in the eye with a sharp stick 2. will do till something better comes along 3. beats hoeing (or picking) cotton 4. will do in a pinch

Acceptance: don't mind if you do

Accident prone: 1. could fall up a well (or tree) 2. could cut his finger with an electric razor 3. a train wreck looking for a place to happen 4. could get thrown by a stick horse 5. got a rubber-lined bathroom, which where most accidents in the home occur 6. would run into the ladder *after* you put it back in the barn 7. could cut himself with a picture of a knife 8. if his windmill breaks down, his cows go thirsty [Since windmills were often out in a pasture by themselves, falling off a windmill while trying to fix it was one of the most dangerous accidents that could happen to a cowboy because it might be some time before help arrived. Anyone prone to accidents (or lazy) would not even attempt the repairs.]

Accompany: might as well come go with me

Accountant: 1. pencil pusher 2. bean counter 3. figure fanatic 4. book balancer 5. debit and credit man 6. tax wrangler

Accountant, good: uses a better grade of beans

Accounted for: 1. all the horses are in the corral 2. the cattle ain't a hoof shy 3. the deck's full 4. all the beans are in the pot

Accurate: 1. hit the nail on the head 2. rang the bell 3. couldn't have said it better myself 4. hit in the black, a reference to hitting a target in the center, which is usually black 5. on the level, as in "Those figures are on the level."

Accurate as: 1. a weather vane [No matter which way the winds blows, the weather vane will always be right.] 2. an echo 3. a mirror image

Accusation: 1. the pot calling the kettle black 2. a fox calling a coyote a chicken thief 3. a horse thief callin' a cattle rustler a crook 4. a chicken snake callin' a hound dog an egg sucker 5. a skunk tellin' a turkey buzzard he stinks

Ace (playing card): 1. bullet 2. arrowhead

Ace blank (domino): often called "Little Johnny" because it's the smallest domino in terms of value other than the double blank

Ace of spades [asa spades]: the big digger

Ache: a painin'

Achievement: 1. earned his spurs 2. earned a place to squat by the fire 3. earned a spot at the bar 4. found his puddle 5. got his crop in the barn

Achilles heel (tendon): heel string

Aching: hurtin' for certain *See also In pain*

Acne scars: 1. looks like his face caught fire and someone put it out with a golf shoe (or ice pick) 2. looks like he was beaten with a barbed wire bat

Acorn-head: a hog that is turned out in the fall to eat acorns and otherwise fend for himself

Acquaintance, casual: someone you know well enough to talk about

Acquainted: 1. we've howdied and shook 2. known him for years in all kinds of weather

Acquainted, casually: 1. we've howdied but we ain't ever shook (or we've swapped howdies) 2. we've watered our horses at the same trough 3. seen him in the mirror behind the bar 4. know him well enough to borrow from but not well enough to loan to 5. we go to the same church but we don't sit in the same pew

Acquainted, well: 1. would know his ashes in a whirlwind 2. would know him if he was barbecued and served for lunch 3. would know him if he'd been through a meat grinder and made into a sausage

Acquiesced: broke down and caved in

Act: play possum

Act intelligent: It's one thing for people to think you're stupid but it's another matter altogether for them to have proof. Former Houston coach Bum Phillips once commented that he didn't want to trade any players who might hurt his team later. He explained, "I don't mind people thinking I'm stupid, but I don't want to give them any proof."

Act now: 1. quick stitches save britches 2. strike while the iron is hot because it's hard to brand with a cold iron

Act premature: 1. bucks before he's spurred 2. broke the barrier [This refers to rodeo cowboys leaving too early and breaking the barrier resulting in penalty time being added to their score.]

Act right: 1. behave 2. straighten up and fly right

Acting big: 1. a bottle-fed colt tryin' to act like a stallion 2. got his big boy pants on 3. acting a little too big for his boots (or britches) 4. acting high and mighty

Acting childish: his didy pin must really be sticking in him *See also Childish*

Acting conspicuously: cuttin' up didoes

Acting foolish: 1. asking a blind man to tell you which horse to buy 2. cuttin' the fool 3. giving away the store 4. ridin' fast and loose, which means he ain't holding on too tight

Acting good: all peaches and cream

Acting pompous: 1. puttin' on the dog for all the world to see 2. big-eyein' around town

Acting prematurely: 1. won't catch many calves if you throw the rope before you build a loop 2. pickin' your peaches before they're all fuzzed up

Acting sick: punin' around

Acting silly: acting his hat size, which means he's acting like his age equals his hat size

Acting smart: acting like he had good sense

Acting strange: 1. his clutch seems to be slipping 2. his tractor ain't gettin' no traction 3. acting like some loco weed got mixed into his feed 4. came unhinged

Action: you can sit up and take notice but it won't do any good if you keep sitting

Action without results: did a heap of stirring but didn't get no biscuits

Actions speak louder than words: when the tailgate drops, the BS stops [This saying comes from coon hunters who like to brag about their dogs. When they go huntin' the bragging stops when the tailgate drops and the dogs jump out of the pickup to go to work. From that point on the action of the dog speaks volumes more than the words of the owner.]

Actions, misleading: has a heart of gold but then so does a hard-boiled egg

Active: 1. feisty 2. full of spit and vinegar 3. his axles stay hot 4. plays a frisky fiddle 5. a goin' Jesse 6. can stir up more dust than Noah's flood could have settled 7. seen more action than a policeman's flashlight [A real active person would move around so much you'd swear he was twins (or even triplets). Remember, a used key is the one that shines and grass don't grow on a busy street.]

Active as: 1. a bobcat tied up in a tow sack 2. a fox in a henhouse 3. an egg-sucking dog in a chicken coop 4. lightning in a jug 5. a blind dog in a packin' plant 6. a worm on a BBQ grill 7. a hen-pecked husband with a harem 8. a four-ball tomcat 9. a calf in clover 10. a bartender's rag on Saturday night 11. a wiggle tail in hot ashes 12. a one-eyed dog in a smokehouse 13. the cinch on a girdle 14. a stump-tailed bull at fly time [This implies that a bull's main defense against biting flies is a swish of his tail. A bull with a stump tail will be very active during fly season.] *See also Busy as*

Active man: *See Male, active*

Active woman: *See Female, active*

Activities: doin's, which is also used for ingredients

Actor: a puppet without the strings

Actor, ham: makes a good line greasy

Acts when ready: he's notional, which means he acts when the notion to do something strikes and not before

Adams apple: bread jerker

Adapted to: a good hand for that

Add weight: flesh up

Add wood: chunk the fire

Addielou (Red River County): pronounced ADD-a-lou

Addled: 1. gone plumb around the bend 2. touched in the head 3. hay brained 4. disoriented

A

Adequate: 1. will do till something better comes along 2. will do in a pinch 3. up to snuff *See also Acceptable*

Admiration: 1. thinks he hung the moon 2. thinks the world of her

Admire: 1. mighty fond of 2. a legend in my mind 3. will take my hat off to him [Texan Bob Wills, the King of Western Swing, was known for never taking off his hat. One exception was at his induction into the Country Music Hall of Fame when he took of his hat in admiration of his many fans around the world.]

Admiring: making eyes at

Admit it: fess up

Adobe: crude bricks made of clay, straw, and water and then hardened in the sunshine; often shortened to 'dobe [Because adobe bricks are of poor quality, the term is also used to mean anything inferior as in "Bubba still wears that 'dobe hat he bought down in Old Mexico."]

Adolescence: 1. between grass and hay, which means he's somewhere between boyhood and manhood 2. in never-never land, which means he never wants to do kid things and his parents never let him do anything adult 3. graduated from Humpty Dumpty to hanky-panky

Adroit: 1. got more moves than a belly dancer on a roller coaster 2. can turn his hand at almost anything 3. got more moves than a possum on roller skates

Adult: someone who has stopped growing except in the middle

Advance warning: According to Gib Lewis, former speaker of the Texas House, prewarned is prearmed.

Advantage: 1. playing with a deck he stacked 2. got the cavalry on his side 3. paying the right preacher 4. built his teepee inside the fort 5. fightin' a three-legged (or blind) bull 6. got a leg up on everybody 7. got an ace in the hole [A really big advantage would be having an ace in the hole with Smith and Wesson stamped on it.]

Advantage, unfair: baited the hole

Adversary: 1. the fly in my ointment 2. the burr under my saddle 3. the nail in my boot 4. the worm in my apple

Advice: 1. when you're up to your neck in manure, don't open your mouth 2. never put all your eggs in one basket or all your whiskey in one woman 3. never play leap frog with a unicorn 4. never play poker with anyone named Ace 5. when your hand is in a bobcat's mouth, don't pull his tail [Sam Houston used a variation: "My rule is when my hand is in a lion's mouth never to strike him on the nose."] 6. sometimes the squeaking wheel gets replaced, which is a variation of the old saying "the squeaking wheel gets the grease" 7. a worm is the only animal that can't fall down 8. keep your wagon between the ditches 9. don't change horses in the middle of the stream 10. never buy anything that has a handle, eats, needs painting, or has babies 11. never eat at a place called Mom's 12. advice is usually only good for passing on *See also Business advice*

Advice for speakers: when you're done pumping, let go of the handle

Advocate: hold to

Affirmative: 1. you-bet-cha 2. I reckon [If someone asks if you'd like to go to a honky-tonk, I reckon would be a strong answer in the affirmative.] *See also Yes*

Affirmative, strong: 1. hell yes or hell, I reckon 2. yes siree bob

Afflicted: down in, such as "He's down in his back." *See also Ill*

Afflicted, seriously: eat up with, as in "My wife is eat up with jealousy just 'cause I had one dance with that little ol' gal."

Afraid: 1. a'feared 2. fraidy cat 3. scared half out of my wits 4. scared half (or plumb) to death 5. has cold feet no matter how hot the country 6. spends most of his time in the shadow of mama's apron 7. his heart was beatin' like a drummer with the hiccups 8. was scared of his own shadow 9. my insides are boogered [Texan Audie Murphy once said, "Seems to me if you're afraid or living with some big fear, you're not really living, you're only half alive."] *See also Scared; Scary*

After: 1. gunning for 2. got my sights on 3. got 'em in my cross hairs 4. lookin' to find

Afternoon: 1. shank of the day 2. cow time, which means cows generally come home late in the day

Afternoon, late: dark thirty [This expression means thirty minutes before dark. In the days before daylight savings time, dark was considered the end of the afternoon. Parents used dark thirty as a way of telling kids to come home before dark. Note: Some people use dark thirty to mean thirty minutes after dark.]

After while: 1. directly 2. toreckly

Against: 1. agin 2. goes against my raising 3. goes against my grain 4. dead set not in favor of 5. can't sit still for that 6. powerful opposed to

Against the odds: 1. sawing against the grain 2. swimming against the tide 3. bucking the odds

Age spots: 1. old lady freckles 2. liver spots

Age, approximate: odd years old, as in "She's 40-odd years old." [Also used as some odd.]

Aggravate: get his goat

Aggravated: gave 'em holy hell

Aggressive as: 1. a snake oil salesman 2. a used car salesman 3. an old-time Methodist circuit rider 4. an insurance peddler 5. a condo time-share salesman 6. a television evangelist

Aggressive: 1. a loose hoer, which means when he gets to hoeing weeds he can tear up a fair-sized pea patch or ruin several acres of cotton 2. hornin' the bush 3. eatin' fire 4. smokin' his wheels *See also Female, aggressive or Male, aggressive*

Agile: 1. loose jointed 2. nimble footed 3. fragile footed 4. could open a beer while standing up in a bass boat during a hurricane and helping a friend net a big one

Agile as: 1. a champion cuttin' horse 2. a snake on a hot concrete road 3. a kid in a cactus patch

Aging: 1. getting on in years 2. the spring has gone out of his chicken 3. getting long in the tooth [This is a reference to the gums in older horses receding, giving the appearance that their teeth grow longer as they get older.] 4. blooming for the pasture, which refers to his (or her) hair getting gray 5. she once got a twinkle in her eye when she was in a romantic mood, now it's just her contact lens in backwards *See also Elderly; Old*

Agitate: 1. pull his crank 2. stir him up

Agitated: 1. flusterated 2. flustrated 3. havin' a dog fit 4. got the all-overs 5. gave my crank a good pull 6. runnin' around like a June bug on a hot griddle

Agitated as: 1. a pack mule in a hailstorm 2. a frog under a milk bucket 3. a short dog in tall grass 4. an English teacher at a cowboy poetry convention

Agitated highly: 1. all fire and tow, which means he's ready to explode 2. a double duck fit

Agitator: 1. stirring the fire with a saber 2. forking manure into the well 3. rocking the boat 4. raising waves on the sea of tranquillity

Agree: 1. can dance to that tune 2. can ride on that range 3. would vote for that and lend a hand stuffing the ballot box 4. would do the same thing if I was in his boots 5. seein' eye to eye 6. chewing off the same plug of tobacco *See also In agreement*

Agreeable: 1. just as soon do that as not 2. might as well since it's too wet to plow and the hogs are too small to kill 3. might as well, we can't dance and it's too wet to plow 4. took to that like a bear to a honey tree 5. whatever suits you tickles me plumb to death

Agreement, changed: the pigs ran through the deal, which comes from the fact that anything pigs ran through would be greatly changed

Agriculture: pronounced agger culture

Agriculture college: cow college

Agua Dulce (Nueces County): pronounced Ogg-Wa-DOOL-Cee; means "sweet water"

Aguilares (Webb County): pronounced Ag-u-LARE-ess; named for a family of settlers who arrived in the 1870s

Ahead marks: special marks given in school when you answered a question someone else missed

Ailments, imaginary: 1. higulcian flips 2. epizoodicks

Aim, good: 1. got prayerful aim 2. shoots seein' eye bullets

Aim, poor: 1. couldn't hit the side of an outhouse if he fired from inside it 2. couldn't hit the side of a barn with a scatter gun at ten paces 3. couldn't hit a bull in the butt with a bass fiddle

Aimless: as a cow patty bobbing along in a back water eddy

Air crap (krap): Air Force cadet

Air out: unscheduled, surprise midnight yell practice imposed on freshmen

Alamo: The "Shrine of Texas Liberty, pronounced AL-a-mo, never A-LAM-Oh; an Alamo expert is an Alamoligist

Alba (Wood-Rains County): pronounced AL-bah, not All-bah [Also known as Simpkins Prairie and Albia. When the MKT Railroad reached the site in 1881, the first shipment to the town was telegraph equipment. When the equipment was installed, one of the first messages received told of the assassination of President James Garfield.]

Alcohol: *See Champagne; Liquor; Tequila; Whisky*

Alcoholic: 1. suffers from Anheuser's disease 2. favorite drink is the next one 3. only time he ever refused the offer of a free drink, he didn't understand the question 4. works his way down from bottoms up 5. whenever he gets in trouble he tries to use a corkscrew to pull himself out of it 6. not one who drinks too much, but one who can't drink enough *See also Drunk*

Alcoholic, reformed: *See Drunk, reformed*

Alcoholics Anonymous: soberness refinery

Alcoholism: panther colic

Aldine (Harris County): pronounced ALL-dean; named for a prominent local farm family

Aledo (Parker County): pronounced A-LEAD-oh; originally Parker's Station but that name caused confusion for postal authorities so a railroad executive suggested Aledo after his hometown in Illinois

Alert: 1. never missed a bet or overlooked a blonde 2. eagle eyed 3. on the ball 4. knows the sound opportunity makes when it comes knocking 5. keep your ear to the ground and your eyes peeled 6. you don't get kicked in the backside by someone who is in front of you, which basically means don't let the enemy sneak up behind you 7. bright eyed and bushy tailed 8. sleeps with one eye wide open and the other on alert *See also Be alert*

Algoa (Hitchcock County): pronounced Al-GO-ah; originally named Hughes, the name was changed by the late 1880s [Origin of the name is unclear but one story is not true. The name did not came from the *Algoaian*, a British tanker that was blown ashore during the great hurricane of 1900. The town was clearly named Algoa prior to that tragedy.]

Alice (Jim Wells County): original petition was for the name Kleberg in honor of Robert Justice Kleberg, but that name was taken so it was changed to Alice in honor of Alice Gertrudis King Kleberg, Robert's wife and the daughter of Richard King, founder of the world famous King Ranch [In 1948 the town made the headlines when 202 votes were "discovered" in the Precinct 13 ballot box. Those votes gave Lyndon Johnson the victory in the Democratic primary for U.S. senator.]

Alike: 1. poured out of the same mold 2. squeezed from the same udder 3. drained from the same crankcase 4. poured out of the same milk bucket 5. cut from the same hide 6. two peas in the same pod 7. mixed in the same bowl 8. cut from the same bolt 9. punched out with the same die 10. cut from the same herd 11. out of the same flock *See also Identical*

Alike, almost: 1. same bull, different pasture 2. same song, different verse

Alike, virtually: 1a, as in "If Earl Campbell ain't the number one running back ever, he's 1a."

Alimony: 1. is like making payments on a pickup truck that got hit by a train 2. the high cost of leaving 3. leave home pay 4. a case of wife and debt 4. is like buying oats for somebody else's mule

Alkali: a soluble mixture of salts in arid regions that is capable of neutralizing acids; also called salt

Alkali-flat: a stretch of land, usually flat, that is overrun with alkali

Alkalied: said of a man who got sick drinking water laced with alkali

All: 1. everybody and the dog (or cook) 2. everything under the sun

All alike: 1. all from the same herd of cats 2. all tarred with the same brush, which comes from the days when sheep were marked with colors using a tar brush 3. ain't a plug nickel's difference between 'em

All in a hump: holus-bolus

All inclusive: bar none, as in "Dewey, Cheatem, and Howe is the worst law firm in Texas, bar none."

All my life: all my born days

All or nothing: it's the whole hog or no hog

All overs: 1. the kitters 2. long underwear

All right: 1. hunky-dory 2. Jim dog dandy 3. okeydokey

All the way: 1. clear (or clean) to, as in "He went clear to the county line tryin' to outrun the sheriff." or "He was cut clean to the bone." 2. plumb, as in "He went plumb to Florida looking for a job."

All together: 1. everybody is in the same pew (or stew pot) 2. all in the same fix

All work, no play: all hominy and no ham

All y'all: *See Y'all*

All-Around Cowboy: ultimate prize for a rodeo cowboy [The All-Around Cowboy is the one who wins the most money in two or more events. Contestants may apply their points—each dollar won equals one point—from 100 rodeos toward their yearly standing.]

Alleytown (Colorado County): pronounced ALLEY-tun; named for Ransom Alley, a surveyor whose family was one of Stephen F. Austin's "Old Three Hundred"

Allow: to declare, as in "If you ask me, I'd allow that Bill Clinton has plumb screwed up the office of the president." or "Bubba allowed he might just vote Republican come next election."

Alma (Ellis County): pronounced AL-mah, not Aul-mah

Almost: 1. close but no cigar 2. like to, as in "I like to forgot to get baby's formula." 3. pert near, as in "I pert near forgot my anniversary." 4. nearly 'bout 5. in a little of 6. mighty nigh 7. nigh on 8. plumb nearly, which can be used together such as "I was plumb out of Texas and nearly out of Arkansas before the law caught up to me."

Almost, but not quite: pert near but not plumb

Almost died: 1. came close enough to heaven to smell an angel's breath 2. came close enough to hell to smell the smoke

Almost empty: 1. runnin' on fumes 2. runnin' on memories

Almost finished: 1. hoeing in the short rows [from the days when cotton choppers considered the job almost done when they made it to the short rows] 2. the fat lady is clearing her throat (or reaching for the song book) 3. turn on the air-conditioner in the bus, which means the ball game is all but over and the visiting team is about ready to leave 4. all over but the shouting 5. don't lack much

Almost none: hardly any a'tall

Alone: 1. stewing in his own juice 2. playing solitaire 3. playing a lone hand 4. on his own hook 5. Lone Rangering it 6. lone wolfing it 7. all by his lonesome 8. cooking solitary chili, which means he's cooking only enough for one

Aloof: 1. high headed 2. hifalutin' 3. uppity as a mountain goat 4. can strut sitting down [This is how attorney

Temple Houston once described the prosecutor in a case he was defending.]

Alpine (Brewster County): pronounced AL-pine [Originally named Murphyville in honor of the man who owned the nearby springs that supplied water for the steam locomotives of the Southern Pacific Railroad; eventually named for Alpine, Alabama.]

Also: 1. at that [This is usually said to add emphasis to something already said, such as in "You're ugly and fat, at that."] 2. on top of, as in "He's mean on top of being stupid."

Altavista (Jim Hogg County): pronounced Al-ta-vist-ah; named for the Jones-Alta Vista Ranch, which purchased and used the town site

Alternate: 1. change about 2. swap around 3. turnabout is fair play

Alternative: 1. more than one way to break a dog (or a mother-in-law) from sucking eggs 2. more than one way to win a pretty girl's heart 3. every coin has two sides 4. every record has a flip side except a prison record 5. instead of biting the bullet, try getting the lead out 6. the hind tit is better than no tit at all 7. there's more than one way to dress a calf's head 8. when you are up to your nose in manure, try breathing through your ears

Altoga (Collin County): pronounced Al-TOE-gah, although some of the old-timers prefer Al-toe-gee; original request was for the name All Together but postal authorities shortened it

Aluminum foil: tin-foal

Alumni: not an athlete but an athletic supporter

Alvarado (Johnson County): pronounced Al-va-RAY-do; named by Sheriff A. H. Onstoot for Alvaredo, Vera Cruz, Mexico, where he had fought during the Mexican War

Alvord (Wise County): despite how it looks, the correct pronunciation is AL-void; originally called Nina, the name was changed to honor the president of the Fort Worth and Denver Railroad

Amarillo (Potter County): when properly pronounced, the name rhymes with gorilla, not Brillo; it's Am-a-rill-ah, which means yellow in Spanish. [Amarillo is the helium capital of the world, and they've got the monument to prove it. It's been said that in Amarillo you can be waist deep in mud and still get dust in your eye.]

Amateur: 1. jake leg 2. tinhorn 3. greenhorn 4. shade tree, as in "He's a shade tree proctologist." *See also Tenderfoot*

Amateur night: *See New Year's Eve*

Amazed: 1. his eyes bugged out like a frog that had been stepped on by a Clydesdale 2. his eyes stuck out like a cowcatcher on a train (switch engine) 3. slack-jawed

Amazed (oath): 1. I'll be dipped in snuff (or tobacco juice) 2. I'll be switched (or jiggered) 3. shuck me nekkid (naked) 4. cut off one of my legs and call me I lean

Amazing: 1. that'll blow your dress up 2. don't that beat all 3. that'll blow your hat in the creek 4. it'll pop your eyeballs out of their sockets far enough to get a rope on 'em 5. that'll snap your girdle 6. a real whistle bringer, which is derived from the fact that a lot of people whistle when something amazing happens 7. that'll cock your pistol 8. that'll melt your butter 9. been to three county fairs, two rodeos, and a goat roping and I ain't never seen anything like that 10. beats all I ever saw or heard tell of 11. a sight to behold 12. takes the cake 13. the beatenest thing I ever saw 14. the best I ever helt, smelt, felt, slept with, or stepped in *See also Astonishing; Exciting*

Ambition, strong: got the bar so high it'd take an eagle two jumps to get over it

Ambition, lacking: keeps the bar on the ground

Ambitious: 1. always looking for new ranges to ride (or fields to plow) 2. a real barn burner 3. thinks he can break every ornery bronc in Texas 4. will take on all comers if the big ones will line up and the little ones will bunch up 5. whittles with a big knife 6. keeps his wick turned up high, which basically means he's trying to be a shining light

Ambrose (Grayson County): pronounced AM-brose; named for Ambrose Bible, the local settler who donated most of the land for the original town site

Amen corner: a pew near the pulpit, usually reserved for the most devout (and vocal) members of the congregation

American: a real Texas pronunciation is Murkin [Texan Lyndon Johnson, while serving as president, often opened his speeches with, "Ma fella Murkins."]

Ammonia Coke: country remedy for headache where you squirt a little ammonia in a Coca Cola [Don't even think about trying it!]

Among: 1. amongst 2. in the thick of 3. in the heat of 4. in the heart of

Amount, large: *See Large amount*

Amount, small: *See Small amount*

An hour by sun: an hour after sunrise or an hour before sunset

Anahuac (Chambers County): correct pronunciation is ANNA-wack although some of the old-timers still say Anny-ock [A small town on Trinity Bay near Houston where the Texas revolution took seed. Also known as the alligator (gator) capital of Texas.]

Ancestry: bark of the family tree

A

Ancestry, clouded: got some shady branches on his family tree

Andice (Williamson County): pronounced ANN-dies, not Ann-dis [Rev. William Isaac Newton applied for a post office and suggested the name Audice in honor of his son. Someone in the post office misread the application and Andice became the name.]

Anemic: 1. tick proof 2. Dracula safe 3. if he cut his finger he'd have to get a transfusion before he could bleed

Angelica: jellico weed

Angelina County: pronounced Ann-ja-LEAN-ah; named for an Indian woman who supposedly acted as a guide for Spanish explorers; the only county in Texas named for a female

Anger: 1. makes your mouth work faster than your mind 2. can't be angry and reasonable at the same time any more than a horse can buck and eat oats at the same time

Angers: 1. chaps my hide (or butt) 2. boils my blood 3. pops my cork 4. fries my patience 5. gets my dander (dandruff) up 6. gets a rise out of me quicker than a snake can stick out his tongue 7. makes me want to kick a stump barefooted 8. makes my butt dip snuff (or crochet a buttonhole) 9. tweaks my beak

Angoras: *See Woolies*

Angry: 1. hopping' mad 2. enough to eat the sights off a six-shooter, which means someone is almost angry enough to start shooting but not quite *See also Female, angry; Male, angry; Upset*

Angry, but in control: chewin' his tobacco ninety to nuthin' [very angry but not enough to spit out his tobacco and fight so he just chews faster and spits more]

Angry as: 1. a preacher with the devil camped out in his backyard 2. a rooster in an empty henhouse 3. a teased rattlesnake (or cottonmouth water moccasin) 4. a bobcat in a mud hole 5. a sore tailed bear 6. an alligator with chapped lips

Angry female: 1. her fangs are flashing and her nails are twitchin' 2. gettin' ready to throw a hissey fit 3. wearing war paint instead of makeup 4. her purr turned to a growl 5. stoked up hotter than the coals in a depot stove 6. hotter than a pot of boiling collards *See also Female, angry*

Angry male: 1. ready to pit his bird, which is a reference to cock fighting 2. riled up 3. foaming at the mouth 4. gettin' ready to burn some powder (shoot someone) 5. got his holster tied down 6. bellerin' and pawing the dirt 7. got his hat set at a fighting angle 8. got his teeth set like a stubborn mule 9. putting on his raking spurs 10. so hot under the collar all the hair on his neck was singed off *See also Mad; Male, angry*

Angry words: 1. war words 2. preaching your own funeral [about to talk yourself into a fight that will be your last; a slight variation to the old saying "hot words lead to cold slabs"]

Animals: critters if they're friendly, varmints if they ain't

Annona (Red River County): pronounced Ann-own-ah; originally named Walker Station, after founder George W. Walker [In 1884 Walker himself suggested the name be changed to honor "a beautiful Indian girl." Walker then became Annona, but no Indian maiden by that name has ever been identified. Some have speculated the post office made a mistake and the name should have been Ramona, the Indian heroine in Helen Hunt Jackson's romantic novel by that name published in 1884.]

Announce: 1. put it on a billboard 2. tell it to someone going to a ladies' club meeting (or a church social) 3. tell somebody it's a secret

Anson (Jones County): pronounced ANN-sun; originally named Jones City in honor of Anson Jones, the last president of the Republic of Texas but was later changed to Anson

Ant: horned frog food [Horned frogs, which are actually lizards, are almost extinct, but those that remain prefer a diet heavily laced with juicy red ants.]

Ant bed: *See Metroplex*

Antiaircraft artillery: buzzard busters

Antifogmatic: *See Whiskey, strong*

Anticipation, strong: 1. makes my ears pop just thinking about it 2. makes my pacemaker run in overdrive

Antioch: the numerous settlements with this name are all pronounced ANTE-ock

Anton (Hockley County): pronounced ANT'n; named for J. F. Anton, an executive of the Santa Fe Railroad

Anxiety, high: wound up tighter'n a two-dollar watch

Anxious: 1. sittin' on the well, which means he is anxious to bring it in 2. raring to go 3. pawing the dirt 4. got buck fever 5. foaming at the trough 6. champing at the bit 7. got ants in his pants

Anxious as: 1. the third monkey scratching on Noah's gangplank 2. a kid on Christmas Eve 3. a dry steer scenting fresh water [On a trail drive, cattle had to have water at least once a day and preferably twice. During dry spells, the herd often had to go days without drinking. When they finally got near water, they would catch the scent and become anxious, even stampede.]

Anxious bench: special bench in the front of a church reserved for those who are real "anxious" about something

Apologetic: got his hat in his hand, which is a reference to the fact that a lot of country boys don't never take off their hat unless they're fixin' to apologize for something

Appealing: 1. strikes my fancy 2. tickles my fancy

Appearance: 1. the man makes the cowboy, not the duds 2. clothes do not make the man, especially if it's an apron

Appearance, bad: 1. looks like he was inside the outhouse when lightning struck it 2. looks like an unmade bed 3. looks like he was rode hard and put up wet 4. looks like he spent the night in a dishwasher 5. looks like he was shot out of a cannon and missed the net 6. looks like the mill ends of hell, which refers to the mill ends produced in sawmills 7. looks like he was pulled through a knothole backwards 8. looks like a stump full of brush frazzled rats 9. looks like the offspring of a scarecrow 10. looks like he got caught in the gears of a combine and drug for three acres 11. looks like death sitting on a cracker 12. looks like something the cat drug in 13. look like you were chewed up, spit out, and stepped on *See also Looks*

Appearance, deceiving: 1. just because someone looks like they are in the fast lane, it don't mean they ain't just hitchhiking 2. just because a chicken has wings don't mean she can fly 3. like a duck, what you can see looks calm but underneath he's paddling as fast as he can 4. like a vulture, looks scary but he's harmless 5. you can find a lot of thread on a small spool 6. you can't tell how fast a rabbit can run by looking at his ears

Appearance, good: 1. looks like he ought to be entering a plea, which refers to the fact that most people dress up when appearing in court 2. always looks like he just stepped out of an air-conditioned room 3. looks like a picture out of a wish book (mail order catalog) 4. looks good enough to give a sermon 5. looks good enough to marry a banker's daughter *See also Looks*

Appetite, large: 1. eats more than a roundup crew 2. if he was a pissant, he could eat a bale of hay

Appetite, small: 1. eats like a hummingbird on a buttermilk diet 2. don't eat enough to stoke a sparrow

Apple out: when vine crops (maypops, pumpkins, etc.) shed their blooms

Apple slump: deep dish apple pie made with molasses for sweetening

Apply: dab it on

Appreciate: pronounced 'preciate to most Texans

Appreciation: 1. would take kindly to it 2. will dance naked at your next wedding if you'll do that for me 3. never look a gift horse in the mouth [Refers to checking the teeth to determine approximate age. Looking a gift horse in the mouth would show very little appreciation, especially if you did it in front of the person who gave you the horse.]

Appreciative: would appreciate that as much as Travis and the boys would have appreciated a Gatling gun or two at the Alamo

Apprehensive as: 1. a crippled fly in a spider's web 2. a pregnant woman in her tenth month 3. a doctor operating on a lawyer who specializes in malpractice cases 4. a cow waiting to be milked on a cold morning ('cause she knows his hands ain't gonna be warm)

Approximately: pert near, as in "He's got pert near 500 head of cattle."

April: shearing time, which is when sheep are sheared for their wool

Aquilla (Hill County): pronounced A-QUILL-ah; originally called Mudtown but the name was changed to match that of a nearby creek

Aransas Pass: pronounced a-RAN-sus; the Shrimp Capital of the World, located across Redfish Bay from Port Aransas

Archer County: pronounced ARE-chur; named for Branch T. Archer, commissioner in the Republic of Texas [County seat is Archer City, made famous in Larry McMurtry's *The Last Picture Show*.]

Arduous: *See Difficult; Hard to do*

Area, large: big as all of hell and half of Texas [No one knows for sure how big hell is, but it is assumed to be larger than Texas, say about the size of Alaska.]

Argument: 1. cuss fight 2. a fallin' out 3. a hen fight 4. like a county road, you never know where it will go 5. when arguing with a fool make sure he ain't doing the same thing

Argument, stupid: as two bald-headed men fighting over a fine-tooth comb

Argument closed: time to back the hearse up or start the hearse, both of which are used to close an argument you lost because the implication is that disaster is imminent

Argumentative: 1. would argue with a sign post, lamp post, goal post, fence rail, or wooden Indian 2. could start an argument in an empty henhouse

Arid land: 1. got about as much water as a secretarial pool 2. would take 50 acres to support one middlin'-sized jackrabbit 3. steamboats would rise a cloud of dust in the riverbed 4. birds build their nests out of barbed wire 5. only swimming hole is the water left in a cow track after a thunderstorm *See also Drought; Dry; Land, dry*

Armadillo: pronounced arm-a-dill-a. [The nine-banded armadillo is official mascot of the state of Texas. Also referred to as "opossum on the half shell" and "Hoover Hog," from the depression, when a lot of Texans couldn't afford pork so they ate armadillos. Today, armadillos are frequently called road bumps.]

Armadillo eggs: jalapeño peppers stuffed with pimento cheese

Arneckeville (De Witt County): pronounced ARNIE-ka-ville, although some use ARE-neck-ville

Around the house: around the place

Arrange: fix, as in "Would you fix the dinner table?"

Arrived: 1. blew in with the weather (or tumbleweeds) 2. struck town 3. lit and stayed

Arrived unexpectedly: came in under the radar

Arrogant: 1. riding a high horse 2. too big for his britches (or overalls) 3. snot nosed 4. biggedy 5. got more crust than a pecan pie factory *See also Aloof*

Arroyo: a narrow gorge with dirt walls that are usually very steep [A dry creek bed is frequently referred to as an arroyo.]

Arsenic: knife-blade medicine *See also Doping a horse*

Art (Mason County): originally called Willow Creek; changed to Plehweville, which was rejected by the post office department. Local postmaster Ely W. Deckart wrote to the department and someone there suggested he use the last three letters of his name.

Arthritis (arthur-EYE-tus): the big miseries

Artist, poor: couldn't draw a conclusion

As they ran: In the old days in Texas, if you bought cattle as they ran, you did so without counting them and, in effect, trusted the count of the seller.

Asafetida ball: worn on a string around the neck and chewed on periodically to ward off evil spirits and to deter the flu bug; pronounced fetiddy

Ash: wish ash tree

Asherton (Dimmit County): pronounced ASH-er-tun; named for Asher Richardson who founded the town

Ashtola (Donley County): pronounced Ash-TOE-la; originally named Southard [When postal authorities requested a change postmaster W. A. Poovey wanted Poovieville, but he was overruled.]

Ashtray: fingernail clipping holder

Askew: 1. totally haywire 2. all cattywhampus 3. scattered every which way

Asleep: looking for light leaks (or pin holes) in his eyelids

Asleep, sort of: just resting my eyeballs, as in "How could I have been snoring when I was just resting my eyeballs?"

Asparagus: sparrowgrass

Aspermont (Stonewall County): pronounced ASS-per-mont, never A-spear-mont [A.L. Rhomberg donated the land for the town and provided the name, which is Latin for "rough mountain."]

Aspiration: 1. just a little pebble who wants to be the whole beach 2. just a little tadpole tryin' to be the big frog in the pond

Assembled, poorly: 1. put together with spit and baling wire 2. Southern engineered 3. jerry-rigged, which, in Texas, is pronounced jury-rigged

Assets, good: got a pen full of baby donkeys [In the old days, baby donkeys were a great asset because they could either be sold or kept so they could one day replace old donkeys that wore out.]

Assistant: 1. right-hand man 2. range boss, which was the ranch owner's assistant 3. hazer, which is a rider who assists a calf roper or steer wrestler in a rodeo

Assisted: propped him up

Associated: 1. in cahoots with 2. in the same hitch 3. eatin' out of the same feed bag 4. singing off the same song sheet 5. riding on the same range 6. marching to the same beat 7. dipping ink from the same bottle *See also Involved*

Association dip (or chew): a dip of snuff or chaw of tobacco that is very large, which is preferred by many members of the Professional Rodeo Cowboy Association

Association cowboy: a member of the Professional Rodeo Cowboy Association

Association saddle: *See Rough-out saddle*

Assume: makes an ass out of "u" and me

Assumption, wrong: *See Presumptuous*

Astonished (oath): could a knocked me over with a hummingbird tail feather

Astonishing: 1. beats all I ever saw or heard tell of 2. a sight to behold 3. takes the cake *See also Amazing; Exciting*

Astrodome: Miracle on Main Street, because it was built on Main Street in Houston. [When the stadium first opened, a Houston sportswriter claimed it was something God might build if he had the money.] *See also New Orleans Super Dome; Texas Stadium*

Asylum: 1. booby hatch 2. loony bin 3. nutcracker suite 4. the loco motel 5. Holler Day Inn 6. loco lockup 7. Terrell Hilton, which refers to the state hospital located in Terrell, Texas 8. La Cain't A, a takeoff on La Quinta motor hotels.

At all: pronounced properly as a'tall

At her mercy: got me caught in the rustle of her dress

At his mercy: got me by the short hairs

A

At last: finally (pronounced fine-ly)

At risk: 1. ridin' a short horse in tall brush, which means there's a good chance you'll end up on the ground picking stickers out of your backside 2. dancin' with the sheriff's mistress, which means if you get caught you're liable to end up shot or in jail or both *See also Risk taking; Risky*

Atheism: a fair weather religion

Atheist: has no one to talk to when he's alone

Athens (Henderson County): first named Buffalo, then Centerville, and finally Athens after the city in Greece; known as the Black-Eyed Pea Capital of the World.

Athlete: pronounced ath-a-leet

Athlete, inept: plays like he ought to be in a game where the mothers make the uniforms

Athlete, stupid: can do anything with a football except autograph it; baseball or basketball can easily be substituted for football

Athlete, superior: the bus don't leave till he's on it

Athletic supporter: 1. jewel box 2. marble sack 3. nut cup

Atlanta (Cass County): pronounced At-lanna, the second "t" is silent; small town in East Texas not far from Marietta named for Atlanta, Georgia, the former home of many of the early settlers

Attack: 1. plow into 'em 2. crawl his hump 3. try 'em on for size 4. give 'em both barrels, which refers to a double-barreled shotgun 5. light into 'em

Attacked: 1. like grandma after a chicken snake with a chunk of firewood 2. like conventioneers on a free buffet 3. like grasshoppers on a corn field 4. like a chicken hawk on a fat fryer 5. like a horned toad on a bed of red ants 6. with arms flailing like the blades on a windmill

Attempt: 1. like a steer, I can try, which refers to the fact that even though a steer has been castrated he can still try 2. try your hand at, as in "I'm gonna try my hand at writing a novel someday."

Attempting the impossible: 1. trying to hit a five-run homer 2. trying to bathe five kids in a two-kid washtub [In the country, if you had a large washtub and two small children, it was possible to bathe both the little ones at the same time to save water. There never has been, however, a washtub large enough for five kids at one sitting.] 3. tryin' to square the circle [This saying originated long ago when mathematicians tried to build a square that would have exactly the same area as a circle. The math boys never made it—it can't be done. The saying eventually found its way to the country, though a lot of folks who used it probably never knew what it meant.] *See also Impossible*

A⊤**M Attention:** atten-hutt

Attention getter: 1. will get your attention faster than a cross-eyed javelin thrower 2. will get your attention faster than a cross-eyed man at a turkey shoot

Attention span, small: got the attention span of a gnat [Mosquito, chigger, housefly, or almost any other small insect can be substituted.]

Attentive: *See Alert; Be alert*

Attire: *See Clothes*

Attracted to: 1. like a hawk to a prairie dog 2. like lightning to a lightning rod 3. like a bug to a light 4. like steel to a magnet 5. like a pig to slop 6. like flies to molasses (or honey) 7. took a liking to 8. took a shining to 9. like a kid to a horse 10. like a pack mule to a bell mare 11. like a moth to a flame 12. like a counterfeit quarter to a magnet 13. like a chicken to a new pie pan

Attractive,   somewhat: leans toward, as in "Bubba leans toward handsome."

Aubrey (Denton County): pronounced AW-bree; originally named Onega but the name was changed when Aubrey was drawn out of a hat

Auctioneer: a person who can pick your pocket with his tongue

Aurora (Wise County): pronounced A-ROAR-ah, the small town where a man from Mars is supposedly buried in the cemetery

Austin (Travis County): pronounced AWE-stun, the site of the Texas state capital, which was originally Waterloo; bills itself as the "live music capital of the world"

Austonio (Houston County): pronounced Aus-TONE-ee-oh, which is a combination of Austin and San Antonio. While San Antonio is sometimes pronounced San Ann-tone, this town is never Aus-tone.

Austwell (Refugio County): pronounced Aus-well, the "t" is silent; named for founder Preston R. Austin and his partner Jesse C. McDowell

Auto racing fan: gear head

Automobile dealership: house, as in Ford house or Pontiac house [Generally used only for American-made brands since Toyota house or Porsche house just don't sound right. Foreign vehicles are sold in stores.]

Automobile dents, minor: whiskey dents [These are the small, unexplained dents and dings you find in your car the morning after a night at the local honky-tonk. The term is also used for any small dent you find even if you haven't been to a honky-tonk.]

Automobile repairs: *See Solution, temporary*

Automobile, fast: will pass everything but a gas station

Automobile, large: 1. land cruiser 2. land yacht

Average: 1. run of the mill 2. fair to middlin' 3. nothing to write home to mama about 4. everyday wash 5. just one of the herd *See also Common*

Average person: someone who is as close to the bottom as he is to the top

Avinger (Cass County): pronounced AV-in-gurr; named for Dr. H. J. Avinger, who operated a store at the site of the town

Avoca (Jones County): pronounced Ah-VOCK-ah; originally called Spring Creek; name changed when the site was moved three miles up the railroad tracks to Avo

Avocado: alligator pear

Avoid: 1. plow around the stump 2. dance around it 3. take a different trail 4. ride around the swamp 5. stay away from that like you would a swamp if you were drunk 6. good not to mess with, as in "A drunk with an attitude and a gun is a good man not to mess with."

Avoid a subject: don't go there

Avoid trouble: 1. don't get between a dog and his bone 2. if you run your car on chicken manure, you won't have any trouble with siphoners 3. don't go around kicking sleeping dogs 4. never get between a politician and a TV news crew

Avoided: 1. slipped the noose 2. ducked that so much I'm beginning to quack 3. dodged a bullet

Avondale (Tarrant County): pronounced AH-vun-dale, not AVON-dale

Awalt (Gregg County): pronounced A-walt; named for the first minister of the Pine Tree Cumberland Presbyterian Church, Solomon Awalt

Awesome: a rolling ball of butcher knives [Darrell Royal once said his Texas team was not a rolling ball of butcher knives after they lost to Texas Tech.]

B

Awhile: a spell, as in "Sit a spell and take a load off."

Awkward: could fall down just thinking about walking

Awkward as: 1. a crippled sow or a cow on crutches 2. a duck out of water 3. an elephant tryin' to use a typewriter 4. a blind bear in a briar patch

Awkward situation: 1. in-laws on a honeymoon trip 2. a mother-in-law who's a bad cook 3. a father-in-law who's a good shot

Azle (Tarrant County): pronounced A-zul [There's a rumor the name means something that rhymes with "bass hole" in German, but city fathers and experts in the German language say that is not correct. The rumor was probably started by folks in a rival town.]

B

B.O.I.: "Born On the Island," referring to people who were actually born on Galveston Island

B.Q. (band queer): Aggie band member

B.R.C.: bedroom check

B.Y.O.B.: Bring Your Own Bottle, which relates to private clubs in dry areas that sell setups but you have to bring your own bottle, usually in a paper bag

Baby: 1. a sucker that gets an even break 2. when baby is happy, everyone is happy 3. little dumpling, which is usually said of a baby that's pudgy and sweet

Baby, ugly: *See Ugly baby*

Baby chick: biddie

Baby cow: no such thing; it's a calf

Baby growth chart: As a baby grows it goes through several identifiable stages: Stage 1: arm youngun—so small it has to be held at all times when not in a crib. Stage 2: lap baby—has grown enough that you can rest it on your lap for a few minutes at a time. Stage 3: knee baby—big enough to bounce on your knee and almost ready to walk. Stage 4: sit alone baby—old enough to sit on a pallet all by himself while you cook supper. Stage 5: porch baby—has just learned to walk, and you can let him wobble around the porch while you sit in the rocker and knit. Stage 6: yard baby—has gotten good enough at walkin' that you can let him wander around the yard while you're hoeing in the garden. Stage 7: teenager.

Babysitter: 1. teenager that gets paid for talking on the phone and eating leftovers 2. old, gentle horse that is kept around for the kids to ride 3. old cow that stays with the new calves while their mamas go off to graze

Bachelor: 1. been saved by the bell but never the wedding bell 2. would shuck his hide to get out of a wedding date 3. one fly that won't ever get caught in a spider's web 4. a lone ranger that never gets in a marryin' mood 5. a good ol' boy that's footloose and fiancée free 6. ain't ever married 'cause he's looking for the perfect woman 7. been turned down more than an army blanket 8. favorite dish is one that is already washed 9. a man who leans toward women but not far enough to alter his stance

Bachelor, confirmed: 1. would chew off his own arm to get out of a matrimonial trap, which is a reference to a coyote that will chew off his leg to get out of a steel trap 2. only way he'll ever get married is under the influence

of a shotgun 3. only ring you'll ever get from him is one around your tub

Back cuss: essentially means if someone starts cussing you, then cuss them right back [When sufficiently provoked, a real Texan will never be out-cussed.]

Back out: azzle out

Back it up: 1. put your money where your mouth is 2. put your cash where your crower is

Back pain: down in the back, as in "Bubba is shore down in the back after lifting the engine out of his pickup by hand."

Back plait: process of weaving a harness snap into a twisted rope

Back to basics: go back to the chicken pen and learn how to scratch

Backlog: *See Complication*

Backseat driver: only person not bothered by a back seat driver is a hearse driver

Backslider: *See Sinful person*

Backwards: 1. often pronounced bassackwards 2. got the tail waggin' the dog 3. got your wagon before your horse 4. got your hind part before your front part 5. got your zipper on the wrong side 6. got your hindsight first

Backwoods: upbrush country

Bacliff (Galveston County): pronounced BAY-cliff; originally called Clifton-by-the-Sea; the post office required it to be shortened since the original name wouldn't fit on the rubber stamps used to cancel postage stamps

Bad: would drive a preacher to cuss (or to the bottle)

Bad baby: 1. when the doctor slapped him, he slapped back 2. he was rotten before he was ripe

Bad breath: *See Breath, bad*

Bad bull: a bad joke

Bad day: if today was a fish, I'd throw it back

Bad person: 1. needs to turn over an entire book, not just a new leaf [The "entire book" is, of course, the Bible.] 2. ought to jack up the jail and put him under it 3. lower than a snake's belt buckle (or navel) 4. got a reserved seat in hell and he's headed that way in the devil's hand basket [J. Frank Dobie once described a bad person as, "mean enough to suck eggs and cunning enough to hide the shells."] *See also Evil person; Mean person; Wicked*

Badger fights: a prank often pulled on a tenderfoot or newcomer in West Texas. He would be invited to a fight between a badger and a dog and be given the "honor" of pulling the "badger" out of the pen. However, the badger would turn out to be a concoction of crackers, water, and other substances to resemble excrement. When the laughter subsided, the tenderfoot would be invited to buy a round of drinks.

Badlands: brushy, rocky, generally no account land that ain't fit for nothing but occupying space; often has lots of erosion and in the far West frequently has buttes and peaks

Baffled: 1. buffaloed 2. ain't got a clue 3. bumfuzzled 4. in a fog 5. don't even know what planet he's on

Bag balm: a salve used to treat sores and irritation on a cow's udder; also makes an excellent treatment for chapped lips

Bait: food for man or horse

Bait the hole: process of placing a couple of bales of hay or other "bait" at a particular location in a lake or river. The theory is that fish will find the large quantity of food and hang around, which makes catching them easier because you don't have to hunt for them. This method is often used by fishermen who want to catch their limit quickly so they can get back to drinking.

Bake a cake: build a cake

Balch Springs (Dallas County): original pronunciation was Bawlk Sprangs, which is how founder John Balch pronounced his name; eventually evolved into BAWL-ch Sprangs

Balcones Heights (Bexar County): pronounced Bal-CONE-ees Heights

Bald headed: 1. hitch-headed, which means he has about as much hair as a ball on a trailer hitch 2. chrome dome, because many bald heads shine like they were chrome plated 3. seen more hair on a crystal ball 4. his hair departed in the middle 5. a hair on the head is worth two in the brush 6. parts his hair with a towel 7. hair looks like it was parted by a bolt of lightning 8. bald men are discriminated against because they have to pay full price for a haircut 9. anyone can grow hair but it takes a real man to keep it worn off, implying they wear it off on the headboard 10. God made a few perfect heads and then put hair on the rest *See also Hair restorer, good*

Baler table: table on the hay baler where the hay was placed before it was moved into the actual baler *See also Pitchfork*

Baling wire: thick, strong wire used to hold a bale of hay together [This versatile wire is also used to repair almost anything around a farm from windmills to false teeth.]

Balling gun: a gun-like device used to put pills down a cow's throat

Ballinger (Runnels County): pronounced BAL-in-ger, not Ball-in-ger; originally called Gresham, then Hutchings, and finally changed to honor William P. Ballinger, a Galveston lawyer and major investor in local railroads

Balmorhea (Reeves County): pronounced Bal-Mur-Rah; name derived from three local promoters named Balcolm, Morrow, and Rhea

Balsora (Wise County): pronounced Bal-ZOR-ah; originally called Wild Horse Prairie in recognition of the numerous mustangs who ran wild on the surrounding prairies

Bandage, large: 1. conversation starter, especially if it's on your forehead 2. big enough to be used for a decapitation

Bandana: a square, brightly colored (often red and blue) piece of cloth; one of a cowboy's most versatile pieces of equipment; usually of cotton but silk is preferred since it is cooler in summer and warmer in winter. Some uses include: mask when riding in a sandstorm or robbing a bank; washrag or dish towel; headband; tie-down for your hat; filter for foul water; napkin; bandage for you or your horse; sling; tourniquet; flag on the end of a load that hangs way out the back of your pickup; polishing rag; handkerchief; wallet (when tied shut with a piece of string); blinders for your horse; emergency diaper; also called neckerchief or kerchief *See also Wild rag*

Bandera (Bandera County): pronounced Ban-DARE-ah [The town and county were named for nearby Bandera Pass, which translates into flag pass, but the origin of the name is unknown. The town bills itself as The Cowboy Capital of the World.]

Banged tail: horse whose tail has been cut off below the bony part

Banging: 1. like an outhouse door with the latch broke 2. like a gate with one hinge rusted off 3. like a screen door in an orphanage

Bangs (Brown County): some old-timers still call it Baings; named for its location in the Samuel Bangs survey

Bangy: a cow with brucellosis

Banker: 1. a pawnbroker that made good 2. someone who'll loan you money when you don't need it

Banker axiom: *See Lawyer idiom*

Banker, stupid: loaned out all the money then skipped town

Banker, tight: gives you the same amount of credit as a sharecropper gets in a New Orleans whorehouse

Bankrupt: 1. been run over by the plowshare of financial ruin 2. stuck my boot into the stirrup of financial ruin and got drug all the way to the poor house 3. lost everything but my name and my conscience *See also Went broke*

Banquete (Nueces County): pronounced Ban-KEAT-ee, not ban-qui-tee; named for a four-day celebration commemorating the completion of a road that linked San Patricio, Texas, and Matamoros, Mexico

Baptist: 1. dipper 2. dunker 3. plunger (all of which refer to the Baptist practice of immersing for baptism) 4. a hell expert [It's been said that Baptists learn as much as possible about hell so they'll be familiar with where their Methodist friends go after death.]

Baptist, backslider: 1. dippin' didn't take 2. was dipped in muddy water

Baptist, devout: 1. a hard-shell, foot washing Baptist 2. deep water Baptist

Baptist, drinker: *See Bar, concealed*

Baptist, fundamentalist: hard-shell Baptist

Bar: 1. booze parlor 2. drinking resort 3. booze bungalow 4. saloon 5. beer (or wine) shed

Bar, concealed: a Baptist bar; refers to a belief, widely held by proponents of liquor by the drink, that many Baptists will go to the polls to vote against liquor by the drink, then go home, open their concealed bar, and have a drink to celebrate their victory. This belief gave rise to the phrase "closet-drinking Baptist."

Bar bit: the simplest of bits since it consists only of a straight metal bar

Bar ditch: 1. a small canal along the side of the road created when the road was built to handle water runoff when it rains 2. also called borrowed ditch, because it was created when the dirt was borrowed to make the road

Barbecue: one of the big three in Texas, along with chili and chicken-fried steak [In Texas, barbecue is not an adjective; it's a noun referring to barbecued beef brisket. The term is only used as an adjective when some other meat, such as chicken, is barbecued. It's been said Texans will barbecue everything except ice cream and watermelon.]

Barbecue coma: what happens to most Texans if they don't get a barbecue fix at least once a week

Barbecue sauce: called correction fluid because it has covered up more mistakes than all the maternity dresses ever made

Barbecue, good: *See Fried chicken, good*

Barbed wire: 1. bobbed war or bob war 2. the devil's necklace 3. Satan's necktie 4. sticker wire [When barbed wire was first sold, it was advertised as being "steer strong, feather light, and dirt cheap."]

Barber shop: clip joint

 Bareback riding: a rodeo event where a contestant must ride a pitching (bucking) bronc with one hand for eight seconds; no stirrups or reins allowed. A bareback rigging is used, which consists of a double-thick, sheepskin-lined leather strap cinched around the horse's withers to inspire bucking action. The contestant holds onto a suitcase-style handle attached to the pad. If his free hand touches anything, no score is awarded. When the gate opens, the cowboy must "mark out" the horse with his smooth-rowled spurs over the animal's shoulders or be disqualified. The contestant gets higher points by keeping his toes pointed outwards to highlight his spurring action. A perfect score is 100 points, 50 for the horse and 50 for the man. Contestants draw for the horses to be ridden, and since half the score comes from the action of the animal, cowboys hope for a "good draw," which is a horse that will buck wildly and allow a better chance at a high overall score.

Bareback riggin': *See Bareback riding*

Barefooted: 1. an unshod horse 2. a bootless cowboy 3. clear-footed

Barely made it: made it by the skin of my teeth, as in "beat my wife home by the skin of my teeth"

Bargain: 1. dicker 2. do a little horse tradin'

Barrel, oil: unit of measure in the oil industry; a barrel of oil equals 42 gallons

Barrel horse: a highly trained horse, usually a quarter horse, used in barrel racing

Barrel racing: a rodeo event where a cowgirl rides her horse in a cloverleaf pattern around three barrels set in a triangular pattern. This is a timed event and the time begins when the contestant crosses the timer line and ends when she crosses it again after completing the ride. If a rider misses a barrel, she must either repeat the course or take a "no time" for the ride. There is no penalty if either the rider or the horse touches a barrel but if it's knocked plumb over, there is a five-second penalty.

Barrel rein: same as a roping rein

Barren: 1. not enough topsoil to make a good dirt dauber's nest 2. not enough trees to make a wooden penny, much less a nickel *See also Arid land*

Barrett (Harris County): pronounced BARE-it, not Bah-rehet; named for former slave Harrison Barrett.

Barrier: space allowed for the stock's head start in timed rodeo events *See also Breaking the barrier*

Bartender: 1. beer (or whisky) wrangler 2. bar dog 3. stays on the sober side of the bar 4. snake charmer, which is a reference to some people seeing snakes when they have too much to drink

Bartender, good: lead-fisted drink slinger, which implies his hand is so heavy he can't help but pour strong drinks

Baseball fan: seam-head

Baseball hitter, strong: can hit one out of any park, including Yellowstone

Baseball pitcher, inept: worked two years to straighten out his curve

Baseball pitcher, strong: 1. throws so hard, the baseball looks like an aspirin 2. could throw a lamb chop past a wolf 3. can throw a baseball through a car wash and not get it wet

Baseball-type cap: *See Gimmie cap*

Bashful: blushes every time he remembers he was in bed naked with a woman the day he was born

Basket dinner: a church social where dinner is served on the ground

Basket meeting: a protracted church meeting, frequently lasting several days, where there's dinner on the ground and preaching all around; name comes from the fact that most people bring their food in a basket of some sort

Basket name: what a child is called before being given its proper name when christened

Bass, large: any bass over ten pounds (that has not been filled with two or three pounds of lead sinkers) is a "hawg"

Bastrop (Bastrop County): pronounced BAS-trup for the town and the county; named for Baron de Bastrop, who obtained permission from the Spanish to create a German settlement at the site

Bat roost: Gathright Hall, Texas A&M

Bateau: small, homemade wooden boat used in Northeast Texas; usually 14 to 16 feet long and 2 feet wide with two compartments, a live well (generally covered with lattice) to hold fish that are caught, and a minnow well to hold the bait

Bath: dipping

Bath, quick: soiled-dove shower or whore bath [Instead of actually taking a shower or bath, you simply load up with deodorant and perfume.]

Bathtub: dipping vat

Bathroom limb: a tree limb low enough that you can sit down on it and do your business

Batt: *The Battalion,* the Texas A&M student newspaper

Battery, strong: could use that thing to jump-start a nuclear submarine

Battle: a flat sided bat or paddle used to beat clothes clean

Battlin' board: a board in a stream used to beat clothes on with a battle

Batwing chaps: chaps with very large flaps that resemble the wings of a bat and are attached with rings or snaps. Texas cowboys usually prefer this style because they offer protection yet are easy to get on or off; also called Texas wing chaps.

Bay color: color scheme of a horse with black tail, mane, and legs and a brown coat

Bayou: in Southeast Texas, low land filled with water; in North Texas, low land's called a gully or a draw because there's usually no water in it

Baytown (Harris County): although it is one word it's pronounced as two, BAY-town

Be aggressive: shell the beach

Be alert: 1. keep one eye on the cow's tail [When cows were milked by hand, about the time you had the bucket full of fresh, foamy white milk, the old cow would swish her tail through a pile of manure and half of it would land in your milk bucket. The only way to prevent that is to keep your eye on the cow's tail.] 2. keep the cows milling so they won't stampede [Being killed while trying to turn a stampede was a leading cause of death among old-time cowboys. The cattle were generally kept milling in an effort to prevent stampedes.] 3. keep a weather eye on 'em 4. keep your eyeballs peeled *See also Alert*

Be aware: every shut eye ain't sleeping and every good-bye don't mean he's gone

Be brief: 1. give me the bare bones 2. give me the bacon without the sizzle

Be calm: *See Calm down*

Be careful: 1. don't plow too close to the cotton 2. don't throw out the baby with the bath water 3. hook an unbroken horse to a wagon and you are liable to lose a wagon 4. keep the powder dry 5. don't sit with your back to the window, which was a common caution for old-time gunfighters since a back to an open window presented an easy target to back-shooters and bushwhackers 6. you were too hard to raise to take chances 7. always whistle some before drifting into a strange camp, which refers to the days of the Old West when a man could turn up dead if he went unannounced in a strange camp 8. don't dig up more snakes than you can kill 9. everything that comes from the cow ain't butter so watch

what you spread on your bread 10. never step between a man and his spittoon 11. before you take a bite out of something, make sure it won't bite you back 12. can't always tell which dog'll bite you 13. play 'em close to the vest, which is the best way to play your cards in a poker game *See also Advice; Careful; Caution*

Be cautious: don't celebrate till you're out of the woods 'cause the posse might be hiding behind the last tree

Be creative: *See Innovative*

Be discreet: 1. don't hang your dirty wash on someone else's line 2. don't make love by the garden gate because even if love is blind, the neighbors ain't 3. kiss an ugly girl and she'll tell the world

Be happy with what you got: count your blessings and ignore the pain

Be observant: can't tell which way the train went by looking at the tracks

Be on time: if you're late to church, you have to sit on the front row

Be patient: 1. the watched clock moves slower than molasses in January 2. can't catch a pop fly till it comes down 3. a watched pot never boils 4. every bell you hear ain't the dinner bell 5. don't cross the river till you come to it 6. hot will cool if greedy will let it, which refers to sampling cooked food before it is cool enough to eat 7. don't count your chickens till they hatch 8. don't count the crop till it's in the barn 9. can't measure a snake until it's dead 10. sit tight, everything will come out in the wash

Be prepared: 1. can't sell from an empty wagon 2. keep your ducks in a row 3. keep your saddle oiled and your gun greased 4. if you're gonna run with the big dogs, be prepared to hike your leg in tall grass 5. if you're gonna run with coyotes, better learn to like the taste of chicken feathers 6. keep your traps set *See also Plan ahead*

Be quiet: 1. hobble your lip 2. don't rattle your spurs 3. hush your mouth 4. you don't have to explain what you don't say 5. every fish ever caught had his mouth open 6. keep your 'tater trap shut 7. can't put a foot in a closed mouth 8. little birds shouldn't chirp much in hawk country 9. God gave you two ears, two eyes, and one mouth so you ought to be able to figure out which he expected you to use the most 10. pipe down 11. rest (Aggie) [When Lyndon Johnson was in the U.S. Senate, he had a sign in his office proclaiming, "You ain't learning nothing when you're talking."]

Be selective: 1. admire a large horse, saddle a small one 2. feed the horses you ride

Be smart: 1. keep your head up and your backside down 2. brains in the head save blisters on the feet 3. don't send your dog to the butcher shop or your daughter to the mall 4. hunt where the ducks are 5. don't store your meat in your brother-in-law's freezer

Be specific: 1. scrape off the scab and get to the meat 2. don't dance all over the floor 3. don't ride all over the range 4. cut to the quick [On January 24, 1990, a member of the Dallas Mavericks entered the game wearing his uniform shorts backwards. Following the game, he told reporters, I've been praying to the Lord to show me a way to get more recognition. In the future I'll be a little more specific. That goes along with the old country saying "God's mighty smart but he ain't no mind reader."]

Be still: get your nest built [This is generally used for sleeping partners who are thrashing around in bed trying to get comfortable. It can, however, be used in any instance where someone is moving around too much to suit you.]

Be sure you're right: once you cut off a hound dog's tail you can't sew it back on [Davy Crockett left this piece of advice: "Be sure you're right, then go ahead."]

Be thorough: whitewash don't poison termites

Be wary: keep your eyes skinned, which means keep them open

Be yourself: blaze your own trail [If you follow another man's tracks, you don't know if he knew where he was going or not, which is a slight variation to "Another man's tracks might just as well lead to hell as heaven."]

Beans: 1. the thundering herd 2. Mexican (or Arkansas) strawberries 3. frijoles 4. shrapnel, when cooked with chili; motherless, when cooked without pork 5. artillery (Aggie)

Beans, pinto: 1. red beans 2. rock beans, which refers to the fact that tiny rocks often get mixed in with the beans when harvested

Beans in the pod: snap beans

Bear grass: tough, coarse grass

Bear it: buck up

Beard, heavy: he could raise rabbits in his beard

Beard, long: looks like he swallowed a gray horse [If the beard is some color other than gray, substitute the correct color for the horse.]

Bearing down: busting the traces

Beat: 1. whip him like a redheaded stepchild 2. like a farmer would a stubborn mule 3. tie his ears in a bow knot 4. knock the stuffing out of him 5. take the starch out of him 6. collect his tail feathers 7. burn his barn 8. knock him cold enough to skate on 9. shear his pin 10. nail his hide to the barn wall 11. clean his plow (or sharpen his hoe) 12. give him a what-for lesson

Beatable: 1. the bigger they are the harder they fall so make sure they don't fall on you 2. even the meanest bull can be dehorned

Beaten: 1. feel like someone got after me with a hoe handle 2. knocked the enamel loose from my eye teeth 3. feel like I was whipped with a slippery elm (or bois d'arc) fence post 4. all my nuts, bolts, and screws are loose 5. a fat lip never bolstered anyone's confidence 6. feel like I was whipped with a windmill wrench [Because of its size and weight, the windmill wrench found its way into much of the language of older Texans who had to contend with those particular tools when the need arose.]

Beaten, severely: 1. feel like I did a piñata imitation 2. got beat so hard, the wax popped out of my ears (or my ears started smoking) 3. got licked in spades [Spades are the highest ranking playing cards, thus anything in spades is the best or worst it can be.] 4. beat so bad it took a week to get the sawdust out of my beard, which is a reference to the practice of putting sawdust on the floor of honky-tonks, where fights are not that uncommon 5. hung my hide on a fence, which means you got beaten badly and everyone knows it 6. kicked my butt so hard I could taste boot leather 7. knocked me just this side of heaven 8. knocked my toenails loose 9. hit me so hard my liver turned a cartwheel 10. gave me an all-world butt kickin' 11. hit me so hard my kids will be born shaking 12. pounded my head so far down I had to unzip my pants to blow my nose

Beating around the bush: 1. wolfing around the pot 2. hemmin' and hawin'

Beaumont (Jefferson County): pronounced BO-mont; name came either from a man named Jefferson Beaumont or from a French word meaning "beautiful hill"

Beauty: 1. is in the eye of the beer holder 2. is only a light switch away

Beauty measure: Clydesdale Scale. This is the number of Clydesdale horses that would be required to pull you away from a woman. Therefore, if a pretty girl rates a 7 on the Clydesdale Scale, it would take seven of the giant horses hitched to your back to pull you away from her. There is also the Reverse Clydesdale Scale, which is the measure of how many Clydesdales would have to be hitched to your butt to drag you over to her house for a free meal. A 1 on the Reverse Clydesdale Scale would mean she is fairly ugly but a good cook. Conversely, a 10 would mean she's so ugly she'd make a freight train take a dirt road and her cooking is so bad it ain't fit for slopping hogs. [Both the Clydesdale Scale and the Reverse Clydesdale Scale can be used by ladies to describe their preference in men.]

Bebe (Gonzales County): pronounced Beeb, not Be-Be since the final "e" is silent [According to legend, the local residents were struggling with selecting a name when a traveling drummer for the Bee Bee Baking Powder company happened to blanket the town with posters and suggested the name to the postmaster.]

Become: make, as in "I believe Betty is gonna make a hairdresser."

Bed: a night spot

Bed, crowded: they're sleeping heads and tails

Bed a field: create rows for planting

Bedtime: roosting time

Bed springs, used: redneck television antenna when nailed to the roof of a cabin or trailer house

Bedding: straw, wood shavings, or other material used to make the floor of a horse stall a little softer and more comfortable

Bedias (Grimes County): pronounced Ba-DEE-us; named for the Bidai Indians

Bedraggled: 1. drag-assed 2. looks like a shedding rooster after a rainstorm

Bedtime: roosting time

Bee sting: a small amount of Brahma blood in a cow

Bee sting hump: a very small hump on top of a cow's withers like a Brahma cow

Bee yard: an area where beehives are kept

Beef club: In the days before refrigeration, families would band together and each would supply one live cow. Each week, one steer would be slaughtered and the meat divided among the families. This allowed for fresh meat regularly without worry about spoilage.

Beefs: finished (fattened) steers that are ready for slaughter

Beehive: bee gum

Beer: 1. cowboy Koolaid 2. Colorado Koolaid (Coors) 3. belly fertilizer, which implies that if you drink beer you will grow a big belly 4. fertilizer for raisin' hell 5. kidney wash (or flush) 6. something you don't wanna reload with if your nerves are shot

Beer, disguised: Baptist tea, which is beer served without the foam in an iced tea glass [Baptist tea is most frequently served in dry areas of Texas where beer is illegal.]

Beer, non-alcoholic: like making love in the bottom of a boat, damn close to water

Beer drinker, serious: 1. can hold more beer than a gopher hole 2. drinks like he was weaned with beer *See also Coffee drinker, avid*

Beer foam: calf slobber; also used for meringue on pie

Beer, bad: 1. ought to be poured back into the horse where it came from 2. coyote slobber 3. panther pee

Beeville (Bee County): pronounced as "ville" rather than "vul"

Begin: 1. "Take it away, Leon" [This is a reference to Bob Wills. When he was ready to get started playing a tune, he would ask Leon McAuliffe to "take it away, Leon."] 2. commence to 3. cut loose with 4. set in, as in "You be home before darkness sets in." 5. scratch a fiddle, which means begin playing 6. get on with the opera *See also Start*

Begin an oil well: spud it in

Begin slow: gotta learn to ride before you can do any cowboying

Beginning: 1. the get-go 2. first rattle out of the box 3. the ball's open 4. trigger time, which means it's time to pull the trigger and get started 5. got a toe hold

Beginning to understand: beginning to see some daylight [You've been in the dark but you're finally beginning to understand, so some light is being shed on the subject.]

Behavior, foolish: cuttin' the fool

Behind: 1. put on a postage stamp and mail yourself to catch up 2. coming up short in the keeping-up department 3. bringing up the rear like the tail of an old cow

Belief, strong: hide bound about that

Believe me (bleeve me): 1. if I'm lying, I'm dying 2. if I tell you there will be a dance, you can tune your fiddle 3. if I say a flea can pull a plow, you can hitch him up 4. if I say a katydid can pull a freight train, you can hitch him up and clear the tracks 5. if I say a jackass can lay an egg, you can start gathering twigs for a nest 6. if I tell you it's gonna come a rain, you can set out the catch barrel 7. if I tell you it's Halloween, you can put on your mask 8. if I say it's Christmas, you can hang up your stocking 9. if I say a hen dips snuff, you'll find the can under her wing *See also Absolutely; Guaranteed; Fact; Trustworthy; Yes*

Believed: 1. lapped it up like it was the gospel 2. took it, hook, line, sinker, and bobber

Bellowing: like a new made steer

Bells (Grayson County): original name was Gospel Ridge because of all the churches in the area, but when all the bells started ringing they made so much noise the name was changed

Belly, large: banjo-belly

Belly robber: term frequently applied to the ranch cook *See also Cook*

Belton/Temple area: Centroplex

Bench: plain rising up from a lowland area

Bend over: 1. hunker down 2. rest on your haunches

Benedict: an Aggie that got married

Benhur (Limestone County): named for the epic novel *Ben Hur*, written by Lew Wallace, former Union general in the Civil War

Bergheim (Kendal County): pronounced BURG-heim

Bessie's Bottoms: area north of Jefferson, Texas, where a former prostitute called Bessie was murdered. At the time of her death, Bessie was the mistress of Abraham Rothschild who was distantly related to the famous Rothschilds of Europe. Rothschild was tried for the murder, but a jury that is thought to have been bribed set him free.

Best: 1. pick of the litter 2. top rung on the ladder 3. nickel plated 4. cream of the crop 5. top drawer 6. on the blue chip list

Bet: risk, as in "I'd risk all my egg money on you not being able to eat six saltine crackers in one minute."

Betrayed: 1. sold 'em down the river 2. sold the horse right out from under him 3. let down her milk to the wrong man [You can't take a cow's milk; she has to let it down to someone she trusts.]

Better, slightly: a tick above, as in "Mary Lou's Yankee brother is a just a tick above being absolutely worthless."

Bettie (Upshur County): named for "Aunt Bettie" Anderson, an early settler

Between: betwixt

Between the eyes: 1. between the runnin' lights 2. in the middle of his peepers

Beverly Hills (McLennan County): Yes, there is a Beverly Hills, Texas, which is a suburb of Waco; pronounced Heals instead of Hills in Texas.

Bevo: Longhorn mascot of the University of Texas

Beware: 1. something that sounds too good to be true is probably illegal 2. dead hornets can still sting 3. dead snakes can still bite

Bewildered: kerflummuxed

Bewitched: pixilated

Bexar County: pronounced Bear or, for the old-timers, Bay-are *See also San Antonio*

Beyond hope: a gone goose

Bible: marryin' book

Bible cake: a cake made from a recipe in scriptures; for example, for eggs it would be Jeremiah 17:11, "As the partridge sitteth on eggs and hatcheth them not." Any ingredient needed for a Bible cake, a favorite at church socials, can be specified by a different scripture.

Bible puncher: 1. preacher 2. religious person noted for frequently quoting the holy text

Bicycle chain: roller chain

Bicycling: rodeo practice of spurring with one foot, then the other, which somewhat resembles the action of riding a bicycle

Biddies: baby chickens

Big: 1. bigun 2. bigger 'n Dallas 3. could shade an elephant

Big as: 1. a Brazos riverboat 2. the side of a barn 3. a killing hog 4. a four-bit cigar 5. all of Texas or all of outside *See also Large*

Big building: *See Building, large*

Big headed: his head is getting too big for his toupee

Big mouth: *See Mouth, large*

Big person: 1. fills up a room like he was wearing it 2. looks like half of him ought to be rotating over an open spit, which refers, of course, to barbecuing a side of beef 3. Big Tex wears his hand-me-down jeans [Big Tex is the giant cowboy who greets visitors to the Texas State Fair in Dallas. His jeans size is 256.] *See also Large person*

Big spender: big butter and egg man. When Texas Guinan owned her famous nightclub in New York, she often greeted guests with Hello, Sucker. One night she asked a sucker where he was from and he said he was a dairy farmer from Wisconsin. For the entire evening Texas referred to him as her big butter and egg man. The saying, which may or may not have been a Guinan original, eventually became a country favorite to describe a big spender.

Big Spring (Howard County): correct pronunciation (and spelling) is Big Spring. However, generations of Texans, including a lot of people from the town itself, have grown up saying Big Springs. It has been rumored that schoolteachers will accept either spelling. The name came from a large natural spring that inspired people to settle in the area.

Big trouble: *See Trouble, big time*

Big, strong, and stupid: big as a gorilla, strong as a gorilla, and about half as smart as a gorilla

Bigamist: rasslin' two alligators at the same time

Bigamy: 1. two rites that make a wrong 2. one wife too many, which, some people believe, can also be used for monogamy

Bikini: 1. a bait wiggler 2. a troll suit

Bikini, small: doesn't have enough material to make a petticoat for a pissant

Binoculars: 1. bring-'em-up-close glasses 2. cheaters

Bird dog: an Aggie without a date who becomes a third wheel by joining another Aggie and his date

Birdfoot violets: rooster heads

Birome (Hill County): correct pronunciation is what Nero might have said as he watched Rome burn, BYE-rome; named for Bickham and Jerome Cartwright, who owned the land on which the town was located

Biscuit: 1. sourdough bullet 2. hot rock 3. gravy sponge

Biscuit, broke: biscuit made by pinching off the dough with fingers as opposed to using a cutting instrument such as a can or glass

Biscuit, cut: biscuit formed by cutting dough with a biscuit cutter, tin can, glass, etc.

Biscuit, failed to rise: squatted but forget to jump

Biscuit, good: melt-in-your-mouth, light-as-a-feather good (also used for anything delicious)

Biscuit, hard: could cut a diamond with its edge

Biscuit, heavy: could double for an anvil or a shot put

Biscuit, large: 1. belly breakers 2. cathead biscuits 3. hoghead biscuits 4.

would only take nine of them to make a dozen 5. the Confederacy could have used them for cannon balls

Biscuit, scratch: one made using nothing from a refrigerated container, the kind grandma used to make

Biscuit block: a large block of oak (or ash) on 3 or 4 legs about waist high used for beating biscuit dough and forming the biscuits

Bit: 1. one-eighth of a dollar [In the early days of the Republic of Texas, coins where scarce so dollar coins were cut into eight equal parts (bits). The bits where then used as if they were coins. This process, which may have originated in England, had a defect in that one bit equaled twelve and a half cents, which was not a manageable amount. Thus, bits were generally used in combinations of twos since two bits equaled twenty-five cents, four bits equaled fifty cents, six bits equaled seventy-five cents, and eight bits equaled a dollar. This system eventually led to the most famous high school cheer of all time.] 2. metal device used to control horses *See also Bar bit; Curb bit; Mexican bit; Pelham bit; Snaffle bit; Spade bit; Spanish bit*

Bit house: an early store or saloon where everything sold cost one bit (12.5 cents)

Biting rig: combination bridle, harness pad, and cupper used to help teach a horse to flex at the poll

Bitter: as gar broth

Bivins (Cass County): pronounced BIV-ins, not Bye-vins; named for J.K. and Frank H. Bivins, owners of a local sawmill

Black as: 1. pitch or tar 2. the inside of a pocket (or coffin) 3. a cow's tongue 4. the ace of spades 5. the devil's riding boots 6. the bottom of a dry well 7. the inside of an unopened coffee can 8. midnight

Black baldie cow: a cow that is black everywhere except her head from the ears forward, which is white

Black chaparral: *See Chaparral*

Black motley-faced cow: a black baldie with black spots on her head

Black pepper: dirt

Black tape: tape used to fix anything from hemlines to electric lines

Black waxie: black, rich farmland running from around Denison to the Temple area [Before 1900 Eastern insurance companies would usually make loans only in this area of Texas.]

Black-eyed peas: cowpeas

Blackstrap molasses: *See Sorghum*

Blackwell (Coke-Nolan Counties): pronounced Black-w.l., not Black-well; originally called James or Jamestown but when the Orient Railroad came to town, the name was changed to honor a stockholder in the line

Blame: 1. tie the can on him 2. put the saddle on him 3. tie the knot in his tail 4. fault, as in "You can't fault him for stealing that goat 'cause his kids need milk and they ain't seen their mother since she run off with the preacher."

Blanco (Blanco County): pronounced BLANK-oh; both the county and the town, which is the county seat, are named for the nearby Blanco River

Blanket: 1. lap robe 2. soogan

Blanket (Brown County): named for nearby Blanket Creek; creek supposedly named by a group of surveyors who came upon some Tonkawa Indians who had spread their blankets over some bushes to dry them after a rain shower

Blanket, thin: 1. hen skin blanket 2. can lay under it and count the cracks in the ceiling

Blanton (Hill County): pronounced BLANT-un

B

Blaze: white marking on the muzzle of a horse that extends from the forehead to the nostrils

Bleecher: blonde cheerleader

A&M Bleed meet: Texas A&M upperclassmen, also called dew-heads, reprimanding fish for "head-ins"

Bleeding: 1. like a stuck pig 2. like a dehorned bull 3. like a chicken with its head cut off

Bleiblerville (Austin County): pronounced BLI-ber-ville; named for Robert Bleiber who owned a store at the site

Bless his heart: a magical Texas phrase that allows you to say something really tacky about someone without seeming to be tacky, as in "That ol' Bubba, he ain't got the sense God gave a screwdriver, bless his heart."

Blessing (Matagorda County): The founder of the town was so happy over the arrival of the railroad he wanted to name the town Thank God, Texas, but the post office refused so he settled on Blessing.

Blewett (Uvalde County): pronounced BLUE-it; believed to have been named for John Blewett Smyth, a Beaumont entrepreneur who used the local bituminous limestone to develop a new paving material for roads

Blind as: 1. a bat 2. a fence post 3. a post hole 4. a snubbin' post 5. a coil of bobbed war

Blind bucker: a horse that loses his head and bucks into anything, like fences, gates, etc.; not a favorite ride of cowboys

Blind gunner: cupid

Blinds: area behind the engine and in front of the first car on a train

Blink: bat an eyelash

Blinking, quickly: eyelids batting like a Baptist preacher in the front row at a striptease

Blivit: sound made when you put ten pounds of manure in a five-pound sack and hit someone with it

Blonde: 1. palomino 2. straw haired

Blood worm: internal parasite in a horse

Bloodroot: corn flower

Bloody: looked like he'd been rasslin' a dozen horned toads [A popular legend has it that horned toads can spit blood when excited. The truth is, they expel the blood through their eyes. No matter how they do it, if you handle a horned toad, you may come away looking like you were in a knife fight with an octopus.] *See also Cut up; Knife fight victim*

Blow, misdirected: a mislick, as in "I swung hard at ol' Billy Fred, but it was a mislick. He then proceeded to whup the fire out of me."

Blower: provides air for the stacks on a locomotive

Blowing: like a bull snake at a barking dog

Blowing a stirrup: when a bronc rider's foot slips out of the stirrup; not always a disqualification, but always a penalty; usually results in the cowboy being thrown

Blue as: pinkeye medicine

Blue moon: the second full moon in a month, which is very rare

Bluebonnet flower: *See Sacrifice*

Bluff: 1. rattling his saber or the more modern version, rattling his rockets [While serving as president, Lyndon Johnson said, "I am not going to rattle our rockets. I am not going to bluff with our bombs. I am going to keep our guard up at all times and our hand out."]

Blurry as: a new moon in a thick fog

Blush: 1. reddened up 2. turned red in the face 3. the only thing that cannot be counterfeited 4. man is the only animal that can or needs to blush

Boastful: as full of wind as a corn-eating horse

Boat: The two happiest days in a man's life are the day he buys a boat and the day he sells it.

Boat, flat bottomed: john boat

Body, squatty: 1. built like a rain barrel 2. built like an apartment refrigerator 3. built like a deep freeze chest 4. built like a refrigerator up to the handle

Boerne (Kendal County): pronounced BURN-ee; originally named Tusculum, the name was changed to honor Ludwig Boerne, a German poet and political activist

Bogata (Red River County): pronounced Ba-GOAT-ah, no kidding. When the post office rejected Maple Springs as the name, postmaster J.E. Horner suggested Bogota after the capital of Columbia where his hero Simon Bolivar won a victory in 1814.

Body brush: a brush with firm but not overly stiff bristles that is used for brushing a horse's body

Body lice: cooties

Bog spavin: an unsoundness of a horse's leg that causes the hock to swell

Bogging them in: said when a rider fails to spur (scratch) the horse

Boil: risin'

Boiled over: term applied to a horse in a rodeo that tries to start bucking before the chute is opened

Bois d'arc: pronounced bow-dark [The wood from the bois d'arc tree is very hard and very straight, which makes it perfect for fence posts if you can find a way to cut the trees down. In the early days of Texas, before concrete was used, bricks made of bois d'arc wood were used to pave streets. They became obsolete when someone discovered they were very slick when wet. Bois d'arc was favored by Comanche Indians for use in making bows. Also called Osage orange. The fruit of the bois d'arc tree is called a horse apple.]

Bold as: 1. a blind burglar 2. a 400-pound ballerina

Boling (Wharton County): pronounced BO-ling, named for Mary Boling Vineyard, daughter of Robert Boling, who had the town plat surveyed

Bolivar (Denton County): pronounced Bowl-le-ver, not Bo-la-ver [The county is Dent-un. Soon after his arrival in the area, Henry Austin, a cousin of Stephen F. Austin, established a cotton plantation on the Brazos River and named it Bolivar, the name subsequently used when a community was established nearby.]

Boll weevil (bow-we-vul): 1. insect that eats and ruins cotton 2. also used to describe people who screw things up

Bolt turning rules: righty tighty, lefty loosy

Bomarton (Baylor County): pronounced Bo-Murr-ton; this small town, not far from Seymour, was named for W. H. Bomar, an early settler

Bon Weir (Newton County): pronounced Bahn we're; the name was derived from B. F. Bonner, manager, and R. W. Wier, surgeon, of the Kirby Lumber Company

Bone yard (dominoes): where extra dominoes (widow or kitty) are placed; can be located anyplace on the table outside the field of action

Bonham (Fannin County): named for Alamo hero James Butler Bonham; family descendants insist the name is pronounced Bone-um. In Texas, however, the town name and the name of the Alamo hero are always pronounced Bon-um.

Bonita (Montague County): pronounced Bow-neat-ah; name came either from Bonita Hansen, daughter of a railroad engineer, or

B

from the Spanish "bonita" which was suggested by a surveyor who was taken by the beauty of the area

Bono (Johnson County): pronounced BOW-no, which is supposed to be Latin for "good"

Book, dull: has about as much action as a snake's hips [This saying could also be used for a dull movie or television program.]

Book, poor: biggest problem is that the covers are too far apart

Book, sultry: can produce more heat than a Mexican cookbook

Book, worn: has more wear on it than a *Playboy* magazine on a troop ship

Booster pump: a pump on a water well that delivers water when the wind isn't blowing hard enough to turn the windmill

Bootless: sock-footed

Boots, pointed toed: cockroach killers, so called because you can get the roach in the corner

Boots, repaired: had my boots retreaded, which means they got new half soles

Boots, worn: 1. could stand on a dime and tell if heads or tails was up 2. soles so thin you could read a small print Bible through them in bad light 3. so thin you could see the wrinkles in my socks

Booze: *See Beer; Champagne; Liquor; Tequila; Whiskey*

Borden County: county seat is Gail; both the town and the county were named for Gail Borden, the famous inventor who was a printer in Texas during the revolution

Border-blaster: extremely powerful, unregulated radio stations that were once located just across the Texas border in Old Mexico [These stations, some of which were reported to generate almost a million watts, could be heard all over Texas and a good portion of North America. The famous disk jockey "Wolf Man" Jack made his reputation on one of these stations.]

Bore: 1. only time he lights up the room is when he leaves 2. can stay longer in an hour than most people can in a week 3. has the personality of an empty glass (or a dishrag) 4. got all the sparkle of a bottle of champagne left open for a week

Bored: 1. enjoyed about all this I can stand 2. a frog in a skillet would have more fun 3. a wooden Indian in a forest fire would have more fun

Borger (Hutchinson County): pronounced Bore-gurr, although some folks in neighboring towns have been known to call it Booger

Boring: 1. downtown dull [a reference to there usually being very little to do in the downtown section of a small country community] 2. as much fun as staking out Grant's tomb *See also Dull*

Boring as: 1. a nudist colony without a peephole in the fence 2. a fishing trip with a game warden 3. a balloon race at night (no one can see what is going on) 4. a school play your kid isn't in 5. scraping dead flies off flypaper 6. the unemployment line

Born loser: 1. if he was the last man on earth, the last woman on earth would be his sister (or mother-in-law) 2. if he quit smoking, he'd get hit by a truck 3. if he bought a pumpkin farm, they'd cancel Halloween 4. if he bought a Christmas tree farm, they'd cancel Christmas (or Santa Claus would die)

Bosal (bozal): a leather or rawhide strap around a horse's head just above the mouth; used when riding or breaking an unruly horse; also called nose hitch

Bosque County: pronounced BOS-key and is Spanish for "woods;" the county seat is Meridian

Boss: 1. arena director, the person in charge of the arena where a rodeo is held 2. lead steer 3. big auger 4. range manager 5. ramrod 6. honcho 7. big biscuit in the pan 8. roost ruler 9. wagon boss [When the boss is around, it's good advice to work hard, look worried, and keep a hobble on your lip.] *See also Important person; Leader*

Boss, unreasonable: don't have ulcers but he is a carrier

Boston (Bowie County): pronounced BOSS-ton, never Baastun; a small town in East Texas not too far from Naples

Bother: *See Pester*

Bothersome: worrisome

Bots: internal parasite in a horse

Bottle/can opener: church key

Bottom man: in boot making, the man who does the mounting, lasting, hand-welt sewing, and attaches the soles and heels

Bounce: has more bounce than a volleyball game in a nudist colony

Bourbon: corn liquor

Bourbon, in coffee: coffee lace or laced coffee

Bovina (Parmer County): pronounced Bow-veen-ah [originally called Bull Town because trains traveling through the area usually had to stop and chase cattle off the tracks. When the post office was established, they wanted a name that sounded a little more sophisticated so they settled on a variation of bovine, which means cattle and is generally pronounced bow-vine. However, the name of the town is never pronounced Bowvine-ah.]

Bovine: cattle, buffalo, elk, moose, etc.

Bowie (Montague County): If you want to be laughed out of Texas, just say Bow-ee instead of the

correct Boo-ee; named for Alamo hero James Bowie, as was Bowie County.

Bowie knife: *See Knife, Large*

Bowl: tub

Bowlegged: 1. saddle warped 2. banjo legged 3. couldn't catch a pig in a ditch or a phone booth 4. a yearling calf could run under him without touching either leg 5. warp legged 6. can't sit in an arm chair 7. looks like she's been carrying watermelons between her legs 8. could stand over a barrel and not touch the sides

Bowlegged as: a barrel hoop

Box turtle: *See Terrapin*

Box party: party where the young ladies prepare a meal and pack in a box (or basket) and young men bid for the right to eat the meal with the young lady

Box stall: a stable large enough for the horse to turn around in

Boxelder (Red River County): pronounced BOX-el-der; named for the trees along the banks of nearby creeks

Boy: 1. hen wrangler 2. whistle britches 3. frying size 4. muchacho [Like a canoe, a boy works best when paddled from the rear.]

Boy, young: his daddy was a pistol and he's a son of a gun, but he ain't loaded yet

Braggart: 1. big talker, little doer 2. wind-belly 3. flannel mouth 4. all gurgle and no guts 5. truth stretcher 6. blows harder than a middlin' hurricane 7. talked himself out of a place at the bar 8. trying to build a reputation on what he's planning to do tomorrow 9. if BS was music, he could play the Philharmonic 10. even brags about the number of sit-down holes in his outhouse [Texans have long been known as braggarts. One Texan went off to fight in the Civil War claiming "I can beat the damn Yankees with a broomstick." When he returned after the war, minus an arm and so much the worse for wear, someone asked him about his boast. "I could have beat 'em with a broomstick," he replied, "'cept I couldn't get 'em to fight with broomsticks."]

Bragging: 1. struttin' your okra 2. only blow your own horn when you're in a band [Remember, the hen that lays the biggest egg usually does the least cackling.]

Brake club: a heavy oak club used by a railroad brakeman to turn the brakes on a railroad car in the days before air brakes; also used to beat tramps and hobos trying to "hitch" a ride on the train.

Brakie: railroad brakeman

Brand: 1. marking livestock with the brand that represents your ranch or the one you're working for 2. a cow's return address because if a neighbor finds a stray with your brand on it, he's supposed to either return it or ask you to come and get it [Most cowboys prefer brands big enough to be read in the moonlight.]

Brand, unreadable: a quien sabe (kin savvy) brand, which is any complicated or ornate brand that can't be easily read by anyone except the owner; *quien sabe* is Spanish for "Who knows"; also known as a fool brand

Brand, registered: To be legal, a brand must be registered in the brand book at the county courthouse. If you run cattle in more than one county, your brand must be registered in each county in which you operate.

Brand book: the book in the county courthouse where local brands are recorded. [When doing genealogy research, if you find your ancestors were involved in ranching in Texas, be sure to check the brand book in the county where they lived to determine what brand they used.]

Branding chute: a narrow chute designed to hold cattle while they are branded

Branding iron: a metal rod with a handle on one end and the brand formed on the other [The brand end is heated in a fire and then used to singe the design in the animal's hair. The surface of the brand that actually touches the animal is the burning surface. Today, old branding irons are collector's items.]

Brand new: brand spanking new

Brashear (Hopkins County): pronounced Bru-shear, not Brashear; named for Joseph Brashear, who surveyed the site

Brassiere: 1. flopper stopper 2. over-the-shoulder boulder holder 3. double-barrel slingshot or catapult 4. marble pouch

Brassiere, large: could use her bra for a bowling ball bag

Brave: 1. could win an Audie Murphy act-alike contest [Famous Texan who became America's most decorated hero in World War II.] 2. can't be stampeded, which is how many early Texas Rangers were described, and it probably holds true today 3. not afraid to go to hell alone [One of the most famous Texas Rangers of all time was Jack Hays. Chief Flaco of the Lipan Indians once said of Hays, "Me and Red Wing not afraid to go to hell together. Captain Jack Hays brave, not afraid to go alone." Perhaps the best description of brave is he's kin to William Travis. He was the acting commander of the Alamo. In his famous letter, called the most patriotic in American history, Travis said, "I shall never surrender or retreat." He didn't.]

Brave as: 1. a rodeo clown 2. a high school teacher 3. the man that ate the first oyster (or egg) 4. a bigamist [Surely any man with more than one wife is the bravest of them all.]

Brave enough to: 1. eat in a boom-town café, which were notorious for serving food that wasn't exactly pleasing to the palate 2. marry a woman who's been widowed three times 3. break up a fight between two red-headed women

Bravery: 1. true grit 2. a condition brought on by necessity or a few cold beers 3. what you have to have when you run out of options

Bravery, sort of: even a rabbit will kick a coyote when it's dead

Brazoria (Brazoria County): pronounced Bra-ZOR-e-ah; the town was established by John Austin, who selected the name "for the single reason that I know of none like it in the world"

Brazos (County and River): pronounced BRAZ-us; the name is of Spanish origin and means "arms" or "arms of God"; county seat is Bryan

Bread: 1. gun wadding 2. white bread 3. light bread 4. deal (Aggie)

Break a horse: tame or gentle it

Breakaway: 1. tying a rope to a saddle horn with a string lighter than the rope so the string will break at a calculated time 2. barrier across the roping box 3. jerk line to the roper's belt

Breakfast: the most important meal of the day 'cause if you ain't home by then you're in big trouble

Breaking the barrier: In timed events in rodeo, there is a rope barrier designed to give the calf or steer a head start. If the contestant rides through the barrier before it is released, he "breaks the barrier" and is penalized ten seconds. The rope barrier is called a breakaway.

Breast collar: *See Martingale*

Breast harness: harness across front of horse to keep saddle from working backwards

Breasts: 1. bobbers 2. begonias 3. kitties

Breasts, false: 1. hidden persuaders 2. flat fixers 3. flyin' under false colors, which is derived from ships flying a flag other than the correct one

Breasts, large: 1. the eighth and ninth wonders of the world 2. bra busters 3. quite a pair to draw to 4. carrying a big rack 5. only dates mountain climbers 6. they call her melon 'cause it looks like she's carryin' a couple of honeydews in her shirt

Breasts, small: 1. chicken breasted 2. her chest looks like two BB's on an ironing board 3. no bigger than moles on a chigger 4. could put her bra on backwards and not notice the difference 5. looks like a bed without pillows 6. don't wear an A cup, she wears a saucer 7. wears a thimble cup bra

Breath, bad: 1. could smell it over the phone 2. wolf (or coyote) breath 3. smells like he used a skunk tail for a mustache [Remember, no matter how bad the breath smells, it is still better than having no breath at all.]

Breath, strong: 1. as gasoline, kerosene, No. 2 diesel, turpentine, or Clorox 2. enough to use as a clothesline and hang all the wash in Texas on it 3. as if he had supper in a coyote den 4. could light the stove just by breathing on it 5. so strong he can't wear his false teeth 'cause they might dissolve

Breathing hard: puttin' out enough air to run a gin whistle

Breckenridge (Stephens County): pronounced BRACK-in-ridge [The original name was Picketville, which may have been in honor of rancher and noted cowboy Bill Pickett. When the county was organized, the name was changed to honor Vice President John C. Breckinridge although someone didn't know how to spell the name correctly.]

Breeding: hooking up a live steam locomotive to a dead steam locomotive, via a pipe, to provide steam to run the blower and the atomizer in the engine; the railroad equivalent of jump-starting

Breetching: harness around a horse's rear end to keep the saddle from working forward; also the part of a work harness that lets the animal back a load

Bremond (Robertson County): pronounced BRE-mond; named for railroad financier Paul Bremond, who believed he was guided by the spirit of Moseley Baker, a hero of the Texas Revolution

Brenham (Washington County): pronounced BREN-um; originally Hickory Grove, the name was changed to honor Dr. Richard F. Brenham, a hero of the Republic of Texas; the home of the little creamery that makes Blue Bell ice cream

Bridge gang: group of men assigned specifically to maintain and repair railroad bridges

Bridle [fresno]: 1. leather strapping that connects the reins to the bit 2. head gear that allows a rider to instruct a horse to go forward, stop, or turn to either side

Bridle chain: a short chain used to attach the reins to the horse's bridle

Bridle ring: the ring at each end of the bit where the reins or bridle chains are attached

Brief interval: whip stitch

Bright as: 1. a pewter button 2. a fresh minted penny

Bright person: have to put him in the closet to get the sun to come up

Bring: 1. fetch it with you 2. tote it along for the ride

Broadcast sewn: crops planted by throwing the seed randomly rather than using a planter [Frequently, seed thrown from a tow sack using the step and throw method which is throw seed, take a step, throw more seed.]

Broaddus (San Augustine County): pronounced BROAD-us

Broadview (Lubbock County): named by railroad executives who got a broad view when they looked out the windows of their private cars

Broadway (Crosby County): name suggested by Shorty Reynolds, a store owner, because it described the wide prairies

A&M **Broccoli:** tree tops

Broke (financial condition): 1. if it cost a nickel to use the toilet, I'd have to use the sink 2. if Cadillacs were $10 apiece, I couldn't afford the hood ornament off a Chevette 3. can't even entertain a doubt 4. broke as Lazarus and he had a dog 5. down to my last chip 6. couldn't take the first hand in a penny ante game 7. couldn't change my mind or pay attention 8. if a trip around the world cost a dollar, I wouldn't have enough to get to the Texas state line 9. what happens when you have more yearnings than you do earnings 10. got cobwebs in my billfold See also Destitute; Poor; Poverty

Broken: 1. broke down 2. as a busted trace chain 3. out of whack 4. out of kilter

Broken, almost: borderline broke

Broken, often: been broke more than all the Ten Commandments put together

Broken mouth: a cow with one or more missing teeth

Broker: somebody who helps make you broker

Bronc: short for bronco; generally a mean, often vicious, unbroken horse

Bronc, wild: the wildest bronc is always the one you rode somewhere else and none of the "witnesses" are handy

Bronc buster: *See Bronc rider*

Bronc halter: *See Saddle bronc riding*

Bronc rider: a cowboy who breaks horses as a steady business; sometimes called a twister or bronc buster. [To make a living, a bronc rider is said to need a light head and a heavy seat.]

Bronc rider, good: 1. sits up there in the saddle like he was going to Sunday school in a rocking chair 2. can stick to a saddle like a postage stamp to a letter

Bronchitis: brownkitties

Bronco: simply bronc to most Texans

Bronco (Yoakum County): pronounced BRONK-oh, not Bronco; the name was suggested by a traveling salesman after he saw a cowboy riding a bucking horse

Bronco steer: term used to describe a crazy, wild steer

Bronte (Coke County): pronounced Bront, not Bront-E or Bront-A; originally called Oso but when a suggested change to Bronco was rejected this name was selected in honor of British novelist Charlotte Bronte

Broodmare: female horse used for breeding

Brookeland (Sabine County): pronounced BROOKE-lan since the "d" is silent; named for John C. Brooke, who served as first postmaster

Broom: dirt mover

Broom sedge: straw stalks left in the field after harvesting

Broom tail: 1. a wild mare 2. a Western range horse, usually of uncertain breed, that is frequently not kept in the best of shape [The name comes from the fact that the animal's tail usually looks like a broom.]

Broome (Sterling County): pronounced Broom since the "e" is silent; named for rancher C. A. Broome

Brown bag it: 1. take your lunch to work in a brown paper sack 2. take your favorite sippin' whiskey into a Bring Your Own Bottle (B.Y.O.B.) joint

Bruni (Webb County): pronounced BREW-knee; named for Italian immigrant Antonio Bruni who owned a store in the area

Brush, thick: 1. so thick the snakes had to crawl around it 2. so thick a starving coyote wouldn't go in there after a wounded rabbit 3. rabbits had to climb a tree to look out

Brush arbor: a temporary shelter used for revivals

Brush popper: a cowboy who goes after cattle in thick brush

Buck: refers to the jumping action of a horse; a lot of Texans say pitch, as in "That old nag can pitch with the best of 'em."

Buck acher: term used to describe someone who shakes when very scared

Buck dancing: a cross between a jig and a tap dance (also called buck n' wing)

Buck fever: what happens when you get so excited, you freeze; usually refers to hunting deer but can be used anytime someone locks up

Buck Naked (Parker County): No, this is not a nudist colony. In fact, it's not even a town anymore. A promoter started the town on three acres near Weatherford back in the 1970s, but it didn't last long. However, there's some talk the town may be reorganized somewhere else, and if that comes to pass, it'll be pronounced Buck Nekked.

Buck rake: a plow used to pick up hay from windrows and move it to the baler

Buck rein: four-strand, looseplait, rope made of a combination of cotton, sisal, and polyester

B

Buck strap: a leather loop attached to a saddle horn that is used as a hand hold by bronc riders

Buck-toothed: could eat corn through a picket fence

Buck-kneed: a condition where the horse's knees are bent forward

Buckeroo: a cowboy who generally favors fancy boots, outlandish dress, and lots of silver ornaments on himself and his horse; from the Spanish vaquero [Buckeroos are generally found in places like Colorado and Hollywood.]

Buckeroo roll: large, rolled-up cuff on the legs of a buckeroo's jeans

Bucket, for catching water: 1. drip pot if it's catching water inside the house from holes in the roof 2. rain catcher if it's catching water outside during a rain

Bucket, wooden: piggin

Bucket calf: calf raised on a bottle or a bucket with a nipple attached

Bucking strap: strap around a horse's belly that helps to make him jump during a rodeo event without causing any injuries

Buckle, large: big enough to use as a satellite dish

Buckle bunny: female rodeo groupie who pursues cowboys wearing championship buckles; also called buckle chaser

Buda (Hays County): This one is a little strange. The "Bu" is pronounced like the "beau" in beautiful. Said correctly, its Beau-da not Boo-da. A sign as you leave town says "Keep Texas Budaful," which makes a lot more sense when you know the proper pronunciation. The name is a corruption of "viuda" which is Spanish for "widow." Buda is home of Texas Hatters.

Budget: 1. like a girdle, it takes care of the bulge in one place and it pops out somewhere else 2. like a girdle, there usually ain't enough to cover everything

Budget, small: poor boying it

Buffalo (Leon County): The town bills itself as the crossroads of Texas. Each time the Dallas Cowboys played the Buffalo Bills in the Super Bowl the name was temporarily changed to Blue Star.

Buffalo butt: condition in a cow where the conformation of her butt is very poor

Buffoon: scoggin

Bug Tussle (Fannin County): Yes, there really was a town in Texas named Bug Tussle, but it's gone now. There are several suggestions for how the town was named, but many believe it came from the fact that there was little to do in the area other than have picnics and watch tumble bugs tussle with each other.

Bug-eyed: a condition where a horse's vision is impaired by protruding eyes

Building, fancy: fancier then a two-story outhouse

Building, haunted: a voodoo palace

Building, large: 1. big enough to hold an indoor deer hunt 2. the rough riders could have held maneuvers inside it 3. could use it as a hanger for the *Spruce Goose* [The *Spruce Goose,* the world's largest plane, was built out of wood by Texan Howard Hughes. The plane only flew one time and today is in a museum in California.]

Building, ugly: has all the earmarks of an eyesore

Built well: ain't much to look at but it's hell for sturdy

Bula (Bailey County): The same rules used for Buda apply here; it's Beulah, not Boo-la. It is believed the town was named for either the daughter of R.A. Oakes, a Methodist minister, or the wife of postmaster W.H. Thorn.

Bull: 1. adult male bovine capable of reproducing 2. cow brute 3. top cow 4. superfluous conversation which can be good or bad (Aggie) 5. military officer (Aggie)

Bull chain: twisted link chain like the portion of a snow chain which grips the snow

Bull dogin': *See Steer wrestling*

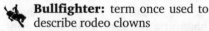 **Bullfighter:** term once used to describe rodeo clowns

Bull riding: premier rodeo event that has been called the longest eight seconds in a cowboy's life. Each bull rider provides his own strap for bull riding, which is usually a sisal (grass) or Manila rope with a suitcase handle woven into it. The rope is wrapped around the bull and held in place by the bull rider's hand in the handle. A large cow bell attached to the rope helps aggravate the bull. When the chute opens, the bull comes out determined to shed the rider, and more often than not he's successful. Spurring is not required but it does add to the total score. A perfect score, which has never been recorded, is 100 points, 50 for the bull and 50 for the rider. When the horn sounds, the cowboy gets off as best he can. If possible, a pick-up man rides up and the contestant leaps onto his horse. Most of the time, the cowboy hits the ground and the rodeo clowns move in to protect the contestant by distracting the bull. The most dangerous part of a bull ride is the cowboy becoming "hung up" in the rigging, unable to free his hand. Since half the score comes from the animal, rodeo bulls are often as famous as the riders. Contestants hope for a "good draw" one with lots of action especially a "spinner" that twists and turns as he jumps. *See also Bullrider's crunch*

Bull rigging: *See Bull riding*

Bull ring: Saturday disciplinary drill for the purpose of removing demerits

Bull session: talk fest

Bull wagon: a double-decker cattle truck

Bull whackers: men who drove oxen and were known for rough ways and rougher language; also called an ox-driver

Bullrider's crunch: grasping the hat brim with a firm, rough hold; used by a bullrider to "set" his hat just before the gate opens

Bullrider's bull: a bull that always gives a challenging ride and produces a high score for those few cowboys able to stay on for the full eight seconds

Bully: 1. big behaver 2. got a carload of big behavior 3. they don't make britches as big as he behaves

Bulverde (Comal County): pronounced Bull-VER-dee; named for Luciano Bulverdo, an early landowner in the area

Bumpkin: just arrived on a load of watermelons (or cantaloupes)

Bumpy as: a 25-pipe cattle guard *See also Handy*

Buna (Jasper County): The same rules used for Buda apply; it's Beau-na, not Boo-na; originally Carrolla after the wealthy Carrol family from Beaumont but the name was changed to honor Buna Corley, a cousin of the family

Bunavista (Hutchinson County): pronounced Bwa-na-vista. The town was established to house government employees during World War II.

Bunch quitter: 1. a horse that habitually quits the remuda and heads off on his own 2. a cowboy who is unreliable and has no sense of loyalty

B

Bunched up: 1. like wild turkeys in a hailstorm 2. like hogs at a trough 3. like cows in a thunderstorm

Burdened: 1. saddled with 2. got an anvil in his shorts 3. heart's heavier than a windmill wrench 4. hitched with a dead mule 5. got a dead chicken hanging around his neck [When Bill Clements ran for governor the first time, he said, "I'm gonna hang Jimmy Carter around John Hill's neck like a dead chicken." He did and it turned out to be more of a burden than Hill could handle.]

Burkburnett (Wichita County): pronounced Burk-burr-net; named for Burk Burnet, founder of the legendary 6666 ranch, which is still going strong today

Burlap bag: 1. tow sack 2. feed sack 3. gunnysack 4. croaker sack

Burned like: 1. a cockroach caught in an electric chair 2. an empty shuck

Burner: a small leather pad that helps prevent wear and tear in the honda on a rope

Burnet (Burnet County): It's Burn-it, durn it, so learn it. Burnet County, however, is pronounced Burr-net.

Burning: *See On fire*

Burro: 1. Colorado mockingbird 2. Mexican canary

Bury: 1. funeralize 2. put to bed with a shovel 3. plant 4. move 'em into stone city

Bus (Greyhound): dog (or gray dog), as in "I'll come for a visit soon as I round up enough money to ride the dog."

Bushland (Potter County): pronounced BUSH-l'nd; originally named for W. H. Bush of Chicago, who owned the land

Busier than: 1. a one-armed stripper 2. a one-armed man in a poison ivy patch

Business: bidness [In Texas, all commerce is bidness, as in the oil bidness, the cattle bidness, the computer bidness, etc. According to Jerry Jones, owner of the Dallas Cowboys, bidness is a contact sport.]

Business, bad: don't even have to lie to the IRS

Business, good: 1. a land office bidness, which refers to the early days of Texas when there was lots of cheap available land and the land office was frequently the busiest around, except for the saloon 2. doing better than a hotel in a boomtown [In boomtowns, bed space was generally very scarce and often rooms were rented in eight-hour shifts, which meant the hotel owners were cleaning up.] 3. doin' better than a boomtown café or saloon, either one of which probably did even better than a boomtown hotel

Business, small: a shirttail outfit

Business advice: 1. never sign anything in the glow of a neon light [Neon lights generally glow in bars and honky-tonks where people are prone to drink, and in gambling casinos, so if you use that light to sign something, such as a contract, you may wake up in the morning wishing you'd used invisible ink.] 2. never enter into a deal with someone who has less money than you have *See also Good business practice*

Business opportunity, good: better than having the neon concession in Las Vegas

Business practice: "Never try to out-trade a man and never let a man out-trade you if you can help it," said Texan Hugh Roy Cullen, who never was out-traded in his life.

Business sense, poor: 1. couldn't run a pumpkin stand if you gave him the pumpkins and the sheriff stopped traffic on the interstate 2. does precision guesswork

Businessman, deceitful: if you buy milk from him you better check it for minnows [Roy Bean once sold milk in San Antonio, Texas. When several customers reported finding minnows in their milk, Roy explained that his cows had been drinking from a nearby creek and must have swallowed the minnows. The excuse didn't hold water, so Roy quickly headed west to become a judge in Pecos, Texas.]

Businessman, going nowhere: on the corporate stepladder

Businessman, small time: just a peanut operator

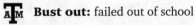 **Bust out:** failed out of school

Bustamante (Zapata County): pronounced Boo-sta-MONT-eh

Bustin' the middies (middles): plowin' between the furrows to get up weeds and loosen the soil to let water soak in

Busy: 1. catching 'em faster than I can string 'em 2. got weeds growing faster than I can hoe 'em 3. hens are laying eggs faster than I can gather 'em 4. just weaving and working, working and weaving 5. got her trottin' harness on

Busy as: 1. a chicken drinking out of a pie pan 2. a zipper in a tight skirt, which has to work all the time just to stay together 3. a pair of jumper cables at a Fourth of July picnic 4. grandma with one hoe and two snakes 5. a barefoot boy on a red ant bed 6. a one-eyed cat watching three mice 7. a one-armed paper hanger 8. a one-legged man in a butt-kicking contest 9. a windsock (or windmill) in a whirlwind 10. a prairie dog after a big rain 11. a coyote chasin' four rabbits 12. bees in a honeysuckle patch 13. an old hen with a young chick 14. a New Orleans bartender during Mardi Gras 15. a termite with a tapeworm 16. a long-nosed weevil in a cotton patch 17. a fiddler's elbow See also Active as

Busybody: gets around so much she runs into herself

Busy day: a handful day, as in harvesting

Busy work: 1. rat killing 2. everyday knitting

Butt, big: See Rear end, large

Butter: 1. cow grease 2. skid grease 3. axle grease (Aggie)

Butter knife: the ultimate tool for a housewife or the inexperienced handy man; a butter knife can be used as a screwdriver, pry bar, putty knife, scrapper, nail puller, and much more

Buy a new vehicle: trade cars (or pickups), as in "I think I'm gonna go down to the Ford house and see if I can trade trucks."

Buzzards: the county hygiene society

Byte: loop in the end of a rope produced when a knot is tied

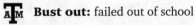 **C.:** Memorial Student Center, Texas A&M

C. F. S.: chicken-fried steak

C.I.A.: College of Innocent Angels

C.Q.: call to quarters, which is mandatory study time

C.R.A.: Central Rodeo Association, which primarily sanctions rodeos in the Southwest. Though not as prestigious as the PRCA, the Central Rodeo Association still puts on fine rodeos and is an excellent organization for cowboys who have to make a living with a regular job. The CRA holds its finals in November at Sulphur Springs, Texas.

C.R.S.: Can't Remember Stuff (expletive deleted)

C.S.A.: Confederate States of America

C.T.: Corps Turd (Corps members)

Cabbage: dead rabbit

Cactus (Moore County): established as an ordnance works in the 1940s; engineers suggested the name, claiming cactus was all they could see on the landscape

Cactus watering schedule: If you have some potted cactus, you may wonder when it should be watered since cactus isn't supposed to need much water. The solution: simply watch the Arizona weather news. They have a lot of cactus so if it rains there, it is an indication that Mother Nature is watering the plants and you should do the same.

Caddo (Stephens County): pronounced CAD-oh, not Kaydough; named for the Caddo Indians

Cadence: Section 1, the Standard

Cadillacking: term used to describe a low-priced car that idles very smoothly

Café: 1. feed lot 2. chili parlor or joint 3. feed trough 4. eatin' ranch 5. greasy spoon 6. greasy sack outfit 7. feed ground 8. grub corral 9. beanery 10. ptomaine tavern

Cajun (in Texas): a bugalee

Calculate: 1. put a pencil to it 2. cipher it

Caldwell (Burleson County): pronounced CALD-w'll; surveyed by the noted George B. Erath and named for Mathew Caldwell, one of the signers of the Texas Declaration of Independence

Calf: 1. cattle of either sex that are less than one year old 2. (dominoes) the smallest non-double in a suit such as six-one which is the calf in the six suit

Calf, motherless: dogie, which is also used for orphan

Calf fries: mountain oysters, prairie oysters, or Oklahoma oysters [The terms are also used to describe lamb,

pig, or turkey fries, all of which are the testicles from the animal that are removed during castration, rolled in batter, and deep fried.]

Calf puller: a mechanical device with a crank and a rope (or chain) used to assist in the birth of a calf

Calf roping: considered by many to be the oldest rodeo event. Once the calf clears the barrier, the cowboy must rope the calf, dismount, run down the rope, and catch the calf. While his horse backs up to keep the rope taut, the contestant throws the calf and ties three legs with a piggin string, which is a six-foot length of rope. When the tie is completed the cowboy throws up his hands, then the calf must remain tied for a full six seconds or the cowboy gets no score. The winner is determined by lowest elapsed time. A contestant has two choices when throwing the calf. Legging the calf means it is toppled by lifting its legs; flanking the calf means it is thrown by grabbing the shoulder and flank.

Calf-kneed: a condition in a horse where the knees are bent backwards which is the opposite of buck-kneed

California saddle: *See Center-fire saddle*

Call his bluff: check his hole card

Call me: 1. give me a holler (or shout) 2. call the house

Call to quarters (CQ): mandatory study time

Callisburg (Cooke County): pronounced KAL-is-burg; this town, near the Butterfield Overland Mail route on the Mormon trail, was established by Lyman Wright and named for Sam Callis, a blacksmith and early settler

Calm: 1. a hotbed of tranquillity 2. so calm she could thread a needle in an earthquake

Calm and collected: don't ever turn a hair [This saying comes from horseback riding. A horse's coat becomes ruffled and requires currying after being ridden. If a horse isn't ridden he stays calm and his hair doesn't turn.]

Calm as: 1. a pup sleeping in the spring sunshine 2. a horse trough in a drought 3. a post hole 4. a dry river bed 5. a plate of spit 6. a boot in the closet 7. road kill 8. a pound of calf liver on a platter 9. the bottom of a dry well 10. a root cellar

Calm down: 1. don't get your shorts in a knot 2. don't bust your bloomers 3. wash off the war paint 4. reset your hat 5. don't go off half cocked 6. hold your horses 7. ease up on the reins 8. simmer down 9. put the safety on 10. choke your motor 11. pull in your horns 12. tap off your temper 13. holster your gun 14. set your hammer 15. cool your heels 16. turn your burners down 17. don't get your tail over the dash [Remember, the man who loses his head is usually the last to miss it.]

Calm them down: gentle the hogs

Calories: weight lifters

Came up empty: had buzzard's luck

Camel: goats of the devil (Indian)

Camp: old-time Texas cowboys would say "in camps" even if there was only one camp

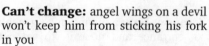 **Camp Verde** (Hemphill County): pronounced Camp VUR-dee; originally a U.S. military fort that was home to camels sent to Texas in an experiment to determine if the beasts could replace horses in the desert Southwest

Camp wagon: forerunner of the chuck wagon, used to carry supplies on cattle drives prior to the Civil War

Campus cop: KK

Campusology: a set of facts about Texas A&M that freshmen (fish) must memorize

Campusology question: a question to a fish relating to campusology on something he should know about Texas A&M

Can/bottle opener: church key

Can't be done: 1. can't unring a bell 2. can't take it back once you spit it out, which refers to not being able to take back something you said 3. can't take back a rock once it's been thrown 4. can't reuse a burned-out light bulb *See also Impossible*

Can't change: angel wings on a devil won't keep him from sticking his fork in you

Can't do that: anymore than Tarzan could swing on greased vines

Can't find anything: wouldn't want to be hangin' from a rope he was looking for

Can't remember: have slept since that happened, implying that once you go to sleep you forget everything that has previously happened

Canaan (Harrison County): pronounced CAN-un

Canadian (Hemphill County): named for the Canadian River [In 1888 a rodeo was held at the cowboys' reunion and it has been going strong ever since. Canadian is the county seat.]

Cane: walkin' stick

Canebreak splitters: term applied to cattle brought into Texas from Louisiana

Cane stalks: country firecrackers [When green cane stalks are pitched into a fire, they "pop" loudly at each joint.]

Canter (horse): three-beat gait of the horse, which is a moderate collected gallop

Cantle: the raised rear portion of a saddle

Cantle-boarding: rodeo term used when a cowboy stretches back to the cantle

Canton (Van Zandt County): pronounced CANT-un; county seat [Home of the internationally known First Monday Trade Days and the only Chevrolet dealership in the state without a salesman; named for Old Canton, which was in Smith County]

Canyon: a deep valley with steep sides

Canyon, box: a mountain gorge with an entrance and no exit; to get out you have to go back the way you came, which makes a box canyon a convenient way to trap wild horses or other stock

Canyon, cross: a canyon that is bisected by another canyon

Capabilities, limited: *See Limited capabilities*

Cap: *See Baseball-type cap; Gimmie cap*

Capable: 1. ain't no slack in his rope 2. a good judge of horseflesh 3. got a lot of arrows in his quiver 4. could track a bumblebee blindfolded in a blizzard 5. could milk a rattlesnake into a Dr Pepper bottle 6. up to snuff *See also Competent*

Capitol of Texas: *See XIT*

Caps (Taylor County): town was founded on an acre of land that was given to Ira and Anna Rollins as a wedding present; originally called Border's Chapel; residents gathered in 1905 to select a new name and, according to the legend, someone threw a cap up in the air and yelled, "let's call it caps" and the idea was accepted

Car: *See Automobile*

Car knocker: railroad car repairman

Caradan (Mills County): pronounced CARE-a-dan, not Car-a-dan; named for two early pioneers, S. L. Caraway and Dan T. Bush

Card player: luckier with cards than with horses 'cause he don't ever get to shuffle the horses

Cardboard: pasteboard

Cards (playing): devil's calling cards *See also individual cards such as Ace, Two, Three, etc.*

Care for: take him under your wing

Care to: see fit, as in "If you see fit, we'll go hunting."

Carefree: 1. footloose and fancy free 2. don't give a hoot or a holler 3. maintains a spit and whittle attitude [This refers to those gentlemen who have nothing to do in life but spit tobacco juice and whittle on limbs.]

Careful: 1. watches his step when the chips are down (as in cow chips) 2. never lets his alligator mouth overload his mockingbird behind 3. never runs against the rope 4. never rides more than one horse at a time 5. plays his cards close to the vest 6. doesn't get his wing feathers wet, which, for some birds, would mean they couldn't fly until the feathers dried, making them vulnerable to predators *See also Advice; Be careful; Caution*

Careful as: 1. a big chested girl in a string bikini 2. a fry cook in a nudist colony 3. a buck naked cowboy crawling through a barbed wire fence 4. a small boy trying to wrap a large scorpion in a Kleenex 5. a cat on a marble table 6. a toupee wearer in a windstorm 7. a welder in a gasoline refinery 8. a frog in a thumbtack factory *See also Walk carefully*

Careless: 1. shoots from the hip, which means he doesn't take time to aim 2. shoots first and asks questions later if he has the time

Careless behavior: ain't no way to run a railroad

Caress, rough: a love lick

Carmelites: cheap cigarettes made of tobacco rolled in corn shucks, which means they burn very fast

Carp: a Southern game fish that is fun to catch but is not considered good to eat. If you must try to eat one, here's a recipe: Clean the carp thoroughly and cut off the head. Baste liberally with a lemon-butter sauce, place on a cedar shingle, into oven, and bake for thirty minutes; remove from oven, throw away the carp, eat the shingle.

Carpenter, poor: 1. couldn't drive nails in Jell-O 2. only way he can avoid hitting his thumb is if he holds the hammer in both hands and his wife holds the nail

Carpenter's level: whiskey stick

Carpetbagger: Yankee opportunist who came South after the war to seek his fortune with all his belongings in a bag made of carpet

Carrizo Springs (Dimmit County): first "r" is silent for Ka-RIZ-oh Sprangs; the town, which is the county seat, was named for nearby springs

Carry: 1. pissant it [This is a reference to having to carry something heavy using brute force and small, pissant-sized steps, as in "We had to pissant the piano down the hall to the bedroom"] 2. tote, as in "tote the watermelon"

Carry a grudge: lay for

Carry through: 1. stay on till you hear the buzzer [refers to rodeo riders who must stay on the bull or bucking bronc till they hear the buzzer signifying they have ridden for eight seconds; said to be the longest eight seconds in history] 2. you don't get lard lessen (unless) you boil the hog 3. the hooked fish ain't caught till he's on the stringer 4. follow the trail to the end

Cash: cash money to a Texan

Cash (Hunt County): originally named Sylvia for the sister of Edward H. R. Green who was president of the Texas Midland Railroad. The residents wanted to rename the town Money for local store owner John A. Money, but that was rejected so they settled for Cash.

Cash on delivery: cash on the barrel head

Cash poor: land rich [had all his money tied up in real estate before the bottom fell out of the market; now he's a millionaire on paper, but he couldn't loan you thirty-five cents to call a cab]

Castrate: 1. steeralize 2. trim up the calves (or pigs)

Castrator: pig or calf trimmer

Cat: 1. mobile mouse trap 2. mouse wrangler 3. cheese wrangler 4. the other white meat 5. just a ball of fur with fangs and claws [According to the old country saying, cats are like Baptists; they raise hell but no one can ever catch them at it.]

Cat, male: a ball bearing mousetrap

Catalog: *See Mail order catalog*

Catch: 1. hem 'em up 2. set the hook 3. throw a loop on 'em 4. drop a loop on 'em 5. corral 'em

Catch barrel: a barrel used to catch rainwater

Catch colt: accidental foal, which means it wasn't sired by the herd stallion

Catch pen: a general use pen where cattle are gathered and held until moved or shipped

Catch rope: a working rope rather than one that's worn on the saddle for show

Catfish: 1. tourist trout 2. a bottom-dwelling, scavenging game fish that's said to be all mouth and no brains, which is why folks in Texas often compare politicians to catfish

Catfish bait: 1. dough bait [meal (preferably cotton seed meal) and molasses mixed together and formed into a small ball. The molasses helps hold the meal together and adds a scent, it is widely believed, catfish can't resist.] 2. stink bait [a repugnant concoction that originally consisted of long-dead minnows compacted and tied in a little sack. The theory is the stench attracts the catfish.]

A︱M Catsup: blood

Cattle: 1. beeves and bovines 2. mortgage on the hoof, which refers to the fact that many a rancher depends on cattle profits to pay the mortgage on the ranch

Cattle, female: she stuff

Cattle, poor: 1. would take half a dozen head to make one shadow 2. could use carbon paper and brand three or four at the same time 3. nothing between the horns and the hooves but hide 4. not much more than a backbone on four legs 5. so thin we have to tie 'em together with rawhide to keep 'em from fallin' apart 6. Ace Reid specials [Ace was a Texas brush popper who was a pretty fair hand at drawing, and most of his cartoon cows were poor and scrawny-looking critters.]

Cattle, shiny: cattle that are fat and fit, which means they'll bring the highest prices at market

Cattle, without horns: muley cows

Cattle pens: See Catch pen; Loading chute; Milking pen; Shipping pen; Chute crazy; Stockyards; Working pen

Cattle prod: 1. stingin' stick 2. hot shot

Cattle feed, sweet bran: sweet feed

Cattlemen: There are three types of cattlemen: those who have been broke, those who are gonna go broke, and those who stay broke.

Caught: 1. lassoed 2. corralled 3. fenced 4. run to earth 5. like a chicken snake in a picket fence [This refers to a chicken snake slithering through a picket fence to eat some eggs, then

discovering he can't crawl back through until the eggs are digested. In other words, he is caught.]

Caught off guard: they ate me up before I knew they were hungry

Cause: the anvil our trouble was forged on

Cause him trouble: 1. drop him in the grease, which basically means put him in a bad situation and let him cook awhile 2. mix a little misery into his tranquillity

Caused trouble: 1. stirred up a hornet's nest or a den of snakes 2. woke up a bear, which refers to a hibernating bear 3. muddied up the water 4. stirred up the manure 5. tipped over the outhouse

Caution: 1. protect your nest 2. keep the food in the wagon 'cause the dogs are loose 3. "Be sure you're right, then go ahead," said Davy Crockett. 4. shoot low, they might be riding Shetlands 5. don't rein the horse when he's jumping 6. never spur a swimming horse 7. don't believe everything you read on tombstones 8. never insult an alligator until you have crossed the river 9. the fewer knots you get on your head the better off you are 10. give a lyin' drunk a wide berth [There is an old country saying: "The three most fatal things in the Old West were smallpox, bad horses, and ignorance enough to argue with a liar full of whiskey."] See also Advice; Be careful

Cautious: 1. keeps his seat belt on in a car wash 2. wears a belt and suspenders 3. looks both ways before crossing a one-way street 4. wears a cast-iron athletic supporter

Cautious as: 1. a small dog with a big bone 2. a bobcat on a barbed wire fence 3. a fat fryer on Sunday morning 4. a turkey near Thanksgiving

Cautious, overly: 1. put a safety belt on his commode seat 2. would ride a mile to spit

Cayote (Bosque County): pronounced Ki-YOTE, just like coyote, which is what the name of the town would have been if someone in the post office hadn't made a clerical error

Cayuse: a scrawny horse of uncertain ancestry; the name comes from the Spanish word *caballejo*

Cayuga (Anderson County): pronounced Kay-OOH-ga; original name was Wild Cat Bluff; in the 1890s, the postmaster requested the change to honor his native home in New York

Cavalry: 1. manure spreaders 2. jocks

Cavesson: bridleless noseband for a horse

Cavy: saddle horses on a roundup

Cedar chopper: woodcutter in the Texas Hill Country

Cedar hacker: woodcutter in West Texas

Cedar brakes: a growth of scrub cedar trees in a broken, barren landscape

Celebrate: 1. put the big pot in the little pot and fry the skillet 2. shoot out the lights, which refers to the habit of cowpokes shooting out saloon and town lights when they were on the prod (celebrating) 3. let's rodeo, which is an advertising line once used by the Nocona Boot Company 4. raise a little cain and pray for a crop failure 5. kick up your heels 6. honky-tonk till you drop 7. paint the whole town and the front porch 8. shoot the anvil [This refers to packing the blacksmith's anvil with powder and setting it off in celebration. This was usually done in towns too small to have a cannon.] 9. gonna sing all day and eat on the ground 10. cut your wolf loose

Celebrate a little: hold the gunfire to a bare minimum

Celebrated: hallelujahed all over the saloon, town, south forty, or entire prairie

Celebrated too much: really lived it up, now he'll never live it down

Celebrating early: cackling before the egg is laid

Celeste (Hunt County): pronounced Sa-LEST, named for the wife of a Santa Fe Railroad official

Celina (Collin County): pronounced Sa-LINE-ah; established by John T. Mulkey and named for his hometown of Celina, Tennessee

Cemetery: 1. bone orchard 2. stone city 3. stone orchard 4. grave pasture 5. buryin' pasture 6. the last resort

Center: smack dab (or square dab) in the middle, as in "After five sad songs in a row, Bubba put his fist smack dab through the middle of the jukebox."

Center City (Mills County): pronounced Sinner City [Originally Hughes Store, the name was changed when a survey identified an oak tree in the town as being the exact center of the state. Although the center of Texas was later proven to be in McCulloch County, the residents elected to keep the name.]

Center-fire saddle: a saddle with the rigging ring mounted to the tree and only one cinch in the center of the saddle [The design permits the saddle to rock on a pitching horse; popular with dally men and California cowboys; also called California saddle or single-rigged saddle.]

Centroplex: the Belton/Temple area of Texas

Cereal, hot: mush

Ceremony, formal and pompous: Moose lodge ceremony

Certain: 1. lead pipe cinch 2. sure as shootin' 3. guaranteed natural fact 4. if I'm not right I'll eat my hat, band, feathers, and all 5. only things that are certain are death, taxes, and Texas 6. a lock nut gut cinch 7. if I ain't right, I'll kiss your backside in a department store window and give you half an hour to draw a crowd and sell tickets 8. can write that on the wall in ink 9. can paint that on the barn in waterproof paint *See also Fact; Guaranteed; Positive; Reliable; That's a fact*

Chain joints: links used to repair (join together) broken chains

Chalk numbers: numbers written on a cow with chalk at an auction sale; one number is the age; the other number is the months pregnant [Cows with good solid mouths are marked 6 years old because you can't tell when a cow is over 6 years.] *See Grease stick*

Challenge: 1. If you want it, come and take it. In 1835 when the Mexican army demanded the citizens of Gonzales return a small cannon, the demand was answered with "Come and take it." The Mexicans withdrew. 2. jump if you feel froggy

Challenging as: 1. tryin' to turn a pair of boots back into an alligator 2. tryin' to mate a bobcat and a bobwhite quail (or a mockingbird and a buzzard) 3. trying to cross a wet prairie in a wide-wheeled buggy

Chamber pot: 1. thunder mug 2. Arkansas fire extinguisher

Champagne: 1. bubble water 2. whoopee water 3. giggle water 4. French firewater

Chance, fat: *See Chance, slim*, which raises the question, how come fat chance and slim chance mean the same thing?

Chance, slim: 1. have a better chance of being hit by a shooting star 2. as much as a steer in a packin' plant 3. have two chances, slim and none and slim is saddling up to leave town 4. have two chances, slim and fat 5. about the same chance as that of the Baptist church opening a brewery 6. don't hold my breath waitin' for that to happen 7. playin' with a cold deck 8. as much chance as a red ant at a horned frog convention 9. as much chance as a hog in a sausage factory 10. as much chance as a grasshopper in a chicken house 11. ain't got a Chinaman's chance [This saying originated during the California gold rush when Chinese workers truly didn't have much of a chance to prosper or even survive.]

Change (coins): 1. egg money 2. scalp money

Change for the worse: that muddied up the playground

Change subjects: 1. punch a different button on the jukebox so we can dance to another tune 2. put the bridle on another horse

Changeable: 1. chicken one day and feathers the next 2. droughts usually end with a flood 3. a ladder works both ways

Changed husbands: found a new dasher for her churn

Changing: the tide is turning

Chaos: three truckloads of bean pickers without a foreman

Chaparral: 1. terrain covered with scrub oaks and thorny evergreen bushes, common in South Texas [Frequently, the bushes will appear almost black, and they are then referred to as "black chaparral."] *See also Roadrunner*

Chapped lips: look like you been using an Oklahoma credit card [When you siphon gas and get some on your lips they burn and look like the world's worst case of chapped lips.] *See also Bag balm; Siphon hose*

Chaps: *See Batwing chaps; Hair pants; Shotgun chaps; Woolies*

Chaps guard: a small knob or hook on the shank of the spur which prevents the rowel on the spurs from snagging the chaps

Character: 1. what you have left when you've lost everything else 2. is easier kept than recovered 3. better to go to heaven in rags than to go to hell in a silk suit 4. like embroidery, is made one stitch at a time 5. like a glass, even a small crack shows 6. strong enough to bend

Character, lacking: will stand for anything you'll fall for

Charge: 1. go a hornin' 2. Remember the Alamo, the battle cry at the Battle of San Jacinto

Charming: 1. could charm a bird out of a tree 2. could charm the gloss off a photograph 3. could charm a pea out of its pod 4. could charm the pants off the queen mother 5. could charm paper off a wall 6. could charm the chrome off a bumper hitch 7. could charm the gold out of your fillings 8. could charm the air out of your tires

Chased: went after him with intent to BBQ

Chastise: give 'em what for

Cheap as: 1. suntan oil in a snowstorm 2. a two-week-old newspaper 3. used chewing tobacco 4. used bubble gum 5. dirt, which refers to the days when Texas land sold for as little as fifty cents an acre 6. an umbrella in a drought 7. a Christmas tree in January

Cheapskate: 1. still using his third grade underwear 2. tied lightning bugs to the branches of the Christmas tree to keep from buying lights 3. his idea of charity is offering $500 to the family of the Unknown Soldier 4. wouldn't pay a nickel to see a monkey make love to a football 5. wouldn't a paid a dollar for a box seat at the Battle of San Jacinto 6. drove his wife slowly through an automatic car wash on their honeymoon and told her it was Niagara Falls 7. wouldn't pay a dime to see a pissant eat a bale of hay 8. wouldn't pay a nickel to see a termite eat a California redwood *See also Frugal; Miser; Stingy*

Cheated: 1. been screwed, blued, and tattooed 2. got the short end of the stick 3. hornswoggled 4. paid for an Indian and got a goatherd [This refers to the days when bounties were paid for dead Indians and some poor goatherds were passed off as Indians. In the 1920s the Texas Bankers Association offered a reward of $5,000 for DEAD bank robbers. Famous Texas Ranger Frank Hamer was convinced petty thieves were being set up and shot as bank robbers for the reward money. He claimed the bankers were, "paying for Apaches and getting sheepherders."]

Cheater: 1. on a first name basis with the bottom of the deck 2. always seems to know both sides of the cards 3. when you play with him you have to play fair 'cause he knows what cards he dealt you 4. made his living selling swampland in Lubbock 5. a scale thumber, which means whenever he's weighing something he always finds a way to add his thumb to the scale

Check everything: 1. run all the traps 2. round up the usual suspects

Check it out: give it the smell test, which means check everything out to be sure nothing smells bad

Cheek-by-jowl dry: a county where the sale of alcoholic beverages is prohibited by law

Cheekpiece: part of a bit that is not in horse's mouth

Chemical aging: process to break in a synthetic rope

Chemical warfare: stink bombers

Chemise: shinny shirt

Chest: 1. brisket 2. barrel

Chest of drawers: frequently pronounced as chester drawers [Mary Margaret Davis of the *El Paso Times* said she was fourteen years old before she knew chest of drawers had more than two words.]

Chewing tobacco: chew backey [Chewing tobacco is an art. When you start you'll notice a collection of tobacco juice in your mouth that you have to do something with, and spitting it out is much preferable to swallowing it. With practice you'll be spitting well enough to drown house flies on the wing. However, always remember the three rules of chewing: 1. Practice a lot before trying to drink a beer while chewing. 2. Always spit downwind. 3. Around other chewers, never drink from any can you didn't personally open.] *See also Pickup aerodynamics*

Chewing tobacco unit of measure: plug or chaw

Chicken: 1. yard bird 2. clucker 3. settin' hen 4. rooster bait 5. Arkansas pheasant 6. Sunday dinner on the hoof, which refers to rural families having fried chicken after church on Sunday 7. low or dirty tricks (Aggie)

Chicken, good: 1. could hatch a petrified dinosaur egg 2. would starve to death trying to hatch a lost golf ball

Chicken, poor: couldn't lay an egg if she was sittin' on a vacuum cleaner and it was running

Chicken, Southern fried: what God would eat if he had chickens in heaven. To prepare properly, start with a Southern chicken (they're the most tender) and cut into manageable pieces. Remove the wing from the breast, cut the breast into two pieces, and separate the drumstick from the thigh. Dip in your own special batter and deep fry until golden brown and every single drop of blood is gone. When prepared properly by a Texas grandmother fried chicken will "straighten your teeth, smooth your skin, and make childbirth a pleasure."

Chicken fighting: a minor skirmish that involves a lot of flapping of the arms and legs but very little actual contact [Chicken fighting usually occurs

when two people are angry but neither is willing to risk the loss of any blood.] *See Male, angry*

Chicken-fried steak: abbreviated as CFS in many Texas country cafes

Chicken-fried steak, good: *See Fried chicken, good*

Chicken hawk: hen hawk

Chicken processor: chicken packer

Chicken rib meat: harrikin

Chicken stew, with pastry: chicken slick

Chicken stew, with rice: chicken bog

Chicken wire: mesh-type wire created from small diamond shapes of wire rather than continuous, straight strands like barbed wire. This wire is more suited to keeping chickens penned up since they would go through a regular, straight strand fence. This wire is occasionally called net wire.

Chicota (Lamar County): pronounced Sha-COAT-ah; originally Center Springs [Robert Draper opened a store and trading post and the Indians who traded with him told stories of Checotah in the Indian Territory. Draper decided to use the name even though he didn't know exactly how to spell it.]

Chiggers: red bugs [Pound for pound, the Texas chigger is the meanest critter on the face of the earth.]

Child: 1. tricycle motor 2. patch-seated kid 3. little britches 4. button cowboy 5. towhead 6. papoose 7. little shaver 8. pullet 9. yard (or house) ape 10. rug rat 11. curtain climber 12. whippersnapper 13. fryin' size 14. short-tailed rooster

Child, arrogant: snot-nosed kid

Child, injured: it'll heal before you get married, which is advice many Texas mothers have given their children

Child, mean: 1. his mother killed three or four peach trees cuttin' switches to whip him with 2. his mama used to give him a bath by carryin' him down to the creek and beatin' him on the rocks 3. the only hell his mother ever raised 4. the worst crop his daddy ever raised 5. was harder to raise than corn in an aquarium 6. hate to have a litter of those

Child, redneck: a handle jiggler [Whenever an indoor toilet doesn't shut off properly, a country mother will look straight at one of the kids and say, "Somebody go jiggle that handle."]

Child, small: no bigger than an uppin' stone [a small block used by proper ladies to mount a side saddle]

Child, underage: still in warranty, which means parents are responsible for fixing anything they break [According to law, the warranty expires when the little darlings reach 18 years of age.]

Childhood: when the baby grows from an armful to a handful *See also Baby growth chart*

Children, spoiled: she raised three "only" children, although any number of children can be substituted

Children, twins: a matched pair of dueling pistols

Children, ugly: parents had to rent kids to make home movies

Childress (Childress County): pronounced CHILL-driss, not Child-res; named for George C. Childress, considered to be the author of the Texas Declaration of Independence

Chili: 1. bowl a red 2. Texas red 3. national dish of Texas [Not all Texans enjoy chili. In the April 1983 issue of *Esquire* magazine, Paul Burka quoted the following chili recipe from former Texas governor Allan Shivers: "Put a pot of chili on the stove to simmer. Let it simmer. Meanwhile, broil a good steak. Eat the steak. Let the chili simmer. Ignore it." Rumor has it that sales of the magazine in Texas went down sharply.]

Chili, good: according to some knowledgeable Texas chiliheads, the chili ain't no good a'tall if it don't make your ears ring and your nose run *See Fried chicken, good*

Chili, hot: 1. sinus medicine, which refers to really hot chili having the ability to open clogged sinuses and make your nose run 2. armor piercing 3. could eat through a crowbar 4. two-, three-, or four-alarm warm 5. would cauterize your hemorrhoids, which implies chili is just as hot coming out as it is going in 6. had to keep it on a pile of cracked ice to keep the cast-iron pot from melting 7. will melt the fillings out of your eye teeth 8. would melt the enamel off your molars 9. have to keep it in the refrigerator to keep it from burning down the house 10. as a mouth full of red ants [The hottest chili could be freeze dried and used for gunpowder.]

Chili, mild: 1. false-alarm chili 2. flame-retardant chili

Chili, with beans: 1. chili with shrapnel 2. Texas red with Mexican strawberries 3. rocks in the red sea 4. tourist chili

Chili, without beans: real chili the way God intended it to be made

Chile piquins: small red peppers, very hot, that once grew wild in the Texas brush country

Chillicothe (Hardeman County): pronounced Chill-a-coth-ee; name is supposed to be Shawnee for "the big town where we live."

Chimney, clay and straw mixture: 1. cal & clayed 2. wattle & daub

Chin chain: chain under the chin of a cattle halter

Chinaberry: umbrella tree (also used for *magnolia tripetela*)

Chinking: mud or clay, mixed with straw, that was used to fill the cracks between logs in cabins [Chinking works very well until it becomes extremely dry and starts to drop out in chunks.]

Chinks (chaps): knee length chaps, often decorated with fringe. These chaps, often called "high water chaps" are relatively new and primarily used by buckeroos, but the popularity is spreading to other working cowboys. Chink comes from the Mexican word chincadera, which means "sawed off."

Chinquapin (chinkie-pin): the edible nut of a dwarfed chestnut tree

Chinquapin (Matagorda County): pronounced CHINKY-pin; this town, which is surrounded by swamp, was probably named for a type of tree that grows in the area

Chiropractor: alignment specialist

Chitlins: small squares of hog intestines that are deep fried until crisp [Chitlins are a favorite country dish, although some folks who cook 'em don't actually eat them. According to an old legend, the smell of them cooking is so bad it drives all the flies out of the house and keeps 'em out for up to two weeks. Also called chitterlings. Regardless of what they're called, I'd rather eat an RCA radio than even one of these suckers.]

Chitlins strut: a social, usually a fund-raiser, where most of the food served is chitlins, okra, cornbread, collards, and sweet taters and the most common drink is either iced tea or moonshine. The strut is a type of clogging dance that can get rowdy; also called "okra" strut.

Chitterlings: *See Chitlins*

Chivalrous: picks up a lady's hanky even when she ain't pretty *See also Gentleman*

Choate (Karnes County): pronounced Shh-oat; named for James Monroe Choate, a prominent local rancher

Choctaw (Grayson County): pronounced CHOCK-taw; originally Dugan's Chapel; it is believed the name was changed by officials of the Texas and Pacific Railroad when the tracks reached the area

Choice: druthers

Choice, difficult: the horns of a dilemma, as in "I'm on the horns of a dilemma tryin' to choose Betty Sue or Bobby Lou to take to the dance."

Choked up: got a lump in my throat big as a fishin' bobber

Chore, big: 1. got a lot of cotton patch to hoe 2. got a lot of calves to fix 3. a lot of corn to shuck 4. a big barn to raise 5. a big hole in the fence 6. a big garden and a dull hoe

Chore, unpleasant: would rather pick stickers out of a skunk's butt than do that

Chow call: soupy

Christoval (Tom Green County): pronounced CHRIS-ta-vul; the name is believed to be a Spanish version of Christopher for early settler Christopher Columbus Doty

Chrome: country term for a horse or cow with a lot of color

Chrysanthemums: white and yellow Octobers

Chuck: food

Church: 1. a gospel mill 2. doxology works

Church, small: they pass a saucer instead of a plate

Church goer, infrequent: a two-fer, which implies he only goes to church twice a year, on Christmas and Easter *See also Religious, sometimes*

Church goers: 1. steeple people 2. Bible thumpers

Church offering, unusually large: a stranger in our midst, meaning someone gave a larger offering than usual

Church service: 1. preachin' 2. prayer meeting 3. Sunday go to meetin'

Church service, fervent: a singin' and shoutin' meeting

Church stick: a long stick with a fox tail on one end that was used to tickle people who had fallen asleep in church

Chute crazy: cattle that are nervous and apprehensive about entering a narrow branding or loading chute

Cibolo (Guadalupe County): pronounced SIB-a-low, although some say C'willow. [The name, which is Spanish for buffalo, came from nearby Cibolo Creek, a favorite watering hole when the buffalo roamed Texas.]

Cicada: 1. locust 2. jarfly

Cider, fermented: hard cider

Cigar: sea-gar

Cigar, large: could smoke it in the shower, the idea being that it is so big the fire end wouldn't get wet

Cigarette: 1. cancer stick 2. coffin nail

Cinch: a wide band, usually woven horsehair or mohair, that goes under the horse's belly to hold the saddle in place; also called girth; from the Spanish cincha which means girth

Circle Back (Bailey County): the name is from a local ranch that branded cattle with a circle on their back

Circled: took roundance

Cirrhosis: roaches of the liver

Cistern: water storage structure, usually about 20 feet deep, 6 to 8 feet wide, with bricked walls [A cistern is not a well but rather is designed to catch water run-off from the roof of the house.]

City boy: raised on concrete

Civil War: the War of Northern Aggression to a true Southerner

Claimed: allowed as how

Clarendon (Donley County): pronounced CLAIR-en-dun; the county seat, named for the Clarendon Land Investment and Agency Company, an English firm that invested heavily in the area

Clarify: 1. cut the deck a little deeper 2. put another log on the fire 3. shuffle and redeal 4. throw a new loop 5. run that flag a little higher up the pole 6. stir that chili a little more 7. chew it a little finer 8. chew the bark off and get down to the wood 9. sand through the varnish and get down to the wood 10. put a little more butter on that biscuit 11. crack that nut a little closer to the meat

Clarksville (Red River County): pronounced CLARKS-vul; the county seat, named for founder James Clark

Class horse: an event at a horse show

Class reunion: a liar's convention where everyone gets together to see who is falling apart

Class set: a set of push-ups equal to your graduation year (93 push-ups for 1993, 94 for 1994, etc. [This tradition presents the Aggies with their own year-2000 problem. Will cadets scheduled to graduate that year have to do 100 push-ups or none? Only time will tell.]

Clattering: 1. like two skeletons making love on a sheet of galvanized iron 2. like a cowboy dancing in a washtub with his spurs on *See also Noisy*

Claws: 1. dinner hooks 2. paw fangs

Clean as: 1. a hound's tooth 2. a fresh boiled white shirt 3. a preacher's sheets 4. a new mirror 5. a whistle 6. a new barn. The only time a barn is really clean is when it's brand new and unoccupied.

Clean living: live your life so you wouldn't have to worry if the FBI taped your phone line and then played the tapes in church (or court)

Cleaned up: shined up

Clean shaven: 1. bald faced 2. nekked faced

Clear as: 1. mother's milk 2. glass 3. a bell

Clear brush: grubbing brush

Clear footed: a horse with a clear and clean gait

Clear the top water (poker): To get rid of those players barely hangin' on, you make a large raise that the other players can't call and they must fold their hand.

Clear underbrush: swamp it

Clean up, country style: sweep the yard [Country folks often don't have much grass in their front yard so to clean up around the place, they just sweep up everything, dirt, leaves, trash, twigs, bones, and all.]

Cleburne (Johnson County): named for Confederate general Patrick Cleburne who pronounced his name Clay-burn; the name of the town, however, is pronounced KLEE-burn

Clerk: counter hopper

Clevis: a loop that pins in a hitch to provide an attaching mechanism for a log chain or other device

Clicks: like a set of $20 false teeth

Climb a tree: 1. skin it 2. shinny up it, as in "Bubba, shinny up that tree and get the cat down 'fore he falls and hurts himself."

Cling: 1. like East Texas mud to a rusty shovel 2. like a tick to a dog's (or mule's) ear 3. like manure to a boot 4. like a dirt dauber's nest to the side of a barn *See also Hang on*

Clock, old: so old the shadow of the pendulum has worn a hole through the back of the case

Clorox bottle, empty: An empty Clorox bottle is one of the most versatile tools in rural Texas. It can be used as is for a flower vase or an emergency gas can; it can be sealed and used for a trotline float; you can cut the bottom straight off and use it for a funnel or seedling cover; you can cut the bottom off at an angle and use it for a water bailer or grain scoop.

Close: 1. within hollerin' distance 2. a holler and a half away 3. just two whoops and a holler away 4. just down the road apiece 5. could chunk a rock and hit it 6. enough to share a snap (or buttonhole) 7. enough to be Siamese twins 8. within earshot 9. enough to raise a blister 10. as two fleas on a frozen dog 11. nigh, which is the opposite of yonder *See also Nearby*

Close at hand: if it had been a snake it would a bit you

Close call: 1. didn't lose nothing but some confidence 2. that bullet went by close enough to raise a blister 3. missed me by a cat hair 4. came within a peg of getting hit [Peg comes from old-time dry good stores where yard goods were measured by pegs on a counter that were one inch apart.] 5. came within a lash of winning [Lash is short for eyelash.] 6. almost got the dollar knife, which in the old country carnivals was a pocketknife worth about a dollar that was usually the best prize

Close finish: 1. finished in the money but it wasn't top money 2. had to develop the picture to see who won 3. made the picture but he wasn't the star, implying he was in the photo finish but he didn't win.

Close to the ground: could trip an ant (or a tumble bug)

Closed: 1. nailed shut 2. like a covered coffin 3. like a bank vault on the Fourth of July 4. as a judge's mind

Closed mind: gathers no new ideas

Clothes: 1. duds 2. riggin'

Clothes, fancy: 1. Sunday go-to-meeting outfit 2. looks like a page out of a mail order catalog 3. looks like the joker out of a deck of cards 4. bib and tucker outfit

Clothes, inside out: wrong sideouten

Clothes, skimpy: 1. wears barbed wire clothes, which means they protect the property without obstructing the view 2. wears dresses that start late and end early 3. wears less in public than grandma did in bed *See also Dress, skimpy*

Clothes, tight: tighter than a first day bride's clothes *See also Jeans, tight*

Clothes, worn: brush frazzled

Cloudburst: *See Rain, heavy*

Cloudy: 1. clabbered skies 2. not enough sun to warm a baby rattlesnake

Cloudy: muddy skies

Club: 1. big stick 2. hoe handle 3. ax handle *See also Walker Colt*

Clubs (playing card suit): 1. dog foot 2. puppy tracks

Club-footed: reel footed

Clumsy: 1. tangle-footed 2. shot himself in the foot 3. got two left feet 4. an accident looking for a place to happen 5. like a big, friendly dog in a small room; every time he wags his tail he breaks something *See also Accident prone*

Clumsy as: a longhorn bull in a Neiman Marcus china department

Clutch: *See Settin' of eggs*

Clute (Brazoria County): pronounced Cloot, not Clu-tee

Coachwhip snakes: Texas term for any of a number of harmless snakes that are thin like a coach whip

Coahoma (Howard County): pronounced Ka-HOME-ah, not Co-a-home-ah; some say it's Indian for "good place to live," but others believe the Indian word means "signal" since the town is located near Signal Mountain

Coast artillery: big guns

Coasters: longhorn cattle that ran free on coastal ranges and offshore islands

Coasting: in bareback riding (rodeo), completing a ride with your feet just resting on the horse's shoulders instead of spurring, which won't win you any points with the judges

Coat hanger: Oklahoma dipstick [If you lose the dipstick from your old pickup, a coat hanger will usually get you by but be careful about trusting the readings.]

Cocked up on three legs: stance of a horse when he is sleeping while standing; the weight is on three legs and he is resting the fourth leg and is usually very relaxed

Cockfight: rooster fighting, never chicken fighting

Cockleburs: porcupine eggs

Cockroach: *See Roaches, large*

Coffee: 1. belly wash 2. up and at 'em juice 3. muddy water 4. break fluid 5. tank water 6. coal oil or coal squeezin's 7. dope (Aggie) [An experienced country boy knows not to ever wash the coffee mug 'cause it ruins the taste.]

Coffee drinker, avid: 1. would walk barefooted through a mile-long cactus patch for a cup of coffee 2. would rassle the devil himself for one more cup 3. would go to hell when he died if that was the only place they served coffee [Note, these sayings can also be used to describe an avid beer drinker or an avid Dr Pepper drinker.]

Coffee, cool: saucered and blowed, which refers to the café practice of pouring coffee into the saucer, blowing on it till cool, and then drinking it straight out of the saucer

Coffee, decaffeinated: unleaded

Coffee, strong: 1. will grow hair on your saddle horn (or chest) 2. range coffee 3. couldn't drive a nail into it with a sledgehammer 4. could use it to stop leaks in your truck radiator 5. strong enough to float a horseshoe, anvil, windmill wrench, or Colt pistol 6. doesn't have to be poured, just walks into the cup

Coffee, thick: 1. you take a bite of it rather than drink it 2. too thick to drink and too thin to plow

Coffee, weak: 1. town coffee 2. has to have help to get out of the pot 3. won't even hold a spoon straight in it 4. won't float a horseshoe much less an iron wedge

Coffee with cream: 1. with the socks on 2. whitewashed 3. blonde coffee

Coffin: 1. dust bin 2. dirt box 3. pine overcoat 4. eternity box 5. buryin' crate 6. forever bed 7. planter box

Coins: hard money

Cold (illness): nose runner [Some people starve a cold, some people feed a cold, but a lot of others follow the Jack Daniels theory and try to drown it.]

Cold (weather): 1. my teeth chattered and they were in a jar on the dresser 2. the tobacco chewers were spittin' brown ice cubes 3. four below no longer referred to cows 4. only place you could get warm was on the front row of church when the preacher was talking about the flames of hell (or people were going to church just to hear about the flames of hell) 5. the hogs had to eat slop through a straw 'cause their jaws were frozen shut 6. lawyers were standing around with their hands in their own pockets 7. teeth were chattering like dice in a crap game 8. so cold the wolves were eating the sheep just to get the wool

Cold as: 1. a knothole in the North Pole 2. a witch's tit in a brass bra in an Amarillo snowstorm 3. a cast-iron (or brass) commode in the shade of a glacier 4. a well digger's shovel in Dalhart 5. a witch's caress 6. as a banker's heart 7. a mother-in-law's kiss 8. a frozen bullet or anvil 9. an outhouse seat in January 10. a possum in a deep freeze 11. a bartender's heart 12. hell with the furnace off 13. a pawnbroker's smile 14. a week-old enchilada 15. sheared sheep in a snowstorm 16. an ex-wife's (or ex-husband's) heart

Cold blooded: 1. as a frozen snake 2. as a grand jury foreman 3. as an ex-wife's lawyer 4. one drop of his blood would freeze a cat (any small animal can be substituted for cat) 5. could get frostbite on your fingers if you took his pulse

Cold enough to: 1. freeze the balls off a billiard table 2. freeze boiling water so fast it'll make warm ice cubes 3. freeze all the water outside the tea kettle 4. make a third degree Mason drop a degree 5. freeze the tail off a brass monkey 6. freeze the stink out of manure 7. freeze the horns off a billy-goat (or longhorn steer) 8. freeze ducks to a pond 9. make the eagle on a silver dollar shiver 10. make cows give ice cream

Collard sandwich: cold collards in corn bread or a biscuit

College Station (Brazos County): name came from the fact that it was the site of Texas Agriculture and Mechanical College. Although the college has since become Texas A&M University, the name of the town has not changed. According to supposed research done at the University of Texas, the name wasn't changed because parents of Aggies had to be spotted two or three letters to spell college but they had no chance at spelling university. Thus, if the name had been changed, the students would have stopped getting care packages from home.

Colleyville (Tarrant County): this one is a "ville" not a "vul"; the name evolved when a community grew up near the property of Hilburn (or Liburn) Howard Colley, a popular physician in the area for more than forty years

Colmesneil (Tyler County): pronounced Kol-mis-neal although it is usually pronounced so fast the first "l" becomes silent; occasionally called Colmesneil Junction, from a conductor on one of the first Texas and New Orleans trains to reach the area

Colorado City (Mitchell County): pronounced Col-a-ray-da City [This town has been pronounced with a "ray" rather a "rah" (like the state of Colorado) for generations, but now some newcomers to the area are trying to change it to sound like the state of Colorado. If you're really an old-timer, you might pronounce it Col-a-ray-der.]

Colorado County: pronounced like the state of Colorado (Col-a-rah-doe)

Colt: a male horse not over three years old

Comanche moon: September moon, which comes from the Comanche tradition of raiding during September

Comanche Trail: the trail from the Staked Plains in West Texas down to Old Mexico, which was favored by the Comanche Indians

Combine: harvesting machine that automatically separates the seeds from the stalk and discharges the waste; used for wheat, maize, rice, and other stalk crops

Combiner's lunch: *See Sawmill lunch*

Come along: a mechanical device that can be hooked up to a fence wire to take the slack out by stretching the wire; can also be used for various other projects such as pulling out old fence posts or a neighbor's pickup that is stuck in a bog

Come back: y'all come back now, ya' hear

Comedian: does a ten-minute routine every time the refrigerator light comes on, which is derived from a quote by Texan Debbie Reynolds

Comfort (Kendall County): pronounced Kum-fert [The original German settlers wanted to name the town Gemutlichkeit, a German word that conveys coziness and tranquillity. After giving the matter some thought, they decided on Comfort, the Anglo term that came closest to the original German phrase.]

Comfortable: snug as a bug in a deep-pile rug

Comfortable as: 1. an old boot 2. a warm bed on a cold morning 3. a pair of old boots that know your feet

Coming of age: struttin' and gobblin' time

Commencing: the pot's beginning to simmer or the chili's beginning to bubble

Commerce (Hunt County): local residents chose the name hoping their town would become a center for commercial enterprise since it was at the juncture of several trade routes

Commitment, lacking: just won't stay hitched

Committed: bound and determined, as in "That Bubba is bound and determined to open a septic tank business." [The difference between being totally committed and just involved is the difference between having bacon and eggs for breakfast. The chicken that provided the egg is involved, the pig is totally committed.]

Committee, small: a pulpit committee, which is generally a small

committee in charge of hirin' and firin' preachers

Committed, somewhat: not on the bandwagon but running beside it

Common: run of the orchard (or mill)

Common as: 1. pig tracks in a barnyard 2. cow chips in a pasture 3. broken dreams in Hollywood 4. corn bread 5. dirt 6. rocks 7. cow patties 8. everyday wash

Common knowledge: even the chickens under the porch know that

Common sense: horse sense [Of course, having a lot of horse sense doesn't keep a man from acting like a jackass. Texan Sam Rayburn once said, "Having good common sense ain't enough. You have to exercise it."]

Common-law marriage: 1. hitched but not churched 2. united with a cotton patch (or saw mill) license

Commotion: 1. ruckus 2. like a lizard in a pile of dry leaves 3. like there's a chicken snake in the coop

Community loop: extra large loop, said to be big enough to rope an entire community

Community standing, improving: the bottom rail is gettin' close to the top

Como (Hopkins County): pronounced KO-mo; originally named Carrolton but the locals decided to change it to avoid confusion with a town of the same name near Dallas. They decided on Como because some of the settlers were from Como, Mississippi.

Comp time: swap work

Company, failing: on its last legs and wobbling

Company, large: takes a week and a half for gossip to travel from one end to the other

Compatible: 1. goes together like red beans and ham hocks 2. like chili and beer 3. like bourbon and Coca Cola 4. like chili and pepper 5. like biscuits and gravy 6. like a gun and a holster 7. like a kid and candy

Competent: 1. top hand 2. could hunt a whisper in a whirlwind 3. right smart of a windmill fixer 4. could string ten miles of barbed wire blindfolded in a blizzard 5. can read and write, figger and fight, whup or throw down 6. could track a hornet in a hurricane *See also Capable*

Competition: 1. if you can't beat 'em, confuse 'em 2. if you can't dazzle 'em with brilliance, baffle 'em with bull ...stuff

Complain: 1. bellyache 2. a hit dog hollers 3. a squeaking wheel gets the grease 4. a squeaking windmill (or gate hinge) gets the oil 5. a banging gate gets the new latch [You have heard the old saying, I used to complain about having no shoes until I saw the man with no feet. A different version is, I used to complain about a flooded basement till I saw a man with a flooded attic.]

Complainer: 1. would complain about the service in a self-service café 2. would complain if they hung him with a new rope

Complete: 1. lock, stock, and barrel 2. the whole shootin' match 3. it takes eight bits to make a dollar 4. hook, line, sinker, and bobber

Complete, almost: don't have any loose ends but we got some loose edges

Complication: 1. muddied up the water 2. turned over the creek 3. gummed up the windmill works 4. more to it than meets the eye 5. makes the cheese more binding 6. woke up the Indians 7. backlog went plumb out [Backlog, in this case, refers to the large log used in kitchen fireplaces in the country. A big log was placed at the back and usually burned all night, providing flames for cooking and heat for sleeping. Even if it burned up completely, there would always be enough embers to start a fire the next morning. Since matches were usually in short supply in those days, if the backlog went completely out and left no embers, it was a major complication.]

Compliment: *See Good person*

Compliment, sort of: she's a lot nicer than she is ugly

Composed: as cool as the center seed in a cucumber *See also Keep your composure*

Composure: no matter what, never let 'em see you sweat

Composure, lost: come apart at the seams

Compromise: aim high and settle

Computer: 1. brains in a box 2. electric thinker

Con man: 1. snake oil salesman 2. lightning rod salesman 3. condo time-share salesman 4. could talk you out of the shirt on your back and then convince you to buy it back

Concan (Uvalde County): pronounced CON-can; according to local legend the name is from "coon can," a Mexican card game that was popular among the local residents

Concarned: ding busted

Conceit: pulps you up but it don't prop you up

Conceited: 1. thinks the sun comes up just to hear him crow 2. thinks the manure from his cows don't stink 3. hangs a mirror on the bathroom ceiling so he can watch himself gargle 4. has his x-rays retouched 5. suffers from "I" strain 6. joined the navy so the world could see him

Concentrate: 1. keep the cobwebs out of your head 2. defog your brain 3. unclutter your mind [In 1974 Dallas Cowboy rookie Clint Longley, from Abilene, Texas, filled in for an injured Roger Staubach and led the team to one of the most memorable comebacks of all time against arch rival Washington. Fellow Cowboy Blaine Nye said, "It was a triumph of an uncluttered mind."]

Concho: silver button on a saddle, bridle, halter, etc.

Concluded: put two and two together

Concrete: see-mint to a Texan

Concrete (DeWitt County): pronounced KON-cret; named for adobe concrete that was used in early buildings

Conditions worsening: haven't hit the panic button but we did have one installed

Conference: 1. prayer meeting 2. powwow 3. making medicine 4. treaty talks

Confess: 1. own up to 2. spill the beans (or your guts) 3. acknowledge the corn, which generally means confess to a lie 4. let the cat out of the bag

Confessed: fessed up, as in "He fessed up to paintin' those cuss words on the side of the water tower."

Confession: hurryment

Confidence, large: would sign up for a fiddle contest and start learnin' how to play as he walked out on the stage

Confident: 1. thinks he's bulletproof 2. cock sure 3. would take on Pecos Bill with one arm tied behind his back [Pecos Bill is the Texas equivalent to Paul Bunyon.]

Confidential: 1. keep it close to the vest 2. keep it under your hat 3. keep it between me and you and the gatepost (or snubbin' post)

Confirmed: 1. according to all accounts 2. got it from the horse's (or mare's) mouth

Conform: 1. walk the line 2. toe the mark

Confrontation: 1. set to, as in "Blackie and Billy Jack had a real set to and the blood was flowing like beer from a busted barrel." 2. a prayer meeting without the preacher or the choir 3. a shoot-out [In 1969, when No. 1 Texas played No. 2 Arkansas for the National Championship of collegiate football, Longhorn coach Darrell Royal referred to the game as a shootout. Since then major sports confrontations have frequently been referred to as a shootouts.]

Confused: 1. buffaloed 2. don't know if he's gettin' up or goin' to bed 3. can't find the right wagon to load 4. barking up the wrong tree 5. driving the wrong herd to market 6. getting your horse before your cart 7. don't know if he's commode-hugging drunk or taking communion at church 8. mind is in a fog

Confused as: 1. a mosquito in a nudist colony (he knows what to do but he doesn't know where to start) 2. a woodpecker in a petrified forest 3. a coyote with a rubber chicken 4. a termite in a yo-yo 5. a little kid who dropped his chewing gum in the chicken yard 6. a rooster crowin' to the ground 7. a mouse in a maze 8. a fish on a stringer 9. a goat on Astroturf or shag carpet 10. a frog in a blender *See also Mass confusion*

Confusing: 1. Greek (or algebra) to me 2. would stump a rocket scientist 3. a real mare's nest

Confusing situation: 1. confusion reigned like manure at a horse show 2. don't know which way to send the scouts

Congress: like a county fair, nothing gets more attention than the bull

Conniption fit: a sort of tantrum that you throw whenever someone does something to you. "Bubba had a conniption fit when I dropped the Evinrude on his ingrown toenail." A snotslingin' conniption fit is twice as bad as

a plain one and a foamin' at the mouth conniption fit is the worst of all and usually indicates blood is about to be spilled. *See also Hissey fit*

Conscience: 1. like an old toothless hound dog, it might not bite you but you can't keep it from barking 2. like a baby, it has to go to sleep before you do 3. something that works best when you're being watched

Conscience, lacking: 1. don't have any more conscience than a cow in a stampede 2. got about half as much conscience as a tomcat

Consecutively: hand runnin', as in "He's been sick for four days hand runnin'."

Conservative: 1. never bites off more than he can chew 2. never puts more on his plate than he can say grace over 3. never plants more garden than his wife can hoe 4. like an old cow, he chews more than he bites off

Consistent: never changes horses in the middle of a stream

Conspicuous: 1. sticks out like a thumb mashed by a ball peen hammer, which is a Texas version of sticks out "like a sore thumb" 2. stands out like a cactus in a rose garden 3. stands out like a possum in a dog show

Conspicuous as: 1. a pink saddle 2. fender skirts on a fire truck 3. ballet shoes on a bay mare 4. a pimple on a cheerleader's nose 5. a rusty link in a chrome chain, which is the only link that gets noticed

Conspiracy: the big dogs are ganging up on the little dogs

Constipated: 1. my plumbing's backed up 2. got a peach pit in my pipes 3. feel like I swallowed a stopper

Construction, poor: *See Assembled, poorly*

Consultant: 1. someone you hire to tell you what you already know 2.

someone who'll borrow your watch to tell you what time it is

Contagious: catchin'

Contemptible: sorry

Contented as: 1. a barbershop cat 2. a boardinghouse pup 3. a buffalo in a dirt wallow 4. a turtle on a log 5. a hog in mud 6. an old dog next to a warm fire

Contest: 1. real rodeo 2. a cuss-off [In the Old West, cowboys actually got together, on occasion, to hold cuss-offs to determine who could sulphurize the air (cuss) the best. Although the winner wasn't held in as high esteem as, say, the best all around cowboy, he was still admired by his peers.]

Contestant's card: *See Professional Rodeo Cowboy Association*

Continue: meanwhile, back at the ranch

Continued: 1. went right ahead 2. kept right on plowing

Contrary: if he falls in a river and drowns, look for the body upstream

Contribution, poor: contributed about as much as one poor pullet would to a trainload of hungry troops

Control: 1. keep a tight hold on the whoa reins 2. shorten the stake rope 3. ride a close herd on 4. keep the fences up 'cause a loose mare is always looking for a greener pasture 5. hold down the fort 6. take the slack out of the rope

Control yourself: 1. keep the lid on your can 2. keep your buttons snapped 3. hobble your emotions 4. stake rope (or ground hitch) yourself 5. put a governor on your carburetor 6. tighten your reins

Controversy, nonviolent: a cussin' or spittin' match

Convenience store: ice houses to a lot of old-timers [In the days before home refrigeration, folks would get their ice from the local ice house. One day the operator of an ice house in Dallas got the idea that folks coming in for ice might also buy other products such as eggs or bread. From that idea sprang the world's first 7-Eleven store, and an entire new industry was born.]

Convenient: mighty (or powerful) handy, as in "A pocket on a shirt is mighty handy." *See also Handy*

Conversation: 1. chin music 2. squaw talk 3. lip exercising *See also Talk*

Conviction: 1. sticks to his guns 2. tends to her knitting 3. keeps his fields plowed

Convince: bring 'em to your lick log, which infers to convince others your opinion is best *See also Lick log*

Convinced: 1. got him on my stringer 2. got him on my hook 3. got him singing off my song sheet 4. got him in my back pocket

Convincing: 1. could make a well believe it's a windmill 2. could make a cow give up her calf without a beller

Convincing as: 1. a spade flush 2. the business end of a .45

Cook: 1. steak charmer 2. bean masher 3. belly cheater 4. biscuit roller 5. biscuit shooter 6. pot wrangler 7. oven boss 8. dough puncher 9. bean masher 10. a Cajun cook is a flame thrower 'cause everything he prepares comes out blackened

Cook, good: could make a meal out of a bone's smell

Cook, inept: 1. tried to smoke a turkey but the bird wouldn't stay lit 2. took homemaking classes in school but dropped out after they covered thawing 3. can't open an egg 'cause it don't have no pull tab 4. puts dark meat in her chicken salad, which is something you just don't ever do in the South

Cook, inexperienced: 1. cooks peas and turnips in the same pot 2. where there's smoke, she's cooking 3. when she cooks banana pudding she don't peel the bananas 4. if it wasn't for pepper and ketchup, we'd starve

Cook, poor: 1. if she'd been cooking for the Yankees, the South would have won the war 2. takes an hour and a half to cook minute rice 3. her biscuits could kill a cat if thrown hard enough 4. can scorch water trying to boil it 5. could use one of her pancakes to patch an inner tube 6. her chili tastes like it was cooked in an old boot 7. her cooking would gag a sword swallower 8. you can taste feathers in her chicken-fried steak 9. the best thing she makes for dinner is reservations 10. flies commit suicide in her kitchen 11. gave some scraps to a stray dog and it paralyzed him

A&M **Cookies:** dry cush

Cooking: kissing don't last, cooking does

Cool as: the other side of the pillow

Cooling board: where you lie after you die

Coon biscuit: large biscuits made with deer meat in the center

Coon-footed: a horse with long pasterns which throw the fetlocks low

Coonie: *See Possum belly*

Coonin' a log: when the water is so high you have to sit down and sort of frog hop across a stream on a log

Cooper (Delta County): although spelled Coop-er it's pronounced Cup-er; named for L.W. Cooper who was instrumental in organizing the town in Northeast Texas not far from Klondike

Copperas Cove (Coryell County): pronounced quickly so the "a" is silent for Coppers Cove [The original application was for the name Cove; that was rejected so the residents settled for Coperas Cove, which related to the mineral taste in the water from a nearby spring, and the spelling has evolved to Copperas.]

Cooperate: 1. will sit still for that 2. will help corral that horse 3. will help plant that crop 4. will help raise that barn

Cooperation: 1. we all can't play the same instrument, but we all can play in the same key 2. we don't all have the same voice, but we can all sing the same song 3. sometimes you have to go along to get along

Cooperative effort: a load is much lighter when several mules are carryin' it

Coordination, poor: 1. has to pull over and come to a stop before he can pass gas 2. has to pull over to the side of the road before he can blow the horn

Cooter-back road: a dirt road with an arch (crown) in the middle to allow for rain to drain off

Copperhead snake: diamondmouth copperback, which is obviously taken from cottonmouth water moccasin and diamondback rattlesnake although the origin of the derivative is unknown

Copulation: 1. naval engagement 2. mattress thrashin' 3. leg rasslin'

Cordele (Jackson County): pronounced COR-deal; originally Sandy Creek, then Brushy Creek, then finally changed to honor the hometown of the postmaster, which was Cordele, Georgia

Cordwood: cordwood is a piece of firewood about 24 inches long, which fits nicely in most fireplaces. [If you have a stack of wood four feet high, four feet wide, and eight feet long, you have a cord of wood.]

Core: 1. the nubbin' 2. the heart

Corkscrew anchor: screw-like device used to stabilize corner posts

A&M **Corn:** horse feed

Corn coverings: shucks

Corn bread: Arkansas wedding cake

Corn bread and clabber: redneck malt, made by crumbling corn bread into a glass of buttermilk

Corn doger: cornmeal cake fried in a pan until crispy

Corn fritter: flapjacks made with cornmeal

Corn on the cob: 1. roastin' ears 2. sweet corn 3. fresh corn 4. garden corn

Corn toll: a percentage of your corn paid to the man who grinds it into meal; toll was paid in lieu of cash payment

Corner post: brace and stretch post

Cornered: like a frog in a blender, you got nowhere to turn to

Cornpone: corn bread made without milk or eggs; originated after the Civil War when milk or eggs were often in short supply

Corona: a saddle pad with a large colorful roll around the edge; not as popular as they were back in the fifties and sixties

Coronet: the section of the pastern over the hoof of a horse

A&M Corps happy: said of someone who is obsessed with the corps at Texas A&M

Corpus Christi (Nueces County): usually just CORE-pus; means "body of Christ" in Spanish

Correct: 1. hit the nail right on the head 2. hit the bull in the eye or hit the bull's eye 3. got your saddle on the right horse 4. got your boots on the right feet 5. mighty shoutin' right *See also Yes*

Corrective action: 1. get the train back on the track 2. get the horses hitched to the right wagon 3. pick up all the pieces of the puzzle 4. buy a new deck of cards 5. get the wagon (or ox) out of the ditch 6. put some oil on those troubled waters, which is a reference to old-time sailors believing that spilling oil on rough sea would calm the water

Corrigan (Polk County): pronounced CORE-a-gun; named for Pat Corrigan, who was the conductor on the first train that arrived after the railroad was completed in 1883 [Corrigan's grandson Douglas gained immortality when he took off from New York to fly to California and twenty-nine hours later landed in Ireland! He was forever after known as Wrong-Way Corrigan.]

Corsicana (Navarro County): pronounced Core-sa-can-ah [Corsicana is the county seat; Texas Revolution hero Juan Antonio Navarro was given the honor of naming the town, and he chose Corsicana as a tribute to the island of Corsica, his parents' homeland.]

Cost, unreasonable: 1. higher than my pocketbook 2. costs a pretty penny

A&M Cottage cheese: 1. clabber cheese 2. duck butter

Cotton, chop it: thin it out

Cotton, hoe it: clear out weeds and grass

Cotton, poor: bumblebee cotton, which is cotton that is so low a bee can stand on the ground to suck a blossom

Cotton, table it: put cotton on the baler table

Cotton Center (Hale County): pronounced as if it were Cott'n Sinner

Cotton country: a rural area where cotton farming is the primary enterprise

Cotton field: cotton patch

Cotton ginning time: packin' time, from the days when cotton was packed in bales

Cotton grades: from very best to absolute worst are: middlin' fair; good middlin'; strict middlin'; middlin'; and strict low middlin' *See also Quality, fair*

Cotton picker, bad: a pull dew, which is usually a group of cotton pickers that don't pick much

Cotton picker, good: keeps cotton goin' in his sack all the time

Cotton raking: using a rake to move cotton from the hopper (when the volume is low) into the gin stands

Cotton remnants: leftover cotton after picking a crop; not enough to make a whole bale; also called "scrap cotton"

Cotton scales: stillards

Cotton waste: stringy, shredded cotton that isn't good for much except perhaps as kindling to start a fire

Cotulla (LaSalle County): pronounced Ka-TWO-la; named for Polish immigrant Joseph Cotulla

Cough: the croup

Cough, hacking: graveyard cough

Count corral: corral where cattle were gathered for counting before being shipped or sold

Count rocks: dominos that add up to five or ten, the only ones that count [The count rocks are: blank-five; ace-four; two-three; double-five; six-four.]

Counter brand: when branded cattle were sold, a new brand was placed on the other side of the cow and a bar was burned through the original brand

Counterfeit, poor quality: couldn't fool a blind man

Country boy: 1. redneck 2. good ol' boy 3. goat roper 4. foaled in the country 5. bubba 6. wears boots because of his roots 7. went barefooted so long that when he finally did get a pair of shoes he wore 'em out from the inside ["When someone says he's just a country boy, you better keep your hand on your pocketbook," said Lyndon Johnson. In other words, just 'cause someone is a country boy, don't assume he's a country bumpkin.]

Country boy, dressed up: can see the hanger creases in his suit, which means country folks don't care to wear suits unless they have to, such as to a marryin' or buryin'

Country boy, smart: he may not eat possum, coon, armadillo, or jackrabbit, but he knows where to find 'em if another Depression breaks out

Country girl: 1. redneck girl 2. good ol' girl 3. heaven in blue jeans

Country music: Texas is the capital, Nashville is the county seat

Country people: 1. ranch-raised folks 2. raised on dirt 3. range folks

County employee: courthouse barnacle

County seat: the seat of government for a particular county; where the county courthouse is located and where all primary business concerning county activities, such as courts, is transacted

Courageous: 1. works the high wire without a net 2. got Brazos River water in his veins 3. knows how to die standing up 4. got more guts than you could hang on a fence 5. got enough guts to fill a number three washtub 6. got a double backbone 7. would fight a rattlesnake with one hand tied behind his back and give the snake three bites head start 8. would go down the cliffs of hell without a safety rope *See also Brave; Fearless*

Courthouse bench (or steps): liars' bench, which is a reference to the old-timers who don't have much to do but sit on a bench down at the courthouse and tell lies all day

Courting: 1. is like dying, you got to do it yourself 2. jularkin' 3. fixin' to make himself lady-broke 4. sparkin' [In Texas, when two youngsters are sweet on each other, a smart mother will have 'em shell beans so they can get some work done while sparkin'. That same mother wouldn't want 'em huskin' corn 'cause that's usually done in the barn.]

Cover it: 1. like green on grass 2. like white on rice 3. like stink on manure 4. like fur on a cat 5. Mother Hubbard it [a dress that covers everything but touches very little]

Covered: 1. like a low water crossing in a flash flood 2. like a dew on a lawn 3. like it was under grandma's quilt 4. like an anvil at the bottom of a stock tank, which would be covered with water 5. like a hardwood floor under wall-to-wall carpet

Cow: 1. generic term used to indicate cattle of either sex at any age 2. bovine 3. (dominoes) the largest non-double in a suit. Six-five would be the cow in the six suit.

Cow, barren: a cow that hasn't had a calf in the last several months and probably isn't going to; considered open and a "cull"

Cow, hornless: muley

Cow, milk type: cows that are "punched" while sitting on a stool

Cow, wild: could go through a barbed wire fence like a fallin' tree through a cobweb

Cow, worthless: coffee cow, only produces enough milk to keep the coffee blonde

Cow bird: a small white bird that spends all its time pickin' ticks off cows or peckin' through manure, which is why they are frequently compared to politicians

Cow boss: person in charge of a ranch's cattle operations

Cow cake: cattle feed made of heated and pressed cottonseed and formed into cakes (usually 100 pounds)

Cow camp: an area away from home where cowboys set up a temporary residence while gathering cattle; also called a roundup camp

Cow chips: dried cow droppings; often used as fuel for a fire when wood was in short supply

Cow country: an area where more cattle are raised than crops; the opposite would be farm country

Cow cousins: families, usually related, that were close enough to share a cow for milk but were not officially related

Cow driver: Texas term for one who drove cattle to northern markets

Cow droppings: 1. cow chips 2. meadow muffins 3. cow pies 4. cow flop 5. prairie coal [When wood was scarce, as it often was on the plains, dried cow chips were used for cook fires on trail drives. In West Texas, it is sometimes called Throckmorton firewood.]

Cow fever: term applied to those who were infatuated with becoming a cowboy

Cow-hocked: when a horse's feet are wide apart and the hocks are close together

Cow hunt: early Texas term for cattle roundups

Cow paper: When cash money was short, commerce was often conducted with a promissory note, mortgage, or even an I.O.U. and, regardless of the form, the documents were referred to as cow paper.

Cow pasture pool: golf

Cow shed: open front barn often used as a milking shed

Cow stomp: a shady spot where cattle gather to get out of the sun and stamp their feet to keep away the flies

Cow tipping: a game usually played by youngsters or drunks. Since cattle sometimes sleep standing up, the object is to sneak up on the animal without waking it and tip it over on its side. When successful, the cow isn't hurt, but its heart may skip a beat when it wakes up on the ground and thought it was standing up.

Coward: 1. got henhouse ways or his breath smells like hen feathers, both of which mean he's "chicken" 2. if he was melted down, he couldn't be poured into a fight 3. fraidy cat 4. afraid of his own shadow or afraid of a worm's shadow 5. paper backed 6. yellow as mustard but without the bite 7. always wears white underwear 'cause he never knows when he might need a white flag 8. only time he'll stand his ground is if he's buried standin' up 9. electric socks couldn't warm up his cold feet 10. someone who thinks with his feet when danger comes calling *See also Afraid; Scared*

Coward, extreme: in Texas, the supreme definition of coward is first cousin to Moses Rose. In 1836, as legend has it, William Barret Travis, convinced the Alamo would fall, gave an impassioned speech to the men, then drew a line with his saber and invited all who wanted to stand and fight to cross the line. All but Moses Rose crossed the line and died for Texas independence. *See also Afraid; Scared*

Cowardice cure: if your knees start knockin,' kneel on 'em

Cowbell: a copper bell worn by the bell cow, which is the one the others follow when it's feeding time; not to be confused with a bull bell, which is larger and has a bigger clapper

Cowbelles: country version of the Junior League; Western women who band together to stage social and fund-raising events

Cowboy: 1. stands on his own two feet by sitting on a horse 2. saddle warmer 3. leather pounder 4. bronc buster 5. goat roper 6. buckeroo 7. kicker 8. wrangler 9. cowpuncher 10. cow chaser 11. chuck wagon tailer 12. brush popper 13. waddie 14. a lover, a fighter, and a wild bull rider 15. someone who is paid to outthink a cow

Cowboy, experienced: 1. wore out his share of saddles 2. as cattle-wise as a calf's mother

Cowboy, female: 1. wranglerette 2. buckerooette 3. kickerette 4. a lover, a fighter, an' a wild barrel rider

Cowboy, good: 1. can ride anything with hair on it 2. top hand 3. expert at the 3 R's [riding, roping, [w]rangling] 4. a three-jump cowboy, one good enough to stay on a pitching horse for three jumps 5. when he gets in trouble, he lets his horse do the thinking 6.would do to ride the rough string [Every ranch outfit had a string of rough horses that were barely broken, much less suited for everyday riding. The best cowboys had the job of getting the kinks out of horses in the rough string.] *See also Good person*

Cowboy, old: a cowboy who hands out good advice 'cause he's too old to set a bad example

Cowboy, poor: 1. a corral cowboy, which means he spends more time around the corral talking cows than he does cowboying 2. couldn't ride a tame stick horse 3. couldn't ride a charley horse 4. couldn't ride a nightmare without getting thrown out of bed 5. would get throwed by a good rocking chair (or wheelchair) *See also Tenderfoot*

Cowboy, smart: 1. knows better than to get off a swimming horse and grab him by the tail [In swimming a river with a horse, the intelligent rider will slide off to the side and hold on to the saddle horn while helping the horse kick. This method allows the cowboy to easily swing back into the saddle when the river is crossed. On the other hand, if you hold onto the horse's tail and let him tow you across the river, he will probably run off when he gets to the other side, leaving you to shake yourself and walk home.] 2. he's horse smart, which means he knows a lot about how horses work [You can substitute cow, sheep, or pig. Do not, however, substitute women 'cause there's no such thing as a cowboy who knows a lot about how a woman works.]

Cowboy, talking: A cowboy can talk a lot better when he's kicking clods and scratchin' in the dirt like a chicken in a dung heap.

Cowboy code: 1. your word is your bond 2. do what you were hired to do 3. feed the neighbors 'cause you might be hungry yourself sometime 4. return strays if you want yours returned 5. never borrow another man's horse without permission 6. if your dog starts killin' the neighbor's calves, you shoot the dog so the neighbor won't have to

Cowboy cool: the temperature of the beer after all the ice in the cooler melted while you were participating in a rodeo

Cowboy limousine: Chevy Suburban

Cowboy pencil: a stick of wood. When a cowboy needs to do some drawin' or cipherin' while out on the range, paper and pencil are usually not available. In such cases, any small stick or tree limb can be used to write in the dirt.

Cowboy requirements: all you need is guts and a horse, and if you have enough guts, you can steal a horse

Cowboy snaffle: long shank snaffle

 Cowboy's cowboy: 1. a real hand 2. winner of an event in the National Finals Rodeo

Cowboyed: performed duties of a cowboy

Cowboy up: 1. said when cowboys saddle up and get ready to ride 2. said when city boys dress up like cowboys for a night out at the honky-tonk

Cowpuncher: term originated from the days when cowboys rode train cars loaded with cattle. Since cattle ride better standing up, the cowboys would walk through the cars and punch the animals with a long pointed stick to keep them from lying down. This prevented down cattle from being trampled or suffocating. The term is often abbreviated to just puncher.

Cowrisma: a country boy with charisma. During the 1990 governor's race in Texas, *Time* magazine claimed Clayton Williams had "cowrisma." Apparently, it didn't help at the ballot box because Ann Richards beat him like he was a rented mule.

Coyanosa (Pecos County): pronounced Ki-NO-sa

Cracked open: like an egg laid by a tall chicken

Crackers: shingles

Crap out: a session of exhausting physical activity

Crave: 1. got a hankerin' for 2. got a hurtin' for

Crayfish: 1. mud bugs 2. East Texas or Louisiana lobsters

Crazy: 1. a few bricks shy of a load 2. ain't playing with a full deck 3. his guitar ain't tuned right 4. his porch light's on but nobody is home 5. been eatin' loco weed with his Wheaties 6. got a screw loose in his thinker assembly 7. vertical hold is out on his television set 8. his cinch is loose 9. half a bubble out of plumb 10. if you put his brain in a mockingbird it would fly backwards 11. a few logs short of a cord 12. his genes are loose 13. ain't parked too close to the curb 14. a few fish short of a full stringer 15. a few pickles shy of a full barrel 16. a few peaches short of a full bushel 17. a few spokes are missing from his wheel 18. his biscuit is a little short of baking powder 19. his elevator don't stop at all the floors 20. don't have both oars in the water 21. got cobwebs in his attic *See also Idiot; Insane; Nutty; Strange person*

Crazy, very: slap-assed crazy

Crazy as: 1. an outhouse rat 2. a bed bug 3. a loco'd calf 4. a lizard with a sunstroke 5. a goat at mating time 6. a road lizard 7. a March hare 8. a parrot eatin' stick candy 9. a bullbat [Often in the late afternoon the bullbats fly in various directions giving the impression they are crazy, which they may very well be.]

Crazy look: 1. loco was camped out in his eyeballs 2. eyeballs are fogged over like a frosted windshield

Create: do up

Created excitement: raised a storm

Credit: 1. living on his jawbone 2. tick, as in "Bubba got his new hat on tick."

Credit, bad: 1. can't even borrow trouble 2. the cork's been hammered into my bottle [A bartender would set the bottle on the bar and let you drink until your credit ran out, then he'd hammer the cork into the bottle with the ball of his hand. You didn't get any more to drink till the tab was paid.]

Credit, misapplied: lightning does the work, thunder gets the credit

Creek bed, dry: arroyo

Creek, flooded: water in the creek got so high you had to look up to see the bottom, or you could see under it, both of which imply you were under water *See also Water, deep*

Creep: a small horse pen where a colt can be fed without interference from the mare

Creosote bush: greasewood

Crescent wrench: monkey wrench

Cresson (Johnson County): pronounced Cress-un, not CRE-son; named for John Cresson who was the leader of a wagon train that stopped in the area

Crest: the top of a horse's neck where the mane is located

Cribbing: a bad habit where a horse bites a fixed object, pulls back with its head, and sucks in air

Cribbing up: process of righting a derailed train engine and putting it back on the tracks [In the old days, this was generally done using numerous 2x6 wood levers and plenty of men with strong backs.]

Crick in his getalong: *See Hitch in his getalong*

Crick sand: a country version of quicksand

Crime, small: chicken larceny

Criminal: 1. high line rider 2. rides a crooked trail 3. desperado 4. lowlifer 5. drygulcher 6. backshooter *See also Crook*

Criminal, small time: 1. chicken rustler 2. Saturday night sinner, which means he leads a good life till he goes out on Saturday night and gets drunk 3. a bounty on his head wouldn't cover the cost of a bullet to shoot him

Criticize: 1. badmouth 2. sulphurize his reputation

Crockett (Houston County): pronounced CROCK-it; named for Texas hero Davy Crockett, who is believed to have camped in the area on his way to the Alamo

Crook: 1. his family tree has a lot of horse thieves hanging in it 2. got more ways to take your money than a room full of lawyers 3. knows his rights better than his wrongs *See also Thief*

Crooked: 1. if he swallowed a ten-penny nail, he'd spit up a corkscrew 2. will have to be screwed into a coffin when he passes on 3. has to screw on his socks 4. can't tell from his tracks if he's a coming or a going 5. a snake would break his back tryin' to follow his trail 6. could sleep in the shadow of a post hole auger

Crooked as: 1. a barrel of snakes 2. a barrel of fishhooks 3. a dog's hind leg

4. the devil's backbone 5. a snake in a cactus patch

Crop, laid by: a crop that has been cultivated and is waiting for harvest

Crop, promising: got a good season in the ground

A&M Crop failure: satirical expression for an expensive automobile

Crosscut saw: a misery whip. This refers to the whip action that occurs when a crosscut saw becomes jammed and springs back into place, causing misery to the person working the saw. Anyone who spent any time in an East Texas sawmill learned firsthand about a misery whip.

Cross-eyed: 1. gotch-eyed 2. can stand up in the middle of the week and see two Sundays 3. can watch a tennis match without moving his head 4. when she cries the tears roll down her back 5. so cross-eyed her eyeballs could swap sockets

Cross hobble: hobbling a horse by connecting a front foot to the rear foot on the opposite side, which can easily cause the animal to stumble

Crow hop: a mild form of bucking where the horse uses short, stiff-legged jumps

Crowd, quiet: Frank Luska of the *Dallas Morning News* once said of a crowd at a Dallas Mavericks game: "One guy walked out. He heard his tire leaking air in the parking lot."

Crowd, small: 1. not enough people to make a good combine crew 2. Frank Luska described a crowd at a Texas Ranger game as being "only a few more than Custer's last stand."

Crowded: 1. can't swing a dead cat without hitting someone 2. as a Baptist tent revival 3. the barn's full and the corral is fillin' up fast 4. packed to the rafters 5. thick as yellow jackets on a spring nest 6. there's an hour wait for the bathroom 7. the dance floor is full 8. somebody left the gate open, which implies that the pasture is full of cows because the gate to the pen was left open 9. have to grease your hips to turn around 10. crammed in like pigs in a trailer 11. couldn't stir 'em with a stick 12. everyone in the zip code was there

Crowell (Foard County): pronounced KROW-ul, rhymes with growl; named for George T. Crowell who owned the land the town was built on

Crude: rough hewn

Cruel: 1. would tie two cats together by their tails and hang 'em on a clothesline 2. would steal a kid's candy and eat it in front of him 3. would steal pencils from a blind beggar

A&M Crunchie: army cadet

Cry: 1. bawl 2. squall 3. catterwall 4. spill some tears

Cry a lot: 1. shed enough tears to short out the jukebox in a honky-tonk 2. more than the onion chopper in a Cajun restaurant 3. enough to fill a number three washtub (or a rain barrel) 4. put out more water than a patio fountain

Crystal City (Zavala County): pronounced CRIS-tul City; name came from several local springs with flowing water said to be crystal clear.

Cuero (DeWitt County): pronounced Q'AIR-oh; named for nearby Cuero Creek [The Spanish originally named the creek Arroyo del Curero (Creek of the Rawhide) because the Indians would slaughter cattle that got stuck in the mud. The Turkey Capital of the World.]

Cultivator: a plow used to get out weeds and grass. A cultivator you walked behind was a walking cultivator or a hill burner.

Cuney (Anderson County): pronounced COON-ee not Cun-ee; named for Cuney Price, the son of

C

H. L. Price, who was influential in organizing the town

Cunning as: a repossession wrecker driver [No matter how well you hide the car, he's always cunning enough to find it.]

A&M Cup: china

Cupboard: kitchen safe

Cupid: blind gunner

Curb bit: a bit specially designed to exert a lot of pressure on the horse's mouth; preferred by cowboys since it does not have to be removed for the horse to graze

Curb chain: small chain under a horse's chin that applies pressure to the nerves in the chin

Curb strap: strap attached to the bit that passes behind the horse's chin

Cure: sure as an eggshell full of red pepper will cure a dog from suckin' eggs

Curious: came to town to see the fat lady [The traveling carnival shows made regular stops in country towns. The carnival always included, among other oddities, a fat woman, and the country boys were always curious to see just how fat she was.]

Curious as: 1. a kitten in a new room 2. a calf in a new pasture 3. a bra with three cups

Curling iron: beau catcher

Curry: brush a horse's coat

Currycomb: a comb with blunt teeth that removes loose hair and dirt from a horse's coat

Cush: leftover corn bread plus onions, eggs, and water, mixed together and cooked in a frying pan until it has the consistency of oatmeal

Cuss him: give him a Confederate talkin' to [Confederate soldiers had a penchant for expressing their views with "colorful" language.]

Cuss words, clean: 1. heck fire 2. shoot fire 3. goldarn 4. consarned 5. dad blast it 6. bull pucky 7. hell's bells 8. son of a buck 9. dad blamed 10. fiddlesticks

Cussed a lot: 1. ran out a string of profanity so hot it would a fried bacon 2. cussed enough to singe all the grass within ten yards 3. enough to melt the ears off a Baptist preacher 4. made the air sulfurous with profanity 5. fluent in the bull whacker's language 6. can cuss a gate off its hinges, a wheel off a wagon, or the feathers off a buzzard 7. could out-cuss a veteran mule skinner on his best day

Cusser: 1. naughty tongued 2. tough mouthed 3. flannel tongued 4. keeps a Civil War tongue in his mouth [Many of the soldiers in that fight were notorious cussers. For Confederate soldiers, if they didn't cuss before they joined up, they sure did by the time the fight was over.]

Cussing: 1. airing out his lungs 2. taking the strain off his liver

Cut banks: a hillside or bank that drops off sharply; very dangerous to horse and rider

Cut in half: in Texas, you never cut anything in half, you always cut it half in two.

Cut it short: 1. scissor it off some 2. trim the fat and get to the meat 3. bob tail it 4. take a shortcut to the main point

Cut N' Shoot (Montgomery County): always pronounced Cut n' Shoot, never Cut and Shoot. A fight started either about a local preacher who was a little too fond of the female members of his congregation or over the design of new church steeple. In either case, the participants used guns and knives.

Cut off: 1. gelded 2. lopped off

Cut out: separate specific cattle from the rest of the herd

Cut proud: term describing a gelding who still goes through the motions of a stallion even though he's been fixed

Cutthroat (dominoes)**:** 1. three-handed Mexican dominoes 2. four-handed count dominoes where each person plays for himself and keeps his own score (under the watchful eye of his opponents, you can be sure)

Cut up: 1. required more stitches than a patchwork quilt 2. got himself fricasseed 3. got himself skewered 4. looks like he was used as a razor blade tester *See also Bloody and Knife fight victim*

Cut up, severely: got more stitches than a patchwork quilt

Cut your partner off (dominoes)**:** play in such a way as to block your partner [When you do that, you better be sure to go out or domino to keep relations with your partner civil.]

Cute: darlin'

Cute as: 1. a bug's ear 2. a white-faced calf 3. a speckled pup 4. a paint horse 5. a newborn colt (or puppy)

Cutter: 1. a thin, worthless cow whose future has a lot of bologna in it 2. a showoff 3. a hay cutter

Cutter bull: a male calf that has become sexually mature. Some cowboys refer to a cutter bull as being nothing but horns and testicles.

Cutting horse: a horse specially trained to remove selected cattle from a herd

Cutting horse, good: 1. could cut the bakin' powder out of a biscuit without breaking the crust 2. could cut fly specks out of a pepper shaker 3. could cut a prairie dog out of his hole 4. could cut the eye teeth out of a rattlesnake 5. could cut the seeds out of a watermelon and not break the rind 6. could cut fleas off a mongrel dog

Cutting torch: blue tip wrench

Cynic: knows everything but don't believe anything

D

D.M.S.: Distinguished Military Student

D.P.S.: Department of Public Safety

D.S.: Distinguished Student

Dadgumit: damgotit

Daingerfield (Morris County)**:** pronounced Dain-gur-field, not Danger-field; the county seat got its name from Capt. London Daingerfield who was killed in an Indian fight in the area

Dainty as: 1. a June bride 2. a blown glass bell

Dairy farmer: owes everything he has to udders (sorry, I just couldn't resist)

Daisetta (Liberty County)**:** pronounced Day-SET-a, not Daisey-etta; Newt Farris named the town in honor of Daisy Barrett and Etta White

Dalhart (Dallam/Hartley Counties)**:** pronounced DAL-hart; the name is a combination of Dallam and Hartley since the town is on the line that separates these two counties

Dallas (Dallas County)**:** also called "Big D" or the Manhattan of the West [Dallas is said to be where the East peters out, which means Fort Worth is where the West begins. Dallasites prefer to say Dallas is where the cotton pickin' ends and culture begins. No one is positive about who Dallas was named for but it was probably either vice-president George Mifflin Dallas or an early settler named Joseph Dallas. Either way, the word is Scottish for "place on the plains."]

Dally: wrapping a rope around the saddle horn several times so it will be secure without having to tie a knot [In a rodeo, the dally is used in team roping but not in calf roping since a hard, fast tie is necessary to hold the calf. Dally comes from the Spanish *dar*

la vueltra which means "give a turn." A cowboy who uses this method is called a dally man. These cowboys can often be identified by one or more missing fingers on his dally hand since the wrap can be very dangerous.]

Dally horn: a saddle horn that's a little taller than normal to allow for easy dallying

Dam: female parent of a horse

Damn: pronounced day-um in Texas, as in "Frankly may dear, I don't give a day-um."

Danbury (Brazoria County): pronounced as if it were two words, Dan Berry; named for D.J. "Uncle Dan" Moller, a local rancher

Dance (noun): 1. wingding 2. shindig 3. hoedown 4. hoe dig 5. properly pronounced daince in Texas

Dance (verb): 1. hugging set to music 2. boot scooting 3. shake a hoof 4. rubbin' bellies 4. scratching or polishing belt buckles 5. bone shuffling

Dance, enticing: showin' her linen, which means parts of her undergarments are showing while she moves on the dance floor

Dance close: 1. hog rasslin' 2. hold the girl so close you're almost behind her

Dance fast: 1. movin' to a frisky fiddle 2. smoke your boots

Dance hall fever: condition prevalent among those who like to dance and have a good time, primarily at a Texas honky-tonk; often considered a highly contagious disease

Dancer: 1. hoofer 2. two-stepper 3. boot scooter 4. buckle polisher

Dancer, expert: can dance to the national anthem or "Dixie"

Dancer, good: 1. slings a mean ankle 2. goes through more buckles than most people do underwear 3. a dress-tail popper [This implies she's is so good out on the dance floor that she can make the tail of her dress pop like a bull whip.]

Dancer, large: looks like a waltzing rhino

Dancer, light-footed: could tap dance on a light bulb

Dancer, poor: does a whole lot better at intermission than she does on the dance floor

Danciger (Brazoria County): pronounced DANCE-a-gurr; named for the Danciger Oil and Refining Company

Dancing: 1. a contact sport before some darn fool invented line dancing 2. hog or pig rasslin' [The difference between rassling and dancing is that some holds are barred in rassling.]

Dancing around: like a drunk spider [This is an old country saying and yet years of research have failed to uncover a single person who will admit to actually ever seeing a drunk spider.]

Dancing like: a bobber on a line

Dandelion greens: peckerwaller

Dandelion puffball: snuff ball

Dandy brush: a brush with stiff bristles

Danevang (Wharton County): pronounced DAN-a-vang, which is Danish for meadow

Danger sign: 1. a horse running with an empty saddle, which in the Old West usually meant the rider had either been thrown or shot off 2. the flag is flying upside down [A flag flown upside down is supposed to be a danger or help-needed signal. Usually when the Texas flag is flying white stripe down, it means some Yankee didn't know how to fly it.]

Dangerous as: 1. opening the latch on a wire gate [In less modern times, gates in Texas were constructed by attaching barbed wire to a stick or pole. The gate would be closed by stretching the wire taut and latching the pole in loops of wire on a fence post. If you let the pole slip when opening the gate, it would whip back and strike you, usually in the chest or belly 2. lightning striking your zipper 3. wetting on a 'lectric fence [Any male who has ever made that mistake knows just how dangerous and painful it can be.] 4. walking into a lion's cage with a pocket full of pork chops 5. a copperhead under your comforter 6. a skunk (or scorpion) with his tail up 7. a hornet (or yellow jacket) with his tail down 8. tryin' to put your foot down while it's in your mouth 9. sleeping in a waterbed with long toenails 10. playing with a cocked cannon 11. a walking rocker on a high porch [A walking rocker is one that moves just a smidgen (little bit) each time you rock back and forth.] *See also Hazardous; Risky*

Dangerous person: 1. bad medicine 2. due a wide berth 3. will whip or tree anyone who gets in his way 4. a very good person not to mess with

Dangerous situation: 1. smoking in a fireworks factory 2. using rocket fuel in your coal oil lamp 3. trying to milk an alligator, fraught with danger at both ends 4. a bad time to have your gun jam 5. running out of room on the dance floor 6. cattle are getting mighty thirsty, which is a reference to cattle being hard to control when they are thirsty 7. driving on black ice [Black ice is a layer of ice on a busy highway that is thin, almost invisible, and extremely dangerous to drive on.] 8. sittin' in the electric chair and prayin' for a power failure 9. a black widow in your boot 10. courtin' the sheriff's daughter 11. playin' poker blindfolded 12. walkin' under a Ferris wheel [A lot of country boys chew tobacco all the time, even when on a ride. If they're near the top of the Ferris wheel when they need to spit, which is often the case, they naturally just spit out the side of the gondola. If you happen to be walking underneath, you get splattered.]

Danglers: *See Jinglebobs*

Darco (Harrison County): pronounced Dar-co; named for lignite that was mined in the area and used as a decolorizer in the refining process

Daring: 1. would play basketball in a mine field 2. would shoot craps with the devil 3. ain't afraid of hell, high water, or a pretty girl 4. would arm wrestle King Kong 5. got grit in his gizzard and sand in his craw 6. a fugitive from the law of averages [This is how Audie Murphy, one of the most daring Texans of all time, once described himself. Unfortunately, the law of averages finally caught up with him when he later died in a plane crash.]

Dark: 1. pitch black 2. so dark you could feel it

Dark, barely: first dark, when you can't see the horizon any longer

Dark, completely: slap dark

Dark as: 1. pitch 2. a pile of black cats on a moonless night 3. a lighthouse with the bulb burned out 4. the inside of a boot when it's filled up with foot 5. night under a wash pot (or skillet) 6. the inside of a cow (or black bear) 7. a wolf's mouth 8. the bottom of a deep well *See also Black*

Dark moon: interval between old and new moon

Dark night: 1. so dark, if you lit a match, you'd have to light a second one to see if the first one was burning 2. so dark the bats are flying on autopilot 3. couldn't see your hand in front of your face 4. couldn't find your nose with both hands 5. as dark as it would be to a blind flea on a black cat under a bushel of wet charcoal 6. raindrops had to ask directions to find the ground

Darling: pronounced darlin' in Texas

Darrouzett (Lipscomb County): pronounced Dare-ah-zet; originally named Lourwood but name was changed to honor John Louis

Darrouzett, who was an attorney for the Santa Fe Railroad

Daughters, all married: all daughtered out

Dawn: 1. rooster time 2. crack of day 3. break of day 4. newborn day 5. first light

Dawn, cloudy: the new day was stillborn

🅰️🅼 **Dawn duck:** off-campus student at Texas A&M; also called Day Doger

Dawn lilies: garden house lilies, often planted around the outhouse

Dawn to dusk: cain't see to cain't see, which is how long country folks have to work to stay ahead of starvation

Day shift: day herding

Day, good: any day you wake up with a pulse [An old-timer once remarked that every day when he woke up, the first thing he did was check the obituaries to see if his name was listed. If it wasn't, he knew it would be a good day. That same man also wondered how people manage to die in alphabetical order.]

Daydream: turkey dreams

🐎 **Daylighting:** a condition where you can see daylight between the rider's rear end and the seat of the saddle during a rodeo, which indicates the rider is having trouble staying on; also called seeing daylight

Dead: 1. shook hands with eternity 2. morgue-aged 3. on a stony lonesome 4. just coyote bait 5. pushing up bluebonnets 6. don't have the pulse of a pitchfork 7. ready for a cold slab 8. answered the last roll call 9. turned up his toes or turned belly up *See also Died; Died suddenly*

Dead as: 1. hell in a preacher's backyard (or a parson's parlor) 2. a bearskin rug (or a mink coat) 3. a lightning bug in the cream pitcher 4. a

drowned cat in a goldfish bowl 5. a rotten stump 6. a doornail or doorknob 7. a wooden Indian 8. a sardine in a can 9. a fly in molasses 10. a 6-card poker hand *See also Died; Died suddenly*

Dead double (dominoes): refers to a double that can never be played because all other six dominoes in the group have been played

Deadly combination: jealous wife and an active imagination

Deadning: an area where trees have died either naturally or by girdling which means large areas of bark have been removed. A deadning is considered highly dangerous during storms because dead limbs are easy prey to high wind.

Deaf as: 1. a cow skull 2. a granite rock 3. a snubbin' post

🅰️🅼 **Dean's team:** mythical list of Texas A&M students who passed less than 12 hours in a semester

Debilitated: whipped down

Deceive by flattery: honey funk

Deceived: 1. pulled the wool over their eyes 2. hoodwinked

Deceiving: Gib Lewis said of changing the Texas constitution, "It's one of those things that sounds good and tastes bad."

Deception: he wet in my boots and told me it was rainwater

Deck of cards: 1. railroad Bible 2. California prayer book [This saying originated during the California gold rush when a lot of people who didn't find gold turned to card playing as their "last prayer" in the search for an easy fortune.]

Dedicated: 1. goes the whole hog 2. will stay with you till the last drop of sweat 3. married to, as in "married to his job" 4. likes his job as much as a chicken likes working with eggs

Dedicated as: 1. a preacher tracking sin 2. an Aggie football fan

Dee ring: d-shaped rings that the saddle cinches are attached to

Deep: 1. goes all the way to bedrock 2. goes all the way to the bottom of the well 3. goes so far down the other end of the hole could be a cup on a Chinese golf course [In Terlingua, Texas, where the world championship chili cook-offs are held, the outside toilets were said to be so deep you could listen in on Chinese conversations.]

Deep as: a West Texas oil well [Some of the deepest wells in the world were drilled in oil-rich West Texas.]

Deep well: 1. water comes out boiling, which implies the well is deep enough for hell to heat the water 2. have to strain the rice out before using the water, implying the well goes all the way to China

Deer, large: could make a rocking chair out of the horns

Deer camp: where deer hunters sleep, eat, drink, play cards, and talk about the one that got away. While most deer camps are rundown old shacks that ought to be condemned, some are four-bedroom, well-equipped cabins that you'd be proud to live in year round.

Defeated: 1. got saucered and blowed 2. got blown plumb out of the tub 3. got my tail feathers trimmed

Defender, staunch: will stand in the hedge and take up the gap, which is how Texan Leon Jaworski was described in a eulogy after his death

Defunct as: 1. Aunt Bessie's corset 2. ethyl gasoline *See also Obsolete*

Dehorned cattle: those whose horns have been removed

Dekalb (Bowie County): pronounced Da-calb, not DEE Kalb [According to legend, when Davy Crockett visited the area he asked about the name and was told there wasn't one. He was asked to suggest a name and he came up with De Kalb after Prussian Baron de Kalb.]

Delay: 1. put it on the back burner 2. put it on the back shelf 3. drag your feet awhile

Delicate as: frost on a moonbeam

Delicate situation: 1. got a fly in the ointment 2. got a blonde hair in the butter

Delicious: 1. larrupin' good 2. powerful good 3. sets your lips to rejoicing 4. better than mesquite grass to a longhorn steer 5. better than cow's milk to a newborn calf 6. best I ever wrapped a lip around 7. pure dee good eatin' 8. chin lickin' good *See also Taste, good*

Delirious: 1. got snakes in his boots 2. got spiders in his shorts

Delmita (Starr County): pronounced del-MEET-ah [According to legend, N.G. Pena held a lottery to determine the name of the town. Each of his seven sons drew one letter of the alphabet and the seven letters were combined to form the name.]

Demerits: rams

Democrat: Will Rogers, one of the favorite sons of Oklahoma and a great fan of Texas, once said, "I am not a member of any organized political party. I am a Democrat." According to the old country saying, not all Democrats are horse thieves, but all horse thieves are Democrats.

Democrat, devout: yellow dog Democrat, which means he'll vote the straight Democratic ticket even if there is a yellow dog on the ballot

Demote a cowboy: put him on the haying crew, fence crew, or thrashing crew, all of which are jobs a real cowpoke considers a demotion

Denial: Texan James B. McSheehy once said, "I deny the allegations and defy the alligator."

Denison (Grayson County): pronounced DEN-a-sun; named

for George Denison, a vice-president of the Katy Railroad

Dentist: 1. enamel driller 2. tooth doctor 3. tooth fairy 4. jaw breaker 5. jaw cracker [A dentist's office is a jaw cracker suite.]

Dentures: store-bought teeth

Denver City (Yoakum County): originally named Wasson since it was surrounded by the Wasson ranch [When oil was discovered, the name was changed to honor the Denver Production and Royalty Company, which financed petroleum development in the area.]

Departed: 1. left out for parts unknown 2. left out in a hurry 3. cut a hole in the atmosphere 4. took off for some high riding 5. hightailed it *See also Leave*

Departing: If you don't think I'm leaving, you just count the days I'm gone.

Dependable: 1. solid as bedrock 2. plows a straight row all the way to the end 3. as grandma's gravy, which is always good

Deport (Lamar County): pronounced DEE port; named for Col. Dee Thompson, who founded the town supposedly so he would have a place to water his horses

Depressed: 1. my heart is as heavy as a bucket of hog livers [This refers to the fact that when hogs were killed, the livers were generally saved in one bucket. If you had a lot of hogs to kill, the bucket got heavy to tote.] 2. my heart is as heavy as a bushel basket full of ball bearings 3. in low cotton, which is the opposite of someone doing well being in high or tall cotton 4. feeling so low you couldn't get a jack under me

Depressing as: homecoming at an orphanage

Depression soup: *See Soup, thin*

Deranged: *See Crazy; Insane*

Derringer: a very small pistol, usually with two barrels, named for the inventor. These pistols packed a lot of wallop in a small package that could be easily concealed on your person, such as in a vest pocket or a purse. Since these guns were small and powerful they were favorites of cardsharps and tinhorn gamblers. The range and accuracy were poor, but they were very useful if all you had to do was hit some old cowhand sitting on the other side of a poker table. Also called a stingy gun.

Desdemona (Eastland County): pronounced DES-da-mona the settlement was originally Hogtown since it was located on Hog Creek. The name was changed to Desdemonia to honor the daughter of the justice of the peace, then altered by postal officials in 1901 to Desdemona, probably for Othello's wife.

Desirable: 1. better than a fifty-yard-line ticket at the Super Bowl 2. as a snow cone in hell 3. would give half the King Ranch for it [The King Ranch is one of the world's largest, occupying 850,000 acres in Texas alone, not to mention the foreign holdings.] 4. would give my war pension for it 5. would give up some body parts for that 6. worth riding through blisters for

Desire: 1. want it so bad I could spit (or taste it) 2. got a yearn for 3. got a hankerin' for [When asked why he purchased the town of Luckenback, Texas, Hondo Crouch replied, "I wanted it for the same reason a dog buries a bone, so no other dog'll get it."]

Desk, large: 1. would have to be a distance runner to chase a secretary around it 2. looks like the deck of an aircraft carrier

Desolate: 1. looks like hell with all the inmates out to lunch 2. where rattlesnakes wouldn't pitch their tent 3. a gone-yonder county

Desperate: 1. you're huntin' hungry [If you go hunting when you're hungry, you'll tend to shoot at anything and take chances you might not otherwise take, which frequently means you come home still hungry.] 2. playing dead to call buzzards 3. grabbing at strings (or straws) 4. need that more than a dry land farmer needs rain, which is something a farmer always needs 5. grabbing at sunbeams

Desperate as: an Aztec witch doctor without a virgin on sacrifice day

Desperation: a drowning man will grab at anything, even a double-edge sword

A&M Dessert: 1. cush 2. cush plate is a dessert plate

Destination: 1. jumping-off place 2. gettin'-off place 3. halting place

Destitute: 1. the bank won't let me draw breath 2. ain't got a tail-feather left 3. scraping the bottom of my last barrel 4. my boot soles are so thin, if I scratched a match on 'em I'd set my socks on fire 5. if eagles were a dollar a pound, I couldn't afford a humming-bird drumstick 6. grew up so hard we had to take turns eating, and my turns came on Monday, Wednesday, and Friday 7. if money was leather, I couldn't half sole a katydid 8. so bad off I couldn't buy a pair of pants for a pissant 9. have to fast twice a week to keep from starving to death 10. ain't got a pot to pee in, a bed to slide it under, or a window to throw it out of *See also Broke; Poor*

Destructive: could tear up one of the great pyramids with a crowbar

Detergent: washin' powder

Deteriorated: gone to the dogs, to hell, to pot, or to seed

Determination: the good Lord willing and the creeks don't rise [A variation is the good Lord willing and the wash don't fall off the line, which means she wouldn't have clean clothes to wear. We all know that women,

unlike cowboys, don't go anywhere unless their clothes are clean.]

Determine the loser: figure out whose train got robbed

Determined: 1. shore 'nuff means business 2. hell bent for leather 3. will do it if it means hairlipping the governor and every mule in Texas (or every cannibal in the Congo) 4. dead set on 5. gonna do it, come hell or high water 6. will do it by hook or by crook [Davy Crockett said, "I'm determined to stand up to my lick log, salt or no salt."]

Developing: 1. something's brewing, cooking, or stewing 2. it's taking shape like a growing girl 3. the coffee is getting ready to boil

Device: 1. contraption 2. thingamajig 3. dofunny

Devil: 1. boogerman 2. old heck 3. old scratch

Deviled egg: dressed egg

Dewalt (Fort Bend County): pronounced DEE-walt, although if you get in a hurry and forget the "t" you're OK; named for local plantation owner Thomas Waters Dewalt

Dewclaw: a useless toe (claw) on an animal, usually a dog

Dewlap: the loose skin that hangs from the front of a cow's neck

Diagonally: 1. catty corner 2. catty-whampus 3. antigogglin 4. antigodlin

Diamond: 1. a hunk of coal that made good [Most girls will tell you the only thing harder than a diamond is getting one.]

Diamonds (playing card suit): glass cutter [In some cases the "gl" in glass is dropped, especially if you have a winning hand in diamonds.]

Diaper: 1. three-corner pants 2. hippins

Diarrhea: 1. Aztec two-step 2. Montezuma's revenge 3. green apple nasties 4. the Mexican water trot 5. Mexican two-step 6. Arkansas travels

D

7. the backdoor trots, which obviously is a reference to trotting out the back door and heading to the outhouse in a hurry [During the war Rebels believed that whiskey was a sure cure for the Tennessee quick step, and some of their descendants still believe it.]

Diboll (Angelina County): pronounced DIE-ball; named for J. C. Diboll, a local landowner

Dice: 1. bones 2. devil's play bones 3. painted rocks (or marbles)

Dice player: shooter, which is derived from shooting dice in a crap game

Did the impossible: caught lightning in a bottle

Did you ever: jevver, pronounced as one word in Texas

Didn't say anything: never said pea turkey or didly squat

Didn't show up: if he was here he was dressed like Claude Raines (the invisible man)

Didn't mean to: didn't go to do it or didn't aim to do it

Died: 1. woke up shoveling coal for the furnaces of hell 2. gave up the ghost 3. went over the river 4. fed the buzzards 5. quit the earth 6. gave up his guitar for a harp 7. headed for the last roundup in the sky 8. finished his branding 9. loped off into the sunset 10. cashed in his chips 11. roped a cloud and rode off to the great beyond 12. the fire went out in his boiler (or his pilot light went out)

Died happy: took the undertaker and his helper three days to get the smile off his face

Died suddenly: 1. never knew what hit him 2. didn't have time to kiss his wife or cuss the IRS 3. got got before he knew he was being chased 4. bit the dust and got too large a mouthful 5. lit a shuck for the pearly gates and didn't have time to get a passport 6. bought the farm

Diesel aftertaste: the supposed aftertaste some people believe you get if mesquite wood is used in barbecuing

Diet: the length you go to change your width

Diet, successful: lost a third grader [This means he lost about sixty-five pounds or roughly the weight of a child in the third grade. The grade can be adjusted if you lose more or less weight.]

Difference: Someone once said that the difference between men and boys is the price of the toys, which means the amount a male person spends on toys is indicative of whether he is a man or a boy. Another version might be the difference between women and girls is the price of the curls.

Difference, dramatic: only thing they have in common is that neither one of 'em was raised by coyotes

Difference, large: the difference between lightning and a lightning bug

Difference of opinion: in a corral, some people see the horse, some see the manure

Different as: 1. a wolf and a poodle dog 2. a hog and a herring 3. night and day 4. snakes and snails

Different situation: 1. that's another bucket of possums 2. that's another box of worms 3. you got a long shot with a limb in the way

Difficult as: 1. teaching a mermaid to do the splits 2. tryin' to find a needle in a haystack while it's going through a threshing machine 3. taking the shine off a sausage 4. climbing a rainbow 5. settin' cotton picking to music 6. keeping mosquitoes out of a swamp 7. eatin' Jell-O with chopsticks 8. trying to swim up a waterfall 9. puttin' socks on a rooster 10. picking up mercury with a pair of tweezers 11. roping (or riding) a lightning bolt 12. sneaking the crack of dawn past a veteran rooster 13. sneezing with your eyes open 14. trying to hear a whisper in a whirlwind 15. tryin' to get a drink out of a fire hose 16. picking rat droppings out of a pepper mill 17. trying to blow out a gas lamp 18. trying to shovel sunshine 19. making butter out of skim milk 20. digging a ditch in the ocean 21. plowing a wet field behind a drunk mule 22. shearing an elephant 23. catchin' a housefly under a teacup 24. shooting pool with a calf rope 25. getting a cow out of quicksand 26. tryin' to strike a wet match 27. running a marathon with a pebble in your shoe 28. pushin' a wet noodle through a keyhole

Difficult situation: 1. there's a lot more alligators than there is rice stalks in that pond 2. plowin' in sticky mud, which means it'll stick to the blade, making plowing very difficult 3. the log is so crooked it won't lay still in any position 4. like trying to sack up a den of rattlesnakes (or a wildcat with a toothache) 5. tough row to hoe 6. a lot of stumps in the field 7. will separate the cowboys from the greenhorns, which is a Texas variation of separate the men from the boys [The most difficult situation I ever heard about was the ol' boy whose wife caught him cheating on her. When he went to sleep, she got a couple of tubes of super glue and fastened his private parts to his leg. Later that night when her husband got up to go to the bathroom he found out real quick that he was truly in a difficult situation.] *See also Hard to do; Tough job*

Difficult to accept: hard (or bitter) pill to swallow

Difficult to handle: 1. hard to curry 2. hard to keep in a corral

Difficult, somewhat: it's just a little harder to make a banker out of a horse thief than it is to make a horse thief out of a banker

Dig: 1. gopher 2. auger

Dilemma: 1. whether you're hung as a lamb or a lion, you will still be dancin' at the end of a rope 2. whether you die from the chills or the fever, you are still dead 3. don't know whether to wet or go blind 4. don't know whether to go home or go crazy 5. caught between a rock and a hard place 6. caught between the devil and the deep blue sea

Dilemma, environmental: an endangered animal eating an endangered plant

Dilly-dally: polly-foxing

Dilute: water it down

Dime Box (Lee County): founded long before they got a post office, which meant mail service was poor at best. To send a letter, residents would put the stamped envelope and a dime in a box outside Joseph S. Brown's office down at the mill. One a week the letters were collected and delivered to Giddings to be mailed, and the person who made the trip kept the dimes as payment for his trouble.

Dimwit: 1. his coil ain't wrapped too tight 2. she took an umbrella to a baby shower 3. would only be charged half price by a mind reader 4. only time he really knows where he is going is when he takes castor oil 5. has the mental range of a windshield wiper 6. you could pull a slow one on him 7. his roof ain't nailed on too tight (or is short a few shingles) 8. ain't no light on in his attic 9. if brains were dynamite he couldn't blow his nose 10. if he knew half of what he thinks he knows he'd be dangerous 11. undertakes vast projects with half vast ideas 12. has to be watered twice a week

Dine with us: stay and see how the poor folk live, which is said no matter what your financial condition

Dinero (Live Oak County): pronounced Da-nair-oh, which is Spanish for money [According to legend, the name came from rumors of Mexican treasure buried in the area. It has never been found if it ever existed.]

Ding Dong (Bell County): appropriately located in Bell County

Dink: a horse that is known to be a poor bucker, which is not what a contestant in a rodeo wants since half the score comes from the animal

Dinner: the noon meal in Texas

Dinner call: come and get it before the grease sets

Dinner choices: have two choices for dinner, take it or leave it

Dip: 1. smokeless tobacco 2. a strong antiseptic used to control ticks, lice, etc., on cattle and sheep

Diplomacy: 1. lying in state 2. the ability to dive into a cesspool and not make a splash 3. the art of saying things in such a way that no one knows what you said 4. the art of saying "nice doggie, nice doggie" till you can find a rock

Diplomat: 1. can put all his cards on the table without showing his hand 2. can make his wife believe she'd look fat in a mink coat 3. can tell you to go to hell and make you look forward to the trip 4. remembers a lady's birthday but forgets her age 5. can let you do all the talkin' while he gets what he wants 6. puts please before shut the hell up

Direct (Lamar County): pronounced DYE-rect; name supposedly came from a traveling preacher who told the local folks they were going "direct to hell" for selling whiskey to Indians

Direction: "To know where we are going, it's important to know where we have been," said Texan Sam Rayburn.

Dirt road: *See Road, Dirt*

Dirty: broady

Dirty as: an Indian's horse blanket in a drought [The implication is that the only time an Indian's horse blanket got washed was when it rained.]

Disadvantage: 1. playin' with a short stick [When Jimmy Johnson became coach of the Dallas Cowboys, Jim Reeves of the *Fort Worth Star Telegram* said he was working with a short stick, which meant he was at a disadvantage; he later found a much bigger one.] 2. not playing on a level field [If a football field was not level, the theory is that whoever had the lower end would be at a disadvantage because they would be playing uphill. The saying could also be used by the winning team to mean advantage.]

Disadvantaged as: a cat wearing boxing gloves (he won't catch many rats)

Disagree: 1. that log won't float 2. that dog won't hunt 3. that rig won't drill 4. that dipper won't hold water 5. that cat won't flush

Disagreeable: was raised on sour milk and paregoric

Disagreement, large: a large-bore squabble

Disagreement, small: a small-bore squabble

Disappeared: 1. couldn't find hide nor hair of him 2. like he fell into a varmint hole and pulled it in after him 3. faster than a plate of fried chicken when the preacher comes over for Sunday dinner 4. like a short beer 5. he's got the coon and gone

Disappeared suddenly: absquatulated [This term, used by country folk until about the turn of the century, has become archaic but is too good a word to be totally forgotten.]

Disappointed as: 1. a bride left at the altar 2. a coyote with a rubber chicken

Disaster: 1. a real train wreck 2. bottom fell out of the milk bucket (or churn) 3. roof caved in on the hen-house 4. all hell come undone

Disaster, eminent: 1. the firing squad is taking target practice 2. a train wreck is coming

Discouraged: 1. his tail is dragging the ground 2. his dauber is down 3. down in the mouth 5. his face is long enough to eat oats out of a butter churn

Discouraging as: 1. smelling whiskey through the jailhouse door 2. a rice planter up a salt river 3. the bottom check fallin' into the well [A bottom check is used to determine how deep you've dug, and if it happens to fall into the well, you have to fish it out before you can proceed, which is very discouraging to a well digger.]

Discovered: 1. stumbled into 2. fell into

Discovery well: the first oil well brought in a new field. According to one grizzled old roughneck, "They either discover oil or discover there ain't no oil so any well is a discovery well."

Discuss openly: talk turkey

Discussion: 1. holding herd [This was derived from cowboys getting together to decide what must be done with the livestock.] 2. holding court [This generally applies to an old-timer telling stories to members of the younger generation.]

Disgraced: sold his saddle, which was about the most disgraceful thing a cowboy could do

Disgraced the family: up and registered Republican [Texas was a Democratic stronghold for several generations after the Civil War. In more modern times, however, Democrat can easily be substituted here.]

Disguised: gunnysacked, which refers to the old practice of cowboys wearing gunnysacks over their heads when attacking sheepherders

Dish (or disk)**:** a plow that breaks up the ground and turns one lane

Dish, one way: a plow that turns the ground completely over

Dish cloth: dishrag

Dishpan: (roundup) wreck pan

Dish towel: cup towel

Dishonest: if honesty is the best policy, he ain't no policyholder *See also Crooked*

Dish washer: pearl diver

Dislike: 1. don't cotton to 2. can't sit still for 3. don't sit right with me 4. hate that worse than the devil does holy water 5. don't hold with 6. never liked you and always will

Dislike a lot: wouldn't wet on him if he was on fire

Dismiss: show 'em the gate

Disorganized: 1. wakes up in a different world every morning 2. running around like a chicken with its head cut off 3. bounces around like a pecan in an empty wagon

Disorganized as: 1. a wild hog drive 2. a cattle stampede 3. a Chinese fire drill

Disoriented as: a goose in a hailstorm

Dispersed: hogs scattered ever which a way

Dispose of: 1. rid yourself of 2. get shed of

Disposition, sour: raised on pickle juice and vinegar

Disqualified: got both hands on the rigging

Disregard: 1. don't put any stock in 2. pay it no never mind

Disrespectful: offers no more respect than a coyote does to a jackrabbit

Distance: There are varying degrees of distance in Texas: 1. within spittin' distance is extremely close 2. if you can chunk a rock and hit it, it's very close 3. just down the road a piece is close 4. within hollerin' distance is fairly close 5. a holler and a half away is farther than fairly close 6. a see and a half away is starting to get far 7. a rifle shot away is a fairly long distance 8. far enough away that you can't hear the dogs is farther still 9. a fur piece is a long way.

Distance, exact: house to house [It might be 200 miles between Dallas and Austin, but if you live in far North Dallas and you're visiting someone in South Austin, the true distance—the house to house distance—might be 250 miles.]

Distance, long: 1. a fur piece, such as "It's a fur piece from Dalhart to Brownsville" 2. farther than the nekkid eye can see 3. long as a country mile 4. four sights down the road 5. farther away than you can point to 6. three pointin's away

Distance, short: just a rooster step away [A rooster step is an indefinite measure of distance that would be short to a person but might be long to a rooster.]

Distance, small: 1. no piece a'tall 2. just a hoot and a holler away 3. just over yonder

Distance, measure: 1. For short distances use the beer method, which means the distance is measured by the number of beers that would be consumed in makin' the trip, as in "It's a three-beer trip from here to Austin." 2. For longer distances, use the bus change method, which is the number of times you'd have to change buses to get there, as in "It's a three-change bus trip from Dalhart to Brownsville."

Distemper (horse): *See Epizootic*

Distracted: forget the mules, load the wagon

Distracting as: a swarm of gnats [When the small insects get to

swarming, they have been known to stop baseball games, prevent marriages, and provide drunks with some solid food.]

Distressed: *See In trouble*

Disturbance: 1. somebody hauled hell out of its shuck 2. the peace has come undone *See also Commotion*

Disturbed: someone rattled his cage

Disturbing situation: like to killed my soul

Ditch: gully ditch

Dived: like a frog into a stock tank

Diversion: 1. kill a skunk [The theory is that a dead skunk will stink up the place so much that everyone's attention will be diverted.] 2. set fire to the barn or town [The famous western gunfighter Doc Holiday killed his first man in a town called The Flats, Texas, near Fort Griffin. As legend has it, his girlfriend, Big Nose Kate, became concerned the good dentist was going to be hung, so she set fire to the town as a diversion and helped Doc escape. The pair left Texas for good and headed for Tombstone, Arizona.]

Divide: cut it up like a boardinghouse pie [In an old boardinghouse there was generally only one pie to go around, no matter how many guests there were. Thus, the more boarders, the smaller the piece of pie each received.]

Divide and conquer: a log is a log before you split it, but split it and it is no longer a log [Sam Houston once used this analogy when talking about a split in the Democratic party.]

Divining rod: 1. wiggle stick 2. water witch

Divorce: 1. separate the dasher from the churn 2. show your mate to the gate 3. split the blanket 4. past tense of marriage 5. matrimonial recycling 6. holy deadlock

Divorced couple: they took the cure

Divorced man: 1. a gone gander that still has to supply corn to the goose 2. deringed himself

Divorced woman: 1. a grass widow 2. found out the knot he tied was a slipknot 3. drinks doubles but sleeps single 4. born again virgin 5. only support she gets is from her panty hose *See also Changed husbands*

Dizzy: swimmy-headed, as in "After a couple of beers, Ethyl gets swimmy-headed."

Do good: plow straight rows

Do gooder: 1. keeps his halo polished 2. keeps the shiny side up

Do it cheap: poor boy it

Do it quick: 1. get it done in one-half less than no time 2. get it done in less than two shakes of a lamb's tail

Do it right: 1. don't go off half cocked, go off full cocked 2. if it's worth doin', it's worth doin' right 3. can't tell how deep the well is by measuring the pump handle 4. hang your wash on a taut line

Do it your way: sing the song you came to sing

Do it yourself: 1. roll your own 2. paddle your own canoe 3. saddle your own horse 4. hitch your own team 5. if you're looking for a good hand, try the end of your arm 6. milk your own duck [There is an old country saying for do-it-yourselfers. If you cut your own firewood, it will warm you twice. Lyndon Johnson once said, "The best fertilizer for a piece of ground is the boot prints of the owner," which roughly means the land that produces the best crops is the land that an owner works for himself.]

Do-it-yourselfer: Any do-it-yourselfer should be proficient in stobery. A stob is a sort of makeshift wooden stopper or stake, usually made from the branch of a handy tree, that is one of the most versatile items known to mankind. It could be a plug for an oil pan, a bathtub stopper, or a plug for a broken water line, garden hose, or water cooler. A really big stob could be used as an emergency radiator cap if you didn't have too far to go. Anything repaired using a stob has received a stobectomy. After stobs, the most important do-it-yourself tools are spit and baling wire. In Texas it has been said if you have enough spit and baling wire, even Humpty Dumpty could be put back together again.

Do-it-yourselfer, expert: could repair the crack of dawn

Do what you can: if you can't preach, you can pass the plate

Do what you want: 1. if you're feelin' froggy, jump 2. if you got an itch, scratch it

Do your best: put the best dog you got into the fight

Do your part: if you ain't pullin' your weight, you're pushin' your luck

Docked: cutting a horse's tail bone to shorten the tail

Doctor: 1. pill roller 2. medicine man 3. sawbones 4. pill wrangler 5. cut-'em-up

Doctor, poor: 1. treated appendicitis with Pepto Bismol 2. uses a shot glass to listen to your heart instead of a stethoscope

Doesn't matter to me: 1. don't make me no never mind 2. ain't no skin off my backside (or nose) 3. don't have a dog in that fight

Dofunny: *See Dololly*

Dog (dawg): 1. hound 2. flea catcher 3. skillet licker or pot licker [This refers to the practice of letting hound dogs lick cooking utensils clean after use, which saved a lot of washing.] 4. you keep a dog but you only feed a cat, which means a dog is faithful but a cat ain't

Dog, good: 1. a coon whippin' dog [It takes a good huntin' dog to get a coon up a tree but it takes a better dog to whip the coon.] 2. a close tracker, which means he stays on the trail 3. a hard dog to keep under the porch (or wagon) [This refers to the fact that the best dogs were not the ones that spent their time resting under the porch. The phrase is also used to describe a good person.] 4. a meat gitter [This is a dog that will hunt, which means it will help fill the dinner table. A dog that won't hunt is just another mouth to feed.] *See also Hunting dog, good*

Dog, harmless: 1. wouldn't bite a biscuit or chase a cat 2. wouldn't scratch fleas for fear they'd get hurt if they fell off 3. never met a man he didn't lick

Dog, lazy: 1. has to lean against a fence to bark 2. wags his tail up and down 'cause it takes less energy 3. won't even wag his own tail

Dog, small: 1. kiyute 2. lap dog 3. holdin dog 4. arm dog

Dog, smart: 1. knows the difference between being tripped over and kicked at 2. knows dinner is ready when the bell sounds on the microwave oven

Dog, stupid: can get lost under the house

Dog, ugly: someone ought to shave his rear end and make him walk backwards

Dog, worthless: a country store dog [Dogs that hang around country stores don't do much but lay in the sun, eat scraps, and go huntin' with anybody who's going. Such a dog has no loyalty and thus is worthless.]

Dog cuss: verbal assault, usually loud, that involves enough serious cuss words to, as old-time cowboys used to say, sulfurize the air [The saying comes from the fact that a lot of country boys will use their best string of cuss words on an unruly dog since the dog can't cuss back.]

Dog fall: *See Steer wrestling*

Dog name: the most common name for a Texas dog is Damn It, as in "Get in the truck, damn it."

Dog run house: When the pioneers came to Texas they discovered that it got hot in the summertime. To combat the temperatures, cabins were built in two parts with a common roof and an opening in the middle that was arranged in the direction of the prevailing winds. No matter how hot it got, there always seemed to be a breeze in the opening that made life a little more bearable. The opening also proved to be a favorite for the dogs who would run through it when playing or chasing the cat, and the design came to be generally known as "dog run." Also called "dog trot" and "Texas house."

Dogtrot: a fast gait on a horse

Doger: *See Steer wrestling*

Doggin horse: *See Steer wrestling*

Dogwood: bride of the woods

Dohicky: *See Dololly*

Doing good: 1. cooking with gas 2. flying with the big birds

Doing it wrong: you're not holding your mouth right; often said to someone who is trying to do something but just can't quite get it right

Doing nothing: just sittin' around with my teeth in my mouth

Doing poorly: livin' off the back forty; the worst part of a farm, usually heavily wooded with deep ravines and lots of rocks. [Anyone living off the back forty would be doin' poorly.]

Doing well: 1. cooking on the front burner 2. steppin' in high cotton 3. living high off the hog 4. got enough shirts and overalls so I don't have to go to bed while mama washes [If you only had one shirt and one pair of overalls, you'd have to go to bed while mama washed 'em so you wouldn't be runnin' around the place mostly naked.]

Dololly: term used to indicate something for which you don't know the name, as in "Bubba couldn't make it to church 'cause some dololly broke on his truck." Synonyms would be dohicky, doodad, thingamajig, dofunny, flung dung, whatchamacallit, and whoozit.

Domino: 1. bone 2. rock 3. stone 4. tile 5. seed 6. the act of going out in a hand during a game of dominoes 7. give birth

Domino spots: 1. pips 2. dots 3. points 4. spots

Don't argue: won't hear of it, as in "Don't even try to pay for the beer 'cause I won't hear of it."

Don't be surprised: when you walk into a javelina's cave don't be shocked if you get bit on the butt

Don't blame the equipment: it ain't the arrow, it's the Indian

Don't care: my giveadamner is broken

Don't criticize: can't sling mud and keep your hands clean

Don't do it: why don't you quit before you start

Don't forget: what you don't have in your head you got in your feet, which means if you forget something, you have to go back and get it

Don't include me: don't sink the lifeboat with me in it

Don't know: 1. don't rightly know 2. have no more idea than a dead snake has fleas (or than a hog knows when it's Tuesday) 3. don't know anymore than a rabbit knows which briar scratched him *See also Illegitimate*

Don't like it: don't like that and I always will

Don't need it: 1. need that like a hen needs singing lessons 2. need that like a frog needs a face-lift 3. need that like a sinkin' ship needs water *See also Unwanted*

Don't participate: don't mud wrestle with pigs; all you get is dirty and the pigs love it

Don't sit down: stay off your pockets

Don't want to do that: would rather rent a ringworm to wear on my nose

Don't understand: not sure I understand all I know about this

Don't want to: 1. would rather test bulletproof vests 2. would rather give a polar bear a hysterectomy 3. would rather have twins 4. would rather kiss the top of your hind leg 5. would rather eat a coil of barbed wire 6. would rather get a root canal from a plumber 7. would rather get a good case of malaria 8. there ain't enough money to pay me to do that *See also I don't care; Reluctance*

Don't look for trouble: 1. let sleeping dogs lie 2. don't kick the cat 3. if you pull a bull's tail you can expect to see horns

Don't surrender: 1. "Never say die, say damn," said Jim Ferguson, the only Texas governor, to date, to be impeached 2. As William B. Travis said from the Alamo, "I shall never surrender or retreat."

Don't understand: 1. hear you clucking but I can't find the nest 2. can see the fire but I can't find the camp 3. can smell the bacon but I can't find the breakfast table 4. can smell the manure but I can't find the stock pen 5. hear the choir singin' but I can't find the church 6. can feel the heat but I can't see the flames

 Donie (Freestone County): pronounced DOWN-ee, not Don-ee; residents applied for the name Douie but postal officials misread the application

Donkey, female: a jenny

Donkey, male: a jack

Donut: cruller

Doodlebug: 1. pill bug 2. roly-poly

Doodad: *See Dololly*

Doomed: you're a gone gosling

Door-to-door selling: trick-or-treat practice

Doping a horse: 1. put salve on a sore (see blow fly) 2. the old horse trader's trick of feeding a sound but worn-out old horse small amounts of arsenic. That would increase his appetite so he ate enough to improve and get his coat full and shiny. The arsenic was measured on a knife blade so it became known as knife-blade medicine. Unfortunately, the arsenic was highly addictive, and once the process was started it had to be continued. Generally, the person who traded for a doped horse was the big loser.

Double-barrel saddle: *See Double-rigged saddle*

Double-fire saddle: *See Double-rigged saddle*

Double-rigged saddle: a heavy stock saddle with high cantle, large pommel, square skirt, and two cinches; very popular among Texas cowboys to the point these saddles are usually called Texas saddles. Also called Texas double barrel, double fire, or rim fire. These saddles were very popular with cavalry troops from Texas during the War Between the States.

Double in: alarm cry used on the frontier when Indians threatened a settlement [The call meant the men should come in at double speed in order to prepare for a possible attack.]

Double-shuffle: when a pitching horse changes pace or rhythm

Double six (domino): thousand legger

Double-talk: doublespeak

Double-talker: 1. squawks out of both sides of his beak at the same time 2. talks like he's got two mouths

Double wide: a trailer house created by joining two half trailers [A double wide makes settling a divorce a little easier because either party could hook up to his or her half and simply drive off with it.]

Doubtful: 1. pigs'll fly before that happens 2. will be a cold day in hell before that happens 3. as much chance as a snowball in hell 4. a jury wouldn't believe that if three preachers and the governor of Texas gave sworn testimony 5. got about as much chance as a steer does of surviving a trip to a packing plant 6. whales will be blowing sand in West Texas before that happens 7. "That'll be the day," which was John Wayne's favorite line when he played a grizzled old Texas cowboy in *The Searchers*. [A young man in Lubbock, Texas, saw the movie and became so infatuated with the line he used it as the title for a classic rock and roll hit song. His name was Buddy Holly.] *See also Chance, slim*

Doucette (Tyler County): pronounced Do-SET; originally Carroll's Switch but was renamed for Pete Doucette, who was one of the men who bought out Alva Carroll

Dough bait: *See Catfish bait*

Down the road: downstream

Dr Pepper drinker: *See Coffee drinker, avid*

Dragging behind a plow: method of aging a rope by dragging it in the dirt

Dragonfly: 1. mosquito hawk 2. snake doctor

Drainage system, country style: cracks in the floor [If you have enough cracks in the floor, all the rain that comes in through the holes in the roof will drain off.]

Dread: 1. would rather have a wisdom tooth pulled than do that 2. would rather have triplets than do that 3. would rather get a poke in the eye with a sharp stick 4. would rather skin skunks with a dull knife

Dream book: Back in the old days when the policy games were rampant in Texas, one could purchase a Dream book from the numbers man to be used in determining which numbers to play according to your dreams. For example, if you dreamed of taking a long trip, the Dream book would suggest you play the numbers 42, 14, 84. It could be said that dream books were the precursor to calling the Physic Hotline.

Dreamer: 1. rainbow rider 2. to make your dreams come true, you have to stay up nights

Dreamer, big: dreams in Technicolor

Dreary: dreariness

Drench: term used to describe the process of giving livestock liquid medicine orally

Dress, raised: hiked up

Dress, skimpy: 1. peek-a-bosom dress, which is one that isn't all there on a woman who is 2. if she bent over we could see all the way to El Paso 3. so skimpy the hemline and the collar were touching 4. a Texas dress, which is one with plenty of wide open spaces 5. her clothes represent more dollars than sense 6. not enough material in that dress to keep a titmouse dry in a drizzle

Dress, tight: *See Sweater, tight*

Dressage: a riding test for a horse involving several gaits and maneuvers

Dressed fancy: looks like he just stepped out of a bandbox

Dressed up: 1. like a mail order catalog on the hoof 2. like a Dallas banker or a Houston lawyer 3. sporting a fancy riggin' 4. looks like a bob war salesman [Old-time barbed wire salesmen were often well dressed.] 5. wearing his rodeo parade outfit 6. looks like some deck of cards is missing a face card 7. gussied up 8. wearing courting clothes

9. wearing more stars than a clear night in July [Stars refer to silver ornaments worn on hatbands, belts, vests, etc. by old-time Texas cowboys.]

Dresses poorly: 1. only time you see him dressed up is when he has to enter a plea in court 2. when she's dressed up she looks like a sow with side pockets

Dresses, sloppy: 1. wears her clothes as if they were thrown on with a pitchfork 2. looks like she tossed her clothes up in the air and ran under them 3. a full grown mess

Drift fence: in the days before barbed wire, a drift fence was designed to keep cattle from drifting off a range

 Drill and ceremony cadets: Texas A&M cadets who don't sign a military contract but opt to pay a drill and ceremony fee instead

Drink: 1. hist one 2. bend an elbow 3. settle (or cut) the dust 4. wet a beak 5. paint your tonsils 6. take on a talking load 7. wet your whistle 8. wear a blister on your elbow 9. dip your bill

Drink, mixed: drown some bourbon (or another type of liquor), which is derived from mixing liquor and water

Drink, straight: the gulp and shudder method

Drink, strong: 1. snakebite serum 2. extract of barbed wire

Drink a lot: 1. drinks enough to float the battleship *Texas,* a bass boat, a houseboat, a John Deere tractor, or all the logs in East Texas 2. drinks enough to flood an armadillo hole 3. drinks like a poisoned pup 4. only drinks on the days of the week that end in y 5. a cork (or cap) collector [This implies that once he starts drinking he finishes the bottle so there is no longer any need for the closure, be it cap or cork. In the old days someone who drank a lot was said to "throw the cork away" so it couldn't possibly be used again.] *See also Drunk*

Drink chaser (water): fire extinguisher

Drinker, avid: he quit drinking when the funnel was invented, which means he now just pours it in

Drinker, female: when she drinks she goes hug wild

Drinker, male: if they were selling all the beer you could drink for a dollar, he could drink two dollars' worth

Drinkers' advice: if you drink like a fish, swim, don't drive

Drinking and talking: jugin' and jawin'

Dripping Springs (Hays County): pronounced Drippin' Sprangs; named for the nearby springs

Driscoll (Nueces County): pronounced DRIS-cul [Robert Driscoll Jr. organized the town and named it after himself even though there was another community by that name in the same county. Driscoll was a wealthy, influential lawyer and banker, however, and the name of the other Driscoll was changed to Alfred.]

Drive-in movie: passion pit

Drizzling: mizzling

Drooling: your jaw is leaking

Drop (Denton County): residents wanted the name Dewdrop, but when the postal boys rejected that they dropped the dew and settled for what was left

Drop handles: The practice of calling one another by first names

Dropped: 1. like a hot horseshoe or rock 2. like yesterday's oats in a horse corral 3. like a bad habit 4. like spit off a tall building

Drought: 1. the cows are giving powdered milk 2. so dry the Baptists are sprinkling, the Methodists are using washcloths, and the Catholics are giving rain checks 3. only water you could get was dehydrated 4. the catfish are carrying canteens 5. the trees are bribing the dogs 6. so dry, we had to spray the bass for ticks 7. if you put all the rain we've had in the last three years in a teacup, there wouldn't be enough water for a chigger to skin-dive 8. not only did we have to plow under the cotton, we had to plow under the hogs 9. we had to soak the hogs' heads to get 'em to eat slop 10. the crows have to lie on their backs to eat the corn 11. three-year-old catfish haven't learned to swim See also Dry; Dry land; Arid

Drunk: 1. laps up liquor like a fired cow hand 2. his idea of a seven-course meal is a six-pack and a toothpick 3. a snorter and a snoozer 4. still chaser or was still born 5. has to hold onto the grass to lean against the ground 6. on a worm diet [This refers to one who drinks Mexican tequila and swallows the worm in the bottom of the bottle.] 7. booze blind 8. loop legged 9. so drunk he grabbed a snake and tried to kill a stick 10. won't be able to die until the government finds a safe place to bury his liver 11. never gets beaten to the punch 12. always wakes up at the crack of ice 13. would rather pull a cork than punch a time clock 14. couldn't pour whiskey in a barrel with the head out 15. cockeyed 16. glassy-eyed 17. juiced up 18. petrified 19. pifflicated 20. potted 21. tanked up 22. pizzy-assed 23. lit to the gills See also Drunk, extremely; Intoxicated

Drunk, degrees of: 1st degree, you're interesting; 2nd degree, you're irresistible; 3rd degree, you're invisible; 4th degree, you're bulletproof

Drunk, extremely: 1. knee walking, commode-hugging, snot slinging, hymn-singing drunk 2. three sheets and a pillowcase to the wind 3. if he was shot through the head he'd have to sober up to die 4. he's so drunk, if he died and was cremated it would take the undertaker three days to put out the fire

Drunk as: 1. a skunk, pig, or waltzing pissant 2. Cooter Brown 3. a hoe-down fiddler [This refers to the days when cash was short and the fiddlers at a dance were often paid in whiskey, so they were usually drunk by the time the dance ended. Some old-timers claim the more the fiddler drank, the faster he played, which may explain the term "frisky fiddler."] *See also Fiddler's bitch*

Drunk cowboy: 1. so drunk he couldn't find a cow if she was in bed with him 2. can't even scratch himself 3. so drunk they found him singing naked on top of the windmill

Drunk driver: 1. an autopsy looking for a place to happen 2. motorized murderer 3. always wants to drive 'cause he's too drunk to sing 4. puts the quart before the hearse 5. prefers to drive tight rather than sit tight 6. has plenty of hearse power 7. drives a drunk car

Drunk, reformed: 1. gave up the bottle to see what a snake really looks like or to see if elephants come in anything but pink 2. decided to prove that a silk purse could be made out of a sow's ear

Dry: *See Drought*

Dry as: 1. a frog under a cabbage leaf 2. the heart of a haystack 3. dust in a mummy's pocket 4. a blue tick hound dog under a wagon 5. popped corn 6. a powder keg 7. Moses in the middle of the Red Sea 8. a sack of Bull Durham 9. a wooden leg 10. an eagle's nest *See also Arid; Drought*

Dry cereal: scabs

Dry hole: 1. a duster 2. didn't produce nothing but suitcase sand [the sand that inevitably got into an old-time wildcatter's luggage when he packed up and moved on after the well he drilled came in with nothing but dirt]

Dry land: 1. even the catfish have ticks (or flea collars) 2. my three-year-old duck don't know how to swim 3. trees (or bushes) are chasing the dogs 4. land wouldn't support a horned toad family 5. only got a quarter of an inch of rain during Noah's flood 6. was ten years old before I saw a fat cow 7. lizards are carrying army canteens *See also Barren; Drought; Land, dry*

Dry off: shake yourself

Dry wit: rosin jawed

Dublin (Erath County): pronounced DUB-l'n; it is believed the name came from "double in" which was the alarm cry when Indians threatened

Duck-blind camaraderie: the process of those who share the small, often cramped quarters of a duck blind getting well acquainted [Since everyone in a duck blind is armed it is always best that they be friends.]

Duct tape: 1. Texas welding rod, so called because it is used to join pieces of metal that should be welded 2. "90-mile-an-hour tape" because vehicle repairs made with it are supposedly good till you reach 90 miles per hour [Note: Although duct tape was supposedly invented to repair air ducts, recent scientific experiments have proven that duct tape is one of the worst tapes for that purpose.] *See also Excuse, poor*

Dude: 1. Rexall Ranger, which is the modern equivalent of "drugstore cowboy" 2. only horse he ever had was a charlie horse 3. city slicker 4. wouldn't know how to mount a stick horse

Dull: *See Boring*

Dull as: 1. a week-old soda pop with the top off 2. last week's news 3. watching paint dry 4. watching a bumper hitch rust 5. a fisherman who tells the truth 6. rinse water from a Chinese laundry

Dull edge: 1. dull as a widow woman's ax [In the old days, when a woman lost her husband, a lot of her chores went unattended to.] 2. wouldn't cut warm butter 3. wouldn't cut ice cream after it sat out of the freezer all night 4. wouldn't cut the heart of a watermelon

Dull person: 1. no speed and no sparkle 2. his idea of excitement is spending a couple of hours in a Christian Science Reading Room 3. if he was a light bulb, he wouldn't have many watts 4. if he was bacon, he wouldn't sizzle if he was cooked in a blast furnace

Dumas (Moore County): pronounced DO-mus, never Dumb-ass; named for Louis Dumas, president of Panhandle Town site Company [In the 1940s Phil Baxter of Navarro County stopped in Dumas while en route to Denver. After spending the night, he wrote the song "I'm a Ding Dong Daddy From Dumas" which put the town on the map when it was recorded by Phil Harris.]

Dumb: 1. don't have the sense to spit downwind 2. enough to be twins 3. would have to study up to be a half-wit 4. thinks the Mexican border ought to pay rent 5. has the IQ of a cantaloupe 6. never got past the third page of a first grade reader 7. don't know come on from sic 'em 8. half as smart as a wooden Indian 9. could screw up a two-car funeral 10. he's like a catfish, all mouth and no brains 11. don't have sense enough to pour rain water out of a boot 12. about as sharp as a bowling ball 13. someone gave him a pair of cuff links and he went out to have his wrists pierced 14. don't have the sense to pull in his head before he pulls down the window 15. if brains were dynamite he couldn't blow the wax out of his ears 16. was fourteen years old before he could wave good-bye 17. like a pin, his head keeps him from going anywhere 18. couldn't scatter manure with a four-dollar rake 19. couldn't roll a ball down a steep hill 20. don't know manure from wild honey 21. dumb enough to make his doctor the beneficiary in his will 22. not the sharpest knife in the drawer *See also Dimwit; Idiot; Ignorant; Stupid; Uneducated*

Dumb as: 1. a stump 2. a snubbin' post 3. a wagon load (or sled load) of rocks 4. dirt 5. hair on a barber shop floor 6. a screwdriver 7. an armadillo [Official mascot of the state of Texas, the armadillo is considered by many to be one of God's dumbest critters.] 8. a turkey [When it starts raining, a turkey will look up to see where the water is coming from and stand there with his mouth open. If it's a hard, fast rain, the turkey will drown before he realizes what's happening. That's about as dumb as you can get.]

Dumb supper: In the old days, young people, especially girls, would eat corn bread made of equal parts of meal and salt. The meal would be eaten in silence and the person would remain silent for the remainder of the evening. The theory was that the future mate would then appear in a dream carrying a glass of water to quench the thirst brought on by the salt.

Duncanville (Dallas County): pronounced DUNK-an-ville, unless you want to be uncomplimentary, in which case it's Drunken-ville

Durability: 1. the post wears out before the hole 2. will last so long you'll swear it must be stuffed with scrap iron

Durable as: 1. iron underwear 2. half-inch thick rawhide

Durango (Falls County): pronounced da-RANG-oh; originally West Falls. [As the story goes, one day a cowboy rode into town who had recently been in Old Mexico and was so drunk he believed he was in Durango, Mexico. For reasons never explained, the locals decided to change the name of their town, making Durango the only town in Texas named by a drunken cowboy. Believe it or not.]

Duration, long: 1. longer than a month of Sundays 2. long as a coon's age

Duration, short: 1. as long as a rainbow after a spring shower 2. as long as an old man's dream

Dusk: first dark

Dust: 1. house moss 2. dust bunnies

Dust balls: slut's wool, which is usually found under the bed

Dust storm: 1. Panhandle (or high plains) rain 2. dogs (or rabbits) are diggin' holes six feet up in the air 3. blowing so hard you couldn't find the beer cooler on the front seat of your pickup if you were driving it 4. blowing worse than Black Easter [On a Sunday morning in April 1935 the worst sandstorm in history struck most of the Texas Panhandle as well as parts of several other states. The sun was blacked out and millions of acres of valuable topsoil were lost. The day has come to be called Black Easter although it actually happened on Palm Sunday. Some people believe a dust storm means the angels are shakin' the dust out of their sheets.]

Dusted: a cowboy who ends up in the dust after being bucked off a bull or horse

Dusty dark: the time just before good dark when the sky is a dark, grayish blue

Dutch iron: wash clothes and then spread then out under a mattress rather than ironing them

Dutch wash: turn the tablecloth over rather than washing it

 Duval (Travis County): pronounced do-VAL; named for Douglas Duval, a local store owner

Dying: 1. fixing to promenade home 2. fixing to gather up over yonder

Dwelled on: harped on

E

Eager: hot to trot and already saddled

Eager anticipation: his face is lit up like a new saloon (or a new casino in Las Vegas)

Eagle bills: *See Stirrup, closed*

 Eagle Lake (Colorado County): named allegedly from an Indian legend. As the story goes, an Indian maiden had to make a choice between two suitors. To resolve the problem, she supposedly said her hand would go to the first brave to swim the lake, climb a tree, and return with an eagle feather.

Ear cattle: Brahma cross cattle

Ear down: 1. twisting a horse's ear to either keep it from rearing or fighting 2. biting a horse's ear to distract him while being saddled; also called ear twisting

Eardrum: hear drum

Ear head: a single or double split-ear bridle without a noseband, brow band, or throat latch

Ear twisting: *See Ear down*

 Earth (Lamb County): halfway between Dawn, Texas, and Sundown, Texas. According to legend, as the locals were pondering what to name the community, a severe dust storm came up. The name came from the earth (dirt) that was flying everywhere.

Early morning: chicken hollerin' time

Early riser: 1. dew chaser 2. races the crack of dawn to work 3. gets up with the chickens 4. has to pry up the sun with a crowbar 5. gets up almost early enough to meet himself going to bed

Earmarks: practice of cutting away part of the ear in a certain, unique pattern, for identification purposes; often used in conjunction with brands

Earn a living: bring home the bacon

Earrings: ear bobs

Ears, dirty: only time he washes his ears is when he eats watermelon

Ears, large: 1. Texan Howard Hughes observed, "Clark Gable's ears make him look like a taxicab with the doors open." 2. so large he can swat flies with them 3. his head looks like a loving cup

Earthquake, severe: it shook the hail out of the clouds

Ease up: 1. cut me some slack 2. lay back on the reins 3. don't dance me so hard 4. let the hammer down easy 5. give me a little breathin' room

Easily angered: fighty-fied

 East Bernard (Wharton County): pronounced East Ba-NARD

East Tawakoni (Rains County): pronounced East Ta-WOK-a-knee

East Texas: the pine curtain

Eastland (Eastland County): pronounced EAST-lun, with a silent "d"; courthouse is the final resting place for Old Rip the world famous horned frog

Easy: 1. no hill for a stepper 2. no hill for a climber 3. piece of cake 4. no chore for a doer 5. no pond for a swimmer

Easy as: 1. shooting ducks on a pond 2. cutting warm butter with a hot knife 3. shooting fish in a barrel (or dry creek bed) 4. catching fish with dynamite [When a dynamite charge is exploded under water, all the fish in the surrounding area are killed by the concussion. When the dead fish float to the top they can be plucked out of the water, making this the easiest though not the most sportsmanlike method of fishing.] 5. slidin' off a greased pig backwards 6. fallin' off a rollin' log 7. gettin' up after you sit down on a thumbtack (or your spurs)

Easy isn't always best: You can grow more cotton in a crooked row than you can in a straight one. Unfortunately a crooked row is harder to plant and harder to plow.

Easy part's over: all the white meat is gone and there is nothing left on the platter but necks, which refers to the fact that white meat is usually eaten first just as the easy part of a job is often done first

Easy to do: a cakewalk [In rural communities, a cakewalk is usually held at church socials. The ladies bake cakes and they are arranged on the floor. Then everyone who pays an entry fee starts walking around the cakes. When told to stop, the person next to the designated cake wins it. And they say Baptists don't gamble.]

Easy to find as: 1. the pitcher's mound in The Ballpark in Arlington 2. the deck on an aircraft carrier 3. the Alamo [Note, anyone who can't find the Alamo ought not to call himself a Texan.]

Easy to fix: 1. a spit and baling wire job 2. all it needs is a stobectomy *See Do-it-yourselfer*

Easy to use as: 1. a rocking chair 2. a light switch 3. a fork

Easy way out: As former Texas governor Mark White said, "It's easier to burn down a barn than it is to build one."

Eat: 1. table grazing 2. bite a biscuit 3. line your flue 4. put on the feed bag 5. pad your belly

Eat a lot: eating like the Russian army was crossing the Rio Grande

Eat all you want: pitch till you win

Eat anything: 1. eats anything that don't eat him first 2. will eat any critter as long as it has stopped wiggling, implying he will eat anything that has died

Eating irons: utensils

Echo: secondhand noise

🌵 **Ecleto** (Karnes County): pronounced ee-CLET-oh.

Edge stitch: decorative stitching around the edge of a leather product

Editor: 1. someone assigned to keep egg off an author's face 2. would edit the sermon on the mount if he found a dangling participle

Educated: book learned and hog smart (horse can be used in place of hog)

Educated guess: used the SWAG system, which is a scientific wild assed guess *See also Uneducated guess*

Effectiveness: 1. the more straws in the broom, the more dirt you can sweep 2. the longer the rope, the bigger the loop you can build, the reference being the bigger the loop, the more your can rope 3. the softer the leather, the better the feel

Effectiveness, poor: about as much effect as a BB on a bull elephant

Efficient: 1. built the outhouse on the other side of the woodpile [According to country legend, the smartest country boy would build the outhouse on the other side of the wood pile so whoever went out first on a cold morning could stop and pick up some stove wood on the way back and save a trip.] 2. don't lose nothing but the squeal when he kills a hog

Effort: If it's worth doing, it's worth doing well. Texan Mildred "Babe" Didrikson Zaharias, one of the greatest woman athletes ever born, said, "If a game is worth playing, it's worth playing to win."

Effort, different: difference between picking corn and cotton is the amount of the stooping

Effort, futile: 1. rearranging the cannons at the Alamo 2. burnin' green wood for kindling, which means you get a lot more smoke than fire

Effort, large: 1. took all the hands and the cook 2. would have taken God eight days to get it done

Effort, wasted: 1. winking at a pretty girl in a dark room 2. panning for fool's gold 3. closed the barn door after all the horses were out 4. built the windmill after the well went dry 5. buying oats for (or whipping) a dead horse 6. trying to train an old dog 7. can't move a plow by tickling it with a feather 8. banging your head against the outhouse wall 9. shoveling the sidewalk before it has stopped snowing 10. can train a jackass all you want, but it still ain't gonna win the Kentucky Derby 11. trying to find hen eggs in a rabbit cage *See also Wasting time*

Egg: 1. hen fruit 2. hen apple 3. cackleberry 4. omelet shell 5. cackle fart 6. a whole day's work for a chicken 6. cackle (Aggie)

Eggs, large: only takes eight of them to make a dozen

Eggs, poor: her eggs aren't cooked, they're vulcanized

Eggs, small: would take sixteen of 'em to make a dozen [This saying can be used to describe almost anything small.]

Ego: 1. big ideas seldom come from swelled heads 2. if you get too big for your britches, your hat won't fit either

Ego, deflated: 1. fell off his high horse 2. his high horse came up lame 3. someone knocked half the rungs out of his ladder 4. someone pulled the rug out from under him 5. somebody put a dead chicken in his well

Ego, large: 1. a legend in his own mind 2. could strut sitting down 3. considers himself the whole railroad including tracks, trains, and right of way 4. was born on third base and thinks he hit a triple 5. nice thing about him is he never goes around talking about other people 6. a self-made man who worships his creator 7. has

E

calluses from patting himself on the back 8. sing your own praises and you'll be a soloist 9. can't see anything taller than the smoke from his own chili 10. like a ship in a fog, he's always blowing his own horn 11. don't want a feather for his cap, he wants to wear the whole eagle 12. thinks she's the only berry on the bush (or peach on the tree) 13. thinks he's the only show pig in the pen 14. if his head got any bigger, he wouldn't fit through the outhouse door 15. thinks he's the only rooster in the barnyard 16. too big for cowboy britches 17. wish I could buy him for what he's really worth and sell him for what he thinks he's worth *See also Aloof; Arrogant*

Eight (playing card): eighter from Decatur (Decatur, Texas, that is)

El Campo (Wharton County): pronounced El CAMP-oh; originally called Prairie Switch, Mexican cowboys eventually changed the name

Elated: 1. homesteading cloud nine 2. walking around three feet off the ground

Elbow: the top joint of the foreleg on a horse

Elbow grease: ointment for rusty joints

Elderly: 1. ready for a warm corner 2. was around when the Dead Sea was only sick 3. blooming for the pasture, which refers to his (or her) hair getting gray *See also Aging; Old*

Eldorado (Schleicher County): tricky one; it's pronounced El-da-RAY-do; note, it is spelled as one word; the county seat; named by W. B. Silliman who surveyed the town site

Electra (Wichita County): pronounced with a long "e" at the beginning, E-lect-tra. The town is named for the only daughter of oilman W. T. Waggoner. Supposedly, Miss Waggoner was advised of the name on her birthday, making it one of the most unique birthday presents in the history of Texas. According to legend, the Lockheed Electra airplane and the Buick Electra were also named for Electra Waggoner, who herself became one of the most famous ranchers in Texas. After oil was discovered on her daddy's land, it is believed she became the first person to spend $20,000 in a single day at Neiman Marcus in Dallas. And she came back the next day and spent another $20,000.

Electrical problems (car): ain't getting' no fire

Electrician, good: could rewire a lightning bug so it would blink the national anthem in Morse code

Elephant: senior; also called leather legs or zip

Elephant walk: before the annual game with the University of Texas, Aggie seniors gather and wander aimlessly over the campus imitating dying elephants

Elevator music: wallpaper set to music

Elgin (Bastrop County): sometimes pronounced el-gin (and some written sources back this up), but the correct pronunciation is ELG'n. Elgin is the home of some of the best sausage made in Texas.

Elmaton (Matagorda County): pronounced el-MET'n; supposed to be Spanish for "the killer"

Elusive: 1. rarely comes out of the same hole he climbed into 2. got more movements than a Rolex watch 3. as hard to pin down as a ghost's shadow

Elysain Fields (Harrison County): pronounced uh-LEE-z'n Fields. Captain Edward Smith visited the area in 1818 and later claimed he had seen fields of gushing springs and huge trees. A listener said it sounded like the Elysian Fields from Greek mythology so when Smith returned that was the name he chose.

Emaciated: wormy lookin'

Embarrassed: 1. as an old maid baby-sitting a sea captain's parrot 2. as a preacher with a broken zipper 3. looking for a hole to hide in 4. blushed to the roots (of her hair) 5. got caught with his pants down and his boots off 6. his suspenders snapped 7. her garter snapped

Embarrassed reply: hush your mouth; usually said when someone lays an outlandish compliment on you, as in the following exchange. "Ethyl, since you got your teeth fixed an' them warts removed, why you're the prettiest girl in this corner of the county." "Hush your mouth, Bubba, I ain't the prettiest. Cutest, maybe, but not the prettiest." [Note: Hush your mouth is not to be confused with "shut your mouth," which is a reply when someone says something controversial or surprising that you don't necessarily want to hear.]

Embarrassing: 1. a fine how do you do 2. a fine howdy do

Embarrassing situation: 1. even made the moon blush 2. telling a woman her stockings are wrinkled when she ain't wearing stockings 3. having your dress tucked into the back of your panty hose 4. when two eyes meet in the same keyhole from opposite sides of the door

Embellished: 1. put a little extra straw in the brick 2. put a few extra pounds on that fish

Embezzle: 1. books are half a bubble out of square 2. books are out of plumb [Remember, figures don't lie but liars figure.]

Embroidery: needlework

Emergency: 1. hell's bells are ringing 2. the finger is out of the dike 3. got an ox in the ditch 4. the barn's on fire 5. the electric fence shorted out [On a farm or ranch this is a real emergency since electric fences are often just a single strand of wire that would be easy to go through if the power failed.]

Emotion: *See Overcome with emotion*

Emotional: 1. sounds like she's about to have kittens 2. call her jigsaw because every time something goes wrong she goes to pieces

Emotionless: 1. poker faced 2. stone faced 3. if he ever smiled, his face would crack open like a dropped watermelon

Employed: riding for a brand [Ranches are referred to by their brand, such as the XIT, 6666, or Pitchfork. Thus when a cowpoke hired on regular with a ranch, he was "riding for the brand."]

E

Employed, temporarily: 1. round-up hand, which refers to ranches taking on extra help during roundup time 2. working for day wages, which is what cowboys did when they didn't have a regular job

Employee: 1. gave you a job, didn't take you to raise 2. hired hand 3. hired gun 4. field hand 5. hireling

Employee, good: 1. does more by accident than most people do on purpose 2. would take two men, a mule, and a good dog to replace him if he left

Employee, poor: has a sign on his desk proclaiming, "Yes spoken here"

Employee, vital: the grease on the wheels

Employee, worthless: 1. either don't do what he's told or he don't do anything except what he's told [Bum Phillips once used such an expression to describe the two kinds of football players that are worthless.] 2. wouldn't leave a vacancy if he left [There is an old saying in Texas that the most worthless employee is the one who wears a hat, rolls his own smokes, and wears shoes that have to be tied. Such a person will spend so much time chasing his hat when it blows off, fiddling with his makings (the stuff used to hand-roll cigarettes), and retying his shoes that he won't have any time left to work.]

Employee relations: Don't muzzle your ox when it's treading out the corn, which could be interpreted to mean let your employee do his job.

Empty as: 1. a banker's heart 2. a dry hole 3. a brassiere (or girdle) hanging on a clothesline 4. last year's bird nest or last night's beer bottle 5. an ex-wife's (or ex-husband's) head 6. an old maid's dreams 7. a horse corral with an open gate 8. a pickup full of post holes 9. a chicken farmer's bank account

Empty headed: 1. has to talk with his hands to keep from getting an echo 2. could shoot him in one ear and the bullet would come out the other ear without hitting anything 3. his mind is so empty it could double as a vacant lot

Encourage: 1. light a fire in his tail (or overalls) 2. push on the reins 3. set him down on a branding fire 4. jerk his chain 5. pull his string

Encouragement, firm: 1. a kick in the butt is a step forward 2. sometimes kicking a man when he's down is the only way to get him up

Encroachment: gettin' close to diggin' in my 'tater patch

End: puts the rag on the bush [In the country, the rags are washed after all the clothes. Since there usually isn't any room on the clothesline, the rags are hung on a handy bush. Therefore, when the rags are on the bush, the washin' is at an end for that day.]

End (noun): 1. tailgate 2. hind end 3. south end of a northbound mule 4. caboose

End (verb): 1. lose the range 2. wet on the fire and call the dogs 3. snuff out the lamp

Ended: 1. played out 2. knocked down on (from auctions) 3. fizzled out 4. petered out 5. all over but the shouting 6. nothing left to do but kiss the bride, which implies that someone you cared for ended the relationship by marrying another

Ended, abruptly: put the quietus on it [Quietus (kwi-EAT-us) is a favorite Texas word that is used anytime something is halted abruptly, as in "Ethel found out Bubba was fixin' to go huntin' and she put the quietus on those plans quicker than a minnow can swim a dipper."]

Ended early: died on the vine like a watermelon in a drought

Ending: 1. put that in your pipe and smoke it 2. put that in your pan and bake it 3. put your saddle on that and ride it home 4. that's all she wrote

Endless: there's always another: calf to brand, horse to break, fence to mend, squeaking windmill to grease, gate off the hinge, or rat to kill

Endurance: bottom

Endure it: to see a rainbow you got to put up with some rain

Enemy: 1. someone you wouldn't want packin' your parachute 2. when picking enemies, pick lazy ones

Engaged: she's been ringed

Engine, bad: has more pings than a Chinese phone book

 Engineer: crapper builder

Enjoyable: 1. more fun than recess in heaven 2. ain't had this much fun since the hogs ate baby sister 3. had more fun than a one-eyed tomcat in a fish market 4. as much fun as skipping stones on a still pond 4. more fun than playin' in grandma's sheet rows [When grandma hung clean sheets on a clothesline, a row of wet flapping sheets was created that was the perfect place to play until grandma caught ya'.] *See also Fishing*

Enochs (Bailey County): pronounced E-nooks

Entangled: embrangled

Entered: *See Joined*

Enthusiastic: 1. bright eyed and bushy tailed 2. a frisky fiddler

Envious: 1. if you got a heart transplant, she'd have to have one 2. if your house had ants, she'd want termites

Environmentalist: tree hugger

Epileptic: fitified

Episode: go round [Each day's events in a rodeo are referred to as a go round.]

Epizootic: a cowboy's term for distemper (influenza) in a horse

Epsom salts: workin' medicine

Equal: even steven

Equal to: 1. even up with 2. with the best of them, which means you can do a particular thing as well as most people, as in "Bubba can rope calves with the best of them."

Equality: 1. on a mule team, the scenery is the same for all the mules except the leader, which could be a Texan's version of rank has its privileges 2. what's good for the gander is good for the goose 3. stands neck and neck with 4. six of one, half a dozen of the other 5. when it rains, it rains on both sides of the fence [In football, that would be both sides of the line of scrimmage.] 6. every man has an equal opportunity to seek his own level 7. on a gentle horse, all men are expert riders 8. a blind horse can see equally well from either end 9. it's a hoss and a hoss, which is how Darrell Royal described two equally matched football teams

Equestrian: relating to horses or people who ride them

Equine: horse species, which includes horses, mules, zebras, donkeys, etc.

Equipment, old: it's old enough to vote

Equipped: 1. armed to the teeth 2. loaded for bear 3. fitted out

Equipped, improperly: tryin' to cut a big hog with a little knife

Equipped, poorly: 1. can't sell from an empty wagon 2. can't hunt with an empty gun 3. can dance with a straw broom but it's better to use a girl 4. working with sand, which means anything you do won't be permanent

Erase: 1. blot the brand 2. blotch it out 3. wipe the slate clean 4. dust the board

Erin (Jasper County): pronounced AIR-in

Errand boy: 1. a go-fer 2. a shagger, which is someone who shags fly balls 3. a spear carrier

Erred: you really pissed in your whiskey this time

Error: 1. hung the wrong horse thief 2. sat down in your own coyote trap 3. got caught in his own loop 4. ripped his drawers (or britches) 5. pulled your trigger without taking aim 6. laid her egg in the wrong nest 7. put your boot on the wrong foot 8. that deer you shot turned out to be the neighbor's milk cow [Note: Lead goat, bell goat, bell mare can be substituted for milk cow.] *See also Made a mistake; Mistaken; Screwed up*

Escape: 1. head for higher ground 2. jump bail

Escaped: 1. slipped the hobbles 2. broke jail 3. slipped (or spit out) the hook

Escort: carry, as in "Can I carry you to the barn dance next Saturday?"

Essential information: 1. the bare bones 2. the meat without the fat

Estelline (Hall County): pronounced ES-ta-lean; named for Estelle de Shields, daughter of an early settler

Estrus: the period when a mare will accept breeding; also called "heat period"

Etc.: something you use to make people think you know more than you really do

E

Etoile (Nacogdoches County): pronounced E-toil; townspeople chose the name because it is French for "star"

Euless (Tarrant County): pronounced YOU-less, or use-less if you want to be derogatory

Eulogy: a funeralization

Eustace (Henderson County): pronounced YOU-stus; named for Confederate veteran W.T. Eustace, who was very popular among local residents

Evacuated: like red ants pouring out of a burning stump (or log)

Evaluate: 1. size 'em up 2. see what they're made of 3. can't judge corn unless you look inside the shuck 4. don't call him a cowboy till he does some riding and roping 5. don't call it a cutting horse till it gets a calf out of the herd

Evaporated milk: 1. canned cream 2. canned cow

Evasive: 1. when he ain't hemming, he's hawing 2. will beat around every bush in the county

Event, remarkable: a man-on-the-moon event [This means you'll always remember where you were when it happened. The phrase comes from the fact that anyone who was alive and old enough to know what was going on when Neil Armstrong set foot on the moon remembers where he was at the time it happened.]

Event, unsuccessful: folks stayed away in droves

Events: goings on

Eventually: by and by, as in "I'll get that fence fixed by and by."

Everclear: a very powerful, 200-proof liquor that will make you feel like you can leap tall buildings with a single bound or stop bullets with your bare hands; also called see-through liquor [not recommended for rookie drinkers]

Every man for himself: have to skin your own skunk

Everybody: 1. the whole outfit 2. all the hands 3. all the cowhands and the cook 4. the whole outfit including cook, go-fer, and big auger

Everyone suffers: sparrows get hungry just like eagles and mockingbirds

Everything: 1. guts, feathers, beak, and all 2. the whole kit and caboodle 3. hook, line, and sinker 4. the whole she-bang 5. the whole shootin' match 6. the whole enchilada 7. the whole hog 8. the whole load of watermelons (cantaloupes, turnips, strawberries, or manure) 9. the whole hide, including the tail 10. jocks to socks [When Jerry Jones took over the Dallas Cowboys he said he was going to be involved in everything from socks to jocks and he wasn't lying.] 11. the whole nine yards [This refers to the fact that material would usually come in nine-yard bolts so if you got the whole bolt, you got the whole nine yards.] *See also Complete*

Everything is fine: There ain't a bump in the road, as ol' Texan Glenn Raines is fond of saying.

Everywhere: 1. all over hell and half of Texas 2. all over the entire pasture

Evil City: letters addressed to hell would go there, as in "If you address a letter to hell it would be delivered to New York City." [Any city outside of Texas could be substituted.]

Evil man: *See Male, evil*

Evil person: 1. would hate to be the preacher who's gonna have to think of somethin' nice to say at his funeral 2. might paint him into a corner but it won't be the amen corner 3. would steal a widow women's only milk cow 4. will never die in bed 5. don't believe in taking prisoners 6. keeps the ball of sin rolling 7. in cahoots with the devil 8. his reservation in hell was made the day he was born 9. someday he'll be stringing barbed wire in hell 10. his life is a measuring stick for sin 11. only place he'll make a name for himself will be on a tombstone 12. wrath finder 13. one of John the Baptist's snakes in the grass (Mathew 3:7, Luke 3:7) *See also Bad person; Wicked*

Evil, somewhat: just one good scare away from being virtuous

Ewe: female sheep

Ewe-necked: a horse with a concave neck like a female sheep

Exaggerate: 1. stretch the blanket 2. stretch the facts 3. his facts are elastic

Examine close: put a hairy eyeball on it

Exasperated: 1. all put out 2. acting like the pay toilet costs a quarter and you only got a dime 3. at the end of his rope (or tether) 4. dancing in the hog trough, which is said of girls whose younger sister marries before them

Exasperated as: 1. a settin' hen trying to lay a square egg 2. a snake without a pit to hiss in 3. a short tailed bull in fly time 4. a drummer with the hiccups 5. a bridegroom at a shotgun wedding

Exasperating: 1. makes my backside bite a hole out of the seat of my pickup 2. gets my goat 3. wouldn't that cock your pistol 4. that'll rattle your slats (or cage) 5. would make a preacher pack his Bible 6. rips the rag off the bush 7. will take the ink out of your pen 8. will take the starch out of your shorts

Exceeding your limits: boring with a big auger

Exell (Moore County): name came from the XL brand of a local ranch and that's the way it's pronounced

Excellent: 1. dead solid perfect 2. larrupin' good 3. the cat's meow 4. hard down good 5. cream of the crop

Exceptional: 1. beats anything I ever helt, smelt, felt, or fell back in 2. would like to be gathering eggs and find that

in my nest 3. been to county fairs, goat ropings, and world championship rodeos and I ain't never seen anything like it 4. best I ever laid eyes on

Exchanging hard words: 1. a squanderin' off 2. jawin' and joreein'

Excited: 1. got biting ants in his britches 2. his bobbin is wound tight 3. all fired up like a steam locomotive 4. running around like a chicken with its head cut off 5. swallowed his head and chinned the moon, which is a reference to the action of a bucking horse 6. soaring with the eagles 7. bawlin' and squallin' and slinging snot every which way 8. got his tail over the dashboard 9. has to walk sideways to keep from flying 10. eyes shining like two fried eggs in a slop bucket 11. eyes blinking faster than a frog's eyes in a hailstorm 12. eyes big as saucers 13. heart pounding like the devil beatin' tanbark

Excited as: 1. a pullet anticipating her first egg 2. a billygoat in a pepper patch 3. a peach orchard boar 4. a spring lizard in a henhouse (or on a griddle)

Exciting: 1. that'll get the dogs out from under the porch (or wagon) 2. that'll pop the wax out of your ears 3. would set the woods on fire 4. a real stem winder 5. will melt your butter 6. will set folks to talking 7. will put the boys up on the top rail [This refers to rodeo cowboys seeking the safety of the top rail of a fence when a mad bull gets after them.] 8. will give your liver a quiver 9. will put lead in your pencil and make you forget you were supposed to write home 10. will set your tail feathers on fire *See also Amazing*

Exciting as: 1. a wind-fanned West Texas grass fire 2. a fire at the IRS office 3. farting in a flour barrel 4. grandma getting her hair caught in the wringer

Exclamation of astonishment: 1. well, I declare 2. I'll be switched (or jiggered) 3. well shut my mouth 4. well

E

toot my horn 5. don't that beat all 6. well, I swan 7. what in the Sam Hill 8. for cryin' out loud *See also Oath*

Exclamation of displeasure: horse hockey

Exclamation of finality: 1. tears up the whole biscuit 2. slams the barn door or a door slammer

Exclamation of pleasure: boy howdy

Excluded: was invited not to come

Excuse, pending: always keeps a root canal handy in case he's asked to do something he doesn't want to do

Excuse, poor: had to stay home 'cause I ran out of duct tape. The implication is that he was afraid to take his ol' truck out on the road without duct tape to make repairs if it broke down.

Exhausted: 1. plumb tuckered 2. tuckered out 3. played out 4. my get up and go got up and went 5. plumb tared (tired) 6. my tired hurts 7. feelin' mighty white-eyed, which is a reference to the fact that your eyes seem to get bigger and whiter when you are very tired *See also Tired; Weary*

Exhibitionist: shows off parts of her body that some women don't even know they have

Ex-husband: 1. a former pain in the neck (or certain other parts of the anatomy) 2. a man who was given enough rope to skip 3. a man who'll be reminded of the good times every time he sends a child support check

Expect ('spect): 1. look for that to happen 2. betting on it

Expectant as: 1. a bird watching a worm hole 2. a woman ten months pregnant 3. a buzzard circling a dying mule

Expectations, high: every minnow figures to be a whale someday

Expectations, low: 1. if you go hunting with a tomcat, you can't expect to catch nothing but field mice and crippled birds 2. can't expect anything from a hog but a grunt

Expendable: cannon fodder

Expensive: 1. would have to hock the family jewels to make a down payment 2. costs an arm and a leg 3. cost three prices 4. as popcorn at a picture show 5. wallet buster 6. would make Neiman Marcus look like a discount store 7. costs a pretty penny 8. high as a cat's back 9. too rich for my blood

Experience, good: will put some hair on your chest or whipple your crispit

Experience, lacking: 1. needs a few more skins on the wall 2. needs a few more antlers over the barn door

Experience counts: 1. an old coyote knows the shortest way to the chicken coop 2. any broom will sweep but an old broom knows where the dirt is 3. a new hat looks good but an old hat knows the shape of your head

Experienced: 1. if he crows, the sun is up 2. been down the road a piece in all kinds of weather 3. been at the dance quite a spell 4. sits deep in the saddle 5. horse wrangler from way back 6. master hand 7. can plow a long row in a short time 8. better to know the country than to be the best cowboy 9. been to the barn a few times 10. knows how to use hay hooks 11. too old a cat to be fooled by a kitten 12. been doing that since before I shucked my three-corner pants 13. been to more than one rodeo 14. was already ten years old and half a cowboy when he was born

Expert: 1. nobody could give him lessons 2. could rope a jackrabbit with a grapevine 3. a good judge of horseflesh 4. ain't ever been bested in a horse trade 5. could break the orneriest mustang without a bridle [Someone once said an expert is a person who has all the right answers as long as you ask the right questions.]

Expertise: 1. strong suit 2. money crop 3. strong hold 4. trump suit

Expired: *See Died*

Explain: tell them how the cow ate the cabbage *See also Clarify*

Explain fully: 1. put all the cards on the table 2. shuffle all the dominos

Explain it better: 1. put it down where the calves can get at it 2. wring out the rag some 3. chew it a little finer

Exploded: 1. like a full beer can that had been in the paint mixing machine down at the hardware store 2. like a frozen Coke

Explore: 1. plow new ground 2. blaze a new trail

Exposed: been smoked out a' the hole

Expound on: 1. fill it out with meat 2. put some clothes on the skeleton 3. color the picture

Expression, dumbfounded: looks like a car-chasin' dog that caught a Buick

Expression, horrified: looks like he just found out he made love to a leper

Expression, painful: 1. look like you squatted with your spurs on 2. look like lightning just struck your zipper

Expression, shocked: look like you just wet on an electric fence [On a pig farm near Lubbock, Texas, a few years ago I was helping a friend tend to his hogs. Nature called and I asked where to go to relieve myself. The friend pointed to a bush and said water the plants. What he did not say was that his brand new electric fence ran just beneath that bush. Well, since any kind of water is an excellent conductor of electricity, I soon learned the error of my ways. The friend swears I went eight feet straight back and landed with a thud in some pig manure. Thirty minutes later when I finally got my breath back, the friend also swore I had the most shocked expression on my face that he had ever seen. I have never doubted him.]

Expression, strange: 1. look like you're passin' a peach pit 2. look like you just swallowed a fishing lure 3. looks like he's chewing on tin foil

Expression, surprised: look like you just took a big ol' drink out a somebody's spit can

Expression of approval: to who laid the chunk, as in "Bubba can raise cotton to who raised the chunk."

Extra: 1. to boot, as in "I'll give you $50 for the horse if you'll throw in a saddle to boot." [In the old days some country folks used lagnappe (land yap) for to boot.] 2. excess baggage 3. rumble seat rider 4. the eighth man [In poker, some games use seven cards per hand, so eight people can't play since a deck has only 52 cards.] 5. two hours on the Bull Ring (Aggie)

Extra dominoes: 1. widow 2. kitty

Extra effort: if you work around here, you better soak your screws [This saying comes from working with wood. If you put forth the extra effort to soak screws in a light lubricant or even thick, soapy water, they will go into hardwood much easier than unsoaked screws. Therefore, anyone who soaks his screws is putting out extra effort.]

Extra money: 1. rat hole money 2. cotton picking money 3. wild hare stake 4. scalp money 5. egg money

Extraordinary: 1. a real doozey 2. a lollapalooza

Extremely: 1. all get out, as in "He's happy as all get out." 2. plumb, as in "I'm plumb tired." 3. big time, as in "He's got the mumps big time if you know what I mean." 4. big boy, as in "He has big boy trouble with the IRS."

Extremist: 1. fire eater 2. firebrand

Ex-wife: 1. a wife lasts for the length of the marriage, an ex-wife lasts forever 2. if you want to keep the beer real

E

cold, keep it next to the heart of an ex-wife 3. only thing more expensive than a wife is an ex-wife

Eyeballer: someone who is nosy and always seems to be looking into other people's affairs

Eyelids, held shut (in the morning): sleepy eyed

Eyes, beady: eyes are closer together than an earthworm's

Eyes, large: 1. doe eyes 2. bug-eyed 3. calf eyes

Eyes, bloodshot: 1. got more lines than a road map 2. looks like a red spider built a web in his sockets 3. looks like some sack of Bull Durham is missing its string [Bull Durham tobacco is packaged in a small cloth bag with a red string that is used to draw it closed.] 4. look like two tomatoes in a glass of buttermilk

Eyes, sunken: 1. look like two rabbit pellets in a snow bank 2. look like two cigarette burns in a saddle blanket

Eyes, small: BB eyes

Eyes, soft: as ribbon cane syrup on a tin plate

Eyes, wide open: pop-eyed

Eyes in back of head: very common on Texas women, especially those with children. The standard answer for mama when asked how she knew something was going on behind her back is, "I've got eyes in the back of my head."

Eyesight, good: can spot a gnat at fifty yards and tell if it's a male or female

Eyesight, poor: 1. couldn't read the big line on an eye chart if you spotted him half the letters 2. don't take him long to read a newspaper 'cause all he can make out are the headlines 3. taking Braille by correspondence course 4. lost his glasses and couldn't look for them till he found them *See also Sight, impaired*

4 H: youth organization for rural children dealing in livestock, home economics, leadership, farm skills, etc. [The four H's stand for Health, Heart, Hands, Head.]

F.F.A.: Future Farmers of America.

F.T.S.: Texas version of PMS; it means fixin' to start

Facade: 1. all vine, no watermelon 2. all hat and no cattle, which means he dresses like a rancher but he don't own any cows

Face, large: got enough chins for three faces

Face, skinned up: got bicycle face [In the late 1800s the bicycle was becoming very popular but a lot of people didn't understand how to ride or how to stop. This prompted many doctors around the nation to report they were treating a new malady they named bicycle face.]

Face cards (playing cards): 1. paint cards 2. court cards 3. royalty

Face the music: if you can't face the music you'll never lead the band

Fact: 1. that's how the cow ate the cabbage 2. if it ain't true, God's a possum 3. if it ain't true, you can wet in my hat 4. if it ain't true, there ain't a cow (or oil well) in Texas 5. if it ain't true, may a wild steer hook my gizzard 6. can take that to the bank and borrow money on it 7. can bet the farm (or the railroad) on that 8. that's the name of that tune 9. if I ain't tellin' you the absolute truth, then I'm grass and God's a lawnmower 10. if it ain't true, grits ain't groceries 11. if that ain't the truth, you can cut up grandma for catfish bait *See also Believe me; Certain; Guaranteed; Reliable*

Facts: There are two kinds of facts in Texas, plain facts and true facts. Plain facts are ones that are true most of the time but not always. True facts are positively true until proven otherwise.

Failed: had buzzard's luck, which is a reference to the fact that a lot of time when a buzzard goes looking for supper he comes up empty

Failed to speak: he was squattin' when he should have been squawkin'

Failure: 1. set out to be a swashbuckler but he buckled before he swashed 2. didn't pan out 3. didn't make the grade 4. blames everything on the weather or his raising 5. fell off cloud nine into a thunderstorm 6. got caught in his own loop 7. made it into the fast lane then shifted into reverse 8. put his bucket down the well of financial security but the rope broke 9. sat down in his own bear trap 10. hitched his wagon to a falling star 11. his cotton didn't come up 12. he started out with nothing and has most of it left 13. made his mark in the world but someone erased it 14. aimed to do right but he was a poor shot 15. aimed high but he was shooting blanks 16. her cake was all dough

Failure, sort of: he made it to the fast lane but couldn't get off the shoulder

Fair: middling good

🔹 **Fair Play** (Panola County): according to legend, name came from the way locals were treated at John Allison's store

🔹 **Fairlie** (Hunt County): pronounced FAIR-lee not Far-lee or Fair-lie; apparently named for Fairlee Webster, who is believed to have lived in the area

Fairy duster: *See Huajillo*

Faithful: dance with who brung ya' [Darrell Royal, former coach of the Texas Longhorns, made the saying famous in 1965 after his 'Horns, previously ranked No. 1 in the nation, had lost three games. When asked if he would change his offense, Royal replied, "We're going to stick with what we've been doing. There's an old saying, 'You dance with who brung ya.'" Of all the quotes Royal gave us, this is the one most often repeated.] *See also Loyalty*

Faithful as: an old hat [Outside of his horse, there was nothing more special to a cowboy than his hat. He used it as a rain bonnet, sun shield, a fan for the cook fire, as well as an emergency water bucket and feed bag. A cowboy often became mighty attached to his hat and treated it like an old friend. More than a few range riders actually drowned while tryin' to retrieve their favorite headgear after it had blown into a swollen river. One cowboy claimed he had a hat that had outlived a dozen pair of boots, three saddles, and one or two horses. He said the best thing about that old hat was that it never did forget the shape of his head. Because the hat was always ready to go where the cowboy went, never drank any of his beer, never ran off with his best girl, never broke a promise, and never let the cowboy down when the goin' got tough, a lot of old-time cowboys considered their hat to be their most faithful friend.]

Fake: 1. a sheep in wolves clothes 2. big barker, little biter

Fake as: 1. a three-dollar wig 2. eyelashes (or other parts) on a Las Vegas showgirl 3. a hooker's affection 4. a tin quarter

🔹 **Falfurrias** (Brooks County): pronounced Fal-FURE-us. No one knows exactly where the name came from, but the romantic explanation is that the word is Indian for "the land of the heart's delight."

Fall, serious: took a head-over-rainbarrel spill

Fallen angel: fell out of heaven and landed in the devil's lap

Fallen hide: a hide taken from a cow found dead on the range

F

False as: 1. election returns in Jim Wells County [In 1948, 202 votes mysteriously appeared in Jim Wells County to give Lyndon Johnson a victory, by 87 votes, in the race for U.S. Senator. No one ever explained how 202 people managed to vote alphabetically.] 2. Chamber of Commerce statistics 3. entries in a truck driver's log book

False impression: anyone looks tall when surrounded by midgets

False teeth: 1. store-bought molars 2. synthetic molars 3. store teeth 4. like stars, they come out at night 5. Roebucks, which refers to the days when false teeth were ordered by mail from Sears

False teeth, good: The best false teeth are those which, when dropped into a spring while getting a drink, can be fished out by tying a chicken bone to a string and dropping it in the water. Really good false teeth will just naturally clamp down on the bone so you can pull 'em up.

Familiar with: if his ashes were used for making lye soap, I'd know which bar he was in *See also Acquainted*

Family, sorry: would vote dry, then move away [In Texas, the drinking laws are about as confusing as Chinese arithmetic. In some places you can get liquor by the drink and in other places you can't. Usually, the right to drink is settled by a local option election, and the sorriest of families would all vote dry even if they knew they were moving away.]

Famished: *See Hungry*

Fan, electric: store-bought air

Fanatic: someone who sticks to his guns, whether they are loaded or not

Fancy: cotton to, as in "She really cottons to big diamonds and little bathing suits."

Fanning the horse: rider takes off his hat and fans the horse's neck. It's usually done when the cowboy thinks he has bested a real tough ride. The practice started back in the '30s and gradually died out, but it's enjoying somewhat of a comeback lately.

Far away: 1. yonder, which is the opposite of nigh 2. a three-greasin' trip, which means you'd have to grease the wagon three times to get there and back 3. right smart piece, as in "It's a right smart piece from El Paso to Texarkana." 4. so far you'd have to ride a pregnant mule to get there so you'd have a way back 5. would have to pack a lunch to get there 6. would take fourteen dollars in postage to get them a letter 7. so far away overnight mail from the post office takes a week to be delivered *See also Rural*

Far side: the right side of a horse

Farewell: hasta luego

Farm name: in the old days, a farm was usually named for the original or previous owner, such as "the Owen's place in Seymour"

Farm country: rural area where crop raising is the primary enterprise. If one particular crop is predominate in the area, the reference would be to that crop such as "Lubbock County is cotton country." The opposite would be cow country.

Farm laborer: 1. hand 2. hoe hand 3. field hand

Farmer: 1. Agro-American 2. plowboy 3. sod buster 4. tractor wrangler 5. plow wrangler 6. plow chaser 7. butter and egg man 8. pumpkin roller 9. clod hopper 10. mule man; mule trailer; mule follower; all of which refers to the days when farmers plowed behind a mule instead of on a tractor [Remember, a farmer doesn't have to go to work, he wakes up surrounded by it.]

Farmer, expert: 1. knows everything there is to know about cows, sows, and plows 2. only thing he can't do around a farm is lay an egg

Farmer, inept: 1. got his tractor hung in reverse and unplowed fifteen acres 2. don't know if he's plowin' or playin' dominoes

Farmer, lazy: don't raise nothing but hogs 'cause hogs don't need plowin' or hoein'

Farmer, small time: 1. a wool hat boy, which means he can't afford a felt hat 2. a broadcast farmer, which means he can't afford planting equipment so he has to sow his crops by broadcasting the seeds by hand

Farmer, smart: signed his crop [When a farmer in Weatherford, Texas, was having trouble with people stealing his watermelons, he put up a sign for all to see proclaiming: "Beware. One watermelon in this patch has been poisoned." The sign worked and the thefts stopped though no melon had actually been poisoned. Unfortunately, the plan backfired when the farmer went out one morning and noticed another sign: "Now there are two poisoned watermelons."]

Farmer, stupid: shot his mule 'cause the cotton rows came out crooked [A more modern version might be he sold his tractor because the rows came out crooked.]

Farmer, successful: made a whale of a crop

Farmer, unlucky: 1. only time he gets rain is when the crops are ready to harvest, which is about the only time a farmer doesn't want rain 2. don't ever get nuthin' but bull calves and girl babies [This means he never gets cows to help build his herd and he never gets boys to help out around the farm.]

Farrar (Limestone County): pronounced FAIR-ah, although some people say Fair-are; named in honor of Lochlin Johnson Farrar, a local settler

Farrier: person who cares for horses' feet, including shoeing and doctoring

Fart off: to insult another person; the perpetrator is subject to quadding by the offended person

Farwell (Parmer County): pronounced FAR-w.l.; named for Charles B. and John V. Farwell, who headed the Capitol Syndicate that received more than three million acres in return for building the Texas State Capitol

Fashion conscience: 1. if she was a hen she'd lay pastel colored eggs 2. dresses up to do the dishes 3. wears high heels to mow the lawn

Fast: 1. double quick 2. in the wink of an eye 3. in a heartbeat, as in "He can pick your pocket in a heartbeat" 4. going hell bent for leather 5. passed me like I was up on jacks in the garage 6. burning rocket fuel 7. could outrun the beaters on an electric mixer *See also Quick*

Fast as: 1. greased, chain, or double geared lightning 2. a duck on a June bug or a hen on a grasshopper 3. a cat with his tail on fire 4. bad news traveling at a church social 5. small town gossip 6. a shooting star 7. a tomcat shot with a boot jack 8. a turpentined cat 9. a hoop snake [This is a large reptile that curls himself into a loop, bites his own tail for balance, and rolls quickly out of harm's way. They are so fast no one has ever actually seen one.] 10. a pig after a pumpkin 11. a canned cat [This refers to the country prank of tying a can on a cat's tail to see him run.] *See also Quick as*

Fast horse: can run from sunup to sundown in about half an hour

Fast person: 1. can blow out the lamp and get into bed before it gets dark 2. can beat a bull to a hole in the fence 3. takes him fifteen minutes to draw to a halt 4. can stay neck n' neck with a jackrabbit 5. gets there in one-half less than no time 6. can gather up over yonder before you can bat an eyelash 7. could outrun a six-legged

F

bobcat 8. even sleeps fast [As Bobby Layne, the legendary quarterback from the University of Texas once said, "You don't need much sleep if you sleep fast."] 9. can play pitcher and catcher at the same time 10. so fast he can run down a rumor 11. when he stops it takes his shadow ten minutes to catch up 12. can catch his own echo 13. runs like a scared ghost 14. he's a bullet with feet *See also Quick*

Fast start: 1. quick out of the gate (or chute) 2. quick off the blocks

Fast worker: could have bailed fast enough to keep the *Titanic* afloat

Faster than: 1. a prairie fire with a tail wind 2. a whirlwind can snuff a match 3. a six-legged jackrabbit 4. a minnow can swim a dipper 5. a three-legged chicken [There was once a Texan who liked the drumstick when fried chicken was served. The only problem was both of his two sons also liked the drumstick. To resolve the situation, the man asked the Texas A&M University to breed some three-legged chickens. Six months later, the university delivered six of the unusual birds but, unfortunately, no one can catch these three-legged chickens.]

Fat: 1. hen plump 2. beef plumb to the hocks 3. heavy in the middle and poor on both ends 4. 20 pounds (or a dozen biscuits) away from a sideshow in the circus

Fat, loose: shakin' fat

Fat as: 1. a boardinghouse cat 2. a killing hog 3. a poisoned pup 4. a grub line coyote 5. a town dog [In the country, dogs often have to fend for themselves, but in most rural towns there will always be someone willing to share scraps with any old stray dog that happens along.] 6. a prize winning hog 7. a full possum 8. a coon in a corn field 9. a sausage salesman at a country fair

Fat man: 1. never seen anything that big without John Deere stamped on it 2. looks like he ate his brother 3. he don't care what you call him as long as you call him at meal time 4. has to sit down in shifts 5. a walkin,' talkin' tub a lard 6. a cellulite silo 7. got enough tallow for two head of cattle 8. suffers from hand to mouth disease 9. his energy has gone to waist 10. got a figure like a depot stove 11. can pinch an inch on his forehead *See also Obese; Male, fat; Rear end, large*

Fat woman: 1. warm in winter, shade in the summer 2. puts her pantyhose on with a crowbar (or a winch) 3. split her dress up the side and you could make a tent for an entire Gypsy family 4. don't wear nothin' but Mother Hubbards, which are dresses that cover everything but touch nothing but the shoulders 5. her housecoat would fit around a small house 6. she's built for comfort rather than speed 7. she ain't fat, just short for her weight *See also Rear end, large*

Fate: 1. some days you get, and some days you get got 2. some days you're the ball, some days you're the bat 3. some days you're the bug, some days you're the windshield

Father: the parent who has to endure childbirth without an anesthetic

Fathered: pappyed

Fatigued: 1. feel like I've been pullin' a dull saw all day 2. all out of snuff 3. plumb tared

Fattening day: first Saturday after payday, which is traditionally the day folks go to town and stock up on groceries

Fattening food: don't bother to eat it, just apply directly to the hips and thighs

Faucet: hydrant

Favor: If you'll do that for me, I'll give you the first silver dollar I find rolling uphill with spurs on.

Favoritism: playing brother-in-law [This saying comes from the theory that one would show favoritism to his sister's husband. The saying can be used to indicate favoritism even if in-laws are not involved.]

Favors: 1. resembles 2. limps, as in "Bubba sure favors his right leg ever since that ol' girl threw him out the window at the honky-tonk."

Fawmching: sulking

Fearless: 1. would walk through the valley of the shadow of death blind-folded and barefooted with one arm tied behind his back 2. the only things a cowboy was afraid of were a right-eous woman and being afoot 3. sweats ice water [Old-time Texas Ranger Bill McDonald was said to be so fearless "he'd charge hell with a bucket of water."] *See also Brave; Courageous*

A&M **Feather legs:** one who uses chicken practices

Feeble minded: touched in the head

Feed 'em and lead 'em: horse show people. [The term comes from the fact that many show people just feed their horses and lead them around the ring.]

Feeder mules: young mules that were broken but not in good condition [These mules would be fed out (put a bloom on) over the winter so they could be sold in the spring or early fall.]

Feeding time: the time to feed the stock after the day's work is done and before you eat

Feeler: the person who uses a pole to "feel" the bottom of a river so those about to be baptized won't fall into a hole or run into a rock

Feeling bad: 1. feel like I was run down, run over, and wrung out through a little bitty wringer 2. feel like I was sent for and couldn't come 3. feel like I was chewed up and spit out 4. feel like I was shot out of a cannon and missed the net 5. feel like I was eaten by a billygoat and puked over a cliff *See also Sick*

Feeling good: 1. if I felt any better, I'd have to be twins 'cause one person just couldn't stand it 2. if I felt any better I couldn't stand it and the sheriff wouldn't allow it 3. feel good all over more than any place else 4. feel so good I could do the hokey pokey all by myself

Feeling sorry for himself: 1. got his tail beneath his hind legs 2. his bottom lip is sagging so much he's picking up gravel as he walks 3. licking his wounds

Feelings, hurt: cut me to the quick

Feels good as: 1. fresh washed sheets on a bed 2. takin' off a pair of tight boots after a hard day's work [An old cowboy finally saved up enough money for a pair of handmade boots. Unfortunately, when they arrived, they were about a size too small. Three or four months later the cowboy ran into the boot maker and told him the problem. Naturally, the boot maker offered to stretch the boots but the cowboy refused. "After 14 or 15 hours of bustin' horses, punchin' cows, mending fences, and chasing strays, the best thing I have to look forward to is gettin' them damned tight boots off.]

Feet: 1. the spur end, referring to the fact that spurs are always worn on the feet 2. the forked end, referring to legs resembling a very large two-pronged fork 3. dirt movers, which is an expression that comes from the habit of country folks kicking some dirt while they stand around and chew the fat (talk)

Feet, cold: 1. when he gets under the electric blanket, the street lights short out 2. when he takes off his shoes the furnace comes on

Feet, large: 1. has to put his britches on over his head 2. has a large understanding 3. so big he has to go to a crossroads to turn around [Remember,

F

you can't have a big building without a big foundation.]

Feet, stinking: 1. put Odoreaters in his boots and they evaporated 2. always sits on the front row in church so if the sermon runs long, he can take off his shoes and inspire the preacher to a quick conclusion

Fell: 1. got his spurs tangled 2. ate some gravel (or asphalt) 3. joined his shadow in the dirt 4. like he'd been hit between the eyes with the butt end of a quirt (or scatter-gun) 5. like a wormed apple in a whirlwind 6. like a flour sack off the back of a wagon 7. like an eagle in a wind shear

Female: 1. ol' slick legs 2. belle 3. gal 4. darlin' 5. little lady 6. sweet thing 7. filly 8. heifer 9. sage hen 10. skirt 11. honky-tonk angel 12. pullet, which can be used for any female, regardless of age, although it is generally used for younger ladies 13. something the world would be a lot worse off without 14. the best thing on earth to squeeze 15. someone who's fully armed when she's fully naked *See also Girl*

Female, active: keeps her dance card full

Female, age of: a lady's age is like the speedometer in a used car—you know it's been set back but you don't know how far

Female, aggressive: comes on like a mouthful of hot gumbo (or red beans) [If you have ever taken a mouthful of very hot gumbo, you know it gets your attention real quick just like an aggressive female does.]

Female, aging: used to get a romantic twinkle in her eye when she was in a romantic mood, but now it just means her contact lens is in backwards

Female, angry: madder than an old hen in a wool basket

Female, anxious (sort of): itching for something she ain't willing to scratch

Female, attractive: 1. could make a glass eye blink 2. captured my heart and about three or four other organs 3. looks so good she could make a bishop kick a hole in a stained glass window

Female, conniving: 1. she takes you by the hand so she can tug on your heart strings 2. didn't learn to cook because she was hungry 3. always dragging her rope trollin' for some poor ol' cowboy that don't know no better 4. always smells tired [Just before her husband gets home she dabs some Pine Sol on her neck and sprays Lysol under her arms so she'll smell like she's been working all day.] 5. ain't lookin' for a husband, she's looking for a diamond mine 6. may have a short rope but she can still throw a big loop (and there is always, it seems, some man who is willing to get caught in it) 7. made it to the top because her dress didn't *See also Looking for a husband*

Female, crazy: a cup and a saucer short of a set

Female, dangerous: 1. can shoot as well as she cooks 2. would dip her man's boxer shorts in catnip and then buy a mountain lion for a pet 3. might turn your head but it would be on a spit over an open flame 4. plays with fire [Note: When a woman plays with fire, it's a man that usually gets burned.]

Female, deceiving: 1. if she's an angel she's wearing invisible wings 2. if she was a hen, she'd eat your feed and then lay her eggs under the neighbor's porch [This is a country version for she'd let you buy the drinks all night and then go home with the bartender.]

Female, desirable: 1. can ride any horse in my string 2. can eat crackers in my bed 3. can put her shoes under my bed 4. can squeeze my toothpaste anywhere she wants 5. would make a man plow through a stump 6. would make a cowboy forget his horse 7. so desirable, I'd give an alligator a hysterectomy without antiseptic just for the opportunity to hold her hand 8. don't have any trouble findin' a rake to gather her hay crop

Female, easy: 1. she's called "radio station" because anyone can pick her up, especially at night 2. call her Ford 'cause she's the best pickup 3. such a pushover, you can fool her even if you play your cards wrong

Female, evil: she'd make Bonnie Parker look like an MYF counselor [MYF is Methodist Youth Fellowship and Miss Parker was the Bonnie in the Bonnie and Clyde crime duo.] *See also Male, evil*

Female, fat: *See Female, large and Fat woman*

Female, flirtatious: 1. been in more laps than a napkin, which is how the legendary Mae West once described herself 2. never met a lap she didn't like

Female, gentle: only hits you with the soft end of the mop

Female, hard: only thing that will make an impression on her is a diamond

Female, high spirited: if she was a horse, she'd be hard to break to a halter

Female, ignorant: IQ is about equal to her bra size

Female, inept: 1. bought cosmetics for a makeup exam 2. she went to the Community Chest for a mammogram 3. when she puts on her bikini she takes off her brain 4. don't think she can be overdrawn at the bank 'cause she still has checks left

Female, irate: your butt is crabgrass and she's the goat

Female, jealous: *See Jealous woman*

Female, jilted: 1. her heart's been broken more than the ten commandments 2. her heart broke into more pieces than a crystal ball dropped out of an airplane 3. took up with the

wrong ol' boy and he took her for a short ride

Female, large: 1. if she was a stripper, her G string would be as wide as a tow strap 2. has to put on a girdle to get into her kimono 3. built like a pillow 3. gained so much having the baby that her stretch marks look like tank tracks

Female, lazy: *See Lazy woman*

Female, lying: 1. don't even tell the truth in her diary 2. usually starts lying about her age when the mirror starts telling the truth

Female, made up: got fresh paint on her cheeks, new chalk on her nose, and fresh slobber on her spit curls. [Unfortunately, her husband will probably never notice it.]

Female, mean: 1. her emery board is a whetstone, which implies she sharpens her nails rather than manicures them [Some people use whampus cat (or kitty) for "mean female" although no one seems to know exactly what it means. The Itasca, Texas, high school uses Whampus Cat as its team mascot and Bill McMurray, in his book *Texas High School Football* explains, "It's said this nickname came from a fan of an opposing team when he referred to Itasca playing like whampus cats." A good guess is whampus is derived from whomp us, and any female that'll whomp you is certainly mean. *See also Mean woman*

Female, middle age: too young for Medicare and too old for men to care

Female, promiscuous: 1. sleeps around so much, she'd catch fire if she didn't sweat 2. the inscription on her tombstone will read: "The only time she ever slept alone" 3. she's a widow woman who always seems to want her weeds plowed under 4. the original Frito lay 5. you have no chance to be the first one but you stand a good chance of bein' the next one 6. got

F

round heels, which implies the heels on her shoes have been rounded, making her an easier pushover

Female, proud: 1. a real honey but none of the bees know it 2. thinks she's the only peach on the tree

Female, respectable: an all-standing tough ol' gal which, from a country boy, is high praise

Female, restless: a hard old gal to keep down on the farm

Female, rowdy: would rather listen to some trash than sweep some up

Female, seductive: 1. got more moves than a water wiggle 2. can give you such a hot feeling it'll melt the fillings in your teeth *See also Walk, seductive*

Female, shallow: like an Easter egg, she's mostly trimmings

Female, shapely: 1. built like a brick outhouse [This is a common saying although few people built their outhouse out of bricks because you often had to move the location of the facility, especially if the prevailing winds changed.] 2. like the song says, nuthin' sure would look good on her 3. got more curves than a barrel full of snakes 4. could qualify for the Swedish bikini team 5. Coke bottle figure 6 would take first place in the halter class 7. her figure would raise steam from an icy heart 8. would make a freight train take a dirt road 9. her hips got more motion than an ocean

Female, shy: won't even bend over in the garden 'cause the potatoes have eyes

Female, skinny: has to wear suspenders to hold up her girdle *See also Skinny woman*

Female, small: if she was gold plated you could use her for a watch fob

Female, smart: has horse sense [She knows when to say nay.]

Female, stubborn: got a body like a marble statue and a head to match

Female, stupid: 1. has to sneeze every now and then to keep the dust from building up on her brain 2. they call her the last frontier, 'cause all she has between her ears is space *See also Stupid woman*

Female, tired: looks like she's been ironing all day in high heels with a cold iron

Female, tough: 1. shaves her legs with 80-grit sandpaper 2. shaves under her arms with a chain saw

Female, ugly: 1. ain't two faced 'cause if she was, she wouldn't be wearing that one 2. can't help being ugly but she could stay at home 3. her necklace ought to be a flea collar 4. a dead hog that has been lying in the sunshine for two weeks could beat her in a beauty contest 5. wouldn't be fit for a drunk cowboy to take up with *See also Ugly woman*

Female, underage: 1. jail bait 2. forbidden fruit 3. Huntsville honey [Hunstville, Texas, is where the main unit of the Texas prison system is located.]

Female, unmarried: 1. bell chaser, as in wedding bell 2. home wrecker 3. keeps her hair combed and her purr tuned

Female, vain: used so many mud packs, she could drain a Louisiana swamp

Female, young: better use what mother nature gave her before father time takes it away

Female confidence: the ability to walk past a mirror and not sneak a peek

Female equality: As Ann Richards said in her 1988 Democratic keynote address, Ginger Rogers did everything Fred Astaire did and she did it backwards in high heels.

Female florist: a lady who loves to show off her bloomers

Female gathering: 1. hen party 2. quilting bee 3. shower practice, referring to women holding showers for friends who are getting married

Female liar: *See Liar, female*

Female magician: she can, as if by magic, turn any ol' dirty, rundown, ramshackle, rat-infested house into home sweet home [I'd like to see Houdini try that.]

Female power: ability to wrap a man around her little finger without twisting his arm

Female superiority: Houston's Liz Carpenter said it best, in a speech supporting Texas State Treasurer Ann Richards, with, "Roosters crow, hens deliver."

Female wardrobe: a woman is like a salad, everything depends on the dressing

Feminist, devout: arrow proof [This means she doesn't have to worry about being struck by one of Cupid's arrows.]

Fence, good: 1. horse high, pig tight, bull strong, and goose proof 2. a wire fence strung tight enough to pick a tune on

Fence, screeching: the sound a fence makes as it gives a little when livestock runs into it

Fence crawler: cattle or horses that attempt to get out of a pen by "climbing" the fence

Fence line: property line where a fence is constructed

Fence gap: a place in a fence that can be let down, usually not close to a gate

Fence row: line of trees growing up in the fence line where you drag broken down equipment that is not worth repairing

Fence sitters: cowboys who observe the actions from the top rail of a fence rather than as a participant; can pertain to rodeos or ranch work

Fence stretcher: *See Come along*

Fenders: 1. the body parts on a pickup most likely to get damaged 2. wide pieces of leather along the stirrups on a saddle

Feral: a wild horse

Ferocious: savagerous

Fetching stick: stick used in an old-time dry goods store to "jostle" something on a high shelf just enough so it will fall and you can catch it; also called a reaching stick

Fever, high: 1. got so high his hair was sweatin' 2. got so high you could fry an egg on his forehead 3. so high his eyes were almost hard boiled

Feverish: felt like my hat was full of hot coals

Few: pickin's are powerful slim

Fiador: a hackamore throat latch, or knot, that exerts pressure at the rear of a horse's jaw; usually pronounced "Theodore" by cowboys

Fiddler, bad: he plays the fiddle like the strings were still in the cat *See also Musician, poor*

Fiddler's bitch: the fiddler's dog that hangs around the stage and gets drunk by drinking out of the glasses set on the bandstand by folks who are out on the dance floor

Fiddlin: drive a stake in the ground and fiddle (saw) on it [This is supposed to make fishing worms come to the surface. The process is talked about a lot more than it is actually practiced.]

Fidgeting: like a three-legged cat tryin' to bury manure on a frozen lake

Fidgety: antsy

Field: open land that has been plowed for planting; a pasture is land that has not been plowed

Field, small: patch of ground

Fifty-dollar bill: *See Ulysses S. Grant*

Fifty-gallon drum: one of the most versatile things you can have around the place. You can cut one half in two (end to end) and make a BBQ pit or a matched pair of hog troughs. You can cut one half in two (around the middle) and make a pair of matched planters. You can leave it as is, take the top off, and use it for cooking sour mash or for a trash can. You can weld a whole bunch of 'em together and make a first-rate pontoon boat that'll float real good till the barrels rust out.

Fifty-yard line: 1. line dividing the rodeo arena into two equal part (seven through the arena isn't always 100 yards long) 2. center line of a football field

Fifty cents: four bits

Fight: 1. a bloodletting 2. a two-man square dance 3. a Pecos promenade [This refers to the old days when fighting was not uncommon out west of the Pecos. If it hadn't been for a fella named Judge Roy Bean, things might have got plumb out of hand.]

Fight, big: a teeth-gnashing, knock down, drag out fight

Fight, short: 1. will be a two-hit fight—I'll hit you and you'll hit the ground 2. had me licked and whipped before he even had time to get good and mad

Fighter: 1. if you're gonna beat him, it will be after the fight 2. if you wanna fight him, bring your lunch 'cause it will take all day 3. will kick your backside till your nose bleeds 4. could whip his weight in wolves or bobcats 5. would fight a buzz saw and give it three turns head start 6. will fight at the drop of a hat 7. will whip you or get whipped trying 8. will make you think you've been in a sack with a wildcat

Fighter, poor: 1. couldn't fight his way out of a paper sack 2. couldn't whip a crippled kitten 3. couldn't beat his way out of a spider's web 4.

couldn't whip a 90-year-old blind, paraplegic grandmother

Fighting: 1. raised more dust in five minutes than Noah's flood could have settled 2. only the absence of shooting irons prevented a killing 3. go at it bucktooth and hangnail, which is the Texas version of "fought tooth and nail" 4. locking horns 5. fur (or feathers) was flying in all directions 6. crossed sabers

Figure, fair: somewhere between oh boy and obese

Filled up: like an airline seat holding a 400-pound passenger

Filly: female horse not over three years old

Final act: 1. the door slammer, which means the door to further opportunities is closed 2. the deal killer, which is the act that finally kills the deal

Final review: the last military review of the year at A&M where every member of the corps passes in review and is promoted; seniors then review underclassmen

Finalize: 1. tie up the loose ends 2. round up the strays 3. dot the i's, cross the t's, and run it by a lawyer 4. put the last nail in that coffin

Financial condition, poor: 1. like a dog chasin' his tail, we're both tryin' to make ends meet 2. runnin' a poor string of horses [This comes from cow country where it is said that a ranch is no better than its horses. A ranch with good horses can get by even if the cowboys are only average quality. It follows that a rancher running a poor string of horses is having financial problems.] *See also Bankrupt; Rich; Went broke*

Financial genius: somebody who can earn more money than his wife can spend

Find: 1. smoke 'em out 2. flush 'em out 3. hunt 'em up if you have to turn over every cow patty (or rock) in Texas, which is the Texas version of "leave no stone unturned"

Finders fee: bird dog money

Fine as: 1. frog hair split three ways 2. dollar cotton

Finger, index: 1. trigger finger 2. pointer

Fingernail: 1. claws for a male; love hooks for a female 2. hammer magnet, which refers to people often striking their finger while hammering a nail

Fingernail polish: 1. claw paint 2. finger paint

Fingernails, long and sharp: if she came after you with both hands, you'd think you had been attacked by a flock of flying screwdrivers

Finished: 1. stick a fork in him 'cause he's done 2. over and done with 3. the prom, rodeo, dance, or hoedown is over 4. that's the old ball game 5. turn out the lights, the party's over [This is the title of a Willie Nelson song made famous by Dandy Don Meredith, the former Dallas Cowboy, during his broadcast days on Monday Night Football.]

Finished it: put the pin in the party hog

Finishing: playing out the string

Fire ants: imported South American ants that hurt worse than a scorpion, are as tenacious as an angry water moccasin, and are harder to get rid of than a deadbeat brother-in-law

Fire bread: bread cooked over an open fire instead of in a stove or Dutch oven

Fire engine: fire trucks in Texas

Fire starter, poor: wore out three hats tryin' to get one little ol' camp fire to blaze

Fired often: he's been fired more than Custer's pistol

Firefly: lightning bug

Fireman: smoke eater

Firm as: bedsprings in a $100 mattress

Firm but fair: like a watermelon, he's got a big heart but it's hidden under a mighty thick skin

First: first rattle out of the box, which refers to rolling dice out of a box

First light of day: 1. peep of day 2. morngloom 3. comin' light (day) 4. bust of day

First Monday: traditionally, a trade day in rural Texas. The farmers and ranchers come to town to do their business. Also called swap day or trade day. The most famous first Monday is at Canton, in northeast Texas. What started as a farmers market is now the largest flea market in the state. If you go, wear your most comfortable shoes.

A&M First sergeant: Top-Kick

First things first: 1. the water won't clear up till you get the hogs out of the trough 2. can't kill the snake till you get the hoe in your hand 3. to eat pecans you gotta crack the shells 4. can't steal second base if you're not on first 5. gotta catch it before you can hang it, which refers to calf roping—you have to rope the calf before you can tie it

Fish (noun): the size of the fish makes it a keeper but the fight in the fish makes it a leaper *See Catfish*

Fish (verb): 1. drown some worms, minnows, or crickets 2. wet a hook 3. bait a line

A&M Fish: freshman

Fish, fighting: jerked so hard on the line he pulled down my drawers (or britches)

Fish, large: 1. when I pulled him into the boat the water level in the lake dropped three inches 2. measured 14 inches between the eyes [Any number between 10 and 20 can be used since anything under 10 would be too small and no one would believe anything over 20.] 3. could use the scales for roof shingles 4. would have to dislocate both shoulders to describe how big it was [Remember, the biggest fish are always caught by the tale.]

Fish, medium sized: too small for the wall; big but not big enough to stuff and hang on the wall as a trophy

Fish, old: found the Mayflower anchor when we cut him open

Fish, small: could have it stuffed and use it for a key chain

A&M **Fish answers:** Freshmen (fish) are permitted to give only four answers to upperclassmen as follows: 1. Yes, sir 2. No, sir 3. No excuse, sir 4. I hesitate to articulate for fear that I may deviate from the true course of rectitude. In short, sir, I am a very dumb fish and do not know, sir (to be said as fast as possible)

A&M **Fish day:** the one day each year when sophomores and freshmen change roles

A&M **Fish privilege:** Fish do not have the privilege to think, like, want, or feel.

Fisherman: 1. a jerk on one end of a line waiting for a jerk on the other end 2. bait killer 3. line runner, which refers to fishermen who prefer to use a trotline 4. bass buster [Any other kind of fish can be substituted, such as crappie buster or catfish buster. Younger fishermen are junior bass busters and really young children are sunfish busters.]

Fisherman, active: 1. his trotline never gets dry 2. his hooks never rust in the tackle box

Fisherman, avid: a foaming-at-the-mouth fisherman [Foaming at the mouth is a reference to someone having rabies, which means they are sure enough crazy. Therefore, a foaming-at-the-mouth fisherman is just plumb crazy about fishing. The foaming mouth analogy can be used for anything.]

Fisherman, clever: 1. fishes with drunk worms [A really clever fisherman would dip his worms in tequila until they got good and drunk. Then when he put the worm on the hook it would be so brave that it would bite the fish!] 2. fishes with chewin' tobacco [An equally clever fisherman simply feeds the tobacco to the fish and then knocks 'em over the head when they come up to spit.]

Fisherman, expert: completed the graduate program at the Oklahoma school for fishhook baiters, which makes him a Master Baiter

Fisherman, illegal: talks to the fish [This is a reference to old-time telephones that had a magneto and hand crank to supply the power. When the magneto was eventually replaced by a battery, the old phone could be used to talk to the fish by removing everything but the magneto, electrical lines, and the crank. When the lines were put into the water and the crank was turned, an electrical current was created which would stun the fish, causing them to quickly float to the surface where they could be harvested. In some places men who use the tactics are said to be fish pickers 'cause they pick their catch off the top of the water much like a cotton picker might pick cotton.]

Fisherman, inept: 1. biggest thing he ever hooked was the back of his lap 2. couldn't drown a plastic worm 3. don't know his bass from a hole in the ground 4. knows the two days fish are always biting, yesterday and tomorrow 5. couldn't catch a fish in a baited hole (or at Sea World) 6. went ice fishing and came home with 200 pounds of ice [He almost drowned when water filled the kitchen after his wife tried to cook his catch.]

Fisherman, lazy: 1. never married 'cause he couldn't find a rich, good lookin' woman willin' to clean fish, which means he was also a stupid fisherman 'cause no rich, good lookin' woman ought to have to clean fish

Fisherman, liar: all fishermen except me and you are liars

Fisherman, lucky: 1. fishes with a silver hook 2. was born with a silver hook in his mouth 3. could catch his limit in the Dead Sea 4. could tie his line into a loop and lasso fish if he ran out of hooks 5. uses a magnetic hook 6. could catch fish with rotten line and a straight hook

Fisherman's creed: it ain't how deep you fish but how you wiggle your worm

Fishing: 1. the most fun you can have with your clothes on 2. a bad day fishing is better than a good day working 3. the best excuse on earth for drinking in the daytime 4. the best way to separate men and truth

Fishing, good: the fish are so hungry you have to hide behind a tree to bait your hook to keep the bass from jumping out of the water and taking the worm out of your hand

Fishing, poor: even the biggest liars weren't catching anything

Fishing rodeo: term used to describe a cowboy who makes a legal catch in the roping events

Fishing trip, lousy: the only fish we caught were the Dolphins on TV

Fist: 1. the five of clubs 2. Arkansas soup bone

Fist fight: knuckle-buster

Fit, good: 1. fits like scales on a fish 2. like bark on a tree 3. like ugly on an ape 4. like sardines in a can 5. like hide on a horse 6. like feathers on a duck 7. like a hand in a glove 8. like hot lead in a bullet mold

Fit, loose: like a choir robe on a skinny person [Robes often come in one-size-fits-all variety, which means they'll fit you whether you weight 103 pounds or 301 pounds.]

Fit, poor: 1. fits like a sock on a duck's beak 2. like a boot on a bull 3. like pantyhose on a pig 4. like a housecoat on a hog 5. like a bikini on a mermaid 6. like daddy's hat on the head of a patch-seated kid 7. like a big ring on a little finger 8. like socks on a rooster 9. like a hog in a saddle

Fit, tight as: 1. wax in a candle mold 2. ski pants on a fat woman *See also Tight as*

Fit as: a fiddle *See also Out of shape*

Five (playing card)**:** nickel or buffalo nickel

Five-gaited horse: one that is trained to perform in five gaits: the walk, trot, canter, slow gait, and rack

Flabbergasted: beflustered

Flag, Texas: *See Texas flag*

Flank girth: the rear girth on a double-rigged saddle

Flank strap: strap, lined with sheepskin, that circles the flank of a horse or bull and encourages the animal to buck without causing pain

Flanking: *See Calf roping*

Flapping: like a runaway window shade

Flask: tickler

Flat as: 1. a panhandle prairie 2. the deck of an aircraft carrier 3. a pancake 4. a mashed snake 5. an ironing board 6. a red wagon run over by a Peterbuilt 7. a tromped on cat

Flat iron: smoothin' iron

Flat deck: single deck cattle truck

Flat footed: term used when the angle of a horse's foot is less than 45 degrees

Flat rock: *See Rock, flat*

Flattery: 1. artificial sweetener 2. like French toilet water; smells good but you ain't supposed to drink it 3. is like chewing gum, enjoy it for a while but don't swallow it 4. resembles friendship about as much as a wolf resembles

F

a dog [John Wayne described flattery as "the phony express."]

Flea market: jockey lot

Flea bit: a gray horse with tiny red spots roughly the size of a chicken's eye about every 4 or 5 square inches

Flea trap: a cowboy's bedroll

Flee: 1. hightail it 2. skeedaddle out of here 3. cut a hole in the wind

Flew apart: like a two-dollar suitcase in a train station

Flexible: 1. can dance to whatever tune the band is playing 2. goes whichever way the wind is blowing

Flick team: term used for a group of friends, usually women, who get together to attend a movie

Flighty: always flyin' up the creek

Flimsy as: 1. a three-dollar suitcase 2. a house of cards 3. a Kleenex shirt 4. cheesecloth socks

Flinch (card game): Baptist poker

Flip: an elastic hand catapult, sort of like a forkless slingshot, that uses only one piece of rubber with a leather pouch attached

Flirt: 1. wishful winking 2. attracts a man before he's married, distracts him afterward

Flirtatious: can sit on your lap while you're standing up

Flirtatious, innocent: don't matter where you get your appetite so long as you take your meals at home

Flirting: sidled up to him

Floating a horse's teeth: term used for filing sharp points off a horse's grinding teeth

Floating around: like milkweed in a spring breeze

Floccillation: picking at the bed covers

Flomot (Motley County): pronounced FLO-mot; located so close to the Floyd County line that residents opted to make their name a combination of the two counties

Flood: 1. water was hub deep to a Ferris wheel 2. had enough water to make Noah's flood look like a baby's bath water 3. enough water to float the rock of ages 4. so much water we had to use a skin diver to grease the windmill *See also Creek, flooded and Water, deep*

Floozy: in Texas, not necessarily a prostitute. Any painted-up, flirtatious, skin-showing woman with a wiggle in her walk, wickedness on her mind, and whiskey on her breath will be a floozy, according to the fine ladies of the First Baptist Church. A floozy is transformed into a hussy when she steals another woman's boyfriend or husband.

Flop: *See Texas hold 'em*

Flow tank: the tank that receives the crude oil as it flows from the well *See Settling tank*

Flowed: 1. like the Brazos River at flood stage 2. like the water from a flash flood over a low water crossing 3. like beer at a bachelor party

Flowella (Brooks County): pronounced Flo-ella; name came from the flowing well that was at the center of the town when it was first platted

Floydada (Floyd County): pronounced Floy-DAY-da; the name is a combination of the county name and Ada Price who was the mother of local rancher W. T. Price

Flung dung: *See Dololly*

Flush (poker hand): 1. all blue, used even if the cards are red or black 2. caught five from the spade litter [Naturally, clubs, diamonds, or hearts can be substituted depending on your hand.]

Flushed: jilted or ceremonies when jilted

Flustered: 1. in a lather 2. walleyed 3. foaming at the mouth

Flyswatter: 1. emergency tea strainer 2. fly flapper 3. fly brush, which was a homemade brush used by many country folks to shoo the flies off the food

Fly, open: *See Zipper, open*

Flying jenny: merry-go-round

Foal: newborn or young horse, colt or filly, less than a year old

Foaming at the mouth: frothin'

Foard City (Foard County): both the town and the county are pronounced like the cars, Ford, not Foe-erd

Foddering time: the time to strip dried leaves from standing corn stalks

Fodice (Houston County): pronounced FOE-dice. Although the name probably originated from a misspelling of Fordyce, Arkansas, the more popular version is the name originated when someone yelled "fo dice" in a crap game down behind the local post office.

Fog, thick: 1. so thick you couldn't cut it with a chain saw 2. so thick the farmers had to mount foghorns on their tractors

Follow: 1. ride in his dust 2. run in his ruts 3. tail 'em like a coyote after a lost calf 4. eat some of his dust 5. bird-dog 'em

Following: traipsing after

Food: 1. vittles 2. grub 3. chuck, which refers to food from a chuck wagon on a trail drive 4. groceries

Food, bad: 1. would make a buzzard gag 2. would make a maggot puke 3. could be used as a fly repellent *See also Taste, bad*

Food, good: best I ever lapped a lip over *See also Taste, good*

Food, poor: 1. ain't fit for nothing but a slop bucket or a garbage disposal 2. don't feed that to the hogs unless you want dead hogs

Fool: 1. yoakum 2. yahoo 3. you can educate him but you can't make him think 4. you can teach sense to a smart man but not to a fool [If you have to be a fool, be a rich one.]

Fool, startenated: means he's been a fool since he was born

Fool, total: tomfool or he's eaten' up with tomfoolery

Fool head: an invisible second head on Southerners that tends to come off easily, as in "Billy Fred laughed his fool head off when I fell into the well."

Fooling me: 1. passing gas and tryin' to blame the dog 2. tryin' to sell me possum hide for rabbit fur

Foolish: 1. would jump into the river to get out of the rain 2. would pick a fight with a skunk or a porcupine 3. would buy hay for a nightmare 4. would buy a square hula hoop 5. if he was a mouse, he'd build his nest in a cat's box 6. could get held up through the mail

Foot: 1. wheel 2. hoof

Football: 1. Elbert Hubbard called it "a sport that bears the same relation to education that bullfighting does to farming" 2. a three-hour commercial with occasional interruptions for play

Footlog: a tree across a stream that can be used as a makeshift bridge

For a long time: 1. till all the cows in Texas have been BBQ'd 2. till the cows come home 3. till hell freezes over thick enough to skate on

For sure: sure as the world, as in "I'm gonna get my wife a job next week sure as the world." *See also Absolutely; Certain*

Force: 1. put (or hold) his feet to the fire 2. give him a dose of convincing

Forced play (dominoes): when you have only one play and you have to make it, even if it opens up the opportunity for your opponents to score

F

Ford lover: would rather have a sister workin' in a whorehouse than a brother driving a Chevy

Forefathers: foreparents

Forefooting: roping a horse by the fore feet (front feet)

Foreigner (furiner): can't even laugh in English

Foreman: 1. segundo 2. bullwhacker, which was an old-time ox driver 3. bell goat *See also Boss; Leader*

Forest: big thicket

Forever: 1. as long as ducks (or pigs) go barefooted 2. till somebody slides home from first 3. for good, as in "I'm yours for good, unless I get a better offer." 4. until there's enough frost in hell to kill snap beans on the vine 5. until the devil asks for forgiveness

Forgetful: thin minded

Forgot: 1. misremembered it 2. slipped through the cracks [may have originated in the days when wood planks were used as flooring; anything that slipped through the cracks in the planks was generally forgotten until new flooring was installed]

Fork: 1. to mount a horse 2. the forward part of a saddletree

Fort Worth (Tarrant County): properly pronounced Foat Wurth; the town that bills itself as "Where the West begins," which naturally means Dallas is where the East peters out. It was named for General William Jenkins Worth, who never visited the site. Folks in that town have been known to claim "You can't be a cowboy unless you were born in Fort Worth." Also called Panther City and more commonly Cow Town since it was once a major shipping point for cattle. Some people even refer to it as Town of the Cow.

Fortunate: 1. they tried to hang him but the rope broke (or they would have hung him but nobody had a rope) 2.

good fortune follows him around looking for a place to happen 3. fell into the outhouse and discovered a gold mine 4. always toted her ducks to a good market *See also Lucky*

Forty acres: nickname for the University of Texas at Austin [The original campus comprised forty acres. Today it is more than 300 acres.]

Forward seat (horse): riding in such a way to keep weight over the withers; used for jumping; also known as "hunt seat"

Foster mother: *See T.A.M.U.*

Fought: 1. locked horns 2. went at each other tooth and nail

Founder: inflammation of a horse's hoof that can cause lameness; also called "laminitis"

Four (playing card): Henry Ford or simply Ford

Four get: When the famous Chicken Ranch was open near La Grange, Texas, they had an $8 Aggie special. Aggies called it four get: get it up, get on, get off, and get out.

Four-wheel-drive vehicle: 1. 4 x 4 (pronounced four by four) 2. what I'd like to be buried in 'cause I ain't never seen a hole they couldn't get you out of

Fourable: an oil field term for four lengths of pipe

Fox ears: very small, well-defined ears on a horse, which is considered a good quality

Fox trot: 1. a dance your grandparents used to do 2. the short gait of horse when he's passing from a walk to a trot

Foxfire: fungus that forms in decaying wood, which causes a strange, eerie glow *See also Glows*

Fractious: 1. gravel in his gizzard (or craw)

Fragile as: 1. a hand blown glass bulb 2. a sopapilla

Frail: has to be propped up to cuss

Frazzled: good Texas word with several meanings such as well worn (for clothes), messy (for a room), tense (nervous)

Frazzlin: special word with no particular meaning; generally used, somewhat in a derogatory manner, to group things together, as in "I'm fixin' to whup every frazzlin one of you worthless Yankees."

Freckles: 1. looks like she swallowed a quarter and broke out in pennies 2. got more spots than a turkey (or guinea) egg

Fredericksburg (Gillespie County): pronounced Fred-ricks-burg; named by German immigrants in honor of Prince Frederick of Prussia

Fredonia (Mason County): pronounced Fra-Doan-ya

Free: ain't got nothing left to lose, which infers that a man who has lost everything is free from worrying about losing anything else

Freedom: like cheap soap, loses its strength when it's watered down

Frenzied: 1. runnin' around like a sage hen 2. crazy as a half-grown bird dog

Fresno: used to build highway roadbeds (mule pulled)

Friction fire: occurs when the insurance policy rubs too hard against the mortgage papers [Some people refer to friction fire as Jewish lightning, which is considered derogatory.]

Fried chicken, good: so good it'll straighten your teeth, smooth your skin, and make childbirth a pleasure [This description, or something similar, can be used to describe good barbecue, chili, chicken-fried steak, gravy, or other good food.]

Friend: 1. pardner 2. sidekick 3. shotgun rider 3. running buddy 4. compadre 5. kemosabe, which is how Tonto referred to his Texas friend The Lone Ranger 6. can chew tobacco off my plug anytime 7. sidekick 8. amigo 9. "long as I got a biscuit, you got half" is a sign someone is a sure 'nuff friend 10. stick together through thick and thin, lose or win 11. someone who will talk about your faults in private 12. someone who has never heard your story before 13. a real friend will tell you when you have broccoli on your teeth or when your zipper is open 14. would back you till a chicken got a toothache 15. as close as cloves on a Christmas ham 16. will stick by you till they're chopping ice in Death Valley (or hell's a glacier) 17. thick as feathers in a pillow [Note: The word Texas comes from the Indian word tejas (pronounced tay hoss, never te jays), which means friend or ally.]

Friend, best: will help you out when both your arms are broken and your nose needs picking

Friend, fair weather: like your shadow, you only see 'em when the sun shines

Friend, faithful: 1. will ride with you till hell freezes over then go a little piece on the ice 2. will stay with you through all kinds of weather 3. will stay with you when everybody else has abandoned you except the sheriff, which means he'll still be your friend even if you get arrested

Friendless: a one-buggy man [This means when he dies the only buggy in his funeral procession will belong to the undertaker. A more modern version would be one-car man, which means one car would be more than enough to take all his friends to his funeral.]

Friendly: 1. neighborly 2. his porch light is always burning 3. his welcome mat is always out 4. keeps the latch string on the outside [This is a reference to the days before doorknobs when a string attached to a latch was used to open doors. The friendliest people always kept their latch string on the outside so anyone could open the door.]

Friendly advice: 1. don't buy friendship, you might lose it to a higher bidder 2. friendship is like a dollar, hard to get, easy to throw away 3. can't cultivate a friend by diggin' up dirt around him [Remember, friendship isn't something you get, it's something you give.]

Friendly as: 1. a pink-eyed rabbit 2. a pup in a box

Friendly, somewhat: only friendly up to the pockets, which means he'll be your friend until you need to borrow some money

Friends: 1. get along like two pups in a basket 2. so close they use the same toothpick 3. close enough to share a buttonhole

Friendship: is like a cow's milk; you can't take it, it's got to be given [Bum Phillips, former coach of the Houston Oilers, explained, "A cow has got to let her milk down. She's gotta give it to you; you can't take it away from one, you ain't strong enough." Lyndon Johnson said, of friendship, "Never overlook an opportunity to do an honest favor for an honorable friend."]

Friendship, questionable: friendly as a bootlegger [In the old days a bootlegger was usually known to be friendly only when you were buying his whiskey. When you ran out of money he went looking for new "friends."]

Frightened: 1. come down with a case of the runs and he did 2. scared witless *See also Scared and Scary*

Friendswood (Galveston County): usually said quickly so that the "d" becomes silent; Frens-wood

Frightening: 1. would stand up the hair on a mink coat, stuffed animal, bearskin rug, or buffalo lap robe 2. will make you ruin your shorts 3. hair

raisin' 4. would scare you out of ten years' growth *See also Scary*

Frigid: his (or her) side of the waterbed froze solid as a glacier

Frijole: Mexican dried beans, usually pinto beans

Frijole chomper: eats a lot of Mexican food

Friona (Parmer County): pronounced Free-ona; originally called Frio. A sign outside the town offers some friendly advice: "You're now leaving Friona: take a smile with you." It's located just up the road from Muleshoe.

Frisky: 1. feeling his oats 2. got steam in his boiler (or locomotive)

Frisky as: 1. a cutting horse 2. a pig in a new pen 3. a fresh born colt 4. an unsaddled horse, which, according to Darrell Royal, is how football players feel when they cross the fifty-yard line

Frog: a student who enters Texas A&M at mid-term of his first year

Frog, large: pond chicken, because its legs look like they came from a chicken when they're in a frying pan

Frosting: icing in Texas

Frugal: 1. crawls under the gate to save the hinges 2. won't take cold showers because goose pimples use up more soap 3. gets out of the bed to turn over to save wear and tear on the sheets 4. so cheap he has a three-legged dog (which doesn't run around much and thus doesn't need to be fed as often) 5. can squeeze a dollar till George Washington's nose starts to bleed 6. has short arms and deep pockets 7. tight as a tick 8. chews close and spits tight 9. closed fisted 10. a cardboard walker, which means he fills holes in the bottom of his boots with cardboard rather than spending money for new soles 11. when he blinks his eyes, his toes curl up 12. so tight he names all his dollar bills like they were pets 13. still has his elementary school lunch money 14. learned Braille so he could read after dark without turning on a lamp *See also Cheapskate; Miser; Stingy*

Frugal, but courteous: quick to tip his hat to a lady but slow to tip anyone else

Frustrated: in a lather

Frustrated as: 1. a pickpocket in a nudist colony 2. a chicken drinking out of a pie pan 3. a gelding in a mare corral 4. a rubber nosed woodpecker or a woodpecker in a petrified forest 5. a young rooster in a pen full of old veteran roosters, which means the young one spends more time pecking for food than entertaining the hens 6. a small hog in the big hog's pen, which means the big hogs would crowd out the little hog at the trough 7. a chicken snake in an empty coop 8. a de-clawed cat trying to climb a shade tree 9. the seventh baby pig when mama has only six teats

Frustrating as: tryin' to eat soup with a fork

Full: 1. stuffed to the gills 2. chock full 3. brim full 4. full as a tick 5. to the limits of my springs 6. gorged to the eyelashes 7. two notches full, which means he had to loosen his belt two full notches 8. I could bust a beetle on my belly 9. you'll need a wheelbarrow to get me from the dinner table to the den

Full as: 1. a tick on a dog's rear (or ear) 2. a bloated toad 3. an egg

Full house (poker hand): full boat or the boat is floating

Full moon: 1. full-grown moon 2. Indian moon [Indians often attacked during periods of full moon.]

Fulshear (Fort Bend County): pronounced FUL-sure; named for Churchill Fulshear since the town was developed around his plantation

Fun: 1. more fun than a tick in a blood bank 2. as much fun as watching a nearsighted rooster in a strange henhouse

Fun as: 1. feeding monkeys at the zoo 2. chasing armadillos

Funeral: 1. buryin' 2. plantin'

Funeral food: In Texas, when someone dies it is customary for friends and relatives to gather at the deceased's home after the funeral. Naturally, the bereaved family can't be expected to cook, so neighbors and friends pitch in to provide the food. Traditional Southern funeral food includes: Southern fried chicken, baked ham, green beans, baked beans, vegetable casseroles, Jell-O salad, homemade hot rolls, deviled eggs, iced tea to drink, and a variety of cakes and pies for dessert.

Funeral parlor: the only business with a permanent layaway plan

F

Funny: 1. a heap of hilarity 2. knee slapper 3. laughed so hard I almost popped a gizzard string (a supposed tendon in the stomach)

Funny as: 1. a three-legged mule tryin' to pull a buggy 2. a one-armed stripper

Furious: got blood in his eye

Furnishings: fixments

Futile: 1. shootin' spit wads at a battleship 2. bear hunting with a broomstick [Davy Crockett once said, "I might as well have sung psalms over a dead horse."] *See also Wasting time; Useless*

Futile as: 1. arguing with a mother-in-law (or tryin' to borrow money from a father-in-law) 2. a bird hunting for worms on Astroturf 3. talking Chinese to a deaf pack mule

Futility: 1. a bull snake tryin' to make love to a buggy whip 2. a turtle tryin' to mate an army helmet

Future, uncertain: only thing he can count on is his fingers

G

G.T.T.: 1. In the years following the Civil War, a lot of Southerners migrated to Texas in an attempt to escape the harsh Reconstruction policies. It was customary for those leaving to put up a handmade sign that read simply G.T.T. so all the neighbors would know they were "Gone To Texas." 2. Because Texas afforded plenty of places to hide, outlaws and assorted criminals would often flee to the Lone Star State. When the local sheriff got wind that the wanted man had left for Texas he would simply mark the warrant G.T.T. and the case was closed. There were even cases where outlaws marked their own wanted posters G.T.T. in hopes the sheriff would quit looking for them, and in some cases it worked.

G.Y. hat: *See Garrison hat*

Gadget: 1. dohicky 2. thingamabob 3. whangdoodle 4. dodad 5. whatchamacallit

Gain weight: 1. put on tallow [Tallow, a cowboy's word for fat, is the solid rendered fat of cattle and sheep used in the manufacture of soap, candles, and lubricants.] 2. bottoming out, which means, in this instance, his (or her) rear end is growing

Gainesville (Cooke County): pronounced GAINS-vul; named for U.S. General Edmund Pendleton Gaines, who was sympathetic toward Texas during the revolution; the sight of the "Great Hanging" during the Civil War when a number of Union activists where hung for plotting to overthrow the government in Texas

Gait: the pace of the horse; natural gaits are walk, trot, and canter

Gait impediment: hitch in the getalong

Galena (Smith County): pronounced ga-LEAN-ah

Galded: what your foot is when a new shoe blisters it

Gallop: a fast three- or four-beat gait, which is the fastest run of the horse. A three-beat gait equals 10 to 12 miles per hour. An extended gallop, four-beat gait equals 12 to 16 miles per hour.

Gallus gate: *See Gate*

Galveston (Galveston County): Gal-va-stun. When you visit this city on the Texas coast, you might say you're going to visit a "gal with a vest on," which is the romantic notion for how the town was named. A less romantic notion is that the town was named for a viceroy of Mexico named Galvez. *See also B.O.I.*

Gamble: buck the tiger [According to Ramon F. Adams, this term was derived from old-time traveling faro dealers who carried their gambling paraphernalia in a box with a tiger painted on the side.]

Gambler: 1. risk taker 2. crap shooter 3. wildcatter 4. would bet on the sun coming up if the odds were right 5. an Amarillo Slim starter kit [Amarillo Slim is a world famous Texas gambler] 6. cut him open and he'd bleed green felt, which means he spends his time leaning on the felt of a crap table 7. the ice in his dice is never cold

Gambler, avid: it's money, marbles, or chalk, which basically means he'll bet anything

Gambler, busted: picked clean as a Sunday chicken

Gambler, honest: could shoot dice with him over the phone

Gambler, inept: 1. once lost ten dollars in a stamp machine 2. loses money on instant replays *See also Poker hand, worthless*

Gamblers advice: 1. never bet the farm if you can't afford to lose it 2. a full house divided wins no pots 3. a faint heart never filled a flush (or an inside straight) 4. never bet with scared money [This is a favorite saying of former Dallas Cowboy coach Jimmy Johnson. Scared money is money you can't afford to lose, which means if you bet with it, you'll be too scared to be a good gambler.]

Gambling: the best way to get nothing for something

Game blocked (dominoes): a condition that exists when no more dominoes can be played

Game roosters: roosters used in cockfighting

Ganado (Jackson County): pronounced Ga-NAY-do. According to legend, when the railroad reached Jackson County, an official aboard the first train looked out a window, saw a large herd of cattle grazing by the tracks, and decided to name the local station Ganado, which is Spanish for livestock.

Gandy dancer: railroad track worker

Gap: 1. hole in the fence or hedge 2. wire gate

Garage: car shed, which comes from the days when the garage was usually detached from the main house

Garden: Generally, in Texas, gardens are for vegetables while flower boxes or planters are for flowers. A Texan is usually so proud of his garden that it's a high insult to refuse an invitation to inspect it. Never refuse any home-grown vegetables if offered.

Garden City (Glasscock County): name was supposed to be Gardner after a local merchant, but post office officials misread the application

Gardener, inept: 1. would fertilize Astroturf 2. only thing he can grow in his garden is tired 3. couldn't grow pole beans in a pile of horse manure

Gardener, smart: never plants more garden than his wife can hoe

Garlic, wild: ramp

Garrison hat: a billed hat worn by Texas A&M cadets on special occasions; usually referred to as G.Y. hat

Garrulous: talking up a storm

Gas station: *See Service station*

Gas wrench: cutting torch

Gaskin: muscles in the upper portion of a horse's hind leg

Gate opening protocol: 1. Never open a gate without permission unless it's on your own property. 2. If you open a gate, close it behind you.

Gate, gallus: a gate made of two posts, the taller the better, with a third pole across the top

Gate, plank: a gate made from wood planks

Gatesville (Coryell County): pronounced GATES-vul; residents took the name from nearby Fort Gates

Gather: 1. bale 'em up 2. rustle 'em up 3. round 'em up 4. wrangle 'em up 5. put a lot on 'em

Gathering: turn out

Gaudy: tacky

Gave me pause: knocked me back a peg or two

Gave up: 1. this old dog is done hunting 2. threw in the towel 3. cashed in his chips 4. sold his horse, which refers to an old-time cowboy selling his horse and giving up the good life of the open range 5. let her milk down, which refers to a milk cow giving up and letting you take her milk 6. hollered calf rope 7. unhooked the horses 8. pulled on the whoa reins 9. quit on account of my health, I wanted to keep it

Gear, low: granny gear, so called because in old model cars with standard transmissions, granny almost never got out of low

Gelding: male horse that has been castrated and cannot reproduce

G

[Horses that have been gelded can be kept with the mares; stallions must be kept separated from the mares.]

Genius: a crackpot that hit the jackpot

Gentle: wouldn't harm a hair on a dog's head

Gentle as: 1. a horse on a merry-go-round 2. a fawn, lamb, kitten, or ladies horse 3. a mother nursing a baby

Gentleman: 1. has never heard the other person's joke 2. will help an old woman across a busy street when no one is looking *See also Chivalrous*

Gentleman farmer: only thing he raises is his hat when a pretty girl walks by

Gently: 1. treat it with kid gloves 2. pull the reins too tight and the horse will buck

Genuine (gen-u-ine): 1. real McCoy 2. pure-d 3. dyed in the wool 4. sure 'nuff, as in "He's a sure 'nuff cowpuncher."

Georgia stock and heel sweep: a plow used to clean out the middle of a row; also used to make rows in a garden because it doesn't go as deep as other plows

Get attention: 1. hit 'em between the eyes with a 2x4 2. knock him over the head with a singletree, which is what you use to hook a horse to a wagon 3. put a shotgun in his ear

Get busy: 1. shake a hoof 2. get on with the dancing, branding, plowing, or rat killing 3. can't plow a field by turning it over in your mind 4. a coyote don't catch no rabbits while sittin' in the shade 5. don't worry about the mule goin' blind, just load the wagon 6. get up and git instead of sittin' down an' sittin' 7. never get a hit with the bat sittin' on your shoulder 8. shake the cat out of the quilt [This comes from quilting bees. When a quilt was finished, one young lady would hold each corner and then a cat would be pitched on it.

The girls would shake the quilt until the cat ran off, and whichever young lady was closest to the cat when he departed would be the next to marry.]

Get close: sidle up

Get control: 1. curry the kinks out of that bronc 2. stop the hemorrhage 3. teach 'em to fly in formation 4. get everybody dancing to the same tune (or singing out of the same song book) 5. better flag down the train 6. cut the ground out from under 'em

Get down to business: 1. money talks, BS walks 2. talk is cheap but whiskey costs money 3. get down to the brass tacks

Get even: 1. turn about is fair play 2. whatever goes around, comes around

Get: fetch, as in "Will you fetch the beer?"

Get going: 1. giddyup 2. kick some manure off your boots 3. move your shadow 4. pull the trigger [John Wayne would probably say, "Head 'em up and move 'em north."]

Get help: 1. call in the cavalry (or Marines) 2. organize a posse 3. rustle up a threshin' crew, which refers to the practice of neighbors pitching in to help one another thresh their crops

Get involved: gotta be in it to win it

Get it done quickly: get past the house before the dog starts barking [This basically means get something done before someone starts complaining. An example might be "Let's get that tax increase bill past the house before some taxpayin' dog starts barking."]

Get it out in the open: smoke it out of the hole

Get out: 1. adios the joint 2. put some distance between you and here 3. gather up your shadow and haul it out of here

Get out of here quickly: 1. don't let the door hit you where the good Lord split you 2. cut the chain on the anchor and row so fast the friction makes the water boil

Get prepared: hunker down

Get ready: 1. rosin up the bow, which refers to using rosin on the bow of a fiddle before playing 2. fix bayonets 3. comb your fur and tune your purr 4. cock your pistol 5. soap your saddle 6. cinch the riggin' 7. sharpen your hoe, which refers to the fact that you can chop more cotton with a sharp hoe 8. grease your holster and file your sights, which refers to gunslingers getting ready for a shoot-out 9. build a fire in the branding pen 10. mount up

Get ready for trouble: circle the wagons

Get rid of: 1. get shed of 2. shuck it

Get rid of him: loan him some money [According to the old country tradition, the best way to get rid of someone is to loan him some money that you expect to be repaid.]

Get serious: 1. get down to the nut cuttin', which is a reference to castrating bulls or pigs 2. get down to cases 3. talk turkey

Get started: 1. get to plowing, hoeing, branding, or roping 2. pull the trigger 3. open the gate 4. pull the string 5. pop the cork 6. drive a stake [In almost any construction job, the first thing you do is drive a stake to provide a starting place.]

Get to the bottom of it: 1. get down to where the water hits the wheel 2. get down to where the hogs are gruntin'

Get to the point: 1. don't tell me about the labor pains, just show me the baby 2. quit coyotin' around the rim 3. quit dancing me all over the floor 4. skip the gristle and get to the bone 5. go around that pig and get to the tail 6. shell down to the corn 7. sand through the veneer 8. split open the watermelon 9. skin down to the bone 10. cut to the quick

Get to work: 1. quit spittin' on the handle 2. get some manure on your boots 3. bees that make the honey don't hang around the hive 4. a mosquito don't get slapped on the back till he gets to work 5. can't plow a field by turning it over in your mind

Get up: 1. hoist your carcass 2. cool that chair, which is a reference to chairs getting warm when you sit in them 3. will never stumble over anything worthwhile sitting down

Getalong: an unknown body part on a Texan that serves little purpose other than to impede progress when injured from a hitch. For example, "Bubba couldn't play in the game Friday night 'cause he had a hitch in his getalong."

Getting angry: 1. his sap's rising 2. his blood is simmering, which indicates it's about to boil

Getting behind: 1. catching them faster than I can string 'em 2. roping them faster than I can brand 'em

Gettin mad: he's cloudin' up and fixin' to rain knuckles

Getting old: 1. feeling his corns more than his oats 2. can still paint the town but he can only give it one coat at a time 3. had to stop having birthdays 'cause he couldn't find a cake that could stand up under the weight of the candles

Getting worse: going to hell in a hand basket [John Connally once said he decided to run for governor because he was concerned Texas was "going to hell in a hand basket" after Republican John Tower got elected to the senate.]

Gets into trouble a lot: never has any trouble finding the deep end

Ghost: 1. booger 2. ol' smokey 3. spook

 Giddings (Lee County): technically GIDD-ings but many say

GIDD-uns; named for either Jabez Deming Giddings, a railroad stockholder, or DeWitt Clinton Giddings, a Confederate veteran and noted banker

Gift, perfect: give a gift that keeps on giving—a female cat

Gig line: the alignment of shirt, belt, and trousers on the uniform of a Texas A&M cadet

Gilchrist (Galveston County): pronounced GILL-crist. The town was named for Gibb Gilchrist, a young engineer who rerouted the railroad to the area after a hurricane. Gilchrist eventually became president of Texas A&M and later chancellor of the A&M college system.

Gillespie County: pronounced Ga-LES-pee; named for Capt. Robert A. Gillespie, a Mexican War hero

Gimmie cap: baseball-type cap that got its name "gimmie" from the fact that feed stores, implement dealers, and other merchants once gave them away for advertising purposes. Although most people now sell gimmie hats, a real Texan wouldn't think of buying one. The gimmie cap's curved bill was started by farmers and ranchers who had to stick their entire head into the mailbox looking for a government check that never seemed to come.

Ginger, wild: monkey jugs

Ginseng: sang

Girdle: 1. pot holder 2. waist basket 3. an aid for overdeveloped areas 4. holds a woman in when she goes out [A lot of women claim that taking off a girdle after a hard day is the second best feeling in the world.]

Girl: 1. filly 2. sweet thang 3. little darlin' 4. little dumplin' 5. little lady 6. muchacha See also Female

Girl, cute: could make you jump a nine-rail fence, rassle a boxcar load of bobcats, and dance across Texas with a grizzly bear See also Female, desirable

Girth: 1. circumference of a horse's body as measured just to the back of the withers 2. strap (leather, canvas, or cord) used to hold the saddle on; it is usually pronounced girt in Texas See also Cinch

Give birth: 1. domino 2. put another cowboy on the range

Give him a chance: let him alone and he'll come home to his milk

Give it a try: 1. cut your wolf loose 2. let the big dog eat 3. take a stab at it 4. give it a good crank 5. give it a shot 6. see if you can dance to that tune

Give it up: fork it over

Give me some room: scrowge over

Give me the facts: tell it with the bark (or hair) on

Give orders: scatter the riders (or hands)

Gizzard string: stomach tendon, supposedly

Glad: proud, as in "I'm proud to meet you."

Glance at: cut your eyes to

Glanders: a highly contagious venereal disease among horses, mules, and asses; in rare cases it can be transmitted to humans and can be fatal

Glasses, thick: looks like he's staring at you through the walls of an aquarium

Glistens: like hoarfrost in the morning sunshine [Hoarfrost is a country word for frozen dew that coats the ground and plants with a thin layer of ice crystals. It glistens in the morning sun like a basket full of diamonds.]

Glove compartment: glove box

Glows: like foxfire at midnight [Foxfire is a fungus that forms in decaying wood, which has a strange, often eerie glow.]

Glum: as a tongue-tied parrot

Go ahead: 1. let her rip 2. turn it loose 3. plow straight and don't look back 4. open the gate

Go ahead and do it: go right ahead on [Remember, it's easier to get forgiveness than permission.]

Go for it: 1. kick for the moon whether you hit the mark or not [During the Texas Revolution, Colonel James Walker Fannin Jr. used this phrase, but he never got much chance to make the kick. On Palm Sunday, 1836, Walker and about 400 of his men were shot down in cold blood by Mexican soldiers, after having surrendered a week earlier.] 2. shoot the moon, which is a reference to the domino game called "moon" 3. don't settle for half a shebang, get the whole shebang

Go gitter: a cowboy who forgot to hobble his horse

Go into business for yourself: If you don't give it a try, you'll always work for the man who did.

Go round: a single performance in a rodeo. Each go round includes all the events in the rodeo, usually with from 10 to 20 cowboys competing in each event. An entire rodeo generally consists of one to ten go rounds.

Go to bed early: 1. go to bed as soon as it's dark in the churn 2. go to bed with the chickens so you can get up with the rooster

Go with God: vaya con dios

Goal line: alumni line, according to Darrell Royal

Goat hipped: a horse with poor confirmation in its rear end

Goat roper: a term coined in the seventies that was intended to be derogatory toward cowboys. However, whoever invented the term obviously didn't know that goats are damned hard to rope, and any cowboy who can do it is a pretty good hand.

Gober (Fannin County): pronounced Go-Burr, not Goo-ber; originally called Grittersville, the name was changed to honor J. F. and William Gober, who built the first mill in the area

God: 1. Sky King 2. Foreman of the Grandest Jury 3. the Judge

Goes together: 1. like Shiner Bock and barbecue 2. like biscuits and molasses 3. like cowboys and country music 4. like lips and lipstick

Going nowhere: soap-tracked and spinning his wheels

Going too fast: hung in overdrive

Going well: 1. going great guns 2. cotton's high 3. runnin' with the big dogs

Gold digger: a violation to the law of gravity 'cause it's easier to pick her up than it is to drop her

Golden grain tobacco: called "Hoover Dust" because it sold for a nickel a sack during the Great Depression

Goldthwaite (Mills County): when pronounced properly, the "d" in Gold is all but lost but the "th" is not; it's Goal-tha-wait; named for Joe G. Goldthwaite, the railroad executive who held the auction for town lots

G

Golf: 1. the game that turned the cows out of the pasture and let the bull in 2. a game where the player's lie can correct the lay of the ball

Golf course, long: have to reckon in the curvature of the earth measuring distances

Golfer, honest: one that's being watched

Golfer, lucky: could hit into a sand trap and grass would grow under his ball before he got there

Golfer, unlucky: could putt toward a hole and it would heal over before the ball arrived

Goliad (Goliad County): pronounced GO-lee-add; the town in

South Texas referred to as Fort Defiance by some old-timers. During the Texas Revolution, Colonel James Walker Fannin Jr. christened the Goliad mission Fort Defiance. His defiance didn't last long since Fannin and his men were captured and executed. The presidio at Goliad is La Bahia, pronounced La Ba-hay-ya.

Gonzales (Gonzales County): pronounced Gon-ZAL-is, the county seat

Good: 1. anything that good ought to be against the law 2. crackerjack 3. bueno 4. couldn't beat it with a stick 5. top drawer 6. esta bien 7. shiny, as in "The way I rode that bull wasn't too shiny but it worked." 8. whale, as in "He's a whale of a horse." *See also Delicious*

Good bull: something funny or positive

Good draw: *See Bareback riding*

Good day: a nekkid-on-the-back-porch sort of day [An old saying in Texas goes, "As long as there's a God in heaven, a Democrat in the governor's mansion, and a pulse in my arm, it's a good day." The saying was most popular in the days when the Democratic Party had a choke hold on Texas.]

Good enough: *See Acceptable; Adequate*

Good fences: *See Neighborly*

Good grief: good honk

Good loser: "You can be a good loser but you should bleed a little," said former TCU coach Dutch Meyer.

Good luck: 1. hope all your kids are born nekkid 2. keep your wagon between the ditches 3. may all your cattle be fat, your wife skinny, and your kids obedient 4. draw a good bull [This refers to rodeo cowboys drawing for which bull they will ride. The better the bull the better the chance to make a good ride.]

Good morning: buenos dias (also used for good day)

Good night: buenas noches

Good ol' boy: For generations in Texas, "good ol' boy" was a term of endearment. It meant a man was fiercely loyal to his country, his state, his family, his friends, and his God. A good ol' boy never missed a chance to help someone who was down or come to the aid of a friend in trouble. There was a time when male Texans wanted to earn the label good ol' boy. Unfortunately, modern politicians have gotten hold of the phrase and screwed it up like they do most things. Today, when strangers hear that someone is a good ol' boy they frequently assume that he's a bad guy and not to be trusted to do the right thing.

Good old days: when a stocking would hold all a kid wanted for Christmas

Good person: 1. will stand without hitching [Texan John Nance Garner once said to the Reverend Billy Graham, "I hear you will stand without hitching. I am glad of that. Out in my country a cow horse wasn't worth a damn unless he would do that. Most of the time there wasn't anything to hitch him to." Garner's country was South Texas, in and around Uvalde.] 2. pick of the litter 3. don't have any faults God would pay attention to or the devil would be interested in 4. if he was a dog, someone would have stolen him when he was a pup 5. sits tall in the saddle 6. can march in my parade 7. the best that ever drew a breath 8. an uncommon common man *See also One of a kind; Trustworthy; Dog, good*

Good shot: could shoot the eyes out of a mosquito at 250 yards [Almost any small critter could be substituted for mosquito. Also, the distance can be raised or lowered depending on your mood.] *See also Aim, good*

Good-bye: 1. adios 2. so long, Red Ryder 3. glad you got to see me

Goodnight (Armstrong County): named for ranching legend Charles Goodnight, who founded the famous JA Ranch

Goose down: cultivated thermo filling for bedding and clothing

Goose-rumped: a horse with a narrow, drooping rump similar to that of a goose

Goree (Knox County): pronounced GORE-ee although some will say GO-ree; originally called Riley Springs, the name was changed in honor of Robert D. Goree, a local pioneer and Confederate veteran

Gorman (Eastland County): pronounced Gore-mun; early name was Shinoak but was changed to honor Patrick Gorman, road master for Texas Central Railroad. Gorman claims to be the Peanut Capital of Texas.

Gossip: 1. moccasin talk 2. clothesline chatter 3. horseback opinion 4. scandalization 5. fence talk, referring to neighbors gossiping about other neighbors over the back fence 6. tongue exercise 7. the difference between news and gossip is whether you're hearing it or telling it 8. travels faster over grapevines that are sour 9. is like slinging fresh manure at a clean white wall, it may not stick but it leaves its mark

Gossip (person): 1. has a keen sense of rumor 2. believes in the old adage that you can't believe everything you hear but you can repeat it 3. like red beans, will talk behind your back

Gossipy: 1. loose tongued 2. leaky mouthed 3. will peel your eye and bend your ear back 4. like two geese on a new feed ground

Got away: slipped the bridle or noose

Got happy: spirits rose like a corncob in a cistern

Got married: 1. belled his mare 2. licked him in 3. got him hitched to a double harness

Got next to: sidled up to

Got no response: drew a blank

Got religion: rassled the devil and won

Got things to do: 1. like an old chicken, got scratchin' to do and eggs to lay 2. gotta kill a chicken and churn

Got what he deserved: his chicken came home to roost, or as Jennifer Chariton said, his chicken came home to roast

Gotten fat: gone to pot

Gourd hole: mud hole

Government (gover-mint): the public tit, which implies it is there to nurse everyone [John Nance Garner said, "That government governs best which governs least." Someone else said the government ought to be like a digestive system, when it works properly you hardly know it's down there.]

Government employee: 1. nurses on the public tit 2. dips his finger in the public lard bucket 3. cooks with public grease

Grab hold: 1. grab a holt 2. cabbage on to it

Grab the apple: a bronc rider who grabs the saddle horn to keep from being thrown and gets disqualified

Grabbing leather: riding with one hand on the saddle horn, something a Rexall Ranger would do

Graciously: kindly

Grades: plain old horses of no particular breed

Grain bin: galvanized metal cylindrical grain storage building

Grand Prairie (Dallas County): locals often claim the first name says it all about life in this Dallas suburb

G

Grand Saline (Van Zandt County): pronounced Gran' Salean, not Sa-line; small town often referred to as Salt City because a considerable portion of America's salt supplies are produced in the area

Granbury (Hood County): should be straightforward and simple, Gran-bury but some people try to add a "d" for Grand-bury which is incorrect; named for Hiram H. Granbury, a Confederate general from Texas who was killed in action at the battle of Franklin, Tennessee

Grandma: cheek pincher

Granny race: when a midwife (granny woman) hurries to get to a house before the baby arrives

Granny frolic: party to celebrate the birth of a grandchild

Granny-woman (or granny-doctor): an elderly lady who is so wise in the use of herbs and home remedies that everybody for miles around comes to her when they're sick. An accomplished granny-doctor could poultice the shell off an armadillo.

Grannying: taking care of children

Grant, Ulysses S.: "Useless" S. Grant to most Southerners [Some Texans don't carry fifty-dollar bills, the ones that feature a picture of Grant, because they don't want a Yankee president loose in their billfold. Many Texas gamblers don't carry them because they consider them unlucky, probably because they feature Grant's picture.] *See also Penny*

Grass: cemetery carpet, as in "I believe the cut worms are gonna kill the cemetery carpet in our front yard."

Grass, medium high: belly deep to a big dog

Grass, short: belly deep to a ground squirrel

Grass, tall: belly deep to a big horse

Grasshopper counterweight: oil field term for "grasshopper" shaped counterweight used on pump jacks

Grassland (Lynn County): You might expect Texans to pronounce this as if it were two words, Grass Land. Not true. It's pronounced quickly as one word Grasslan. The "D" is optional depending on how fast you're talking.

Grateful: 1. much obliged 2. you've got a good turn coming whenever you need it

Grave: 1. cold storage 2. a one-size-fits-all hole in the ground

Gravel rash: *See Injured slightly*

Graveyard: marble orchard

Graveyard cleaning: *See Party, dull*

Gravy: 1. Texas butter [This is gravy made by throwing some flour into steak grease and letting it brown. When it begins to bubble you add some water and stir till thick and delicious. It's called Texas butter because Texans will often use gravy in places a lot of other people would use butter, such as on biscuits, bread, mashed potatoes, etc.] 2. lube (Aggie)

Gravy, good: sloppin' good *See also Fried chicken, good*

Gravy, poor: 1. couldn't cut it with a Bowie knife 2. had more lumps than chunky peanut butter

Gravy, red eye: gravy made by mixing boiling water and strong black coffee with the juice from fried ham. The gravy is stirred until the liquid is well mixed with the juices and small pieces of ham that were left in the skillet. This delicacy was supposedly named by Andrew Jackson, when he remarked that the gravy looked like the "red eyes" of his cook, who had gotten very drunk the night before.

Gravy, thickenin': gravy made by mixing flour and milk into the juice left from cooking meat, usually sausage.

Stir the mixture and cook until it is good and thick. Another Southern delicacy.

Gray headed: blooming for the retirement pasture

Gray horse: coloration comprised of black and white hairs that are interspersed to produce a gray appearance

Greasy as: fried lard

Greed: as we say in Texas, "Pigs get fat, hogs get slaughtered"

Green as: 1. fresh grass 2. mint money 3. a gourd

Green broke: a horse that has been broken but not worked much *See also Newlyweds*

Greenville (Hunt County): pronounced GREEN-vul; named for General Thomas J. Green, a former member of the Republic of Texas army

Greeting: "How's ya' mama and them?" [This is usually said with sincerity to a close friend. "Them" in this case generally means everyone else in the immediate family. If you want to include other than family members in the greeting, use "How's ya' mama and them and everybody." Note: this greeting is never used when addressing strangers.]

Grin, wide: 1. as the wave in a slop bucket 2. could swallow a banana sideways 3. like a cat that ate an eagle

Gringo: a derogatory Mexican term for an Anglo

Grinning: 1. like a possum eating persimmons (or yellow jackets) 2. like a small dog with a big bone 3. like a barrel of possum heads 4. from his butt to his eyebrows 5. like a mule eating prickly pear cactus [When a mule eats cactus he holds his lips apart, which gives the impression he's grinning.]

Grip, strong: 1. like vice grip pliers 2. like a snappin' turtle

Grip, unsafe: a hospital hold

Grits (gree-uts): East Texas ice cream [Grits are made of dried, ground corn cooked in boiling water and served with butter and gravy; a staple of the Southern breakfast table. Only Yankees and foreigners would put sugar on their grits in public. Also called "little hominy."] *See also Hominy*

Groady: something filthy, gross, or very dirty

Groesbeck (Limestone County): pronounced GROWS-beck; named for Abram Groesbeck, a director of the Texas Central Railroad

Grosvenor (Brown County): correct pronunciation, no joke, is Groves-VEEN-er, which actually rhymes with "weiner"

Ground ball: worm killer

Ground-cuckoo: *See Roadrunner*

Ground, hard: packed down dirt

Ground hitch: to immobilize a horse by dropping one end of an open rein on the ground; if the horse tried to move, it would eventually step on the rein and stumble

Ground hog: whistle pig

Growing: 1. beginning to feather out 2. gettin' some size to him 3. blossoming out 4. growin' so fast his shadow can't keep up

Growing fast as: 1. a crack in a frozen windshield 2. a fertilized weed 3. popcorn in a popper

Growing up: getting a little hair on his belly

Grub liner: cowpoke who shows up in time to eat and then leaves before it's time to work; a professional grub liner is a saddle tramp

Grubbin hoe: *See Hoe*

Gruene (Comal County): pronounced Green; a small town near New Braunfels where the local honky-tonk, Gruene Hall, bills itself as the oldest in Texas

Guadalupe (Victoria County): proper Texas pronunciation is GWAD-a-loop, not with an "a" sound on the end as it would be in Spanish; some people say it with such a slur that it sounds like War-loop

Guarantee, country style: if it breaks, you get both pieces

Guarantee a test: term used on a bull that means seller hasn't fertility-tested the animal but will guarantee it to be fertile if the buyer wants to test him

Guaranteed: 1. can bet your bottom dollar 2. lead pipe cinch 3. can bet the ranch and all the cattle (mineral rights) on it 4. sure as grass will grow in a crack *See also Certain; Reliable; Trustworthy*

Guaranteed open: seller guarantees that a cow is not pregnant

Guilty: 1. got caught with his paw in the cookie jar 2. caught red-handed

Guilty as: 1. sin 2. a kid with his hand in the cookie jar

Guitar (get-tar): 1. getfiddle 2. getbucket

Guitar player: 1. picker 2. picker and grinner [Texan Waylon Jennings once claimed he plays a "stuttering guitar."]

Gulch: a very deep gully

Gullet: 1. throat 2. underside of the saddletree [A properly fit saddle is one where you can put three fingers (no more or less) between the gullet and the withers on the horse.]

Gullible: 1. would buy hair restorer from a bald barber 2. believes all of the people all of the time 3. would buy a soundtrack album from a silent movie [Remember, man is the only animal that can be skinned more than once.]

Gully: a narrow ravine created by the erosion of water runoff *See also Bayou*

Gully dirt: dirt in a gully that doesn't produce a crop *See Worthless*

Gun: equalizer [When Samuel Colt invented his famous Colt .45 shootin' iron it is said he made all men equal.]

Gun, powerful: would stop a Plymouth at 100 yards

Gunsel: country term for braggart, tenderfoot, or fool

Gustine (Comanche County): pronounced GUS-teen; named for Samuel Gustine, the town's first postmaster

Gut shot: western term for someone shot in the stomach; highly feared in the Old West because it almost always meant a slow, painful death

Guts: insides

Gutted snow bird: a very thin animal (or person)

 Gymekhana: horse games that are not part of a rodeo

Gyping: a cowboy's word for deceiving

H

H.E.B.: 1. grouping of the towns of Hurst, Euless, Bedford, all located in the mid-cities between Dallas and Fort Worth 2. chain of grocery stores in Central and South Texas founded by H.E. Butt

H.O.T. Heart of Texas, frequently seen on signs in and around Waco

Habits: are like a half-full waterbed, easy to get into and almost impossible to get out of

Hack: 1. short, rapid jerks on the reins to make the horse back up in a fast manner 2. a hickory-handled steel axe-like tool used to "hack" pine trees to get the gum

Hackamore: a bridle without a bit that is used to train a horse; from the Spanish word *jaquima*

Hackamore bit: a combination mechanical hackamore and bit

Had all I can stand: 1. at the end of my tether 2. enjoyed about all I can take of that 3. had a good full dose of that 4. had a bait of that

Had difficulty: was hard put (pressed) to do it

Hail: usually pronounced as two syllables in Texas, HAY-ul; small pieces of frozen precipitation that can range from pea to softball size [When a car lot is struck by a hailstorm, they usually try to get rid of the damaged vehicles by staging a "hail of a sale."]

Hair: light when you're young, then it turns dark, then it turns loose

Hair, oily: 1. looks like it was combed with buttered toast 2. enough oil on his hair to grease a wagon train 3. enough oil on his hair to grease a Greyhound bus

Hair, bad: when she goes to the beauty parlor she has to use the emergency entrance

Hair, messy: looks like you combed your hair with a skillet

Hair, unruly: don't need conditioner, it needs a therapist

Hair pants: chaps made from leather with the hair left on

Hair restorer, good: will grow hair on a doorknob (or saddle horn)

Haircut: roach your mane

Haircut, first time: rinktums, said of a small boy who gets his first store-bought haircut

Haircut, soup bowl: where mama placed a soup bowl on the head and cut off all the hair that hung down under it

Haircut, poor: a white sidewall haircut [The barber shaves a band all around the head fully exposing the ears, which then appear to be circled with a white stripe much like a white sidewall tire.]

Hairdo, wild: 1. asylum hair 2. looks like he stuck his finger in a light socket

Hairy: 1. big crop of locks 2. sportin' enough hair to braid a well rope

Hairy chest: 1. got plenty of man feathers 2. got enough hair on his chest to weave a Comanche blanket

Hale Center (Hale County): pronounced Hail Sinner

Halfway (Hale County): pronounced Haf-way; name is taken from the fact the town is halfway between the county seats of Plainview and Olton; home of the world famous Halfway Baptist Church (think about it)

Halter: headgear used to tie up or lead a horse

Hames: two curved strips of wood (or metal) that form the collar on a draft animal

Hankamer (Chambers County): pronounced HAN-comer; named for I. A. Hankamer, co-owner of the Hankamer-Stowell Canal Company

Hand: 1. mitt 2. paw 3. lunch hook

Hand me: reach me

Handbag: pocketbook

Handicapper, poor: would have trouble picking his own father out of a Chinese parade if he were carrying an American flag, which is how a reader once described Blackie Sherrod's ability to pick a winner in a horse race

Handle carefully: 1. like you were tryin' to get a fishhook out of a baby's bottom 2. like you were trying to wrap a vinegarroon scorpion in tissue paper 3. like you were trying to put braces on a rattlesnake's fangs 4. like you were trying to tie a bow tie on a bear 5. like you were carrying an egg in a teaspoon

Handle: 1. pig tail 2. business end 3. blister end; you don't wear blisters on your hand holding a hammer by the head

Hands, large: could pick the nose on King Kong (or the Jolly Green Giant)

H

Hands, quick: 1. could steal hubcaps off a moving car 2. could steal the needle out of a running sewing machine

Handshake, firm: 1. shakes hands like he's clubbing a snake at a garden party 2. shakes your hand like it's a pump handle

Handshake, weak: 1. makes you think you're holdin' a limp dishrag 2. wouldn't dent a marshmallow

Handsome: got magazine face, which means his face would look good in a fancy magazine

Handwriting, illegible: chicken (or hen) scratching

Handwriting, poor: 1. can't read his own handwriting when it gets cold 2. couldn't even be a doctor

Handwriting, small: could write the constitution on a matchbook cover

Handy as: 1. a two-story outhouse in a snowstorm (if the snowdrifts cover the ground floor, you'd still have someplace to go) 2. a box of stoppers on a submarine, which would come in handy in case that sucker sprung a leak 3. indoor plumbing 4. a heart transplant 5. sliced bread 6. electricity 7. a milking machine on a cold morning 8. a Braille Bible to a blind preacher 9. a pocket on a shirt 10. the top rail on a fence 11. a ladder on a windmill 12. a cattle guard [This is an opening in a gate protected by a series of pipes spaced far enough apart to prevent livestock from crossing. You save a lot of time not having to open and close gates so they are very handy.]

Handyman, good: *See Do-it-yourselfer*

Handyman jack: *See High lift jack*

Hang on: 1. like a scared kid to a mother's skirt tail 2. like an Indian to a red-eye jug 3. like a tick to a dog's ear 4. like a snappin' turtle, which, if legend is correct, means you'll hang on till it thunders *See also Tight grip*

Hanging: *See Lynching*

Hanging on, strongly: like a tick to Dracula

Hanging on, barely: like a rusty muffler on an old pickup

Hangover: 1. feel like the Baptist bell choir is practicing inside my head 2. my head is banging like a Chinese gong

Happy: 1. tickled half to death 2. content with all creation 3. absolutely edified 4. chock full of glee 5. doing double back flips 6. swelled up with elation 7. couldn't blow the smile off his face with dynamite *See also Elated*

Happy (Swisher County): the town without a frown; name came from nearby Happy Draw, which was supposedly named by thirsty cowboys who were very "happy" to find the spring in the draw

Happy as: 1. a short cowboy dancing with a tall cowgirl 2. a blind man at a Braille striptease 3. a kid pullin' a pup's ears 4. a pig (or hog) in slop 5. an armadillo digging grub worms 6. a hound in a tannery 7. a pig in a peach orchard 8. a street cleaner in a one-horse town 9. a coon in a cornfield 10. a one-eyed dog locked in a smokehouse 11. a wettin' dog with a mile of fence posts 12. a colt in clover 13. a gopher, groundhog, prairie dog, or armadillo digging in soft ground 14. a cow in a field of belly high clover 15. a wet dog behind a kitchen stove 16. a blowfly on manure 17. a wife who sees a double chin on her husband's old girl friend 18. a weasel in a henhouse 19. a toad frog under a dripping faucet 20. a cat in a creamery

Harassing: bein' ugly with me

Hard and fast: a catch rope tied to saddle horn

Hard as: 1. the hubs of hell 2. a frozen turtle shell 3. nails 4. a frozen worm 5. bois d'arc wood 6. an iron horseshoe 7. bricks 8. a rock 9. a frozen cannon ball 10. Superman's kneecap

11. pig iron 12. yesterday's corn bread 13. a lightard knot [This is the center of a pine stump that contains a concentration of pine pitch. When fully dried, the center of the stump takes on the characteristics of hardened blue steel.]

Hard labor: splittin' gum logs in August with a dull ax [There may not be any hotter job on earth.]

Hard part's over: time to lick the calf [If you have ever seen a cow giving birth, you know that by the time she gets around to licking the calf, the hard part is over.]

Hard times: been sandpapered, which means he's had a rough time

Hard to do as: 1. eating red beans with a pitchfork 2. wearing out a crowbar (or ax) 3. trimmin' the whiskers on the man in the moon 4. putting spilled toothpaste back into the tube 5. pushing a wheelbarrow with rope handles 6. getting all the coons in the county up one tree 7. threading a needle in the dark 8. putting boots on over wet socks 9. catching a sand bass in a sock 10. cutting a hog with a dull knife 11. dodging rice at a wedding 12. flying with water wings 13. scratching a porcupine's back 14. scratching your ear with your elbow *See also Difficult; Tough job*

Hard to find as: 1. bird droppings in a coo-coo clock 2. ticks on a cue ball 3. a water lily in a desert 4. an elephant at the North Pole 5. ears on an earthworm 6. third base in a football game 6. lips on a chicken 7. a snake's (or worm's) shadow

Hard to sell: harder to sell than measles

Hard worker: 1. works as hard as a cold nosed bird dog 2. a goin' Jesse 3. is hell on boot leather and cheap saddles 4. can wear out several pairs of gloves in a single day 5. works from can't see to can't see [This refers to the farmer or rancher who begins work before sunup and works till after sundown.] *See also Worker, good*

Hardheaded: 1. knothead 2. if his head had a point, he could etch glass 3. you could use his head as a ball peen hammer 4. unwilling to be confused with the facts 5. follows the straight and narrow minded path 6. couldn't put a nail in his head with a .22-caliber nail gun 7. you could turn him upside down and use him for a rock crusher 8. as a Texan [According to the old saying, you can always tell a Texan, but you can't tell him much.]

Hardtack: made of cornmeal worked into a ball about the size of a golf ball and hard as a rock. When ready to cook, soften up by boiling in water then fry in a skillet or bake in a Dutch oven.

Hardware: buckle, harness rings, dee rings, conchos, and all other metal parts on leather tack

Harmless: 1. toothless 2. his horns have been sawed off 3. bark is worse than his bite 4. wouldn't harm a sand flea 5. gum mouthed, which implies he has lost all his teeth and thus his bite wouldn't hurt 6. no skin off your moccasins (or boots)

Harmless as: 1. a bowl of oatmeal 2. a shadow 3. an empty paper bag

Harmonica: 1. French harp 2. mouth organ

Harness leather: oil-tanned leather with very little stretch

Harness snap: mechanical fastener

Harvest: barn it

Has faith in: 1. puts a lot of stock in 2. sets a lot of store by

Haslet: a form of stew made of organs from hog including heart, liver, lights (lungs) with red pepper, sage, and onions

Haste: *See Hurry*

Hat: 1. Stetson or John B, which are references to John B. Stetson, who is

H

credited with inventing the western-style cowboy hat, even though he was a Yankee 2. war bonnet 3. sombrero 4. portable feed bag, which refers to cowboys sometimes using their hats to feed the horses

Hat, crooked: sloshed on

Hat, large: 1. big enough to shade you and your horse 2. big enough to catch a bobcat under 3. a ten-gallon hat [The term gallon is actually derived from the Spanish *galon*, which were decorations Mexican vaqueros wore on their hats, and Texas cowboys followed suit. Some people credit Sam Houston with first using the phrase "hand me my ten-galon hat," which meant he had ten galons on his hat, not that it would hold ten galons of liquid. If the truth were known, the biggest hat in Texas wouldn't hold much more than five gallons.]

Hat, small: 1. a stingy brim 2. wouldn't shade half a head 3. couldn't use that to water a pissant

Hat, special: marryin' and buryin' hat, which basically means it is only worn on special occasions, such as a wedding or a funeral [The same expression could also be used for a special jacket, belt, or pair of boots.]

Hat, tight: have to stick your head in a boot jack to get it off

Hat crease: personalized shape in the crown of your hat

Hat crease, homemade: a crease created at home using the steam from a teakettle [Since the steam is impossible to control, the crease almost always comes out like a bull rider's crush, and in many cases the hat gets scorched and burnt and ends up in the trash. Always get your hat creased by a professional and don't forget to tip the one that does the creasing.]

Haughty: 1. too big for his britches 2. actin' mighty biggety 3. never learned

to swim 'cause he thinks he can walk on water *See also Aloof*

Having a baby: gone to the pen

Hawaii: pronounced Hi-wa-ya by many old-time Texans

Hawg: *See Bass, large*

Hawleg: nickname for the original Colt revolver because the shape supposedly resembled the leg of a hog; also called a thumbbuster

Hay: horse manure seeds

Hay shoveler: derogatory term for a farmer

Hazardous as: 1. wading in quicksand over hell 2. grabbing a branding iron by the business end, which is the end that gets hot in the fire 3. a rattlesnake (or a bobcat) in your bedroll 4. a rattlesnake on your running board 5. stomping on a red ant hill barefooted 6. milking a wild longhorn cow 7. hollerin' "snake" at a quilting bee (or church revival) 8. kicking a loaded polecat 9. trying to separate two cats tied together by their tails 10. a tail hold on a grizzly bear, longhorn bull, wildcat, or polecat 11. trying to brand a mule's ear 12. trying to ride a cyclone with the bridle off *See also Dangerous*

Hazer: *See Steer wrestling*

Head: noggin

Head shaking: like a dog killing a garden snake

Head full of notions: been pondering so long I ain't had time to think

Head gate: stockade head holder for a cow

Head shy: a horse that is sensitive to being touched on the head

Head start: a good sling

Head to toe: hair to heel

Ⓐ Ⓜ Head-ins: dumb or stupid acts

Headache: 1. feel like an anvil was introduced to my noggin 2. if a horse's head hurt this bad we'd have to shoot him 3. would have to be dead three days before my head would stop hurting

Headache, severe: 1. had to keep my eyelids shut to keep my eyeballs from popping out 2. a diamond cutter 3. a skull (or brain) crusher 4. so big it wouldn't fit in a horse corral 5. so strong it would kill a rhinoceros

Headache medicine: easin' powder

Header: *See Team roping*

Heading for trouble: your ox is heading for the ditch

Headstall: headgear that holds the bit in the horse's mouth

Headstall buttons: used to keep headstall loops in place on a bosal

Headstrong: 1. bull headed 2. bull necked

Health, good: 1. fit as a fiddle 2. feeling frisky 3. feel like I was raised in a hothouse (or incubator) 4. doin' fine as long as I got a pulse and my plot down at the cemetery is still empty

Health, poor: 1. feel (or look) like death warmed over 2. would have to get better to die 3. doctor said he didn't know what ailed him but he'd know more after the autopsy *See also Ill, gravely*

Healthy town: had to hire a stranger to shoot himself so we could start a cemetery, which is a favorite saying of the folks in Van Horn, Texas

Heard a secret: a little bird told me

Heard about: got wind of

Hearing, good: 1. could hear a termite sneeze in a thunderstorm 2. could hear a worm cough 3. could hear the sun set or the moon rise

Hearing, impaired: 1. deaf in one ear and hard of hearing in the other 2. couldn't hear a gin whistle if he was sitting on it when it went off 3. couldn't hear a rattlesnake buzzing if he was wearin' it for a necktie 4. couldn't hear a pin drop if it was a cattle pen dropped off a cliff onto a tin roof barn

5. couldn't hear a train if he was laying on the tracks 6. he's left eared, which means he can hear only in his left ear [Obviously, if he can only hear in his right ear then he's right eared.]

Hearne (Robertson County): pronounced Hern, which rhymes with urn; never Hern-EE

Heart: 1. ticker 2. blood pump 3. Cupid's target

Heartbroken: 1. she threw a rock through the windowpane of my heart 2. broke my heart so bad it took two bottles of whiskey to splint it, implying someone went on a drunk after being jilted 3. my heart was broken into more pieces than an empty milk bottle dropped on a concrete sidewalk 4. my heart's so broken all the spit and half the baling wire in Texas couldn't put it back together again

Hearts (playing card suit): valentines

Heat, severe: frazzles you up and frazzles you down

Heat period (horse): *See Estrus*

Heaven: 1. Texas [It has been said that when Texans get to heaven they have to be chained up to keep them from trying to go back home. Native daughter Tanya Tucker in her song "Texas (When I Die)" sang, "When I die, well I may not go to heaven, 'cause I don't know if they let cowboys in. If they don't, just let me go to Texas, 'cause Texas is as close as I've been."] 2. the last roundup 3. sweet by and by 4. happy hunting grounds 5. Sky Range 6. Angeltown 7. Spiritville 8. the Golden Range 9. God's South Forty

Heaves: a serious respiratory disease in horses

Heavy as: 1. a full-grown anvil 2. the anchor from the USS *Texas* 3. a frozen bear 4. the front end of a John Deer 5. a tow sack full of ball bearings 6. a mother-in-law's baggage when she's moving in 7. an elephant tusk with the

H

elephant attached *See also Light (weight)*

Heavy enough to: 1. flatten wagon springs so much the running boards would be scraping ground 2. pancake a ball bearing 3. squash a Caterpillar (earth mover type)

Heel cattle: catching cattle by the back feet with a rope

Heel flies: only living thing that could get the best of a wild longhorn. The flies would attack the back of the leg and lay their eggs just above the hoof. To protect themselves when the flies attacked, the longhorns would run to water and drown the suckers. If there wasn't any water, they'd run anyway trying to shake the flies loose.

Heel knot: large knot at the base of a bosal

Heel rope: hard-lay nylon rope used to catch cattle by the back feet

Heeler: a working style of stock dog *See also Team roping*

🔺 **Heidenheimer** (Bell County): pronounced Hide-'n-hammer although Hide-'n hi-mer is also used

Heifer: young female cow

🔺 **Helena** (Karnes County): pronounced HELL-in-a; named for Helen, the wife of founder Lewis S. Owings

Hell: 1. fire and brimstone range 2. the devil's playground 3. Satan's suite (or palace) 4. heaven's junkyard 5. a Texas measure of extreme, such as hotter'n hell; colder'n hell; crazier'n hell; meaner'n hell; or bigger'n hell

Hellacious: a favorite word in Texas that can be used for something severe or intense that is either good or bad. Examples are "They had one hellacious fight down at the Dew Drop Inn last night." or "She gave me one hellacious kiss goodnight."

Hello: Texans say hidee or howdy, pardner

🅰️🅼 **Helmet liner:** pot

🔺 **Helotes** (Bexar County): pronounced Hell-OH-tus, as in "Come on down to Helotes and say hello to us;" name is Spanish for "green roasting ear of corn"

Help: 1. hep, as in "You gotta hep me fix this fence." 2. lend a hand 3. take a turn 4. turn a hand 5. catch my saddle [This was a phrase often used by a cowboy when he got thrown by an unruly horse and needed help catching the horse so his saddle could be saved.]

Help her up: tail her up, which is derived from grabbing the tail of an old cow and helping her get to her feet

Help, unwanted: too many cooks spoil the chili (or stew)

Helpless: 1. hog-tied 2. couldn't do nothing but let the mainspring run down, which means had to let events run their course

Helpless as: 1. a mute in handcuffs 2. a cow in quicksand 3. a cat up an East Texas pine tree 4. a grasshopper (or worm) on a red ant bed 5. a fox in a forest fire 6. a clay pigeon

Hemorrhoids: hammer-royeds [According to the old Texas tale, hemorrhoids are like Yankees who come to Texas to visit. If they come down and then go back up home, no problem. If they come down and stay, that's a problem.]

Hemp: cultivated rope material

Henpecked: 1. jumps when she hollers frog 2. steers clear of the henhouse so the roosters won't chase him 3. his wife even complains when he makes too much noise in the kitchen

🔺 **Hereford** (Deaf Smith County): pronounced Hur-furd, not Hereford; named for the breed of cattle that is raised by the thousands in the area

Heroism: steppin' into the breach [Remember, when there is heroism to be done, someone still has to hold the horses.]

Hesitated: blinked, as in "Bubba blinked and everybody at the poker table knew he was bluffing."

Hiccup cure: the best known cure for hiccups is to go to a turkey shoot for blind men

Hickey: 1. love bite 2. monkey bite 3. passion strawberry 4. blood blister

Hico (Hamilton County): pronounced HI-co, not Hick-oh; named for the Kentucky hometown of John R. Alford, who founded this town just down the road from Dublin

Hidalgo (Hidalgo County): pronounced He-DAL-go; named for the nearby Hidalgo Bluffs that overlook the Brazos River

Hide-behind bird: a rare bird that will sneak up and hide behind you. They are so quick that when you turn around for a look, they're gone and only tracks remain. It's been rumored that some tourists have gone home believing there actually is such a critter.

Hidden well: a psychic couldn't find it

High as: 1. an East Texas pine 2. a hen's behind when she's in a dead run

High enough to: see the lights of Palestine (as in Palestine, Texas)

High heels: *See Shoes, high heels*

High Island (Chambers County): name came from the location, which is on top of a high, natural salt dome

High lift jack: extremely large bumper-type jacks

High risk: like playing a poker hand with your eyes shut

Highway heat waves: witch water

Hill burner: *See Cultivator*

Hillbilly: 1. hick 2. hayseed 3. cedar chopper 4. yokel

Hillister (Tyler County): pronounced HIL-is-ter. Local historians seem to agree the name resulted from a mistake by postal authorities but they can't agree on what the name should have been. Perhaps it was Hollister, the name of a local railroad official, or the name could have been in honor of the Hallister brothers who operated a local sawmill.

Hillje (Wharton County): pronounced HILL-gee; named for Fred Hillje who bought land and brought in German and Czech settlers

Hillsboro (Hill County): pronounced HILLS-bur-ah; named for Dr. George W. Hill, the first settler in the area

Hind leg: a phrase that baffles Yankees because, on a Texan, the hind leg is invisible. The phrase generally means I don't believe you, as in "The dog drank the beer, my hind leg."

Hinder: 1. put a stob in his spokes 2. chock his wheels 3. loosen his cinch 4. put a little sugar in his gas tank 5. put a stob in his exhaust pipe

Hissey fit: a tantrum you throw when you don't get your way. "Lizza Lou threw a hissey fit when her daddy wouldn't buy her a new welder." A wall-eyed hissey fit would be a lot worse, and a snot slinging, foot stomping hissey fit is the worst of all. *See also Conniption fit*

Hysterical: slap happy

Historian, amateur: a shade tree historian

Historical event, minor: historical speed bump

Hit: 1. whallop 2. whomp 3. lambast 4. crack his head 5. rattle his teeth 6. knock his gizzard loose 7. tattoo him 8. slap him a new hat size 8. give him a stinging lick

Hit, hard: 1. took two and a half days to get his breath back 2. he'll have to look out through his ear hole to see

H

anything 3. enough to knock his head down into his jeans so he'll have to open his zipper to peek out 4. a gizzard loosener, which means you ought to get your breath back in a day or two

Hit, medium hard: a stinging lick, which means your head will stop ringing in a couple of hours

Hit, soft: wouldn't bruise a peach

Hit in the mouth: got kissed in the eyeteeth

Hit on the head: conked him

Hitch in his getalong: 1. a cow or horse with something wrong that causes an unusual gait 2. a person who walks funny due to some medical problem [occasionally called crick in his getalong] *See also Getalong*

Hoard: ground squirrel it

Hoarfrost: *See Glistens*

Hobbled stirrups: stirrups that are tied down under the horse's belly

Hobbles: a rope loop around a horse's legs to keep it from wandering off

Hock: bottom joint on a horse's hind leg

Hockheim (De Witt County): looks like it should be Hockheim, but it's actually Hoe-heim; named for Valentine Hoch, an immigrant who settled in the area

Hoe (noun): 1. cotton chopper 2. weed killer

Hoe (verb): chop it *See also Cotton*

Hoe, cotton: a wide hoe used to cut weeds and thin out the cotton crop

Hoe, grubbin': half as wide as a cotton hoe with a special handle used for clearing land and digging up sprouts

Hoe cake: cornmeal baked on the blade of a hoe held over a fire

Hoe user: hoer (think about it)

Hoedown: a country celebration [The name came from cotton choppers who were told to put the "hoe down" and go to the party.]

Hog: 1. slop chaser 2. rooter 3. ham (or breakfast) on the hoof

Hog head: railroad engineer

Hog wallow: a shallow depression in the dirt thought to have been caused by the wallowing of wild hogs [Large wallows are buffalo wallows, although they are somewhat rare today.]

Hogged: a horse's mane that is cut very, very short

Hold on: *See Hang on*

Hold on, tightly: freeze onto it

Holding hands: armed up

Hole: a cadet's room

Hole in a sock: grass hole, so a toe can come out for grass, don't you know

Hole, small: 1. crawling through that hole would be like reliving your birth 2. about as big as a cat hole, which is the small hole often cut into a door to allow cats to come and go as they please without someone having to get up and open the door [An even smaller hole would be a spit hole, which was often cut into the flooring of cabins to be used to dispose of tobacco juice when no spittoon was available. A hole that is smaller yet would be a peephole.]

Holes, numerous: got more holes than a cabbage leaf after a hailstorm

Hollered: 1. like a stuck pig 2. like a baby pig caught under a gate 3. like a cat shot with a boot jack [This is rumored to be one of the leading causes of death among Texas house cats.]

Hollow: holler

Home girl: been back under the chicken coop looking for eggs farther than she's been away from home

Home ranch: cowboy term for ranch headquarters

Home remedy: Poultices have been used by country grandmother types to cure just about anything that might ever ail you. Of course, some grand-mothers make better poultices than others, but the best ever recorded was the little old lady that could poultice the hump off a camel's back. Another could use a hot Coke bottle to suck the venom out of a snake through his tail. [This comes from an old cure for boils. Someone, usually a grandmotherly type, would heat up a Coke bottle and slap it over the boil. As the bottle cooled, a vacuum was created that would draw the poison out of the boil. Speaking as one who has endured the cure, trust me on this one, don't try it.]

Home remedy, expert: would be the envy of a rain forest witch doctor

Home, cheap: a shotgun house, which means it was built by firing the nails out of a shotgun rather than using a hammer

Homeless as: a poker chip

Homely: 1. as a buck-toothed buzzard 2. when she was a baby her daddy had to tie a T-bone steak around her neck to get the dogs to play with her 3. hate to have a litter of 'em 4. has to sneak up on a sink, a dipper, or a glass to get a drink of water 5. has to sneak up on a mirror to fix her hair 6. ain't exactly a parlor ornament 7. a hoss fly wouldn't look at her twice 8. her husband would rather stay home than kiss her good-bye 9. her face would look good in a bridle *See also Ugly*

Hominy: corn kernels that are boiled until they are three or four times their original size; sometimes called big hominy *See also Grits*

Homesick: wishin' she was back under mama's bed playin' with the kittens

Honda: small loop on one end of a rope used as a slip ring when forming a large loop; used for roping

Hondo (Medina County): pro-nounced HON-dough; from the Spanish word for "deep" given to a

nearby creek [A local sign proclaims: "This is God's country, please don't drive through it like hell."]

Honest as: 1. a baby's smile 2. the day is long 3. a mirror image 4. the horse between your legs

Honest man: 1. plows a straight row 2. a square (or straight) shooter 3. so honest he don't have to worry about having a poor memory 4. his word is as binding as a hangman's knot 5. could shoot dice with him over the phone

Honesty: *See Absolute honesty*

Honeydew melon: mush melon

Honey Grove (Fannin County): Legend has it Davy Crockett named the town when he camped in the area and almost every tree was filled with honey.

Honeymoon: 1. the calm before the storm 2. the period between the bridal toast and burnt toast 3. the last time the husband gets to work the controls on the electric blanket or the furnace [The honeymoon usually ends when he finds out he married a big spender and she finds out she didn't.]

Honk a horn: Texans don't honk a horn, they blow it

Honky-tonk: a Texas saloon fre-quently located on the outskirts of town where the beer is always cold and the women are always willing—to dance. In addition to having a jukebox, a honky-tonk always has live music at least a few days a week. When you're going out for a night of drinkin', dancin', and fightin' at local honky-tonks or juke joints, you are going "jooking." *See also Juke joint; Saloon, dangerous*

Honky-tonk, dangerous: a hold 'em and hit 'em joint where they search you, and if you aren't carrying a knife, they rent you one. Some enterprising owners of dangerous honky-tonks have found a way to get rich. They charge $3 dollars to get in and $10 to get out.

Honky-tonk, friendly: a squeezin' and pleasin' joint

Honky-tonk angel: a lady who frequents honky-tonks hoping to find a husband of her own but who often ends up with someone else's for the night

Hoochiecoochie girl: grandpa's exotic dancer

Hooey: a halt hitch wrap tied with piggin' string used to secure three feet of calves roped in the calf rope event in a rodeo

Hoolihan: a loop thrown backhanded when roping horses

Hoolihaning: occurs when a dogger leaps onto a steer in such a way as to knock the animal down without having to twist it to the ground with the customary wrestling hold [This practice is generally barred in rodeos.]

Hooves and horns: said of a very thin cow [If you tell a waitress to knock the hooves and horns off and put it on a plate, you want your steak rare.]

Hopeless: 1. ain't got a prayer 2. following a cold trail 3. can't put out a barn fire with a dipperful of water 4. buckin' a losing game

Hopeless as: 1. whipping a dead horse 2. trying to fill up a bottomless pit 3. arguing with the angel of death

Hopeless situation: got about as much chance as a pig in a dog race

Hopping around: 1. like drops of water on a hot griddle 2. like a migrating bull frog

Horn: 1. something you blow in Texas instead of honking 2. the pommel (knob) on the front of the saddle

Horned toad: 1. horny toad 2. horned frog [The truth is these little prehistoric-looking critters are not any kind of frog or toad, they are lizards.]

Horse: 1. something that is uncomfortable in the middle and dangerous at both ends 2. the hardest thing on earth filled with hay [To ride a horse, put one leg on each side and keep your mind in the middle. Never ride a horse named Widow Maker, Whiplash, Undertaker, Bone Crusher, or Autopsy.]

Horse, cutting: *See Cutting horse*

Horse, fast: 1. runs so fast he has to keep knockin' the rabbits out of the way 2. would make Man O' War look like a pony in a kid's ride 3. a Secreteriat starter kit

Horse, gentle: 1. as easy to ride as a rocking chair (or a stick horse) 2. so gentle you could use him on a merry-go-round

Horse, good bucker: 1. gut twister 2. bucks like a balloon with the plug out, which refers to the wild motion a balloon makes when the air is escaping 3. could pitch off a plaster saddle

Horse, independent: don't have to give him his head 'cause he takes it when he wants it [Giving a horse his head refers to releasing the pressure on the reins to allow the animal to pretty much do as he pleases.]

Horse, mean: 1. will kick you into a funeral home 2. will stick a hoof in your hip pocket 3. will kick you high enough for St. Peter to brand your backside 4. will pitch you so high an eagle will build a nest in your back pocket before you come down 5. cinch buster [A horse that rears and falls backwards, often breaking the cinch.] 6. a bucker and a snorter 7. will throw you so high you'll need a parachute to get back down 8. can throw you so high you'll knock a couple of bricks out of the Pearly Gates 9. could buck your whiskers off

Horse, poor: 1. two-bit nag 2. he don't do nothing but burn hay 3. would rather eat a biscuit than run like Sea Biscuit

Horse, rawboned: a horse with large bones that don't appear to be covered with enough skin

Horse, rear end: 1. get up end, referring to the fact that a horse uses its rear legs to get himself up 2. horse's patoot

Horse, scared: boogered up and bailing out

Horse, scrawny: ain't nuthin' but buzzard bait

Horse, small: could shoe him with lock washers

Horse, sound: a horse free of blemishes and ailments

Horse, tame: could stake him to a hairpin (or toothpick)

Horse, unbroken: 1. bronc (bronco) 2. mustang

Horse, well-trained: if he jumped off a cliff, he'd stop three feet before he hit bottom if I yelled whoa.

Horse, wild: 1. could buck off a plaster cast or buck you into a plaster cast 2. only way to ride him is try to hang on till the mainspring runs down 3. have to catch him and show him he's caught

Horse, worthless: a jughead, which means he ain't nuthin' but a hay burner

Horse apples: *See Bois d'arc*

Horse head stirrer: a wooden device that resembles a stick horse with a blade; used to make apple butter

Horse rustler: a horse thief, although in Texas they were frequently called horse wranglers

Horse sense: 1. stable thinking 2. usually found only in a stable mind 3. what keeps a horse from betting on people 4. what keeps a woman from being a nag

Horse sense vs. a Ph.D.: a country boy with horse sense is content with the notion that if it looks like manure and smells like manure, it probably is

manure. The guy with the Ph.D. has to taste it to verify the hypothesis.

Horse stocking: white markings as high as the knee or hock *See also Sock*

Horse thief: there are two kinds: one who steals to make money and one who steals just because he needs a better horse

Horse trade: In the old days, it was the act of trading horses. Today, it is bickering between two people when one person is trying to obtain ownership of something the other possesses.

Horse wrangler: the man (or young boy) assigned to take care of the horses and have them ready for work [considered the lowest level of cowboyin' and usually reserved for youngsters and beginners]

Horseshoe: a good luck piece if nailed open side up over the door to your place [If nailed open side down, all the good luck will run out. Of course, the horseshoe with the best luck is the one on the winning horse.]

Horseshoe pitching: barnyard golf

Horseshoer, good: could put iron shoes on a horsefly

Horses in a corral: the stookers are hemmed up

Hospital: sick pen [On many ranches a separate pen was maintained where sick and diseased cattle were kept away from the healthy stock.] *See also Hospital, psychiatric*

Hospital, expensive: only thing they don't charge for is the ink in the pen you use to write the check to pay your bill

Hospital, psychiatric: nerve hospital [In the old days, a lot of people were hard put to admit that friends or relatives could have psychiatric problems serious enough to require hospitalization. A mental problem, no matter how serious, was generally referred to as a nervous breakdown,

H

and the hospital they went to for a cure was called a nerve hospital.]

Hospitality: ability to make your guests feel like you want them to stay without interfering with their plans to leave [If your hospitality gets to runnin' thin, you can always use the old country hint, "I guess we'll get on to bed so you folks won't feel like you have to stay any longer."]

Hostler: the man who gets the railroad engines out of the roundhouse and ready to go on the road

Hot: 1. the cows are shaded up, which is a sure indication the temperature is high 2. spitting brown steam, which is a reference to tobacco juice spitters 3. had to feed the chickens cracked ice to keep them from laying hard boiled eggs 4. blisters are poppin' out on my boots 5. potatoes are baking in the ground 6. corn's poppin' on the stalk 7. makes hell look like an ice plant 8. so hot, I saw a bird pulling a worm out of a hole and he was using pot holders 9. so hot I saw a rattlesnake crawl into a campfire looking for shade under the coffee pot 10. so hot the chickens were pluckin' themselves 11. so hot the mercury in the thermometer evaporated

Hot, very: 1. blistering hot 2. burnin' up, as in "I wish I hadn't wore three pair of longhandles 'cause I'm burnin' up." 3. could fry a steak on your bald spot

Hot as: 1. a burning boot (or stump) 2. high school love 3. honeymoon sheets 4. a Cadillac bumper in July 5. a two-dollar pistol on Saturday night 6. a bed of mesquite coals in a BBQ joint 7. a fresh forged horseshoe 8. road tar in August 9. a Palacios parking lot 10. a fox in a forest fire 11. a café griddle 12. a depot (or bunkhouse) stove 13. a June bride in a feather bed 14. a sinner on a preacher's knee 15. hell's door handle, the hinges of hell, the hubs of hell, hell with the blower on, or the devil's roasting prong

Hot enough to: 1. melt diamonds 2. boil mercury or melt the mercury in a thermometer 3. roast marshmallows on the dashboard of a pickup truck 4. dissolve the shoes on a horse 5. boil spit on a sidewalk 6. melt leather with it still on the cow 7. boil water inside a watermelon on the vine 8. wither a fence post 9. melt dirt 10. sunburn a horned toad 11. buckle pavement on the interstate 12. hard boil an egg in a stock tank 13. fry an egg on the fender of your pickup 14. use the glove box in my truck as an oven 15. loosen the bristles on a wild hog

A M **Hot sauce:** hot stuff

Houlihan: *See Steer wrestling*

House: 1. casa 2. hacienda 3. wickiup 4. wigwam

House with a loft: a story and a jump

House without indoor plumbing: three bedrooms and a path (to the outhouse)

Housekeeper, good: 1. pushes a mean broom 2. hell on dust and spiderwebs

Housekeeper, inept: waxed the carpet

Houston (Harris County): pronounced Ewe-ston; named for Texas hero Sam Houston; also called Bagdad on the Bayou. It was the first word spoken from the surface of the moon when the spacecraft touched down and Neil Armstrong radioed, "Houston, tranquillity base here. The Eagle has landed."

How are you feeling? How in the health are you?

How are you: 1. how ya' doing 2. how in the world are you 3. como esta *See also Greeting*

How's that again? 1. lick that calf again? 2. come again?

Huajillo: a small-leafed shrub with clusters of pink flowers (*calliandra*

eriophylla); also called false mesquite and fairy duster

Huckabay (Erath County): pronounced HUCK-a-bee; named for John A. Huckaby, one of the founders and the first postmaster

Hug: love their neck, a frequent instruction for Texas children when the grandparents come calling

Huge: *See Large*

Hugging: They were so twisted up together you couldn't tell where the boy stopped off and the girl commenced.

Huh: a multi-purpose interjection used for surprise, skepticism, suspicion, doubt, disbelief, incredulity, bewilderment, and even contempt

Humble: It's hard to be humble when you're from Texas.

Humbled: 1. got his hat in his hand 2. got knocked down a peg or two *See also Ego, deflated*

Humid: 1. I'm sweating setting 2. my upper lip is mildewing, which is a reference to people sweating on their upper lip when it's very humid

Humiliate: fluff-off

Humility: when you say grace before eatin' crow

Humorous: would bring a grin to the face of a stuffed owl

Hump in his back: a horse that is humped up so bad the saddle will not set down squarely on his back and he is certain to buck (not a good thing)

Hump it: traditional position for Aggie yells

Humped up: like a country girl on an organ stool

Hung up (on a bull): *See Bull riding*

Hung over: got the whistleberry thumps and skull cramps

Hungry: 1. feeling gant 2. so hungry he's become left-handed, which implies you are so hungry that your cerebral polarity has changed 3. my stomach thinks my throat has been cut 4. my belly button is rubbin' a blister on my backbone 5. could take up the slack in my stomach and wipe the sweat off my brow 6. is something you don't get better at with practice 7. my teeth itch 8. my stomach is playin' a recital 9. could eat the blades off a windmill 10. could eat a handful of ball bearings 11. could eat a saddle blanket after a day's riding 12. just fry the skillet and throw away the handle 13. a sign once seen in a ranch kitchen: "If you're hungry, grab a plate. You have my best wishes. But before you pull freight, be sure to wash the dishes." *See also Starving*

Hungry as: 1. a goat on a concrete pasture 2. a wolf with a toothache 3. a woodpecker with a sore pecker (or a headache) 4. a moth on a nylon sweater 5. a toothless coyote

Hungry enough to: 1. eat a chicken, feathers, beak, cluck, and all 2. eat a horned frog backwards. If you look at a horned frog, you'll notice the horns point to the rear, so he would be hard to eat backwards unless you were very hungry. 3. eat the skirts off a Mexican saddle 4. eat a longhorn steer, hide, horn, hooves, and beller 5. play dead and try to attract a vulture 6. eat the stuffin' out of a rag doll 7. eat the tail off a dead skunk 8. eat a plumber's rag

Hunt seat: *See Forward seat*

Hunter, avid: keeps a taxidermist on retainer

Hunter, inept: 1. a bush shooter [This means he saw the bushes moving and fired away without really knowing what he was shooting at. Bush shooters have killed a lot more cattle than deer or antelope.] 2. won't shoot skeet 'cause he don't want to clean 'em *See also Bird hunter, dumb*

Hunter, inexperienced: 1. nothing but a sign shooter [This comes from the practice of shooting at innocent

H

signs along the highway. The theory is that anyone who would shoot at signs wouldn't be much of a real hunter. The favorite targets for sign shooters are deer and cattle crossing signs.] 2. hasn't learned that everything that goes "moo" ain't a moose

Hunter, poor: only thing he shoots are pool, craps, and bull

Hunting dog, good: 1. braggin' dog 2. flushes a covey of quail, chases 'em down a prairie dog hole, and then lets 'em out one at a time for the shooter

Huntsville (Walker County): pronounced HUNTS-vul; named for Huntsville, Alabama, former home of the founders. Sam Houston is buried in Huntsville and his life is commemorated with one of the tallest statues in the state.

Hurricane deck: the back of a bucking horse

Hurrying: didn't stop for water, wood, or wolves

Hurry: 1. spur the flanks 2. hit the ground runnin' 3. get the lead out 4. come a whipping 5. get high behind (like an old hen in a hailstorm) 6. fan the fat (use the spurs) 7. jingle your spurs 8. rattle your hocks 9. ride like a deputy sheriff 10. lay the quirt to 'em 11. get into high gear 12. like a house afire 13. don't spare the horses 14. use that rowel 15. come at a double trot 16. pop some leather 17. hurry 'cause early don't last long 18. flap your chaps 19. put a hip-hop in your getalong

Hurt, bad: my butt and all the fixtures are broke

Hurting: punishing, as in "I wore my boots without socks and the blisters that were raised are sure punishing me."

Hurts: smarts

Husband: 1. running mate 2. my bigger half 3. the ball and chain 4. warden 5. my kid's daddy 6. the old man 7. honey doer [A wise man once observed that husbands are like state fairs, they get bigger and better every year. A wise woman once observed that some husbands are angels, the rest are still alive.]

Husband, cunning: carries a doctor's prescription for pantyhose in case his wife ever finds a strange pair in the glove compartment of his car

Husband, henpecked: 1. molts twice a year 2. him and his wife will never join a nudist colony 'cause she wouldn't be wearing no skirt for him to hide behind 3. wears the pants in the family but has 'em on under his apron 4. only time he gets to open his mouth is when he yawns 5. still takes orders from his first wife 6. gets his money the hard way, he asks his wife 7. washes dishes even if they are paper plates 8. only time he puts his foot down is on a spade in his wife's garden

Husband, inept: his wife said she'd like to be seen in something long and flowing so he pushed her into the Brazos River

Husband, lazy: 1. married his first wife's sister so he wouldn't have to break in a new mother-in-law 2. his idea of helping out around the house is starting the lawn mower for his wife

Husband, smart: bought his wife the finest china so she wouldn't throw any of it at him when she's angry and she won't ever trust him to wash it

Husband, ugly: his wife goes out drinkin' and carries his picture so she'll know it's time to stop drinking when he gets good looking [could also be reversed and used for ugly wife]

Husband, unfaithful: 1. he ain't married but his wife is 2. out doin' what he hopes his wife is home doin' without

Hush your mouth: *See Embarrassed oath*

Hussy: *See Floozy*

Hutto (Williamson County): pronounced HUTT-oh, home of the fighting Hutto Hippos

Hypochondriac: 1. his car always smells like BenGay 2. holds his breath when driving past a hospital 3. can tell you exactly how many chicken pox he had 4. takes so many vitamins and iron pills, when he dies his heirs will argue over the mineral rights to his body 5. thinks ingrown toenails are catching

Hypochondriac, dead: his tombstone will read "I told you I was sick"

Hypocrite: his religion is in his wife's name

Hysterectomy: where they get rid of the baby carriage and leave the playpen

Hysterical: slap happy

I

I agree: 1. you're preaching to the choir 2. I'm here to tell ya'

I declare: 1. I swan 2. I'll be darn

I don't know: search me

I guess so: hell, I reckon

I don't care: 1. don't give a bedbug's behind about that 2. don't mean any more to me than a hair on my backside

I might: don't know but what I won't do it

I suppose: 1. I reckon 2. I 'magin

I would appreciate it: I'd take it kindly, as in "I'd take it kindly if you'd get me a Dr Pepper."

I'm not lying: hope to get kicked to death by a crippled grasshopper if I ain't tellin' the truth

I'm ready: my hair's set [After a hog is slaughtered, it is boiled in hot water, which stands the hair on end, or sets it, then the hog is ready for scraping.]

I've been there: been on the cow's side of the fence

Iago (Wharton County): pronounced EYE-a-go

Ice, thin: chicken foot ice [the first little layer of ice that forms on a stock pond when it freezes over; normally has small crack-like imperfections, which are said to resemble chicken feet]

 Ice cream: cold cow

Ice house: *See Convenience store*

Iced tea drinker, avid: grew up with a ring across his nose, referring to drinking from Mason jars [also used for moonshine drinkers]

Idalou (Lubbock County): pronounced I'd-a-lou. Historians argue over the origin of the name. It may have come from Ida and Lou Bacon, early settlers, or Ida and Lou Bassett, daughters of the vice-president of a livestock company. No matter which is correct, it is somewhat amazing that one little town had two sets of Ida and Lou.

Idea: a young impulse [J. Frank Dobie once explained the difference between having an idea and thinking. He said, "thought employs ideas, but having an idea is not the same thing as thinking. A rooster in a pen of hens has an idea."]

Idea, good: 1. neon light idea 2. an idea that was cooked on the front burner

Idea, possible: don't know if it's a hunch or a gas pain

Identical: 1. spittin' image of 2. dead ringer for 3. scissored from the same piece of cloth *See also Alike*

Identified: 1. read his iron 2. checked his dog tags 3. read his scars

Idiot: 1. chucklehead 2. lunkhead 3. IQ is equal to one-half his hat (or boot size) 4. churnhead 5. could keep him busy for half a day by asking him to find the top of a ball bearing or the corner in a round room 6. his limits are limitless 7. could get trapped on an escalator in a power failure 8. about three fourths of a halfwit 9. would have to study up to be a crash dummy 10. got the IQ of a dust mop 11. sawdust head 12. ain't got a lick a sense 13. went to the tattoo parlor and asked for a pair of boxer shorts on his chest so he could have a chest of drawers 14. won't buy a dictionary 'cause he's waiting for the movie 15. almost froze to death at the drive-in movie waiting to see "closed for winter" *See also Dumb; Ignorant; Stupid*

Idle: 1. about as busy as a pickpocket at a nudist colony 2. no busier than a saddle maker at a dog show 3. about one-half as busy as a ghost town undertaker or telephone operator 4. just standing around with his teeth in his mouth 5. has as much to do as a hibernating bear 6. got nothing to do but stand around and scratch his seat

Idle talk: bat chatter

If: 1. a hog had wings he'd be an eagle 2. a pig had wings, he'd be a chicken hawk 3. a frog had wings he wouldn't bump his behind when he jumped 4. the biggest word in the dictionary [If ifs and buts were candy and nuts what a merry Christmas we'd have, as Texan Don Meredith was fond of saying on Monday Night Football.]

If I was you: pronounced fize-you

If it's worth doing, do it right: The best stove wood is always the stove wood that is farthest away, which means if you're gonna get the best wood you gotta do it right and walk a little farther.

Ignorance: is a lot more expensive than an education

Ignorant: 1. if he knew two languages he'd be bi-ignorant 2. a mite shy in schoolhouse learning 3. don't know cream from cantaloupe 4. don't know his hiney from a gin whistle 5. don't know rock salt from bee honey 6.

couldn't find an egg under a setting hen 7. couldn't dig fish bait in a worm farm 8. don't have the sense God gave a screwdriver, goose, grasshopper, saddle horn, or sack of flour 9. would play Russian roulette with a single-shot derringer 10. has the IQ of hanging beef 11. cut down his only shade tree for firewood [While the firewood might keep you warm for a little while, the entire summer will be mighty hot without that shade tree.] 12. don't know chicken manure from chicken salad 13. don't know pinecones from pineapples 14. has a photographic mind but nothing ever develops 15. thinks Dairy Queen is a royal cow 16. couldn't get the same answer if he counted his nose twice 17. don't know beans from rocks *See also Dumb; Idiot; Stupid*

Ignore him: 1. play like his mother didn't have any children that lived 2. don't give him a second thought and only half a first thought 3. pay him no never mind 4. like a bus driver does a hitchhiker

Ignore it: 1. turn a blind eye to it 2. don't take any stock in that 3. let a sleeping dog lie

Ill: 1. took sick 2. green around the gills 3. riding the bed wagon, which refers to cowboys who became sick on a trail drive and had to ride the bed wagon rather than their horse 4. feelin' mighty shy of bein' half well 5. feelin' mighty puny 6. took down with miseries [Any specific illness such as the flu, gout, pneumonia, etc. can be substituted for miseries, which is an undiagnosed disease.] *See also Ill, gravely; Looks sick; Sick*

Ill, gravely: 1. time to get the chickens out of the hearse 2. so far under the weather the only way back is through heaven (or hell), which infers someone is going to die and the only way to return is to be reincarnated 3. paid the wrong preacher 4. got one boot in a pine box 5. his last hope is a faith healer 6. looks like about one more clean shirt is all he'll ever need *See also Health, poor*

Ill, not too seriously: 1. not supposed to pick up anything heavier than a biscuit or a nightgown for about two weeks 2. fit as a fiddle but just a little bit out of tune

Ill, seriously: crippled sick

Illegal: 1. on the hot side of the law 2. ain't square (or plumb) with the statutes

Illegitimate: 1. a descendent of a long line his mother heard in a honky-tonk 2. brush colt 3. camp meeting baby 4. woods colt 5. oil field colt 6. the baby didn't come early, the wedding came late 7. his parents ate supper before they said grace 8. her parents planted the corn before they built the fence 9. was born on the wrong side of the blanket

Illiterate: 1. can't read writing or write reading 2. signs his name with a holler 'cause he can't even make a mark 3. if he knew two languages he'd be bi-illiterate 4. if you write him a letter, write slow 'cause he can't read fast 5. doesn't go to football games 'cause he can't read the words spelled out by the band at halftime

Illness, relapse: a sinking spell

Imagination: what a wife sits up with when her husband is out late

Imaginative: imagineer, which is how Hondo Crouch described himself

Imitating: walking in someone else's boots (or tracks)

Immature: 1. acts his shoe size instead of his IQ 2. half baked 3. a fuzzy thinker 4. happiest when he's playing with a string of spools [On the frontier, mothers tied empty thread spools together as a toy for the kids.]

Immobile: got the mobility of a speed bump

Immoral: 1. suffers from a lapse in the code of decency 2. never could decipher the code of ethics 3. got leaky morals 4. got the morals of an alley cat 5. morals are about as loose as ashes in a whirlwind

Impartial: 1. totes water on both shoulders 2. a fence walker [As a general rule, if a man sees both sides of a dispute, he don't have any money in the deal.]

Impartial as: a sad country song, which don't care whose heart it breaks

Impatient: 1. chomping at the bit 2. fighting the bit [Generally, a horse that is fighting the bit is either ready to run or ready for you to get off.]

Imperial (Pecos County): pronounced im-PEER-e-ul; an irrigation center that got its name from the Imperial Valley area of California, which was also known for its irrigation system

Important person: 1. big frog in the pond 2. tall hog at the trough 3. tush hog 4. big buck at the lick 5. big brick in the wall 6. when he does something, it sets folks' tongues to wagging, which is a reference to people talking about anything an important person happens to do 7. name spends as much time on the front page of the paper as the name of the paper *See also Boss; Leader*

Impossible: 1. can't sweep sunshine off the porch 2. can't unscramble an egg 3. can't hitch a horse with a coyote 4. can't fit two pounds of manure into a one-pound sack 5. can't make a silk purse out of a sow's ear 6. can't make moonshine out of mare's milk 7. can't drop a cat on his back 8. can't dip well water with a tea strainer 9. can't keep the dew off the grass 10. can't teach a longhorn steer to sing the Aggie war hymn 11. can't put a quill back in the goose 12. can't pull a ten-horse load with four Shetland ponies 13. can't put a duck egg in an eagle's nest and get an eagle 14. can't scratch a wet match 15.

I

can't straddle the fence and keep your ear to the ground 16. can't pole vault with a pitchfork 17. crops don't grow by moonlight 18. can't throw a big loop with a small rope 19. can't cook in cold grease 20. can't make butter from skimmed milk 21. can't pee in a naked man's pocket 22. even the smallest anvil won't float [Texans usually take the attitude that nothing is impossible, but some things take a little longer than others to get done.] *See also Attempting the impossible*

Impossible, almost: 1. will take a heap a doin' but it can be done 2. to tree that coon you'll need all the dogs

Impossibility: 1. trying to hit a three-run homer with no one on base 2. trying to measure water with a tea strainer 3. can do that the day after a rooster lays an egg 4. tryin' to lead a cow downstairs [For reasons best known only to cattle, you can lead a cow up all the stairs you want, but you better have a different plan for getting her down 'cause no force on earth can make a cow walk down any stairs. Speaking as one who once led a jersey milk cow up two flights of stairs to the top of the school building, you can trust me on this one; you cannot get them back down the stairs.]

Impotent: 1. ain't got no lead in his pencil 2. ain't got no sting in his stinger 3. his Evinrude won't crank

Impractical: makes as much sense as an artificial wart

Impractical as: 1. carrying a settin' hen to Sunday school 2. giving a hug by mail 3. trying to carry water in a peach basket

Impressed: 1. showed 'em a thing or two 2. blew her dress up

Impression, false: 1. just because his breath smells like bananas don't mean he's Tarzan 2. just 'cause a hog has hair don't mean he can grow sideburns

Impression, strong: made more of an impression than a three-legged man in a butt kicking contest

Impressionable: has a head like a doorknob, anyone can turn it

Improbable: 1. would take a big woman to weigh a ton 2. would take a big biscuit to weigh a pound

Impudent: got a lot of gall

Impulsive: jumps at the drop of a hat, anybody's hat

In a bind: up against it (a stump)

In a hurry: in a sweeping trot

In a quandary: up against a stump

In agreement: 1. singing off the same page 2. singing the same song in the hymnal 3. hitched to the same plow (or wagon) 4. chewin' off the same plug

In contention: 1. in the hunt 2. in the game

In control: 1. holding all the aces 2. got the bull by the horns 3. got the key to the gate 4. got the cattle gathered and penned 5. holding all the trump cards 6. holding all the count rocks (dominos) 7. owns the deer lease, which means he gets to call the shots. [Like they say in Russia, we got 'em by the Baltics.]

In danger: 1. flying with one wing 2. dancing in a mine field 3. fishing in troubled waters 4. dancing with the devil and they are playing his tune 5. you're not only behind the eight ball, you're behind the whole rack 6. juggling hand grenades and the pins are comin' loose 7. walking a high wire and the net has a big hole in it 8. tied to the tracks and the train is on time 9. cussin' a range cook [For a cowboy, cussing the cook was very dangerous. If the cook didn't simply whip the stuffin' out of the cowboy, he almost certainly saw to it the cowpuncher went hungry.] *See also Dangerous; In trouble; Trouble*

In demand: like an Easter egg at an orphanage

In disarray: everything is all boogered up

In disrepair: misfixed

In error: 1. pulling the wrong pig's ears 2. tryin' to milk a bull

In every direction: 1. everwhichaways 2. seven ways from Sunday

In good shape: sittin' pretty

In heat: in season

In love: 1. got her brand on my heart 2. got Cupid's cramps 3. wearing Cupid's hobbles 4. got calico fever 5. got my stake pin in her court

In pain: hurtin' worse than a parakeet caught in a badminton game. Since badminton is normally played with a little plastic birdie, if a real parakeet happened to fly into a game in progress, he would be hurtin' for certain by the time he flew out. Hummingbird can be substituted for parakeet.

In poor condition: it'll take a faith healer to repair it

In the country: out back yonder

In the hole (dominoes): in moon, if your score falls below zero, you're in the hole

In the rear: eatin' drag dust, referring to riding drag on a trail drive

In the whiskey row: *See Whiskey row*

In trouble: 1. your biscuits are burning 2. staring down the barrel of a real dilemma 3. parachuted into a volcano 4. holding a pair of threes against a full house 5. in a wild bull's pasture without a tree 6. up a creek without a paddle and the boat is leaking 7. bucking in the rodeo without a pick-up man 8. kicked over a hornet's nest 9. the slop hit the fan, implying that slop would be spread everywhere in a hurry 10. got your tail in a crack 11. plowing in a bad row of stumps 12. in a pickle 13. dippin' snuff out of a can of rat poison 14.

in a hell of a fix [While serving as secretary of war for the Republic of Texas, Thomas J. Rusk is credited with saying, "We are in a hell of a fix. Let's go to the saloon, have a drink, and fight our way out of it."] *See also Trouble; In danger*

In trouble, big time: 1. got your tit in a wringer and it's wash day at the orphanage 2. a Gypsy fortune teller offered to refund my money 3. don't worry about biting the bullet, just go on and swallow it 4. got so many problems, if something else happens it'll be two weeks before I can worry

Inappropriate: ain't fittin'

Inbreeding: the family tree don't have many branches

Incentive: 1. added money [In a rodeo the purses are made up of contestant entry fees and "added money" contributed by the rodeo committee.] 2. boot, as in "I'll throw in a set of new tires to boot if you'll buy my old pickup."

Inclined: 1. got a mind to, as in "I've got a mind to go along with you on that." 2. got a good notion to, as in "I got a good notion to drink that six-pack of beer all by myself."

Inclined, somewhat: 1. got half a mind to, as in "I've got half a mind to paint the barn and surprise the missus." 2. got half a notion, as in "I've got half a notion to start looking for a job."

Include: 1. deal me in 2. set another place at the dinner table

Incompatible as: 1. a .45 shell in a shotgun 2. water and oil 3. Aggies and Longhorns

Incompetent: 1. couldn't be crew chief on a sunken submarine 2. couldn't drive a nail into a snow bank with a sledgehammer 3. couldn't ride a nightmare 4. couldn't split enough firewood to fry an egg 5. couldn't cut a lame cow from the shade of a mesquite tree

I

Incomplete: 1. a kiss without a squeeze 2. not fully baked 3. that deer's only half skint 4. takes more than one act to make a circus

Inconsequential: just a flea on the dog of life

Inconsequential as: 1. a bee sting to a honey lovin' bear 2. a grain of sand on a beach 3. a wart on a frog

Inconsistent: 1. runs hot and cold 2. king of the crawfishers 3. wishy washy

Inconspicuous as: 1. a blanket Indian on a reservation 2. a tree in a forest 3. a cow chip in a pasture 4. a peach (or pecan) on a tree

Incorrect: 1. barking up the wrong tree 2. cutting (or skinning) the wrong cat *See also Mistaken; Wrong*

Increase workforce: when a woman is having trouble getting pregnant, put more men on the job, which is how Burton Smith explained he was going to address construction delays at the Texas Motor Speedway

Indebted to: 1. beholden to, as in "I'm beholden to you for helpin' pull my pickup out of that bar ditch." 2. would rather owe it to you than beat you out of it 3. I'll dance at your next wedding for that

Indecisive: 1. like a grasshopper, he's liable to jump one way as another 2. don't know whether to fish or cut bait 3. don't know whether to ride or rope 4. don't know whether to brand or go bowling 5. has a four-year-old son who ain't been named 6. just a fly-up-the-creek, which means he changes his mind and probably never will make a decision

Indelible: 1. tattooed on 2. branded on

Independence (Washington County): originally called Cole's Settlement, the name was changed after Texas declared independence on March 2, 1836

Independent: 1. would rather leave some hide on a fence than stay corralled 2. takes no sass but sarsaparilla 3. saddles his own horse 4. rides his own trail 5. totes her own skillet 6. paddles his own canoe or rows his own boat 7. cooks his own beans (or chili) 8. rolls his own loop 9. pulls his own teeth 10. keeps his forked end down (stands on his own two feet)

Independent as: 1. a dog (or hog) on ice 2. a mule on a dance floor

Indian: 1. hair raiser 2. whiskey warrior 3. land moccasin, as opposed to a water moccasin, which is a snake 4. buffalo hunter 5. barebacker, referring to the fact that Indians didn't need saddles to be expert horsemen

Indian summer: a spell of warm weather that comes after the first frost

Indicative: 1. where there's cows there's cow chips 2. the tongue always seeks the tooth that hurts 3. if the saddle squeaks, it ain't paid for [This refers to cowboys buying their saddles on time. The leather wouldn't be broken in fully and stop squeaking before the bill was paid off.] 4. if it winks, it'll screw [This phrase comes from the oil patch. Wink, in this case, is the very first little turn of a tight bolt. When you get that first little wink you know you can unscrew the entire bolt.]

Indifferent: don't give didly squat

Indiscreet: will talk ropes in the house of a man who was hanged

Individualism: every pot has to stand on its own bottom [Some people follow old wagon tracks, others blaze their own trail.]

Individualist: one duck you won't ever get in a row

Indolence: he's grown to the chair

Indoor toilet: peeslapter or pee splasher

Indoors: can't get rained on indoors. Bum Phillips believed so strongly in that principal that he wouldn't wear his hat when the Oilers played at home inside the Astrodome.

Industrious: his kindling box is always full

Inebriated: *See Intoxicated; Drunk*

Ineffective: 1. "It had no more effect than a pint of whiskey split five ways," said *Houston Chronicle* columnist Leon Hale. A fifth of a pint wouldn't be enough whiskey to affect anyone very much. Now a whole pint, that's a different story. 2. as a scarecrow covered with bird droppings [Not only was the scarecrow ineffective keeping the crows away, the birds actually used it as a perch to decide which row of your corn they'd eat first.] *See also Scarecrow, good*

Inefficient: 1. got too many colonels and not enough cavalry 2. too many chiefs and not enough Indians 3. too many cooks and not enough chili meat

Inept: 1. couldn't get a hooker a date on a troop train 2. couldn't hit sand if he fell off a camel 3. could walk himself to death in a revolving door 4. would put a bucket under a natural gas leak 5. only opens his mouth to change feet 6. would pay extra for an air conditioner on a motorcycle 7. in a battle of wits, he'd be unarmed 8. tried to drown himself in a shower 9. couldn't hit the floor if he fell outa bed 10. walks around with his zipper unbuttoned [Lyndon Johnson once said of his staff, "They aren't walking around with their zippers unbuttoned," but he didn't explain how you unbutton a zipper.]

Inevitable: 1. girls get better looking when it's almost closing time 2. a fox will fool with chickens till he feels buckshot in his behind 3. if he's a rooster, he'll crow 4. if he's a dog he'll bark and bite 5. every turkey has his Thanksgiving 6. a horse's tail will catch cockleburs 7. a bird in the hand leads to messy fingers 8. chickens will come home to roost sooner or later 9. what goes around comes around 10. a man who was born to drown would drown in a desert 11. there's always someone to take the slack out of a troublemaker's rope 12. chips happen 13. if the stable (or barn) is gonna get clean, somebody is gonna get dirty 14. if you drill enough oil wells, you will learn the sound of suckin' air a dry hole makes 15. if you sit down in a cactus patch, you can count on pullin' stickers out of your butt 16. no matter how hard the winter, spring always comes 17. only way to keep from growing old is to die young *See also Accept the inevitable*

Inevitable, almost: sunshine always follows a storm, unless the storm was at night

Inexperienced: 1. next time he does that will be the first time 2. still wet behind the ears 3. bench warmer 4. so green he could hide in a lettuce patch *See also Rookie; Tenderfoot*

Inexperienced as: Ned in the first reader [In case you don't remember, poor ol' Ned didn't know how to do anything.]

Inez (Victoria County): pronounced EYE-nez. *See also Telferner*

Infatuated: got his hat set for her

Inflation pressure: when the price of syrup goes to a dollar a sop, the biscuit stays mighty dry

Infuriated: was spouting steam from every joint

Ingenious: he could split something down the middle and still get the biggest half

Initial: *See First*

Injured: 1. took hurt 2. my gears are out of mesh 3. my dauber's dented 4. feel like I was booted over a seven-foot fence 5. crippled up 6. stove up 7. got a broken spoke

Injured, seriously: hurt all over worse than any place else

Injured, slightly: 1. got the gravel rash, which usually occurs when you walk out of a honky-tonk and fall down drunk on the gravel parking lot 2. cut up some but I ain't gushing blood 3. hurtin' some but it's not as bad as rivet burns [This refers to the rivets on a pair of blue jeans. If you sit too close to a fire while wearing jeans, the rivets get very hot. When you stand up you get burned in places that are hard to scratch when they start healing.]

Innocent as: 1. a newborn colt, lamb, calf, or armadillo 2. little Red Riding Hood 3. a fresh laid egg

Innovative: "If you want to catch a mouse you got to make a noise like a cheese," said Texan Charles Tandy, founder of Tandy Corporation.

Insane: 1. slipped a cog 2. snapped a link in his trace chain 3. touched in the head 4. addled in his thought box 5. a little shy in the hat size 6. cross threaded 7. got a slip in his differential *See also Crazy*

Insignificant: 1. the small end of nothing whittled down to a point 2. chicken feed 3. small potatoes 4. just one blade on the windmill 5. don't amount to a hill of beans 6. just a drop in the bucket (or Gulf of Mexico) 7. wouldn't even be a pimple on a frog 8. nothing to write home to mother about [During his ill-fated 1992 presidential campaign, Texan H. Ross Perot defined insignificant as "one mosquito at a picnic for ten thousand people."]

Insignificant as: 1. dirt under a gnat's fingernail 2. gas passed in a whirlwind (it'll be long gone before anyone notices) 3. ice to a polar bear 4. a minnow in a stock tank

Insignificant person: 1. just a small spoke in a big wheel 2. just one more hand on the range 3. don't drive the train or blow the whistle 4. a little frog in a big pond

Insomnia: mind over mattress

Insomniac: gets less sleep than a man with three daughters and two back doors

Inspect, closely: go over it with a fine-toothed comb

Installment buying: buying on time, which means by the time you're sick and tired of the thing, you own it

Instantly: sudden like

Instead of: pronounced sted-uf

Instructions, lacking: can't do what I ain't been told any more than I can go back to where I ain't been

Insubordination: saddle your hoss before you sass the boss

Insult: 1 would trade you for a flea-bitten old hound dog and then shoot the dog 2. she don't sweat much for a fat woman

Intellectual: can listen to the *William Tell Overture* and *not* think of the Lone Ranger

Intelligence, average: 1. knows enough not to wet on an electric fence 2. knows enough to come in out of the rain 3. knows enough to pour rainwater out of a boot 4. can tell a mule from a racehorse 5. wasn't in the top half of his class but he was one that made the top half possible

Intelligent: 1. his mama didn't raise a pretty boy but she didn't raise a dumb one either 2. uses his brain to keep blisters off his feet 3. may have been born at night but it wasn't last night 4. got more facts than a mail order catalog *See also Smart*

Intelligent, very: 1. has a total lack of ignorance 2. smarter than a tree full of wise old owls

Intend: aim to, as in "I aim to get the fence mended one of these days."

Intend to marry: got her cap set for him

Intends to stay: pitched out his anchor

Intercept: head 'em off at the pass

Interfering: 1. dipping your quill in my ink bottle 2. branding my cows 3. messing with what comes under the heading of my business 4. hanging your wash on my line 5. tryin' to put your leg in my shorts 6. dippin' snuff out a my can

Intermittent: on and off like a firefly's light (or a refrigerator light)

Interoffice romance: 1. don't cut your heifers out of the company corral 2. don't dip your quill in the company inkwell 3. don't work the breedin' stock and don't breed the workin' stock

Interrupted: another county was heard from

Interrupting: 1. who's robbing this train, me or you 2. who mashed your button 3. who rattled your cage

Intimidate: 1. read him the riot act 2. melt his backbone 3. tie a knot in his pistol barrel

Intimidated: 1. as an oilman in a banker's office 2. as a hen in a coyote den

Intoxicated: 1. knee-walking, snot slinging drunk 2. floored and frenzied 3. couldn't see through a ladder with two tries 4. couldn't hit the ground with his hat in four tries *See also Alcoholic; Drunk*

Investigate: take a look see

Investor (oil business): pigeon

Investor, poor: don't know a stock from a sock

Invincible: 1. bulletproof 2. armor plated 3. wearin' a blacksmith suit, which is a suit of armor

Invisible body parts: *See Eyes in the back of the head; Fool head; Getalong; Gills; Gizzard string; Hind leg*

Invitation, Texas style: 1. y'all come 2. come see us 3. come by the house

Invitation to return: y'all come back now, ya' hear

Inviting trouble: 1. itchin' for a lickin' 2. cruisin' for a bruisin'

Involved: 1. in the hunt 2. got his finger in the pie 3. got his iron in the fire 4. bogged in it all the way to his saddle skirts 5. up to his eyeballs in it 6. got some hogs in those bottoms *See also Among*

Involved deeply: went whole hog

Iron: smoothin' iron

Iraan (Pecos County): although some will argue, the proper pronunciation is Ira ann, never EYE-ran. When the town was laid out a contest was held to find a name and the winner was to receive a choice lot. The owners of nearby Yates Ranch, Ira and Ann Yates, combined their names and won the lot. It was probably only a coincidence that a huge oil field had recently been discovered on the Yates Ranch.

Ireland (Coryell County): pronounced IRE-lan; named for former Texas governor John Ireland

Irons: *See Eating irons*

Irrational: 1. took leave of what little sense he had 2. plowin' blindfolded which, for a farmer, would be very irrational behavior

Irrelevant: 1. nothing but squaw chatter 2. horse feathers

Irresistible as: 1. jackrabbit liver to a channel cat 2. a can on a sidewalk (you just can't resist kicking it)

Irresistible to women: has to fight 'em off with a wet tow sack

Irretrievable: 1. can't get words back once you've spit 'em out 2. can't get the cigar back once you've smoked it 3. can't get back spit from the ocean

Irrevocable: once you make a steer, you can't turn him back into a bull

Irrevocable as: 1. a flushed toilet 2. a death sentence half an hour after the hanging

Irritated: 1. my stinger's out 2. my dauber's down 3. got a thorn in my paw 4. gettin' ready to come apart at the seams 5. got a burr under my saddle 6. got a thorn in my side 7. got my tail feathers ruffled *See also Angry; Mad*

Irritating: 1. grates on my nerves 2. cocks my pistol 3. primes my stinger 4. gets my dander up 5. chaps my butt 6. sticks like a thorn in my short ribs 7. galls me

Irritation: sore spot

IRS: Infernal Revenue Service *See also Lawyer axiom*

Is that right? 1. pronounced zat-right 2. sure enough? Primarily used as a reply when somebody tells you something that's hard to believe. His response would then be hell yes, yessiree-bob, or you-bet-cha.

Isn't it: pronounced idinit

It's over: 1. pick up the hymnals, the preachin's over 2. pull down the shades 'cause there ain't nuthin' left for the neighbors to see 3. that's the opry 4. that's the ball game 5. might as well call the dogs and pour the coffee on the fire

Italian hemp: the core to each of the three strands of a grass rope

 Italy (Ellis County): pronounced IT-a-lee or IT'ly; this town, which bills itself as the biggest little town in Texas, is home of an EYE-talian (Italian) festival every June

 Itasca (Hill County): pronounced Eye-TAS-ca; named after Lake Itasca in Minnesota

Itching: like I spent the night in a bed of chiggers or a poison ivy patch

J

Jack (playing card): 1. hooker 2. junior

Jack Daniels: 1. Black Jack 2. Tennessee sippin' whiskey

Jack squat: term used in place of "absolutely nothing" as in "Bubba's old pickup is worth jack squat."

Jackalope: a cross between a jackrabbit and an antelope; an animal that runs so fast no one has ever seen one

 Jacksboro (Jack County): pronounced JACKS-bur-ah; named in honor of William H. Jack and his bother Patrick, who were veterans of the Texas Revolution

 Jacksonville (Cherokee County): this one is a "ville" not a "vul"; named for three Jackson families who were early settlers

 Jacobia (Hunt County): pronounced like Jacoby; named for an early settler whose exact name has been lost

Jagged: jaggedy

Jail: 1. hoosegow 2. booby hatch 3. calaboose 4. clink 5. pokey 6. can 7. juzgado 8. cross bar hotel

Jailhouse deer: a deer shot by a poacher, the implication being he will go to jail if caught

Jake joint: a saloon during the oil boom days that served Jamaican ginger, a popular drink during Prohibition

Jakeleg: a condition where the feet and legs are "paralyzed" by the effects of strong drink

Jalapeño pepper: 1. pronounced (hal-a-peen-ya) 2. Mexican bullet 3. napalm seeds 4. Mexican or the devil's strawberries

Janitor: floor flusher

Jar heads: Naval and Marine cadets

Jaws, strong: 1. like a bolt cutter 2. like the beak of a snappin' turtle

Jealous man: 1. his wife has to bring home a note from the preacher to prove she went to church alone 2. the only time he trusts his wife to go out with the girls is when she takes a Girl Scout troop camping 3. he trusts his wife about as far as he could throw a baby grand piano 4. he's been bit by the green-eyed monster, which is a term Shakespeare used to describe jealousy that became a favorite among country folks for some reason 5. he wouldn't trust her if she had a date with the Pope

Jealous woman: 1. if you go home to her with a hair on your coat, you'd better have a horse to match 2. someone who sits up with her imagination when her husband is out on the town 3. she wouldn't trust her husband if he was in solitary confinement in a Mexican jail

Jeans, cowboy cut: have zippers instead of buttons; extra room in the seat and thigh to make it easier to get on and off a horse; higher back pockets so you won't have to sit on them when riding; and extra wide space between the front belt loops to better accommodate that world champion bull rider buckle if you happen to win it

Jeans, stacked: when jeans are very long and they bunch up around the boots, they are said to be stacked

Jeans, tight: 1. her jeans were so tight, I could hardly breathe 2. looks like they were tattooed on 3. if she gets goose bumps she'll bust some seams 4. looks like she was melted down and poured in them 5. she has to carry her handkerchief in her mouth 6. looks like they were painted on 7. it took two hours of wiggling to get 'em on 8. she'll bend a crowbar gettin' 'em off 9. if she ever drops her purse, she'll have to walk off and leave it 'cause she can't bend over to pick it up 10. Swift and

company never packed a ham that tight. Most of the preceding can also be used for tight dresses, tight shorts, or tight sweaters.

Jeopardy: *See Double jeopardy*

A͟M Jell-O: wiggle

A͟M Jelly: sweet stuff

A͟M Jelly fritters: gun-wadding

Jerk line: a rope and windlass device used to teach a horse to back up

Jerking pole: a young sapling left standing under a brush arbor so anyone struck with the "jerks" will have something to hang onto

Jerks: emotional, sometimes violent spasms that strike worshipers who are overcome with religion during protracted church meetings or brush arbor meetings

Jerky: dried meat, usually beef, venison, or buffalo, that was dried in the sun or in the smoke of a fire to preserve it

Jermyn (Jack County): pronounced Ger-man; named for J. J. Jermyn, son of coal magnate Joe Jermyn of Pennsylvania

Jerry rigged: temporary repair; also called Johnny rigged

Jiba (Kaufman County): pronounced He-ba

Jigger boss: buckeroo boss

Jilted: 1. her bass spit out the hook 2. dropped him like a hot horseshoe 3. changed everything about her but her name 4. she's haunting my pillow 5. dodged the ball and chain 6. got over her in less than one half the time you can hold a hot branding iron 7. she quit him like a dead horse does a wagon *See also Female, jilted or Male, jilted*

Jimmy: GMC pickup

Jimsonweed: cow-lily

Jinglebob: small ornaments, frequently pear shaped, hung from spurs so they "jingle" when you walk; worn for show, never when working

Jitney: old-time term used to describe a worn-out or broken-down automobile

Joaquin (Shelby County): pronounced Wha-keen; named for Joaquin Morris, the grandson of Benjamin Franklin Morris who donated 100 acres for the town site

Job: something people do between fishing trips

Job, unfinished: 1. still got some creeks to cross 2. still got some syrup to sop

Job, unpleasant: if you have to drink from a spittoon, do it in one quick gulp, which basically means if you have something unpleasant to do, get it over with quick as you can

Jockey lot: flea market

Jody: marching chant such as in "I don't know but I've been told. Eskimo women are mighty cold" or "Hut-two-three-four, I love the Cadet Corps"

Joggle board: a wide strong board suspended between two objects for children to play on

Johnny cake: cornmeal cake made from a mixture of meal and water and baked until brown and crispy

Johnson bar: the reverse lever on a steam locomotive

Johnson-type halter: rope halter put together with rope hardware (rope joints)

Join: 1. put my marbles in with yours 2. jump into bed together, as in "We jumped into bed together and opened a café" 3. throw in with 4. stick your oar in his pond 5. tie in with 6. fall in with 7. wiggle on in 8. pick a spot on the company stringer 9. take a hand 10. drop your rope in with 11. wade on in 12. throw your sombrero (or hat) into the ring 13. mosey on up to the trough

Join in: 1. pitch in 2. a dog enjoys the hunt a lot more if he does some of the barking 3. grab a knife and do some skinning

Join the bird gang: a phrase which originated to mean jump off a train that was about to derail

Joined: 1. sidled up with 2. hitched to 3. galvanized together

Joke, funny: 1. a real knee slapper 2. a real hooter 3. ain't laughed that much since grandma got her hair caught in the wringer

Joke, old: the first time I heard that I laughed so hard I kicked a slat out of my crib

Joked: 1. fed 'em a load of corn 2. scalped his goat

Joker (playing card): 1. bloke 2. bluke 3. bug 4. court jester

Jooking: 1. playing a musical instrument, usually a piano or guitar, in a roadhouse or whorehouse 2. going out for a night of honky-tonking *See also Honky-tonk*

Joshua (Johnson County): for generations the town has been pronounced Josh-a-way, but recent newcomers are saying Josh-a-wa

Jourdanton (Atascosa County): pronounced Jord'n-ton; named for Jourdan Campbell, one of the founders

Judge: hizoner

Judge, poor: lets 'em go faster than the law can catch 'em

Judgement: 1. don't judge a man by his arrows but by how he shoots them 2. don't judge a woman by the size of her biscuits but by how they taste 3. can't judge a man or a car by the sound of the horn

Judgement, poor: 1. selling his horses to buy horse feed 2. buying feed for a mechanical bull

Jughead: a horse without horse sense

Juke joint: a bar that resembles a honky-tonk except there is no live music, only a jukebox; a true Southern juke joint must have a pool table or two *See also Honky-tonk*

Jukebox: 1. cowboy stereo 2. honky-tonk angel's best friend 3. a no-armed bandit [A slot machine is a one-armed bandit but at least you have a slim chance of winning something when you drop your money into the slot. With a jukebox, you might get a dance but you have no chance to get your money back if you don't.]

Jumped: 1. quit the earth like a dynamited stump 2. like he got a cattle prod caught in his coveralls 3. like a bull out a chute 4. like a fish on a hook 5. like a frog trapped under a bucket 6. like a frog's leg in a frying pan 7. like he sat down on a hot horseshoe 8. like he stepped on the sun 9. swallowed his head or sunfished, which are terms associated with a pitching horse that jumps and turns from side to side

Jumps: 1. like a cockroach on a hot griddle 2. like an armadillo [When an armadillo is frightened his natural instinct is to jump first and then start running. If an armadillo is scared by a car, he jumps straight up, which is why most are killed by a bumper or grill rather than by being run over.] 3. like a whang-doodle *See Whang-doodle*

Jumpy: 1. fiddle footed 2. horsey 3. got a gut full of bed springs 4. dancin' like a bobber 5. hearin' hoof beats 6. as a cat on ice 7. got a frog in her bra 8. got a scorpion in his shorts

Juning around: a June bug connected to a child's leg by a length of tobacco twine

Junior: 1. second classman 2. serge-butts

Junior, without rank: slick-sleeve; also used for sophomores without rank

Junk: plunder

Jury: 1. twelve people who decide who had the best lawyer 2. one thing that don't work right when fixed

Just arrived: 1. right fresh from 2. new to these parts 3. just struck town 4. ain't been here long enough to draw breath

Just reward: got what was comin' to him

Justins: boots made by the Justin Boot company, Fort Worth, Texas

K

Kack: cowboy slang for saddle

Kamay (Wichita County): At first glance you might think the pronunciation would be like the famous soap Camay, but you'd be wrong. When the town was founded in 1912, it was originally named Kemp for Joe Kemp. He, along with W. Munger and R. Allen formed the K-M-A Oil Company. In 1938 the name K-M-A was proposed, but the postal authorities rejected it and Kamay became the name. It is, however, pronounced as if the initials had been accepted, Kay-em-a.

Kamey (Calhoun County): pronounced KAY-me; named for J.W. McKamey, local citizen and store owner

Kanawha (Red River County): pronounced Ka-NOY-ee; named for the Kanawha River in West Virginia

Karnack (Harrison County): pronounced KARH-nac; named for an Egyptian village that was supposedly near Thebes and the same distance from the Nile River as this town is from Caddo Lake

Katemcy (Mason County): pronounced Ka-TEM-see; named for Comanche chief Ketemoczy

Katy: nickname for the Missouri-Kansas-Texas Railroad

Katy (Harris County): Since this town was on the Missouri-Kansas-Texas Railroad line, many assume the town name came from the nickname of the railroad. In fact, the town was named for Katy Mares who owned Katy's, a popular saloon.

Keep active: 1. if your pot's boiling, the flies won't come around 2. keep your plow moving 3. it's better to wear out than to rust out

Keep alert: keep a weather eye peeled

Keep busy: 1. hold your nose on the grindstone 2. tend to your knitting

Keep still: take a little coma practice

Keep trying: 1. church ain't over till the choir sings amen 2. keep plugging 3. keep shooting, you'll eventually hit something 4. pitch till you win 5. keep going till the cows come home (or till hell freezes over) 6. keep plowin' till the mule dies or the ground freezes 7. keep dealing 8. even if you're down, you can still swing from the floor 9. another try is better than an alibi 10. you gotta start from scratch and keep on scratching 11. it's OK to give out but don't ever give in 12. a steam kettle keeps singing even though it is up to its neck in hot water 13. saddle sores eventually heal and only your best girlfriend will ever see the scars, which implies you should keep riding despite the pain of saddle sores *See also Persevere*

Keep up: pack your backside with powder and fire yourself on up here with the rest of us

Keep your composure: whatever you do, never let 'em see you sweat

Keep your mouth shut: don't want to hear a peep outa you, a favorite saying of Texas mothers

Keeping bad company: 1. if you bed down with hound dogs, you'll wake up with fleas 2. if you make friends with the devil, you'll wind up on his prong

Keeps a low profile: keeps his head low in the herd; can be said of a horse or a cowboy

Keepsake: something you never put in a garage sale

Keester: old-time safecrackers' word for the interior door of a safe; also called a duster

Kennard (Houston County): pronounced Ka-NARD

Kennedale (Tarrant County): pronounced Kin-a-dale; named for Oliver S. Kennedy, who platted the town and donated land to the Southern Pacific in hopes of luring the railroad to the town

Kerchief: *See Bandana*

Kerens (Navarro County): pronounced as if the second "e" is silent, it's Kerns

Kermit (Winkler County): When President Theodore Roosevelt made a tour of the West in 1910, which included Texas, local residents named their town for the president's son Kermit, who was frequently mentioned in news stories.

Kerosene: 1. coal oil 2. called lamp oil by some old-timers

Kerosene lamp: coal oil lamp

Kerrville (Kerr County): pronounced with a "ville" not a "vul" for KURR-ville; named for James Kerr, a leader in the Republic of Texas

Kettle, large: wash-pot used for just about everything from washing (boiling) clothes, to making lye soap, to giving the small kids their Saturday bath

Kicks wildly: kicks like a bay steer, which is the Texas equivalent of "kicks like a mule"

Kid: *See Child*

Kidding: 1. you're shucking me 2. pullin' my leg 3. hooraying me 4.

wetting in my boots and telling me it's raining 5. rawhiding 6. hurrahin' *See also Joked*

Kilabrew: hydraulic-dump fertilizer transport trailer

Kill: 1. dry gulch 2. blow out his lamp 3. snuff out his candle 4. rid the ground of his shadow 5. shoot daylight into him, which means shoot a hole into him so daylight can get through 6. pull him up by the roots 7. give him a ticket for the hereafter then punch his ticket 8. dispatch him to hell

Killeen (Bell County): pronounced Ka-LEAN; named for Frank P. Killeen, assistant general manager of the Sante Fe Railroad

Killer: 1. widow maker 2. orphan maker 3. home wrecker 4. everything he touches turns to rigor mortis 5. funeral maker 6. he don't believe in life after birth 7. didn't cut those notches in his gun for whittling practice

Killing time: 1. just grazing 2. just sittin' on the dresser

Kind: 1. has to hire someone to kick his dog 2. wouldn't hurt a flea (or chigger) 3. got kindness enough to kill a cat 4. got a heart as big as all outdoors

Kind hearted: 1. would buy crutches for a lame duck 2. has a heart as soft as summer butter

Kind of: kind a like

Kind, but dumb: whole hearted but half-witted

Kindling: 1. lighter wood 2. starter wood for a fire [The best kindling is pine knots because they're so rich in turpentine. If you can't start a fire with pine knots, you got no business having a fire.]

King (playing card): 1. cowboy 2. killer 3. big bull

Kingsville (Kleburg County): a "ville," not a "vul" for KINGS-ville; named for Richard King, founder of the King Ranch

Kiomatia (Red River County): pronounced Ki-MISH-ee; named for the Kiomatia River, which is Indian for "clear water"

Kiss: 1. swap spit or slobber as in "Quick, get me the mouthwash 'cause the dog just swapped slobber with me." 2. a mouthful of nothing that tastes good and sounds like an old milk cow pulling her foot out of a mud bog *See also Incomplete*

Kiss, long: was wet enough to water a Shetland pony

Kiss, quick: a Yankee dime, which is about all a Yankee girl's kiss would be worth to many Southern boys

Kissing cousins: people who are very close but not actually related by blood

Kitty: *See Extra dominoes*

Knees: 1. prayer bones 2. lower joint in the foreleg (horse)

Knickknack: 1. a feather duster target 2. dofunnies 3. dohickies 4. dust magnet

Knife fight victim: got so many holes you could put a garden hose in his mouth and use him for a lawn sprinkler *See also Bloody*

Knife: 1. pig sticker 2. cowboy (or Texas) toothpick 3. two blader 4. Bowie 5. lock blade 6. Case knife 7. pocket skewer

Knife, dull: 1. could ride all the way to town on the sharp side of the blade without a saddle or even a blanket 2. could let the baby teethe on that blade 3. this knife's been to breakfast, which means it was dulled cutting the food

Knife, large: 1. Arkansas toothpick 2. Bowie knife [a large knife with a single-sided blade, tapered point that's sharp on both sides, and a strong guard. Designed by James Bowie, the original knife was lost when the Alamo fell.]

K

Knife, lock-blade: a folding knife that "locks" in place when open to prevent accidents

Knife, sharp: you could use the shadow of the blade as a razor

Knife, small: 1. apple peeler 2. a bubblegum knife [This is a reference to the small toy knives that were once prizes in bubblegum machines in general stores.]

Knife, switchblade: Mexican Express card [Although switchblade knives have been outlawed in most of the United States, they can still be purchased in Mexican towns along the Texas border.]

Knife with illegal blade: 1. Dallas special 2. Texas special

Knippa (Uvalde County): the "K" is not silent; it's pronounced Ka-NIP-ah [A sign in town proclaims: "Go ahead and blink, Knippa is bigger than you think." That may be true but just to be safe don't make it a long blink.]

Knock lightly: peck

Knocked down: 1. dusted his pants 2. he went down like a power line in a hurricane or a scarecrow in a whirlwind

Knocked out: 1. laid out cold as a wedge 2. he dropped like an anvil fell on his head [windmill wrench, cotton bale, tractor, or most anything heavy can be substituted for anvil]

Knot, tight: a Case knot [a knot tied so tight you have to use a Case knife and cut the rope to get it undone. Generally, a Case knot is tied by someone who doesn't know how to tie a tight knot properly so it can be undone without ruining the rope.]

Know him well: know where all his warts are

Know your worth: every ol' sausage knows if he was made from a hog or a dog

Knowing without doing: is like plowing without sowing

Knowledgeable: 1. plenty savvy 2. didn't just come in on a load of firewood (wintertime) or cantaloupes (summertime) 3. knows more about it than a whiteface calf knows about sucking 4. knows more about it than a jackrabbit knows about running 5. knows enough to keep his mouth shut when he's up to his chin in a pile of manure 6. knows more about that than he does about the back of his hand 7. what he don't know ain't worth learning *See also Common knowledge; Intelligence; Smart*

Kopperl (Bosque County): pronounced Cop-rul

Kosciusko (Wilson County): pronounced Ka-SHOE-sko; named by Polish immigrants for Tadeusz Losciuszko, who was a hero of the American Revolution and the Polish insurrection

Kosse (Limestone County): pronounced KOSS-ee; named for Theodore Kosse, the chief engineer for the Houston and Texas Central Railroad

Kountze (Hardin County): pronounced Coo'nts; named for Herman and Augustus Kountze, backers of the Sabine and East Texas Railroad line

L

Laboring: like an idiot with a short pencil

Lacking: 1. a bit shy 2. on the stingy side

Ladies man: 1. woman or skirt chaser 2. could charm the pants off the Mona Lisa 3. sowed more wild oats than all the wheat farmers in the Panhandle could combine *See also Womanizer*

Ladle: dipper

Lagnappe: in the old days some country folks used lagnappe (land yap) for to boot or extra amount

LaFayette (Upshur County): pronounced La-Fee-ette; named for LaFayette Locks, the son of an early setter

La Grange (Fayette County): pronounced La-GRAINGE; Fayette County was named for Marquise de Lafayette and La Grange, the county seat, was named for his chateau [The town was once home to the Chicken Ranch, which was celebrated as the "Best little whorehouse in Texas."]

Lajitas (Brewster County): pronounced La-HE-tus; Spanish for "little white rocks," which is a reference to the Boquillas flagstone of the area

Lake: a fisherman's farm

La Marque (Galveston County): pronounced La Mark; originally known as Highlands, but the postmistress changed it to La Marque, which is French for "the mark"

Lamasco (Fannin County): pronounced La-MASS-co; name was derived from Law, Mason and Scott, who were three early settlers

Lamb fries: *See Calf fries; Brave as*

Lame: 1. sore footed 2. short booted, implies he's wearing boots that are too small, which certainly causes sore feet

Lamesa (Dawson County): pronounced La-ME-sa, Anglo version of la mesa, which describes the flat terrain

Lancaster (Dallas County): pronounced quickly as one word, Lank-a-stir and not, as many believe, as two words Lan Caster

Land: 1. a piece of ground 2. a spread 3. an acre accumulation

Land, dry: 1. had to buy dehydrated water at the 7-Eleven 2. had to put postage stamps with paper clips 3. takes twenty years for a nail to rust 4. only time we see rain is when they show pictures of it on television [A man in West Texas swears that one year it was so dry when it finally did rain he had three and a half inches of mud in his rain gauge.] *See also Drought*

Land, fertile: 1. can plant a horseshoe nail and grow a horseshoe 2. could plant a beer can and grow a Japanese car 3. could plant a penny and grow a copper tea kettle 4. could plant cow chips and grow a herd of longhorn cattle 5. could plant a nail and grow a crowbar 6. could plant a whisper and grow a rumor 7. could plant some wind and grow a windmill 8. could plant a toothpick and grow a railroad tie 9. chickens that don't catch the corn on the fly just wait and eat it off the stalk in a day or two 10. could plant a feather and grow a pillow

Land, flat: could stand on a tuna fish can and see another 100 miles away [Some people in West Texas claim they can stand on a tomato can and see another one in Kansas.]

Land, poor: 1. godforsaken country 2. can't grow anything but broken dreams 3. tumbleweed territory 4. can't grow anything but Johnson grass and jimson weed 5. would have to put fertilizer around the bottom of a pole to raise a flag 6. couldn't raise your voice on it 7. a piece of ground so sorry the only thing that ever gets raised on it is taxes, implying that taxes are raised on worthless land as well as good land. *See also Arid; Barren*

Land, rich: can't ship anything to another county 'cause the seeds refuse to leave

Land, rich as: the dirt in an old abandoned cow pen (or feed lot)

Land, steep: 1. our land was so steep we could look up the chimney and watch the cows come home 2. so steep grandpa fell off the corn field

L

Landscaping: the bush bidness

Langtry (Val Verde County): pronounced LANG-tree [This is the town where the infamous Judge Roy Bean dispensed his "Law West of the Pecos." Bean was obsessed with the English actress Emille "Lille" Langtry, so generations of Texans have assumed Bean named the town in her honor, which is incorrect. The town was already named by the time Bean arrived. The name was in honor of George Langtry, an engineer and supervisor for a Chinese work crew that helped build the local railroad. Bean did, however, name his saloon "The Jersey Lilly" in honor of the actress even though he did misspell the name.]

Lannius (Fannin County): pronounced LAN-us; originally called Stephenville but the name had to be changed when they got a post office since the name was already taken

Lard: pig salve

Lard bucket: the bucket where lard was collected and stored

Large: 1. a picture of it would weigh five pounds 2. enough to store hay in 3. enough to burn diesel, which refers to the days when anything that burned diesel was large, such as a truck or a tractor *See also Big*

Large amount: 1. a whole pocket full 2. a barrel full 3. a wagon load 4. right smart of, as in "He's got a right smart of trouble from his mother-in-law" 5. got more of those than hell has sinners or heaven has angels 6. got more of those than there are liars in Washington

Large person: 1. fell down and rocked herself to sleep trying to get up 2. his shadow would weigh ten pounds 3. takes a big loop to rope him 4. blazes a wide trail 5. fills up a huddle 6. takes a big stick to knock him down 7. looks grained up and ready to ship to market 8. was born on the 8th, 9th, and 10th of September 9. ought to bed down with the night herd 10. you think he never will get through gettin' up 11. has to curl up to lay down in a boxcar 12. large enough to be a quartet 13. like a train, he takes a while to get going and a while to stop 14. big as a gang plow 15. fills up a room like he was wearing it 16. could go bear hunting with a switch and give the switch to the bear 17. looks like he ought to have "John Deere" stenciled on his butt 18. when he tries to walk, he gets in his own way *See also Big person; Fat*

Lariat: from *la reata*, which is Spanish for rope; refers to a rope made of horsehair but the term is rarely used in Texas

Lariat rope: used to rope a cow; in Texas it's called a catch rope

Las Vegas: Lost Wages, Nevada [There's the old story about the Texan who went to Las Vegas in a $35,000 Cadillac and came home in a $250,000 bus. If you're planning a trip to Las Vegas, remember you get better odds by flushing your money down a toilet and hoping the pipes are stopped up. Cowboys who visit Las Vegas for the National Finals Rodeo refer to the city as "Helldarado."]

Lasso: from the Spanish *lazo reata*, which means slack rope [In Texas and on the rodeo circuit, the word rope is generally used instead of lasso, which is considered a "dude" or Yankee term.]

Last: 1. the tail end 2. the end of the trail 3. the hind tail

Late night: just this side of bedtime

Latexo (Houston County): pronounced La-TEX-oh; acronym for Louisiana Texas Orchard Company, which purchased land and platted the town

Last chance: If you don't win this time, the giant sucking sound you hear will be your chances going down the drain, to paraphrase Texan Ross Perot.

Last one in is: 1. a rotten egg 2. an old maid

Last place finisher: he got the pig's tail [When country folks slaughter a pig they use virtually every part except the tail and the squeal, so the tail would be a perfect prize for a last place finisher since nobody else would want it.]

Lasts long as: an appendix scar

Latigo: very strong, almost weather-proof, oil-tanned leather that has very little stretch or give [Latigo straps run through the cinch on a saddle.]

Lattice well: *See Bateau*

Laudable: proud, as in "You shore did a proud thing when you made an honest woman out of Mary Ann."

Laugh hard enough to: 1. bust a gut 2. shake a tonsil loose from the roots

Laugh, hearty: 1. like a double-jawed hyena 2. shake your belly

Lavernia (Wilson County): pronounced La VERN-ah

Lavish: *See Quantity, large*

Lavon (Collin County): pronounced La-VON; named for Lavon Thompson, son of E. C. Thompson, who operated the local post office [Beware the local speed traps!]

Lawbreaker: 1. careless with the statutes 2. even ignores the law of gravity

Lawman: 1. law bringer 2. badge toter 3. star strutter *See also Highway patrol; Police*

Lawsuit: something you go into as a hog and come out of as sausage

Lawyer: 1. law wrangler 2. statute wrangler (also used for judge) 3. legal eagle 4. legalized con man 5. ambulance chaser [Lyndon Johnson once said, "In Texas there is a saying that a town which can't support one lawyer can always support two." As we say in Texas, the only difference between a dead lawyer and a dead armadillo laying on the road is skid marks in front of the armadillo.] *See also Wasteful*

Lawyer, experienced: 1. been through more briefs than a BVD inspector 2. could find a loophole in the ten commandments

Lawyer, good: 1. a real ground hound, which means he can have you back on the ground (street) quickly after an arrest 2. if I ordered a trainload of lawyers and he was the only one that showed up I'd be satisfied

Lawyer, poor: 1. he can have your speeding ticket reduced to a charge of manslaughter 2. thinks he's dressed up when he gets a paternity suit 3. hiring him to settle your problem would be like hiring General William Tecumseh Sherman to hold a barbecue in Atlanta

Lawyer, promiscuous: spends more time taking off his briefs than he does writing them

Lawyer axiom: If you put all the lawyers in Texas in one barrel and rolled it down a hill, there'd always be a son of a bitch on top; also applies to bankers and IRS agents.

Laxative: working medicine

Lay down: 1. sun your heels, which implies the only time your heels see the sun is when you are laying down 2. the "pat hand" in dominoes [You have a lay down when you can immediately play all your dominoes.]

Lay down the law: read 'em the scriptures (or statutes)

Lazbuddie (Parmer County): usually pronounced as two words, Laz Buddy; named for two ranchers, D. L. "Laz" Green and A. "Buddie" Shirley

Lazy: 1. like a blister, never shows up till the work is done 2. instead of

L

shaving her legs she just spreads ice cream on 'em and lets the cats lick it off 3. will starve to death someday 'cause he won't work and he's too lazy to steal 4. keeps hittin' the snooze alarm on her biological clock 5. walks into a river so he can get a drink without having to bend over 6. if his house caught on fire, he'd go outside and pray for rain instead of trying to put it out 7. will never drown in his own sweat 8. ain't afraid of hard work 'cause he can lay down beside it and sleep like a pup 9. would try to pick up a girl on another man's whistle 10. so lazy, her self-winding watch stopped 11. a saw rider, which refers to one man not pulling his weight on one end of a two-man cross-cut saw 12. won't even swat flies 13. she even washes dishes in bed 14. only exercise she gets is jumping to conclusions 15. riding the singletree, which means another horse has to do the work 16. spends most of his time on the loafer's log (or bench) 17. spends his time looking for sundown, shade, and payday 18. too light for heavy work and too heavy for light work 19. if he was a dog, he wouldn't wag his own tail 20. claims he was wounded in the war but no one has ever seen a scar 21. only thing she does fast is get tired 22. a shade follower [When he sits in his rocking chair out on the porch he moves the chair as the sun moves so he's always sitting in the shade.] 23. hangs out more than mama's wash on a line *See also Loafer*

Lazy and cautious: knows hard work never killed anyone but he don't want to risk being the first victim

Lead: 1. shepherd 'em 2. blaze the trail 3. take the bull by the tail

Lead ox: 1. an ox used repeatedly to lead cattle on a trail drive 2. an ox that is necked (tied by the neck) to an unruly steer that refuses to be herded

Lead rope: rope attached to an animal being lead

Lead shank: a tie rope with a harness snap on the end to anchor it to the halter

Leader: 1. bell cow 2. bell mare 3. bell wearer 4. ringleader 5. rules the roost 6. chief cook and bottle washer 7. big buck at the lick 8. tall dog in the pack 9. stud buzzard 10. big duck in the puddle 11. big buzzard on the carcass 12 the head eagle [When former Texas governor Jim Ferguson arrived at a meeting, one of his aides remarked, "All you owls hunt your holes, the eagle is here."] *See also Boss; Important person*

Leader, inept: if he lined up a firing squad, he'd arrange them in a circle

Leader, poor: leadership ain't a snug fit on him

Leaks: 1. holds water like a crocheted handkerchief holds snot 2. like a bottomless bucket

Leaky: 1. so full of holes it wouldn't hold hay 2. sieve bottomed

Learn: 1. wise up on 2. study up 3. practice up 4. get the hang of 5. get posted on

Learned of: got wind of

Learning: beginning to make a hand

A͟M Leather legs: senior cadet at Texas A&M; also called elephant or zip

Leathers: leather bushings on sucker rods

Leave: 1. make some boot tracks 2. drag your carcass out of here 3. head 'em up and move 'em out 4. pull your picket pin and drift 5. hit the trail 6. put the wind to your back and ride 7. pull up stakes 8. skeedadle out of here 9. get along on 10. hit the breeze 11. strike camp 12. put wheels on the whorehouse and haul butt 13. gather up some over yonder 14. fade into the sunset 15. promenade for home 16. vamoose 17. get while the gettin' is good 18. lay down tracks in the direction of outa here 19. run around the barn three times and come back twice 20. move it on down the line

Leave fast: 1. drag your navel in the sand or fill your vest pockets with dirt, both of which imply you should run close to the ground 2. don't let the door hit ya' where the good Lord split ya' 3. jump the dust 4. hightail it 5. light a shuck, which is a reference to dry corn shucks burning very quickly 6. get the hell out of Dodge 7. tear out like a ruptured duck 8. tuck your tail and light out 9. pop some mesquite 10. like a glory-bound bat or a bat out a hell

Leave it alone: 1. let it be 2. let sleeping dogs lie 3. let him play his own hand 4. leave it be

Leave me alone: don't crank my motor unless you want to see it runnin'

Leaving: 1. off like a prom dress 2. goin' to the house 3. feeling mighty temporary 4. not long for this place 5. feel the get up and goes coming on 6. he bought a trunk and packed it 7. pulled his freight and left

Leery: 1. this old crow has eaten enough field corn to know scarecrows sometimes carry shotguns 2. this old fox has raided enough chicken coops to know there ain't no free lunch 3. robbed enough nests to know you can't enjoy eggs if you're picking buckshot out of your behind 4. caught too many coyotes to put my foot in a trap 5. got a twitch in my jaundice eye

Left a bar after one drink: flew off on one wing

Left early: 1. jumped the gun 2. jumped the traces 3. beat the bell 4. beat the clock or gun 5. broke the barrier

Left fast: 1. took off like a goose in a hailstorm 2. headed for the tall timbers in a short time

Left-handed cousins: families that are related by marriage instead of blood

Left him limp: took the starch out of him

Left home: jumped out of the nest

Left in a hurry: 1. vamoosed 2. raised enough dust to choke a buffalo herd 3. took off in such a hurry he didn't have time to take his real name 4. took off like a chicken through a hole in the fence 5. took off like the heel flies were after him

Left side: haw, which was the old mule driver's word for left

Left: 1. struck the trail 2. took to the tall timber 3. took out 4. lit out 5. got off toward 6. left out 7. cut a trail 8. withered from 9. split the breeze 10. he's a long time gone 11. made for, as in "He made for town as soon as he heard the sheriff was on vacation."

Leggett (Polk County): pronounced LEG-it, not Leg-ette [Ralph Leggett was an early settler and store owner who had a sign over his establishment featuring a red horse, so most people referred to the area as Red Horse. When a post office was requested Leggett agreed to use his name.]

Legging: *See Calf roping*

Legs: wheels

Legs, long: 1. high rumped 2. mighty leggy 3. granddaddy long legs 4. lanky legged 5. stilt legged

Legs, thin: 1. spider legs 2. chickadee legs 3. banty rooster legs 4. you ought to sue those legs for nonsupport [said by former Dallas Cowboy Dan Reeves to teammate Don Meredith] 5. looks like he traded legs with a killdeer (or stork) and got the short end of the deal

Lela (Wheeler County): pronounced LEE-la; named for Lela Smith, the sister-in-law of postmaster Bedford F. Bowers

L

Lemonade, sour: would even make the pitcher pucker

Lenorah (Martin County): pronounced La-NORE-ah; originally called Plainview but that name was taken when the townspeople applied for a post office, so they changed the name to honor Lenorah Epley who was the county clerk

Leon day: the day of the year that is exactly six months from last Christmas and six months from next Christmas; Leon is Noel spelled backwards

Lesson for children: bringing up lecture

Let everyone know: put it right out on the front porch [In the country, houses are often few and far between, so when you pass a house you almost always glance at the front porch. Anything on that front porch would be seen by everyone who passes.]

Let go: 1. turn a loose 2. give him his head [This refers to giving a horse his head by releasing a tight hold on the reins so he can run better.]

Let everybody see it: pull back the curtain

Let me do it: let me rock the baby

Let someone else do it: let somebody else catch the snakes or clean the fish

Let them go: 1. set 'em free 2. set 'em loose 3. let her rip 4. open the chute 5. open the cage

Let's discuss it: 1. let's hoe that row 2. got a crow to pick with you

Let's do it: 1. let's do some dancin' 2. let's get at it 3. let's rodeo

Letter, from girlfriend: sugar report

Levelheaded: so levelheaded he has tobacco juice runnin' out of both sides of his mouth

Levelland (Hockley County): pronounced LEVUL-land; originally called Hockley City, the name was changed to a term that accurately described the local terrain

Lewisville (Denton County): this one is a "ville" not a "vul"; named for founder Basdeal W. Lewis

Liar: 1. him and the truth ain't well acquainted 2. truth stretcher 3. don't dance with the facts 4. story don't track with the facts 5. got his facts tangled 6. couldn't get a notary to certify he was alive 7. talks through his hat 8. fork tongued, which comes from the forked tongue of a snake 9. lying through his teeth 10. has to send the dogs to bring the kids home 'cause they don't believe her when she calls 'em 11. believes that truth is scarce so he don't want to use it up 12. thinks truth is like a girdle, made to be stretched 13. never lets the truth stand in the way of a good story 14. a point blank tale teller, which means he'll lie right to your face 15. would tell a lie even if the truth sounded better 16. tells such big lies she has stretch marks around her mouth 17. would rather climb a tall tree and tell a lie in the sunshine than to sit in the shade and tell the truth 18. all her blankets are stretched plumb out of shape, which is derived from the saying that to lie is to stretch the blanket 19. only time he tells the truth is when he admits he's a liar

Liberty (Liberty County): originally founded by settlers who were turned down for inclusion in Austin's colony; first name was Santisma Trindad de la Libertad, which translates into Most Holy Trinity of Liberty, but the name was ultimately shortened to Liberty

Lice: walking dandruff

License plates: tags

Lick log: a fallen tree with several notches cut along the top side. Salt is poured into the slots so cattle can lick it out. The term "lick log" has long been a part of the language of Texas and the South and it has numerous uses including: 1. getting close to the end, as in "We're getting down to the lick log so it's time to stuff the ballot box." 2. interfering, as in "Your cows are on my lick log." 3. joined, as in "He came over to our lick log." 4. in agreement, as in "We're all at the same lick log." 5. threaten, as in "I'm gonna whittle a few holes in you and use your carcass for a lick log."

Lie (noun): 1. windy 2. whizzer 3. yarn 4. ain't square with all the facts 5. tall tale 6. cock and bull tale 7. as shy of the truth as a pig (or turtle) is of feathers 8. corral dust

Lie (verb): 1. pull a sandy 2. tell a windy 3. spin a yarn (or tall tale)

Lie, big: a boldface lie

Lied to: sold me a bill a goods

Lies: 1. there are three kinds of lies: lies, damn lies, and Chamber of Commerce statistics 2. the two biggest liars are "hearsay" and "they say"

Lies, black: the kind meant to hurt or deceive

Lies, white: the kind meant to spare someone's feelings

Life: 1. is like a suitcase, if you cram enough into it something has to give 2. is like square dancing; about the time you get into the swing of things, someone changes directions on you 3. is like a poker game; if you don't put anything into the pot, there won't be anything to take out 4. is like riding a bicycle; you either go or you get off 5. is something that is too short and too full of blisters 6. is like juggling pitchforks; everyone knows when you screw up

Life, boring: if it wasn't for Gamblers Anonymous, Alcoholics Anonymous, and Weight Watchers, he wouldn't have nothin' to do

Life, simple: a five and dime existence [This implies someone lives such a simple life he can purchase anything he wants or needs at a five and dime store.]

Lifeless: *See Dead*

Lifetime: 1. from crawling to crutch 2. from womb to tomb 3. all my born days, as in "I've been a Texan all my born days."

Lift: 1. hist 2. hoist 3. histed

Light a match: scratch a match *See also Zipper*

Light as: 1. a sparrow (or hummingbird) feather 2. an empty eggshell 3. an ant's eyelash 4. a mother-in-law's baggage when she's moving out

Lightard knot: the center of a pine stump that contains a concentration of pine pitch; when fully dried takes on the characteristics of hardened steel and is very hard to cut through

Lighten the load: bury the whiskey and draw a map [This is a reference to the old days when a loaded wagon had trouble making it over rough terrain. It such a case, any spare whiskey was often buried so it could be retrieved later.]

Lighter wood: kindling, generally pine wood that is so dry it catches on fire so quickly you think it exploded

Lightning: sparks from God's camp fire

Like: 1. mighty fond of 2. right fond of 3. cotton to 4. took a fancy to

Like father, like son: fruit don't fall far from the tree

Likeable: when he cashes in his chips, the funeral will be standing room only

Likely to: liable to, as in "If your wife catches you spendin' your paycheck on beer, she's liable to snatch you baldheaded."

Likeness wagon: wagon used by old-time traveling photographers

Lillian (Johnson County): pronounced LIL-yun. [Ironically, the town was named for two different women both named Lillian. J. W. Cunningham purchased land for the town site from G. W. Renfro. When the men discovered that their wives were both

L

named Lillian that became the name of the town.]

Limited capabilities: his pony only knows one trick [Note: if the only trick your pony knows is singing, that ain't bad.]

Limp as: 1. a dishrag 2. an empty glove 3. a bartender's rag 4. a cup towel 5. a neck-wrung turkey 5. a fiddle string without the fiddle

Line, single file: standing heads to tails

Line-back horse: a horse with a black or dark brown stripe running down the base of his withers to his tail. Most line-back horses have black feet, which are extremely tough.

Line camp: small camp, usually on the outskirts of a ranch, where cowboys are assigned to stay while they look after cattle, keep fences up, break ice out of stock tanks, etc.; not considered a plum job

Line the song: when the song leader in church reads the line of a hymn before the congregation sings it

Lingleville (Erath County): pronounced as a "ville" not a "vul" for LING-le-ville; named in honor of John Lingle, an early settler

Lipan (Hood County): pronounced LIE-pan; named for the Lipan Indians who reportedly used the surrounding land as a hunting ground

Lips, attractive: See Mouth, female

Lipstick: pucker paint [Note, lipstick smears are a leading cause of powder burns.]

Liquor: 1. likker 2. firewater 3. whusky 4. red-eye 5. bottled courage 6. rot gut 7. joy juice 8. wild mare's milk 9. nose paint 10. tarantula juice 11. conversation juice, which refers to the fact that many people get talkative when they drink 12. stomach varnish 13. coffin paint 14. gut warmer 15. snakebite medicine 16. mountain lion milk 17. crazy water 18. panther piss 19. tiger milk 20. antifreeze 21. hooch 22. snake venom 23. giggle water 24. witch's piss 25. squaw piss 26. tonsil paint 27. whoopee water 28. embalming fluid 29. courage water 30. stagger juice See also Whiskey; Champagne

Liquor, just right: if it was any better you wouldn't a given it to me, and if it was any worse I wouldn't a drunk it

Liquor, smooth: sipping whusky

Liquor, strong: 1. bumblebee whisky 2. gator sweat 3. will jump your IQ fifty points per swallow 4. will make you act single, see double, and pay triple 5. would melt your tonsils 6. enamel solvent, which implies it will melt your teeth 7. would make a jackrabbit spit in a coyote's eye 8. would make an earthworm bite a catfish 9. brave maker See also Drink, strong; Whiskey, strong; Fisherman, clever

Liquor, weak: has the kick of a 75-year-old pregnant chorus girl

Lissie (Wharton County): pronounced Liss-EE; original name was New Philadelphia

Listen to me: 1. let me tell you 2. mark my words 3. mind you

Listless: could starve to death in a pie factory

Little: 1. puny 2. runtified 3. stingy sized 4. half-pint 5. thimble sized 6. thumb sized 7. poco

Lively as: a coyote with a knot in his tail

Lives close: 1. they just live a howdy and a half down the road 2. just a hop, skip, and a jump from here 3. just a hoot and a holler away

Livestock, lacking: he don't even have a scapegoat

Living above your means: eatin' ham on sowbelly wages

Living dangerously: 1. messin' with your heartbeat 2. wading in a pool of quicksand over hell

Living good: riding a gravy train with biscuit wheels

Living righteous: wouldn't be afraid to sell the family parrot at a church bazaar

Living room: 1. parlor 2. sitting room 3. front room

Lizard-eater: *See Roadrunner*

Llano (Llano County): pronounced LAN-oh; named for the nearby Llano River

Llano estacado: Staked Plains

Loading chute: a ramp with fencing on both sides used to load cattle onto trucks or trains [According to Lyndon Johnson, a loading chute is "Where the cows go out and the money comes in."]

Loafer: 1. charter member of the spit and whittle club [This refers to men who frequent courthouse benches and pass the time spitting tobacco juice and whittling twigs.] 2. will never see manure on his boots 3. coffee cooler 4. porch sitter 5. red flagger [This refers to the person on the road construction gang who does nothing but use a red flag to control traffic.] 6. spends his time looking for sundown and payday 7. thumb twiddler 8. porch preacher *See also Lazy*

Loafing: 1. wasting daylight 2. pirooting, which is a cowboy term for fooling around doing nothing 3. foot dragger 4. spending his days in the porch (or wagon) shade 5. chasing butterflies 6. pussyfooting (or spuddin') around

Lob (dominoes): play a domino when it's your turn

Lobo stripe: a black stripe down the back of some longhorns

Located near: in this neck of the woods

Location, good: it ain't heaven but you can see heaven from there

Lock the door: bolt the door

Locker system: a method used in some private clubs to circumvent liquor laws in dry counties. The waiter would "give" you liquor, supposedly from his personal locker and then charge you handsomely for delivering it. If your favorite brand wasn't in the "locker," you could bring in your own bottle, but you still had to pay for the service.

Log, hollow: gum log

Loggering: holding onto the saddle horn

Loggers: flatheads

Loitered: dallied around town

Lolita (Jackson County): pronounced Low-LEE-ta; named for Lolita Reese, who was the great-granddaughter of C. K. Reese, a San Jacinto veteran [Her grandfather C. K. Reese Jr. was a survivor of the Mier Expedition.]

Loner: 1. lone wolf 2. rides his own range 3. chews his own cud

Lone Star (Morris County): name came from the nearby furnace of the Lone Star Steel Company, which was the inspiration for founding the town

Lonesome as: 1. a preacher on payday, referring to the fact that preachers are not always well paid 2. a windmill on a still day 3. an orphan calf 4. a lighthouse keeper 5. a homely girl under mistletoe

Long: all drawn out

Long ago: 1. when the Dead Sea was only sick 2. before women got the vote 3. when the devil was a pup 4. before the frost melted off hell 5. when snakes walked (or had legs) 6. when Moby Dick was just a minnow

Long as: 1. a country mile 2. a rainy Sunday afternoon 3. a wagon track 4. a West Texas well rope 5. a stake rope 6. plow lines 7. reins on a forty-mule

L

team 8. an old maid's dream 9. a Mormon clothesline

Long distance: 1. fur piece 2. a good piece 3. quite a ways 4. from here to hell and gone 5. as far as an outhouse on a cold morning 6. long as the Texas Oklahoma border [This is the longest border between any two states, measuring over 900 miles.]

Long lasting: it'll outlast the Alamo or dirt

Long lasting as: 1. a pair of steel handled posthole diggers 2. a crowbar 3. a necktie you don't like 4. the scars from a broken heart

Long time: 1. coon's age 2. month a Sundays, which is about seven months in duration 3. quite a spell or a long spell 4. since God knows when, as in "I ain't seen him since God knows when." 5. a right smart spell 6. till hell freezes over 7. till the cows come home 8. till a snapping turtle turns loose 9. longer than a wet week [a week during which it rains every day; nothing seems longer, especially to the mother of five]

Long underwear: 1. longhandles 2. long johns

Long winded: *See Speaker, long winded*

Longe (horse)**:** a horse on the end of a rope moves in a circle while a trainer is in the middle; also called "lunging"

Longneck: a bottle, usually for beer, that has a neck long enough to wrap your hand around to hold the bottle. The theory is if you hold it by the neck, the beer in the rest of the bottle will stay a little colder because the heat from your hand won't warm it up. Whether you believe that or not, it might make an ice-breaking good story the next time you're in a honky-tonk and you see a cute girl holding her beer wrong.

Longneck spoken here: means the establishment serves beer and understands its importance

Longview (Gregg-Harrison Counties)**:** any real Texan will pronounce it slowly as if it were two words, Long View

Look: 1. eyeball 2. look see 3. look-a-here

Look, mean: she looked at me like I had just tracked horse manure (or fish guts) across her clean floor

Look, sweet: you could pour it on a biscuit

Lookalike: 1. dead ringer 2. spittin' image

Look everywhere: 1. search high and low 2. turn over every rock, cow chip, and rotten log in Texas 3. beat all the bushes

Look for: *See Search*

Looking for a husband: 1. draggin' her stake rope 2. trolling for a breadwinner and using a short skirt for bait *See also Female, conniving*

Looking for a job: *See Unemployed*

Looking for trouble: 1. walking around half cocked 2. pawin' the dirt 3. hornin' the bush 4. scratchin' around in the turmoil pen 5. campaigning for a butt kicking

Looks good in action: show bucker, which refers to a horse that bucks best in a rodeo

Looks: *See Appearance*

Looks, bad: 1. looks like he was run over by a switch engine 2. like he hard wintered 3. like he was pulled through a bob war fence backwards by a bobcat *See also Appearance, bad*

Looks, deceiving: 1. powder and paint will make a woman look like something she ain't 2. just 'cause a chicken has wings don't mean it can fly 3. a wagging tail has no control over a dog's mouth, which means even a dog that looks friendly can bite you 4. just 'cause the water is still don't mean it ain't deep 5. any cat would kill you if it was big enough 6. ugly icing don't mean the cake will taste bad *See also Appearance, deceiving*

Looks, good: all combed and curried

Looks like: favors, as in "Dad can't understand why my brother favors the milkman."

Looks sick: 1. peaked lookin' 2. green around the gills *See also Ill*

Looneyville (Nacogdoches County): pronounced LOONY-ville; named for a local pioneer family, the town is located near Loco Creek

Loop: *See Rope loop*

Loose as: 1. a goose, which refers to the loose bowels of your average goose 2. the hide on a Brahma bull [In a rodeo, Brahmas are hard to ride, not only because they are mean but because their skin is so loose it is hard to hold onto in an emergency. One ol' rodeo rider sought to solve the problem when he walked into the arena carryin' a hammer and some shingle nails. When asked what he intended to do, the cowboy replied, "I'm nailing that critter's hide in place so I'll know if I'm sittin' on his back or hangin' onto his belly."]

Loose: 1. uncinched 2. the bridle's off 3. the gate's open 4. limbered up

Loosened up: 1. her personality began to purr and hum 2. his personality erupted like a baby volcano

Lope (horse): western canter

Lorena (McLennan County): pronounced Low-REEN-ah; named for Lorena Westbrook, the daughter of a prominent local family

Los Ybanez (Dawson County): pronounced Los You-BAN-ez

Loser: 1. hitched his wagon to a falling star 2. a clinker 3. couldn't beat a drum 4. don't go home with his tail up 5. should have called a cab instead of the bet 6. like the cow that went dry, an udder failure 7. got the small end of the horn, which is a reference to there being very little in the small end of the Horn of Plenty 8. came up empty handed 9. was left holdin' the empty sack 10. started slow and tapered off 11. when opportunity knocked he was out hunting for a four leaf clover 12. struck out before he even came up to bat 13. got throwed before the horse started bucking 14. every time he makes his mark somebody paints the wall [Darrell Royal said, "There is no laughter in losing." Former Dallas Cowboy Blaine Nye said, "It doesn't matter whether you win or lose but who gets the blame."]

Loser's penalty (mumbly-peg): root the peg

Losing: 1. paying the wrong preacher 2. suckin' hind teat 3. playing second fiddle 4. fightin' a non-payin' proposition

Losing ground: the faster I go, the behinder I get

Losing money: 1. wettin' in the cash box, implying the money is ruined and lost 2. got a hole in the profit sack 3. bottom line is shrinking faster than a grape in a blast furnace or an ice cube in an oven

Losing proposition: feeding a lost dog, which means you'll lose the feed and the dog when his owner shows up

Losing weight: 1. looks like he's evaporating 2. fallin' away to nuthin'

Losses, heavy: had more losses than a swarm of grasshoppers in a chicken yard

Lost: 1. brought in a dry hole 2. finished out of the money 3. a day late and a dollar short 4. took it on the chin 5. got caught nappin' 6. came up on the short end of the stick 7. got a chamber pot instead of a jackpot 8. couldn't find hide nor hair of it

Lost an argument: his thinking packed more weight than mine

Lost as: 1. an outhouse in the fog 2. a turtle at the bottom of a barrel of

L

molasses 3. a goose in a snowstorm 4. an Easter egg 5. a nickel down a West Texas oil well [Some of the deepest wells in the world are in West Texas.]

Lost control: 1. come undone 2. went to pieces 3. come apart like the seams in a fat man's underwear 4. went hog wild

Lost everything: 1. got plucked cleaner than a Thanksgiving turkey or a Sunday chicken 2. lost everything but the rustle in her dress and the snap in her garters

Lost forever: got about as much chance of finding that as you do a gold watch in a border town lost and found

Lost his appetite: off his feed

Lost his baby teeth: shed his colt teeth

Lost his temper: flew off the handle, which is a country equivalent to went ballistic

Lost money: had Las Vegas surgery and got the scars on his bank account to prove it

Lost person: 1. had to run an ad in the paper for someone to come and get me 2. couldn't find him if you combed all of Texas with a fine-tooth comb 3. even his own bloodhound couldn't find him in a week of good weather 4. don't know where I am and got no mother to guide me home *See also Missing*

Lost unexpectedly: got snuck up on

Lot: 1. heap of, as in "He's in a heap of trouble." 2. a sight of, as in "I got a sight of work to do." 3. a posse of 4. beaucoup 5. a whole passel 6. big batch 7. whole slew 8. big litter 9. many a, as in "He's had many a girlfriend." 10. a bushel basket, a gunnysack, or a peck sack full, any of which would be a lot if you were talking about diamonds 11. a big chunk of 12. a plenty, as in "She scared me a plenty." 13. a good many 14. great mess of, as in "He caught a great mess of fish" 15. a full wagon load

Loud as: 1. a hungry calf 2. boot heels on a hardwood floor 3. fresh shod horses on a concrete sidewalk 4. a gin whistle *See also Noisy*

Loud enough to: 1. rattle the rafters 2. wake the dead 3. be heard in the next county 4. embarrass thunder 5. out-roar a buffalo 6. be heard a mile against the breeze 7. scare bulls off the bed ground 8. jar pecans off the tree

Loudmouth: his bark is enough, he don't need a bite

Louisiana: Texans pronounce it Luzy-ann-ah and they call a native a "coonass" *See also New Orleans Superdome*

Love: 1. may not make the world go round but it sure makes the trip more pleasant 2. is like measles, the later it comes the worse it is 3. is like lightning, it's as apt to strike an outhouse as a mansion 4. is like the morning dew, it's just as apt to be on a cow patty as on a cactus rose 5. conquers all things except poverty and a real bad toothache

Love, devout: grade A pasteurized passion

Love, true: is like a circle, it has no end

Lovelady (Houston County): home of the annual "Lovefest" every February The town got its name from Cyrus Lovelady, an early settler.]

Lover: got Romeo blood in his veins *See also Ladies man*

Lovers advice: never make love by the garden gate; love is blind but the neighbors ain't

Loving (Young County): the "g" is not silent and it is pronounced as it appears; named for legendary Texas trail driver Oliver Loving [In 1867, Loving died at Fort Sumner, New Mexico, after being wounded in an Indian attack. His friend and partner, Charles Goodnight, saw to it that Loving's request to be buried in Texas was accomplished. After completing the cattle drive, Goodnight had the remains exhumed and returned to Texas for proper burial. Writer Larry McMurtry used similar circumstances in his book *Lonesome Dove*.]

Low: 1. a scared rabbit couldn't go under it 2. a snake couldn't get under if he'd been run over by a truck

Low as: 1. a snake's navel in a deep wagon track 2. a mole's navel on diggin' day 3. a cockroach's belly

Low-down person: could wear a ten-gallon hat and walk under an armadillo

Lowake (Concho County): pronounced Low-ACHE-ee; the name came from J. L. Lowe and C. G. Schlake; home of some the best steaks in Texas

Loyalty: 1. be true to your own heart 2. stand by your man *See also Faithful*

Loyalty (school): When you are loyal to a particular university, it is said that your blood runs in the color of the school. For example, if you cut an Aggie's arm he would bleed maroon. If you are loyal to two different schools, your blood runs in multi-colors. If you cut MY arm, I would bleed red (Texas Tech) and orange (University of Texas).

Loyalty, gone: he broke his neck jumping off the band wagon

LPG: Liquefied Petroleum Gas

Lubbock (Lubbock County): pronounced LUB-uck, never Lou-bock of Lub-ick; named for Francis R. Lubbock, a governor of Texas and prominent Confederate veteran; the city, which is home to Texas Tech University, is also called the Hub of the South Plains

Lucerne: *See Alfalfa*

Lunging: *See Longe*

Luck: better to have a little luck than a lot of learning [Sid Richardson, famous Texas oilman, once said, "I'd rather be lucky than smart 'cause a lot of smart people ain't eatin' regular." One of H. L. Hunt's sons, Ray, said, "Given the choice between luck and intelligence, always take luck."] *See also Plan ahead*

Luck, turning: everything was going good but it's gettin' back to normal

Luckenbach (Gillespie County): pronounced LUKE'n-bock [When August Engel decided to apply for a post office to be located in his wife's store, he needed someone to run it. His sister agreed to do the job and suggested the town be named for her fiancé, Albert Luckenbach.]

Lucky: 1. if he bought a cemetery, he'd strike oil digging the first grave 2. if he fell into a cesspool, he'd come out smelling like a Tyler rose [Tyler, Texas, bills itself as the Rose Capital of the World.] 3. could draw a pat hand from a stacked deck 4. Lady Luck stays camped on his shirttail 5. could pitch pennies (or marbles) down the neck of a swinging beer bottle 6. could sit on a fence and the birds would feed him 7. relies on a rabbit's foot instead of horse sense 8. if you've got enough luck, you can get by with barbed wire for brains 9. got all his squirrels up one tree 10. always draws the best bull [Rodeo cowboys draw for the bull they ride. The best bull is the one that will buck wildly so the rider can earn more points.] *See also Fortunate*

Lucky, extremely: 1. could fall into septic tank and come out smelling like a Beaumont whore who bathed in Channel No. 5 2. if he fell face down in a fresh cow patty he'd find a diamond ring when he washed his face

Lueders (Jones County): pronounced LU-ders; named for Frederick Lueders, a soldier in the Texas Revolution

Lukewarm: 1. cowboy cool 2. touchin' hot 3. country cold [Country boys frequently buy a six-pack of beer that they expect to drink right away so

L

they don't bother to buy ice. If there's only one drinking, the last beer will be lukewarm (country cold) but still highly drinkable.]

Luling (Caldwell County): pronounced LEW-ling [Historians disagree on who the town was named for. The choices are: 1. a Judge Luling 2. the wife of the man who built the railroad to the site 3. a Chinese worker on the railroad.]

Lunch: dinner to a real Texan

Lye soap: a potent homemade soap made from lard and wood ashes or lye; excellent for washing kids, clothes, and chicken droppings off the porch. It'll also wash off your hide if used before properly cured. Made with 12 pounds of tallow, 10 gallons of water, 3 cans of lye. Sir in pot over open fire to keep from burning. When the lye is fully dissolved, let cool overnight then cut into cakes.

Lynch: 1. cow pasture justice 2. somebody get a rope 3. string 'em up 4. turn an oak into a courtroom 5. give a little necktie party 6. stretch some hemp 7. extra-legal hanging 8. decorate a cottonwood

Lynching: 1. stringing up party 2. Texas tree trimming 3. neck-tie party

M

Mabank (Kaufman County): pronounced MAY-bank; originally called Lawn City, which was a type of dress material sold in the local store. When the community received a post office the name was changed to Lawndale. When the railroad came to town, it literally missed Lawndale by a mile. G.W. Mason and Thomas Eubank, owners of a ranch on the rail line set aside a square mile of land for a town and called it Mabank, a combination of their two names.

Macaroni: dago

Macune (Augustine County): pronounced Ma-QUE'N; named for Charles W. Macune, president of the Farmer's Alliance

Mad: 1. on the prod 2. on the peck 3. on the warpath 4. plumb riled 5. got his dauber down 6. got his stinger out 7. lathered up 8. got a craw full of sand and fightin' tallow 9. her fangs are flashing and her nails are twitchin' 10. spittin' spite 11. all horns and rattles (horns from a bull, rattles from a rattlesnake) 12. boiling over with prejudice 13. walled his eyes and bowed his neck 14. got his dander up 15. got a burr under his saddle (or in his boot) 16. eating fire and spitting smoke 17. so mad he couldn't spit straight 18. her purr turned to a growl 19. hot as Hannah's hairbrush 20. had a fit and fell in it 21. fit to be tied 22. bent plumb out of shape 23. something got him cross legged *See also Angry*

Mad as: 1. a fighting cock 2. a rained on rooster or a wet hen 3. a bullfrog in a thumbtack factory 4. a bull in a red dye factory 5. a rattler in a roadrunner's sights, which refers to the fact that roadrunners will actually stalk, kill, and eat rattlesnakes 6. a red-eyed cow 7. a bear with two cubs and one sore teat 8. a teased snake 9. a wet hornet 10. fogged fire ants

Mad enough to: 1. eat bees 2. chomp a big chunk out of the head of an ax 3. put something on you Ajax won't take off 4. chew nails and spit rivets 5. kick a hog barefooted 6. eat the devil with the horns on 7. bite the head off a rattlesnake 8. bite a bullet plumb in two

Mad grandmother: she's rockin' and rantin'

Mad rush: wild stampede

Made a mistake: 1. misfired 2. wet in your own well 3. zigged when you should have zagged *See also Error; Screwed up*

M

Made love: went to the pea patch *See also Related, sort of*

Made money: got well, as in "He got well in the hog business."

Maguey: a Mexican four-strand rope made of fibers of the aloe (maguey) plant; often preferred by calf ropers, trick ropers, and dally men

Mah: possessive form of ah (I), as in "When ah fell down ah landed on mah new hat an ruint it."

Mail order catalog: 1. wish book 2. sheepherder's bible 3. outhouse bible

Mailbox: country clothesline pole [If the family was too poor to afford regular clothesline poles, they could simply run a line from the front porch to the mailbox.]

Main street: main drag

Maintain control: 1. keep the gate closed because a loose mare is always lookin' for a new pasture 2. hold the fort 3. keep the fence up [As Texan Lee Trevino said, "We all leak a little oil, but the good ones control the flow."]

Maintainer: road grader

Maintainer tour: to ride out and check all the stock, tanks, and windmills

Make a choice: 1. cut one out of the herd 2. pick one out of the litter 3. name your poison [This either means make a choice of drinks or that all your choices are bad.] 4. pick your pasture 5. draw a bead on one 6. choose your weapon 7. in a race, everybody has to pick his own horse 8. you can't sell your chickens and keep the feathers 9. you got to separate the preachers from the chicken thieves

Make believe: play like

Make it better: put a little spit on that apple

Make it easier: sugar the pill

Make it short: 1. cut a few corners off 2. trim the fat 3. knock some links out of the chain 4. short stroke it 5. take the slack out of it

Make love: 1. make whoopee 2. do the nasty thing

Make peace: 1. bury the hatchet 2. smoke the peace pipe 3. sign a treaty 4. let bygones be bygones

Make room: scooch over a little bit

Make the job easier: put the hay down closer to the ground so the goats can get at it

Make up your mind: 1. fish, cut bait, or swim to shore 2. spit or get off the pot

Makeshift: jakeleg

Makeup: war (or love) paint

Making progress: 1. getting the corn ground 2. getting the fields plowed 3. getting the calves branded 4. weedin' and seedin'

Making progress slowly: peckin' away at it

Malakoff (Henderson County): pronounced MAL-a-koff; originally known as Caney Creek [When the town applied for a post office, both names they suggested were taken so some postal official suggested Malakoff, which was a Russian town that gained prominence during the Crimean War.]

Malaria: swamp fever

Male: 1. old hairy legs 2. like a watermelon, you can't tell how good he is till you thump him 3. seldom as smart as his mother thinks or as dumb as his mother-in-law thinks

Male, angry: 1. fightin' with his hat [Country boys will occasionally get so angry they'll take off their hat and wave it in all sorts of motions. They might hit the ground, their knee, a fence, or even whoever they're talkin' to with the hat. In any event, when a country boy starts fightin' with his hat, he's gettin' real angry and about ready to start fightin' with fists or firearms.]

2. would make an untipped New York cab driver look like a Baptist choir boy 3. bent plumb out of shape 4. came on like a mad father with a loaded shotgun

Male, effeminate: got a little sugar in his blood

Male, evil: 1. prefers vice to advice 2. would chase off a widow woman's ducks 3. the one your mama warned you about 4. would steal the air out of a widow woman's tires 5. when he's alone he's in bad company 6. a trigger looking for a finger 7. nothing wrong with him that reincarnation (or cremation) wouldn't cure 8. when he dies, they'll print his obituary under Public Improvements 9. would make Clyde Barrow look like a Baptist choir boy *See Female, evil*

Male, fat: 1. a member of the sprawl of fame 2. well watered 3. his overcoat could be a tent for a Boy Scout troop *See also Fat man*

Male, jealous: *See Jealous man*

Male, jilted: when she took him by the hand he thought she was takin' him by the heart but she was only takin' him for a fool (which surely ought to be the name of a country song)

Male, large: 1. large enough to be a quartet 2. so big it takes a committee of five to look him over 3. people ask him "Where did you put Fay Ray?" 4. big as a John Deere gang plow 5. big enough to hunt a bear with a stick 6. last time I saw anything that big it had a bulldog on the hood [Mack trucks use a bulldog hood ornament on all their trucks.]

Male, large and mean: could be the bouncer in the devil's saloon

Male, lazy: *See Lazy man*

Male, liar: *See Liar, male*

Male, mean: *See Mean man*

Male, promiscuous: 1. like a real estate investor, he believes in gettin' lots while you're young 2. when the wages of sin are paid, he'll be charged time and a half 3. the only people who know he's married are the ones who were at the wedding 4. can find his name in the yellow pages under recreational facilities 5. has all the resistance of a willow tree in a hurricane

Male, short: when he stands up he looks like he's standing in a hole

Male, skinny: 1. can hear his bones rattle when he walks 2. could take a shower in a fountain pen 3. his muscles look like flea bites on a cane pole 4. could use him for a dipstick

Male, sorry: a man without principle so he don't draw much interest

Male, stupid: 1. the only time you'll find him in an institution of higher learning is as a test body in an anatomy class 2. some of the lights in his string are burnt out 3. his brain on the edge of a razor blade would look like a BB on an interstate highway 4. if brains were gasoline, he couldn't run an ant's motorcycle around a cherry pit 5. could mess up a two-car funeral 6. a forthright person—he's right about a fourth of the time 7. don't know the difference between working up steam and generating fog 8. could teach a rock to be dumb 9. used his food stamps to mail a letter 10. food for thought gives him indigestion 11. forgot his twin sister's birthday *See also Stupid man*

Male, ugly: 1. couldn't get a date if he was shipwrecked on an island full of lonely women 2. his mother only loves him on payday 3. could scare night into day 4. could sour milk in the carton 5. if he broke his leg, we'd have to shoot him 6. if ugly was a crime, he'd being doing life without parole 7. could kill waist-high cotton *See also Ugly man*

Malpals: badlands or rough country; from the Spanish *mal pais*, which means bad country

Man: 1. hombre 2. good old boy 3. redneck 4. ol' hairy legs

Man, good: *See Good person*

Man, old: 1. codger 2. old-timer 3. geezer 4. antique yahoo *See also Elderly; Old*

Man, tough: the toughest man west of any place east

Man killer: cowboy's term for a mean, ornery horse that strikes out at everybody

Manageable: it's been whittled down to size

Management, poor: selling his hogs to buy hog feed

Manager, good: 1. nobody circles the wagons better 2. could show the devil how to manage hell

Manchaca (Travis County): pronounced MAN-shack, believe it or not; the fire department and the post office spell the name Manchaca but the school spells it Menchaca. Either way, the pronunciation is the same.

Manila: cultivated rope material

Manipulative: can play you like a $50 fiddle

Manners: eatin' regulations

Manners, good: can yawn with his mouth closed

Manners, poor: 1. will wait on you like one hog waits on another 2. invented the boardinghouse reach, the practice of just reaching for what you want rather than having it passed to you 3. would sop biscuits and slurp coffee out of a saucer at a White House breakfast 4. would pass gas when he was playing the front end of a horse costume

Mano a toro: man against the bull, as in bull riding

Manor (Travis County): pronounced MAIN-er; named for postmaster James Manor

Mantle: fireboard

Manvel (Brazoria County): pronounced MAN-vul; originally called Pomona, the name was changed to honor the president of the Atchison, Topeka and Santa Fe Railroad

Many: 1. more than Carter had oats (or liver pills) 2. thick as fiddlers in hell 3. thick as ticks on a hound dog 4. thick as flies in a garbage dump *See also Lot*

Marathon (Brewster County): pronounced quickly as Mara-thun, not Mara-thon like the race [That means you could run a mara-thon in Mara-thun. Supposedly, the name came from a railroad surveyor who commented that the area reminded him of Marathon, Greece.]

Marble Falls (Burnet County): named for nearby falls [The town was founded by Adam Rankin Johnson, a Texas Confederate hero blinded during the war. He never let his disability slow him down and founded the town after returning to Texas. Johnson was so active in building the town it was occasionally called "Blind Man's Town." Johnson later dictated his memories of Confederate service, and they were published under the title *Partisan Rangers of the Confederate States Army.*]

Mare: female horse over three years old

Marfa (Presidio County): pronounced MAR-fa [Please note, this town is not Martha. According to legend, the name is from *Brothers Karamazov*, a novel by Feodor Dostoevski, which a railroad executive's wife was reading when the train reached the area. The town is home of the famous Marfa Lights, a phenomenon that defies explanation.]

Marital advice for her: 1. it is better to buy a good horse than to marry a man 'cause at least you know the horse won't turn into a jackass 2. a husband is like a fire in a cook stove, he goes out if unattended 3. wear shows where the wife stands and the husband sits 4. marry an ugly man; he won't leave you since he can't do any better

Marital advice for him: 1. marry an ugly woman; she'll leave you but you won't mind much 2. marry a woman with brains enough for two and you'll come out about even 3. never try to drown your troubles if she can swim 4. the husband who treats his wife like a thoroughbred will find she don't turn into a nag 5. a wife is like a baseball umpire, she don't think you're safe when you're out 6. a husband controls his wife like a barometer controls the weather 7. a poor man who marries a rich woman gets a boss instead of a wife *See also Three R's of marriage*

Mark out (rodeo): *See Bareback riding*

Marked: 1. branded 2. ear marked

Marked cards: 1. doped cards 2. branded cards 3. cards that can be read from either side

Marksman: 1. a meat gitter 2. could shoot a yellow jacket off a cactus at 500 yards 3. could shoot the eye out of a gnat at 100 paces 4. could shoot a chigger off a thistle *See also Aim, good*

Marksman, poor: couldn't hit the side of a outhouse if he fired from inside

Marksmanship: triggernometry

Marquez (Leon County): pronounced MARK-a; named for Maria de la Marquez on whose land the town was founded

Marriage: 1. the difference between painting the town and the back porch 2. for better or worse means for good 3. a life sentence that can be suspended by bad behavior 4. like taking a hot bath, once you get used to it, it ain't so hot 5. is like farming, you have to start over again every morning if you want to be successful 6. the leading cause of divorce 7. stops your circulation faster than a tourniquet on a snakebite 8. is

like eating with chopsticks, it looks easy till you try it

Marriage, bad: they were married by a judge but should have held out for a jury

Marriage, perfect: a deaf man and a blind woman

Marriage that lasts: they've been married so long they're on their third bottle of Tabasco sauce [This would be more than twenty years since it takes most people about ten years to use one bottle.]

Married: 1. got hitched 2. trottin' in a double harness 3. welded into a neck harness 4. necked in harness 5. committed matrimony with 6. double hitched 7. yoked up with 8. lassoed 9. holy bedlock

Married foolishly: picked his wife by the glow of a neon light, which implies he was drunk at the time

Married man: 1. private in the honey do army, which means his wife is always saying honey do this or honey do that 2. carryin' her brand 3. roped to a heifer 4. he's broke for domestic work 5. he belled the mare 6. he dropped a rope on her 7. he may not be the best informed, but he is the most informed

Married often: been married so many times she has rice scars

Married up in class: out-married himself

Married well: didn't pick up a crooked stick, which is usually said of a man who marries a good woman

Married woman: 1. double ringed, meaning she has an engagement ring and a wedding ring 2. carrying his brand 3. finally got him in her web 4. chased him till she caught her

Martingale: a strap, usually 32 inches long, that attaches to the saddle to prevent a horse from rearing up his head; also called a breast collar

Martini, Texas style: a regular martini with a pickled black-eyed pea in place of the olive [For an alternative, use the olive but stuff it with a japaleno pepper instead of pimento.]

Mason Dixon Line: dividing line between you'se guys and y'all

Mass confusion: 1. the blind leading the blind 2. like a herd of mules in a hailstorm 3. three lawyers and one case 4. like a sudden shower on an eat-off-the-ground church social, no one knows whether to stay dry or save the food 5. fifteen roofers and only one pickup

Massive: *See Large*

Match, poor: 1. go together like mustard and pancakes 2. go together like scotch and Dr Pepper

Matches: Oklahoma air freshener

Maternity blouse: 1. hatching jacket 2. a slip cover

Mathematician, poor: 1. to him, it's four of one and half a dozen of the other 2. he counts real good till he runs out of fingers and toes

Mattress: redneck ironing board [This refers to putting clothes between mattresses to "smooth" out the wrinkles.]

Maverick: 1. motherless, unbranded calf 2. person prone to doing other than the accepted norm

Maverick (Runnels County): pronounced MAV-rick; named for the Samuel Augustus Maverick, a true Texas legend

Maverick Latin: Maury Maverick, descendant of Sam Maverick, created his own Latin with a favorite saying: *Illigitimi non carborundun* which he translated to mean, "Don't let the bastards grind you down."

Mayday situation: emergency

Maypearl (Ellis County): The name Pearl City was rejected so the locals changed it to Maypearl in honor of Mary Pearl Trammel, the wife of an engineer for the International Great Northern Railroad.

McAllen (Hidalgo County): pronounced almost as two words, Mac-Allan; never say it fast as Micallen

McLean (Gray County): pronounced Mc-CLAIN

McLeod (Cass County): pronounced Mc-CLOUD

Meal, skimpy: as near to nothing as they could find (the kind served in prison)

Meal hound: an Aggie who takes food from a table other than his own

Mean: 1. a bucker and a snorter, referring to a mean rodeo bucking horse 2. a bad Indian 3. an ornery old cuss 4. a scalp hunter 5. two shades meaner than the devil hisself 6. a good man not to mess with 7. a fire eater 8. has a good reputation for cussidness 9. a bad hombre 10. keeps his stinger out all the way 11. cut his teeth on a gun barrel 12. he don't wear a belt gun for ballast 13. if he says giddyup, you better go 14. he's proof there are more horse's butts than there are horses 15. he'll get on you like ugly on an ape 16. his mother had to feed him with a slingshot 17. would just as soon shoot you as look at you *See also Evil person, Vicious; Wicked*

Mean and cunning: mean enough to suck eggs out of a widow woman's basket and cunning enough to hide the shells on a neighbor's porch

Mean and stupid: would take a knife to a gunfight

Mean as: 1. a bulldog on a gunpowder diet 2. a curly wolf 3. an old range cow 4. hell with the hide off 5. a cornered cottonmouth 6. a caged cougar 7. a rodeo bull 8. a pit bull dog 9. eight acres of snakes 10. a mule on a sawdust diet 11. a two-stingered yellow jacket 12. a rattlesnake with a headache 13. an alligator with a gum -boil 14. a mama wasp with a sore stinger

Mean child: so mean, his mama gives him a bath by carrying him down to the creek and beating him on a rock

Mean man: 1. would pitch his bath water on a widow woman's kindling 2. can raise more hell than an alligator in a drained swamp 3. if he went deaf he wouldn't tell his barber 4. was baptized in vinegar 5. would put a rattlesnake in your pocket and ask you for a match 6. would steal the light bulb from the porch lamp at an orphanage 7. would take the manure away from a tumble bug and send him on the wrong road home 8. so low down you couldn't put a rug under him 9. would have to look up to see hell 10. makes a hornet look cuddly 11. if he was baptized all the fish in the creek would die [When Sam Houston, former governor of Tennessee and Texas, was baptized he was told that all his sins had been washed away. He replied, "Lord help the fishes down below."]

Mean woman: 1. if she died, everyone would rest in peace 2. an expert at chunkin' skillets 3. a hurricane with two eyes 4. even whips her husband while he's doing the dishes 5. would send a get well card to a hypochondriac 6. the cake she baked for Santa Claus was made with Ex-Lax 7. makes a junkyard dog look like a miniature poodle in a New York dog show 8. keeps hot water on tap to scald neighborhood dogs with

Meander: traipse

Meaning, hidden: there's more to that than meets the eye

Meaningless: 1. hogwash 2. buffalo chips 3. horse (or frog) feathers 4. a mare's nest 5. that and half a buck will get you a cup of coffee 6. don't amount to any more than what the little bird left on top of the flag pole

Meaningless as: 1. warts on a hog's belly 2. a striptease to a blind man 3. eye shadow on an eagle 4. a silk nightgown on a scarecrow 5. socks to a grub worm 6. pantyhose to a pig

Meanness: 1. cussidness 2. orneriness 3. double cussidness

 Meat: bull neck

Measurement, approximate: use appropriate number of ax handles as in: "He's two ax handles wide" or "He stands four ax handles high" [As a rule of thumb an ax handle measures about thirty inches.]

Meat, rare: *See Rare meat*

Mecate: horsehair rope, usually pronounced "McCartney" or "McCarty"

Mechanic, poor: 1. treats your car with sunshine, which means he leaves it parked outside for several hours hoping the problem will go away 2. he's called "waitin' for parts" because that's all he ever seems to be doing

Mechanical hackamore: a bosal with cheek pieces for leverage

Medical book: doctor book

Medicine, poor: so bad I was sick for three weeks after I got well

Medicine, quick acting: goes through you like corn through a goose

Meet a challenge: take the bull by the tail and face the situation

Medina (Bandera County): pronounced Ma-DEAN-a.

Meeting: 1. powwow 2. prayer session 3. get-together 4. a dog and pony show

Meeting, disastrous: had a dog and pony show but the dog wet everywhere and the pony didn't know any tricks

Meeting over: 1. court's adjourned 2. that's the rodeo (or ball game)

Melts: 1. like a chocolate Easter bunny on a pickup dashboard 2. like a snowball on the devil's prong

Memorial service: a send-off service

M

Memory, poor: 1. for the life of me, I can't recall it 2. his recall needs an overhaul 3. could hide his own Easter eggs 4. can't remember names, but he always forgets faces 5. can't even remember the Alamo 6. can't even remember the first girl he kissed 7. memory is shorter than a chigger's eyebrow

Memphis (Hall County): pronounced MEM-fuss [According to popular legend, several names were rejected by postal authorities. Then a Rev. Brice happened to visit Austin where, by chance, he saw a letter that had been accidentally addressed to Memphis, Texas, instead of Tennessee. The letter was marked "no such place" and the preacher knew they had a name that would be accepted.]

Men: 1. menfolk 2. most men are like barbed wire; they have their good points *See also Male*

Menard (Menard County): pronounced Ma-NARD; originally called Menardville but the name was changed when Menard County was organized and Menard was selected as the county seat

Menopause: minner-paws

Mentone (Loving County): pronounced MEN-tone; originally called Ramsey, the new name was suggested by a French surveyor who was from Mentone, France

Mercedes (Hidalgo County): pronounced Mur-SAY-diz [Local residents were plagued by raids from bandits crossing the Rio Grande. Hoping to inspire Mexican president Porfirio Diaz to use his influence to stop the plundering, they named the town for his wife, Mercedes. It was a good idea but it didn't work and the raids continued.]

Mercurochrome: monkey blood

Mercury: quicksilver

Mercy: *See At his mercy*

Meringue: calf slobber

Merry-go-round: flying jenny

Mesquite: *Prosopis juliflora,* a small, short-trunk tree with killer thorns that grows prolifically in South and West Texas. Texans usually pronounce it Ma-skeet or Mess-keet. The bean pods make excellent feed for cattle and horses, especially in areas where grass and other feed is scarce. Indians used the pods to make a mildly alcoholic drink. The thorns were a particular problem to cowboys trying to round up cattle. Although small, the mesquite trees are almost impossible to get rid of without dynamite.

Mesquite (Dallas County): pronounced like the tree; named after Mesquite Creek

Mesquite, false: *See Huajillo*

Mesquite grass: a rich, native grass in the western part of Texas that gets its name because it often grows in proximity to mesquite trees

Mess: 1. fine kettle of fish 2. the works are balled up 3. a real sow's nest

Mess with: tinker with

Messed up: boogered up

Meticulous: fussy as an old hen makin' her nest [For some reason chickens need to have everything just right before they'll do their laying.]

Metroplex: Dallas/Fort Worth area, which, because of the number of people, is also called Ant Bed

Mexia (Limestone County): the name of this small town in central Texas is usually pronounced Ma-hay-ya, although some of the old-timers still say Ma-hair [Mexia was made famous by the old joke about the two traveling salesmen who were arguing over how to pronounce the name of the town. They decided to settle the argument by asking a local citizen so they stopped at the first place they came to and went inside. A young lady approached and asked if she could help. "Can you us tell how to pronounce the name of this place?" asked one of the men. "Sure," she replied, "it's Dairy Queen." The town is named for the Mexia family since the town site is on land in the family's original land grant.]

Mexican bit: a bit that uses a curb-ring rather than a curb-chain

Mexican iron: *See Rawhide*

Mexican saddle: a heavy saddle with a high cantle and bow and a wide-base, flat topped saddle horn

Mexican Standard Time: *See Punctuality, lacking*

Mexico: 1. Old Mexico 2. land of mañana

Miami (Roberts County): usually pronounced like that other Miami in Flar-dah (Florida) but some old-timers say My-AM-ah

Mico (Medina County): pronounced MIKE-oh, not Mick-oh; name is an acronym for Medina Irrigation Company

Middle: 1. smack dab in the heart 2. down the chute 3. the heart

Middle age: 1. the age when you'd rather skip a night at the honky-tonk than have to get over it the next day 2. when a narrow waist and a broad mind swap places 3. when you lose more hair in the shower than you do in the barber's chair 4. when your actions creak louder than words 5. when your favorite night spot is on the couch in front of the television 6. when you only chase girls who are going downhill 7. for a woman, middle age is when men stop pinching and the girdle starts

Middle buster: a walk behind, double sided plow pulled by four mules; creates rows for planting crops such as cotton

Middle of the road: gunfighter's sidewalk [It's been said gunfighters walked the center of the street so they could watch both sides of town easier.]

Midkiff (Upton County): pronounced quickly as MID-cuf; named for founder John Rufus Midkiff, a Confederate veteran and stockman

Midland (Midland County): the "d" is frequently dropped for Mid-lan [In Texas, whenever you ask someone how they are, they may respond "fair to middlin'." Out in West Texas they may say, "fair to middlin' but not all the way to Odessa." Midland got its name because it is about midway between Fort Worth and El Paso. It's also known as Tall City since its tall buildings offer a strong contrast to the surrounding flat land.]

Midlothian (Ellis County): pronounced Mid-LOW-the-an; originally called Hawkin's Springs [Most historians seem to agree the new name was taken from a site in Scotland and was suggested by a Scottish engineer working for the railroad.]

Might: liable to, as in "I'm liable to do just that."

Might as well: we can't dance, it's too wet to plow, the kids are fed, the pigs are bred, and I never could sing anyway

Miles: the "s" is frequently dropped in Texas, as in "It's 14 mile to town."

Milford (Ellis County): pronounced Mil-ferd; home of about 700 friendly people and 3 or 4 old sore-heads, named by one of the founders for a town near Boston he had read about

Military walk: running from Sbisa Hall to the Rudder Tower Auditorium complex on the Texas A&M campus

Milk: 1. udder delight 2. cow

Milk, canned: a favorite among cowboys, milk in a can wouldn't sour quickly like fresh milk. Some unknown poet summed up the feelings of many cowboys about canned milk with this little poem: Carnation Milk, best in the land; comes to you in a little red can. No tits to pull, no hay to pitch; just punch a hole in the son of a bitch.

A̲M̲ **Milk, chocolate:** mud

Milk, whole: sweet milk

Milk, curdled: clabber

Milk, turning: blinky

Milk a cow: 1. pump a cow 2. shake hands with some teats 3. drain a cow

Milk cow, poor: a coffee cow, which is one that barely gives enough milk to put in the coffee

Milking: 1. burglarizing a cow 2. draining the spigots 3. flushin' a cow

Milking pen: the pen where cows are gathered for milking

Mill worker: lint dodger

Millionaire (oilman): oillionaire

Mind: 1. thinker 2. head filler [A mind is like a parachute, it only works when it's open.]

Mind your own business: 1. tend to your own knitting (or bees) 2. saddle your own horse 3. mend your own windmill 4. use your eyes to look and your sense not to see 5. every man has to skin his own skunk 6. cut your own firewood 7. mend your own fences 8. chew your own tobacco 9. hoe your own weeds 10. stay on your own range 11. turn your tongue in your own coffee 12. if it don't bother you, don't bother it

Mineola (Wood County): pronounced Mini OH-la, which rhymes with payola [There are two possibilities for the origin of the name: 1. Major Ira H. Evans, a railroad official, derived the name from his daughter, Ola, and a friend Minnie Patten 2. Major Rusk, a railroad surveyor, combined his daughter's name with Minnie Patten]

Minnow, poor: a top water minnow, which is a minnow that, once on a fishing hook, swims around the top of the water instead of going deep where the fish are

Miracle: water-walking act [Remember, believe in miracles but don't bet on them.]

Mirando City (Webb County): pronounced Me-RON-do City; named for Mirando Valley

Mirror: looking glass

Misbehaving: acting up or acting ugly

Mischievous person: 1. rounder 2. maverick

Miser: 1. wouldn't loan you a nickel unless the Lord and all the disciples countersigned the note 2. the way to his heart is through your pocketbook 3. so tight he squeaks when he walks 4. still got half of his third grade allowance 5. got four cents out of every nickel he ever made 6. skinflint 7. tightwad 8. wouldn't pay a nickel to see a pissant eat a bale of hay 9. squeezes a dollar until the eagle screams 10. chokes a dollar until George Washington turns blue 11. when company pulls into the driveway, he makes everyone in the family grab a toothpick so it'll look like they just finished dinner 12. mighty tough to live with but he's gonna make a great ancestor *See also Cheapskate; Frugal; Stingy*

Miserable: 1. got misery up to my armpits (or eyeballs) 2. got so much misery, if I was triplets all three of us would be miserable 3. in a world of manure

Misguided: you're in the up elevator but it's on the *Titanic*

Misled: 1. he wet in my boots and swore it was raining 2. he led me down a cold trail

Miss meal colic: term to describe the condition of a thin cow that has not been getting her fair share of the groceries

Missed: 1. off the mark 2. by a country mile 3. a miss by an inch is as good as a mile

Missing: 1. off the home range 2. off the reservation 3. came up absent 4. can't find hide nor hair of him *See also Lost*

Mistake, serious: opened up the door for the machete [This is a reference to the saying "he got his head chopped off," which refers to an employee who got fired. If you make a mistake serious enough to open the door for the machete, you are in danger of being fired if you can't blame someone else.]

Mistaken: 1. roped the wrong steer 2. hit on an empty chamber 3. barking up the wrong tree 4. roping the wrong calf 5. puttin' your saddle on the wrong horse 6. pulled the wrong sow's ear 7. milked the wrong cow 8. got the wrong dog by the tail 9. it's the stallion that picks the mare, not the other way around 10. your calf ain't sucking the right cow 11. doin' a two-step and the band's playing a waltz *See also Error*

Misunderstood: guess I opened the hymnal to the wrong page

Mixed emotions: when your daughter comes home from the prom carrying a Bible—from the Gideons [Dwight Paddlefoot Sloan, a star football player with the University of Arkansas in the 1930s, may have said it best. When Arkansas decided to leave the Southwest Conference and join the Southeast Conference, Sloan, like a lot of Arkansas fans, had mixed emotions. "It's like your mother-in-law driving off a cliff," he said, "in your Cadillac."]

Mixed train: one with both passenger cars and freight cars

Moans: like the enchanted rock [Between Fredericksburg and Llano there is a large boulder that moans whenever the weather changes; it has "enchanted" people for generations.]

Mobeetie (Wheeler County): pronounced Mo-BEAT-ee which is supposed to be Indian for sweet water

Mobil home: 1. trailer house 2. tornado magnet

Mockingbird: state bird of Texas [These birds are notorious for protecting their nests and will not hesitate to attack man or beast. Their have been several instances where mailmen were forced to suspend delivering the mail because they couldn't get to the front door without being attacked.]

Modest: 1. makes her husband wear a blindfold when they shower together 2. can't even tell the naked truth or look at things with a naked eye 3. won't walk over grates in the sidewalk 'cause she don't know who might be down there 4. wouldn't wear patent leather shoes 'cause she's afraid of what might be seen in the reflection

Mohair: Angora goat hair

Molars: bridle teeth

Molasses (ma-lass-is): sometimes called just lasses *See Sorghum; Blackstrap*

Moment: heartbeat

Monahans (Ward County): pronounced MON-a-hans; folks in the surrounding area frequently refer to it as "Money Hans"; originally called Monahan's Well

Money: 1. wampum 2. geetus 3. chunk-a-change 4. dinero 5. the only known cure for poverty 6. like a drunk, the tighter it gets, the more it talks 7. mother's milk of politics [H. L. Hunt said, "Money is nothing. It is just something to make bookkeeping more convenient." Clint Murchison Jr. said, "Money is a lot like manure. If you pile it up in one place it stinks like hell. But if you spread it around it does some good."]

Money, small amount: 1. chicken feed 2. scalp money 3. egg money

Monkey blood: mercurochrome

Monkey rum: *See Sorghum*

Monkey Ward cowboy: a cowboy wannabe decked out in Western clothes purchased from a department store such as Montgomery Ward, which cowboys called "Monkey Ward."

Monogamy: *See Bigamy*

Montague (Montague County): county and town are pronounced Mon-taig, which rhymes with The Hague in the Netherlands; named for Daniel Montague, who donated land for the town

Montalba (Anderson County): pronounced almost like two words, Mont alba; named by founder William J. Hamlett, supposedly for the white on nearby mountains

Montgomery Ward: Monkey Ward

Moocher: 1. will always find him on the dock when someone else's ship comes in 2. always got a mouthful of grin and a handful of thank you [This means he's always borrowing something (lawnmower, chainsaw, etc.) but never offers to pay, and if he happens to bring it back, it won't be clean and may not be running.]

Moon, decreasing: dark of the moon

Moon, full: 1. buttermilk moon 2. full-grown moon 3. Indian moon, from the fact that Indians often attacked during periods of full moon

Moon, increasing: light of the moon

Moonshine: 1. swamp dew 2. homemade lightning 3. bottled lightning 4. Tennessee tea 5. quart juice 6. worm medicine [from the belief that folks who drink a lot of moonshine never have worms. Although this is just a theory, there is a test to check authenticity. Get two glasses and fill one with water and one with moonshine, then drop a live worm into each glass. You will observe that the worm in the water lives and the worm in the moonshine dies leading to the natural conclusion that moonshine is, in fact, worm medicine.]

Moonshine, good: can taste the feet of the farm hand that hoed the corn it was made from

Moonshine, poor: panther spit

Moonshine, strong: goes four or five fights per jug

Moonshiny: old term used to indicate a bright, moonlit night

Moral: nosebag

Morals, high: wouldn't say crap if he had a mouth full of it

Morals, poor: *See Immoral*

Morning: 1. sunup 2. daybreak

Moscow (Polk County): pronounced Moss-cow, not Moss-co [The original request was for the name Greenville, which was rejected. It is assumed the name came from the Russian city.]

Mosquito: 1. skeeter 2. nail ripper [The best description is that a mosquito is pure distilled essence of absolute aggravation that, with a hypodermic-like nose, can make you slap a knot on your own head with your class ring tryin' to kill him. It has been wisely speculated that life in Texas would be a little better if only Noah had swatted a couple of mosquitoes while he was on the ark.]

Mosquito, large: 1. could stand flat footed on the ground and kiss a rooster on the beak 2. half a dozen of 'em could pull a man off a horse 3. so big we catch 'em in mousetraps 4. got an ice pick for a nose that can drill through a rawhide boot 5. so large in Texas that a fisherman swears he killed one and found three wood ticks on the body 6. we don't shoot skeet, we shoot skeeters [Some Texas mosquitoes get as big as a duck, but most rarely get larger than a sparrow.] *See also Get to work*

Mossy: renegade steer

Most: the lion's share

Motel: public bunkhouse

Mother: if mama ain't happy, ain't nobody happy

Mother, good: like an old quilt, she keeps the kids warm but doesn't smother them

Mother, protective: 1. sewed name tags in the clothes her son wore when he left for the army 2. has the longest apron strings in the county, which implies that her kids have trouble gettin' untied

Mother-in-law, lazy: if it wasn't for giving directions she wouldn't get any exercise

Mother-up: said when a cow reclaims her calf after a drive

Motherless: dogie

Motherly patience: like toothpaste in a tube, it is never quite all gone

Motionless: 1. laid there like a sack of flour (or feed) 2. sat still as a frozen anvil

Motivate: spur the horse [A horse that has been spurred is motivated to run.]

Motivational speech: chalk talk [This is derived from sports coaches using chalk and a blackboard to explain how plays are supposed to work.]

Motorcycle: 1. murdercycle 2. suicycle

Motorcycle, Japanese: rice burner to a Harley owner

Mount up: 1. fork your pony 2. strike leather 3. warm your leather

Mountain laurel: calico bush

Mouse: cheese burner

Mouth: a hole under your nose where the firewater goes in and the cuss words come out

Mouth, dry: 1. feel like the Russian army marched through my mouth in their sock feet 2. couldn't raise enough spit to repair anything, which is a reference to making repairs with spit and baling wire

Mouth, female: A famous Texan named Big Foot Wallace once said that a certain young lady had a mouth that looked like a gash cut in a juicy ripe peach.

Mouth, large: 1. bucket mouth 2. gopher trap 3. big enough to hold an andiron 4. can sing a duet by himself 5. mouth looks like a torn pocket 6. gets lipstick on her ears when she smiles 7. big as a grader blade 8. the bigger the mouth, the better it looks closed

Mouthful: 1. beak full 2. dipper full 3. double cheek full 4. looks like he swallowed a pair of lovebirds 5. looks like he threw up his heart

Move: 1. change range (or pastures, camps) 2. got a new bed ground

Move it: get it out from under foot

Moved, slightly: oozed it up

Moves a lot: 1. got tumbleweed blood in his veins 2. moved so much when I was a kid every time we started packing, the chickens would lay down and stick up their feet to be tied [This came from the Depression days when families moved often. Usually, country folks had chickens, and they would load them on the truck with their feet tied.]

Moves crazy: 1. like a full balloon with the air running out 2. like a knuckleball 3. like a straw in a whirlwind 4. like a loco'd calf 5. like a pup looking for a place to lay down (or squat)

Moves slow: 1. as a snail climbing a greased pole 2. would have to speed up to stop 3. about as fast as the Great

Northern glacier 4. as a deadbeat father writing out a child support check 5. pigeons could roost on his hat 6. couldn't catch a fever

Movie: 1. picture show 2. movin' pictures

Movie, frightening: would make the hair on a mink stole stand on end

Movie, sad: *See Sad movie*

Movie, Western: horse opera

Moving fast: ginnin', as in "He was really ginnin' when the sheriff got after him."

Mow the lawn: cut the grass

Mrs: 1. missus 2. ma'am 3. *señora*, in Spanish

Much: a heap sight

Much less: let alone, as in "I can't afford the horse, let alone the feed."

Muck out: clean a horse's stall

Mud hole: 1. loblolly 2. gourd hole

Mud hop: clerk in a railroad

Mud sleeping sickness: a disease that strikes pigs that spend a lot of time in the mud. A mud ball forms on a pig's tail and then grows as he moves around. Eventually, the ball gets so heavy it causes the pig's skin to draw up so tight he can't close his eyes and he dies from lack of sleep.

Muddy enough: 1. to bog a kitten 2. to bog a bird's shadow 3. to bog a horse all the way to the rider's hat 4. to track a coon down the middle of the creek

Muddy road: heavy road

Mudville (Brazos County): pronounced MUD-vul; named after the mud common in the floodplain of the Brazos River

Muenster (Cooke County): pronounced MUN-ster, like the television program [Local settlers were from the Westphalia region of Europe and requested that name for their community, but it was already taken. The residents settled for Muenster, the capital of Westphalia.]

Mule, blue nose: a mule with a black coat rather than the customary brown, gray, or mottled; despite the name, the nose is black

Mule, typey: sound mule without harness marks or other imperfections

Mule, untrained: shavetail, which is also used for a rowdy child

Mule ears: leather straps attached to boot uppers that make the boots easier to pull on

Mule sense: approach a mule the way a porcupine makes love, slow and careful

Muleplex: *See Muleshoe*

Muleshoe (Bailey County): named for the nearby Muleshoe Ranch [Muleshoe is home of a world famous mule statue. However, if you want to get a picture of it, don't go on the weekend when the high school students graduate. Seems the mule has been stolen so many times, the town leaders remove it for that one weekend.]

Muley cow: a cow that naturally has no horns as opposed to one whose horns have been removed

Mumbly-peg: a country game played with a knife, usually outdoors unless it's raining. The first player throws the knife in some fancy way, and if it sticks, the other player must throw the knife in the same manner. The game continues until one of the players thinks of something better to do.

Munday (Knox County): pronounced MUN-dee; originally called Maud but was renamed to honor R. P. Munday, the local postmaster

Munger (Limestone County): pronounced MUNG-er; named for local farmer Henry Martin Munger

Murchison (Henderson County): pronounced MURR-ka-sun;

named for Confederate recruiting officer T. F. Murchison

Music lover: 1. if he hears a pretty girl singing in the bathtub, he puts his ear to the keyhole 2. she applauds when her husband comes home singing at 4:00 a.m. 3. for women, the music they love best is when some other woman plays second fiddle

Music, lively: 1. foot stompin' music 2. music that is connected to your boots

Music, slow: buckle polishing music

Musician, good: 1. can hit every note except the ones in the bank 2. picks on golden strings 3. can make a washtub and a dinner bell sound like a symphony orchestra 4. can play both kinds of music, country and western

Musician, poor: 1. shade tree musician 2. can't take notes, much less play them 3. better practice dodging beer bottles before he tries to play in a Texas honky-tonk 4. the proper pitch for his guitar would be out the window

Mustang: stray horse, usually wild; descendants of the ones that were brought over by the Spanish

Mustang cattle: Texas term for wild, unbranded cattle

Mustang grape: a small red grape that grows wild in some parts of Texas

A&M Mustard: baby

Mustard plaster: fly blister [In the old days, a mustard plaster made the room smell like you'd been raising goats inside the house. When pulled off, the plaster sounded like a cat being tore into.]

A&M Muster: gathering of all former Texas A&M students wherever they may be; held on April 21, which is also San Jacinto Day

My turf: my stompin' ground

My turn: 1. they're playin' my tune 2. they dialed my number 3. it's my turn in the barrel

Mysterious as: a neighbor who keeps the shades drawn shut all the time

N

N: 1. and [Texans rarely take time to say "and." Generally the "a" and the "d' are discarded and only the "n" is left, as in "We're gonna have coon 'n collards for supper."] 2. than [Texans also frequently use "n" in place of than, as in "It was hotter'n hell today."]

N.F.R.: *See National Finals Rodeo*

Nacogdoches (Nacogdoches County): pronounced KNACK-a-DOE-chez; a true Texan will know how to spell this name correctly

Nag: a sorry, often wore out horse

Nail, rusty: could kill a fence post

Naïve: 1. he could be held up through the mail 2. she'd play "Go Fish" with a mind reader

Naked: 1. nekkid [No one in Texas is naked or nude, they are nekkid or even buck nekkid.] 2. runnin' around in the altogether 3. polishing or sunnin' his birthday suit 4. didn't have on enough clothes to pad a crutch 5. ain't got on so much as a stitch 6. without a shuck on 7. got nothing on but the radio (or television) 8. bare behinded 9. stitchless

Naked as: 1. a scalded hog, referring to the process of slaughtering hogs where they are boiled, then all the hair is scraped off 2. a plucked chicken 3. a jaybird 4. a worm

Naked possessor: Texas term for someone who occupied land without title but also without dispute

Naked woman: 1. a doubt remover 2. an imagination killer

Name: handle

Nap: 1. siesta 2. checking my eyelids for leaks

A&M Napping: horizontal engineering

Narrow as: a branding chute (or loading chute)

Narrow escape: 1. by the skin of my teeth 2. barely got out with my hide intact *See also Close Call*

Narrow-minded: 1. wears a blind bridle 2. so narrow-minded his ears rub together [Narrow-minded people are like long neck beer bottles, the less they have in them the more noise it makes coming out.]

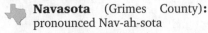 **National Finals Rodeo** (NFR): the "Super Bowl" of rodeos. The NFR is officially sponsored and conducted by the Professional Rodeo Cowboys Association and pits the top fifteen money winners in every event against each other. The winners are crowned "world champion." The highest prize is World Champion All-Around Cowboy. Any NFR winner is considered a "cowboy's cowboy." The first NFR was held in Dallas, Texas, in 1959. It later moved to Los Angeles and then to Oklahoma City. It is currently held each December in Las Vegas.

Native: native-born to a Texan

Natural ability: *See Ability, natural*

Natural as: 1. a duck in water 2. a pig in slop 3. flies on a watermelon rind

Nature calling: 1. if I don't find a sandbox soon I'm gonna have a flooded pocket 2. my back teeth are floating 3. I'm beginning to see yellow

Navajo blanket: a 30" x 60" woven wool saddle blanket

Navasota (Grimes County): pronounced Nav-ah-sota

Navel: where the Yankee shot you, which is how Texas mothers explain the navel to inquisitive children

Navelitis: a disease cased by an almost constant pressure of the navel on the edge of a bar; generally affects only professional drunks and jilted cowboys

Navy man: anchor cranker [A lot of country boys eventually find themselves in the navy, perhaps because many of them grow up without ever seeing much water at any one time.] *See also Submarine crewman*

Near: *See Close*

Near miss: 1. the bullet went by close enough to raise a blister 2. the car went by so close I could smell the driver's breath

Near side: the left side of a horse or a team of animals [When pulling a coach, it was customary for passengers to enter through the near side.] *See also Off side*

Nearby: *See Lives Close*

Nearly: 1. nearbout, as in "It's nearbout ten miles to town." 2. nigh, as in "He ain't got nigh as much cash since he went to Las Vegas."

Nearsighted: 1. could lose a bass fiddle in a phone booth 2. mistook the shampoo for the mouthwash and almost gargled to death 3. can't tell toothpaste from Preparation H

Necessary: 1. you don't get lard unless you boil the hog 2. you can't be a cowboy if you can't ride a horse

Neches (Anderson County): pronounced NAY-chez for the town and Net-chez for the river; Indian word for "friend"

Neck: gozzle

Neck, large: if you put him into a guillotine it'd take three chops to cut off his head

Necked: *See Lead ox*

Neckerchief: *See Bandana*

Necktie: 1. choke strap 2. feel like I was tied to a snubbin' post

Need, desperate: like a scalded dog needs a stock tank

 Needmore (Bailey County): while trying to build the town, the local folks always seemed to "need more" of everything

Needs attention: that ol' hog needs sloppin'

Needless as: 1. perfume for a skunk 2. earrings for a pig

Negotiation: 1. dickering 2. horse trading

Neighborhood, bad: if Diogenes went through that neighborhood with his lamp looking for an honest man, they'd steal his lamp

Neighboring: helping the neighbors with whatever chore needs doing

Neighborly: good fences make good neighbors [If you ever live in the country next door to someone who doesn't keep his fences mended, about the third time you have to chase that neighbor's livestock out of your garden, you will understand what this saying means.]

Neiman Marcus: Needless Markup to some, which makes fun of the traditional high prices in the store [There was a time when anybody who was anybody in Texas did their shopping at Neiman's. Weatherford native Mary Martin, the famous actress, once said she grew up like every other little girl in Texas, "dreaming of the day she got a dress from Neiman Marcus."] *See also Electra*

Nemo (Somervell County): pronounced KNEE-mo [The settlement was originally called Cleburne, Johnson Stop after one of the earliest settlers, Jimmie Johnson. When the town applied for a post office, the postal authorities suggested a shorter name. According to popular legend, when the townspeople gathered to select a new name, one man suggested "Nemo," which he claimed was Latin for "no one." The man argued, "If Jimmie Johnson's name ain't good enough, then no ones' name is." Believe it or not.]

Nerve: 1. got the nerve of a 20-year veteran on the bomb squad 2. got more nerve than a toothache in a molar

Nerve hospital: *See Hospital, psychiatric*

Nervous: 1. got a crick in his neck from lookin' over his shoulder 2. got an itchy trigger finger 3. wound tighter than an eight-day clock on Sunday morning [This is a reference to the old country practice of winding the clock on Sunday morning before going to church.] 4. sweating bullets 5. hearin' footsteps 6. twitchin' and shaking like a wet dog 7. his stomach is balled up in a knot 8. couldn't draw an easy breath 9. chute crazy, which refers to cattle being nervous about entering a narrow branding or loading chute 10. got a belly full of bedsprings 11. jumpy as a bushel basket full of Louisiana hoppin' frogs

Nervous as: 1. a long tailed cat in a room full of rocking chairs 2. a frog in a frying pan 3. a pig in a packing house 4. a whore in church, a soiled dove in Sunday school, or a painted lady at a prayer meeting 5. a settin' hen at a wolf (or coyote) convention 6. a grass widow at a camp meeting 7. a tongue-tied lawyer 8. a declawed cat 9. a fly around a glue pot 10. a porcupine in a balloon factory 11. a worm on a hook 12. a cat in a tennis racket factory 13. a horse on a high wire 14. a boy waiting to be spanked 15. an old hog on a cold morning (*see Cold weather*) 16. a small kitten up a big tree

Nervy as: 1. a 400-pound cat burglar 2. a 350-pound ballet dancer 3. a 300-pound jockey

Net wire: *See Chicken wire*

Nevada (Collin County): pronounced Na-VEY-da, not like the state out west somewhere that allows Texans to gamble right out in the open instead of behind closed doors [The name of the Texas town was, however, taken from Nevada Territory because the founder, John McMinn, had passed through there on his way to the gold fields in California.]

Never: 1. the flames of hell would be as cold as a Popsicle before that would happen 2. in a pig's eye 3. when cows give beer

Never do it: 1. never learn to iron, someone will expect you to do it 2. never pet a polar bear unless he's a rug 3. never put a broom on a bed unless you want bad luck 4. never put the cart before the horse unless you are backing up

Never ending: 1. there is always another fence to mend, field to plow, or well to dig 2. like wiping with a bicycle inner tube

Never-never land: diddy wah diddy

New: 1. fresh, as in "He got a fresh horse." 2. young, as in "He just had a young idea." 3. hot off the press (or fire)

New Baden (Robertson County): pronounced properly as New BAY-dun although some say New Bad-un

New Berlin (Guadalupe County): settled by German immigrants, which explains the name

New Braunfels (Comal County): pronounced New BRON-fells; named for Prince Carl of Solms-Braunfels, who worked to organize immigration of German farmers to Texas

New Deal (Lubbock County): originally named Monroe, the residents changed the name during the days of the Dust Bowl to show their support for President Roosevelt's programs

New development: new wrinkle in an old shirt

New information: a new wrinkle (or ring) on my horn

New invention: new-fangled contraption, as in "Do you have any idea how that new-fangled contraption called the Internet works?"

New Orleans: pronounced as three words, New Are Leans

New Orleans Superdome: to a Texan, it's the Coonasstrodome

New Ulm (Austin County): originally known as Duff's Settlement before German immigrants changed it to honor a city in Wurtemberg, Germany

New Year's Eve: amateur night [A lot of the people who are welcoming in the new year don't normally go out and are not accustomed to partying and may be prone to drinking too much before they begin the drive home.]

Newcomer: 1. pilgrim 2. nester 3. a Johnny-come-lately

Newlyweds: 1. sleeping double in a single bed 2. fresh married 3. new to the halter 4. green broke for matrimony [A "green broke" horse is one that has been broken to accept a rider but has not been trained to ride.]

Newness: novel

News: There is an old saying that a dog biting a man is not news but a man biting a dog is. A modern version is a senator throwing a bull is not news but a bull throwing a senator would be news.

News, bad: sit down news, which means you should ask someone to sit down before delivering it

Newspaper article: a piece in the paper

Neyland (Hunt County): pronounced NEE-lan; named for Robert Neyland, an early settler

Neylandville (Hunt County): pronounced Nee-Land-ville, although frequently the "d" is silent.

Nickel: case nickel, instead of five pennies

N

Nickel count (dominoes): a score of 5 points

Nigh: 1. a Texas term used to mean close 2. left side of an animal, especially a horse or mule

Night: 1. between suns 2. prowling time 3. coon time, which refers to hunting coons at night when they are out searching for food

Night shift: 1. night herding 2. singing shift, which refers to cowboys singing to the cattle at night to keep them quiet

Night work: working between suns

Night, dark: *See Dark night*

Nightfall: sundown [In the foreword for *Sure Enough, How Come* by F. W. Van Emden, J. Frank Dobie wrote, "One time I shot a young Doctor of Philosophy from Harvard for grading down a Texas freshman because he had used the word 'sundown' in a theme. The grand jury did not so much as investigate."]

Nine (playing card): cat card, which refers to a cat having nine lives

Ninety-mile-an-hour tape: *See Duct tape*

Nit-picking: picayunish

Nitro shooter: the person who "shot" a well with nitroglycerine to fracture it and start the flow of oil *See also Torpedo*

Nitroglycerine (oil field): grease

No: 1. no dice 2. does a chicken have lips 3. can a donkey fly 4. can a rattlesnake whistle "Dixie" 5. does dirt taste good 6. does a windmill pump oil 7. does a bull give milk

No doubt: ain't no two ways about it

No good: no account

No hurry: get it done by the second Wednesday of next week

No intention: not about to, as in "I'm not about to loan you my pickup."

No matter what: 1. come hell or high water 2. no matter how the cards fall

No place to go: you're holding a picnic in a landslide

No one: narry a soul

No opening: full handed

No options: we're string haltered

No similarities: 1. about as similar as a French negligee and a flannel nightgown 2. about as similar as a rat and a reindeer 3. no more similar than nylon hose and a garden hose

No such thing: there ain't no such thing as betting too much on a winning horse or being a little pregnant

No way: 1. in a pig's eye 2. fat chance 3. slim chance [As former Houston Astro pitcher Larry Anderson pointed out, "How come fat chance and slim chance mean the same thing?"]

No way out: 1. we're in a box canyon 2. we're in a swamp full of alligators and the drain is plugged 3. there ain't no key for the gate and the fence is too high to climb

No work, no pay: them that don't pluck, don't get no feathers [This saying comes from plucking geese to get feathers for mattresses and pillows. Usually, if you didn't do your share of the plucking, you slept on the ground.]

Nobody can help you: 1. got to chew your own tobacco 2. tote your own skillet

Nocona (Montague County): pronounced No-CONE-ah [Originally called Jordanville but postal authorities rejected that. A Texas Ranger then suggested the town be named for Pete Nocona, the Comanche chief who was Cynthia Ann Parker's husband and the father of Quanah Parker.]

Nod: 1. give 'em a tuck 2. dip your hat

Nogalus (Trinity County): pronounced no-GAL-es [According to popular legend, the name came from the lynching of two horse thieves who were strung up in a tree since the town had no gallows. The town came to be known as Nogallows, which became Nogallis and eventually Nogalus.]

Noise, loud: sounds like somebody knocked over a pyramid of cans [a stack of beer cans emptied during a party or celebration]

Noise, ominous: *See Sound, ominous*

Noisy as: 1. a chicken coop full of fifty chickens and one fox 2. an old wagon on a frozen road 3. a slow moving windmill crying for oil 4. a pair of dancing jinglebobs 5. a calf crying for mama 6. geese on a new feed ground 7. a pig eatin' charcoal 8. a scrub calf in a briar patch 9. wind blowing over a bung hole in an empty barrel 10. a longhorn steer in a dry thicket 11. a restless mule in a tin barn 12. a kid playin' with a coffee can that has one rock inside 13. hailstones on a tin roof 14. a hungry calf *See also Loud, Sound*

Noisy, somewhat: about as much noise as a harelip cowboy tryin' to whistle "Dixie"

Nonaggressive: ain't much for fight, just a little push and shove

A&M Non-reg: Texas A&M student who is not in the corps

Nonchalant: ability to look like a thoroughbred when you just acted like a jackass

Noncommittal: 1. he won't stay hitched 2. he's a fence rider (or straddler)

Nonconformist: 1. maverick [The term originated before the Civil War when financier Sam Maverick took a herd of cattle in settlement of a debt. When his calves started having calves, they went unbranded and came to be called mavericks. Today, anyone who doesn't conform to the norm is a maverick.] 2. he throws a different loop 3.

he two-steps to his own beat 4. he uses German shepherds to hunt coons 5. he wears straw hats in winter [As J. Frank Dobie said, "Conform and be dull."]

None: 1. nary a one 2. not a lick of 3. not a blessed one

None (money): penny one, as in "Bubba said he'd pay me twenty-five dollars for them possum hides, but I ain't seen penny one."

Nonexistent: 1. rooster eggs 2. donkey eggs 3. bull's milk 4. mare's eggs 5. like being a little bit pregnant, there ain't no such thing

Nonexistent as: 1. a nose on a football 2. a jackalope. According to country legend, the world's fastest animal is a cross between a jackrabbit and an antelope. Unfortunately, no one has ever seen a real jackalope.

Nonpaying: riding a free horse

Nonsense: 1. burro milk 2. horse feathers 3. hog wash 4. for the birds 5. bull feathers 6. hooey 7. heifer dust 8. cockamamie 9. rigmarole 10. don't make no never mind 11. buffalo chips 12. ballyhoo 13. bull oney 14. a crock of cow confetti 15. Mexican oats 16. armadillo eggs 17. horse hockey 18. just a load of chicken teeth 19. tomfoolery

Nonsense, political: gobbledygook [The term was coined by Texan Maury Maverick, a descendent of Sam Maverick, while serving in Congress. He used the term, which he said was derived from watching turkeys gobble and gook, to refer to political statements that were ridiculous nonsense, as are most political statements.]

Noon to midnight: evening

Noontime: 1. high noon 2. dead center day 3. lunch time

Nopal (McMullen County): pronounced NOPE-ul; name is Spanish for "prickly pear cactus" which is common in the area

Normangee (Madison County): pronounced Norman-G; originally called Roger's Prairie; name was changed to honor state legislator Norman G. Kittrell

North: Yankeedom, which is roughly described as anywhere north of the Red River

North Texas crush: a Difficult dance requiring practice and timing; done only in the Student Union at the University of North Texas

Norther: 1. a cold front that comes up quickly from the north and is usually associated with high winds and a quick, dramatic temperature drop 2. came on so sudden the front half of the horse was frothy and the back half was frozen 3. boiling water froze so fast the ice was still warm 4. the ducks froze to the stock tank [A classic Texas story tells of the farmer who was out plowing and one of his mules died from sunstroke. While he was off looking for a replacement, a norther struck and the other mule froze to death.]

Nose, large: could store a small dog in that hole

Nose, long: he could suck the guts out of a pumpkin through a keyhole

Nose hitch: *See Bosal*

Nosey: 1. always hunting something to meddle in 2. got her nose in everybody's business but her own

Not able: can't hardly do it

Not communicating: you're preaching to the choir, which implies the preacher's message is not getting through to the entire congregation

Not easy to fool: was born at night but it wasn't last night

Not funny: 1. about as funny as a crutch 2. about as funny as a constipated chicken

Not good at: a terrible hand at

Not himself (after surgery): he's still circling the airport, which basically means the anaesthetic hasn't completely worn off

Not important: ain't no great shakes

Not interested: 1. don't give a hoot or a holler 2. wouldn't touch that with a ten-foot pole 3. wouldn't touch that with your pole 4. don't give a wrap or a hooey (wrap refers to tying up a calf's legs and a hooey is a knot)

Not involved: 1. don't have a dog in that fight 2. out of the revolution 3. he'll have no more to do with that than I will in admitting him to heaven 4. not on my dance card

Not motivated: like a wheelbarrow, he stands still until someone pushes him

Not my fault: 1. didn't light the fuse 2. don't drive the train or blow the whistle 3. didn't string the bow

Not needed: need that about as much as a cow needs a fifth teat

Not practical: 1. you can shear a pig but you'll get a lot more noise than wool 2. you can cut firewood with a penknife but the first flames will be a long time coming 3. a bucket under a bull will get full but it won't be with milk

Not working: 1. the ox ain't plowin' 2. that dog ain't hunting

Nothing: 1. nuthin' 2. not a blooming thing 3. neither hide, nor hair, nor horn 4. just a load of post holes 5. just a tap hole without a beer keg around it 6. what most politicians are good for

Nothing is impossible: 1. cows eat salt blocks one lick at a time 2. never has been a hoss that can't be rode or cowboy that can't be throwed 3. you can carry water in a tea strainer if it's in the form of ice cubes [Texans generally take the attitude that the impossible just takes a little longer than usual to accomplish.]

Nothing realized: I got what the bear grabbed at and missed

Nothing to do: got about as much to do as the vice president [Will Rogers once said the vice president had the best job in the country because all he had to do was get up each morning and say, How's the President?]

Notrees (Ector County): named because there are NO Trees around so that's the way it should be pronounced

Now I understand: the nickel finally dropped [This is a reference to the old days when pay telephones were first perfected, sort of. The cost of a call was a nickel but frequently the coin would hang up in the mechanism requiring several whomps on the phone to get it to drop and complete the connection. Of course, to modernize the saying you'd have to say the thirty-five cents finally dropped, which just doesn't have the same ring to it.]

Nubbin: a tiny, useless ear of corn that grows near the top of the stalk

Nude: *See Naked*

Nudist: one who grins and bares it

Nueces: pronounced New-aces, this Spanish word for nuts is also the name of a Texas river that flows into the Gulf of Mexico at Corpus Christi

Nuisance: he's pain in the back of the lap

Numerous: 1. more than Quaker has oats 2. more than you can shake a stick at 3. as many as Carter has liver pills 4. thick as fleas on a mongrel dog

Numerous as: 1. ants on a dead worm 2. oil wells in Texas 3. hailstones 4. hair on a dog's (or coyote's) back 5. foot-soldiers in the Chinese army 6. relatives at a rich uncle's funeral 7. cow chips on a cattle ranch

Nurse: a pan handler

Nutritionist, poor: He thinks a balanced diet is a cheeseburger in one hand and a burrito in the other.

Nutty as: 1. a Corsicana fruitcake 2. a box of soft-shell pecans 3. a bag of circus peanuts. *See also Crazy*

Nylon fraternity: membership limited to cowboys who have lost a finger while dallying a catch rope

Nymphomaniac: mattress tester

O.P.M.: Other Peoples' Money [This is what was used to finance most oil wells back in the boom days. The legendary "Dad" Joiner used O.P.M. to drill his wells in East Texas. One of those wells struck a virtual ocean of oil that was the largest discovery ever in the United Sates. Unfortunately, Dad expected another dry hole so he had sold out the well three times, which meant he had sold 300 percent when only 100 percent was available. H.L. Hunt came to the rescue when he bought out Joiner and paid off the investors. He then went on to become one of the world's richest men, and it could be argued he did it all thanks to O.P.M.]

Oaf: 1. empty skulled 2. feather headed 3. hollow headed 4. he could make an anvil complicated 5. leather brained 6. sawdust brained 7. mental mummy 8. hamster brain 9. bubble head 10. yahoo 11. rattle brain 12. scatterbrained 13. chuckle head 14. bucket head 15. clabber head 16. mud head 17. lumber head 18. churn head 19. plumb weak north of the ears *See also Dumb; Ignorant; Stupid*

Oakalla (Burnet County): Texans pronounce it Oak-alley.

Oath: 1. I'll be jiggered 2. jumping Jehoshaphat 3. gee wilikers 4. by cracky 5. cut off one of my legs and call me I lean 6. I'll be a suck-egg mule 7. I'll be dipped in snuff (or shellac) 8. don't that twirl your spurs 9. shoot me a runnin' 10. I'll be switched 11. that tears a plank off the wall 12. shoot me for a billygoat 13. slap me naked and sell my clothes 14. flip my garters 15. I declare 16. that takes the cake 17. shut my mouth 18. I hope your mother crawls out from under the porch and bites you 19. fiddlesticks, fiddle-faddle, or fiddle-dee-dee 20. heck fire 21. sakes alive 22. look a here 23. gosh all mighty

Oath, surprised: 1. why, I'll be damned [y-ahl-be-dayamd] 2. shut yore mouth, which is said when someone says something controversial or surprising that you don't necessarily want to hear or believe 3. well, look a here

Obedient: 1. stump broke 2. as a trained pig [Darrell Royal once said, "Every coach likes those old trained pigs who'll grin and jump right in the slop for him." He was referring to football players.]

Obese: 1. looks like he's perfected the boardinghouse reach 2. beef plumb to the hocks 3. heavy in the middle and poor on both ends 4. twenty pounds (or a dozen biscuits) away from a sideshow in the circus 5. the tongue and buckle of his belt are strangers *See also Fat; Rear end, large*

Obligated: 1. obliged to 2. if you give a dance, you gotta pay the band (or at least the fiddler)

Obliged: not one to thump a free melon

Obnoxious: 1. hell bent for trouble 2. believes the only business that happens is his business 3. if she asked for a ride, she'd want to drive 4. a goat-gitter

Observant: 1. quick eyed 2. smart eyed 3. he could spot a mole on a hoochiecoochie dancer from fifty feet in a smoke filled room 4. eagle eyed 5. can spot rat droppings in a raisin pie [Note, housefly can be substituted for rat and any number of words can be substituted for droppings.]

Observe: 1. hide and watch 2. keep your eyes peeled

Obsolete as: 1. a buffalo hunt 2. a drive-in movie 3. an eight-track tape 4. a bois d'arc brick (*see Bois d'Arc*) 5. a horse drawn combine

Obstacle: 1. a stump in the cotton patch 2. a root in the sewer line 3. tall hurdle to jump 4. tall horse to saddle 5. tall fence to climb 6. sprag in the wheel

Obstacle, small: that grass ain't tall for a high stepper

Obstinate: 1. if you don't like where you got it, he'll tell you where to put it 2. wouldn't move camp out of the way of a prairie fire 3. ornery as a rat-tailed horse at fly time 4. you couldn't melt him down and pour him into anyplace he didn't want to go

Obvious: 1. could read that with one eye tied behind my back 2. plain as the nose on your face (or the hand on your arm) 3. don't have to tell a cat what to do with a mouse 4. the cards are all face up on the table 5. if the windmill is running, the wind is blowing 6. plain as rabbit pills in a sugar bowl 7. goes without saying 8. if it had been a snake it would a bit you sure 9. plain as a glass eye on a goat 10. anybody can read that dipstick

Obvious, somewhat: clear as looking through lace curtains

Occasionally: 1. every now and again 2. every once in a while

Occurrence, rare: once in a blue moon

Odd: a horse of a different color

Odd behavior: a strange way to run a railroad

Odd person: 1. his cross hairs ain't lined up 2. there's a few pieces missing out of his puzzle *See also Strange person*

Odds, poor: 1. about the same as those of a turtle tryin' to cross a six-lane highway in rush hour 2. about the same as those of you diving into an empty swimming pool and stopping before you hit bottom *See also Chances, slim; Las Vegas*

Odessa (Ector County): pronounced Oh-DESS-a; named for the major city in the Ukraine [If you ever get out to this town, ask an old-timer to tell you the story of Tessy from Odessy.]

Odor, bad: 1. smells like a bouquet of stinkweed 2. like a burning hay field 3. like a wet dog 4. like fifty-cents-a-gallon perfume 5. like the business end of a polecat 6. like a sewer main with the cork out 7. like a New Orleans whorehouse

Odor, good: 1. like a baby's breath 2. like a perfumed cat (or poodle dog) 3. as rain, which refers to the sweet, gentle odor often associated with a rainstorm 4. sweet as fresh mowed grass

Oenaville (Bell County): pronounced Oh-EEN-a-ville; thought to have been named for Miss Oena Griffin, who was a friend of founder C. D. Johnson

Of: most Texans simply say "a" as in "Bubba went kind a crazy when he found those whiskey dents in his new pickup."

Of course: 1. why yes [This is a traditional Texas reply when the answer is obviously "of course." For an emphatic of course use "hell yea-us" or "damn straight."]

Off center: gee hawed

Off-ox: the ox in the lead team on the left side

Off side: right side of a horse or team *See also Near side*

Offense: the best offense is a good defense [Darrell Royal once pointed out, "You don't lose a game if your opponent doesn't score."]

Office job: sitting down job

Office, large: 1. could hang a stuffed whale on the wall, which is a reference to fishermen liking to hang their trophy catches on the wall 2. big enough to hold deer hunting practice

Office, small: 1. if it was twice as big, it might qualify as a broom closet 2. if you hung a fish on the wall it would have to be a minnow

Offspring, poor: she needs a large apron to cover her children's faults

Often: 1. oft times 2. many a time 3. more than a time or two

Oil (awl): 1. black gold 2. Texas tea

Oil derrick: Texas tree

Oil field: oil patch

Oil field station: Christmas tree

Oil field worker: roughneck [According to Donnis Baggett, a roughneck is either an oil field worker or what an unemployed oil field worker feels after shaving too long with an old blade.]

Oil field worker, inexperienced: a worm

Oil well, dry: duster

OK: 1. mighty fine 2. that'll do nicely *See also Agreeable*

Ol': old, as in "That Jim Bob was a good ol' boy."

Oklahoma: Indian for "dump it here" according to Hal Jay of WBAP Radio in Fort Worth

Oklahoma University: 1. zero U 2. paper-clip U, which is derived from the symbol on the side of Oklahoma football helmets, which, to a Texan, looks like a paper clip

Okra strut: *See Chitlins strut*

Old and fat: ain't seen his feet since a Roosevelt was in the White House [The name of the president can be changed to adjust the age.]

Old Army: 1. the Corps of Cadets 2. the old days 3. the time when the speaker was a freshman

Old as: 1. a rock 2. the Brazos River 3. dirt 4. sin, which implies something has been around since Garden of Eden days 5. black pepper 6. sunshine 7. her tongue and older than her teeth *See also Aging; Elderly*

Old days: 1. horse and buggy days 2. back when granddaddy was a pup

Old-fashioned: 1. from the old school 2. old-timey or ol' time 3. from the good old days

Old Glory (Stonewall County): German settlement originally named New Brandenburg. Due to anti-German sentiment during World War I, the residents were pressured to change the name to something more patriotic, so they named the town after the American flag.

Old man: geezer

Old person: 1. the Dead Sea wasn't even on the critical list when he was born 2. been around since Sitting Bull was a calf 3. was born ten years before Moses 4. living on borrowed time and three payments are past due 5. old-timer 6. codger 7. no spring chicken 8. gummer 9. could have helped dig the well at the Alamo 10. galoot 11. buzzard 12. aged out 13. diehard 14. old fogie 15. when he was born the sun was just a match head and there weren't no moon a'tall 16. was a stowaway on the ark 17. three years older than dirt 18. he used to bang the gong to release the lions in the Roman coliseum 19. when he was born Moby Dick was just a minnow 20. could have been a waiter at the Last Supper 21. got plenty of wrinkles on his horns *See also Elderly; Old-timer*

Old woman: battle-ax

Old-timer: 1. his back goes out more than he does 2. the only exercise he gets is acting as a pallbearer for his friends 3. so old he don't buy green bananas 4. tells it like it used to be 5. can remember when a woman looked the same before and after washing her face 6. been around since before water was wet 7. already waded his deepest water 8. a codger 9. a blessing [In Texas, old-timers are considered a "blessing" by their relatives. "Uncle Glen was such a blessing, I just loved to hear his stories." Some old folks who are still very active will often say "I ain't ready to be a blessing yet."]

Old-timer, country boy: been scraping manure off his boots for more years than you could count, or has scraped enough manure off his boots to fertilize the Rio Grande valley [Either expression means he's been working around farm animals and manure for a long time.]

Olden times: lamp oil days

Older than you: been around since before your daddy met your mama

Oldest: granddaddy of 'em all

Oletha (Limestone County): pronounced Oh-LEE-tha [During prohibition, as many as thirty-six stills were in operation at Oletha.]

Olney (Young County): pronounced AHL-knee, not Ohl-knee [There are two schools of thought as to the origin of the name: 1. to honor Richard Olney, secretary of state under President Cleveland 2. an article in a newspaper concerning noted Texan Roger Q. Mills' activities at Olney, Illinois.]

Omen: invisible handwriting on the wall

Ominous as: a skeleton dangling in an oak tree [This refers to the days when a horse thief was lynched and left hanging in the tree as a warning to other rustlers.]

On credit: 1. on tick 2. belongs to me and the bank, credit union, savings and loan, or mortgage company

On fire: a far [Texas youngsters who hear the story about the wise men coming from afar to see the baby Jesus assume they were fireman.]

On his own: 1. paddling his own canoe 2. on his own hook 3. branding his own cows 4. ridin' for his own brand

On his side: siding with him

On target: 1. where the feathers fly is where the shot will lie 2. you hit the can (or bottle) *See also Aim, Good*

On the make: 1. on the prowl 2. cattin' around 3. pickin' up strays 4. prowlin' the honky-tonks

On top: atop, as in "We had to get the cat down from atop the tree."

On your own: it's root hog, or die [This means an old hog that won't root around for his own food will surely die.]

Onalaska (Polk County): proper pronunciation is Unalaska [Some newcomers are trying to say On-Alaska, which is not correct. Founder William Carlisle named the town after Onalaska, Arkansas, where he had once operated a mill.]

Once in a while: 1. usually pronounced as one word, wunsinawhall 2. ever now and again

Once or twice: a time or two

Once: wunst

One-holer: an outhouse with seating room for one person at a time. It naturally follows that a two-holer and a three-holer would have seating room for two and three persons respectively, although three-holers are extremely rare. According to an old country legend, if you want to confuse someone from Arkansas, just send him into a two-holer; he'll mess up his shorts before he can decide which hole to use. *See also Outhouse protocol*

One-timer: a sparkler, which means he'll burn bright for a minute or two, then go out

One-way dish: *See Plow*

One button: a second lieutenant in the Texas A&M Corps of Cadets

One hundred: a hunard

One iron (golf club): Texan Lee Trevino was once struck by lightning on the golf course. Later, at another tournament, the weather threatened again. Trevino promptly held his one iron over his head, explaining, "Not even God can hit a one iron."

One of a kind person: 1. nobody can hold a candle to him 2. when they made him they broke the mold 3. cream of the crop 4. he was delivered by an eagle instead of a stork 5. if he's not alone in his class it wouldn't take long to call role, which is how Bum Phillips described Earl Campbell *See also Good person*

One or the other: when an old hen cackles, she's either layin' or lyin'

One sided as: a turkey shoot

One time: a flash in the pan

Onions: skunk eggs

Only one: onliest one, as in "I have to find my pickup key 'cause it's the onliest one I got."

Open: 1. the gate's unlocked 2. the latch string is on the outside 3. the breech is open 4. the fence is down 5. the lid's off [In Texas things are rarely open, they are generally wide open.]

Open a business: set up shop

Open a window, slightly: crack it

Open behind: when a horse's hocks are far apart and its feet are close together

Open cattle: expression used to describe cows that are of breeding age but have not been bred

Open-minded: the only thing he sets in concrete are fence posts

Open range days: before barbed wire

Opera: 1. opry 2. a Texas term for a horse breaking when viewed by fence sitters who are observers rather then participants

Operation, minor: one performed on somebody else

Opinion, casual: horseback, back porch, or back fence opinion

Opinionated: 1. he ain't no fence rider or line walker, which means he always has an opinion one way or the other 2. he can't weigh the facts because his scales are full of opinions

Opinions: 1. like noses (or other parts of the anatomy), everyone has one 2. the difference between a rat and a rabbit depends on who is doing the eating [Lyndon Johnson said, "We don't all see everything alike. If we did we'd all want the same wife."]

Opossum: *See Possum*

Opponent, easy: a breather [Every football coach likes to have one or two breathers on his schedule.]

Opportunities, lacking: picking's are mighty slim

Opportunities, plentiful: 1. there are still fish in the lake as big as any that have been caught, maybe bigger 2. everything is fair game 3. the field is wide open

Opportunity missed: was asleep at the switch

Oppose: 1. won't set still for that 2. goes against my grain 3. goes contrary to my raising

Optimist: 1. starts putting on his shoes when the preacher says, "Now, in conclusion." 2. you wouldn't want to borrow money from him 'cause he would expect you to pay it back 3. he only takes one ball to the golf course 4. he only takes one match to light the fire

Optimistic as: a deer hunter (or fisherman) who takes along a camera

Optimistic, overly: 1. don't count his chickens before they hatch, he counts 'em before the eggs are laid 2. would expect to bring home a bird from a wild goose chase

Option: 1. dealer's choice 2. ladies' choice 3. you can stand pat, draw, or get the sandwiches, referring to the options in a friendly poker game

Options, limited: like flipping a coin, you got two choices

Ordinary: 1. plain everyday bowlegged human 2. just an old shoe 3. everyday wash

A&M Ordnance: flaming onions

Organization, poor: a Chinese fire drill is better organized [This term is often used to describe almost any government agency.]

Organized: finally got everybody sittin' in the same pew

Original source: the horse's mouth, as in "Bubba got the news about Ethyl being pregnant straight from the horse's mouth."

Ornery as: 1. a mule colt 2. a snapping sow

Orphan: dogie, which is a motherless and consequently, fatherless, calf

Osage orange: *See Bois d'Arc*

Osceola (Hill County): pronounced Oh-sea-oh-la; named for the Seminole Indian chief

Other side: 1. yonder side 2. back side 3. flip side 4. under side

Other: tuther

Out: 1. like Lottie's left eye [This refers to Lottie Deno, the famous female gambler in Texas during the days of the Old West. Although unable to see out of her left eye, she still managed to win a pot or two. In 1933 famous Texas bank robber Clyde Barrow felt the law was closing in on him and Bonnie Parker when he said, "Sooner or later they'll catch us and we'll be out like Lottie's eye." He was correct.]

Out in the open: 1. out in the broad daylight 2. out of the closet

Out of control: 1. the tail is wagging the dog 2. the herd's stampeding 3. the bridle's off 4. he's a runaway freight train 5. the well's gushing 6. running wild 7. the lid's off 8. he slipped his hobbles 9. a loose hose (or cannon)

Out of danger: out of the woods

Out of date as: 1. a drive-in movie 2. a magazine in a doctor's office

Out of line: doing something they oughten

Out of place: in the wrong cage

Out of place as: 1. a thong bikini on grandma 2. a mule in a buggy harness 3. a crane in a goldfish pond 4. a sidewinder on a sidewalk 5. heavy metal music in a honky-tonk 6. a hiccup at a funeral or a prayer meeting 7. a Methodist bell choir in a honky-tonk 8. a whale in a washtub 9. a white dress on a witch 10. overalls on a rooster 11. a hickey on a nun 12. a cow patty in a whirlpool 13. a snowstorm in July 14. a bow tie on a black snake 15. a dog in a cat fight 16. dirt under a beauty queen's fingernails 17. a ham sandwich at a Jewish picnic 18. a fish out of water

Out of plumb: geehawed

Out of practice: 1. plumb out of the habit of doing it 2. rusty as a twenty-year-old windmill

Out of shape: 1. breathing from memory 2. ain't as much tone in his muscles as there is in a guitar without strings 3. the only things he lifts are a fork and knife 4. it's hard to be fit as a fiddle when you're built like a cello 5. you can lie about being in shape but you can't fool a flight of stairs 6. he looks like someone cut him open and stuffed him with Jell-O [When Abe Lemons was head basketball coach at the University of Texas, someone asked

if he jogged. "Hell no," replied Lemons, "I want to be sick when I die."]

Out of stock: 1. fresh out of 2. the wagon's empty 3. the cupboard is bare

Out of town: off the reservation

Out of trouble, almost: finally got his ends meeting but he ain't quite got 'em tied

Out of work: like a pregnant stripper

Out of your league: 1. you're a dachshund runnin' with a pack of Great Danes 2. you're a parakeet tryin' to fly with eagles

Outdid me: stole my thunder and lightning but left behind a lot of hail

Outdo: 1. will do you one better 2. put the big britches on him

Outhouse: 1. reading room 2. throne room 3. back house 4. closet out back 5. Sears order desk, which refers to the old practice of keeping the Sears mail order catalog in the outhouse *See also One-holer*

Outhouse breeze: Normally, the outhouse is located so the prevailing wind blows the odor away from where you live. An outhouse breeze occurs when the wind changes and blows the smell toward the house. This can be particularly embarrassing if it happens on Sunday when you have the preacher over for dinner.

Outhouse protocol: 1. always knock before entering 2. kill any spiders, snakes, or wasps that you might find inside to save the next user the trouble 3. never remove the Sears catalog no matter how bad you want to order something

Outdoorsman, poor: his idea of roughing it is having to watch black and white television in a motel that doesn't have room service

Outfit: a business, farm, or ranch

Outlaw: 1. bandito 2. horse thief 3. long rider 4. the moon is his sun *See also Crooked; Criminal; Thief*

Outlook, different: the difference between a possum and a pig depends on who's doing the eating

Outmaneuver: wheel 'em and deal 'em

Outrun the law: There's a saying in Texas that goes, "You might be able to outrun his old Chevrolet, but you can't outrun his old two-way," which means even if you can outrun the lawman's car, you can't outrun his radio call for assistance.

Outsmart: out coyote 'em

Outstanding: 1. couldn't beat that with a claw hammer 2. a good farmer is one who is out standing in his field 3. a real humdinger, as in "That new hydraulic jack I got for my wife is a real humdinger."

Over the hill: he's not only over the hill he's over the Guadalupe Mountains [Remember, being over the hill is better than being under it.] *See also Elderly; Old*

Overalls: redneck tuxedo

Overanxious: 1. he rared up to go but he couldn't go because he was rared up 2. it was an early worm that was eaten by the early bird 3. champed at the bit so much he broke off a wisdom tooth at the roots 4. you're runnin' ahead of the dogs 5. you're tossin' the rope before you build a loop 6. you're shopping for maternity dresses before the rabbit died

Overate: 1. over grazed 2. stuffed to the gills 3. as full as an egg 4. took on a nap load [This refers to the habit some have of taking a nap after a big meal.]

Overbearing: acts like he's got a bill of sale on the whole county

Overcome with emotion: his words stuck in his throat like a lure in a fish's mouth

Overconfident: 1. acting a little big for his britches 2. settin' himself for a long fall 3. he thinks he's bulletproof or invisible

Overeater: 1. you're gonna dig your grave with them teeth 2. if you keep eatin' your knees are gonna buckle but your belt won't

Overexerted: 1. split his britches 2. popped her girdle

Overextended: 1. bit off more than he can chew (or swallow) 2. got more on his plate than he can say grace over 3. hung the ivy basket higher than she can reach, which means she won't be able to water the plants 4. weeding a mighty wide row 5. got six pots on a four-burner stove 6. this camper has too much gear to haul around 7. got twenty pounds of fish on a ten-pound stringer 8. feel like a country dog trying to wet on all the fireplugs in town 9. got a big cotton sack to tote

Overflowing: slopping over

Overkill: killed too dead to skin

Overloaded: 1. my cup runneth over with opportunity 2. spread too thin 3. carrying more than a pack horse 4. got more than I can shake a stick at 5. bogged to the saddle skirts 6. my wagon springs are flattened to the axle 7. got more ground cleared than I can plow 8. got himself spread so thin you can see through him if the light's right

Overnight guest: suitcase company [They bring along a change of clothes and toothbrushes in case you invite them to spend the night.]

Overreacting: 1. using dynamite for rat poison, which gets you a lot of dead rats in the rubble pile where your barn once stood 2. using a 2x4 for a flyswatter 3. using a sledgehammer to drive thumbtacks into papier-mâché 4. don't need a bonfire to roast marshmallows 5. usin' a fryin' pan for a flyswatter

Oversported: worn out from too much kissing and petting

Oversexed: 1. ain't no neutral in his transmission 2. whoever turned her on forgot to turn her off

Overwhelming: world beater

Overworked: got too many irons in the fire [When you find yourself in this predicament, you have two choices: 1. get some irons out of the fire 2. get a bigger fire.]

Ovilla (Ellis-Dallas Counties): pronounced Oh-VILL-ah, not the traditional Spanish Oh-vee-ah; name was formed from the Spanish word *villa*

Owensville (Robertson County): This one is a "ville"; named for Harrison Owen, first county clerk. In addition to providing the town its name, Harrison Owen would one day have a 5th great-grandson who would write a book on the language of Texas.

Own: 1. it's carrying my brand 2. it's mine, all bought and paid for 3. it's all mine, lock, stock, and barrel

Owned, but not paid for: it belongs to me and the bank

Ox drover: bull whacker 'cause he could hit the lead oxen's ear with his whip

Ox jobbing: *See Bull riding*

Ozona (Crockett County): pronounced oh-ZONE-ah [Originally called Powell Well after E. M. Powell, who drilled a well near Johnson Draw and put up a windmill. He later offered land and water to settlers, and the name was changed to Ozona to indicate the area had open air or ozone.]

P

P.M.S.&T.: Professor of Military Science and Tactics, Texas A&M

P.R.C.A.: Professional Rodeo Cowboy Association. In the early years it was called the Turtleass; later it was the R.C.A.; now it's the P.R.C.A.

Packed: 1. like pig's feet in a jar 2. like hogs at a trough 3. like cows in a boxcar, which refers to shipping cattle by rail when you pack as many as you can into a boxcar

Paddling: when a horse throws his feet outward as he picks them up off the ground

Paducah (Cottle County): pronounced Pa-DUKE-ah [Early settler R. Potts offered free land for those agreeing to name the town after his hometown in Kentucky. The town is often referred to as The Crossroads of America because U.S. highways 70 and 83 intersect in the town. Each highway runs from border to border across the nation; U.S. 70 runs east to west and U.S. 83 runs south to north.]

Painful as: 1. a hiccup (or sneeze) with a broken rib 2. an anvil dropped on an ingrown toenail *See also In pain*

Paint Rock (Concho County): named for the Indian paintings on the bluffs overlooking nearby Concho River

Paint wagon: where the drinkin' whiskey is kept hidden

Pair: 1. a cow and a calf 2. a duet, as in "She has a duet of kids."

Pajamas: sleeping drawers

Pal: A real Texan almost never uses "pal" to signify friendship. Instead, he'll use words like buddy or pardner. Generally, a Texan uses pal only when he's irritated with something a stranger has done, as in "Listen, pal, if you don't keep your hand off my girl's knee, I'm gonna whup you so bad you'll dog-cuss your momma for bringing you into this world."

Palacios (Matagorda County): pronounced Pa-LAY-shus, the town is on Tres Palacios Bay, for which it is named. *Tres palacios* is Spanish for "three places."

Palatial: makes a king's bedroom look like a ranch bunkhouse [On a ranch, the bunkhouse was not the most well appointed of rooms.]

Palaver: talking something over

Pale: 1. peak'd, as in "Ever since he got that certified letter from the IRS he's been lookin' mighty peak'd." 2. look like you've been on a hayride with Dracula

 Palestine (Anderson County): in Texas it is properly pronounced Pal-a-steen, not Pal-a-stien [There is an old joke about the young Texan who was asked where Jesus was born. After guessing Athens and Carthage, the young man gave up and the Sunday school teacher said it was Palestine. The young Texan replied, "I knew it was somewhere in East Texas."]

Palo Duro Canyon (Randall-Armstrong Counties): pronounced Pal-a Dur-oh Can-yun; name is Spanish for "hardwood," which is a reference to the trees and shrubs found in the canyon

Palo Pinto (Palo Pinto County): pronounced PAL-ah PIN-toe

Paluxy (Hood County): pronounced Pah-LUX-ee

Pampa (Gray County): pronounced PAM-pa, Spanish for "prairie;" named by developer George Tying, of the White Deer Land Company, who thought the area resembled the Pampas of Argentina

Pan, large: roundup pan, which refers to the fact that during a roundup there are generally lots of mouths to feed so the largest pans around were used for cooking *See also Wreck pan*

Pancakes: 1. hotcakes 2. batter cakes 3. hen fruit stir 4. blankets

Pancakes, large: big as hubcaps

Panic: a stampede, which is a reference to cattle panicking and stampeding, a trail driver's nightmare

Panicked: 1. stampeded the herd 2. shot out the lights 3. tipped over the outhouse

Panting: 1. like a lizard on a hot rock 2. like a hound dog that run a coon two counties 3. his tongue was out so far he was lapping up dirt

Pants: 1. britches 2. breeches 3. pantaloons 4. Wranglers 5. blue jeans

Pants, short: high water britches [This refers to the practice of rolling up your pant legs to wade through high water. For a Texan, any pants that don't reach the ground are high water britches.]

Pants, torn in the rear: looks like he ate an alley cat, which implies the cat was clawing and scratching on the way out as well as on the way in

Panty hose: Arkansas tow strap

Paradise (Wise County): You knew it had to be somewhere in Texas, right? This tiny town was a "paradise on earth" for Texas cowboys driving cattle north to the Kansas market, and the name stuck.

Paranoid: puts a safety pin on his back pocket when he goes to church [Pete Gent, former Dallas Cowboy and author of *North Dallas Forty,* said, "A paranoid is someone with all the facts."]

Parent, poor: more worried about his golf swing than his offspring

Parental authority: 1. woodshed diplomacy 2. a mama hen has the right to peck her chicks on the head if they need it

Parents: the folks [In Texas, your parents are generally mama and daddy, no matter how old they are or how old you are.]

Parents, bad: their son was born with a tattoo and it wasn't spelled correctly

Paris (Lamar County): originally named Pinhook, the new

name, in recognition of the French capital, was suggested by an employee of the town's founder

Park bench: 1. spit and whittle bench 2. loafers' log

Parking ticket: bill for landing

Part of: part and parcel of

Parted: like the Red Sea

Participate: 1. if you ain't branding, you can hold a rope 2. if you ain't skinning, you can hold a leg

Participated: had a hand in, such as "He had a hand in lynching the horse thief."

Particular person: 1. would complain if they hung him with a new rope 2. wouldn't steal a chicken if it wasn't a brown leghorn 3. when she checked into heaven she insisted on seeing the upstairs

Partier: born under a honky-tonk moon

Partner: in Texas, it's pardner

Partnership: 1. pardnership 2. in bed together 3. in cahoots

Party (celebrate): staying out with the dry cattle [Refers to dry cows staying out in the pasture rather than coming in to be milked.]

Party (noun): 1. a bee, as in a quilting bee 2. shootaree 3. fiesta 4. fandango

Party, dull: had all the excitement of a graveyard cleaning [Many country churches have an annual picnic at their local graveyard. After eating, everyone turns out to cut the grass, pull the weeds, and right the leaning tombstones. All in all, a graveyard cleaning is an honorable endeavor, but it is a rather dull affair.]

Party goer: 1. hell (or cane) raiser 2. ring tailed tooter 3. Saturday night sinner

Party time: 1. let's rodeo or wanna rodeo 2. let's honky-tonk 3. the honky-tonk moon is up

Party, wild: a tooth kickin' party

A&M **Pass** (food): shoot the food

Passed away: *See Died*

Passed gas: there was a roar in his rumble seat

Passed me: 1. went by like we were set up on jack stands 2. went by in a blur 3. fogged right on by

Passenger: window watcher

Passenger seat (automobile or pickup): In Texas it's the "shotgun seat," which is a reference to the old days when the extra rider on the seat of a stagecoach was riding shotgun for the driver.

Passes gas a lot: 1. they call him thunder pants 2. he can pass more gas in a weekend than a pipeline could carry in a month 3. if they ever perfect a car that'll run on natural gas, he can hook up his rear end to his carburetor and drive around the world

Passion flower: ground ivy

Past, questionable: got blind spots in his back trail

Pastern: short bones above a horse's hoof

Pasture: open land that has not been plowed [it becomes a field when it is plowed]

Patch of ground: a small field of anything

Path to righteousness: the good road is straight and narrow, which is why it's so darn hard to follow

Patience: 1. hot will cool if greedy will let it 2. of an angel assigned to a Texan [Texan Sam Rayburn said the three most important words in the English language are "just a minute."]

Patient as: 1. a circling buzzard waiting for a sick mule to die 2. a cat camped out under a birdbath 3. a settin' hen [She knows that what's comin' is inevitable and there isn't any way

P

she can speed up the process, so she just squats patiently and waits.]

Patriotic: 1. flag waver 2. anthem singer

Patronize: 1. plays up to 2. butters up 3. kisses his foot (or other parts of the anatomy)

Pawelekville (Karnes County): pronounced Pa-VALICK-ville [This little rural community is home for some of the friendliest Polish-Texans in the state. They sell T-shirts proclaiming "Nowhere Else but Pawelekville." The town, originally called Carajal Crossing, was renamed to honor the local Pawelek family.]

Pay attention: 1. pay some mind to 2. set your mind on it 3. cinch your mind to it 4. even a horse wearing blinders can see what's up ahead if he'll just look

Pay up: 1. pony up 2. cough it up

Pay your dues: 1. earn your spurs 2. if you give a dance, you gotta pay the band (or the fiddler) 3. if you're gonna rock you gotta have a big roll

Payment in advance: when I see the money in my hand, the goat'll jump off the wagon [The inference here is that the person selling the goat will keep it in the wagon until he gets paid. The saying can be used when you're selling anything and require payment in advance.]

Peace loving: 1. if God had intended me to fight like a dog, he'd have given me longer teeth and claws 2. more a lover than a wild bull rider 3. believes in evolution rather than revolution

Pear flats: *See Prickly pear flats*

Peas: shot

Peas without pork: motherless peas

Pecan: A pah-con is a nut, a pee-can is a can you use when you don't want to go to the outhouse in the middle of the night. The pecan tree is the state tree of Texas.

Peccary: javelina to a Texan

Peckerwood: woodpecker

Peckerwood sawmill: small sawmill where the operator cuts your logs for a percentage (often 50%) of the lumber produced

Pecking order: measure of a person's vulnerability [Those who are high in the order are always less vulnerable than those below them. For example, "Bubba is so far down in the pecking order at the chicken plant he'll be the first to go if people quit eating chickens."]

Pecos (Reeves County): pronounced PAY-cuss; the cantaloupe (can-a-lope) capital of the world; named for the nearby Pecos River

Pedernales River: correct pronunciation is Purr-din-alice; the name is Spanish for the flint rocks that are common in the riverbed *See also Perdenales*

Pedigree, lacking: his family tree has a lot more nooses than heroes

Peeved: got her nose out of joint

Peg: *See Close call*

Pegging: occurs when a bull dogger sticks a horn from the steer into the ground, which is prohibited

Pelham bit: a combination of a curb bit and a snaffle bit

Pen, ballpoint: still "ink pen" to a lot of Texans so it's clear they are not talking about straight pins, safety pins, or cattle pens

Pencil engineering: arbitrary additions to an incorrect answer that make it look correct

Pencil whip: occurs when the player keeping score fails to mark opponent's scores properly [In a friendly game, pencil whipping is humorous; in a money game it can be deadly.]

Pencil with an eraser: a golfer's best friend

Penelope (Hill County): pronounced Pa-NELL-a-pee; named for Penelope Trice, the daughter of the president of the International-Great Northern Railroad

Penicillin: 1. a wonder drug; anytime the doctor wonders what you have, you get it 2. what you give the man who has everything

Penmanship: hand, as in "Betty sure writes with a pretty hand."

Penitentiary bat: a steel-handled wooden club with a thick, wide piece of leather attached; used to beat prisoners in the Texas penitentiary until outlawed in the 1930s

Penny: 1. copper cent 2. Lincoln-head cent [Some Texans don't carry pennies 'cause they don't want no Yankee president in their pocket.]

People: 1. folks 2. common folks 3. everyday folks

People, good: 1. my kind of folks 2. top shelf folks

Pep rally: yell practice

Pepper sauce: shotgun

Perch (fish): panfish

Perdenales (Travis County): pronounced Purr-din-alice, like the Pedernales River [When the founders located this town near the Pedernales River, they decided to spell it like the river name is pronounced rather than how it is spelled.]

Peregrinus (perry): a mythical animal with the tail of a fox, body of a donkey, head of a stork, and eyes of an eagle; stands for all that makes a man great: pep, power, and pertinacity. The perry is the patron saint of the Laws at the University of Texas.

Perfectionist: Don Meredith described Tom Landry as a perfectionist. "If he was married to Racquel Welch," Meredith said, "he'd expect her to cook." A perfectionist lady might be

one who, if married to Mel Gibson, would expect him to mow the lawn.

Performance, mixed: like the man in the circus act who was shot out of a cannon, he had his ups and downs

Performance, poor: gave it a lick and a promise

Perfume: 1. parfume 2. liquid lure 3. follow-me-boys ointment 4. chemical warfare 5. liquid flypaper, which refers to a woman dabbing on perfume in the hopes of catching a man like flypaper does a fly 6. phoo-phoo water 7. holy water, which means when she puts it on she prays she will smell good enough to attract a man

Permanent: 1. set in cement or concrete 2. can't blot a brand [Once a brand has been burned into the hide of a steer, it's permanent; a brand can be changed by a rustler but it cannot be erased.] 3. carved in stone 4. dyed in the wool, which refers to the fact that once the dye is in the wool, it is there to stay

Permanent as: 1. a temporary tax 2. an autopsy

Permit-holder: See Professional Rodeo Cowboy Association

Perrin (Jack County): pronounced PAIR-in; named for L. W. Perrin, an early settler

Persevere: 1. hard work keeps the fences up 2. the best buck gets the doe 3. if the steer won't come to the branding fire, take the fire to the steer 4. catch a fish, even if you have to dig a canal and drain the tank 5. if steel won't cut it, a diamond will, which is a reference to using diamond drill bits 6. ride her out 7. lick by lick, any old cow can polish off a grindstone 8. if you mind your knitting, you'll eventually have a sweater that will fit someone 9. stick to your guns 10. you can teach an old dog new tricks but it takes more time 11. if she says no, you didn't ask the right question, you didn't ask the question right, or you didn't ask the right person [Spike Dykes, the West Texas sage who also doubles as the head football coach at Texas Tech, was asked to comment after his team beat the University of Texas in Austin for the first time in 22 years. "If you keep scratchin'," he said, "sooner or later you dig up a worm."

Persevering: hanging in like a hair in a biscuit

Persimmons: Ozark dates

Persist: 1. stick to your guns 2. the squeaking wheel gets the grease 3. eight seconds to ride and a lifetime to think about it [This refers to a rodeo cowboys having to ride bulls and bucking horses for eight seconds. Whether they make the ride or get thrown off, they get to think about it the rest of their lives. A variation of this is a football coach, whose team is behind at halftime, saying, "You have 30 minutes to play and a lifetime to think about it."]

Persistent as: 1. a June bug on a screen door 2. a sick kitten sticking by a warm brick 3. a terrier after a rat in the woodpile

Person: body, as in "If our taxes are raised even a little bit it'll be more than a body can stand."

Person, cold: you couldn't warm up to him if y'all were cremated together

Person, controversial: Billy Martin, former manager of the Texas Rangers, was perhaps the essence of controversy. After his accidental death, Randy Galloway, then of the *Dallas Morning News*, wrote: "Billy Martin was one of a kind. He came, he went, he left a long skid mark." Martin himself may have explained why he was so controversial when he said, "I don't throw the first punch. I throw the second four."

Person, educated: got more degrees than a thermometer

Person, good: 1. all wool and a yard wide 2. when the bombs start falling, I want to be in his foxhole

Person, mean: *See Mean man*

Person, not normal: needs to go back into the oven and bake some more

Person, small: could model for the figures on trophies

Person, strange: could be ambassador to the Bermuda Triangle

Person, superficial: an empty bucket makes the most noise [An empty bucket will get dropped and kicked around, which makes a lot of noise, while a full bucket will be handled carefully. The inference is that a superficial person will make a lot of noise while a person with character will not.]

Person, unacceptable: wouldn't have him if his head was strung with gold

Person, useless: his limitations are limitless

Person, worthless: to see how much he'd be missed, stick your finger in a pond, pull it out, and look in the hole

Person of high esteem: all beer and no foam

Person of low esteem: all foam and no beer

Person who gets things done: a tail twister

Personal responsibility: every cat has to lick his own backside

Persuasive: 1. could talk a chicken into jumping up and down on an ax to cut off its own head 2. can convince his wife to be sorry for the girl who left her bra in his glove compartment 3. could convince her husband the cigar butt in the ashtray was his even if he didn't smoke 4. most persuasive of all is the lady who can talk her way out of a traffic ticket when she's stopped by a female cop

Pert: as a ruttin' buck

Pessimist: 1. his glass is always half empty 2. the only thing he'd expect to find on a silver platter is tarnish 3. never puts anything away for a rainy day 'cause he's always expecting a drought 4. always try to borrow money from a pessimist 'cause he won't expect to ever get it back

Pester: 1. worry him a link or two 2. get under his saddle like a cocklebur

Petolia (Clay County): pronounced PATROL-ya; supposedly named for the petroleum deposits in the area

Petronilia (Nueces County): pronounced Petro-neal-a; named for a nearby creek

Pflugerville (Travis County): pronounced FLEW-gurr-ville; named for Henry Pfluger, who brought his family from Germany and settled in the area

Philosophy: horse sense in a dress suit

Phony: talks the talk but he don't walk the walk [This fairly modern saying originated in honor of the late, great John Wayne. A lot of people can imitate his voice but not many can walk like he did.]

Phony as: a marriage license from Wal-Mart

Physician: *See Doctor*

Piano player: 1. ivory tickler, which refers to the days when the keys of a piano were made of real ivory 2. piano pounder, which is how Bob Wills described his piano player, Al Strickland

Pick the best: 1. get the pick of the litter 2. separate the wheat from the chaff [Chaff is the seed coverings and miscellaneous debris that is separated out in threshing.] 3. cull the lot [It's

been said the man who culls the crop of girls spends a lot of nights alone.]

Picket pin: a pin (or stake) that is used to tie a horse when nothing else, like a tree, is available; usually metal but can be wood, with a ring attached

Pick-up line, good: that's the best icebreaker since the *Titanic*

Pickles and onion: sour rabbit

Pickup: 1. pickemup 2. cowboy Cadillac [In Texas it isn't necessary to include "truck" since everybody knows a pickup is something you drive, not something you find in a honky-tonk. It has been said you can't be a real Texan if you don't drive a pickup.]

Pickup, dilapidated: *See Work truck*

Pickup, new: it ain't got the novel wore off yet

Pickup aerodynamics: True pickup aerodynamics is the measure of how well the pickup is designed to prevent tobacco pin-striping and juice blow-back when you spit out the window. A truck with good aerodynamics means you can spit out the window and the juice will land on the Mercedes that's tryin' to pass. Poor aerodynamics means when you spit at certain speeds it "blows back" into the cab or splatters the side of the truck producing "tobacco pin-striping." Bad aerodynamics, especially when your wife is riding in the passenger seat, is when you spit out the driver's side window and the projectile travels around the cab and reenters through the passenger window. Such aerodynamics, if not corrected, are a leading cause of accidents and divorces.

Pickup man: 1. mounted official who assists saddle bronc and bareback riders in the dismount 2. farmer who also runs a few head of cattle on his place

Piece: a chunk

Pig fries: *See Calf fries and Brave as*

Pig salve: lard

Piggin' string: short, soft rope, usually six feet long, a cowboy uses to tie up the legs of the calf in the calf roping event in a rodeo. The term is also used for any small length of rope. When the animal is tied it is said to be "hog-tied."

Piggley Wiggley: Hogly Wogly

Piggy heifer: a heifer bred before her first birthday

Pilot: 1. propeller boy 2. fly boy 3. jet wrangler

Pilot, poor: a hangar flyer [This implies he spends more time around the hangar talking about flying than he does in the air.]

Pilot Grove (Grayson County): originally Lickskillet, the new name was taken from the nearby Pilot Grove Ranch

Pinchback suit: a suit that is made to fit better by pinching together some of the material in the back; the term "pinchback" can also be used for any article of clothing that fits poorly

Pinchers: pliers, from the Mexican word *pinchas*

Pine gum gatherer: a person who harvested pine gum, which was distilled to make turpentine and resin

Pine knot: See Kindling

Pine needles: twinkles

Pine resin: rozzum

Pink as: 1. a fresh-spanked baby's bottom 2. a plastic flamingo

Pinks: pearl gray breeches

Pinnacle: Texas term for any kind of hill, regardless of height

Pint bottle: a slider because its flat design allows you to slide it across the counter

Pioneers: the ones who took the arrows

Pious: 1. preacherfied 2. raised on prunes and proverbs

Pips (dominoes): spots

Piss head: sophomore at A&M

Pistol: 1. six-shooter 2. persuader 3. peacemaker 4. shootin' iron 5. pistole 6. equalizer See also Derringer; Hawleg; Saturday night special; Thumbbuster

Pistol, double action: a pistol with a double action that allows the trigger to be pulled with or without the hammer being cocked

Pistol, large: 1. hogleg 2. thumbbuster 3. so big it runs on diesel

Pistol, single action: the trigger works only when the hammer is cocked

Pistol, small: See Saturday night special

Pitchfork: two types—one with curved tines, used for stacking or pitching hay into a stack; and one with straight tines, used for moving hay such as from a baler table into the baler

Place to sit: 1. a spot to squat 2. a hunker-down spot

Placedo (Victoria County): pronounced PLAS-a-doe

Plagiarism: 1. would publish the Ten Commandments under his name if he could get away with it 2. the art of concealing your sources [If you steal from one person it's plagiarism, if you steal from two or more it's research.]

Plain: 1. unplowed 2. unvarnished 3. without frills, bells, or whistles 4. stripped down model 5. with the bark off 6. unwrapped version See also Obvious

Plain as: 1. day, as in "I saw him kiss her on the mouth plain as day." 2. fresh plowed ground, which infers that no crop is growing, thus the ground is plain 3. the nose on your face 4. the top line on an eye chart 5. the ears on a mule

Plan: aim to, as in "I aim to get that bill paid one of these days."

Plan ahead: 1. build the fence before you buy the cattle 2. build a coop before you buy the chickens 3. drill the well before you build the windmill 4. don't hang the gate till you've built the fence 5. don't buy the saddle till you've got a horse 6. don't start choppin' till you've treed the coon [Burk Murchison has a sign in his office that reads "Well planned is half built." And remember, Noah built his ark before it started raining.]

Plan to stay: 1. aim to stick around a spell 2. brought my toothbrush and a change of underwear

Plank gate: *See Gate*

Planning to stay: wearin' his sittin' britches

Plano (Collin County): pronounced PLAIN-oh, not Plan-oh [Folks from this town are just plain ol' Texans, known for producing legendary high school football teams.]

Play: horse around, which refers to the playfulness of an unbridled horse

Play by the rules: according to Hoyle [In gambling, especially poker, it could be "according to Doyle," a reference to Doyle "Texas Dolly" Brunson, considered by many to be the best high stakes poker player ever to lift a chip. *According to Doyle* was the title of a book published by Brunson in 1984.]

Play dead: play possum

Player: shooter, which is derived from shooting dice in a crap game

Playful as: 1. a calf in clover 2. an unbridled horse

Playing around: horsin' around

Pleasanton (Atascosa County): pronounced PLEASANT-un; the town claims to be "the birthplace of the cowboy"

Pleased: 1. tickled to death 2. my toes are tingling 3. overcome with gratefuls

Pleased as: 1. punch 2. a kitten that lapped up milk from a contented cow

Pleasing: 1. so good it would make childbirth a pleasure 2. tickled my fancy 3. warms your gullet 4. sight for sore eyes 5. will make your skin tight 6. pleases me no end 7. melts my butter

Pleasurable: 1. ain't never had this much fun with my clothes on 2. had as much fun as two hogs in a wallow

Plentiful: as ticks in a wet spring

Plenty: 1. got it in carload lots 2. a whole deck of 3. a whole herd of

Pliers: pinchers [So called because it's hard to use a pair of pliers for very long without pinching your finger.]

Plow: 1. turn some clods 2. go stare at the mule's rear, which refers to the days when farmers plowed behind mules so there wasn't too much scenery

Plow types, old style: *See Buck rake; Cultivator; Middle buster; Dish (or Disk); Dish, one way; Georgia stock and heel sweep; Sulky; Sulky rake; Turning. See also Bed a field*

Pluck (Polk County): originally called Stryker to honor local sawmill owner Henry Stryker [Since making a living at a sawmill was a Difficult proposition, the name was changed to reflect the determination of the locals to be successful. Stryker was so popular, many locals continued to call the town by that name. Incredibly, both names are still used today, which can be confusing for nonresidents.]

Pluck a chicken: dress it, as in "Y'all come on over 'cause granny's gonna dress a chicken and fry it for supper."

Plumb: a popular Texas adjective that can be used to mean extremely, far, pleasurable, or almost anything else. An exaggerated example is "Bubba was plumb crazy to go plumb to Houston for a date with Mary Ann even though she is plumb pretty."

Plumber: pipes doctor

Plumber, good: 1. could plug Niagara Falls 2. could repair a hole in the ozone layer

Plumber, poor: don't make house calls

Poacher: *See Jailhouse deer*

Pocket money: walking around money

Pointblank (San Jacinto County): A French governess for a prominent local family called the community Blanc Point which meant "white point." For reasons lost to history, the words were reversed and eventually Texanized to Pointblank.

Pointed as: the devil's tail

Pointless as: 1. painting manure 2. a June bug arguing with a duck

Poise: 1. the ability to not look conspicuous when you have to sit on the front row in church 2. the ability to raise an eyebrow instead of the roof

Poison: pizzen

Poker: 1. chips passing in the night 2. the key to poker is not in holding a good hand but in playing a bad hand well

Poker axiom: you have to draw to catch

Poker game, small: 1. saddle blanket game [Cowpunchers on the trail never had a table to play cards on so they simply spread a saddle blanket on the ground.] 2. ain't worth the cost of keepin' the lights on [This means the amount of money that changes hands wouldn't cover the electric bill for running the lights. In the old days, a small-time poker game wouldn't cover the cost of the coal oil for the lamp or the candles that would be used up.]

Poker hand, dangerous: a Dixie Hammer [This is a poker hand of any five cards in one hand and a knife in the other. It's unbeatable unless the other fella has a gun, in which case you become living proof that it ain't smart to carry a knife to a gunfight. Also called a Dixie Boxing Glove.]

Poker hand, poor: holding a paregoric

Poker hand, worthless: an Arkansas or hillbilly straight [In normal poker, a straight consists of five cards in any suit in numerical order, such as 3, 4, 5, 6, 7. An Arkansas straight, however, skips one card between the others such as 3, 5, 7, 9, Jack. Such a hand is absolutely worthless.]

Poker raise, large: 1. clearing the top water [In poker, to get rid of those players barely hangin' on, you make a large raise, which clears the top water.] 2. separate the men from the boys [This means the raise is so large only a real man can or will call it. Another way to say it is "we're gonna separate the does from the bucks."]

Poker raise, small: you sent a boy to do a man's job [This expression is generally used when you make a small raise and someone else at the table raises you by a much larger amount.]

Police: 1. po-leece 2. do-right boys 3. bear 4. Federales 5. rangers 6. county mounties 7. badge toter [In the old days when the likes of Bonnie and Clyde were loose in Texas, the police were usually called simply "the laws."] *See also Highway patrolmen; Lawmen; Outrun the law*

Political inefficiency: Texan Don Bowman wrote, "Politicians are like cockroaches. It's not what they carry off, but what they fall into and mess up."

Political office, nonexistent: fiddler general

Political parties in Texas: 1. Republican 2. Democratic 3. Independent 4. lunatic fringe

Political philosophy: "He never met a tax he didn't hike," is Donnis

Baggett's definition of Texas political philosophy.

Politician: 1. baby kisser 2. spoiled by being given a pull on the public teat 3. a promise merchant 4. thinks twice before saying nothing 5. stands for what he hopes most people will fall for 6. repairs his fences by hedging 7. give him a free hand and it'll wind up in your pocket 8. will promise to build bridges where there ain't no rivers 9. got what it takes to get what you got 10. adept at getting money from the taxpayer without disturbing the voter 11. like a bullfrog, what isn't stomach is head and that mostly mouth [When W. Lee "Pappy" O'Daniel ran for governor he couldn't vote because he didn't pay his poll tax, claiming, "No politician in Texas is worth $1.75." He won anyway. O'Daniel is often credited with coining the phrase "Washington is the only lunatic asylum in the world run by its own inmates."]

Politician, ambitious: He's like a country dog in town, tryin' to pee on every post, meaning he's trying to please everyone, which can't be done.

Politician, devious: Donnis Baggett said it best, "He's so slick his socks won't stay up."

Politician, experienced: like a football coach, smart enough to know the rules and dumb enough to think the game is important

Politician, expert: 1. can borrow $20 from you, keep it six months, pay you back only $10, and then convince you that you're even because you both lost $10 2. can stand firmly in midair 3. if he was being chased naked down Main Street by an angry, armed lynch mob, he could make you believe he was leading a parade

Politician, good: can sit on a fence and keep both ears to the ground

Politician, honest: 1. someone money can't buy, but if you do buy him he'll stay bought 2. stands out like a do-it-yourself haircut 3. honest politicians are like eclipses, few and far between

Politician, poor: 1. couldn't get elected if he ran unopposed 2. couldn't get elected fiddler general of Texas 3. a coattail politician [This means his fortunes turn on the fortunes of some other higher up politician.] 4. his credibility has stretch marks 5. they thought he was presidential timber but he turned out to be just bark 6. couldn't get elected if the national guard stuffed the ballot boxes

Politician, ugly: You could use his picture to wean calves off their mothers. There is an old story about a politician being so ugly that some farmers would tie his campaign posters on their cows and the calves would be so scared they would stop sucking and start eating grass. Being a consummate professional, the ugly politician, when told of the use for his signs, simply replied, "I am glad I could be of service to our valuable farmers."

Politician, versatile: 1. has a mind open at both ends 2. takes a firm stand on all sides of the issues 3. once he makes up his mind he's full of indecision

Politician, windy: 1. can give mouth-to-mouth resuscitation over the phone 2. listening to him is like shooting at a moving target, you have to allow for the wind

Politics: 1. "The science of public service," according to former Texas governor Pat Neff 2. those that can, do, those that can't, run for office 3. legalized larceny 4. the art of promising 5. the public goldfish bowl 6. the only thing harder to clean up after than a small boy 7. only thing that makes a man faster on his feet than politics is bigamy 8. the art of keeping as many balls in the air as possible while protecting your own [You can break down politics into poly, which means many, and ticks which means bloodsuckers. Thus politics is many bloodsuckers.]

Poll: the part of a horse's head between the ears

Polled: cattle that have been bred to not produce horns

Polluted area: so polluted you get dirty echoes

Poly grass blend: *See Rope types*

Pommel: front part of the saddle

Pommel string: a rope attached to the pommel used to secure something being carried

Pond, small: 1. tank 2. stock tank 3. dirt tank 4. watering hole

Ponder: cogitate

Pontotoc (Mason County): pronounced PON-a-tock

Poodle: poodle dog

Pool: when local ranchers combine their herds to make working the cattle easier [Riders who tend to the cattle are called pool riders.]

Poor: 1. ate so many rabbits when we were young we'd hide under the porch every time the dogs barked 2. ain't got a pot to pee in or a window to throw it out of 3. if an elephant overcoat cost a dollar, I couldn't buy a jacket for a gnat 4. couldn't even go window shopping, which means they couldn't afford the gas to get to town 5. the only time we had ice was right after a hailstorm 6. I have to stay alive 'cause I can't afford to be buried 7. if he had a $100 bill in his pocket he'd be wearing somebody else's pants 8. the only time he carries any money is when he's an usher in church 9. so poor the wolf wouldn't come to our door 'cause he knew he would end up on the dinner table 10. had to wear a straw hat to Christmas [In Texas you wear straw hats in the summer and felt hats in the winter, thus anyone wearing straw at Christmas would be too poor to buy a felt

hat.] 11. my folks told me Santa got killed in a sleigh wreck 12. the hogs wouldn't eat our slop 13. so poor I had a tumbleweed as a pet (West Texas) 14. so poor I had a pinecone as a pet (East Texas) [Paul Peterman of Celina, Texas, said when he was young they were so poor they ate dried apples for breakfast and dried apples for dinner. Then at supper they drank water and the apples would swell up so much they'd go to bed thinking they were full.] *See also Bankrupt; Broke; Destitute; Poverty stricken*

Poor, but proud: too poor to paint, too proud to whitewash

Poor and mean: would rattle empty dishes just to fool the cats

Poor as: 1. Job's turkey 2. a lizard-eating cat 3. a church mouse 4. a sawmill rat 5. a pineapple farmer in Texas

Poor imitation for: sorry excuse for, as in "Bubba, that poodle dog of yours is a sorry excuse for a bird dog."

Poor quality: 1. crow bait 2. cull 3. ain't worth two bits 4. put together with spit and baling wire 5. plug 6. ain't worth a hoot or a holler *See also Worthless*

Popped: like a firecracker

Popped open: like a morning glory

Popped out: like a spit watermelon seed

Poppers: one or two pieces of leather attached to the end of a quirt or rein. When in use, the leather will "pop," which helps to reinforce what you want the animal to do.

Popular as: 1. an oilman's (or banker's) daughter 2. a lottery winner [If you think you have a lot of friends and relatives now, haul off and win the lottery and see how fast the numbers of both grow.]

Popularity: Bum Phillips said, "No matter how popular you are, the size of your funeral depends on the weather."

Porch: 1. gallery 2. veranda

Pork (fatty)**:** fatback

Pork preserved in salt: salt pork or sowbelly

Pork rind: fish bait

Pork skins: cracklin's

Port Neches (Jefferson County)**:** pronounced Port NET-chez

Portion: batch of

Positive: 1. right sure 2. sure as hell's hot 3. you can tattoo it on your arm 4. you can write it in ink 5. if it ain't true there ain't an Indian in Oklahoma, a pine tree in Georgia, a pretty girl in Texas, or a white tooth in Hollywood *See also Certain; Fact; Guaranteed; Reliable*

Positive, almost: 1. purt-near positive 2. purdy-nigh sure

Positively: as sure as Santa Claus has reindeer manure on his boots

Possessions: 1. belongings 2. plunder

Possessions, dear: wouldn't take for them

Possible: 1. even a blind hog finds an acorn now and then 2. never been a horse that can't be rode or a cowboy that can't be throwed 3. anything is possible if you have the know-how or the money 4. anything is possible if don't matter who gets the credit

Possible bag: a bag you take when hunting so you'll have a place to carry the game. Today, the term can be used for any small bag.

Possum: a Southern game animal that ain't worth nuthin' till it's in a sack. There are lots of possum recipes, but here's the most popular: Clean and dress one middlin-sized possum. Put it in boiling water for half an hour to tenderize. Baste with honey and butter and stuff with sweet potatoes, carrots, and onions. Wrap in tin foil and bake for one hour or until golden brown. Remove sweet potatoes, carrots, and onions and eat them. Give the possum to the dogs.

Possum belly: a green cowhide stretched and fastened under the chuck wagon for holding wood and dried cow chips; also called a "coonie"

Post (Garza County)**:** Cereal magnate C. W. Post wanted to establish an experimental model community so he purchased 250,000 acres in West Texas and brought in 1,200 families to settle the area. He named the community after himself.

Postman: letter carrier

Pot liquor: liquid that remains after cooking vegetables like greens; nonalcoholic, chock full of vitamins, and good for sopping with a biscuit [not to be confused with a pot licker, which is a faithful old hound dog that licks the pots clean after cooking so you don't have to wash 'em]

Potato: tater

Poteet (Atascosa County)**:** pronounced POE-teat; named for Francis Marion Poteet, the first postmaster

Potent: 1. can cure more than patent medicine 2. as a broken bottle of French perfume in a boy's dorm 3. as a mare's breath

Poth (Wilson County)**:** pronounced Poath; named for A.H. Poth, who owned the first gin in the area

Pounding leather: riding fast

Poured out: like hens through a hole in the fence [Anytime you keep hens in a fence they become convinced the pecking is better on the other side, so if even a little hole gets punched in the fence the hens pour out.]

Pouter: thumb sucker

Poverty stricken: 1. ate so many armadillos when I was young, I still roll up into a ball when I hear a dog bark 2. we had to fertilize the sills before we could raise the windows, which is how poor Bum Phillips said his family was *See also Broke; Destitute; Poor*

Powerful: 1. Texas adjective meaning very, immense, considerable, etc., such as "I'm powerful glad to get this check." 2. deeply or intense, as in "I'm doin' some powerful prayin' that the jury will come to its senses and find grandma not guilty."

Powerful person: if he crows, it's daylight [It was said of Houston's Jesse Jones, "When that rooster crows, it's daylight in East Texas." Jones owned considerable land and lumber holdings in East Texas.]

Poynor (Henderson County): pronounced POI-ner; named for D. H. Poynor, a railroad surveyor

Practical joker: 1. his main crop is tomfoolery 2. he'd pull the leg of a wild bull for a laugh

Practice: dry shooting or frying. Dry shooting is learning all about shooting a gun without using any ammunition. Dry frying is learning how to cook without having any grease in the skillet. [Everything gets easier with practice except getting up in the morning and eating crow.]

Praying: talking to headquarters

Praying mantis: devil's walking stick

Preacher: 1. Bible thumper (or pounder) 2. sin buster 3. parson 4. sky pilot 5. padre 6. gospel shooter 7. Bible banger 8. gospel grinder 9. devil chaser 10. gospel wrangler 11. hallelujah peddler 12. pulpit pounder 13. sin killer 14. the Lord's deputy (or a member of the Lord's posse) 15. a member of Heaven's jury 16. hell, fire, and brimstone man 17. hell, fire, and damnation man

Preacher, devout: could talk a whole bowl of mashed potatoes cold [In the country the preacher is often invited over for Sunday dinner. A really devout preacher is one who takes so long saying grace that the entire bowl of mashed potatoes turns cold. The most devout preacher of all can talk an entire turkey cold at Thanksgiving.]

Preacher, emphatic: a suck-back preacher, which is one who frequently "sucks" large gulps of air for emphasis

Preacher, experienced: 1. can estimate the size of the collection within ten dollars just from lookin' at the crowd 2. could count the collection in his mind just from hearing the coins being dropped into the plate [One experienced Baptist preacher could tell a counterfeit coin was dropped in the plate 'cause it had a different ring from the other quarters.]

Preacher, smart: 1. has the ushers pass the plate before the sermon [The larger the collection the less he speaks. Of course, such a plan only works when the congregation knows it in advance.] 2. when visiting, he keeps one eye open saying grace so the children don't beat him to the white meat on the plate of fried chicken

Preaching to the choir: 1. explaining something to someone who knows as much, if not more, about it than you do 2. trying to convince someone who already agrees with you

Prearranged: 1. it's already been cut and dried 2. the wool is already dyed 3. the die is cast

Precarious situation: 1. your pig's sucking hind tit [Occasionally an old sow would have more piglets than she had teats to accommodate them, which meant one or more had to scramble for a place to suck. The baby pig unlucky enough to get the hind teat often had to squirm between mother's legs to get at the spigot. If mama hog changed positions or rolled over, the baby pig between her legs was in danger of being thumped hard or, worse yet, being flung across the barnyard. The same situation also existed for calves who had to sneak up on the mama cow from behind and stick their head between her legs to get to the hind teat. In either case, having to suck the hind teat was a precarious situation.] 2. got the cow staked next to the truck patch [She'll eat most of the crop you intended to sell. In such a precarious situation, the cow gets a full belly but you lose money.]

Precaution: Never eat anything that grows wild around the back porch. In the country, some folks don't always make it all the way to the outhouse when they have to relieve themselves. In fact, many have been known to make it just as far as the back porch, thus any food growing around the porch probably had some strange liquid fertilizer dumped on it.

Precious: a term used by Texas ladies to indicate a high compliment such as "She just looks precious in that new dress." Synonyms would be darlin' and lovely. Antonyms would be sweet and nice, which Texans frequently use to sound nice when saying something really tacky.

Predicament: picklement *See also In danger; In trouble*

Predictable: No matter how warm the sunshine is, the cat will always have her kittens in the barn.

Preference: 1. druthers 2. rather do that than dig for buried treasure 3. beats a poke in the eye with a sharp stick 4. whatever pops your cork 5. whatever blows your dress up 6. whatever winds your clock 7. whatever floats your boat 8. some people object to a fan dancer, others to the fan 9. every fish has its favorite bait

Prefer not to: 1. would rather get under the porch and peck with the chickens (or put on a tin bill and peck with the chickens) than do that 2. would rather give a camel an enema than do that 3. would rather give a rattlesnake a root canal than do that

Pregnant: 1. heiferized 2. sitting on a nest 3. looks like she swallowed a blimp seed 4. flying her flag at half mast 5. a heavy springer 6. her apron is riding high 7. she's been storked 8. got one in the oven 9. got one in the chute 10. was hung by a serpent 11. got a big biscuit in the oven 12. looks like she swallowed her husband's bowling ball 13. wearing her bustle wrong

Pregnant and skinny: looks like a snake that swallowed a basketball

Pregnant with second child: got one bucking and one in the chute, which is a reference to loading rodeo chutes

Pregnant with twins: knocked up squared

Prejudiced as: a father in a baby judging contest

Preparation: the best way to hold cattle in the winter is to do your sleeping in the summertime.

Prepare food: fix [Folks up North may prepare dinner but Texans fix it as in "Honey, don't be late 'cause I'm fixin' chicken-fried steak for supper."]

Prepared: 1. done my homework 2. primed and ready 3. got the rifle sighted in 4. running on a full tank 5. ready for all comers 6. hunkered down and raring to go 7. stays ready so he won't ever have to get ready

Prepared for the worst: never forgot how to pick cotton [If things get bad, he's prepared to pick cotton so he'll at least have a job.]

Presidio (Presidio County): pronounced Purr-SID-ee-oh, which is in one of the oldest continuously cultivated areas in the United States

Presumptuous: just because you donate an organ to the church, don't mean you call the tunes to be played

Pretend: 1. make out like, as in "He made out like he was a cowboy and tried to ride that wild horse." 2. play like, as in "Why don't you play like you're rich and loan me $20?"

Pretend cowboy: just found the hat

Pretending: shooting at the hump [Anyone shooting at the hump of a buffalo, where there are no vital organs, was just pretending to hunt.]

Pretty: purdy

Pretty as: 1. a field of bluebonnets 2. a picture 3. a fresh painted wagon 4. a speckled pup under a wagon 5. a mortgage paid in full 6. a polished pearl 7. dollar cotton

Pretty girl: 1. cheerleader material 2. a real looker 3. a real beaut 4. eyeball pleaser (or soother) *See also Female*

Prevail: *See Persist; Persevere*

Prexy: President of Texas A&M University

Prexy's moon: lights above the dome of the Academic building at Texas A&M University that resemble missiles

Price: 1. worth, as in "What's that shotgun worth?" 2. what ya' asking for it, as in "What ya' asking for the bird dog pup?"

Price, approximate: 1. this side [used for a price that is a little less than an approximate amount as in "Can you believe Bubba paid just this side of $1,000 for that huntin' dog pup?" 2. the other side [used for a price that is a little more than an approximate amount as in "If you want to buy a new, loaded Ford F150 pickup it's gonna cost you something on the other side of $22,000."]

Prickly pear flats: flat, mostly arid land highlighted by a concentration of prickly pear cactus; also called pear flats; not good for much except rattlesnakes, roadrunners, and horney toads

Priddy (Mills County): sounds like a Texan saying pretty; named

for Thomas Jefferson Priddy, who was a preacher and a Texas Ranger

Pride: 1. every old crow thinks her chick is the blackest 2. so thick a Bowie knife wouldn't cut it 3. something that ain't hard to swallow once you chew on it long enough

Prim and proper: 1. Miss Priss 2. as a preacher's wife at a church social

 Primera (Cameron County): pronounced Pre-MARE-ah

Princeton (Collin County): pronounced PRIN-stun; originally named Wilson's Switch; residents later applied for Wilson, but postal authorities rejected it as already taken. The name Princeton was then chosen to honor Prince Dowlin, a local landowner.]

Prioritize: 1. don't chase grasshoppers when the hogs are eating the corn 2. get your ducks in a row 3. don't be baiting rat traps in the barn when coyotes are after the spring calves 4. don't chop firewood till you've built the fireplace 5. you're looking for the thermostat when the roof is caving in from the snow 6. a calf can't bawl and suck at the same time

Prison, maximum security: 1. sunshine has to have a pass to visit 2. a cockroach couldn't get out of that place

Prison, minimum security: where you serve three years at hard tennis (or golf)

Prisoner: he's been penitentured

Pritchett (Upshur County): pronounced PRITCH-it, not Pritch-ette; originally named Lockhart's Switch. When the locals applied for a post office, they requested Pritchard after a local settler. [The post office accepted the application but somehow misspelled the name.]

Private as: 1. underwear 2. your dirty wash

Probable: 1. likely as not 2. in all likelihood

Problem: 1. grasshoppers in the axle grease 2. a fly in the buttermilk 3. got a yellow jacket nest in the outhouse 4. that's the thorn in my side 5. a fly in the ointment 6. a firefly in the milk churn 7. a burr under his blanket 8. a dead cat down the well *See also In trouble; Trouble*

Problem, large: 1. sat down in a bear trap 2. opened a can of worms

Problem drinker: 1. one that never buys 2. gets alligator arms when the tab arrives [Tommy Lasorda once said of Billy Martin, former manager of the Texas Rangers, "When he reaches for a bar tab his arm shrinks six inches."]

Procrastinate: piddle diddle, as in "When it comes to mowing the lawn Bubba can piddle diddle with the best of 'em."

Procrastinator: never puts his best foot forward until he gets the other one in hot water

Profanity: Mark Twain said, "Under certain circumstances, profanity provides a relief denied even to prayer." Sometimes it just feels better to tell someone to go to hell than it does to pray they don't make the trip.

Profession: 1. stock in trade 2. his main (or long) suit

Professional: takes time to sharpen his ax [A real pro would recognize the value of keeping a sharp edge on an ax because it would make choppin' wood much easier. A nonprofessional would keep choppin' even when his ax got dull and would end up taking a lot longer to finish the job.]

Professional Rodeo Cowboy Association (PRCA): governing body of professional rodeo [To join the PRCA, a cowboy must apply for a permit and then compete as a "permit-holder" in the smaller association rodeos. Once a permit holder has earned the required amount in the smaller rodeos, he is eligible for a non-restrictive "contestant's card" that allows him to compete in any event in any sanctioned rodeo, regardless of size.]

Proficient: 1. been doing that since before he could drool 2. right handy with, as in "He's right handy with a fork or a forklift." 3. on a first name basis with, as in "He's on a first name basis with the business end of a hoe." *See also Experienced*

Progress, slow: just staying one day ahead of yesterday

Progressing: made it to the fast lane but I'm still on a farm to market road

Project, special: got a hen on the nest, which is a special project that demands your undivided attention

Promiscuous: free for all *See also Female, promiscuous and Male, promiscuous*

Prone to: bad to do it, as in "Bubba's bad to fight after drinking a six-pack."

Proof: 1. got the deadwood on 'em 2. the lowdown

Proper: fittin'

Proposal, attractive: that'd get the preserves down on the bottom shelf

Prospects, good: got a good season in the ground, which means he's planted a good crop

Prosperous: 1. living high on the hog 2. sitting (or living) in high cotton 3. cuttin' the big jimson 4. sneezes through silk, a reference to someone well off enough to afford silk handkerchiefs *See also Rich*

Prostitute: 1. a John's dear, which is a takeoff on John Deere tractors 2. fallen angel 3. soiled dove 4. pavement princess 5. painted lady 6. trick wrangler 7. flat-backer 8. floozy 9. hooker

Protect: 1. guard that like a farmer does a watermelon patch 2. scarecrow it 3. bury that bone so no other dog'll get it 4. look after it like a mockingbird guarding her nest

Protect yourself: 1. circle the wagons 2. fort up

Protected: 1. bulletproof 2. fired proof, which means he isn't likely to be fired from a job

Protested: raised a bigger stink than a skunk under the church

Protruding: pooched-out, as in "His gut has gotten pooched-out since he went back to drinkin' beer and eatin' possum."

Proud: 1. swelled up like a poisoned pup 2. swelled up like a frog in a churn 3. struttin' like a gobbler at layin' time

Proud as: 1. a peacock in full bloom 2. a dog with two tails 3. a pup with a new collar 4. a goat with four horns

Provider, good: keeps his smokehouse greasy

Provider, poor: 1. the bacon he brings home is just sow's belly 2. don't bring home enough bacon to fill a toy skillet

Provoked: egged me into it

Prude: 1. old iron pants 2. holds out like a Zane Grey heroine

Prudent: don't waste buckshot on a sparrow [This basically means don't waste ammunition killing a sparrow since they are too small to eat and too hard to clean.]

Prunes: wrinkle

Pry: prize, as in "Prize open that beer cooler and hand me a fresh one."

Pry bar: 1. jimmy bar 2. prize bar

Psychiatrist: nerve doctor *See also Hospital, psychiatric*

Pucker string: Tobacco was once sold in small cloth sacks that had a string in the top so it could be drawn shut. When closed, the top of the sack looked "puckered" so the string that held it that was called a pucker string.

The term was used universally to signify any small piece of string.

Puckered: like a wet sheepskin next to a hot fire

Puffed up: like a frog in a cream can

Pull down your dress: stretch your gingham

Pull out: for an underclassman to say words that it is not his privilege to know (or say)

Pull tabs: 1. metal tabs that make beer cans easy to open 2. small leather loops inside boots that make them easier to get on [also called pull loops, pull holes, and mule ears]

Pull up your pants: hitch up your britches

Pulling leather: said of a cowboy who holds onto a saddle with both hands while riding a pitching horse. If a contestant "pulls leather" in a rodeo, he's disqualified.

Pulpit committee: *See Committee, small*

Pump handle: a horse that bucks with a seesaw action, which is usually easy to ride

Pump jack: pumping unit on an oil well that looks a little like a giant grasshopper

Pumper: man in charge of pumping operations on an oil well

Puncher: *See Cowpuncher*

Punctuality, lacking: operates on Mexican Standard Time, which means you tell him when to be there and he gets there when he damn well pleases

Punish: 1. take 'em to the woodshed 2. fix (or clean) his clock 3. clean his plow 4. dust his feathers

Pure: In his book *Texas Proud and Loud,* Boyce House included the best definition: "Pure as the dewdrop that sparkles on the tail of a Texas bull as he rises from his grassy couch and bellows in the face of the rising sun."

Pure as: driven snow

Purple as: eggplant

Purse: pocketbook

Push: mash; in Texas you don't push a doorbell, you mash it

Pussy willow: possum bush

Put a bug in your ear: tell a secret of major importance

Put in writing: 1. script it 2. black and white it

Put it on: like a mud plaster

 Putnam (Callahan County): pronounced PUTT-nam [The locals will not take kindly to your saying Put-nam. Originally called Catlaw, the name was changed in honor of General Israel Putnam, a hero of the American Revolution.]

Putting on airs: stepping high like a rooster in deep mud

Puzzled: 1. buffaloed 2. the windshield of my mind is fogged over

Pyote (Ward County): pronounced PIE-yote [The name may have come from a misspelling of peyote, the hallucinatory cactus that once grew in the area. Another tale indicates the name came from Chinese railroad workers who had difficulty pronouncing the word coyote.]

Pyramid of cans: *See Noise, loud*

Q

Quaker gun: pretend gun

Qualifications, lacking: his bag of tricks has a hole in it

Qualified: 1. earned his spurs 2. made the grade

Quality, fair: 1. fair average quality 2. it ain't bad if you ain't used to much 3. middlin' fair [Although this saying is widely used to indicate fair average quality, that is not a correct usage. The term "midlin' fair" is actually a term in cotton grading used to mean the very best, a long way from average.]

Quality, good: 1. blue ribbon fine 2. best in all creation 3. State Fair winner [This refers to winning entries in the annual contests held at the State Fair in Dallas.] 4. can't beat that with a hickory switch 5. grade A good

Quality, poor: 1. don't make the grade 2. alligator bait 3. piddlin' poor 4. wouldn't even make honorable mention at the State Fair 5. fell apart like a two-dollar wagon

Quanah (Hardeman County): pronounced KWAN-ah; named for the last great Comanche chief Quanah Parker [The word means "sweet odor."]

Quantity: 1. a mess of 2. a dose of 3. a plenty 4. right smart of 5. more than you can shake a stick at *See also Lot; Many; Numerous*

Quantity, deceiving: ain't always the size of the load that counts [A handful of manure wouldn't be worth as much as a wagon load of fertilizer but a handful of diamonds would be worth more than ten truckloads of coal.]

Quantity, large: 1. a whole slew of 2. a sight of 3. a passel of [Another forgotten word from out of the past is lavish, which means large quantity as in "We got a lavish of last year's calendars on hand."]

Quarrel: cuss fight

Quarter: 1. two bits 2. jukebox feed 3. a half-ass, half-brass twelve-and-a-half-cent two-bit piece

Quarter moon: rustler's moon [Many rustlers preferred to ply their trade by the light of a quarter moon. A full moon was so bright, the thieves could easily be seen, and when there was no moon it was too dark to see the cattle.] *See also Moon*

Quarter section: 160 acres of land, which is a quarter of a section, the amount of land that was usually allotted to homesteaders

🅰🅼 **Quartermaster:** blanket-stackers

Queen (playing card): 1. mop squeezer 2. washer woman

Queer as: 1. a three-dollar bill 2. pink ink

Quick: 1. moves mighty sudden like 2. went by so fast I thought I was backing up 3. plenty pronto 4. double fast 5. could thread a needle on a running sewing machine 6. lickety split 7. on the trigger or draw *See also Fast*

Quick acting: 1. goes through you like bunkhouse, bus depot, or mess hall chili 2. goes through you like corn through a goose 3. like a dose of Epsom through a widow woman

Quick as: 1. a minnow can swim a dipper, which Darrell Royal says is how fast a punt return can kill you in a football game 2. beaters on an electric mixer 3. the flames of hell can scorch a tail feather 4. the snap of a bullwhip 5. a hiccup 6. a New York minute 7. a heartbeat 8. heaven's gate slams shut on a horse thief 9. a settin' hen on a June bug 10. you can bat an eye 11. a winter wind can lift a dead leaf 12. a roadrunner on a rattler 13. a hair trigger will get you shot in the foot 14. a hot iron can scorch a cotton dress 15. a Baptist preacher can spot a counterfeit quarter 16. the shake of a lamb's tail 17. wind from a duck's backside 18. a snake through a hollow log *See also Fast as*

Quick look: windshield inspection [In buying land, many people simply drive by and look at it through the window rather than getting out of the car and kicking some dirt.]

Quick tempered: 1. has a fuse shorter than an ant's eyebrow 2. hair trigger temper 3. prone to flying plumb off the handle 4. evil tempered 5. shoots first and doesn't even bother to ask questions later 6. got an easy wire to trip 7. his trigger finger is always itchy or his trigger don't take much pullin'

Quien sabe: Mexican for "Beats the hell out of me"

Quiet: 1. could hear hair grow 2. could hear a worm sneeze 3. could hear the break of day 4. the silence was deafening 5. could smell the odor of dead silence 6. can hear a hummingbird's heartbeat 7. well muzzled 8. prayer time 9. library time 10. talks half as much as an oyster with his shell shut 11. could hear a pin drop on a cotton bloom in the next county 12. could hear a field mouse wetting on a cotton boll 13. could hear the moon rise 14. could hear ants making love 15. could hear toenails growing *See also Be quiet; Keep quiet*

Quiet as: 1. a snowflake on a feather 2. a thief in the dark 3. a deaf mute's shadow 4. a grave at night 5. a church mouse 6. a well greased wagon in sand 7. the rustle of a cotton dress 8. a nightgown dropped on a plush carpet 9. a sick sow in a snowstorm 10. a coon stalking a crayfish 11. a worm's heartbeat 12. a sparrow in a hawk's nest

Quiet type: 1. don't use much kindling to get his fire started, which means he is a man of few words but the words he does use generally count for something 2. never mixes breath and tongue oil

Quietus: to end or stop something, frequently by applying some force or influence, as in "I was all set to join my buddies at the topless bar till my wife put the quietus on that plan when she stole the distributor cap off my truck." *See Ended abruptly*

🗺️ **Quihi** (Medina County): pronounced KWE-he; named for quichie (or keechie), which is a white-necked Mexican buzzard

Quilt: 1. soogan 2. Baptist pallet

Quilting bee: a get-together where several women join forces to sew a quilt, each taking a particular section. Before telephones, quilting bees and church socials were the primary method of spreading gossip.

Quirt: a small whip used to encourage horses

Quirt, loaded: a quirt with a popper attached

Quit: 1. pulled my lariat 2. cashed in 3. threw my spurs away 4. sold my horse and sacked my saddle 5. called it a day 6. threw in (or folded) my hand 7. threw up her dress

Quit drinking: weaned myself off the bottle

Quitaque (Briscoe County): pronounced KIT-a-qway, no kidding [Charles Goodnight gave the town its name, which he believed was Indian for "end of the trail." Some people, however, believe the word is Indian for "pile of manure" to put it mildly.]

Quitting time: time to put the tools in the truck

R

R.H.I.P.: rank has its privileges

R.H.I.R: rank has its responsibilities

R.O.C.: the "rice, oil, and cattle" area around Alvin, Texas, home of the legendary Nolan Ryan

Raccoon: a coon to a country boy

Race: running match

Racehorse, slow: it took that horse so long to finish, the jockey kept a diary

Rachal (Brooks County): pronounced RAY-shell; named for E. R. Rachal, the first tax assessor [maybe the only town in Texas named for a tax man; ordinarily, the tax boys weren't popular enough to get a whole town named for them]

Radiator shop: the best place to take a leak

Rag: 1. redneck gas cap 2. emergency radiator cap

Ragged as: a sheepherder's britches

Railbirds: cowboys who sit on the fence around a rodeo arena to watch the action

Railroad terms: See Blinds; Blower; Breeding; Brake club; Brakie; Bridge gang; Car knocker; Cribbing up; Gandy dancer; Hog head; Hostler; Johnson bar; Join the bird gang; Katy; Mixed train; Mud hop; Roundhouse; Section boss; Section crew; Section hand; Section train; Switch engine; Unbreed

Rain, approaching: 1. comin' up a cloud 2. flies are swarming on the screen, which is said to be a sure sign of approaching rainstorms

Rain, heavy: 1. a frog (or toad) strangler 2. a clear-up rain, which means you got so much rain the water was clear up to the back porch 3. a goose or turkey drowner 4. a gully washer 5. like a cow peeing on a flat rock 6. like somebody knocked over Heaven's water tank 7. a chunk, stump, cob, clod, or fence floater 8. a duck drencher 9. raining cats and dogs 10. pouring bullfrogs and heifer yearlings 11. rained like God pulled the cork 12. a tank destroyer, as in stock tank. On the farm, a really heavy rain may produce enough water to flood the place and wash out of any shallow stock tanks you might have. 13. had to jump into the river to keep from drowning 14. rainin' pitchforks and black cats

Rain, intermittent: 1. a sputtin' and spittin' rain 2. my double barreled shotgun only got wet in one barrel 3. you could count the drops 4. wasn't a runnin' rain, which means there wasn't enough water to run off the road 5. a three-inch rain, as in there was three inches between each drop

Rain, moderate: a degreaser, which means it rained just enough to wash the grease off the road

Rain, prolonged: a root soakin' rain, which means you got so much water the roots of trees were soaked thoroughly

Rain, short: like an old-timer's dance, it was soon over

Rain, soft: angel tears

Rain, sprinkling: a Methodist shower, which is a reference to Methodists sprinkling when they baptize

Rain, very heavy: an anvil mover, as in "After that rain last evening my anvil had been moved a foot and half." [Any anvil, even a small one, is very heavy, so it would take a lot of fast-flowing water to move one. Even though that never happens, use of the saying produces the connotation that you got a lot of rain. A really heavy rain would be an anvil floater.]

Rain after a dry spell: a sittin' in rain [This means you are so happy to finally see rain that you go right outside and sit in it awhile.]

A_M **Raincoat:** poncho

Rain shower: the clouds are crying

Rainbow, partial: sundog

Raining while the sun shines: the devil is beating his wife

Rainy day: a good day to be in bed with a good book or someone who has read one

Rainy: duck weather

Raisin (Victoria County): pronounced Raise-un; named in recognition of local rancher J. K. Reeve's effort to raise grapes

Raising the standard: raised the bar

Raking spurs: running spurs across the top of the shoulder of a horse or bull in a rodeo

Rambunctious: 1. hell raiser 2. feeling his oats

Ran: 1. like a jackrabbit feeling a coyote's breath on his backside 2. like a field mouse in an eagle's shadow *See also Runs*

Ranch, large: 1. measured by MPG (miles per gate) 2. had to have its own zip code 3. a two-horse ranch, which means you'd have to have two horses to ride across it in one day

Ranch, small: 1. an oleo ranch, which means it is a cheap spread 2. a tumbleweed outfit 3. a cocklebur outfit 4. don't have enough beef to hold a BBQ

Ranch horse: a good, reasonably gentle horse that works well around the ranch

Rancher: 1. fluent in hoss talk (or chatter) 2. speaks cow like a steer 3. what he don't know about cattle don't need to be known

Rancher, rich: his cows ain't branded, they're engraved

Range delivered: *See Sight unseen*

Rangerville (Cameron County): pronounced RAINGER-vul; named because the Texas Rangers maintained a camp in the vicinity

Rankin (Upton County): pronounced RANK-in, not Ran-kin [The original name Astoniat was changed to honor Frederick Harrison Rankin, one of Stephen F. Austin's "Old Three Hundred." The area around the town was popular with such noted outlaws as Sam Bass and Bonnie and Clyde.]

Ransation: an old North Texas term for revival

Rapid: *See Quick; Fast*

Rare: 1. ain't seen one of those in a coon's age 2. can't remember when I've seen one of those

Rare as: 1. a smile on a pallbearer 2. a flat tire on a freight train 3. a mermaid in a stock tank 4. a white crow 5. a round trip ticket to Heaven 6. a one-legged hurdler or a pregnant pole vaulter 7. bluebonnets in October 8. icicles in hell 9. wool in a beehive 10. a fat coyote 11. an out-of-state license plate in Hawaii 12. clean socks in a bunkhouse 13. an honest fisherman (or politician) 14. tears at a boot hill burying [In the days of the Old West, it was generally the bad men and outlaws who were buried in boot hill so there weren't a lot of tears shed over them.] 15. a jackelope [This is a Texas jackrabbit that has spiked horns like an antelope. Texas jackrabbits are so big that male antelopes often mistake them for female antelopes during mating season. Fortunately for the jackrabbits, they can usually outrun the antelope so the offspring that would be produced—the jackelope—are extremely rare.] *See also Scarce*

Rare meat: 1. the brand is still smoking 2. seen a cow cut worse than this get well, or I know a vet that could cure this critter 3. just thrown across the fire 4. if I got caught eating this in someone else's pasture, I'd go to jail for rustling 5. all they did was knock the horns off, wipe its butt, and slap it on a platter 6. get me a Band-Aid and I can save the steer 7. I can still see the jockey's whip marks, which implies that the meat is not only rare but that it might not be prime beef

Rascal: 1. yahoo 2. ring-tailed tooter 3. rounder 4. maverick 5. pistol 6. wild turkey 7. wild and wooly 8. corker 9. scoundrel

Rascality: the trouble caused by rascals, as in "The sheriff charged Billy Fred and Bubba with rascality when he caught them tumping over his outhouse."

Rash: prickly heat

Rat bait: rat poison

Rat killing: 1. normal, everyday chores or business 2. a project, usually reserved for rainy days, where puppies get their first hunting lesson [On a rainy day when it is not possible to work in the fields, menfolk gather up the new pups and a couple of bottles and slip off for the barn. Making as much noise as possible, they move bales of hay, saddles, implements, feed troughs, etc. in hopes of flushing out a rat so they can sic the pups on it and teach them how to kill the pests. The theory is that once a dog has killed his first rat he'll continue to kill them for the rest of his life. In actual practice, the success of the project is secondary. What really matters is the men got to have a few drinks outside the watchful eye of their wives.]

Rather: druther

Rations, short: eatin' short, which usually means drinkin' water and suckin' on your thumb

Rattles like: 1. BB's in a boxcar 2. marbles in a washtub

Rattlesnake: a viper common in all of Texas, also called rattler. These snakes range is size from very small, as in the pigmy rattlesnake, to the very large diamondback, which can be six feet or more in length. The popular legend that you can tell the age of a rattlesnake by counting the "buttons" on its tail is not true since the snakes shed the buttons.

Rattlesnake, big: 1. big around as a fire hose 2. so big it needed two coils

Rattlesnake milkweed: *See Texas milkweed*

Ravenna (Fannin County): pronounced Rah-VIN-ah [According to local legend, the name is taken from the numerous ravines in the area.]

Rawhide: 1. skin from a cow that is scraped and then dried in the sun [The name comes from the fact that the leather is not tanned and thus is a raw hide. Rawhide, which expands when damp and contracts when dried, was one of the most versatile products on the frontier. The uses included: ropes, straps, chaps, whips, boot soles, joint material in a corral, repairs to a broken wheel, hinges for a door or gate, and much more. American Indians were known to use playing cards made of rawhide. Also called "Mexican iron" because the closer you got to Old Mexico, the more rawhide you saw being used.] 2. a Texan when he ventured outside the state, especially to the Northwest area (so called because Texans used a lot of rawhide and were themselves considered as tough as the rawhide) 3. adjective used to describe anything in a raw or unfinished state as in rawhide lumber, which is green wood that has not been dried and is not prepared for use by a carpenter *See also Rawhiding*

Rawhide a windmill: using rawhide strips to repair the bearings in a windmill or to hold on the blades

Rawhider: a derogatory term for poor, often suspect drifters who moved around a lot and used a lot of rawhide to hold their gear and themselves together

Rawhiding: using rawhide to whip or beat someone

Raymondville (Willacy County): pronounced Ray-Mon-ville since the "D" is silent; named after developer Edward Burleson Raymond

Razorback hogs: are generally as mean as a bear and more deadly because they travel in packs. These wild hogs, sometimes called "long rooters," have long snouts, long tails, long tusks, and a long squeal. The name comes from the fact the hog's back is long and thin and appears to be sharp enough to shave with. Also called an acorn chaser.

Reach agreement: lick thumbs

Reached his limit: bumped the peg

Reaching stick: *See Fetching stick*

Reacted quickly: didn't take him long to look at a hot horseshoe [This is from the joke about a know-it-all who visited a blacksmith shop. Although warned not to, he picked up a red-hot horseshoe and naturally dropped it very quickly. When asked if it was too hot to handle, he replied, "Naw, it just don't take me long to look at a hot horseshoe."]

Ready: 1. got his holster tied down 2. all brushed and curried 3. combed her fur and tuned her purr 4. all saddled up 5. screwed down and sitting deep in the saddle, which means ready to ride 6. primed and tightly wadded

Ready, always: you'll never find him sitting on his gun hand

Ready as: a rooster with his spurs up

Reagan Wells (Uvalde County): pronounced RAY-gan, not Ree-gun; probably named for John Reagan who is thought to have been the first person to commercialize the mineral waters in the area

Real: 1. sure 'nuff genuine 2. natural born, as in "He's a natural born cowboy."

Real County: There is a real Texas county named Real but it is pronounced Re al, which is Spanish for royal.

Real estate deal, good: got five years free on a four-year lease

Real man: got hair on his belly and gravel in his guts

Realitos (Duval County): pronounced Re-a-LEE-tus

Reappeared: bobbed up again, which is a reference to fishing with a bobber

Rear end: 1. patoot 2. back of the lap 3. part of the chicken that went over the fence last 4. south end of a northbound mule (or horse) 5. bohunkus 6. rump 7. south pasture 8. hindquarters 9. hind tail (or end) 10. tailgate 11.

sitter downer 12. differential 13. behind 14. back porch

Rear end, flat: 1. shingle-butted 2. slab-assed

Rear end, large: 1. looks like two hogs living in the back of her jeans 2. jug butted 3. heavy bottomed 4. something nice to fall back on 5. measures two ax handles wide between the hip pockets 6. her jeans are living proof that 50 pounds will fit in a 25-pound sack 7. if you told him to haul butt, it would take two trips, minimum 8. looks like two baby pigs under a bed sheet 9. got the old office job spread [This implies that those who sit all day will have a larger rear end than those who are on their feet most of the time.] 10. well-reared 11. couldn't sit down in a number three washtub 12. looks like a bag of nickels 13. looks like fifty pounds of used chewing gum 14. the back of her lap looks like two big watermelons in a tow sack 15. his butt is bigger than a river bottom coon [Coons living along a river bottom are often better fed and thus plumper than most other coons.]

Rear end, small: 1. looks like a witch doctor shrunk his hiney instead of his head 2. skinny hipped 3. runt butt 4. hummingbird hiney 5. could fall plumb through an outhouse hole 6. a little hollow cheeked 7. scarce hipped 8. ol' sparrow butt

Reata (riata): rawhide rope, usually braided of four, six, or eight strands but four was preferred for everyday ropes; also called a skin-string

Rebel: maverick *See also Nonconformist*

Rebel yell: a loud, often prolonged yell that originated during the War Between the States when Confederate troops were either charging or celebrating. The tradition of the Rebel yell is still alive in the South and can be heard often when Southerners are celebrating. To practice a Rebel yell, open a car door and then slam it on your fingers.

Recall: 1. I'm minded of 2. that minds me of 3. that brings to mind

Reckless: 1. plowing too close to the cotton 2. filed the half cock off his gun, which means the gun doesn't have a safety

Reckless as: a calf kicking yellow jackets

Reckon: one of the most versatile words in the language of the South, it can be used for suppose, think, guess, believe, calculate, presume, expect, know, imagine, assume, speculate, etc.

Reconcile: let bygones be bygones

Reconcile somewhat: 1. bury the hatchet but don't forget where you dug the hole 2. let bygones be bygones, but remember the Alamo

Record: put it in the tally book [where the ranch recorded its cattle holdings]

Recover: 1. don't cry over spilt milk 2. pick yourself up and dust off the dirt 3. you never fall so far that you can't climb back up

Recovered: 1. gave his pallbearers the slip 2. got the swagger back in his walk and the valor back in his backbone 3. hauled off and got well

Red as: 1. the bottom stripe on a Texas flag 2. a Rebel flag 3. a baboon's butt

Red ass: a tough, traditional Aggie (or practice)

Red beans: *See Pinto beans*

Red candle tradition (UT): burning red candles before important football games

Red eye gravy: *See Gravy, red eye*

Redneck: Some folks, mainly Yankees, use this as a derogatory term meaning "country bumpkin" or "poor white trash." Texans and most people in the South generally use "redneck" to describe good ol' boys who love God, country, cold beer, hot romance, big guns, little government, slow dances, and fast horses, and they'll fight to defend any of 'em.

Redneck, devout: so country, his breath smells like cordwood

Reduce: whittle it down to middlin' size

Reformed hippie: born again redneck

Reformed sinner: got painted into an amen corner

Reformer: someone who wants his conscience to be your guide

Refrigerator: icebox

Refugio (Refugio County): pronounced Re-FURY-oh

Regular as: 1. clockwork 2. a duck goes barefooted

Reins, closed: a single strap looped over the horse's head and each end attached to the bosal; preferred by buckeroos

Reins, open: two separate straps, not connected, with each being attached to a side of the bit; preferred by working cowboys

Reklaw (Cherokee County): pronounced WRECK-law [Residents wanted to name the town in honor of Margret Walker who donated land for the town site. Walker, however, was already taken so they simply spelled the name backwards.] *See also Sacul*

Related: 1. off the same coil 2. out of the same case 3. cut from the same bolt 4. they climb the same family tree

Related, sort of: 1. pea patch kin [This phrase evolved when peas were a mainstay of many country diets. As Donnis Baggett explained in a column for the *Dallas Morning News*: A system of informal farm co-ops evolved back when Texas was a rural state. Some families had more kids than land, and they needed more peas than they could grow. Some families had more acreage than kids, so they needed help to farm it all. Since the needs of one complimented the assets of another, a deal was struck. Two or three families would combine efforts on one garden and split the proceeds. Many of the families involved in these joint ventures were related to each other. And in cases where they weren't, pea patch romances often led to further mergers, takeovers, and stock splits. Hence the term, pea patch kin.] 2. weaned on milk from the same cow (cow cousins) [This means the families were close enough to share a cow but weren't officially related. An even closer version might be weaned by the same wet nurse.]

Relative, strange: if you shook the family tree, he'd be the fruit that fell out

Relatives: 1. kin 2. kinfolk 3. blood kin 4. kissin' kin 5. blood relations 6. the folks

Relatives, distant: we're last cousins

Relax: 1. breathe easy 2. rest your mind 3. sit a spell 4. barn your brain, which is a reference to putting horses in the barn after a ride 5. no one ever got bit by a dog's shadow 6. don't get your shorts in a knot 7. don't get your panty hose in a pile 8. don't get your dandruff up

Release: 1. cut 'em loose 2. let loose all holts (holds) 3. open the cage or cell door 4. jerk off the bridle and turn a loose 5. cut the reins 6. saw off the handcuffs *See Let them go*

Relentless: don't believe in breathing spells

Reliable: 1. if he says a pissant can pull a boxcar, you can hook 'em up 2. you can hang your hat on it *See also Certain; Fact*

Reliable as: the sunrise

Religious freedom: the right to go to church or to go fishing

Religious fanatic: could hear the Pope's confession

Religious person: 1. everything he says is fodder for a sermon 2. cut his teeth on a collection plate 3. camps out in the amen corner 4. a branded and earmarked Christian *See also Reformed sinner*

Religious, but cheap: a clink Christian, which means when the collection passes him you only hear the clink of a few coins being dropped in

Religious, sometimes: a weekend Catholic [A person who was a little less religious would be an Easter Sunday Catholic. And the least religious of all would be a deathbed Catholic, which means he only got religion when he thought he was gonna die. You can substitute the religion of your choice but the implication is clear; the person involved is only religious some of the time.] *See also Church goer, infrequent*

Reluctance: 1. would rather slap my mama than do that 2. would rather take out a polar bear's appendix with a penknife than do that *See also Don't want to; I don't care; Preference*

Remarkable person: got bodacious in his blood [A real remarkable person is double bodacious.]

Remember: 1. keep green the memory of 2. get your recollections started 3. jump start your memory

Reminds me: 1. puts me in the mind of 2. calls to mind

Remote: clear to the back side of nowhere *See also Rural*

Remote control: clicker

Remote location: about fifty miles past the resume speed sign

Remuda: On a trail drive or a roundup, each cowboy requires at least six horses since each one is only good for about half a day's work. Thus he rides two per day then gives them two days of rest. When all the horses for all the cowboys are grouped together, the herd is called a remuda.

Renege (dominoes): occurs if a player fails to follow suit when he can or if a player has a play and is supposed to make it but passes instead. In either case, a renege is against the rules.

Reno (Lamar County): There are two towns named Reno in Texas, one in Lamar County and one in Parker County. They are both pronounced REE-no, almost as two words.

Rent a car: hire a rig

Repair: 1. put the pieces back together 2. spit and baling wire it 3. give it a stobectomy *See also Do-it-yourself*

Repair, temporary: 1. clodhopper or sharecropper repairs [This is mending a fence by using baling wire to connect rusty barbed wire to a rotten fence post.] 2. gave it a lick and a promise 3. whitewash won't strengthen the fence but it makes it look better when the preacher comes calling

R

Repairman, good: could repair the crack of dawn

Repeat: 1. ride over that trail again 2. run that horse by me one more time

Repeatedly: time and time again

Repeater (domino): a domino that, when played, will allow you to score the same points as the player before you. For example, if the player before you had a five count on the end of the string and a blank on the other, he would score five points. If you held the double-blank, you could play it on the blank end and "repeat" the same score.

Repeating: 1. already whipped that old dog 2. already run that horse into the ground 3. already treed that coon

Reprimand: 1. bring 'em down a notch or two 2. cool 'em off a degree or two 2. read 'em the riot act 3. read 'em the ranch (or boardinghouse) rules

Reputation, ruined: his name is mud

Requirement: If you give a dance in Texas, you better hire a band with a fiddle player (and you better pay that band).

Re-ride: In a rodeo, if equipment fails that is not the responsibility of the contestant, he is granted a re-ride.

Reroof: rekivvered (East Texas)

Rescue: 1. save the bacon 2. pull the fat out of the fire 3. snatch victory from the jaws of defeat 4. save his hide

Research: *See Plagiarism*

Resembles: 1. favors 2. takes after 3. a good likeness of

Reserve: ace in the hole (or up the sleeve)

Resist: 1. got up on her hind legs like a frightened mare 2. buck, as in "He'll buck any attempt to close the saloon."

Resolved: 1. it all came out in the wash 2. we finally found the drain plug in the swamp

Respect, earned: *See Friendship*

Respiratory malady: overflow of the flux on the phlegm

Responsibility: it's your blister, you have to sit on it *See also Accept responsibility*

Rest: 1. cool your heels 2. rest your saddle 3. shade up 4. sit a spell 5. take a breather [Remember, if you rest too much you rust.]

Restart it: recrank it

Resting: layin' up

Restless: 1. champing at the bit 2. raring to go

Restless as: 1. a kid in church 2. a hen on a hot griddle

Restrain: 1. keep the lid screwed on 2. keep 'em on the reservation 3. lock 'em up and swallow the key

Restrained: 1. bridled 2. clipped my wings 3. hog-tied 4. hamstrung

Restricted: 1. it's difficult to run with the big dogs when you're chained to the porch 2. hog-tied

Restriction: that cramps my style

Restroom: 1. sandbox 2. necessary room

Results, inevitable: will all come out in the wash

Results, poor: did a lot of grinding but he didn't get much corn

Retaliate: 1. fix his wagon 2. wind his clock 3. what goes around comes around 4. give him a dose of his own medicine 5. give him back his hard times 6. give back as good as you got or better 7. back cuss 'em

Retired: 1. pasteurized 2. turned in his saddle 3. out to pasture 4. joined the spit and whittle club 5. traded his gold watch for a rockin' chair 6. mothballs have replaced his ball bearings 7. wife's gettin' half the money and twice the husband

Retire for the evening, early: went to bed with the chickens

Retraction: eating crow, feathers, beak and all

Retreat: 1. drop back a notch or two 2. come down a rung or two 3. fire and fall back

Retribution: whatever fits around the devil's neck will also fit around his waist [This is an old East Texas saying that roughly means anyone who treats you bad will get a dose of his own medicine.]

Return secretly: circle back

Return to work: get back to your rat killing, rodeoing, or branding

Revenge: put a stinging lizard (scorpion) in his pocket and ask for a match

Reversed: it's bassackwards

Rexall ranger: a tenderfoot who wouldn't know a cow if he found her in his bed; Rexall ranger is a modern version of "drugstore cowboy"

Rhome (Wise County): the "H" is silent for Rome; originally known as Prairie Point; name was changed to honor local rancher Byron Crandall Rhome

Rhonesboro (Upshur County): pronounced RONES-borro, the possum capital of the world and home of the annual possum festival

Rhubarb: pie plant

Ribs: 1. smack bones 2. steer staves

Ribs, broken: his staves are sprung

Rice: swamp seed

Rich: 1. got enough money to burn a wet elephant 2. got enough to pay the Bill of Rights 3. he's got more money than he can keep dry 4. owns controlling interest in half of all creation 5. richer than the dirt in an old cow pen 6. could air-condition hell 7. carries a wad big enough to choke a horse 8. got more money than God 9. in the lap of luxury 10. stiff in the heels 11. eats high on the hog *See also Wealthy*

Rich but inept: 1. born with a silver foot in his mouth [This phrase was immortalized by then Texas State Treasurer Ann Richards in her keynote address at the 1988 Democratic National Convention. She made the remark with reference to George Bush.] 2. tried to order a carpool for his Town Car

Rich child: raised in a floored pen [This comes from hog farmers who can afford fancy floored pens for their hogs.]

Rid: get shed of

Ride: a cowboy's ride is a car or truck; his horse is a horse

Ride, rough: 1. feels like the axles are welded to the frame 2. feels like I'm riding inside a washboard

Ride a horse: 1. flap your chaps 2. work your spurs [To properly ride a horse, put one leg on each side and keep your mind in the middle.]

Ride herd: to herd cattle

Rider, hard: hell on leather

Ridiculous: horse feathers *See also Irrelevant*

Ridiculous as: 1. asking a politician to guard your wallet 2. building a beehive next to a bear's den 3. trying to catch rainwater in a dip net 4. asking a death row inmate to guard the jail 5. pouring water on a rusty hinge

Riding fast: riding fast enough to split a creek wide open

Riding fence: to ride a fence line and make repairs where needed

Rifle: 1. smoke stick 2. meat gitter

Rifle, powerful: 1. kicks hard enough to get meat at both ends [This implies it will kill game with a bullet fired from one end and scrape the hide off your shoulder with the kick from the other end.]

Rig: 1. gun and holster 2. horse, buggy, and harness 3. boat, motor, and trailer 4. a saddle with all the straps and stirrups 5. a still

Rigging: the gear used to secure a saddle on a horse's back

Right side: gee, which is an old-time mule skinner's word for right

Rim fire saddle: *See Double-rigged saddle*

Ring: rang, as in "I gave her an engagement rang."

Ring, graduation: 1. head thumper 2. gold nugget

Ring herd: herd cattle in a circular motion to keep them from scattering

Ringtailed tooter: a rounder with talent

Rio Grande: Texans drop the "e" for simply Rio Grand. Translated it means "big river." An early Texas settler once said of the river, "It is a mile wide and a foot deep, too thin to plow, too thick to drink." During prohibition, the Rio Grande was said to be the only river in the world that was wet on one side and dry on the other.

Rio Vista (Johnson County): usually pronounced as it appears although some old-timers still prefer Rye Vista; home of the world famous "cow pasture" bank

Ripsnorter: a mean, usually aggressive and occasionally drunk yahoo who would be good not to mess with

Rises, fast as: 1. fertilized weeds 2. oil from a gusher 3. gasoline prices in an oil shortage

Rises, slow as: 1. biscuits in a cold oven 2. a hot air balloon in hell 3. smoke off a fresh cow patty

Rising Star (Eastland County): originally called Copperas Creek [According to local legend, the name was changed after D.D. McConnell called the area a "rising star country" because crops thrived there but seemed to fail in other nearby areas.]

Risk, small: 1. gambling with someone else's chips 2. playin' with someone else's money

Risk taker: 1. a riverboat gambler 2. wildcatter 3. blazes his own trail 4. plays dominos with his eyes closed 5. shoots dice over the phone

Risk taking: 1. tap dancing in a mine field 2. bathing with sharks [After one of his players got arrested, former Dallas Mavericks owner Donald Carter lamented "…this is what happens when you bathe with sharks. Sometimes you get bit."] 3. counting the cars in a funeral procession [According to an old country legend, this means you will be the next to be buried.] 4. walking through a forest fire with a wooden leg 5. sawing on the limb you're sitting on 6. puttin' up a lightning rod in a thunderstorm 7. kissing an ugly woman [If you kiss an ugly woman she'll tell the world and ruin your reputation with the other ladies.] *See also At risk; Dangerous*

Risky: 1. riding for a fall 2. playing cards with the devil and there ain't no limit 3. dancing with the devil's girlfriend 4. wading in quicksand 5. out on a limb that's being sawed off behind you [Lyndon Johnson said, "When you crawl out on a limb, you might have to find another one to crawl back on."]

Risky as: 1. sitting on a powder keg and smoking a four-bit cigar 2. driving a gasoline transport with bad brakes

River, dry: 1. the fish raised dust swimming upstream 2. the river had to be irrigated before the kids could go swimming

River, falling: the river shallowed down

River, shallow: 1. a walkin' river [The Rio Grande between Texas and Mexico is said to be a walkin' river because in most spots, illegal aliens simply walk across it. In some places the river is so shallow, they can walk across without gettin' their feet wet.] 2. the lifeguards only have to know how to wade 3. a hog crossin' river [This means the hogs are walking across it. Although hogs can swim, they don't like to.] 4. the water is so low the catfish are getting freckled, which means they are spending too much time in the sun

Riviera (Kleberg County): promoter T. F. Koch suggested the name because he thought the area resembled the French Riviera

Roaches, big: 1. as chocolate eclairs 2. so big you have to have a huntin' license to kill 'em [When Jerry Glanville was the coach of the Houston Oilers he was asked about the advantage of playing in the Astrodome. He replied that one advantage was the size of the cockroaches; players from other cities had never seen roaches that big and thus were distracted from the game. Glanville claimed they were so big his players would ride them out to the team bus after a game.]

Road, crooked: a pea vine road

Road, dirt: Arkansas asphalt

Road, rough: 1. an Oklahoma freeway 2. headache highway 3. a corduroy road 4. rough as a washboard 5. a bad road will call the mile markers liars, which means it seems that miles are longer on bad roads

Road, small: a pig trail

Road-broke: cattle that were accustomed to being herded and thus were easier to handle on a drive; also called trail-broke

Roadrunner: 1. popular, fast, and elusive birds fairly common in South and West Texas; name comes from the fact that the birds would run ahead of riders or wagons on a trail 2. paisano 3. chaparral bird, so called because their favorite habitat is among the chaparral 4. snake-killer (or eater), so called because the roadrunner is one of the few natural enemies of the rattlesnake 5. lizard-bird, so called because a roadrunner will eat a lizard if a rattlesnake isn't handy 6. ground-cuckoo, so called because roadrunners are not considered smart and are believed to act like a cuckoo [This belief spawned the phrase "crazy as a paisano."]

Roanoke (Denton County): pronounced ROAN-oak; named for Roanoke, Virginia

Roaring Springs (Motley County): pronounced Roarin' Sprangs; named for nearby springs said to be so good they "roared" with water

Robbed: 1. picked clean as a dog's bone 2. stole blind 3. took everything but the air in my lungs 4. took everything but the fillings in my teeth See also Lost everything

Robber, inept: put his ski mask on backwards and tried to hold up a police station See also Crook; Thief

Robert Lee (Coke County): named for Confederate general Robert E. Lee but no one knows why the middle "E" was omitted

Roby (Fisher County): pronounced ROBE-E; named for developers M. L. and D. C. Roby

Rochelle (McCulloch County): pronounced Ro-shell; name came from La Rochelle, which was suggested by an early settler from France

Rock, big and flat: if a cow wet on that she could water half an acre [For the uneducated, a cow wetting on a flat rock produces a splatter that gets everything wet for at least half an acre.]

Rock, big: 1. big enough to use as an anchor on the battleship *Texas* 2. big enough to hold down a wagon in a whirlwind 3. would make the rock of Gibraltar look like a kid's skipping stone 4. weighs more than the rock of ages

Rock, flat: skipping stone [This refers to flat rocks being the easiest to skip across a stock tank when you don't have anything else to do.]

Rock Crusher (Coleman County): name originated when the Santa Fe Railroad built a rock crusher in a nearby pasture to provide materials for the track bed

Rock music: music to steal hubcaps by

Rocking chair: gives you something to do but it don't get you nowhere

Rockne (Bastrop County): pronounced ROCK-knee; originally named Lehmansville, then Hilbigville. [Following his death in 1931, residents renamed the town in honor of Notre Dame football coach Knute Rockne.]

R

Rocksprings (Edwards County): this one is "springs" not "sprangs"

Rodeo: a real Texan will always say ROW-dee-o, never row-DAY-oh.

Rodeo events: *See All-around Cowboy; Barrel racing; Bareback riding; Bull riding; Calf roping; Saddle bronc riding; Steer wrestling; Team roping. See also Timed events and Rough stock events*

Rodeo performance: go round, which is each day's events in a rodeo

Rolex watch: in good times, it's a Texas Timex; in bad times a lot of folks try to tell time on a pawn ticket

Roll it up: spool it

Roller chain: bicycle chain

Roller towel: a continuous loop of towel that you keep rolling until you find the cleanest place available to dry your hands

Rolling like: 1. a horse taking a dirt bath 2. a wallowing buffalo

Roma (Starr County): pronounced ROW-ma [Since the town stands on a hill surrounded by other hills, it reminded someone of Rome, Italy.]

Romal: a rope or leather strand attached to saddle horse reins where they were joined; served as a built-in quirt

Romantic as: 1. a river walk, especially a San Antonio river walk 2. the Texas moon [Although it has never been proven to be fact, many Texans believe the moon that shines over Texas is a little bigger and a little brighter than anywhere else.]

Roommate: old lady

Rookie: 1. still wet behind the ears 2. greener 3. greenhorn 4. so green he could hide in a lettuce patch 5. green

as two-week-old corn 6. shorthorn *See also Tenderfoot*

Room, cold: 1. cold enough to hang meat in or use as a deer locker 2. a shiver shack 3. makes a deep freeze look like a steam room

Room, crowded: there ain't enough room left for a shadow

Room, large: could drill a regiment in it

Room, small: 1. you have to leave if sunshine comes in the window 2. if you put the key too far into the lock you'll break the window 3. the furniture is painted on the wall 4. you can't cuss the cat without getting a mouthful of fur 5. the dog has to wag his tail up and down instead of sideways 6. you have to use a crutch and sleep standing up 7. you have to go out into the hall to change your mind 8. you couldn't pucker your lips without accidentally kissing someone

Root hog, or die: you're on your own

Rope: 1. string 2. portable cow catcher [To a cowpoke, a rope was the most versatile of tools. It doesn't rust; need grease, oil, or paint; has no moving parts to break down; and won't boil over in summer or freeze up in winter.]

Rope, long: 1. brag rope, which implies someone is skillful enough to make and control a very large loop, something to brag about, indeed 2. long enough to hang all the wash in Texas on 3. that sucker is so long it's only got one end

Rope, short: *See Piggin' string*

Rope bag: a nylon bag that allows a rope to breathe, which helps it stay softer

Rope can: an airtight container; helps keep a rope stiff

Rope contest: a ropin'

Rope loop, large: a prairie or West Texas loop. The larger the loop, the easier it is to rope something. In West Texas there isn't a lot of brush and trees to get in the way, so you can build a bigger loop.

Rope loop, small: a South Texas loop, with reference to the above entry, in South Texas there are a lot of brush and mesquite trees, which can make using a large loop difficult. The smaller the loop the harder the roping is to get done.

Rope loops: 1. flat loop, used on cattle with horns 2. dipped loop, used on hornless cattle 3. vertical loop, used on horses 4. heel trap, a loop thrown in front of moving cattle 5. mid-air heel loop, used to catch a cow's legs while the legs are off the ground 6. forefoot loop, used on colts

Rope sizes: 1. light, 3/8 inch diameter 2. medium, 7/16 inch diameter 3. heavy, 1/2 inch diameter 4. extra heavy, 9/16 inch diameter

Rope types: 1. poly-grass blend, a catch rope made with a combination of polyethylene and grass 2. poly-nylon blend, a catch rope made with a combination of polyethylene and nylon 3. reata, a braided rawhide rope 4. sash cord, which is machine-braided rope 5. sisal, three strands of white fiber twisted into a strong rope [Note: sisal, often called grass, is grown in Mexico.] 6. silk manila, which is a hand-twisted vegetable fiber rope that is excellent for general ranch work and is considered the best rope by most cowboys

Roper, good: 1. a small-loop man 2. could put a loop over a tick on a mule's back with a barbed wire rope 3. a one-loop man, which means he'll rope his target with only one loop 4. could rope an eagle if they weren't so hard to slip up on

Roper, poor: 1. a three-loop roper, which means it takes him at least three loops to catch his target 2. couldn't get a rope on a steer if he sent the loop registered mail 3. a big-loop roper

Roping rein: a closed loop rein that is usually six feet long

Roping: is like dancing, you got to have rhythm, timing, and a sense of distance

Rosette: leather ornament on saddles and horses

Rosharon (Brazoria County): pronounced Row-sharon [Originally called Buttermilk Station because a local resident would bring a bucket of buttermilk and a dipper for the railroad crew. The new name was derived from George W. Colles' Rose of Sharon Garden Ranch.]

Rosin: a translucent, amber-colored, friable resin that is rubbed on gloves, ropes, and hand holds to reduce slippage

Rotan (Fisher County): pronounced ROW-tan, not Rot-an; originally named White Flat; later changed to honor railroad investor Ed Rotan

Rotary drilling: a revolving platform that grips a length of pipe with a drill bit fastened to it. As the well goes deeper, additional lengths of pipe are added.

Rough as: 1. a stucco bathtub 2. a petrified corn cob 3. a wood rasp 4. tree bark 5. burlap underwear 6. a woman's leg that ain't seen a razor in three weeks 7. barbed wire dental floss 8. a rock seat in an outhouse 9. a peanut patty 10. a bed of broken rocks 11. a cat's tongue

Rough looking: grizzled

Rough-hewn: Davy Crockett once described something rough-hewn as looking like it had been cut out of a gum log with a broadax. Using a broadax on a gum log would surely produce a rough-hewn appearance.

Rough-out saddle: a special, lightweight saddle with stirrups attached in front of the front cinch dee rings. The rear dee rings are moved farther back than on a regular saddle so the cinch is drawn tight in the horse's flank area to inspire bucking. Since it is not needed, there is no saddle horn, something cowboys are mighty thankful for. Also called an association saddle since it is approved for use by the Professional Rodeo Cowboys Association. *See Saddle bronc riding*

Rough stock events: rodeo events where contestants match their talents against the animal itself. The total score is usually 100 points, 50 for the cowboy and 50 for the animal. Rough stock events include bull riding, saddle bronc riding, and bareback riding. Contestants may apply their points—each dollar won equals one point—from 125 rodeos towards their yearly standing.

Rough-string: After all the horses were allotted to a cowboy for ranch work, a roundup, or a trail drive, the ones left over, which nobody wanted, were the rough string; usually no more than half broke.

Rough-string rider: unfortunate cowboy assigned to ride the horse in the rough string

Roughing out: to ride a bronc for the first time

Roundhouse: the circular building in a railroad yard where engines are turned around so they can go the other way

Round Rock (Williamson County): named for a large, toadstool-shaped rock in the middle of Brushy Creek [Legendary bank robber Sam Bass was wounded during a bank robbery in Round Rock and died the next day.]

Rounded as: 1. a dry land terrapin shell 2. the top of a ball bearing

Roundup: 1. cow hunt 2. cow maneuvers 3. when cattle are gathered for working (doctored, castrated, and branded) and or shipping [Generally, roundups are held in the spring and again in the fall.] 4. gathering of all former students at the University of Texas

Routine: 1. just another day at the ranch 2. another day another dollar

Row crop: planted by rows rather than broadcast sown

Rowel: the rotating disk at the end of the spur used to encourage the horse

Rowena (Runnels County): pronounced Row-EEN-ah; probably from the Bohemian word *rovina*, meaning level

Rowlett (Dallas-Rockwall Counties): pronounced Raow-let, not Row-let; named for Dr. Daniel Rowlett, an early settler

Roxton (Lamar County): pronounced ROCKS-tun; originally known as Prairie Mount; the name Roxton is believed to have been derived from Rockstown, a reference to the limestone outcrops in the area

Royalty (Ward County): originally Allentown until oil was discovered in the area and the name was changed to Royalty in honor of the checks most of the residents began receiving

Royse City (Rockwall County): pronounced Royce, as in Rolls Royce; named for G. B. Royse, who platted the town

Rude: 1. evil mannered 2. suffers from hoof in mouth disease 3. even interrupts you when you talk in your sleep

Ruin, eminent: the weevils are in the cornmeal

Ruined (ruint): 1. shot to hell 2. messed with the playhouse 3. gone to the dogs

Ruler: back scratcher

Rule of three rivers: There's an old saying in Texas: "If you're gonna cheat on your wife, you better cross three rivers before you do it." The logic here is simple. Rivers in Texas are few and far between, so if you have gone far enough to cross three of them, your chances of getting caught are greatly reduced.

Rump sprang: a pair of britches or a dress that's stretched out of shape in the back

Run: 1. shake a hoof 2. fog it 3. smoke your boots 4. burn some boot leather 5. scorch the pavement 6. melt your tennis shoes *See also Fast runner; Slow runner*

Runaround: 1. gave me a song and dance 2. crawfished me

Runge (Karnes County): pronounced RUNG-e; named for Henry Runge, a pioneer merchant and banker

Running around: 1. cavortin' around like a fat pony in high oats 2. gallivanting

Running around like: 1. a chicken with his head cut off 2. a scared Mexican quail 3. a water boy with a leaky bucket

Running iron: *See Branding iron*

Running the flag: practice by University of Texas Students of unfurling a giant Texas flag and running it down the field at a football game

Running walk: a slow four-beat gait of a horse that's equal to about six miles per hour

Runs fast: 1. like a house afire 2. so fast the heat in his boots cauterized the blisters on his feet 3. fleet a foot 4. a real road eater 5. splits the wind and skins the ground 6. moves fast enough to catch yesterday 7. like a rabbit in a tunnel 8. like Satan's breath was singeing his neck hair 9. when he stops, it takes his shadow half an hour to catch up 10. like he was gingered up [This is a reference to the old (and highly illegal) practice of making a horse run faster by sticking some ginger in a very private spot just below his tail. The ginger will burn and cause irritation that the horse, in its infinite wisdom, will try hard to outrun.]

Runs fast as: 1. pantyhose in a briar patch 2. a scorched cat 3. water through a sieve 4. a buckshot coyote 5. a rat up a rafter *See also Fast; Quick*

Rural: 1. so far out in West Texas the sun knocks a brick out of the fireplace every time it goes down 2. so far out in the country we have to use a possum for a lap dog 3. sunshine had to be piped (or trucked) in 4. we don't live at the end of earth but we can see the end from my front porch 5. we have to grease the wheel bearings three times to make it to the main road 6. the sun sets between our house and the main road 7. my grandfather started to town to vote for Teddy Roosevelt and got there in time to vote for Franklin 8. we didn't get the Grand Ol' Opry until Tuesday night [An equivalent would be so far out in the country we don't get Monday Night Football till Wednesday morning.] 9. we have to order our moonlight from Sears 10. they hold Sunday school on Monday night 'cause no one can get to the church by Sunday morning 11. nobody else lives in our zip code 12. we have to walk towards town to go squirrel huntin' 13. you can't get there from here 14. we live at 8th and plumb; 8 miles out, plumb in the country 15. we live fifty miles from nowhere by telephone 16. overnight mail takes a week and a half

Rushed away: tore out

Rustler: 1. he raises cattle faster than anyone in Texas 2. his calves don't suck the right cows 3. packs a long rope [This refers to rustlers throwing big loops made from long ropes so they could catch cattle easier.]

Ruthless: 1. doesn't have the conscience of a smuggler 2. don't believe in taking prisoners 3. shoots first and forgets the questions 4. his blood runs colder than Freon in an air conditioner *See also Mean; Vicious*

Ruthless woman: got the heart of a black widow spider [Black widow spiders are common in Texas, and the female of the species is known for eating her mate. That's ruthless.]

 RV's: Ross Volunteers, Texas A&M University

S

 S.M.I.: Sunday Morning Inspection, Texas A&M University

 S.T.B.: shoot the bull

 Sabinal (Uvalde County): pronounced SAB-in-al, not Sabean-ul or SAB-in-all

Sabine (Jefferson County): pronounced Sa-BEAN

Sachse (Collin County): pronounced SACK-see; named for William C. Sachse

Sack: poke

Sack needle: large sewing needle used to sew a closure in a feed sack

Sacrifice: 1. ya' gotta throw a virgin into the volcano 2. throw the rabbit to the coyotes 3. throw him to the wolves 4. throw your doll in the fire [This is a reference to the Indian legend of the origin of the bluebonnet flower. An Indian tribe was suffering a severe drought and their medicine man said the only way to bring rain was for someone to offer his most prized possession as a sacrifice to the gods. None of the adults would comply so finally a little girl threw her rawhide doll into the fire and it was destroyed. Before the flames had died down, it started to rain and the first bluebonnet sprang up in the ashes of the fire.]

 Sacul (Nacogdoches County): pronounced SACK-ul, not Saycull [The original application was for the name Lucas in honor of the family

that had owned the land where the town is located. That name was already taken, so the residents simply spelled it backwards and it was approved.] *See also Reklaw*

Sad: 1. eye watering 2. would jerk tears from a glass eye 3. would produce enough tears to float a wagon 4. would water the eyes of a veteran angel 5. would make an Italian statue cry

Sad as: 1. a country song 2. a hound dog whose family moved off and left him

Sad movie: 1. it brought a lump to my throat big as a fishin' bobber 2. it's a two-box movie, which means you'll need two boxes of Kleenex to make it through

Sad person: 1. so down in the mouth he could eat oats out of a churn 2. got an overdose of woe 3. sad enough to cry a waterfall 4. it would take a river of whiskey to drown my blues 5. the bottom dropped out of his harmony

Saddle, Texas style: double fired or double barreled saddle [Traditionally, Texas cowpokes used a heavy stock saddle with high cantle, large pommel, square skirt, and two cinches.]

Saddlebags: cowboy suitcase

Saddle blanket: a coarse wool blanket, usually doubled, placed between the saddle and horse to help protect the animal's back *See also Navajo blanket*

Saddle blanket game: cowpunchers on the trail never had a table to play cards on so they simply spread a saddle blanket on the ground

Saddle bronc riding: a rodeo event similar to bareback riding except the contestants use a rough-out saddle, which is a stripped down, lightweight saddle. The cowboy grasps a single cotton rein attached to a strong leather bronc halter. The contestant must keep his boots in the stirrups during the ride or be disqualified. The stirrups are usually rounded so the contestant can get his boots out easier after the ride. *See Bareback riding; Rough-out saddle*

Saddle fork: the wishbone-shaped front of the saddletree where the horn, the most important part of the saddle, is attached

Saddle pad: thick single-ply upholstery-type pad placed between saddle blanket and saddle

Saddle-pocket dogies: Texas term for runty cattle, so called because they look small enough to fit in the saddlebags

Saddle pockets: saddlebags

Saddle sack: *See Wallet*

Saddle rigging: dee ring and dee ring attachment to the tree of a saddle

Saddle-seat: riding style where the rider sits back in the saddle in order to highlight the foreleg action of a saddle horse

Saddle skirt: apron

Saddle sores: 1. saddle roses 2. saddle strawberries

Saddle strings: latigo straps on a saddle used to anchor saddlebags, slickers, ropes, etc. to the saddle

Saddletree: frame on which a saddle is made [Originally made of wood, thus the name, but most modern trees are hard plastic. The horn, bars, fork, and cantle are glued and bolted together, then covered with wet rawhide. When dry, the tree is rigid and durable.] *See Sam Stagg tree*

Saddle types: *See Rough-out; Center-fire saddle; Mexican saddle; Rough-out saddle (listed under Saddle bronc riding); Texas saddle*

Saddle up: throw some leather on a horse

Safe as: 1. the inside of a snuff box in granny's apron 2. being in God's back pocket 3. a field mouse in a haystack 4. a worm in a hole 5. a possum (or coon)

in a hollow log [A possum is usually safe inside the log so long as it waits for the dogs to leave before sticking out its head.] 6. an Alamo squirrel [Several squirrels live on the grounds of the Alamo in San Antonio, Texas, and while they are not specifically protected, no one messes with them, perhaps because of the large security guards who patrol the grounds and always seem to be present.]

Safety pin: latch pin

Saguaro cactus: *See Texas movie test*

Salad: rabbit

Salad bar: garden corral

Salado (Bell County): pronounced Sa-LAY-doe; named for nearby Salado Creek, which is one of four creeks in Texas with that name

Salesman: 1. drummer 2. peddler

Salesman, good: 1. could sell a double bed to the Pope 2. could sell ice cubes to Eskimos 3. could sell snowshoes in San Antonio 4. could sell sheep shears to a cattleman 5. sells the sizzle, not just the bacon 6. could sell a furnace to the devil 7. could sell moonshine whiskey at a Baptist prayer meeting 8. could sell clothes hangers at a nudist convention 9. could sell sand to an Arab 10. could sell manure to a feed lot operator 11. could sell carbon paper to Xerox 12. could sell left-handed screwdrivers 13. could sell Bibles at an atheist convention

Salesman, mean: would sell the whistle off the factory and nobody would know when to go home

Salesman, poor: 1. couldn't sell suntan lotion on a nude beach 2. couldn't sell feathers to a plucked chicken 3. couldn't sell Malox on Wall Street 4. couldn't sell $50 bills for $10 5. couldn't sell Popsicles in hell 6. couldn't sell the devil an air conditioner 7. couldn't sell tickets to the ark if it had been raining for two weeks

Saloon: 1. beer joint 2. honky-tonk 3. cantina 4. watering hole 5. road house 6. cow country oasis 7. juke joint 8. hot joint that serves up cold beer

Saloon, dangerous: 1. the Brawl of Fame 2. a hold 'em and hit 'em joint 3. where they check you for guns and if you don't have one they supply it *See also Honky-tonk*

Salt: sand

Salt and pepper: sand and

Salt pork: 1. Cincinnati ham 2. Arkansas chicken

Saltillo (Hopkins County): pronounced Sa-TEA-oh

Sam Stagg tree: Sam Stagg was a Texas saddle maker about whom little is known. He did develop a special saddletree by riveting a metal fork and horn to a wooden tree. The technology has long since been replaced, but Sam lives on in song. However, his name was changed to Sam Stack, probably because he stacked wood and metal to make his tree.

Same problem: same dog, different fleas

San Angelo (Tom Green County): pronounced San ANN-ja-low [Natives usually pronounce it quickly as one word, Snangalo. The exact origin of the name is open for debate, but a strong contender is that founder Bartholomew J. DeWitt named the town San Angela in honor of late wife Carolina Angela. The post office suggested either Santa Angela or San Angelo and the rest is, as they say, history.]

San Antonio (Bexar County): properly pronounced San Anntone or Santone for the old-timers; also referred to as Alamo City or River City. [It's been said that every Texan has two hometowns, his own and San Antonio. Many in the military refer to San Antonio as the "Mother-in-law of the air force" because almost everyone in that branch of the service will spend some time there.]

San Felipe (Austin County): pronounced San Fa-LEAP-eh

San Jacinto (San Jacinto County): correct Texas pronunciation is San-ja-sin-toe, although some misguided souls are attempting to change it to San Ha-SEEN-toe, which is the Mexican version. Shame on them.

San Jacinto Day: 1. April 21, the day the Texans won their independence 2. Aggie Muster Day

San Patricio (San Patricio County): pronounced San Pa-TRISH-e-oh

San Saba (San Saba County): the town and river are pronounced San SAB-a; the mission and presidio are San Sah-Bah

San Ygnacio (Zapata County): pronounced San Ig-nas-e-oh

Sanctimonious: Sunday face

Sand augar: a small whirlwind

Sandbar: vega

Sandstorm: 1. duster 2. black duster 3. black blizzard *See also Dust Storm*

Sank: 1. like a rock with a hole in it 2. like an anvil in a stock tank 3. did a *Titanic* imitation

Santa Anna (Coleman County): pronounced Santa Ann-ah or even Santy-Anny; named for Comanche chief Santa Anna, not the Mexican dictator

Sarcasm: barbed ire

Sash cord: *See Rope types*

Sashay: walk proudly

Saspamco (Wilson County): pronounced Sa-SPAM-co [The name is derived from the initials of the San Antonio Sewer Pipe Manufacturing Company which used clay from the area in manufacturing their products.]

Satisfying: 1. hits the spot 2. fills the bill

Saturday: 1. bath day 2. town day, which comes from the old days when country folks rarely went to town except on Saturday 3. butter 'n egg day, the day country folks go to town to sell butter and eggs 4. tight shoe day

Saturday night special: a small pistol, usually of cheap quality, with a barrel no longer than two inches so it fits nicely in pocket or purse. So named because Saturday night is a time for drinking and partying, and when quarrels erupt somebody always seems to have one of these little pistols handy. These pistols cost about $2 in the old days and tended to heat up quickly when fired several times. This gave rise to the old saying "hotter than a $2 pistol on Saturday night."

Sausage: one of two things you should never see made (the other is a law)

Savagerous: ferocious

Save: salt some away, which is a reference to using salt to preserve meat

Savings and loan officer: Loan Stranger

Savoy (Fannin County): pronounced Sa-VOY; named for Colonel William Savoy, a local settler

Saw (noun): sawdust maker

Saw (verb): 1. seen, as in "I seen who robbed the gas station." 2. spied, as in "I spied a new pickup I'd like to have." 3. laid eyes on, as in "It's the best I ever laid eyes on."

Saw too much: got more than an eyeful (or even a double eyeful)

Sawmill, small: *See Peckerwood sawmill*

Sawmill lunch: Vienna sausage, sardines, or tuna with soda crackers and a cold drink; also used for combiner's lunch

Sawmill worker: dogger

Say grace: ask the blessing

Say it: 1. get a blast off your chest 2. speak your piece 3. spill the goods

Say that again: lick that calf again

Scalawag: Southern whites who joined forces with the Northern carpetbaggers after the War Between the States

Scarce as: 1. hens teeth 2. bird droppings in a coo-coo clock 3. horse manure in a two-car garage 4. a white shadow 5. pig tracks on a linen tablecloth 6. feathers on a frog (or pig) 7. ice water, snow cones, or Popsicles in hell 8. frog fangs 9. grass around a hog trough (or cow lick) 10. trees in Notrees, Texas

Scarecrow, effective: such a good scarecrow the crows brought back the corn they stole last year

Scarecrow, efficiency model: a rubber snake [This comes from the belief that crows are afraid of snakes, so if you put a couple of rubber snakes in your garden, they'll stay away. The theory assumes crows are stupid enough not to notice the "snakes" never seem to move around.]

Scarecrow, worthless: the crows are nesting in its armpits

Scared: 1. boogered 2. panic struck 3. the living daylights out of me 4. his heart skipped more beats than a drummer with the hiccups 5. the fear of God into him 6. into salvation and a Sunday school seat 7. spooked 8. trembling (or quaking) in his boots 9. almost strangled on my heart 10. the dickens out of 'em 11. half out of his wits 12. turned my knees to Jell-O 13. the bejabbers out of me 14. got a mouthful of my own heart 15. my backside puckered so much it bit two pounds of stuffing out of the front seat of my pickup 16. the butterflies in my stomach have butterflies 17. scared the puddin' out of me (make up your own mind as to what puddin' means in this instance) *See also Frightened*

Scared as: a rabbit in a coyote's back pocket

Scared dog: 1. ran with his tail curled up so tight his hind legs were lifted off the ground [This refers to a scared dog running with his tail tucked under rather than flopping in the breeze.] 2. ran like he had a can tied to his tail, which is something very scary to a dog

Scared of the dark? take the broom with you [This is a standard reply of Texas mothers when their children are afraid to go to bed or the outhouse because of darkness. The implication is they can use the broom to ward off the boogie man.]

Scars: 1. hero marks 2. battle tracks 3. wound tracks 4. skewer marks 5. railroad tracks, which refers to scars from wounds that required stitches to close [E. J. Holub, the former linebacker out of Texas Tech and the Kansas City Chiefs, claimed he had so many knee operation scars he looked like he'd been in a knife fight with a midget.]

Scary: 1. boogery 2. it'll cut the curl out of your hair or curl you hair, depending on whether or not your hair was curly to begin with 3. a knee knocker, buckler, or trembler 4. would make you swallow your tobacco 5. enough to clabber a kid's blood 6. enough to harelip the governor 7. a goose pimpler 8. rates high on the pucker scale or carries a high pucker factor 9. made his hair stand on end and he was wearing a toupee 10. had goose bumps big as nickels 11. gives me the hebejebes *See also Frightening*

Scary as: 1. the forked end of a rattlesnake tongue on the back of your hand or a rattlesnake in your sleeping bag 2. a spiderweb you didn't see until you sat down in the outhouse

Scary movie: a white knuckler

Scary situation: 1. seat squirming time 2. made my butt pucker so hard I had to use a crowbar to get my jeans out of the crack

Scattered: 1. all over hell and half of Dixie 2. like cannon balls at the Alamo (or at Gettysburg) 3. like rice at a wedding 4. to all the corners of Texas

Schedule: dance card, as in "I can't see you till Tuesday 'cause my dance card is full till then."

Schertz (Guadalupe County): pronounced Shirts; thought to have been named for William Scherz, a local settler

Scholastic dismissal: one-way corps trip

School: wisdom house

Schulenburg (Fayette County): pronounced SHOE-lynn-berg; named for Louis Schulenburg, who donated land for the railroad

Schwertner (Williamson County): looks like it should be pronounced Shh-wert-ner but it's actually Shh-wet-ner; named for Austrian immigrant Bernard Schwertner, who settled in the area in the 1870s

Science of war: bull tics

Scold: rake him over the coals

Scooter pootin: going from one honky-tonk to another in an evening

Scorpion: 1. stinging lizard 2. vinegarroon, which is a large scorpion that smells like vinegar when squashed

Scoundrel: 1. lower than a snake's belly (or navel) 2. old buzzard 3. stump sucker 4. old galoot *See also Ruthless*

Scratched up: 1. looks like he was sacking bobcats and ran out of sacks 2. looks like he climbed through a barbed wire fence to fight a wildcat in a cactus patch *See also Bloody*

Scratching: 1. like a dog at a flea convention 2. like a hen in a concrete barnyard

Scratchy as: 1. burlap sheets 2. tow sack bloomers 3. asbestos undershorts

Scream: *See Squealed*

Screwdriver: emergency ice pick

Screwed up: 1. shot himself in the foot 2. jumped from the frying pan into the fire 3. traded the devil for a witch 4. put his boot, sock, and foot in his mouth 5. bought a pig in a poke 6. ripped his britches 7. messed in his mess kit 8. dropped his drawers in the wrong parade 9. hollered come on when he meant sic 'em

Screwed up big time: shot himself in the foot with a cannon

Screwing down: when a cowboy sinks his spurs into the cinch and fails to move them in a kicking motion as required by rodeo rules

Scrub hard: use some elbow grease

Seagoville (Dallas-Kaufman Counties): pronounced SEE-ga-ville; named for the town's founder T. K. Seago

Seagraves (Grimes County): pronounced SEE-graves; named for C. L. Seagraves, an official of the Santa Fe Railroad

Seal it: 1. cauterize it 2. weld it shut 3. cork the bottle

Seale (Robertson County): pronounced Seal, not Seal-ee; named for Mike Seale, an early settler

Seamstress, good: 1. can make two pair of underwear out of one feed sack and not have a single letter on either pair, which refers to the lettering on the feed sack 2. keeps her thread galloping and her needles hot 3. uses a frisky needle

Search: 1. beat the bushes 2. fish around for 3. look from floor to ceiling and back again 4. look in all six directions [In Texas, it is said there are six directions: north, south, east, west, up to the moon, and down to hell.]

Seat, small: a hug-me-tight seat [This comes from the days of the horse and buggy when seats were notoriously small. If you picked up your best girl for a ride in the country, she almost had to hug you tight to stay in the seat because there wasn't much room.]

Second table: where the children eat when company comes calling

Secret as: 1. a grand jury investigation 2. an old maid's dreams

Secretive: close mouthed

Section boss: the leader of a railroad section crew

Section crew: a group of railroad workers assigned to work a particular section of track

Section hand: a worker on a railroad section crew

Section of land: 640 acres of land, which equals one square mile; 320 acres is a half section

Section train: a small train that operates only on a portion of a railroad track, often used to transport the section crew

S

Secure: 1. bulletproof and pig tight 2. tied in a double knot with dry rawhide 3. well bolted 4. locked up tighter than a drum

Security system, country style: a mean dog, a loaded shotgun, and enough acreage so no one will ever find where the body is buried

See: lay an eye on

See a lot: 1. he don't wear blinders, which means he doesn't have tunnel vision 2. got more eyes than a peacock's tail, which is a reference to the eye-like designs in a peacock's tail

See ya' later: hasta la vista

Seedbed: an area where a particular philosophy (or religion) is prevalent [Waco, Texas, is a Baptist seedbed.]

Seems: 'pears to me, as in "It 'pears to me that the buck you shot looks a lot like Brother Wilson's bell goat."

Seen enough: 1. got a full eyeful 2. seen about all that I can stand

See-through liquor: *See Everclear*

Seguin (Guadalupe County): pronounced Sa-GEEN [Although it was originally called Walnut Springs, today Seguin is the home of the world's largest pecan; named for Texas hero Juan N. Seguin.]

Select: *See Make a choice*

Self-centered: she's a real foot stomper [Texas ladies, especially rich ones, are prone to stomping a foot whenever they don't get what they want or when things don't go to suit them. It is widely believed that Texas girls are taught to stomp a foot immediately after they take their first step.]

Self-employed: 1. dangling from his own hook 2. if you don't try, you'll always work for the man who did

Self-taught: jakeleg, such as "He's a jakeleg mechanic."

Self-worth: thinks she's the only show pig in the pen

Sell: turn it green

Sells well: 1. does a big trade in 2. does a land office business 3. sells like popcorn at a country fair, beer at a baseball game, or corny dogs at the State Fair 4. sells like hotcakes

Send: dispatch

Senior (all Aggie): 1. zips, which refers to A&M seniors in the corps having privileges such as zippers on their shirts 2. elephant 3. leather legs 4. first classmen 5. slick-shoulder, which is a senior in the corps without rank

Sense danger: hearing hoofbeats or footsteps

Sense of family: knows where his grandparents are buried

Sensible: got good horse sense

Sensitive: 1. thin skinned 2. wears his feelings on his sleeve 3. as a mule with a tick in his ear 4. touchous, as in "He's mighty touchous about his new $10 boots."

Sentimental: 1. would even kiss a ghost good-bye 2. tears up at the drop of a hat 3. even cries at television commercials

Separate the good from the bad: 1. separate the goats from the sheep 2. separate the chicken thieves from the preachers (or the chicken thieves from the chicken pluckers)

Separated: split the blanket *See also Divorced*

Serge-butts: juniors

Serious: playing hardball

Serious as: 1. a snakebite 2. a heart transplant

Serious situation: it's cuttin' time [This comes from the act of cutting bulls to make them steers. For a bull, there ain't no situation more serious than cuttin' time.]

Serious trouble: 1. got a blister on my boil 2. an ox in the ditch

Sermon: the preacher feature

Sermon, long: a growler [This means the preacher talked so long a lot of empty bellies in the congregation were beginning to growl. An empty belly hates a long sermon.]

Serving: helping

Set (dominoes): what happens to you if don't make your bid

Set in his ways: he don't want to be confused by the facts

Set the hair: 1. to a cowboy, it means ride a bronc long enough to take out the roughness 2. to a farmer, it means when a hog is slaughtered, the carcass is boiled to make the hair stand up (set it) so it's easier to scrape off

Set the spinner (dominoes): play the first double

Set the table: 1. fix the table 2. spread the table [The best table spread is one where there isn't much of the tablecloth showing, implying the table is covered with food.]

Set your goals high: eagles don't chase mosquitoes

Set your hat: pulling your hat down snug on your head to keep it from blowing off

Setback: a backset

Settin' of eggs: the number of eggs you gather when you make your daily raid on the henhouse. A settin' of eggs refers to those eggs that you intend to eat, sell, or trade. A clutch of eggs refers to those eggs you gather for hatching purposes.

Settled: ironed out the differences

Settlement: we split the biscuit and both got a half, which means the argument ended when the bounty was divided evenly

Settlement day: the day tenant farmers settle up with the landowner or explain why they can't. Settlement day is frequently the first day of October when the farmers should have had time to harvest and sell their crops.

Settling tank: where crude oil was pumped from the flow tank so the saltwater could be eliminated

Seven (playing card): wake up call, referring to leaving a wake-up call in a hotel for 7:00 o'clock in the morning

Seventy-five cents: six bits

Several: 1. right smart 2. a good many

Seymour (Baylor County): pronounced SEE-more; named for early settler Hart Seymore

Sexy as: 1. a blonde in a Corvette convertible 2. a cowgirl in tight jeans

Shade follower: *See Lazy*

Shagging: 1. delivering on a bicycle 2. chasing down fly balls

Shake hands: 1. tangle mitts 2. a two-fisted reunion 3. press some flesh, as Lyndon Johnson said

Shaking: 1. like a man riding a three-legged horse 2. like a hound dog passin' a peach pit 3. like a wet dog 4. like a hound dog eating razor blades 5. so much I couldn't pour rainwater into a barrel with the head out 6. like a hen in a dust bath [When a hen decides to take a dust bath, she covers herself with loose dust and then shakes all over until the dust is thrown off.] *See also Nervous*

Shallow river: seen dew that is deeper

Shallowater (Lubbock County): George W. Littlefield, a former member of Terry's Texas Rangers, donated the Yellow House Ranch to the Santa Fe Railroad, and the town was named Ripley after a railroad executive; the name was changed to Shallowater in the hopes of luring more settlers.

Shank bit: cheek part of the bit from the mouthpiece down

Sharecropping: farming on the halves (or thirds or fourths, depending on the deal)

Share responsibility: you do the shellin' and I'll do the shuckin'

Sharp: razor edged

Sharp as: 1. a tack 2. a stinger 3. a pup's tooth 4. a mesquite thorn 5. the business end of a bumblebee *See also Knife, sharp*

Sharpshooter: 1. can shoot the grease out of a biscuit without breaking the crust [The term originated from cowboys and buffalo hunters who used the Sharp's rifle.] 2. a Texan's name for a tilling spade

Shaven: slick faced

S

A&M Shave-tail: a new second lieutenant

She's leaving: wearing her it's-all-over coat

Sheep: 1. woolies 2. hoofed locusts [This is a reference to sheep eating grass down to the top of the roots, like a swarm of locusts, and leaving nothing for cattle to graze on. For this reason it was widely thought that cattle and sheep could not graze on the same range until it dawned on someone you could graze the cattle first and let the sheep eat what was left.]

Sheep dip: a foul-smelling medication used to cure just about anything that ails a sheep. Anything that smells or tastes bad is often referred to as sheep dip.

Sheepherder: 1. a man with sheep 2. a cowboy that ain't much of a hand

Sheep raiser: sheep farmer

Sheet rows: wet, clean sheets hung on a clothesline to dry. As the water evaporates, the sheets become lighter and will flap every which way when the wind catches them. A sheet row is a favorite place for children to play (until grandma catches them).

Sheets, clean: fresh straw, said when you change the sheets on a bed

Sheffield (Pecos County): pronounced SHUR-field; named for Will Sheffield, who owned a ranch in the area

Shepherd: 1. flock-minder 2. wooly wrangler

Shiftless person: they call him hydromatic, which was an early term for an automatic transmission

Shifts: tours (pronounced towers) in the early oil fields, frequently 18 hours long

Shindig: country party

Shiner (Lavaca County): pronounced SHINE-ur; named for Henry B. Shiner, who owned the land where the town is located. [Home of the should-be-world-famous Spoetzl Brewery, which produces Shiner Bock, the best darn beer in Texas, bar none.]

Shinnery: a thick growth of small scrub oaks that cover the ground in parts of West and South Central Texas

Shiny: good, as in "Them cows are plumb shiny"

Shiny as: 1. a diamond in a goat's butt 2. an open mussel shell in the light of a Texas moon 3. a coon's (or deer's) eyes in a headlight beam 4. the bottom of a new (or clean) dishpan

Shipping pen: the pen where cattle are gathered for shipping; usually has a loading chute to make it easier to move the cattle into trucks or trains

Shivaree: a Texas wedding celebration

Shiver: a possum ran over my grave, often said when you shiver because someone scratched chalk across a blackboard

Shoat: baby pig

Shocked: could have knocked me over with a feather duster

Shocking as: the business end of a cattle prod

Shod horse: a horse that is "wearin' iron," which means it has horseshoes on its hooves

Shoehorn: slipper slide

Shoes, high heel: 1. stilt shoes 2. calf enhancers 3. knock-me-over shoes

Shook up: 1. all jostled up inside 2. half churned to death

Shook up as: 1. milk in a runnin' cow 2. tequila in a blender

Shoot: 1. burn some powder 2. unravel a bullet 3. uncork a shell

Shoot the anvil: old practice of packing the blacksmith's anvil with powder and setting it off in celebration; usually done in towns too small to have a cannon

Shop at: trade with

Shop rags: red rags, even if they're blue or white or purple

Short as: 1. a deadbeat's memory 2. an ant's eyebrow 3. the hemline of a mini-skirt

Short-lived: lasted about as long as hoarfrost *See also Glistens*

Short-lived as: 1. a bottle at a barn raisin' 2. a pecan pie in a boarding-house 3. a June bug in a henhouse 4. a case of beer on a troop train

Short person: 1. couldn't see over a sway-backed Mexican burro 2. would have to stand on a stepladder to kick a grasshopper in the backside 3. about tail high to a wooden Indian *See also Small man; Male, short; and Small person*

Short shank snaffle: snaffle bit with short cheek pieces

Short time: 1. about as long as you can hold a bear's (or bull's) tail 2. about as long as you can hold a hot horseshoe

Shortcomings: gaps in the fence (or hedge)

Shorts, tight: *See Jeans, tight*

Shorts wheat: the by-product resulting from milling wheat that is primarily used for hog feed

Shot: 1. leaned against a bullet going past 2. plugged 3. ventilated 4. so full of lead his carcass would make a sinker factory

Shotgun: 1. scatter gun 2. bird gun

Shotgun, antique: poke stock

Shotgun chaps: chaps that resemble the barrels of a shotgun because the straight, narrow legs are sewn shut; offer protection for the legs and keep pants legs from blowing up but are more difficult to get off and on

Shotgun wedding, formal: they painted the gun stock white

Should: 1. ought to, as in "You ought to pay that traffic ticket." 2. might oughta, as in "I might oughta go to church someday."

Should not: 1. hadn't oughta, as in "You hadn't oughta do that." 2. ought not, as in "You ought not to mess with a rattlesnake."

Shoulder holster: an ace in the armpit

Shoveler, expert: fills up the back end of the shovel first, which implies he jams the shovel all the way into the dirt, which is the most efficient way to use a shovel

Showdown: when push comes to shove

Show-off: 1. a cutter 2. someone wearing a white hat in the show ring [Most contestants in a horse show wear black or brown hats. Anyone wearing a white one is thought to be purposely drawing attention.]

Shrewd: could give you a head start and still beat you through a revolving door

Shriveled up: like a 200-pound raisin (or prune)

Shrunk: drawed up, as in "When she washed my new shirt it drawed up so much I didn't recognize it for a shirt."

Shuck mattress: a mattress filled with corn shucks instead of feathers

Shuck mop: a mop made by twisting dampened corn shucks into holes in a piece of wood

Shuffle cards: rifle the deck

Shuffle dominoes: mixing up the set of dominoes between plays [One who shuffles excessively is said to be "shuffling the spots off."]

Shut up: 1. hobble your lip 2. put a sock (or stob) in it 3. close your face gate 4. bite down on the bit 5. dally your tongue 6. park (or check) your tongue 7. put a plug in it 8. cork it 9. muffle it 10. bridle your jaw 11. tie

S

your tongue in a square knot 12. put some teeth in that hole 13. holster your tongue

Shut your mouth: *See Embarrassed oath*

Shy: 1. as an old maid skinnin' a polecat 2. she won't even bend over in the garden 'cause the potatoes got eyes 3. as a mail-order bride

Shyster: high binder

Sick: 1. down in the mouth 2. would have to be dead three days to start feeling better 3. the doctor said if I got any worse he'd have to change my prescription to embalming fluid 4. there are folks in a cemetery feelin' better 5. got the whistleberry thumps and the back door trots 6. got the green apple nasties *See also Ill and Ill, gravely*

Sickle-hocked: a curved, crooked hock

Sickness, degrees of: ailing; bad sick; low sick; strict low middlin' sick; get the chickens out of the hearse

Side leather: the leather from only one side of the cow, which means it is half a hide

Side pull: a bosal with reins that attach to the side buttons rather than at the heel knot

Side step: a horse moving laterally rather than forward or backward

Sidewinder: 1. a rattlesnake that makes progress by moving more sideways than straight ahead 2. a horse that twists dramatically after he jumps into the air [Frequently, the horse twists one way and the rider flies off in the other direction.]

Sideways: slaunchways

Sight unseen: range delivered [This means something was bought and delivered to the ranch without being seen and inspected beforehand. A lot of cattle were bought sight unseen as range delivered.]

Sight, impaired: 1. couldn't see through a barbed wire (or pig) fence 2. the only glasses stronger would be a seeing eye dog 3. his lenses are so thick they look like the bottoms of Coke bottles

Signal Corps: wig-wag

Sigsbee's Deep: a deep area near the southern tip of Padre Island

Silent: shut up like a morning glory in the afternoon

Silent as: 1. a shadow 2. a mummy's tomb *See also Quiet*

Silk: a material invented so women could be seen naked in public

Silk manila: *See Rope types*

Silly: 1. air headed 2. fiddle footed

Silly woman: 1. gill-flirt 2. jill-flirt

Silver: fancy conchos and buckles made from silver

Silver belly: a western felt hat in a light silver-grayish color

Silver crappers: ceremony when flushed

Silver taps: solemn ceremony on the A&M campus to honor an Aggie who has died (current student, faculty member, administration). Taps are played three times, to the north, east, and west.

Silver trimmed rig: saddle adorned with silver ornaments; common on buckeroo mounts but never seen on a working saddle

Silverware: 1. eatin' irons 2. grub stakes

Similar to: 1. akin to 2. sort a like 3. kindly like 4. got the same earmarks

Similarities, none: *See No similarities*

Simple: 1. an easy row to hoe 2. an easy fish to clean 3. dead easy 4. anything easier would be against the law

5. no hill for a stepper 6. no tree for a cat with a climbing gear

Simple as: getting stuck in East Texas mud

Simpleminded: 1. like a goose, he wakes up in a different world every day 2. don't know scat from scout 3. don't know a hawk from a handsaw 4. don't know spit from shinola *See also Dumb; Ignorant; Stupid*

Simplicity: anything is simple if you got the brains, the brawn, or the bucks

Sinful person: 1. his dipping didn't take, which refers to Baptists immersing when they baptize 2. a professional sinner 3. it would take a ten-buggy prayer meeting to save him 4. if you melted him down, you couldn't pour him into a church pew 5. went against his raising *See also Bad person; Evil person; Immoral*

Sinful place: 1. double fired or double barreled sin joint 2. palace of sin 3. won't be long till sin's bustin' loose all over this place 4. got sin oozing out of the floorboards (or rafters)

Singer: 1. crooner 2. wailer

Singer, good: Grand Ol' Opry material

Singer, high voice: sings notes so high, you'd swear she had her hair caught in a wringer

Singer, poor: 1. would drive a coyote to suicide 2. couldn't carry a tune in a corked bottle 3. couldn't carry a tune in a box with the lid nailed shut 4. sounds like a death rattle 5. called gate mouth 'cause when he sings he sounds like a swinging gate with a rusty hinge 6. can carry a great tune but can't unload it worth a damn 7. after he carries a tune it has fingerprints 8. no one knows what he did with the money his mother gave him for singing lessons [Big Ed Wilks of Lubbock, Texas, once said, "I was gonna be a singer but I ruined my voice tryin' to cool a bowl of Wolf Brand Chili."]

Singer, very poor: she's been asked not to sing along with the congregation

Singing joyously: kiyoodlin

Single-rigged saddle: *See Center-fire saddle*

Sinner: *See Sinful person*

Sinner, reformed: from now on, the only thing he'll be guilty of is singing too loud in church. That pretty well means he has ruined his bad reputation.

Sipe Springs (Comanche County): properly pronounced Seep Sprangs [It is believed the name came from local springs where water would seep to the surface, but someone either didn't know how to spell or the post office made an error.]

Siphon hose: Oklahoma credit card

Sisal: *See Rope types*

Sissy: 1. he had a drivers license before he was weaned 2. he drives a pink pickup 3. limber tailed 4. powder puff *See also Timid*

Sisters, numerous: had so many sisters he learned to dance while waiting for the bathroom

Sitting: 1. bench rodeoing 2. warming a chair

Situation, delicate: 1. a blonde hair in the butter 2. a fly in the buttermilk (or ointment)

Situation, perplexing: it's too slow for possum and not fast enough for coon

Situation, reversed: 1. now the horseshoes are on the mule 2. now the boot is on the other foot

Situation, sensitive: we got a skunk under the church

Sivells Bend (Cooke County): pronounced Civils Bend; named for early settlers Solomon and Bill Sivells

Six (playing card): shooter, as in six-shooter

S

Six Miles (Calhoun County): originally known as Marekville, then Royal, and finally Six Miles supposedly because that was the distance to the nearest water

Sizeable: *See Large*

Sizzled: like a lizard struck by lightning

Skeleton: bone rack

Skeptic: a person who believes something that looks like manure, smells like manure, and tastes like manure might be custard pudding

Skeptical: 1. wouldn't trust that if it was notarized by the Texas attorney general 2. fishy eyed 3. his confidence is mighty frail

Skeptical as: 1. a turkey in November 2. a fat fryer on a Sunday morning

Skillful: it's not the cards you get but how you play 'em that counts [Lyndon Johnson observed that, "Any jackass can kick down a barn, but it takes a skillful carpenter to build one."]

Skin (noun): 1. hide 2. bark 3. pelt

Skin (verb): peel [Texas cowboys often referred to the hand who skinned the hide off a slaughtered steer as a "peeler."]

Skin specialist: itch doctor

Skin-string: *See Reata*

Skinned up: 1. skint 2. lost enough hide to build a pair of snake leggins (or half sole an elephant) 3. lost so much skin his own mother didn't know him from a fresh hide [one recently removed from the carcass] 4. looks like a strawberry patch [Strawberry, in this case, refers to the superficial skin wounds you get when you slide a little too hard on some rough ground.] 5. looks like he was drug over three miles of gravel road by a runaway horse *See also Face, skinned up*

Skinny: 1. could lay down under a clothesline and not get a sunburn 2. has to wear flippers in the shower to keep from going down the drain 3. could walk through a harp and not strike a note 4. ain't nuthin' but breath and breeches 5. could crawl through the pipe on a depot stove and not get soot on a white shirt 6. had to carry an anvil in his overalls to keep from blowing away 7. built for speed rather than comfort 8. hollow in the flanks 9. have to stand up twice to cast a shadow 10. stuck out his tongue and looked like a zipper 11. can shower in a gun barrel 12. would have to run around in a shower to get wet 13. can run between raindrops and not get wet 14. can run through an automatic car wash without getting wet 15. a walking skeleton or a bag of bones 16. had to tie knots in his legs for knees 17. not much left but skin and bone 18. have to shake the sheets to find her in bed 19. smoke thin 20. looks like he needs worming *See also Thin person; Female, skinny; Male, skinny; Thin*

Skinny as: 1. a lizard-eating cat 2. a rail 3. a hairpin 4. the shadow of a barbed wire fence 5. the running board of a katydid 6. a bed slat 7. a dude's walking cane 8. a leg on a daddy long legs, which is a kind of spider with very thin legs

Skirmish, serious: would have made Gettysburg look like an R.O.T.C. drill

Skirmish, small time: no more action than a Sunday school picnic

Skirt, short: a deep water skirt, which means she can wade in deep water without getting her skirt wet

Skirt leather: bottom leathers on a saddle

Skunk: 1. polecat 2. stink sprayer 3. (dominoes) winning a game before your opponent scores any points

Skygodlin: said of a bronc that runs and bucks seemingly at the same time

Slabs: outside pieces of milled logs usually with numerous knots protruding

Slack: When there are more contestants than can be accommodated during all the go rounds in a rodeo the additional contestants participate in the slack. Frequently the slack is run after the regular go round is completed. Scores and times earned during the slack count toward determining the winners.

Slack tub: a barrel of water a blacksmith uses to cool hot metal fresh off the forge. No matter how thirsty you are, never drink from a slack tub.

Slack-eyed: said of someone who is near death

Slanting: 1. cattywhampus 2. antigoglin 3. out of square (or plumb) 4. slaunchways 5. slantindicular 6. skewgee 7. kittycornered 8. his perpendicular is leaning toward the horizontal 9. the purr is out of his perpendicular

Slap hard: 1. put his head in a sling, as in "Mary Lou slapped Bubba so hard, she put his head in a sling." 2. so hard his head looked like it was on a swivel

Sleep: 1. bag monster 2. sack out

Sleep for a long time: borderline hibernating

Sleep on the ground: use your belly as a cover and your back as a mattress

Sleep soundly: 1. the snores of the righteous 2. like a man with a clear conscious 3. could sleep through a tornado 4. like a dead calf

Sleepy, very: the bag monster has me

Sleeve a cow: internal pregnancy test

Slick as: 1. a watermelon seed 2. a greased doorknob 3. okra 4. owl snot 5. a peeled cucumber 6. a greased ball bearing 7. a quarter dipped in mercury 8. polished ice 9. an eel dipped in axle grease 10. snot on a glass doorknob 11. oil on ice 12. a bull snake dipped in hot butter *See also Politician, devious*

Slick-heeled: a cowboy not wearing spurs

Slick-shoulder: a senior in the corps of cadets without rank

Slick-sleeve: a junior in the corps of cadets without rank

Slide rule: slip stick

Slingshot: 1. bean shooter 2. pea shooter

Slippery as: 1. a pocket full of banana pudding 2. a greased pig 3. owl grease 4. wet mud 5. a boiled onion

Slop bucket: 1. a bucket kept handy (usually in the kitchen) where food scraps are kept until they are fed to the hogs 2. thunder bucket 3. slop jar or pail

Slovenly in appearance: tacky as all get out

Slow as: 1. sucking buttermilk through a straw 2. molasses in January 3. smoke off a fresh cow patty in January 4. cream rising 5. wet gunpowder 6. a petrified porker 7. rush hour traffic in Houston 8. a hound dog in August

Slow down: 1. drag your anchor 2. throttle down 3. drag your boots 4. whoa up a little or give them whoa reins a good jerk 5. put the flaps down 6. throttle back on the afterburner

Slow person: 1. have to set out some stakes to see if he is moving 2. if they decide to hang me, I hope they send him to fetch the rope 3. if he was in a race, you'd have to time him with a calendar 4. moves slower than a milkman or a postman in a nudist colony 5. fell out of the bed last night and didn't hit the floor till morning 6. movin' like a short legged turtle in a molasses spill 7. slower than a flea abandoning a dead dog (the poor ol' flea just don't want to admit he's lost his meal ticket) 8. couldn't outrun a newborn calf 9.

moves like he's got an anvil in his overalls 10. can gain weight walking 11. only got three speeds, slow, slower, and petrified 12. couldn't keep up if he was shot out of a cannon 13. dragging his tracks 14. moving like his shadow is glued in place 15. couldn't get out of the way of a funeral possession 16. only got three speeds, start, stumble, and fall 17. couldn't run out of sight in a whole day 18. moves half as fast as a glacier 19. walks like he's dragging an anchor *See also Moves, slow*

Slowpoke: a dust eater [On a cattle drive, anyone bringing up the rear (riding drags) had to eat a lot of dust kicked up by the herd in front of them. Only the slowest cowboy would ever ride behind the herd.]

Slow talker: thick tongued

Slow walker: so slow, his shadow went to sleep and he walked off and left it behind

Slow-witted: 1. don't know the difference between a shotgun and a grease gun 2. would try suicide with an electric razor 3. could screw up an anvil (or a ball bearing) 4. takes him an hour and a half to watch *60 Minutes* 5. if a duck had his brain it would fly west for the winter 6. don't know manure from mothballs, which is why his closet smells funny and his tomatoes died *See also Stupid; Ignorant*

Small: 1. pissant sized 2. peckerwood sized 3. tee-niney 4. little bitty 5. fryin' size 6. stingy in size 7. hip pocket size 8. pint sized 9. half of a little bit 10. half as big as a minute 11. no bigger than a nubbin (John Wayne's favorite) *See also Eggs, small*

Small amount: 1. drop in the bucket (or Gulf of Mexico) 2. a pissant's mouthful 3. barely enough to fill a tick 4. just a smidgen 5. barely a thimble full

Small as: 1. a bar of soap in a boom town boardinghouse [During the great oil booms of the 1920s and 1930s, boardinghouses were notorious for supplying very few amenities at very high prices. After a few dirty roughnecks got a turn at the one bar of soap that was usually available, there wasn't much left for the rest of the crew.] 2. a frog fingernail 3. the little end of nothing whittled to a point 4. a landlord's heart

Small but active: he may be little but he's wound tight

Small head: could look through a keyhole with both eyes at the same time

Small person: 1. if he was a fish you'd have to throw him back 2. could take a sit-down bath in a half-full bucket 3. stands ankle high to a June bug 4. knee high to a grasshopper, katydid, or Coke bottle 5. has to stand up to look a snake in the eye 6. could take a bath in three fingers of creek water 7. could bathe in a half-full cow track (or wagon track) 8. could drown in a thimble or dipper 9. runtified 10. Pygmy sized

Small space: 1. ain't got room to cuss the cat without gettin' a mouthful of fur 2. had to hang my feet out the window to take off my boots

Small town: 1. one-horse town 2. a jerkwater town 3. so small you can miss it even if you don't blink, which is slightly smaller than a town so small you could miss it if you did blink 4. too small to have a town drunk so everyone took turns 5. a Saturday afternoon town [This refers to a town where everybody goes on Saturday but there isn't much going on any other time.] *See also Town, small*

Smart: 1. his mama didn't raise a pretty boy but she didn't raise a dumb one either 2. sharper than a pocket full of toothpicks 3. a high domer 4. razor sharp brain 5. got a mind like a steel trap [Dallas oilman Ray E. Hubbard said, "Anybody that's got money can hire somebody who's smart to make them money. It's the son of a gun that hasn't got any money that has to be smart."] *See also Intelligence*

Smart as: 1. a thermos bottle [A thermos bottle is smart because it knows how to keep coffee hot and iced tea cold without ever making a mistake.] 2. a bunkhouse rat 3. a whip 4. a tree full of owls

A̲M̲ Smart thinking: head-out thinking; thinking without your head up your butt

Smelled: 1. winded 2. scented

Smells bad: 1. like fresh branded hair 2. like horse sweat 3. like sheepherder's socks 4. stronger than a wolf's den 5. worse than a wet dog, horse, or buffalo 6. like he fell off a manure wagon 7. like a packing house in July 8. like he's got a goat under each arm and a dead fish in his back pocket 9. like he works in a minnow factory 10. all the flies stay on her side of the pickup 11. like the underside of a saddle 12. like he camped out in the stock pens 13. would drive buzzards off a road kill *See also Odor, bad*

Smells bad as: 1. a wet javelina pig 2. an Easter egg in July 3. a mildewed saddle blanket on a sore-back horse that was rode three hundred miles in August

Smells good: 1. makes my mouth water like a patio fountain in a Mexican restaurant 2. makes me drool like a wolf scenting a stray calf

Smile: 1. stretch your lips 2. like a possum eating yellow jackets (or persimmons) *See also Grinning*

Smile, big as: 1. a politician in a runoff 2. a game show host

Smiles: like a ten-year-old pickpocket

Smiles a lot: she knows sunshine is good for your teeth

Smiling: like a dead hog in the sunshine [This saying originated from hogs that were butchered and laid out in the yard of the packin' plant. When the sun got hot, the skin on the hog's face would draw up, giving the impression that the dead hog was smiling.]

Smith: blacksmith, tinsmith, leathersmith, etc., or the action of the process itself

Smithy's shop: blacksmith shop

Smoke signals: signal smoke

Smokey: cannon used by the Texas Cowboys of the University of Texas during football games

Smoking like: 1. a wet wood fire 2. a cook stove with the flue closed 3. a burning tire

Smooth as: 1. butter in molasses 2. a hickory branch without the bark 3. a baby's bottom 4. polished ivory 5. silk

Smooth-mouthed: a horse whose teeth are worn down so much it's difficult to determine the age

Smooth talker: 1. flannel mouth 2. silver tongued 3. cotton mouthed

Snack: a tide over, as in "That candy bar'll tide me over till dinner."

Snaffle bit: a gentle bit with a jointed center bit to better control the horse's direction; excellent for use by young riders

Snake: poison rope

Snake, large: 1. big as a fire hose 2. as a blanket roll 3. biggest one I ever saw without the aid of Jack Daniels

Snakebit: if everything you do turns out bad, you are snakebit

Snake eyes: in dice, a roll where both dice have one pip showing up

Snake-killer: *See Roadrunner*

Snap lead shank: a lead rope that has a harness snap in one end so it can be attached to a halter

Snaring: Texas term for catching cattle with a rope

Sneaky: 1. as a hound stealing eggs or smokehouse meat 2. back prowler

S

Snitch: tattletale

Snores loud: 1. enough to knock wallpaper (or paint) off a wall 2. like a rip saw running through pine knots

Snoring: 1. callin' his hogs 2. laugh and the world laughs with you, snore and you sleep alone

Snow, deep: 1. elbow deep to a ten-foot wooden Indian 2. so deep around the cabin we had to sit down on a shotgun and shoot ourselves up the chimney to get out

Snow, heavy: 1. looks like there was an explosion in a feather pillow factory 2. the angels are puttin' new feathers in their pillows

Snowbirds: Yankees who move to Texas during the winter months; generally found in far South Texas

Snubbing: where an animal is roped and drawn to, or "snubbed" to, a post or tree so it can be controlled

Snuff: 1. sneeze powder 2. worm dirt, so called because it looks like the dirt worms are packed in at bait houses [The preferred unit of measure is pinch.]

Soared: 1. like a flying squirrel 2. like a runaway kite 3. like an eagle on an updraft

Sober as: 1. a watched Puritan 2. a watched preacher 3. a judge in court 4. a corpse

Sociable: as a basket full of kittens

Social gathering: a to-do [Most of them are a big to-do about nothing.]

Social gathering, formal: a peacock parade, referring to all the fancy dresses usually on display

Social life, lacking: a nun in a convent on an island has a better social life

Socorro (El Paso County): pronounced Sa-CORE-oh, not Sock-a-row

Sod: West Texas marble

Soft as: 1. a baby's backside 2. a Tyler rose petal 3. the inside of a calf's ear 4. a summer breeze

Soft drink: 1. cold drink 2. soda water 3. soda pop 4. sody water

Soil: *See Land*

Sold out: he wanted it more than I did so I sold it to him [This implies someone was willing to pay more than you thought it was worth.]

Soldier, dedicated: if he died with his boots on, they'd be polished

Solemn as: a frizzled chicken in a norther

Solution, temporary: 1. a tide-over 2. patching a crack instead of fixing the foundation 3. puttin' Coca Cola in the transmission [Used car dealers are notorious for having temporary solutions to fix large problems with used cars. A little Coke in a slipping transmission gums up the works for a while and makes it seem like the car is fine. Other temporary solutions are sawdust in a slipping rear end and Ivory soap on a leaking gas tank.]

Solved the mystery: we treed the coon

Somebody will do it: there's always someone who will rassle the bear in the circus if the money is right

Son of a bitch stew: stew made from throwing whatever is handy into the pot; also called district attorney or county attorney for obvious reasons. Bashful ladies call it Son-of-a-gun stew.

Soon: directly, as in "I'll get it done directly."

Soothed: 1. salved over 2. tarred over

Sonora (Sutton County): pronounced Sa-NORE-a [Charles G. Adams, founder of the town, named it after Sonora, Mexico, the hometown of a family servant.]

Sop: preferred Texas way to eat gravy or syrup; simply take a biscuit, dip it (or sop it) in gravy or syrup, and eat

Sop gravy: a gravy made by mixing water (no flour) with the juices and some of the fat of fried meat

Sophisticated: he can quote Shakespeare without crediting it to the Bible

Sophomore: dew-head

Sore (noun): a gall

Sore: 1. stove up 2. feel like a cow that was milked by Captain Hook 3. like an old window, full of panes 4. crippled up 5. got a hitch in my get-along [If you're really sore you have a kink in your get-along.] 6. feel like I was chewed up and spit out *See also Injured*

Sore as: a porcupine with an ingrown quill

Sore throat: 1. had hemp fever 2. feel like I had a long drop on a short rope

Sorghum: light colored molasses made from juice pressed out of sorghum cane and cooked [The residue after cooking is "blackstrap," a dark molasses with a sharp, tart taste. Distilled sorghum cane syrup is called "monkey rum."]

Sorting pole: brightly colored, fiberglass pole that resembles a pool cue and is used to separate cattle [Originally, sorting poles were made of hickory and if used too harshly, some cows could be injured. It is considered impossible to hurt a cow with a fiberglass pole although it is not known if the cows concur with that speculation.]

Sougan: a quilt or comforter that's part of a cowboy bedroll

Sound, ominous: 1. a gunshot in a graveyard 2. the Shiner whistle [This is the whistling sound a beer bottle makes when thrown across the dance floor in a honky-tonk. Shiner, if you don't know, is the best darn beer made in Texas. Try some today, but don't throw the bottle.]

Sound, sweet: like notes picked on a golden guitar

Sound, thud: 1. like an ear of corn dropped into an empty wagon 2. like a mule kicking a bale of hay

Soup, thick: as Mississippi mud

Soup, thin: 1. Depression soup, which often consisted of nothing but water and the smell of vegetables 2. made of turkey feathers and deer tracks

Sour: curdled

Sour enough: to pucker a hog's butt

Southmayd (Grayson County): pronounced South-made; named for D. S. Southmayd, who owned the land

Sow belly meat: Arkansas or hillbilly chicken

Spacious: lots of breathing room

Spade bit: a Spanish bit, considered the most harsh to use *See also Spanish bit*

Spades (playing card suit): shovels

Spaghetti: worms

Spanish bit: a particularly harsh bit with a large port that could agonize a horse's mouth if used improperly

Spank: 1. tan his hide 2. warm his britches 3. ruffle his rear end 4. ruffle his tail feathers 5. give him a one-handed salute

Spanking: 1. hiding 2. woodshed lecture 3. a dose of hickory oil (spanking with a hickory switch) 4. dose of strap oil (spanking with a razor strop)

Sparse: slim pickin's

Speak frankly: 1. call a spade a spade 2. shoot from the hip 3. tell it like it ought to be

Speak up: 1. say your piece 2. air your mind

Speaker, experienced: he can give directions without using his hands [A really experienced speaker can describe a pretty girl in detail without

S

using his hands. Go ahead, try it.] *See also Advice for Speakers*

Speaker, long-winded: goes around the pig twice to get to the tail, which means it takes him a long time to get to the point

Speaking engagement, difficult: you're fightin' the food [If you have to give a speech while the audience is eating, you will lose 'cause no one can compete with food.]

Specialty: 1. stock in trade 2. long suit 3. money crop

Specific: *See Be specific*

Speech, kinds of: 1. the Mother Hubbard, which covers everything but touches nothing 2. the French bikini, which touches only the important parts 3. the longhorn, which has two points and a lot of bull in between 4. the chili, which means some meat but mostly beans and mush [Regardless of the type of speech, there are three things that are hard to do: climb a fence leaning toward you, kiss a pretty girl leaning away from you, and give a speech without using your hands.]

Speech, really long: a stem winder, which means you have to wind your watch before it's finished

Speechless: the cat got his tongue

Speechless as: a youngster run over by a calf

Speed trap: a tourist or Yankee trap

Speller, very poor: would misspell his girlfriend's name if he painted it on the water tower

Spend time wisely: do a lot more peckin' than cacklin'

Spends a lot: 1. she could exceed an unlimited budget 2. if Visa ever starts a Hall of Fame, she'll be a charter member

Spent: played out

Spherical: a relatively new term that means a person is a certain thing no matter which way you look at him.

Examples would be "Bubba is a spherical good ol' boy." or "The prosecuting attorney is a spherical son of a bitch."

Spent: all petered out

Spinach: Popeye

Spineless: as a Kleenex

Spinner: 1. a bull that is prone to violent spins during the ride (see *Bull riding*) 2. first double played (dominoes)

Spinning: 1. like a weather vane in a whirlwind 2. like a dog with a clothespin (or snappin' turtle) on his tail

Spirited: 1. got a lot of gumption 2. mighty feisty

Spit hole: a small hole cut in the boards of a plank floor for spitting tobacco juice; common for families that either couldn't afford a spittoon or didn't want to clean a spittoon. In modern times the term is used to describe any small hole.

Spitter, expert: 1. could spit tobacco into the neck of a swingin' bottle 2. could spit tobacco juice through a new broom and not get a single straw wet 3. could drown a housefly at ten paces (any small flying critter like wasp, mosquito, or yellow jacket could be substituted)

Spittoon: gaboon [Unlike what you see in the movies, the spittoon, or gaboon, was usually a box filled with sawdust.]

Splattered: like a country cow wettin' on a city sidewalk

Splint: a bony growth in a horse's lower leg that can produce lameness

Split evenly: went halves

Split open: like a watermelon dropped on a sidewalk

Spoon: shovel

Spraddled out: laying on the ground with arms and legs extended; can also be used for livestock flat on the ground with legs extended

Spread: the land, buildings, and live-stock that comprise a ranch

Spread fast: 1. like a wind-whipped prairie fire 2. like gossip at a church meeting, quilting bee, or ladies club

Spread out: 1. like a sneeze through a crocheted handkerchief 2. like dishes at a church social

Spread quick as: 1. a wildfire in dry grass 2. a rumor in a retirement home

Spring: country water fountain 'cause all you have to do is lay down and dunk your head to get a drink [In some cases a stake is driven into the spring and a dipper is attached to make drinking easier.]

Springing heifer: a cow that's about to have her first calf

Springtime: 1. calf time 2. struttin' time 3. between hay and grass 4. struttin' and gobblin' time

Springy: as curb feelers on a '48 Dodge

Spud in (oil patch): begin drilling a well

Spur (Dickens County): named for the spur-shaped brand used by the Espuela Land and Cattle Company

Spurs: 1. gut hooks 2. can openers 3. grappling hooks [Always wear both spurs so when you get too drunk to walk you can lean back and your friends can wheel you out on the rowels like a two-wheel hand-truck.]

Spurs, cheap: tin belly

Spurs, parts of: button; band; chaps guard; rowel; shank; jinglebobs (optional)

Spur shelf: the small, jutted-out area at the top of the boot heel designed to better hold on spurs

Square dance: 1. stompdown 2. breakdown

Square dancers: do-si-doers

Squashed: smushed

Squat: 1. hunker down 2. set down on your haunches [Never squat when you're wearing your spurs.]

Squatter: a person who occupies land without legal claim or permission

Squatty body: *See Body, squatty*

Squeaks like: 1. a rusty gate hinge 2. a bad speedometer cable 3. an old barn door 4. springs in a fat person's bed

Squealed: 1. caterwalled 2. war hooped 3. squalled

Squealed like: 1. a mashed cat 2. a baby pig caught under a gate 3. a stuck pig 4. a calf in a hailstorm

Squeamish: lily livered

Squeeze: A&M tradition where Aggies "squeeze" their left testicle during tense moments in a football game in order to share "the pain" with the team

Squeeze them down: Charles Goodnight's term for narrowing the width of a cattle herd on a trail drive

Squeezing Lizzie: said of a Rexall ranger who grabs the saddle horn when riding

Squirrel: mountain boomer

Stabbed: skewered

Stabilize: keep the boat from rocking

Stags: Texas term for male cattle that are castrated late in life

Stake rope: a picket-type rope used to tie up a horse

Stakes, high: playin' for the big marbles

Stalled: 1. hemmed and hawed 2. spent half an eternity kicking dirt clods and spitting tobacco juice 3. spit on his hands so much he washed off his fingerprints

Stalling: 1. spittin' on the handle 2. just pitching cards in a hat 3. standin' around with your teeth in your mouth

Stallion: male adult horse that can still reproduce because his manhood has not been lopped off

S

Stamina: 1. got plenty of bottom 2. can ride all day and dance all night 3. can plow all day and play dominos all night 4. can clean house all day and two-step all night

Stampede string: a string attached to a hat so that it hangs down around your neck; designed to catch the hat around your neck if it blows off your head

Stampede string, double loop: a stampede string formed by two strings that run through the brim and are looped over the crown to form a hatband

Stand still: 1. drop your anchor 2. drag your rope 3. ground hitch yourself 4. freeze or petrify your shadow

Stand up: 1. put the forked end down 2. put the spur end down 3. hoist your carcass

Stands out: like an ostrich in a henhouse

Standard: *See Common*

Standards, low: If girls were rated on a scale of 1 to 10, his idea of a perfect 10 would be a 4 carrying a six-pack of beer.

Stanton (Martin County): pronounced STANT-un; originally called Marienfield, the town was renamed to honor Edward M. Stanton, secretary of war under Abraham Lincoln [According to a sign on the outskirts, Stanton is the home of 3,000 friendly people and a few old soreheads.]

Stargazer: a horse that is continuously trying to look back at the rider

Star marking: small white marking on a horse's forehead

Starched shirt: 1. fried shirt 2. boiled shirt 3. petrified shirt

Stare: 1. fix eyeballs 2. would freeze a cat 3. shootin' bullets with his eyes 4. could stare a hole in an oak tree 5. so hot it would make an ice cube feel feverish

Start: 1. pull the starter rope 2. turn the crank 3. pull the cork 4. pit your bird 5. kick the lid off 6. strike up the band 7. pull the gate 8. the ball's open 9. hit 'em north 10. commence to cut loose with 11. crank it up 12. fire it up *See also Begin*

Start early: *See Left early*

Start over: go back to the chicken pen and learn how to scratch

Start slow: gotta learn to ride before you can do any cowboying, which is a cowboy version of "you have to walk before you can run"

Started trouble: pulled the plug on tranquillity

Startled: like he was hit with a church stick [a long stick with a fox tail on one end used to tickle people who have fallen asleep in church]

Starving: 1. getting narrow at the equator 2. feeling mighty hollow 3. got my belt cinched to the last notch 4. stomach is so shriveled it couldn't chamber a single red bean 5. stomach is so empty I echo when I talk 6. a bowl of red beans would look like a T-bone steak 7. so hollow inside, if I fell down, I'd explode like a dropped light bulb *See also Hungry*

Stating the obvious: that's like calling water wet

Statistics, meaningless: it don't make any difference if the average depth of the river is five feet or five inches once you're drowned [Baseball legend Bobby Bragan had some words for folks who fool with statistics to develop percentages: "Say you were standing with one foot in the oven and one foot in an ice bucket. According to the percentage people, you should be about comfortable."]

Status quo: Blackie Sherrod of the *Dallas Morning News* quoted a country preacher who said status quo was "Latin for the mess we is in."

Stay in your territory: keep it shiny on your side

Stay till the end: stay till the last dog dies

Stay away: 1. distance is safer than armor plating 2. if you ain't in gun range, you can't get shot

Stay awhile: 1. stake your horse 2. sit a spell 3. stall your stock 4. pitch camp 5. hole up here awhile 6. ground hitch yourself 7. light and hitch

Stay close: 1. stick to him like tar on a road 2. stick to him like varnish on a dresser

Stay warm: sleep by the fire, kitchen stove, or depot stove

Stay with him: camp on his shirt tail

Stayed too long: 1. frazzled (or wore out) your welcome 2. overstayed the invitation, such as they invited you over for supper and you stayed for breakfast 3. stayed till the last pea was out of the dish

Stays: pickets

Steak, tender: so tender I don't see how it held the cow together

Stealing: 1. thieving 2. ruslin' 3. using a sticky rope 4. brand blotter *See also Crook; Thief*

Steamy as: a fat hog scalded for scraping

Steel bar: jobber

Steer: 1. adult male cattle that have been castrated and cannot reproduce 2. bovine [The difference between a bull and a steer is a bull has his work cut out for him and a steer has had his works cut out. Lyndon Johnson said, "Steers are bulls that lost their social standing."]

Steer wrestling: a rodeo event, also called bull-dogging, that pits a cowboy against a steer one-on-one. A steer, which can weigh 700 pounds or more, gets a small head start. When the steer clears the gate, the cowboy, also called a bull-dogger or simply dogger, rides hard after him. Another cowboy, called a hazer, rides on the opposite side of the steer to assure it runs in a relatively straight line. The contestant's object is to leap off his horse, known as a doggin' horse, grab the steer by the head and horns, and wrestle it down to the ground. The steer must be on its feet before being toppled or there is no score. When the takedown is accomplished, the steer's head and all four legs must be pointing in the same direction or a "dog-fall" is called. When that happens, the steer is allowed to stand up and the cowboy must take him down again, which almost assures he won't win the event. If the steer and the cowboy fall together it is called a "houlihan." The winner of the steer-wrestling event in a go round is the cowboy who legally throws his steer in the least amount of time. [Texans frequently pronounce wrestling as rasslin' but never when they're talking about steer wrestling.]

Step-ins: old term for ladies underwear

Step lively: 1. like a rooster in a bed of mesquite coals 2. like a barefoot boy in a cactus patch

Stephenville (Erath County): pronounced with a "ville" not a "vul"; named for John M. Stephen, an early settler who donated land for the town site

Stepped on: tromped on

Stepping high: like a barefoot boy in a sticker patch

Stick to it: 1. ride it out 2. hang in there

Sticker: goathead

Sticking out: like a cowcatcher on the front of a switch engine

Sticks like: 1. a goathead to a horse's tail 2. ivy to a courthouse wall 3.

manure to a horse blanket 4. stink to manure 5. ugly to a buck-toothed woman 6. mud to a boot 7. melted gum to a horse's tail (or tennis shoe) 8. spaghetti sauce to a silk tie

Sticks out: like a bandaged thumb at a drummer's convention

Sticky as: a blacktop road in July

Stiff as: 1. a new rawhide rope 2. a new baseball glove 3. a frozen (or petrified) rope 4. a starched shirt 5. a bois d'arc two by four 6. an ironing board 7. a table leaf 8. an ax handle 9. a tow bar *See also Rigid*

Stifle: top joint in a horse's hind leg

Still as: 1. a deer in the light of a floodlight 2. a sack of flour 3. a frozen snake 4. a wetting sow

Stilts: tom walkers

Stinger: business end of a bumblebee (or any other critter with a stinger)

Stings: like rock salt shot into your butt [Anyone who has ever tried to steal watermelons from a patch guarded by a farmer armed with a shotgun loaded with rock salt knows exactly how much the salt stings when it hits your backside. If you haven't experienced the sensation, you can trust me on this one, it stings.]

Stingy: 1. the only thing he ever gives is advice 2. would only give you the sleeves off his vest 3. won't even give his wife an argument 4. would skin a flea for the hide and tallow 5. tightfisted 6. wouldn't put an egg in her cornbread 7. if he don't share his whiskey let him catch his own horse [This means if someone drinks all the whiskey by himself, he'll get good and drunk and probably need some help to catch his horse.] *See also Cheap; Frugal; Miser*

Stingy gun: *See Derringer*

Stink bait: *See Catfish bait*

Stinnett (Hutchinson County): pronounced STIN-it; named for Albert Sidney Stinnett, who assisted in purchasing the right of way from the railroad

Stirrup: the footholds on a saddle

Stirrup, closed: taps (*tapaderos*), which are covered (closed) stirrups [Often preferred by cowboys who ride in the brush country. Also called toe finders. The ends of taps are called winds. Fancy, ornately decorated taps are usually preferred by buckeroos but shunned by working cowboys. Taps with long sides and a tapered front are called "eagle bills."]

Stirrup, open: without any covering

Stob: a small piece of wood, whittled to a sharp point so it resembles a short, wide stake [Stobs can be used to fix almost anything that has a hole in it or to replace any kind of stopper.] *See also Do-it-yourselfer*

Stock charge: extra fee paid by rodeo contestants to cover the cost of the stock

Stock contractor: supplies the stock used in a rodeo except the horses supplied by the contestants

Stocks, worthless: ain't good for nothing but wallpaper in the outhouse

Stockyards: a series of pens where cattle from various sources are gathered for shipping or slaughtering

Stomach: 1. grub chamber 2. table muscle

Stomach, full: you could crack a tick on his stomach, which is usually said of children after having a meal at grandma's house

Stomach, large: 1. beer bellied 2. pot bellied 3. stove bellied 4. grass bellied 5. kettle bellied 6. if the way to his heart is through his stomach, it'll be a long trip

Stomach, strong: 1. fireproof innards 2. cast-iron innards 3. asbestos lined belly 4. you could cook chili in his stomach if you could get him to lay still over the fire

Stood out: like a tall man at a Chinese funeral

Stomp: tromp

Stonewall County: Despite his legendary, almost God-like status among Southerners, this is the only county in the South named for Confederate general Stonewall Jackson.

Stop: 1. put the brakes on or set the brakes 2. pull back on the whoa reins 3. hold your horses 4. hang up the fiddle 5. check it 6. head 'em off at the pass 7. nip it in the bud 8. close the candy store 9. call off the dogs

Stop at: go by, as in "Joe Tom, can we go by the drugstore?" [In Texas it is important to remember that when you go by a place you don't actually pass it, you stop there.]

Stop him: spike his cannons [This means drive an iron spike into the touch hole on the breech of a muzzle-loading cannon. Once a cannon has been spiked it is useless, so the artillery has been stopped from doing any more damage.]

Stopped me: 1. put the stopper in my bottle 2. jerked the rug out from under me

Stopped suddenly: stopped quicker than a barefoot bowler

Storage room: plunder room

Storebought: not made at home

Storm cellar: fraid hole

Story, long: a three-drink story

Story, unbelievable: 1. a little gauzy, which means it has holes in it 2. has more holes than a screen door at an orphanage

Story, untrue: don't hang out that wash 'cause it ain't clean

Stout as: 1. a Mexican plate lunch 2. mare's breath *See also Breath, bad*

Stove: lizard scorcher

Stove, potbelly: heating stove

Stove, wood burning: wood stove

Straight as: 1. a fire poker 2. the crow flies 3. a gut with a pup pulling on it 4. a beeline 5. a movie star's teeth 6. a wagon tongue 7. a plumb line 8. a guitar string

Straightaway bucker: a horse that will fool you because he looks easy to ride. No so. This type of horse bucks straight without any twists. However, when he's about to land, he kicks again with his hind legs, frequently sending the rider sailing.

Straighten it out: run an iron over it

Strand, part of a rope: one of the sections of rope material that when twisted together create a rope

Strange as: 1. a three-dollar bill 2. a brassiere in a boy's shower 3. a sidesaddle on a sow

Strange person: 1. not tightly wrapped (or wrapped too tight) 2. three pickles short of a full barrel 3. ain't parked too close to the curb 4. cross threaded 5. his plumb line is crooked 6. his elevator stops a few floors short of the top 7. a few bricks short of a full load 8. his biscuits ain't golden brown 9. got too many birds on his antenna 10. ain't workin' with a full string of lights 11. one taco short of a combo plate 12. don't have enough straw in his bricks *See also Acting strange; Crazy; Idiot; Odd person; Stupid*

Stranger: 1. we've never howdied 2. we ain't on borrowing terms 3. don't know him from Adam (or her from Eve) [Blackie Sherrod of the *Dallas Morning News* wrote, "I wouldn't know him if he walked into this very room and played "Nearer My God To Thee" in whole notes on a bagpipe."]

Straw: 1. broomweed 2. scarecrow stuffing

Strayed: 1. flew the track 2. off the range 3. out of the pasture 4. wandered off the reservation

S

Streets, crooked: 1. if you aren't careful, you'll run down the battery in your car honking at your own tail lights 2. as San Antonio streets [It has been said that the streets of San Antonio, Texas, were laid out by a drunk Mexican on a blind mule in a sandstorm.]

Streets, poor: as Oklahoma streets [It has been speculated that the asphalt used to pave streets in Oklahoma has less tar in it than a carton of cigarettes.]

Strike: *See Hit*

String, short: *See Piggin' string; Pucker string*

String horse: a group of horses assigned to a cowboy or the cowboy's own horses

String dominoes: the line of dominoes played

String rope: short rawhide ropes

Strip: 1. chuck your clothes 2. shuck yourself

Stripper: 1. passion peeler 2. clothes shucker [A guy who married an ex-stripper claimed he had to get rid of their refrigerator because every time she opened the door and the light came on, she started shuckin' herself. That wasn't too much of a problem until the preacher paid a visit and asked for a glass of ice water.]

Stripper well: an oil well that produces less than ten barrels a day

Strong: bull-stout

Strong arm: 1. he could throw a rock through an automatic carwash without getting it wet 2. he could throw a pork chop past a hungry coyote

Strong as: 1. a new well rope 2. battery acid 3. a buzzard's breath 4. a straight flush 5. four acres of garlic

Strong person: 1. could squeeze naphtha out of mothballs 2. can throw horseshoes when they are still attached to the horse 3. even had muscles in his hair 4. could shot-put an anvil across Palo Duro Canyon 5. could knock a tank off its tracks 6. could knock the white out of the moon 7. could tear up an anvil with a toothpick 8. packs quite a whallop 9. could break a trace chain with his teeth 10. could tie a bow knot in an iron horseshoe (or crowbar) 11. plows through stumps 12. could turn a posthole (or gopher hole) inside out with one yank

Strong willed: muscle minded

Strong, silent type: he bores with a deep auger

Strutting: 1. sashayin' 2. flapping elbows like a young rooster in love with his own voice 3. like a tomcat walkin' in sorghum

Strutting promenade: showing off your stuff, especially in a honky-tonk or dance hall

Stryker: *See Pluck*

Stub your toe: stump your toe

Stubborn: 1. thick headed 2. bull headed 3. set in his ways 4. hard nosed 5. would take ten yoke of ox to move him off his position 6. you can explain it to him but you can't understand it for him 7. like a hog, you got to hit him on the snout with a stick to get his attention 8. treat a stubborn man the way you would a stubborn mule you're fixin' to corral; don't try to drive him in, just leave the gate open a crack and let him bust in

Stubborn as: 1. a blue nose mule (or a government mule) 2. a rusty pump, which is mighty stubborn about giving water 3. a two-headed mule

Stuck: 1. bogged down 2. the best four-tree horse team in all creation couldn't budge it

Stuck as: 1. a dollar bill in a miser's wallet 2. a cat in a mud bog

Stuck up: 1. nose is so far up in the air she could drown in a thunderstorm 2. nose is so far up in the air a sparrow tried to build a nest in it

Stud: stallion or male animal used for breeding

Student, poor: 1. had to burn down the school to get him out 2. was only in school for two terms, Johnson's and Nixon's 3. quit school in the sixth grade because of pneumonia—he couldn't spell it

Study: 1. get posted on 2. bone up on

🔺 **Study Butte** (Brewster County): pronounced Stoody-Butte, not Stud-y Butte; named for Will Study, manager of the Big Bend and Study Butte mercury mine

Stuffed: like a Democratic ballot box

Stupid: 1. in a battle of wits he'd be an unarmed man 2. he saw some baby pigs sucking on mama and thought they were blowing her up 3. she don't know if she's washin' or hangin' out 4. he thinks Johnny Cash is change for the pay toilet 5. she thinks Joan of Arc was Noah's wife 6. he ain't the sharpest knife in the drawer 7. if you put his brain in a grasshopper, it would hop backwards 8. she can't pluck a chicken 'cause she can't find its eyebrows 9. if brains were ink, he couldn't dot an "i" 10. if you put his brains on a butter paddle, you wouldn't have enough to smear on a mosquito's back 11. dim witted as a possum *See also Dumb; Idiot; Ignorant; Uneducated*

Sturdy: built like a brick outhouse

Submarine crewman: bubble head on a regular submarine; glow-in-the-dark bubble head on a nuclear powered submarine

Subscribe to a newspaper: take the paper

Substandard: ain't up to snuff

Subtlety, lacking: 1. about as subtle as a rhinoceros in heat 2. about as subtle as a poke in the eye with a sharp stick

Succeed: make good or make room [A famous Texan offered this advice for

success: "If you wish to be successful in life, be temperate and control your passions. If you don't, ruin and death is the inevitable result." Those words came from John Wesley Hardin, one of the most ruthless gunfighters Texas ever produced. However, he said those words after spending 20 years in prison and becoming a lawyer.]

Succeeded: 1. kept his head up and his overhead down 2. it went according to prayer, which is how then Texas A&M head coach Paul "Bear" Bryant described his team's upset of TCU in 1958 *See also Made money*

Succeeded, almost: his ship came in but it docked at the wrong pier

Succeeded, perhaps: got his ends meeting, but they're tied with a slipknot

Success: 1. is the result of backbone, not the wishbone 2. when yearning meets earning 3. is being able to tell the truth at your high school reunion 4. to be a success you have to jump at opportunities as quick as you do conclusions

Successful: doing a land office business

Successful plan: it went off without a hitch

Successful, somewhat: made it to the fast lane but can't get it out of second gear

🏈 **Suck-strap:** back strap on a Garrison hat

Sucker rod: connecting rod from energy source to piston pump in the bottom of a well

Suction, good: 1. could pull a Pecos cantaloupe through an irrigation pipe 2. could back start a Harley Davidson 3. more suction than a bucket full of ticks 4. could pull the chrome off a bumper hitch 5. could pull the wax out of your ears 6. could pull a golf ball through a garden hose [A friend once claimed she had a vacuum cleaner that could suck a cat through a keyhole. She also claimed she had a badly skint-up cat to prove it.]

Suction, poor: 1. wouldn't pull a man's hat off a kid's head 2. wouldn't pull a loose feather off a chicken

Suffered: like a centipede with athlete's foot

A&M Sugar: sawdust

Sugar egg: a kid's treat made by blowing out an egg and filling it with hot, overcooked maple syrup. When cool, break away the eggshell for a perfectly formed sugar egg. Don't tell the kids how you made it and you can keep them guessing for years.

Sugar tit: a small amount of sugar tied up in the end of a cloth; makes a great pacifier for babies

Suicide: punched his own ticket

Suitcase sand (oil patch): *See Dry hole*

Sulking: fawmching, which is a made-up Texas word

Sulky: a turning plow with wheels that you ride on

Sulky rake: a plow used to put hay into windrows

Sullen as: 1. a mule in a mud bog 2. an ox in a bar ditch

A&M Sully: cadet name for the statue of Lawrence Sullivan Ross, former president of Texas A&M University.

Sulphur Springs (Hopkins County): originally known as Bright Star, the name was changed when the nearby Sulphur Springs were being promoted as a health resort

Summer: barefoot weather [Note: summer is never a verb to a Texan.]

Sunburn, bad: turned him into a crispy critter

Sunburned: blistered

Sunday: go to meetin' day

Sunday horse: a cowboy's favorite horse, usually one that looks good and is generally well behaved; primarily used when going to church, calling on a lady, or visiting town

Sunday punch: usually the knockout punch

Sunday quilt: your best one, which is put on the bed for Sunday, in case the preacher comes callin' and decides to spend the night

Sunfishing: when a horse or bull jumps and twists its back end to the side so its belly can be seen; a horse that jumps in this way is a sunfisher

Sunglasses: shade glasses

Sunny: a shower of sunshine

Sunrise: sunup

Superficial: shallow rivers and shallow minds freeze first *See also Person, superficial*

Superior: 1. top drawer 2. a cut above 3. cooked on the front burner [In many early model stoves the front burner produced the highest, most consistent heat.]

Superlative: 1. beats all get out 2. some kind of (sumkahna)

Superstitious notion: an old wives tale

Supervisor: *See Boss; Leader*

Suppose: 1. reckon, as in "Do you reckon the 'Horns will ever win the national championship?" 2. spect, as in "I spect they will if they can keep those pesky Aggies and Red Raiders out of the way."

Surcingle (horse): strap over the girth; designed to prevent the saddle from slipping and to hold the saddle blanket on

Sure thing: 1. a closed savings and loan would reopen just to loan money on it 2. can bet the baby's milk money on that 3. lead pipe cinch 4. can bet your boots (or firstborn child) on it 5.

can take that to the bank and draw interest on it 6. as sure as hell's hot and a Popsicle is cold [According to the old Texas saying, if you gamble on a good deal you may end up with a good deal less, which basically means there ain't no such thing as a sure thing.] *See also Certain; Fact; Guaranteed*

Surplus: we've got more of them than we had buggy whips in the 1920s [Thanks to Henry Ford, the automobile was such an instant success many vendors were caught with a large surplus of buggy whips that suddenly no one seemed to want. Any merchant who had more of something than he had buggy whips was really overstocked.]

Surprised: 1. didn't think I'd ever see the day 2. that blew up her dress 3. could have knocked me over with a hummingbird feather

Surprised as: 1. a young pup with his first porcupine 2. a nearsighted porcupine trying to make time with a cactus 3. a car-chasin' dog that caught a Pontiac

Surprised oath: 1. well I'll be a second cousin to a monkey [This replaces "monkey's uncle" since no real Texan would want to be that closely related to any primate.] 2. well, look a here 3. shut my mouth *See also Embarrassed oath; Oath*

Surprised to see: look what the cat drug in

Surprising: 1. that'll make the back of your dress roll up like a runaway window shade 2. that'll put a kink in your hair

Surprising as: a bolt of lightning out of a blue sky [Although lightning normally occurs in association with storms, there have been lots of instances when it suddenly comes out of a perfectly blue sky. There is no greater surprise, especially if the bolt hits you.]

Surrender: 1. holler calf rope (or uncle) 2. enjoyed all this I can stand 3. run up a white flag

Suspicion: 1. dresses too good to be a Bible salesman [This is a reference to old-time door-to-door Bible salesmen. They never had much luck and thus were never dressed too well. You would, therefore, be highly suspicious of anyone well dressed who claimed to be a Bible salesman.] 2. think we got a one-armed man in the game [Country folks are just naturally suspicious of a one-armed man in any sort of game because they seem to win more often than they lose.]

Suspicious: 1. there's a fox in the chicken coop 2. the stove is cold but the woodpile is shrinking, implying someone is stealing wood 3. found tracks in his front yard, implying that another man had been prowling around with his wife 4. don't trust his own memory 5. only believes half of what he sees with his own eyes *See also Skeptical*

Suspicious as: a goat eyeing a new gate

Swallow: a swig

Swallowing his tail: said of a bucking horse that keeps his head down as if he were trying to swallow his tail

Swamp: sunk land

Swamp, dry: so dry a million bullfrogs ain't learned to swim

Swamp cattle: Texas term for runty cattle, especially in the southeast part of the state near Louisiana

Swamp fever: infectious anemia in horses

Swamp sucker: a low-life person

Swap work: helping someone who will then, in turn, help you, as in "Bubba did some swap work with his father-in-law; Bubba built the fence and his father-in-law carried the beer."

S

Swayge down: *See Swelling, reduced*

Swear to: give (or take) a paralyzed oath

Sweater, tight: fills up that sweater like hot wax fills up a candle mold *See also Jeans, tight*

Sweating: 1. so much it took the whole family to help her get her pantyhose on 2. like a plow mule 3. like a pig 4. like a fish out of water 5. like a polar bear on the equator 6. like a tallow candle 7. like a heifer in heat 8. like a cotton chopper on election day

Sweep: run a broom over it

Sweet: would cause a cavity in an elephant's tusk (or ball bearing)

Sweet as: 1. a watermelon's heart 2. a mother's kiss when you're sick

Sweet bread: cake made with molasses instead of sugar

Sweet milk: regular milk, as opposed to buttermilk

Sweet person: a spoonful of honey (or a sugar cube) wouldn't melt in her mouth

Sweet potato pie: new-ground pie

Sweetening, long: molasses

Sweetening, short: sugar

Sweetwater (Nolan County): While Fort Worth claims to be where the West begins, Sweetwater claims to be where the "best begins." Texas actually has three towns with names that mean sweet water: Sweetwater, Texas, is located west of Abilene just a little less than halfway between Dallas and El Paso; Agua Dulce, pronounced ag-wa-dul-se, Spanish for sweet water, is located in South Texas not far from Corpus Christi; Mobeetie, Indian for sweet water, is a small town in the Texas Panhandle northeast of Amarillo.

Swelling on the head: a pump knot, which is a reference to being hit with a pump handle

Swelling, reduce: swayge down, as in "I hope my sprained ankle will swayge down so I can be in the game this week."

Swimmer, good: moves through the water like a lizard being chased by a cottonmouth

Swimmer, poor: 1. only time he gets near water is when he uses it as a chaser 2. swims about as good as an anvil

Swimming hole: an area in a nearby creek or stock tank deep enough for swimming [A private swimming hole is one where you can go skinny-dipping and no one will see.] *See also Wash hole*

Swindled: 1. got sheared like a spring lamb 2. sold me a bill of goods

Swing: one of those rare words in Texas that sounds the same in the present and past tense—it's swang

Swing you up: an old punishment in Texas prisons. Your hands would be put through holes in a wide board about two feet apart and strapped in. Then you'd be raised off the ground until only the toes of one foot would touch the ground. You'd be left there until you'd learned your lesson.

Switch: 1. something momma whipped you with 2. bushy end of a cow's tail, which is sometimes referred to as cocklebur magnet

Switchblade: *See Knife*

Switch engine: the train used when switching cars from one track to another

Switch off: cut off

Swollen: pooched out

Swollen up: like the head of a horse that was snakebit on the nose

Syrup: reg

T

T.A.M.U.: Texas A&M University; also known as Foster Mother to the students

T.C.S.: Transportation Corps

Tabasco sauce: Cajun catsup

Table count (dominoes): the spot count on the exposed ends only

Tac officer: military officer who teaches tactics at Texas A&M University

Tack: equipment used to handle, work, and ride a horse; includes halters, bridles, harness, saddles, etc.

Tack room: the room where horse gear is stored

Tackle box beer: the one beer you put into the tackle box so you can drink it when you catch your first fish

Tacky: a favorite Texas word that has multiple uses: 1. outlandish or inappropriate attire, as in "Mary sure looked tacky in those green knock-me-over shoes and purple pedal pushers." 2. rowdy behavior, as in "I've never seen Fred when he wasn't acting tacky." 3. causing embarrassment to another person, as in "Bubba was so tacky to Mary she cried herself to sleep." 4. something sticky, as in "After Bubba dropped the watermelon, the back porch was so tacky the cat got stuck on it and we had to call in some firemen to get it loose."

Tactful: 1. can tell you to go to hell and make you look forward to the trip 2. can step on your boots and not mess up the shine 3. could give you a shot and you wouldn't feel the needle

Tahoka (Lynn County): pronounced Ta-HOE-ka

Tailing up: twisting the tail of an unruly cow until the pain encourages it to get to its feet

Take: 1. carry, as in "Carry that with you." 2. run, as in "I gotta run my wife down to the beauty parlor."

Take a break: 1. sit in the shade a spell 2. shade up

Take a chance: 1. you can't make an omelet without breaking some eggs 2. you have to go out on the limb if you want the best fruit 3. play turtle, which implies that a turtle only makes progress when his neck is out

Take a look: eyeball the pasture

Take a seat: drag up a chair

Take action: 1. it's time to plow 2. shoot or give up the gun 3. work or hold the light 4. paint or get off the ladder 5. haul off, as in "Haul off and get to work." [Texan Trammell Crow, often called the nation's landlord, said, "There is as much danger in doing nothing as doing something." Former Texas Agriculture Commissioner Jim Hightower said, "The water won't clear up till you get the hogs out of the creek." And thinking about it ain't doing it. A steer in a pen full of cows can think about it but there's nothing he can do about it.

Take aim: 1. fill your sights 2. get your cross hairs on it

Take care of things: hold down the fort

Take care of your own business first: 1. clean your finger before you point it at someone else 2. clean your own barn before you complain about the smell coming from your neighbor's barn

Take charge: 1. take the bit in your mouth 2. take the bull by the tail and face the situation

Take for granted: you don't miss the water till the well runs dry

Take it easy: cool your nerves

Take it to the limit: see how close you can get to the fire before ya' get burnt

Take over: get the drop on 'em

Take the cure: get divorced

Take turns: 1. let all the reindeer play 2. swap about

Taking a chance: buyin' a tired horse [This is a reference to the old horse trader's trick of taking a spirited horse out for a long ride just before offering him for sale to someone. The horse would get tired and settle down long enough for the deal to be made, but anyone buyin' a tired horse was taking the chance that once the animal got his wind back he'd be just as hard to handle as ever.]

Taking his licks: said of a cowboy who spurs down each time the horse kicks up its back legs

Taking liberties: fudging

Talk: 1. jaw 2. chew the fat 3. shoot the breeze 4. verbal lather 5. speak your piece 6. auger 7. cuss and discuss 8. chin music 9. parlay 10. shoot the bull 11. visit, as in "The sheriff wants to visit with you awhile."

Talk, meaningless: got a good line but there ain't no clothespins on it [This means he's got a lot to say but not much of it is worth holding onto.]

Talk, serious: talking turkey

Talkative: 1. when she dies the undertaker will have to put a stob in her tongue to shut her up 2. she could talk the legs off a baby grand piano 3. his tongue is tied in the middle and waggin' on both ends 4. she can talk tomatoes out of a can 5. if silence was golden, he couldn't earn a plug nickel 6. a man of few words but he uses them often 7. could talk for half an hour after he told you all he knew 8. can talk till you're blue in the face 9. could talk the ears off a brass monkey 10. got a tongue like a bell clapper 11. could talk the loincloth off a wooden Indian

Talked: spilled the beans

Talker: chin wagger

Talker, good (almost)**:** got a silver tongue but it is only plated

Talker, persistent: like an echo, always gets in the last word

Talker, persuasive: 1. could talk the devil into an amen corner 2. could talk a wagon out of a ditch

Talking big: spreading more manure than all the cats in Texas could cover up

Talking nonsense: 1. squaw chatter 2. just bumpin' your gums

Talks a lot: 1. they call her hurricane mouth, she talks 75 words a minute with gusts to 100 2. will bend your ear into a bow knot 3. could talk water into a boil at 20 paces 4. his tongue is plumb frolicsome 5. ain't exactly hog-tied when it comes to making chin music 6. windy mouthed 7. can talk the hide off a longhorn bull 8. oiled tongue 9. long-winded 10. faucet mouth 11. runs off at the mouth 12. has verbal diarrhea 13. had to have her tongue retreaded

Talks big: 1. mouth fighter 2. always seems to have the ammunition to shoot off his mouth 3. all gurgle, no guts

Talks fancy: 1. using words that run about eight to the pound 2. uses a big crop of words 3. silk tongued

Talks fast: 1. waggin' his chin 2. talks a blue streak 3. talks fast but listens slow 4. tongue runs like a machine gun 5. tongue runs faster than a Singer sewing machine 6. can talk fast enough to confuse the devil

Talks slow: takes him three and a half hours to describe a two-hour movie

Talks without thinking: 1. he's like a catfish, all mouth and no brains 2. puts his mouth in motion before his mind is in gear 3. shoots from the lip 4. shoots off his mouth so much he has to eat bullets to reload 5. got hoof in mouth disease 6. must be your rear end talking 'cause your mouth knows better

7. thinks by the inch and talks by the yard, which frequently makes you want to move him by the foot

Tall: 1. his feet caught fire and his boots burned plumb up before he smelled the smoke 2. his boots froze off before he even knew his feet were cold 3. wears his pockets high 4. a long tall drink of water 5. when he stands up you look him in the belly button 6. lean and lanky 7. long tall snuff dipper 8. built high above his corns 9. the sky comes up to his collar bone 10. need a stepladder to look him in the eyes 11. a real menace to low flying aircraft and high flying birds

Tall and skinny: 1. his Adam's apple drops six inches when he swallows 2. looks like two eyes mounted on a cane pole

Tall as: 1. a widow woman's weeds 2. a giraffe's navel 3. the Alamo door

Tall enough to: catch ducks with a crescent wrench

Tall person: 1. if he fell down, he'd be halfway home 2. has to duck low flying birds

Tall tale: a highly embroidered story

Tall tale, Texas style: The difference between a fairy tale and a Texas tale is that a fairy tale begins with "Once upon a time…" and the Texas tale begins with, "You ain't gonna believe this."

Tallow: the fat rendered from cattle that had many uses including making candles and greasing wheels

Tally: to count stock and record the number

Tally book: the book where cattle records, such as number of head, are recorded; usually small enough to fit into a shirt pocket

Tally man: the cowhand detailed to count the cattle

Tame a horse: ride the sap (or starch) out of him

Tame as: 1. a lap dog 2. yesterday's dishwater

Tan (tayun): looks like he was scrubbed with saddle soap

Tan, partial: a farmer's tan [Farmers spend a lot of time outside and generally wear a shirt under their overalls. They almost always a have a deep tan on their neck and forearms, which makes them look partially tanned when they take their shirt off.]

Tanbark: bark that is beaten into small pieces then used in tanning process

Tangled up: 1. like a bushel basket of wire clothes hangers 2. like a pickle barrel full of loose fishhooks

Tantrum: runnin' jumpin' fit *See also Conniption fit and Hissey fit*

Tap: water hydrant

Taps: *See Stirrups, closed*

Tar bucket: a bucket hung from the rear axle of a wagon to hold tallow, resin, or lubricants used to grease the wheels

Tarnation: *See Universe*

Tarzan (Martin County): Although this town was named for the ape man invented by Edgar Rice Burroughs, it is pronounced Tar-zun rather than the more common Tar-zan.

Taste, bad: 1. like rinse water from a Chinese laundry 2. would gag a maggot 3. would harelip a hyena 4. like the sole of a two-year-old boot with the manure still on 5. like runoff water from a packin' plant 6. like wallpaper paste 7. like week-old dishwater 8. half as good as hog slop 9. like stump (or branch) water 10. even a hog (or hungry dog) wouldn't eat it

Taste, good: 1. handy to swallow 2. tickles my tonsils 3. she put a good scald on it 4. it'll make your tongue slap your brains out (or slap an eyeball out) 5. if it was any better, I'd rub it in

T

my hair 6. it'll make your teeth shake 7. makes you want to slap your granny

Taste, strong as: a garlic milkshake

Tastes, simple: I was weaned on corn bread and iced tea

Tax evasion: you'll never hear him say "I declare"

Tea: stud; Note, there is no Aggie term for "iced tea" because it hasn't been available on campus since the guy with the formula for ice graduated.

Teach: learn, as in "He had to learn his dog how to hunt birds."

Teacher: 1. live dictionary 2. wisdom bringer 3. schoolmarm. An old saying goes "those that can, do; those that can't, teach," which is a slur against one of the bravest classes of folks on earth, considering the challenges of life in our modern schools. A better saying might be "those that can, teach; those that can't, get a job."

Teacher, good: An educator once said the three things to remember when teaching are 1. know your stuff 2. know who you're stuffing and 3. stuff them elegantly.

Teacher, poor: 1. couldn't teach a chicken to peck 2. couldn't teach first grade reading at Rice University

Team roping: the only rodeo event in which two contestants work together as a team. This event involves skill, timing, and usually a fair amount of luck. The "header" throws his rope first and catches the steer around the head and horns. He then dallies (wraps) his rope around the saddle horn and when it becomes taut turns the steer to the left. The "heeler" then ropes the steer's hind legs and dallies his rope around the saddle horn. Time stops when both riders' horses are facing the steer and the ropes are taut. A five-second penalty applies if only one hind leg is caught.

Teased: pulled my leg plumb out of the socket

Teasippers: derogatory name for University of Texas Students; often shortened to "Sips" by A&M students because, according to rumor, they can't spell the whole word

Teenage: 1. growing-up years 2. parental plague

Teeter-totter: seesaw

Teeth: 1. nut crackers 2. meat grinders

Teeth, missing: 1. bite hole 2. has so many teeth missing he talks with an echo

Teeth, strong: could bite a chunk out of a railroad spike

Tehuacana (Limestone County): pronounced Ta-WOK-an-ah; the name means "the three tongues" in Indian

Tejano: Anglo Texan

Telephone cable spool: poor boy's coffee table

Telephone (Fannin County): located between Bells and Dial; the town was named because the only local phone was in Pete Hindman's general store

Telephone operator: 1. call girl 2. endangered species

Telephone pole: highline pole

Telephone static: there's a dead cat hanging on the line somewhere

Telferner (Victoria County): pronounced TELF-ner, the middle "er" is silent [The town was named for Joseph Telferner, an Italian count who became a railroad financier in Texas. The town was originally on the New York, Texas & Mexican Railway line. Two other towns on the line, Edna and Inez, where named for Telferner's daughters.]

Tell him off: 1. tell him how the cow ate the cabbage 2. give him a tongue whippin'

Tell it all: wring it out

Tell me more: put some more kindling on that fire

Telling the truth: you ain't just whistling "Dixie"

Temper: 1. the only thing you can lose and still have 2. so well tempered he can lose it three or four times a day and not run out *See also Quick tempered*

Temper tantrum: *See Tantrum*

Temperamental: touchy as a teased snake

Temple (Bell County): part of the Centralplex; self-proclaimed Wildflower Capital of Texas although that would be hard to prove to anyone who has ever been to the Hill Country in the spring

Temporary as: 1. a movie set 2. a cloud 3. affection from a fallen angel

Tempt: bait the hole

Temptation: a character check

Tempting as: 1. a country pond to a tired mallard 2. a lump of sugar to a horse

Ten count (dominoes): dime [The ten count dominoes are six-four and double five.]

Tenaha (Shelby County): pronounced TIN-a-hay; means "muddy water" in Indian

Tender as: a grandmother's bosom

Tenderfoot: 1. skim milk cowboy 2. no more a cowboy than hell is a storage shed for black powder (or rocket fuel) 3. soda fountain puncher 4. couldn't cut a lame cow out of the shade of a scrub oak tree 5. never been closer to a horse than a mounted cop 6. never been closer to a horse than a milk wagon 7. never been closer to a cow than an encyclopedia picture *See also Cowboy, poor; Inexperienced*

Tense: 1. wound tight as a pea vine through a picket fence 2. his slack is twisted into a knot 3. his nerves are tighter than rope clotheslines after a soakin' rain 4. had to slap himself to sleep 5. nerves are ratcheted plumb down 6. got knots in his gizzard string 7. his nerves are beginning to poke through his skin 8. wound up so tight a tornado couldn't stick a straw in me [In actual practice, tornadoes have been know to skewer fence posts and telephone poles with straw.]

Tenuous: he's got a shaky caboose

Tequila: 1. Ta-kill-ya 2. Mexican gasoline (or milk) 3. cactus juice 4. worm medicine

Terlingua (Brewster County): pronounced ter-LING-wah, the one-time chili cook-off capital of the world [The most popular interpretation for the meaning of the word is "three languages" for Spanish, English, and Indian, all of which were spoken in the area when Terlingua was a booming mining town. When the world championship chili cook-offs are held, the outside toilets at Terlingua are said to be so deep you can listen in on Chinese conversations.]

Terminal market: a centralized livestock market serving as a hub for a region

Terrain, rough: horse killing country [In the early days of Texas the terrain was said to be OK for men and dogs but hell on women and horses.]

Terrapin: term frequently used for flat-back water turtles; Texans, however, use it to describe box-back land turtles. If they can't remember terrapin, they just use "box" turtle.

Terrible: turrable

Test him: 1. see what kind of warp his backbone has 2. give him a gut check 3. try him on for size

Testified: swore a paralyzed (or petrified) oath

Texarkana (Bowie County): pronounced Tex-are-CAN-ah [Since the town sits on the Texas/

Arkansas line, the name is a combination of the two states.]

texas: the upper or third deck on a steamboat; the waiter assigned to that deck was a texas tender

Texas (Tex-is): John Steinbeck said in *Travels with Charley,* "Texas is a state of mind. Texas is an obsession. Above all, Texas is a nation in every sense of the word." Robert Ruark said, "Texas is what you are, not what you were or might be." Carl Sandberg said, "Texas is valor and swagger." *See also Friend; Heaven; Texas axioms*

Texas, parts of: Roughly counter-clockwise, the major parts of Texas are: 1. Panhandle 2. High Plains 3. South Plains 4. Far West Texas 5. West Texas 6. Staked Plains 7. Trans Pecos 8. Southwest Texas 9. South Texas 10. The Valley 11. Lower Valley 12. Lower Coast 13. Gulf Coast 14. Upper Coast 15. Piney Woods 16. Big Thicket 17. Hill Country 18. Deep East Texas 19. East Texas 20. Central Texas 21. Northeast Texas 22. North Central Texas 23. North Texas 24. Northwest Texas.

Texas, size of: 1. 267,339 square miles 2. 170 million acres 3. 6,300 square miles under water 4. 801 miles north to south 5. 773 miles east to west

Texas axioms: 1. Never ask a man where he's from. If he's from Texas he'll tell you. If he isn't, you wouldn't want to embarrass him. 2. Never let the truth stand in the way of a good story. 3. Other states were carved or born, Texas grew from hide and horn.

Texas Cowboys: service organization at the University of Texas

Texas fever: a particularly deadly fever that was carried by ticks. Texas longhorns had built up a natural immunity to the fever, but they carried the ticks with them when they were driven up the trail to places like Kansas. As the longhorns were mingled with other cattle, the ticks and the fever were spread through cattle that were not immune, which eventually led to Texas cattle being quarantined before they could enter some other states.

Texas flag: The Texas lone star flag was adopted January 25, 1839, by the 3rd Texas Legislature. Today, the Texas flag is considered one of the most recognized symbols in the world. If you doubt that, think about this. When was the last time you saw the state flag of Oklahoma, California, New York, or any state flag other than Texas being waved in the stands at a sporting event? The Texas flag is a true rectangle. Each of the stripes is exactly the same size although, because of an optical illusion, they appear to be of different sizes. Each stripe touches both of the other two. The colors stand for qualities any Texan ought to strive for: red for bravery, blue for loyalty, and white for purity.

Texas flag, salute to: "Honor to the Texas flag! We pledge our loyalty to Texas, one and indivisible."

Texas flag, use of: 1. When the flag is displayed horizontally, the blue stripe is always to the viewer's left and the red stripe is at the bottom. To help remember this, Keven McCarthy of KLIF radio in Dallas came up with the following rhyme: "It's white over red or the spirit is dead." 2. When flown with the American flag from the same pole, the American flag should be on top but both flags should be approximately the same size. 3. When flown with the American flag but on separate poles, the Texas flag should be the same size as the American flag and flown on the left. 4. The most common misuse of the Texas flag occurs when it is displayed vertically, such as on a wall behind a speaker. When displayed properly, the red stripe will be to the viewer's right even though it doesn't look correct. Numerous ad agencies have displayed vertical flags incorrectly in television commercials, and when George Bush celebrated his victory in the governor's race two flags were hung wrong in his election night headquarters.

Texas gate: a crude gate invented after barbed wire came into general use [The gate consisted of three (or four) strands of barbed wire with each end wrapped around widely spaced fence posts. One side was wired to a fixed post with wire that served as hinges. The other side was connected to a fixed post with a wire loop that could be removed when the gate was opened and reattached when closed.]

Texas Hold 'em: the most popular poker game and the game played in the World Series of Poker held each year in Las Vegas. Each player is dealt two cards and there is a round of bets. Then three cards, called the flop, are turned over in the middle of the table and there is another round of bets. Two more cards are turned up one at a time and bets follow each turn. Every player can use his own two cards and the five cards in the middle to make the best possible hand.

Texas house: *See Dog run house*

Texas Independence Day: March 2, the day Texans declared themselves free from Mexican rule. The dramatic action came only after influential Texans, such as Stephen F. Austin, had attempted to negotiate a peaceful settlement to the differences between the Anglos and the Mexican government. Mexican president Santa Anna, however, had declared himself a dictator and would accept nothing but complete submission. The Texans chose to fight rather than submit to despotism.

Texas martini: *See Martini, Texas style*

Texas milkweed: a weed, *Asclepias texana*, which J. Frank Dobie claimed could be mashed and spread on a snakebite or swallowed to combat the effects of a rattlesnake bite; also called rattlesnake milkweed

Texas movie test: the saguaro cactus watch. Saguaro is the tall cactus with big limbs that usually grow out and up at a right angle to get the appearance of giant stick people. If you see a saguaro in a "Texas" movie, you should know someone is peeing in your boot and telling you it's raining. Saguaro never has and never will grow in Texas, a fact that has always escaped moviemakers. And they are not alone. Not along ago, a national magazine did a story on a town in the Texas Hill Country. The story was fine, but the photograph showed saguaro cactus everywhere. The souvenir crowd has fallen victim to the saguaro fraud, and many now sell trinkets from Texas that feature that type of cactus. There ought to be a law!

Texas oath: I'm Texas born and Texas bred. When I die, I'll be a Texan dead.

Texas Panhandle: skillet handle country

Texas saddle: *See Double-rigged saddle*

Texas skirt: a square saddle skirt as opposed to the rounded, Spanish-style skirt

Texas Stadium: half-Astrodome

Texas symbols: 1. bird, mockingbird 2. dish, chili 3. flower, bluebonnet 4. grass, sideoats gamma 5. mascot, armadillo 6. motto, friendship 7. song, "Texas Our Texas" 8. tree, pecan 9. gem, topaz 10. stone, palmwood

Texas tie: fastening a rope to the saddle horn by a hard-and-fast roper

Texas weather: The weather in Texas proves God has a sense of humor. The late Harold Taft once reported on some strange events related to the Texas weather. When he finished the report, Mr. Taft sort of shook his head and commented, "Texas weather will do anything to get into the news."

Texas wing chaps: *See Batwing chaps*

Ⓣ Texas Women's University students: Tessies

Texan, professional: a Texologist

Thalia (Foard County): pronounced THAIL-ya, rhymes with fail ya [When the post office rejected the original name, Paradise, it was changed to Thalia, which is supposed to mean "blooming" or "luxuriant."]

Thank you: 1. much obliged 2. muchas gracias 3. 'preciate it 4. bless your heart, a favorite of grandmothers

Thank you note: a bread and butter letter

Thankful: shore much obliged

That explains it: that accounts for the milk in the coconut [This is an expression used when something you don't understand, like how the milk gets in the coconut, is finally explained.]

That's a fact: that's the name of that tune

Thawed: unfroze it

The: thuh [Once preceded the name of most diseases in Texas such as "the rheumatism" or "the arthritis."]

There is still time: it's only thunder, which means it has not started raining yet so there is time to finish the job [In his book *If I Tell You a Hen Dips Snuff*, Don Bowman used the expression "cut your peaches, girls, thunder ain't rain."]

Thick as: 1. molasses in winter 2. bunkhouse chili 3. Red River mud

Thick headed: 1. if he got shot between the eyes, it'd take the bullet half an hour to make a hole 2. you could hit him up side the head with a tire iron, and he wouldn't holler till tomorrow morning

Thick skinned: if he ever had to have an operation, the doctor would have to use a hack saw

Thicket: a forest with so much underbrush that passage for man or large animal is virtually impossible. Real bad thickets are so choked that snakes and rabbits have to go around and the owls inside have never seen daylight.

Thief: 1. would steal anything that isn't too hot or too heavy to carry 2. no watermelon patch is safe when he's around 3. careless about which horse he saddles 4. a brand blotter 5. what he wouldn't steal a hound dog pup wouldn't carry off 6. he'd swipe flies from the web of a crippled spider *See also Criminal; Crook; Stealing*

Thief, expert: 1. could steal the saddle off a nightmare 2. could steal the hubcaps off a moving car 3. could steal the fillings out of your teeth while you were eating corn on the cob 4. could steal your shadow 5. nobody can give him lessons on sneaking or thieving

Thief, fast moving: was traveling so fast he didn't have time to pack his real name

Thief, petty: chicken larceny is his long suit

Thief, sneaky: he could steal your shoes while you were walking in them

Thief, stupid: 1. held up a bus load of tourists on their way *home* from Las Vegas 2. couldn't even steal a kiss from an old maid 3. would try to hold you up with a caulk gun

Thighs, large: ol' thunder thighs [This implies her thighs are so large it sounds like thunder when they bang together as she walks.]

Thin as: 1. hen skin 2. a fiddle string 3. a mashed snake 4. a rail 5. a whisper 6. a bat's ear 7. an ant's eyelash *See also Skinny*

Thin but strong: sneaky strong, which means he's a lot stronger than he looks

Thin person: 1. skin flaps on his bones like a quilt on a ridge pole or clothesline 2. if he turned sideways, you could paint stripes on him and use him for a yardstick 3. can put his T-shirt on from either end 4. his body don't look lived in 5. gant up 6. has to get out of the tub before he pulls the plug so he won't go down the drain 7. skin poor 8. lean flanked 9. don't even have enough meat on his bones to qualify as a class project in anatomy school 10. if he drank a Big Red, he would look like the world's biggest thermometer 11. would have to be twins to cast a shadow 12. too thin to send out in a high wind 13. a mop handle with legs *See also Skinny*

Thingamajig: *See Dololly*

Think about it: 1. study on it 2. whip the devil around the stump awhile

Think ahead: 1. once the manure is in the milk, it's too late to grab the cow's tail, which refers to a milk cow swishing manure into the milk 2. don't close the barn door if the mare is already out because she might come home 3. set your pace by the distance left to go and not by the distance already covered

Think alike: you're readin' my mail

Think: 1. scratch your jaw 2. use your head for something besides a hat rack

Thirsty: 1. could drink enough to lower the water level in the Brazos River half a foot 2. have to prime my mouth to spit [When Pat Neff ran for governor of Texas, part of his platform included favoring prohibition, and he promised to take away all the alcohol and make the state so dry Texans would have to prime themselves to spit.]

Thirsty as: 1. a mud hen on a tin roof 2. a cowboy in a new dry town, which means the cowpuncher hasn't had time to find a local bootlegger

Thirsty enough: 1. to spit cotton 2. to drink water from a cow (or wagon) track 3. to drink branch water 4. to suckle a she bear 5. to drink Sheep Dip (a brand of English whiskey)

This one: this right here [This is used to indicate a particular thing. For example, a district attorney might hold up a gun for the jury and say, "This right here is the gun Bubba used to murder the jukebox down at the Arm 'N Dillo saloon." Another example would be the young mother of three who holds up a pail of dirty diapers to show her husband and says, "This right here is the reason you're getting a vasectomy."

Thought: 1. racked my brain 2. figured 3. studied on it 4. ciphered on it

Threaten: 1. gonna hit you so hard it'll raise a knot on your head so big you'll have to stand on a stepladder to scratch it 2. gonna hit you so hard you'll wear out bouncing 3. gonna flail the hail out of you 4. gonna slap you nekkid 5. will knock your eyeballs out of their sockets 6. fixin' to cut you three ways, high, wide, and deep 7. your scalp is in serious jeopardy 8. will beat you like a tied-up goat 9. there'll be a new face in hell for breakfast tomorrow 10. gonna put something on you Ajax won't take off 11. will turn you ever which way but loose 12. will cloud up and rain on your parade 13. gonna rid the ground of your shadow 14. gonna pull you through a knothole so you can relive your birth 15. gonna knock you cross-eyed 16. gonna stomp a mud hole in you and walk it dry 17. gonna open a can of whupass and pour it all over you 18. gonna beat the stuffing out of you and tell God you fell off a horse 19. you better not pee into the wind, pull the mask off the Lone Ranger, or mess with me 20. gonna knock you so cold by the time you wake up your clothes will be out of style 21. gonna tie you in a knot and hang you on a fence 22. gonna slap you like a rented mule 23. will kick your

T

butt so high you'll have to unbutton your Wranglers to tell if it's day or night 24. gonna knock you so far into the ground you'll take root and sprout 25. we're fixin' to have a butt kickin' and you're gonna supply the butt

Threaten, maternal: 1. if you can't listen, you can feel, referring to kids who can't listen can feel a spanking 2. will peck you on the head like a mama bird

Three R's of education: 1. readin' 2. 'ritin' 3. 'rithmatic

Three R's of ranching: 1. riding 2. roping 3. 'rangling

Three R's of marriage: 1. romance 2. rice 3. rocks

Three Rivers (Live Oak County): name comes from the fact the town is located near the Atascosa, Frio, and Nueces Rivers *See also Rule of three rivers*

Thrilled: *See Excited; Happy*

Throat: gozzle, as in "I got some deer sausage stuck in my gozzle and like to choked plumb to death."

Throckmorton firewood: *See Cow droppings*

Throw (thow): chunk, as in "I wouldn't trust her as far as I could chunk her."

Throwing up: 1. driving the porcelain bus 2. laughing at the linoleum

Thumbbuster: nickname for the original Colt revolver, which tended to be very large and heavy; name comes from the fact the hammer on the early models was so hard to pull you could bust your thumb getting your gun cocked; also called a Hawgleg

Thunder: 1. the angels are bowling 2. so loud it knocked me out of the shower

Tie: a kiss for your sister [Even a kiss for your sister can be nice. When the Baylor Bears tied for their first conference football championship in half a

century, their coach, Grant Teaff, said, "...when you haven't kissed your sister in fifty years, it can be mighty nice."]

Tie hack: a person who hews (cuts) railroad ties

 Tie man: a cowboy who ties his rope to the saddle horn

Tie strings: thongs, either leather or rawhide, that run through the leather rosettes or metal conchos on saddles and are used to help hold the saddle together and to secure items tied to the saddle

Tied: 1. hobbled 2. hog-tied

Tight as: 1. the eyelet holes in a woman's corset 2. the skin on a sausage 3. beeswax 4. a 38 bra on a 44 frame 5. paper on a wall 6. a fiddle string 7. bark on a bois d'arc tree 8. a cinch on a fat horse 9. a fat lady's stockings 10. Dick's hatband 11. a drum 12. a wood tick in a dog's tail 13. a block in a vise 14. skin on a catfish 15. a $10 face-lift 16. a clam with lockjaw 17. last year's bikini

Tight fit: fits tight as a cow's foot in a mud bog

Tight grip: 1. like a cowpoke holdin' the reins of a pitchin' horse 2. like a tick on a pup's ear 3. like a kid with a silver dollar

Tight jeans: *See Jeans*

Tighten up: 1. cinch your slack 2. draw the knot closer 3. shorten your stake rope 4. ratchet it down

Tightwad: 1. makes a nickel go so far the buffalo gets sore feet 2. swimming was invented when he came to a toll bridge 3. could back up to a wall and suck a brick out

Tilden (McMullen County): pronounced TILL-den [In 1887 Samuel J. Tilden became the first candidate to win the popular vote for U.S. president only to lose in the electoral college. Residents chose the name so

Tilden would have at least one small victory.]

Tilling spade: sharpshooter in Texas

Timber: pine curtain [East Texas, the piney woods section of the state, is located behind the pine curtain.]

Time consuming: 1. will take longer than it did for Noah's flood to dry 2. will take a spell to tend to 3. you'll be a long time doing it 4. could waltz across Texas before you could get that done

Time enough: there is always time for one more dance

Time isn't right: it's too wet to plow

Time to leave: 1. wet on the fire and call the dogs or pour the coffee on the fire and call the dogs 2. put the chairs in the wagon [On the frontier, chairs were often in short supply, so when families went calling they often carried their chairs so they'd have a place to sit. When the man of the house announced, "put the chairs in the wagon," everyone knew it was time to go home.] 3. put the bricks in the buggy, which relates to the old custom of placing heated, wrapped bricks in the floor of the buggy to keep the feet warm during a trip 4. let's get the hell out of Dodge [This phrase probably originated in the days of trail drives. After weeks on the dusty trail, Texas cowboys were known to have a big time when they reached towns such as Dodge City, Kansas. When the celebrating got out of hand, as it frequently did, the Texans wanted to "get the hell out of Dodge" before the marshal or the lynch mob arrived.]

Time, exact: straight up, as in "It's straight up 6:00 o'clock."

Time, indefinite: a spell, as in "Sit a spell"; also used for awhile

Timed events: rodeo events where contestants compete against the clock and are judged by elapsed time rather than points. Timed events are barrel racing, calf roping, steer wrestling, and team roping. Contestants may apply their points—each dollar won equals one point—from 100 rodeos toward their yearly standing. *See also Breaking the barrier*

Timeless as: Buddy Holly's music. [Note: Buddy Holly is buried in Lubbock, Texas, his hometown. If you visit the grave, it is customary to leave behind a guitar pick as a token of respect.]

Timer line: *See Barrel riding*

Timid: 1. a handwringer 2. weak kneed 3. wouldn't knock a hole in the wind 4. may make a lover, but he'll never make a fighter 5. pantywaist 6. sissy britches 7. a shy dog don't get no biscuits 8. afraid of his own shadow 9. his moist palms are developing mildew 10. has the personality of a custard pudding 11. got the guts of a butterfly 12. the only bull he'll ever take by the horns is the one on a can of Schlitz Malt Liquor *See also Sissy*

Timid as: 1. a whipped pup 2. a lamb

Tinker with: fiddle with

Tioga (Grayson County): pronounced Tie-OH-ga [According to legend, railroad crews who drank at a local spring named the place Tioga, which is supposed to be from a New York Indian tribe meaning "swift current or water." Tioga was the hometown of the late Gene Autry, the singing cowboy. Autry once offered to buy the town if they'd rename it "Autry Springs" but the offer was declined.]

Tired (tared): 1. ran out of rocket fuel 2. feel like an empty shuck 3. feel like I got an axle draggin' in the dirt 4. give out 5. worn to a frazzle 6. dog tired 7. been through the wringer and hung out to dry 8. a mite wilted 9. feel like I pumped a handcar across Texas 10. my mainspring has run down 11. my get up and go got up and went 12. winded 13. tongue is hangin' out like a piggin string 14. played plumb out 15. too pooped to pop 16. feel like I was run down, run over, and wrung out through a little bitty wringer 17. could sleep on a barbed wire fence without a blanket 18. my getalong has got along all it can 19. more wore out than a flour-sack dress 20. rubbed a blister on my chest with my chin *See also Weary*

Tired as: 1. a cat (or mule) that walked a mile in East Texas mud 2. a boomtown whore

Tires, worn: so thin you can see the air inside

Tiresome: as a nagging woman or a barking dog

Tissy: a tantrum, often unprovoked, that borders on a neurotic fit *See also Hissey fit; Conniption fit*

To each his own: 1. even a buzzard is cute to another buzzard 2. a cow chip is a buffet to a fly

Tobacco: tobaccer to a lot of old-timers

Tobacco pin-striping: *See Pickup aerodynamics*

Toco (Lamar County): pronounced TOE-co, not Too-co; originally called Shady Grove, which is still used by some of the local old-timers

Toe finders: *See Stirrup, closed*

Toes, large: nutcrackers

Together: 1. in the same boat (or canoe) 2. hitched to the same wagon 3. plowin' the same row 4. swimming in the same swamp

Together, secretly: got lost in the same place together

Togetherness: 1. thick as thieves 2. in cahoots with

Toilet seat: commode saddle

Told a secret: he put a bug in my ear

Tolerate: abide, as in "Bubba can only abide rock music when he's under the influence of Jack Daniels."

Tom Green County: named for Texas revolutionary war hero and Confederate general Thomas Green; the only county in Texas named for an individual using more than just the last name

Tom Thumb snaffle: unbalanced short shank snaffle *See also Bits*

Tomato: love apple

Tomorrow: mañana [Texans describe Old Mexico as the land of mañana.]

Tongue-tied: his tongue got caught on his eye teeth and he couldn't see what he was saying

Too close to the problem: when you're sittin' in it you don't smell it

Took off: like a cut cat

Toothbrush: 1. molar mop 2. ivory tickler 3. enamel scrubber [It is widely believed the toothbrush was invented in Arkansas where a lot of folks only have one tooth, otherwise it would have been called a teethbrush.]

Toothless: slick gummed

Toothpicks: timber

Tornado: cyclone to old-timers

Tornillo (El Paso County): pronounced Tor-KNEE-ya

Torpedo: long, small metal cylinder a nitro shooter would fill with nitro and drop into an oil well to "shoot the well"

Toss: Texans don't toss anything, they pitch it

Total price: When buying a new vehicle, the total price will include tax, title, and license fees. Texans frequently use "including tax, title, and license" to indicate the absolute total price. The phrase can be used for almost anything from the "all you can eat" price at a barbecue joint to the price of a new pair of boots. Two instances where the saying should not be used are wedding costs and attorney fees. In both cases, there never seems to be anything close to a total price because the charges seem to just keep on coming.

Totin' privileges: a term used to mean when you work for a plant you can "tote home" the leftovers or scraps. In the meat processing industry, workers were once allowed to "tote home" the beef skirts because those parts were not generally used. Today, those beef shirts are known as fajitas. [Note: make sure you have permission before using "totin' privileges" or your boss will have two words for you—grand theft.]

Touchy: 1. raised on sour milk 2. as a teased snake

Tough: 1. leathery 2. case hardened 3. hard boiled 4. hard shelled

Tough act to follow: like elephants in a parade

Tough as: 1. the back end of a shooting gallery 2. calluses on a barfly's elbow 3. a trail drive or bunkhouse steak 4. a boot heel 5. a wagon load of wet rawhide 6. an old boot 7. a knot in a pine board 8. a cast-iron washtub 9. a sow's snout

Tough job: 1. will take a lot of river water to float that boat 2. tying a knot in a mountain lion's tail 3. herding cats 4. like trying to drive a swarm of bees through a snowstorm with a hickory switch See also Difficult; Hard to do

Tough person: 1. when he yells scat you better hunt your hole 2. got fur on his brisket 3. cut his teeth on a gun barrel 4. mite salty 5. gritty 6. gaunt and grizzled 7. uses barbed wire for dental floss 8. uses sandpaper for toilet tissue 9. hunts wildcats with a switch 10. even got a tattoo on the roof of his mouth

Tough town: the chief of police had to hire a bodyguard

Toupee: his hair ain't homegrown

Tourist, poor: came to town with one shirt and a $10 bill and didn't change either

Tourists: comers and goers

Tow: a flax or hemp fiber used to set off a muzzle loading rifle

Town, boring: 1. all we had to do was sit around and watch boats rust 2. spent three weeks there one weekend [This means the town is so boring a weekend seems like three weeks long. A soldier from San Antonio was once transferred to a small base somewhere out west, and he claimed he did a two-year tour there one month.]

Town, fictitious: 1. Snakenavel, Texas 2. Possum Trot, Texas 3. Numbnut or Nosepick, New York 4. Wierdsville, California 5. Bunfuzzel, Egypt 6. Chicky Butte, China 7. Chittlin Switch, South Carolina 8. Gorillaville, Georgia 9. Frogs Eye, Louisiana 10. Coonskin, Kentucky 11. Grittsville, Mississippi 12. Panther Spit, Arkansas 13. Okra, Oklahoma 14. Frostbite, Montana

Town in a difficult location: Abe Lemons, onetime basketball coach at the University of Texas, said of Fayettville, Arkansas, "you can parachute in but you can't parachute out."

Town, poor: only thing you hear after dark is the hardening of arteries

Town, rural: located miles and miles from the middle of nowhere See also Rural

Town, small: 1. had to widen the street to put a stripe down the middle 2. their street sweeper uses a Hoover vacuum 3. nothing but a wide place in the road 4. only need one department store Santa Claus 5. where there ain't much to do but plenty of people to talk about it when you do it 6. only thing that goes out after 10 p.m. is the lights 7. only use first names in the local phone book 8. don't blink or you'll miss it 9. last time they held a boxing match, both fighters had to use the same corner 10. a fixin' to town 11. don't even have a cannon in the park 12. no baby arrives unexpectedly 13. if anyone turned on an electric blanket, the streetlight would go out 14. too small to support a town drunk so everyone takes turns [In Pyote, Texas, they have a sign with "Entering Pyote" on one side and "Leaving Pyote" on the other. In another small Texas town, the "slow down" and "resume speed" signs are on the same pole.

Town, strict: the young girls can't buy a bra without a prescription

Townspeople: 1. paper collar Comanches 2. the manicured tribe

Toy: a play pretty

Toyah (Reeves County): pronounced TOY-ya

Trace chain: chain used to attach mules (or horses) to a wagon or plow

Tracker, good: could track a minnow through a swamp

Trade talk: time to taw down

Traffic signal: traffic signals in Texas are red lights even though they also have green and yellow lights

Trail-broke: *See Road-broke*

Train, short run: puddle jumper

Traipse: In Texas, traipse is generally used to mean "wander about," as in "We had to traipse all over town lookin' for a pair of boots that'd fit over Bubba's big feet."

Transfer: 1. moving camp locations 2. change brands

Trapped like: 1. a lizard under a cow patty [If a lizard happens to be in the wrong place when a cow gets rid of yesterday's oats, he is surely trapped.] 2. a minnow in a bucket 3. a calf in a pen 4. a cat up a tree 5. a treed possum 6. a 50-pound catfish in a 40-gallon aquarium 7. like a yearling in a cattle truck

Travel fast: keep the news behind you [This saying originated in the days when news traveled slow from one place to another, usually in mailbags on a train.]

Travel time: windshield time

Treated poorly: treated me like I was a mistress at a family reunion

Tricked: 1. hoodwinked 2. bamboozled 3. hornswoggled 4. pulled the wool over their eyes 5. took the bait like a bass taking a fancy lure 6. double clutched him

Trickham (Coleman County): According to legend, a local saloon owner submitted the name "Trick 'em" because of his habit of tricking local cowboys by selling them watered-down whiskey. The postal authorities rejected the name so it was changed to Trickham.

Tricky as: trying to braid a mule's tail

Tried but failed: 1. did a lot of stirring but didn't make no gravy 2. did a lot of shootin' but didn't get any meat 3. they carried him out on his shield

Tried hard: 1. bucked till he buckled 2. popped a gut 3. gave it all he had 4. ran a good race 5. buckled up and buckled down

Trifler: one who cheats on a lover, especially a male

Tripping: oil field slang for pulling the pipe out of the hole

Trivial: 1. wouldn't be noticed if it was tied to the saddle of a galloping horse 2. wouldn't get any more notice than one cactus in a desert

Trouble: 1. got a skunk by the tail 2. got an ox in the ditch 3. got hell to pay 4. your goose is cooked 5. in a pickle 6. your butt's in a sling 7. in a heap of trouble 8. knee deep in manure 9. it's Katy bar the door 10. up to my armpits in alligators and can't find the drain for the swamp 11. got my tail in a wringer 12. got a dead cat down the well 13. a washtub full of misery 14. it's cut a switch or woodshed time [Trouble is like a muddy creek. Be patient, don't stir it up, and it will soon clear.] *See also In trouble*

Trouble, big time: 1. parachuting into a live volcano 2. sitting on a hornet's nest 3. sittin' in the middle of a stampede 4. trapped on a high bridge by an unscheduled train [In the old days, the easiest way across a big river or deep ravine was the railroad bridge. Though it was usually prohibited, a lot of people would simply learn the schedule and cross at times when no trains were due. However, since the bridges were just large enough for the train, if you happened to be about halfway across the bridge and an unscheduled train suddenly appeared, you were, indeed, in big trouble.]

Trouble brewing: storm clouds are gathering

Troubled: 1. got a passel of hassles 2. in a mell of a hess

Truck: kidney pounder

Truck patch: a small field where you grow vegetables that you truck into town to sell

True: 1. natural fact 2. it came from the horse's mouth 3. got it straight from the mare's mouth

Trust: trust everybody, but always cut the cards

Trustworthy: 1. a good man to go to the well with 2. can carry the key to the smokehouse 3. could trust him to count the collection in church [A favorite saying of former first lady Lady Bird Johnson is "He'd do to run the river with." Swimming a river on a horse can be dangerous, so cowboys often made the run with a friend who could be trusted.]

Truth: 1. be sure your story is wider than it is tall 2. the gospel 3. the range word 4. dead open fact [Some say Texans have such a high regard for the truth they use it sparingly so as to not use it up, which is why Texans never let the truth stand in the way of a good story.] *See also Certain; Guaranteed*

Try: 1. give it a whirl 2. dance it around the floor 3. sling it on the wall and see if it sticks 4. throw it in the creek and see if it floats 5. run it up the flagpole and see if anyone salutes 6. take a crack (or stab) at it 7. wing it 8. try it on for size 9. see how your luck holds 10. a baby coon can't sit in the den and learn to catch frogs 11. run it down the well and see if it holds water

Try again: 1. squeeze off another round 2. take another shot 3. go back to the well 4. reset your hat and give it another ride 5. take a new hold 6. take another swing around the dance floor

Try everything: 1. run the full length of the rope 2. try every trick in the book 3. if you can't ride 'em and you can't bulldog 'em, you can always rope 'em [Bones Irvin, an assistant under Bear Bryant at A&M, said it another way for football. "Some days you can't tackle 'em, and some days you can't block 'em, but you can always fight 'em."]

Try hard: 1. give it your best shot 2. go for the gusher 3. do your dead level best

Try something new: 1. plow some new ground 2. try a new dance or a new partner 3. if the fish ain't biting, change bait

Trying the impossible: trying to shovel sunshine

Tube cleaners: Texas A&M students in the Medical and Veterinary Corps

Tulia (Swisher County): pronounced TOOL-ya

Tumble bug: doodlebug

Tumbleweed: bushes originally imported from Russia around the turn of the century in hopes they would help hold down erosion. It's a Russian thistle that doesn't become a tumbleweed until its thin stalk breaks off and the plant dries out and becomes brittle. Then when the wind gets it, as it frequently does in Texas, the bush is set in motion and the tumbling starts. The bushes don't do jack squat to prevent erosion, but they have found their way into the folklore of the state. Many people actually believe the weeds were sent by God so the good folks in West Texas could easily tell which way the wind was blowing. Others believe that God invented tumbleweeds so the children of poor families could have a pet.

Turkey (Hall County): originally called Turkey Roost after the wild turkeys that roosted along nearby Turkey Creek; name was shortened when locals applied for a post office [Turkey is the home town of Bob Wills, the king of western swing music. The annual Bob Wills Festival is worth the trip.]

Turkey fries: *See Calf fries; Brave as*

Turn it to aces, duces, etc. (dominoes): refers to playing in such a way that only an ace, duce, or any other one suit can be played

Turn off: 1. cut off 2. kill, as in "Kill the lights"

Turn over: tump over, as in "Billy tumped over his milk at the breakfast table this morning, and the cat lapped it up."

Turned around: 1. spun around like a windmill in a whirlwind 2. turned about

Turned out bad: went sour on me

Turned out good: came out of the deal smelling like I was dipped in Four Roses [Four Roses was a pungent brand of toilet water in the Old West that could easily cover up the scent of a cowboy just off the range.]

Turning: a walk behind, single-sided plow pulled by two mules; it turned over the ground but did not create rows for planting

Tush hog: the big boar hog that was the leader of the herd; now used for leader, boss, or V.I.P

Tuxedo: 1. monkey suit 2. scissortail outfit

Tuxedo, Texas style: a George Strait tuxedo. A lot of good ol' boys in Texas are just not comfortable in a regular tuxedo, which presents a problem on those rare occasions when they have to attend formal events. Several years ago Texan George Strait, a pretty fair country singer, provided a perfect alternative for all Texans. George appeared on stage to accept an award. From the waist up he was dressed in a regular tuxedo. From the waist down, he wore his jeans and boots. If you're invited to any event where this type of tuxedo will not be accepted, that is one of those events you'd be better off not attending.

Twelfth man: Texas Aggie tradition where cadets stand during football games in readiness to go into the game if needed

Twenty-five cents: two bits

Twilight: first dark

Twine: 1. strang 2. runt rope

Twister: *See Bronc buster*

Twitty (Wheeler County): pronounced TWIT-ee. This Texas town provided country singing legend Conway Twitty with his last name. The first name was taken from Conway, Arkansas.

Two (playing card): 1. duck 2. duce 3. two spot

Two-holer: outhouse with seating room for two *See One-holer*

Two-man job: double barrel chore

Two-o-one file: the military file on Texas A&M University cadets kept in the Trigon

Two percenters: Texas A&M students who do not have "the spirit"

Tying: throwing and tying a steer

Tyrant: old war horse

U.T.: THE University of Texas

Ugly as: 1. grandpa's toenails 2. homemade soup, soap, or sin 3. hammered manure 4. second place 5. a cancer-eyed cow 6. a fresh foaled moose 7. the west end of an east bound mule 8. a mud fence

Ugly baby: 1. so ugly, his mother made him put on an Elvis mask before she'd nurse him 2. the stork had to get drunk before he could deliver her 3. when his daddy saw him he grabbed a shotgun and went down to the zoo to kill a stork 4. his mother took him everywhere she went so she wouldn't have to kiss him good-bye 5. his mother had morning sickness after he was born 6. his mother had to be drunk before she'd breast feed him which explains why, fifteen years later, he thought Jack Daniels came from cows

Ugly child: 1. if she ever gets kidnapped they'll never put her face on a milk carton 'cause it would ruin the milk business 2. he ought to sue his parents for damages

Ugly enough to: 1. clabber a mud hole 2. gap lightning 3. make your eyes fog over 4. scare a maggot off a bloated buffalo carcass

Ugly female: 1. the tide wouldn't take her out 2. coyote ugly, which means if you woke up with her asleep on your arm, you'd chew off your arm rather than wake her up 3. wasn't hit with the ugly stick, the whole danged tree fell on her 4. has to slap her legs to get them to go to bed with her 5. couldn't get a date if she was cooking naked for a deer camp (or lumber camp, or cattle drive) 6. a two sacker, which means if you put a sack on her head you ought to put on two in case one falls off 7. would make a freight train take a dirt road 8. looks would stop a courthouse clock 9. would scare

night into day 10. would turn a funeral procession down an alley 11. would wilt knee-high cotton 12. would scare a drunk man sober 13. looks like something the cat drug in and the dog won't eat 14. got a face built for a hackamore 15. whenever her husband goes out on the town he always takes her picture with him so he'll know to stop drinking when she gets good looking *See also Female, ugly; Homely*

Ugly male: 1. when he was born, the doctor slapped his mother 2. when he was a baby his mother fed him with a slingshot 3. has to soak his clothes in catnip to get the cat to play with him 4. if he was an armed robber, he wouldn't need a ski mask 5. looks like he left his teeth in a fruit jar at home 6. his mother had to borrow a baby to take to church 7. whipped with an ugly stick 8. his cooties keep their eyes closed 9. if you look up ugly in the dictionary, you'll find his picture 10. couldn't get a date at the Chicken Ranch with a truckload of fryers [The Chicken Ranch, one of the world's most famous whorehouses, was once located near LaGrange, Texas. The place got its name during the Depression when the girls would accept chickens instead of cash. The Chicken Ranch was immortalized by the Broadway play and movie *The Best Little Whorehouse in Texas.*]

Ulcers: what you get from mountain climbing over molehills

Unable: 1. can't cut the mustard 2. can't do that any more than a steer can take care of a heifer

Unable to answer: don't start me lying [This essentially means don't ask me that question 'cause if I answer it I'll have to tell you a lie.]

Unacceptable: 1. that dog won't hunt [Although long a popular phrase, it reached star status when used by Ann Richards in the 1988 Democratic National Convention to indicate the

Republican policies were unacceptable.] 2. can't sit still for that 3. that bucket won't hold no milk (or water) 4. that boat won't float 5. that horse won't trot 6. that cat won't flush

Unafraid: 1. ain't a scared 2. meant to worry about it but didn't have the time

Unappreciative: checks every tooth in the mouth of a gift horse

Unassuming: couldn't get in the spotlight if he was breakin' out of prison

Unattached: 1. footloose and fancy free 2. unbridled 3. got a loose stake rope

Unattainable: that's one possum you won't get into a sack

Unattractive: 1. as a tow sack shirt (or skirt) 2. a real eyesore 3. looks like 40 miles of bad road

Unavailable: 1. out of pocket 2. off the range 3. dance card is full

Unavoidable: 1. gotta play the hand you're dealt 2. gotta dance to the tune the band plays 3. no matter how warm the sunshine is, the cat always has her kittens in the barn 4. there are some things a man can't ride around 5. that's the way the cow chip crumbles

Unbelievable: 1. beats anything I ever saw or heard tell of 2. sounds a might farfetched to me

Unbreed: disconnect the pipe used in breeding a locomotive

Uncertain: 1. absolutely buffaloed 2. don't have a clue 3. don't have anymore idea about that than a pig knows what day of the week it is

Uncertain (Harrison County): There is some uncertainty about how the town got its name. It may have been because riverboat pilots were "uncertain" about landing there; local fisherman may have been "uncertain" if they'd be able to sell their catch; or the townsfolk were "uncertain" if they would be able to sell alcohol after they

incorporated. Another possibility, perhaps probability, is that the local residents where uncertain about a name so they took the easy way out.

Unchangeable: 1. set in concrete 2. cast in bronze 3. written in ink 4. you can take the boy out of the country but you can't take the country out of the boy 5. you can take the Texan out of Texas, but you can never take the Texas out of a Texan

Unclear: 1. about as clear as Red River mud 2. about as clear as fog in a river bottom

Uncomfortable: 1. as a goat head in a condom 2. as a barbed wire G string

Uncommitted: 1. won't stay hitched 2. like a grasshopper, you never know which way he'll jump [Red Adair, world famous Texas oil well firefighter, has a sign on his desk proclaiming, "I said maybe, and that's final."]

Uncompromising: 1. dead tough no matter what the game or odds 2. won't bend as much as a crowbar

Unconcerned: it's all water off a duck's back to him

Unconscious: out like a cat hit with a boot jack

Uncontrollable: 1. a hard dog to keep under the porch 2. can't check him with a 3/4 hemp rope and a bois d'arc snubbing post

Uncoordinated: 1. can't shuffle dominos 2. can't plow and chew tobacco at the same time 3. can't shower and sing at the same time 4. can't walk and breathe at the same time 5. his egg got shook, which means he has been uncoordinated since birth 6. couldn't even twiddle his thumbs

Uncoordinated as: 1. a drunk getting out of a sunken bathtub 2. a hog on ice

Uncouth: 1. picks his nose at state dinners 2. ain't particular where he spits

Undecided: 1. like a midget in line at a nudist colony, I don't know which way to turn 2. the jury's still out 3. didn't swim or sink, he floated 4. straddling the fence 5. hangin' fire [This is a reference to a breech loading cannon that has a fire in the breech but hasn't gone off.]

Undependable: he's in and out like a dog's hind leg

Underbid (dominoes): when you make a lot more than you bid; there is no penalty

Underbrush: Texas term for undergrowth or brush

Underdog: one of the most dangerous animals on earth

Underestimated: you're callin' an alligator a lizard

Underlip: a horse's bottom lip

Understand: 1. savvy 2. see the light 3. get your meaning 4. get your drift 5. 'nuff said 6. comprende 7. it finally soaked in 8. hear tell, as in "I hear tell she's on the prowl."

Understand fully: you're preaching to the choir

Underwear: 1. scanties 2. long johns 3. unmentionables 4. underdrawers

Undressed: shucked himself

Uneducated: 1. couldn't count to 20 with both boots and his socks off 2. don't know gee from haw, which refers to mule team driver's terms for right (gee) and left (haw) 3. couldn't pour rainwater out of a boot with the instructions printed on the heel 4. don't know cow chips from computer chips 5. ain't got a lick of sense. *See also Dumb; Ignorant; Stupid*

Uneducated guess: used the WAG system, which is a wild-assed guess *See also Educated guess*

Unemployed: 1. my spurs are rusting 2. don't have nuthin' to do and a lot of time to do it in 3. riding with the chuck line [This refers to out-of-work cowboys riding with the chuck wagon hoping for a meal.]

Unequalled: nothing could hold a candle to it

Unexpected: it just came out of the blue

Unexpected as: 1. a fifth ace 2. a seagull in Colorado

Unfaithful: 1. bobbing around 2. got a lot of strings on her fiddle (or guitar) 3. won't even dance with the one that brung her

Unfamiliar with: 1. not too well versed in 2. not posted on 3. don't know as much about that as the devil does the scriptures 4. it's news to me

Unfinished: still got some branding (or hoeing) to do

Unfinished job: a kiss without a squeeze

Unflinching: got the nerve of a riverboat gambler [Anytime a gambler on a riverboat flinched he usually lost a bet or his life or both. As a result, riverboat gamblers were famous for having nerves of iron.]

Unforgettable: 1. won't forget that if I live to be 125 years old 2. wouldn't forget that if I had a brain transplant

Unfriendly: they don't put their horses in the same corral

Unfriendly as: 1. fire ants 2. a mule on a sawdust diet

Ungrateful: he never said kiss my foot much less thank you

Unhappy affair: this has been about as cheerful as a coroner's inquest

Unimportant: 1. don't make no never mind 2. a no account

Uninformed: he's speaking from a pulpit of ignorance

United States, northern part: the rust belt

United States, southern part: the sun belt

U

Universe: tarnation, as in "He's the best shot in all tarnation."

Unkempt: 1. looks like she fell face-down in a briar patch and the cows trampled her 2. looks like he dried his clothes by climbing in the dryer and turning it on

Unknown: 1. never saw or heard tell of it 2. don't know who in blazes it is 3. wouldn't know him if he bit me on the leg 4. don't rightly know 5. ain't got the foggiest notion 6. wouldn't know him from Adam (or her from Eve) 7. don't know that any more than a pig knows he's pork 8. if it ain't a mystery, it's guesswork 9. don't know any more about that than a sow does about bikini bathin' suits

Unknown as: 1. Whistler's father 2. Ameilia Earhart's co-pilot

Unless: lessen

Unlikely: farfetched, as in "It'd be pretty farfetched to think they'd ever bring back the Southwest Conference."

Unlucky: 1. if he'd been a dog on Noah's ark he would have ended up with both fleas 2. if he bought a cemetery, people would stop dying 3. could get a cavity in a porcelain crown 4. paying the wrong preacher 5. been in more holes than a grave digger during a smallpox epidemic 6. put his hat on a bed, which refers to the old country belief that anyone who puts his hat on a bed will have bad luck 7. playing with a cold deck 8. my luck come unraveled 9. my cup is empty but my slop bucket is overflowing 10. if he started selling light bulbs the sun would stop setting 11. the flowers are blooming but they're in someone else's garden 12. if it wasn't for bad luck I wouldn't have no luck a'tall 13. if he bought a flower shop, they'd outlaw Mother's Day 14. dropped a basket full of mirrors 15. snakebit 16. if I bought a truckload of pumpkins in October, they'd cancel Halloween 17. he couldn't win a bet on a football game if he had tomorrow's paper [Temple Houston, noted attorney, gunman, and son of General Sam Houston said, "If I started to hell with a load of ice to sell, the damn place would freeze over before I could get there."] See also Born loser

Unmarked: slick eared, which is a reference to livestock whose ears are not marked

Unnatural: a chicken and a coyote might sleep together, but the chicken will keep one eye open

Unnecessary as: 1. two tails on a tomcat 2. three horns on a steer 3. axle grease on a jackrabbit

Unpopular: 1. was voted most likely to have an autopsy 2. whenever he plays horse, someone else plays the front end and he plays himself 3. if he rode through town in an open convertible, the townsfolk would have to have a lottery to decide who got the privilege of throwing rocks at him

Unpredictable: 1. can't tell what's gonna happen no more than a car-chasing dog knows what he'd do with a car if he caught it 2. you never know which way the cat will jump 3. you never know which way the pickle will squirt 4. changes his mind more often than he changes his underwear

Unpredictable as: Texas weather. As the saying goes, only fools and new-comers predict the weather in Texas.

Unprepared: 1. riding without a rope 2. ain't got all your dogs barking 3. hunting buffalo with a BB gun [About the only way a buffalo could die from a BB gun would be if he ate it and choked to death.]

Unprotected: 1. unarmed 2. his bulletproof vest is in the wash

Unqualified: couldn't pass muster

Unrelated as: 1. chalk and cheese 2. a bull and a ballerina

Unreliable: 1. won't do to tie to 2. don't tote level 3. will be late to his own funeral 4. wouldn't want to hitch him to your wagon 5. couldn't trust him with the key to your wife's chastity belt 6. only count on him when the goin' is easy *See also Untrustworthy*

Unrepairable: as a broken windowpane

Unrestrained: going hog wild

Unsafe: 1. held together with a lick and a promise 2. held together with a cobweb

Unseen: never laid eyes on

Unsettled: wishy-washy

Unsteady: 1. wobbles like a newborn colt (or calf) 2. his knees are drunk *See also Shaky*

Unsure: *See Indecisive*

Unsuccessful: starving to death in the land of plenty

Untouchable: couldn't touch her with a ten-foot pole

Untrustworthy: 1. has to have someone else call his hogs 2. trust him as far as you can throw a bale of hay, post hole, anvil, or full-grown bull 3. you can let him walk in the parade, but don't let him carry the flag 4. don't bunk with him if you value the gold in your eye teeth 5. never trust a rooster handler [From cock fighters often betting on the other man's bird then disabling their own fowl so it would lose.] *See also Unreliable*

Unusual: 1. not your average garden variety 2. beats anything I ever saw

Unwanted: 1. need that like a hog needs a packing house 2. need that like I need a third foot 3. need that like a mermaid needs a bicycle 4. need that like a duck needs an umbrella 5. need that like I need a boil on my butt 6. need that like a chicken coop needs a fox 7. got no more use for it than a sow has for an extra set of teats

Unwanted as: 1. a snake at a garden party 2. a frog in the water can 3. a cow chip in the punch bowl at a wedding reception 4. a hailstorm to a farmer 5. a blown-over outhouse 6. a wart on a pretty girl's nose

Unwelcome as: 1. an outhouse breeze 2. a porcupine in a nudist colony 3. a rattlesnake in a prairie dog town 4. a quitter on a trail drive [According to country legend, there wasn't any room on the chuck wagon for a quitter's bedroll.]

Up to date: there ain't no flies on him

Upbringing: your "raisin'" in Texas

Upfall: opposite of downfall

Uppin stone: *See Child, small*

Uppity: *See Aloof; Arrogant*

Upset: 1. walking mad all over 2. pitching and squealing 3. having a walleyed fit 4. hopping mad 5. her fangs are itching 6. spoiling for a fracas 7. gathered up her skirts and left 8. took his ball and went home 9. threw the cards in the fire 10. ate the dice 11. nose is out of joint 12. got a clod in her churn 13. got his tail over the dashboard [If a horse got his tail over the dashboard of a buggy, he'd try to run away.] *See also Angry; Female, angry; Mad; Male, angry*

Upside down: like an armadillo on the Interstate, which refers to dead animals in the Interstate usually being upside down

U

Upstaged: stole his thunder and his lightning

Urgent: that needs tending to

Urinate: 1. water the grass or horses 2. kill a tree (or some bushes) 3. drain your crankcase, dragon, snake, lizard, or radiator 4. see a man about a dog or a horse 5. go see if the horse has kicked off his blanket 6. milk a rattlesnake 7. shake the dew off the lily

Use sparingly: don't burn all the kindling on one fire

Used often: as a roller towel in a bunkhouse

Useful: *See Handy*

Useful as: 1. a lock on the outhouse door 2. a long sermon on a cold Sunday morning [The church is always warm as a depot stove, so on a real cold Sunday morning the longer the preacher talks, the longer you get to stay inside and keep warm.] 3. a pullin' chain at calf time [If a cow is having trouble delivering a calf, a pullin' chain is used to help. Without a pullin' chain you have to let nature take its course.]

Useless: 1. got no more use for that than Noah had for a foghorn on the ark 2. ain't nuthin but a slop-jar load 3. tie a dollar to it and throw it away so you can say you lost something *See also Worthless*

Useless as: 1. a milk bucket under a bull 2. a two-story outhouse (you wouldn't want to be on the ground floor if someone was doing their business upstairs) 3. tits on a boar hog 4. a screen door on a submarine 5. combat boots at a track meet 6. a saddle without a horse 7. a steam engine without water 8. a cowboy without a horse 9. a windmill without wind 10. speaking Chinese to a jackass 11. wet powder 12. trying to rodeo on a stick horse (or rocking horse) 13. a kiss over the phone 14. a side saddle on a sow 15. a comb to a bald man 16. a needle without an eye 17. an airbag on a saddle 18. a well without a bucket [If you've ever been real thirsty and come up on a well only to discover there isn't a bucket handy, then you know a well without a bucket is nothing but a big useless hole in the ground.] *See also Worthless*

Useless person: 1. deadwood 2. more ornamental than useful

Usin' horse: *See Ranch horse*

Utility bill: light bill

Utopia: hog heaven

 Uvalde (Uvalde County): pronounced u-VAL-dee for the town and the county

 V

V.I.P. 1. a tree shaker 2. a big bug

Vacillate: 1. crawfish 2. changes his mind as often as he does his socks 3. shilly-shally

Vacuum: dust sucker

Vain: 1. wouldn't go to a funeral unless he could be the corpse 2. even checks his toupee for gray hairs 3. wish I could buy her for what she's worth and sell her for she thinks she's worth

Val Verde County: pronounced Val VER-dee; named for the Battle of Val Verde, which was a Confederate victory during the Civil War [This is the only town in Texas named for a battle.]

Valentine (Jeff Davis County): The town got its name because the crew of the Texas and New Orleans Railroad completed tracks to the location on St. Valentine's Day in 1882. A postmark from this little town is very popular on cards, and it is so simple to do. Simply address your card and put on the proper postage. Then put that card, in the envelope, in a larger envelope and mail it care of Postmaster, Valentine, Texas 79854-9998. The postmaster will open your letter, apply the Valentine cancel to your card, and send it on its way to your sweetheart. Be sure to mail early since Valentine is a little out of the way and mail service is slower than it would be from a larger city.

Value: worth, as in "What you reckon that old pickup of yours is worth?"

Valuable: 1. as a herd of pregnant racehorses 2. worth his weight in oil leases 3. wouldn't take a purty for it 4. as the front door key to Fort Knox

Value, lacking: like owning a sawmill that don't make 2x4s [Any sawmill that didn't make 2x4s, the most popular size of cut lumber, would not be worth much.]

Value, poor: the cheapest oats are the ones that have already been through the horse once

Van Alstyne (Grayson County): pronounced Van All-steen, not Van All-stine

Van Zandt County: pronounced Van Zant, the "d" is silent; Canton is the county seat

Vandal: a terrorist on a limited budget

Vaquero: Mexican cowboy

Vara: a unit of measure used in early Texas and still found on many old maps. One vara equals thirty-three and a half inches.

Varied: checkered, as in "He's had a checkered career."

Vegetarian: a person who won't eat anything that can reproduce

Verbal insult: float-out

Varmint: *See Animals*

Venus (Johnson County): pronounced VEE-nus; named in honor of the daughter of a local physician

Veribest (Tom Green County): pronounced Very-best [The town was not named because someone thought it was the very best place in Texas. The name actually came from the old "Very Best" brand of canned goods.]

Very: 1. powerful, as in "I'm powerful glad you weren't hurt in the accident" 2. mighty, as in "I'm mighty happy over the election results" 3. plumb, as in "I'm plumb proud to accept the nomination" 4. durn, as in "I'm durn glad to see you" 5. dead as in "He's dead in love." 6. downright, as in "He's downright bodacious."

Very few: 1. precious few 2. precious little

Veterinarian, good: he could cure a bearskin rug or a stuffed owl

Vibrant: has lots of spizerenctum

Vice, minor: 1. bug hunting [This means he committed some insignificant crime such as stealing flowers from the neighbors to take to his girl.] 2. what he did ain't half as bad as singing too loud in church

Vice president: According to John Nance Garner, the vice president is a spare tire on the automobile of government. Of course, Garner also said "The vice presidency isn't worth a bucket of warm spit."

Vice versa: vicy versey

Vicinity: 1. in these parts 2. hereabouts 3. this neck of the woods 4. round about here

Vicious: 1. don't believe in taking prisoners 2. full of natural cussidness 3. part volcano, part tornado, and all earthquake 4. give you as much chance as a wolf would give a sucklin' lamb 5. got snake blood in his veins 6. a rattler would die if he bit him 7. will rub cockleburs in the hair of an orphan girl 8. rides roughshod over everybody 9. favorite tune is *Deguello* (de-gwa-ya) [This is the Mexican song signifying "no quarter will be given" that was played during the siege of the Alamo.] *See also Ruthless*

Victory: we rolled over 'em like a cow peeing on a flat rock

Victory, sloppy: "Old ugly is better than old nothing," said Darrel Royal.

Vidor (Orange County): pronounced VIE-dur, not Ve-door; named for lumberman Charles Shelton Vidor

Vienna sausage: vi-EEN-ers

View, pleasant: a sight for sore eyes

Vindictive as: an IRS agent

Vinegarroon (Val Verde County): pronounced Vin-a-ga-roon; named for the vinegarroon whip scorpions in the area, which emit a vinegar-like odor when frightened or squashed. Vinegarroon was established by the famous Judge Roy Bean after he was run out of San Antonio, supposedly for selling watered-down milk. When the railroad bypassed Vinegarroon, Bean moved to Langtry and established his "Law West of the Pecos."]

Violin: fiddle, in Texas

VIP: tree shaker

Virtue: keeps him bored stiff

Virtuous: pure as driven snow

Visit: set a spell and take a load off

Visitor, infrequent: comes around about as often as Elvis does

Voice, deep: 1. so low you can smell socks on his breath 2. so deep he has to wear an athletic supporter for a chin strap 3. sounds like an ungreased wooden gin screw, which produces a low moan when it turns

Voice, gravelly: 1. sounds like he gargled with axle grease 2. like a crow with the croup

Voice, high: 1. talks like a mockingbird trill 2. like the screech of a locomotive when there's a cow on the tracks

Voice, poor: 1. sounds like a buzz saw cutting through a cast-iron skillet 2. sounds like she has one foot in a bear trap

Voice, rough: sounds like a rusty gate hinge

Vomit: threw up his toenails (or socks) *See also Sick*

Vote: cast lots

Voting: Lyndon Johnson once said, "We don't care how they vote so long as we get to count 'em."

Vulnerable: a sitting duck [A duck that is sitting is much more vulnerable than one that is flying.]

Vulnerable as: 1. a trailer house in a tornado [It seems whenever tornadoes strike, trailer houses (or mobile homes) take the worst beating.] 2. a 200-pound highline walker on a 100-pound test line

 W.P.R.A.: Women's Professional Rodeo Association

Waco (McClennan County): pronounced WAY-co, never Wack-oh unless you want to be derogatory; named for an Indian tribe that once lived in the area

Waddie: an extra cowboy who fills in where needed

Waggie: a female cadet

Wait: 1. slack up on the reins 2. hold your horses 3. keep your shirt (or bra) on

Wasting time: piddling around

Waiting: just sittin' on the well; a country expression that means you're waiting for an oil or water well to come in

Waitress: 1. biscuit shooter (or dealer) 2. grub quarterback, which refers to a waitress picking up food from the cook and handing it off to the customer 3. menu mama 4. steak (or chili) slinger 5. tip wrangler

Walk: 1. on the boot leather express 2. footin' it 3. doin' a sidewalk sashay 4. pounding the pavement 5. legging it 6. hoofin' it 7. jingling his spurs 8. moseying 9. pi-eyeing 10. afoot [To a cowboy, a man afoot was no man a'tall.]

Walk carefully: 1. like a chicken with an egg cracked inside 2. like you're tryin' not to wake the twins 3. like you were walkin' through a feedlot wearin' a brand new pair of white shoes 4. like your bones were made of rubber

Walk far: used up enough leather to half sole the Confederate army

Walk funny: 1. like a duck out of water 2. like a drunk roadrunner 3. like he's knee deep in ice water 4. like she's holding a cantaloupe between her legs

Walk leisurely: poke along

Walk proudly: sashay, as in "I'm gonna sashay down to the barbershop and show off my new boots."

Walk quietly: tippytoe

Walk slow: *See Slow walker*

Walk softly: cat foot it

Walk, seductive: 1. got more moves than Allied Van Lines 2. got more moves than a snake caught in a steel bear trap 3. if she was in a harness she'd make plowin' a pleasure [This is a reference to the old days when plowing was done by walking behind a plow all day and the only scenery was the back end of a flea bitten ol' mule.]

Walker Colt: Texas Ranger Samuel Walker liked the revolutionary new pistols made by Samuel Colt, but he thought some changes were needed. He suggested the guns have a stationary trigger and a trigger guard. He also urged Colt to make the pistols bigger and heavier so they could be used as clubs when the ammunition was gone. Colt incorporated the changes in a new model that became known as the Walker Colt.

Walking: ridin' shanks mare

Walking-beaming: a bucking horse that lands alternately on his front feet and hind feet

Walking rocker: one that moves just a smidgen (little bit) each time you rock back and forth. If you're not careful, it'll walk right off the porch.

Wallet: Texas term for saddle sack used to carry grub tied to a saddle

Walleyed: a horse whose eyes have light colored irises

Wal-Mart: Wally World

Wamba (Bowie County): pronounced Wam-bee despite the way it is spelled

Wandering: 1. sloshing around 2. moseyin' around 3. strayed off the trail 4. got saddle itch

Want: 1. give half of all creation for 2. would trade all the mineral rights in Texas for it *See also Desire*

Want to know: would give my upper plate to know that [Upper plate refers to false teeth, which means if you'd give up your teeth, you must really want to know it.]

Want to stay young: don't want to be a blessing *See Old-timer*

War bag: a sack, often tied to a saddle, that was used for storing personal belongings

War bridle: an emergency rope bridle that fits in the mouth and over the ears and is used to control an unruly horse

War song: the bridal march

Warm: hot off the griddle

Warm as: 1. a depot stove 2. a grandmother's blanket 3. a turtle on a log 4. a fresh biscuit 5. a fat woman in a feather bed 6. a road lizard 7. worm dirt 8. a baby chick in a wool basket

Warm embrace: an all-squeezin' hug

Warn: 1. shake a rope (or big stick) at 'em 2. send up a smoke signal

Warning: 1. gonna pull you through a knothole so you can relive the moment of your birth 2. will get on you like stink on manure 3. will knock you into the middle of next week 4. will grab your tongue and turn you inside out 5. will grab you and tear along the dotted line 6. will skin you and tan your hide (or nail your hide to the barn door) 7. wring your neck 8. better give your soul to Jesus, cause your butt belongs to me 9. you'll cuss the day you were born 10. if you know a prayer, now's the time to say it 11. gonna cut out your gizzard and eat it (or feed it to my dog) 12. you better hunt a storm cellar 'cause I'm coming after you like a

W

cyclone 13. will snatch you baldheaded
See also Threaten

Wash (warsh)**:** 1. do, as in "If you'll do the dishes, I'll take you to a moving picture show." 2. another term for gulch or ravine

Washcloth: warsh rag

Wash hole: an area of a creek where the family usually bathed in good weather; also doubled as a swimming hole

Wash your hair: wash your head [Texans use this phrase because you might be able to wash your hair and not your head but you can't wash your head without washing your hair in the process.]

Washerwoman loop: a large, flat loop

Washing (warshing)**:** suds busting

Wasp: 1. mud dauber 2. dirt dauber 3. hornet 4. yellow jacket 5. stinger bringer

Wasted a loop: a rope throw that missed the mark

Waste of time: 1. a wild goose chase 2. a kiss over the phone (which is like a straw hat, it ain't felt)

Wasted effort: like getting your teeth cleaned before you have 'em pulled. *See also Effort, wasted*

Wasteful as: a trainload of lawyers going off a bridge with two empty cars [Texan Lamar Hunt, who owns the Kansas City Chiefs, once said, "My definition of utter waste is a busload of lawyers going over a cliff with three empty seats." He made the remark because of all the lawyers involved in the dispute between the national Football League and the Oakland Raiders.]

Wasting breath: talking to Noah about high water

Wasting money: 1. burning rocket fuel in a coal oil lamp 2. throwing good dollars after bad 3. might as well flush it down a toilet (or chunk it in an outhouse hole) 4. putting a $100 saddle on a $20 horse 5. buying pearls for a pig 6. buying horse feed after the horse died 7. buying hay for a mechanical bull 8. ought to put handles on his cash

Wasting time: 1. burning daylight 2. whistling at the moon 3. barking at a knot 4. picking at a wart 5. fishing with an empty hook 6. might as well talk Egyptian to a pack mule 7. putting silk stockings on a sow 8. chasing an eagle's shadow 9. playing solitaire with a deck of fifty-one 10. dilly-dallying around 11. just chewing and whittling 12. arguing with a wooden Indian, a favorite saying of Sam Houston 13. following an empty wagon waiting for something to fall off 14. kick all you want but, unless you're a mule, it won't do any good 15. ain't ever gonna find a watermelon in a pumpkin patch 16. beatin' your head against a brick wall 17. salting the ocean 18. peeing on a forest fire (or trying to put it out with a teacup) 19. ironing with a cold iron 20. tryin' to catch butterflies in a basketball net 21. just sittin' there rustin' 22. grabbing at sunbeams 23. shuckin' a nubbin [A nubbin is a tiny, useless ear of corn that grows near the top of the stalk which would be a waste of time to shuck.] *See also Effort, wasted*

Wasting your breath: 1. hollering down a rain barrel, armadillo hole, or empty well 2. preaching to the choir

Watch (noun)**:** time dispenser *See also Rolex*

Watch (verb)**:** 1. keep tabs on 2. keep your eyes peeled (or skinned) 3. be on the lookout 4. keep a weather eye open

Watch, occasionally: keep half an eye on 'em

Watch over: mind, as in "Will you mind the kids while I go to the store for diapers?"

Watch what you say: 1. keep an eye on your tongue 2. mind what you say

3. never use sharp words in case you have to eat them later

Water: 1. branch water 2. well water 3. spring water

Water, deep: 1. the water was about ankle deep if you were standing on your head 2. the water got so high we were shooting ducks in the parlor 3. we were catching catfish in the kitchen mousetrap *See also Creek, flooded*

Water, muddy: 1. too thick to drink, too thin to plow, which is often said of water from the Red River 2. catfish had to swim backwards to keep from getting mud in their eyes

Water, poor: have to chew it up before you can swallow it

Water, shallow: 1. wouldn't float a kitchen match (or a toothpick) 2. seen dew deeper than that 3. sweat more water than that after mowing the lawn *See also River, shallow*

Water cooler: swamp breeze air conditioner

Water flow, heavy: big trickle

Water gap: where a fence crosses a creek

Water moccasin: usually just "moccasin" because Texans know where they come from

Tₐₘ **Water pitcher:** bucket

Watery: loose, as in "Her stew is always real loose."

Wavering: waffling

Waving: wagging his mitt

Waxahachie (Ellis County): pronounced Wauk-sa-hatch-ee, not Wack-si-hatch-ee or Wax-si-hatch-ee [This is another one a Texan ought to know how to spell correctly. The local Chamber of Commerce folks like to think the name means "cow creek" but a lot of other people believe it might just mean something we call "cow chips." Comedian W.C. Fields was a collector of unusual words, especially town names. Waxahachie was one of his favorites and he even used the name in one of his movies. Unfortunately, he mispronounced it.]

Way bill: a Texas term for a journal kept on a trail drive, which was often required when the owner of the herd wasn't along on the drive

Weak: 1. weakified 2. raised on skim milk 3. built on butter 4. couldn't lick his upper lip 5. limp as a dish rag 6. pantywaist 7. couldn't pull his hat off 8. all his starch is in his shirt 9. paper backed 10. feather legged 11. got the personality of custard pudding *See also Sissy*

Weak as: 1. a two-day-old calf 2. a kitten *See also Sissy; Timid*

Weakling: a weak sister even if he's a he

Wealthy: 1. got so much money he uses an imported anaesthetic instead of a local 2. has so much money, when she goes out to celebrate she paints the town multicolored instead of just red *See also Rich*

Weanling: a weaned foal

Wear-leather: small pieces of leather used to protect the braid in the eyes of honda or reins; also called a boot

Weary: 1. feel like a whipped pup 2. could sleep on a barbed wire fence 3. could sleep standing up in a snowstorm 4. tongue was flapping in the dust 5. ready to rock on the porch 6. been run down, run over, and wrung out 7. tail (or dauber) is dragging in the dirt 8. petered out 9. plumb tuckered 10. played out *See also Tired*

Weary as: a small pup walking in deep mud

Weather, bad: 1. the weather got wholesale 2. the skies muddied up 3. didn't have this kind of weather when Lyndon Johnson was president [The implication is, of course, that while a Texan was president, he didn't allow bad weather in Texas.] *See also Norther*

W

Weather, clearing: 1. breaking up 2. fairing up 3. moderating 4. clearing off 5. lettin' up

Weather, cold: 1. kitchen weather [This comes from the old days when the warmest place in the house was next to the kitchen stove.] 2. hog killin' time, which is the first cold spell of the winter season [In the days of deep-freezes, meat was kept in a smoke-house. The hogs generally weren't butchered until the temperatures were cold enough to keep meat longer. This saying, however, can cause some confusion. Several years ago a young journalism student from the North got a job with a Texas newspaper. His first assignment was to write headlines. When given a story on weather that mentioned it was hog killing time he wrote what he thought was the perfect headline. It read "Farmers, protect your hogs."]

Weather, hot and dry: sick dog weather [This is a reference to a sick dog's nose being dry and hot instead of cold and wet as usual.]

Weather change coming: 1. prairie dogs are building banks [When prairie dogs build up banks around the mouth of their holes, it is thought to be a sign that heavy rains are on the way.] 2. cattle are drifting toward the fence, which means a blue norther is coming [When cattle sense a severe cold front is coming they naturally begin to drift away from the weather. They will drift till they come to a fence and then bunch up in a tight group and hope for the best.] 3. we're in for some weather, which usually means a storm of some sort is on the way [This prediction is often made by someone with arthritis who can sense the coming weather change in his or her afflicted joints; after the storm the weather is fairing up when it begins to return to normal.]

Weather determination: 1. call in the dogs and see if they're wet so we'll know if it's raining outside 2. thick shucks on corn mean a hard winter is coming

Weather tip: If it starts to rain and the chickens run for cover, it won't rain long. If the chickens stay put and continue to peck while it rains, you are in for a long wet spell. The reason is if it's only gonna rain for a short while, the chicken won't want to get wet. On the other hand, if it's gonna rain for a long time, the chicken knows she's gonna get wet sooner or later so she might as well keep eating. *See also Texas weather*

Weatherford (Parker County): pronounced Weather-furd; "watermelon capital of Texas"

Weatherman, poor: only thing he can predict correctly is darkness at night

Weches (Houston County): pronounced WE-chez, not WAY-chez

Wedding ring: one-man band

Wednesday: pressure cooker day [This comes from the famous Reo Palm Isle in Longview, Texas, back in the days before fast food. Wednesdays were ladies days in that legendary Texas honky-tonk, and the crowds were always large. Traveling salesmen were known to go a day and a half out of their way just to be in Longview on Wednesday. The term "pressure cooker day" came from the fact that while a lot of housewives were dancing and drinking away the afternoon, their husband's supper was cooking at home. Many a husband enjoyed a fine meal and assumed his wife had been home all afternoon cooking it because she was exhausted.]

Weesatch (Goliad County): pronounced WE-satch [The town's founding fathers decided to name the town "huisache" after a brushy-type tree that grows in the area and is known for its honey-producing blossoms. Either the founding fathers didn't know how to spell the name or they didn't think anyone else would know how to pronounce it.]

Weight gain: gained so much weight his appendix scar is now more than a foot wide

Weight gain, uncontrollable: 1. can gain a pound or two just watching food commercials on television 2. can gain weight just driving by a store that sells beer

Weight gain denial: they just ain't making 36 jeans as big as they used to

Weimer (Colorado County): pronounced WHY-mer; originally called Jackson but changed supposedly on the suggestion of one of the founders who had visited Weimer, Germany

Weinert (Haskell County): pronounced WHY-nert, never We-nert; named for Texas Senator Ferdinand C. Weinert

Welcome: a Texas welcome is "Make yourself at home."

Welcome (Austin County): named by a German immigrant in recognition of the friendliness of the local residents

Welcome as: 1. a pardon to a death row inmate 2. Santa Claus in an orphan's home 3. a cloudburst to a dry land farmer

Welder: blacksmith

Well, deep: so deep it must a been dug by a banker who dropped a nickel down a gopher hole

Well acquainted: know him better 'n I know my old broom

Well behaved: got a double portion of manners

Well dressed: 1. more ornamental than useful, which refers to the fact that someone who is dressed up isn't ready for work 2. looks like the judge set the trial date 3. looks like he's going to a wedding or a preaching

Well endowed: 1. a bank walker [This comes from the days of skinny-dipping when the boy with the biggest equipment would walk the bank to show it off.] 2. a four-button man [This means he is so well endowed he has to loosen four buttons on his jeans to relieve himself; a one- or two-button man would not be as well endowed.] 3. when he's tired, he leaves three tracks 4. had to use a gunnysack and baling wire for an athletic supporter

Well endowed, not: used a peanut shell and a rubber band for an athletic supporter

Well informed: hears things before God gets the news

Well off: *See Rich*

Went bad: went back on his raisin', which is often said of preachers' kids who turn out bad

Went broke: 1. lost everything but the air in my tires 2. lost everything but the fillings in my teeth 3. they took everything but the dirt under my fingernails, which was often said by a farmer when the bank repossessed his land 4. bought a one way-ticket on the express train to financial ruin *See also Bankrupt*

Went crazy: 1. spun a bearing 2. threw a rod 3. slipped a cog 4. blew a gasket 5. warped his head 6. went hog wild 7. come unbuckled 8. his common sense come unraveled 9. sprang a leak in his crankcase 10. that joker went wild *See also Crazy*

Went home: went back to the barn

Went too far: went to the well once too often

Went to work: har'd on (hired on), as in "Bubba har'd on down at the chicken processing plant 'cause he heard you could buy chickens for half price once they'd been dropped on the floor."

Went wild: 1. came unbuckled 2. broke his trace chain 3. pitched for the moon

W

Weslaco (Hidalgo County): pronounced WES-la-co, an acronym for the W.E. Stewart Land Company

West (McLennan County): named for local businessman Thomas M. West [Despite the name, West, Texas, is south of Dallas in Central Texas. If you happen to go through West, stop and check out the Czech Stop.]

West Tawakoni (Hunt County): pronounced West Ta-WOK-a-knee

Western show: 1. horse opera 2. wild west show 3. rodeo

Westphalia (Falls County): pronounced West-FAIL-ya; immigrants from the Westphalia province in Germany provided the name

Wet: enough to bog a snipe

Wet as: 1. a drowned rat 2. a fish in water 3. a rooster under a drain spout 4. a kid in a mud puddle 5. the bottom of a stock tank 6. an old woman's hanky after a sad movie

Wet stock: livestock brought into Texas from Mexico illegally; so called because the animals got wet crossing the Rio Grande

Weathers: castrated sheep

Whang-doodle: a Texas-sized kangaroo-like animal with a large flat tail. Its habitat is the Palo Duro Canyon area, and its tail allows the critter to jump off the rim of the canyon and make a nice soft landing hundreds of feet below. The whang-doodle is so rare, some people consider it a mythical critter. It is also possible that people who actually see a whang-doodle don't remember the sighting when they sober up.

Whampus cat: The Itasca, Texas, high school uses Whampus Cat as its team mascot and Bill McMurray, in his book *Texas High School Football* explains, "It's said this nickname came from a fan of an opposing team when

he referred to Itasca playing like whampus cats." A good guess is whampus is derived from whomp us.

Wharton (Wharton County): pronounced WART-un; named for Texas pioneers William H. and John A. Wharton

What did you say? 1. Come again? 2. Excuse me? [Both are used when you think you heard something you didn't want to hear.]

What's happening? 1. What in the Sam Hill's going on? 2. What in blue blazes are you doing?

Whatchamacallit: *See Dololly*

Whatever: 1. whatsomever 2. everwhat, as in "Everwhat you want to do is fine with me and any ol' gal I'd go out with."

Wheelbarrow: East Texas buggy

Wheeler-dealer: a major player when it comes to putting together big, often complicated, and always high dollar deals. Some of the more famous Texas wheeler-dealers include Sid Richardson and his nephews, the Bass brothers; Clint Murchison and Clint Jr.; Red McCombs; Tom Hicks; Jerry Jones; Glenn McCarthy; and a fella named Lyndon Johnson. When John Connally was asked if he was a wheeler-dealer he replied, "If it means I could enter a horse trade and come out without losing, I guess I'm guilty."

Wheeler-dealer, smart: always structures a deal where the only thing at risk is O.P.M. (other peoples' money)

Wheeler-dealer axiom: we're not here to rob or steal, just to wheel and deal

Wheeler-dealer starter kit: an individual who puts together small, low-dollar deals hoping to one day make enough money so he can play with the big boys

When: Texans rarely just say "when"; usually it's "whenever," as in "I'll buy you the biggest steak in town whenever you're ready."

Whetstone: grindin' stone or rock

Whichever: everwhich

Wife, ideal: if you fell asleep watching football on TV, she'd remove your chaw of tobacco so you wouldn't choke to death

While: whilst

Will fit parts: parts that are not original replacement parts but which "will fit," so to a country boy they will work

Whipped: like a red-headed stepchild

Whipping: woodshed lecture

A̶M̶ Whipping out: the ritual introduction shouted when a freshman cadet offers his hand. "Howdy, Fish (name) is my name, sir."

Whipping tail head: the portion of a cow between the rear end and the tail

Whirlwind: a sand auger

Whisky: 1. coffin varnish 2. tonsil paint 3. tarantula juice 4. cowboy cocktail 5. firewater 6. whusky 7. gut warmer 8. jig juice 9. jig water 10. glee medicine 11. giggle water 12. grief remover 13. snakebite medicine 14. lamp oil 15. scamper juice 16. conversation fluid 17. snake oil juice 18. tornado juice 19. spider killer 20. redeye 21. tongue oil. 22. a strong drink that makes other people interesting 23. confidence water. The right amount of whiskey will make you believe you're an eight-foot-tall, bulletproof gift God gave to the women of earth 24. it's easier to put up with the smell than it is to listen to it 25. whiskey talks loudest when it is let loose from the jug 26. the stuff that makes you tipsy also makes you tip your hand [There are three kinds of whiskey: hugging, singing, and fighting.] *See also Champagne; Liquor; Tequila*

Whisky, bootleg: it's in the barn not in bond (or bonded in the barn)

Whiskey, fast acting: you have to drink it quick before it etches the glass

Whiskey, good: smooth as a moonbeam

Whiskey, poor: 1. tastes like something that came out of a jackass with a kidney problem 2. tastes like the scum off pond water

Whisky, strong: 1. enough to make a muley cow (or jackrabbit) grow horns 2. enough to make a grasshopper fight a surly wolf 3. enough to draw blood blisters on a boot heel 4. enough to take the moss off your teeth 5. that'd cause a bullfrog to spit in the eye of a great white shark 6. will remove warts from people you have to look at 7. antifogmatic [This was a popular country term for whiskey around the turn of the century.] *See also Drink, strong; Liquor, strong*

Whiskey row: When you are close to having enough points to win a game, you are "in the whiskey row." The game of straight dominoes, for instance, is usually played to 250 points. When you get within fifty points you are in the whiskey row. When you are in the short whiskey row, you are within twenty points and really close to winning.

Whisper: funeral talk

Whistle pig: ground hog

Whistling woman: according to an old country saying, a whistling woman and a crowing hen will come to a bad end

White as: 1. bleached bones 2. driven snow

White man: 1. paleface 2. white eyes

Whitesboro (Grayson County): pronounced Whites-bur-ah; named for Ambrose B. White, the first settler; home of Ken's Clip Joint barbershop

Whitewright (Grayson County): named for investor Jim Whitewright, who purchased the land

W

and had it surveyed [Like the sign says, Everything is all right in Whitewright.]

Whitharral (Hockley County): pronounced Whit-har'l; named for Dr. Whitfield Harral, who donated land for a school and a cemetery

Whittling: a therapeutic exercise in Texas that requires one pocketknife, reasonably sharp; one piece of soft wood or a small tree limb; a bench to sit on; and someone to talk to. Spitting is optional.

Who: who all, as in "Who all's goin' to the poker game?"

Who knows: quien sabe (kin savvy) [Any ornate brand that can't be read is said to be a quien sabe brand.]

Who made you mad? Who licked the red off your candy?

Who won: who beat, as in "I didn't see the fight, who beat?"

Who's in charge: 1. Who's skinning this cat? 2. Who's runnin' this railroad?

Who's to blame? Who robbed the train?

Whon (Coleman County): pronounced as phonetic spelling for Juan, the name of a Mexican cowboy who lived in the area [Many believe it was spelled Whon so newcomers wouldn't have to wonder how to pronounce it.]

Whoozit: *See Dololly*

Whore: 1. alley bat 2. lady of loose virtue 3. painted lady 4. honky-tonk angel 5. fallen angel 6. angel flying too close to the ground 7. mattress buster

Whorehouse: 1. chamber of commerce 2. bawdy house 3. parlor house 4. bordello 5. cat house 6. pleasure palace 7. house of ill fame 8. sporting house 9. hurdy-gurdy house 10. joy parlor 11. Chicken Ranch, which, according to some, was the "Best Little Whorehouse in Texas."

Wichita Falls (Wichita County): pronounced WITCH-a-taw

Falls; new home of the Dallas Coboys training camp [Always include "Falls" so no one mistakes this town for one in Kansas.]

Wicked: 1. if he walked through the valley of the shadow of death, he'd fear no evil cause he'd be the meanest critter in the valley 2. if he didn't like the tune, he'd shoot the piano player 3. Western Union won't deliver to him because he might shoot the messenger 4. the devil's got a mortgage on his soul 5. kin to a rattler on his father's side and a black widow on his mother's side *See Evil person, Mean person*

Wide open spaces: where a man or a horse can swish his tail

Widow: in Texas, it's almost always widow (wid-ah) lady

Widowed, three times: wore out three dashers but never had but one churn [The number of dashers (husbands) can be changed to suit the needs but the number of churns is always one.]

Wife: 1. running mate 2. better half 3. bitter half 4. ball and chain 5. warden 6. my kid's mama 7. the wife 8. the old lady

Wife, smart: knows how to make a man out of a jackass

Wife, ugly: *See Husband, ugly*

Wife, understanding: gives you all the rope you want but never forgets how to tie a hangman's noose [Lee Trevino said his wife doesn't care what he does when he's away so long as he doesn't have a good time.]

Wife, unfaithful: 1. a baby got caught in her trap, which means the father was not her husband 2. can't buy a wedding ring small enough to stay on her finger, which implies the wedding ring comes off when she goes out 3. didn't figure her husband would miss one or two peaches off the tree

Wife, wasteful: can throw more out the window with a teaspoon than her husband can carry in the door with a shovel

Wiggle like: 1. a lizard (or a frog) in a skillet 2. a fish on a line 3. a worm on a hook 4. a worm in a bed of mesquite coals

Wild: 1. running loose in the streets 2. uncurried 3. fuzztail 4. bucking in eight directions at once

Wild as: 1. a peach orchard boar 2. a turpentined cat

Wild cat bluff: *See Cayuga*

Wild cattle: old Texas term for black (or Spanish) cattle

Wild rag: a large silk scarf, similar to an ascot [A wild rag is both decorative and functional since it serves to prevent wind from blowing down your neck.]

Wildcatter: Everett Lee DeGoyler said there were two kinds of wildcatters, the silver spoon boys and the rabbit foot boys. The silver spoon boys had money before they got in the oil business, and the rabbit foot boys made their money from oil.

Willing: game, as in "He's game for a little poker."

Willingness: if you want butter, you gotta be willing to churn the milk

Wimp: he could be kicked to death by a grasshopper

Win at all costs: Former Dallas Cowboy Walt Garrison once said, "If you can't beat 'em, cheat 'em; if you can beat 'em, cheat 'em for practice."

Wind, cold: 1. the breath of a glacier 2. raw as a whip

Wind, strong: 1. blowin' too hard to haul rocks 2. blowin' so hard a chicken laid the same egg three times 3. blows through you like you're wearin' crocheted underwear 4. tomatoes wouldn't grow 'cause the wind kept blowing the sunshine off the vines 5. you could spit in your own eye 6. blew so hard it knocked John Wayne off his horse at the drive-in movie 7. blowin' hard enough to turn a prairie dog hole inside out 8. blowing like perfume through a high school dance 9. blew the feathers off an eagle 10. windmill breaker or spinner [In West Texas the wind blows so hard they use a piece of iron for a kite and some trace chain for a tail. They also use an anvil connected to a steel pole with a log chain as a weather vane. The wind stopped blowing one day in Lubbock, and it took everybody two hours to learn how to walk straight up.]

Windrow: row of cut hay ready to be picked up and moved to the cultivator

Windbag: could blow up the Goodyear blimp

Winded: 1. couldn't gather enough breath to blow out the candle on a kid's birthday cake 2. couldn't gather enough wind to blow a smoke ring

Windies: cattle driven out of canyons

Winding sheets: what they wrap you in when you die

Window, open: 1. pneumonia hole 2. (on pickup) juice hole

Window shade: roller shade

Winds: *See Stirrup, closed*

Windy as: a fifty-pound sack of whistling lips

Wingate (Runnels County): pronounced WIN-gate, not WING-ut; named for W. J. Wingate, an attorney from Ballinger, Texas

Wink: is as good as a nod to a blind mule

Wink (Winkler County): originally Winkler, after the county, but that name was taken when the town applied for a post office so the local citizens simply shortened the name [Hometown of the great Roy Orbison.]

Winkler County: named for Clinton McKamy Winkler, former

W

colonel in the famed Hood's Texas Brigade [Kermit is the county seat.]

Winner: 1. the bell ringer 2. chip dragger 3. went to the big dance and came home with the pretty girl

Winning a contest: trophy picking time

 Winona (Smith County): pronounced Wa-KNOWN-ah

Wire: war, as in bobbed war

Wire cutters: 1. range pliers 2. war pliers, which refers to the range wars that were fought over wire cutting

Wisdom: a double portion of horse sense

Wisdom versus experience: According to an old company adage, wisdom comes from good decisions, experience comes from bad ones.

Wisdom versus foolishness: A wise cowboy learns by watching others get thrown, a fool has to taste the corral dirt for himself.

Wise: book learned and horse smart

Wise man: holds his tongue when arguing with a woman, a fool, or a drunk

Wish: 1. may all your kids be born nekkid 2. may the wind at your back never be your own

Wish book: mail order catalog

Wishbone: pulley bone

Wishful thinking: pie in the sky

Wit, dry: rosin-jawed

Witch: 1. broom rider 2. broom wrangler 3. rides a pitchin' broom

With certainty: without fail, as in "Bubba, you better pay me back that ten dollars without fail."

Withers: the part of a horse's back where the neck joins the body

Without a leader: rudderless

Wobbled: 1. like a drunk on a bicycle 2. like a model A Ford with a flat tire 3. like a red wagon with three wheels 4. like a three-legged horse

Woman, attractive: *See Female, attractive*

Woman, mad: hell on high heels *See also Female, angry*

Woman trouble: got too many hearts in the fire

Womanizer: 1. skirt (or petticoat) chaser 2. AWOL—after women or liquor (or a wolf on the loose) 3. will change everything about you but your name

Women: 1. women folk 2. the fair sex or the spare sew to some chauvinists 3. are like cow patties, the older they are the easier they are to pick up 4. are not like horses because the wilder they are the easier they are to pet

Womb: oven

Won: 1. put another feather in his hat 2. struck pay dirt 3. put another notch in his gun 4. put another scalp on his belt 5. got the buckle, which refers to winning rodeo cowboys receiving trophy buckles

Won, barely: out sorried 'em or won ugly, both of which mean that neither team played well but somebody had to win

Won at poker: sheared the flock

Won big: 1. raked in all the chips 2. if you were gonna take a photo of the finish, you'd need a wide angle lens, which is a horse racing reference to the winning horse finishing far ahead of the other horses

Won everything: a clean sweep of the whole shebang

Won't do it: my momma didn't raise any children dumb enough to do that

Won't work: 1. that boat won't float 2. that dog won't hunt 3. that chicken won't lay 4. that bucket wouldn't hold water 5. that motor won't crank

Wood, quick burning: breakfast wood [Some wood, like dry pine, burns very quickly allowing only enough time to cook breakfast and not enough time to cook a large meal like supper.]

Wood, slow burning: supper (or dinner) wood [Some wood, such as oak and hickory, burns slow and thus provides enough fire to cook an entire supper.]

Woolies: chaps with sheepskin fronts and leather backs, primarily used in colder climates since they are warmer than other chaps. When made with goatskin instead of sheepskin they're called "Angoras."

A/M Worcestershire: Winchester

Word, versatile: *See Reckon*

Words, big: 1. got double barreled syllables 2. two-bit words 3. words that run about two dollars to the pound 4. couldn't pronounce that if you gave me a running start

Work: 1. make hay while the sun shines 2. tend to business 3. like a dog trying to shake off a pinching worm 4. wore fingernails clear down to the knuckles 5. works from can't see till can't see 6. hard at it [As Henri Castro, an early Texas colonist, said, "Begin your day with labor and end it with laughter."]

Work casually: keeps banker's hours or he's got a banker's watch [Both imply he doesn't work all day. Since banks generally close early in the afternoon, it has long been perceived that a banker's day is short although people in the industry say it ain't so.]

Work hard: 1. it's the yeast that raises the dough 2. it's better to have two tired arms than one empty stomach 3. luck don't jump on a man sitting in the shade 4. can't climb the ladder of success with your hands in your pocket 5. you're better off bent from hard work than crooked from trying to avoid it [Bobby Layne, perhaps the most competitive football player Texas has ever produced, once said, "If a man has

to work past noon, the job was too big for him in the first place." On the other hand, Lyndon Johnson said, "The more you work the luckier you get." Then, of course, there is the old country adage "Hard work keeps the fences up."]

Work hard as: 1. a sugar mill jackass 2. a sled dog

Work late: 1. burn the midnight oil 2. ride the night herd 3. ride the sunset rounds 4. night hawking 5. put the sun to bed

Work truck: 1. a dilapidated, beat-up old truck, good for nothing except getting you to and from work if you live close to your job 2. a beat-up old truck you keep around the place to use for hard jobs, like hauling rocks, so you won't get scratches and dents on your new pickup 3. any truck owned and used by a farmer or rancher since those boys buy trucks to use, not to look at

Worker, good: 1. top hand 2. strikes one match and burns daylight and midnight oil 3. could gather all the county's crops by dark 30, which can be either 30 minutes before or 30 minutes after dark 4. a real plow horse 5. keeps his corner up, which means he keeps his property in good order or he does his share of the work 6. active in the harness 7. works so hard he has to be careful not to drown in his own sweat 8. hell on leather, which means he can wear out a saddle or a pair of boots real quick 'cause he works so hard 9. if you give him a job to do, you can color it done *See also Employee*

Worker, poor: 1. got more wishbone than backbone 2. like a cockroach, ruins everything he steps in 3. bottom hand (as opposed to top hand) 4. thinks dirt under the fingernails causes cancer 5. could wear his work shirt to a church social, which implies he doesn't get it dirty 6. only time he holds his end up is when he sticks his head in the sand 7. all back and no brain 8. when he walks up it's about the same as three

W

good men leaving 9. won't last till the water boils [After killing the hogs, the carcass is boiled in hot water. Anyone who didn't make it till the water boiled wouldn't be around long.] 10. does the work of two people, Laurel and Hardy 11. a really poor worker does the work of three people, Larry, Moe, and Curly *See also Employee, worthless*

Worker, quiet: *See Quiet worker*

Worker, slow: 1. like a cow's tail, always behind 2. they call him pockets because his spends most of his time sittin' on his

Workers: 1. the wagon pullers 2. the infantry (or the Indians)

Working chute: a restraining device used to hold a cow while you work on it

Working end: 1. the business end 2. blister end [No one ever raised a blister holding a hammer by the head.]

Working hard as: a little train on a big track

Works good: 1. a going jesse 2. like an automatic milking machine 3. like a pair of $50 teeth

Working pen: the pen where cattle are castrated, branded, and doctored

Worm: wiggle tail; night-crawler; red wiggler

Worn out: frazzled or raveled out

Worn out car: rattletrap

Worried: 1. something is eating on me like a caterpillar on a leaf 2. something is sleeping on my pillow with me

Worried as: 1. a duck in a desert 2. a camel in the Klondike 3. a frog in a frying pan 4. a pig in a packing plant

Worrier: hand wringer

Worrier, incurable: holds onto anxiety like it was an heirloom

Worry him: 1. like a banty rooster worries a bulldog 2. drop him in the grease and let him feel how hot it can get in the kitchen

Worrying: walking a hole in the carpet

Worse off: jumped from the frying pan into the fire or from the skillet into the deep fryer

Worthless: 1. no account 2. not worth diddly squat (or just diddly) 3. plumb no account 4. gone to the dogs 5. not worth a bucket of warm spit, how Texan John Nance Garner described the vice presidency of the United States 6. ain't worth a crying dime 7. good for nothing 8. not worth a plug nickel 9. ain't worth his feed 10. plumb sorry 11. ain't worth a Continental damn 12. not worth the spit on a postage stamp 13. ain't worth a tinker's damn 14. ain't nuthin' you'd want to work up a sweat getting *See also Useless*

Worthless and heavy: good for nothing but a trotline weight

Worthless as: 1. a bow without an arrow 2. a nail without a hammer 3. a canceled stamp 4. a four-card flush 5. a broken boot jack 6. half a haircut 7. one boot 8. an unloaded gun 9. a screen door on a submarine 10. a moral victory—it might make you feel good for a short while but it don't change the standings 11. sour manure 12. a pickle barrel full of feathers 13. last year's calendar 14. a dead possum's tail *See also Useless as*

Worthless group: a sorry lot

Worthless person: 1. ain't worth the oxygen he uses up 2. ain't worth killing 3. ain't worth the powder to blow him to hell 4. nothing but buzzard bait 5. never raised nothing but hell and hot air 6. too dumb to work and too lazy to steal 7. total sorryness

Worthy: 1. earned his saddle 2. earned all he ever got 3. earned his spot at the bar

Wounded: 1. lost enough blood to paint the back porch 2. skewered 3. shot up some 4. if he was cut any

worse, it would qualify as an autopsy
5. **got shishkebobbed** *See also Shot; Skinned up*

Wrangler: *See Horse wrangler*

Wrangling: rounding up, saddling, and riding range horses

 Wrap: dally, which is derived from wrapping, or dallying, a rope around a saddle horn

Wrapped tightly: wrapped tight as a mummy

Wreck: cowboy term for any accident that involves horses or other livestock

Wreck pan: receptacle where cowboys tossed their dirty plate, cup, and irons (utensils). The pan was then filled with water and soap and the items washed. If there were a lot of cowboys and the receptacle was very large it was called a "wreck tub."

Wrecker driver, good: in the "haul" of fame

Wrench, crescent type: Oklahoma socket set

Wrestling: pronounced ras-lin

Wrinkled as: 1. an old or burnt boot 2. the horns on an old steer 3. a cheap suit in a cheaper suitcase

Wrinkles: knowledge lines

Write fast: 1. smoke the lead 2. scorch the paper

Writer: 1. ink slinger 2. word wrangler 3. pen pusher 4. paper waster 5. wild bull slinger, which is a fiction writer

Wrong: *See Error; Incorrect; Mistaken*

 Wylie (Collin County): pronounced WHY-lee; named for W. D. Wylie, a railroad right-of-way agent

X I T: pronounced as three separate letters, X I T, never as "exit" [Refers to the brand of the ranch that was formed with the three million acres of Panhandle land the state of Texas traded in return for the building of the state capitol in Austin. It has to be one of the biggest trades in the history of the world.]

X-ray: bone picture

Xerox: often pronounced x-rock in Texas, perhaps because country folks refuse to believe that a word which starts with an x could sound like it starts with a z

Yack: country term for a stupid person

Yahoo: a rowdy buckaroo

Yam: Although the terms "yam" and "sweet potato" are used interchangeably, there is a difference. When sweet potatoes are candied they become yams.

Yank: jerk to a country boy

Yankee: 1. blue belly 2. bluecoat 3. blue butt [For a lot of Southern country boys there is no such thing as a Yankee. There are only Damnyankees. Being one of those Southern country boys, I was ten years old before I knew damn Yankee was two words. To many folks in the South you're either a Southerner or a Yankee, which explains why some country boys refer to people from Colorado, California, or Oklahoma as Yankees.]

Yankee, galvanized: a Rebel who was captured during the war and agreed to fight Indians in the West in return for a pardon

Yankee dime: Many use "Yankee dime" to indicate a quick kiss. For others, the term is derogatory to Yankees. As the story goes, following the war for Southern independence, Yankee troops would demand credit from the few remaining Southern stores and then hardly ever pay back as much as a "Yankee dime." Many Southerners still use phrases like "He ain't worth a

Yankee dime" to describe someone who doesn't pay his obligations.

Yankee test (for a group)**:** To identify the Yankees in any crowd, have the band play a stirring rendition of "Dixie" and then check the audience for goose-bumps. Anyone who doesn't have them is usually a Yankee.

Yankee test (for an individual)**:** Ask the person what he thinks of any of the following poets: Nathan Bedford Forrest, J. E. B. Stuart; James Longstreet, John Bell Hood, Albert Sidney Johnston, or John Morgan Hunt. If the person doesn't immediately correct you by replying each man was a Confederate general and not a poet, he's a Yankee.

Yard eggs: eggs found in the yard rather than in a nest; usually considered inferior to nest eggs [Yard eggs, of course, are laid by yard birds, which are chickens.]

Yearling: a calf that is a year old; often used for a child that is about a year old

Yeehaw: a cowboy's exclamation generally used when something good has happened or is expected [Yeehaw could be used when somebody rides a really mean bull or the local beauty queen agrees to go out with you.]

Yell: 1. beller 2. holler 3. squall like a shoat 4. blattin' 5. yelp 6. bray like a mule 7. war hoop 8. whooped out 9. like a bluejay protecting her nest 10. caterwall

A&M **Yell leaders:** cheerleaders at A&M

A&M **Yell practice:** Aggie equivalent of a pep rally; held before and after the game

Yellow: 1. yaller 2. yeller [Of course yellow is actually pale green for those who speed through a traffic light when it's yellow.]

Yellow as: 1. a no-passing stripe 2. the sun's insides 3. the stripe down a coward's back 4. a summer squash

Yellow jaundice: 1. yeller jaunders 2. liverish

Yellow legs: cavalry troops who fought Indians on the frontier, so called because of the yellow stripes down their legs

Yells a lot: 1. he's a hollerin' master 2. yells more than a little leaguer's mother

Yes: 1. Does a one-legged duck swim in a circle? 2. Does Howdy Doody have wooden toes? 3. Does a chicken have a pecker on his head? 4. Does a bear sleep in the woods? 5. Is the pope Catholic? 6. Is a snake's belly low to the ground? 7. Does a wet horse (or dog) stink? 8. Does a cat have a climbing gear? 9. Does a fifty-pound sack of flour make a big biscuit? 10. Does a fat man sweat? 11. Does the sun set in the west? 12. Does a hog love slop? 13. Is a duck's butt waterproof? [In case you don't know, the answer to all of the above is yes.]

Yes, definately: 1. yes siree, Bob 2. you sure as hell got that right 3. I'm here to tell ya 4. you betcha 5. darn tootin'

Yo creo que—hell yes: derived from the Mexican idiom *Yo creo que, si* which means "I think so, yes" [This expression, from the El Paso area, is a bit stronger.]

Yoke: a wooden frame used to hold bulls or oxen to a wagon

Yokum: a lie

You: Texans usually pronounced it ya', as in "How ya' doing?" or "Where ya' been?"

You all: Y'all. The national word of Texas, don't y'all know. Y'all is a unique phrase that some Texans use for either singular or plural. When talking about one person, they use y'all; when taking about a group of people, they use all y'all, which is the absolute plural of y'all.

You are welcome: replaced with "Ah, it weren't nuthin', ma'am," when a lady says thanks for a good deed

You can do it: 1. even a brown and red hen can lay a white egg 2. the smallest dog can bury the biggest bone 3. a small horse can throw a big cowboy

You didn't fall in did you? traditional Texan's question asked of someone who has been in the bathroom a long time

You understand? You hear? as in "Don't call me again, ya' hear?"

You'll regret it: will wish you hadn't done it

Your turn to celebrate: your time to howl

You're absolutely correct: 1. ain't that the truth 2. you hit the nail square on the head 3. you ain't just a whoofing

You're late (for a meal)**:** you missed the blessing [This is a reference to someone arriving for dinner after the blessing had been asked but before all the food was gone.]

You're welcome: you bettcha, which is a good country response when someone says thanks

You're wrong: 1. you got another think coming, as in "If you think I'm gonna go to the dance with you, you got another think coming." 2. you're pullin' on the wrong string [This saying may be a reference to the old-time country carnival game where you paid a nickel and then pulled a string to see what prize you won. More often than not the prize wasn't worth anywhere near a nickel.]

Youngster: 1. whippersnapper 2. his teeth ain't wore down much 3. hen wrangler 4. can still remember what his momma's milk tasted like, which means he hasn't been weaned long 5. still wet behind the ears 6. a spring chicken 7. whistle-britches

Your choice: 1. whatever trips your trigger, melts your butter, or pulls your string 2. grab a skinnin' knife, grab a leg, or grab your butt and haul yourself out'a here

Your problem: 1. it's your possum so you skin it 2. it's your itch so you scratch it

Your responsibility: 1. if your dog trees it, you gotta eat it 2. you can't get some other dog to do your barking 3. you got to learn to butt with your own head

Your turn: it's your bat (or bet)

Your: yore

Z

Zebra: 1. half painted (or dressed) horse 2. an umpire horse

Zero: 1. ought 2. nuthin', as in "They whupped us 40 to nuthin'"

Zero U: Oklahoma University

Zip: a senior at Texas A&M; also called elephant and leather legs

Zipper: 1. barn door 2. match starter [If nothing else is available you can almost always strike a match on your zipper, but it's best if you exercise caution so you don't start a fire that might be painful to put out.]

Zipper, open: 1. the barn door is open 2. the corral gate is open 3. the lid to the snake cage is open 4. the lizard pen is open 5. your cotton is blooming, which means your zipper is open and your white briefs are visible 6. it's snowing down south 7. XYZ, which translates into check your zipper

Zoo: critter corral

The End: It's time to pick up the hymnals.

Mysteries and Ghost Stories

Best Tales of Texas Ghosts

Ghosts Along the Texas Coast

Phantoms of the Plains: Tales of West Texas Ghosts

Spirits of San Antonio and South Texas

Spirits of the Alamo

The Great Texas Airship Mystery

Unsolved Texas Mysteries

Unsolved Mysteries of the Old West

When Darkness Falls: Tales of San Antonio Ghosts and Hauntings

Humor and Trivia

A Treasury of Texas Trivia

At Least 1836 Things You Ought to Know About Texas But Probably Don't

Bubba Speak: Texas Folk Sayings

First in the Lone Star State: A Texas Brag Book

Fixin' to be Texan

From an Outhouse to the White House

The Funny Side of Texas

Good Times in Texas: A Pretty Complete Guide to Where the Fun Is

I Never Wanted to Set the World on Fire, But Now That I'm 50, Maybe It's a Good Idea

Just Passing Through

More Wild Camp Tales

Only: The Last Dinosaur

Pete the Python

Humor and Trivia (cont.)

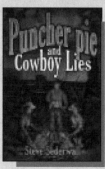

Puncher Pie and Cowboy Lies

Rainy Days in Texas Funbook

Texas Wit and Wisdom

Texas Highway Humor

That Cat Won't Flush

This Dog'll Hunt

This Dog'll Really Hunt: An Entertaining and Informative Texas Dictionary

Wild Camp Tales

History

A Cowboy of the Pecos

Alamo Movies

Battlefields of Texas

Daughter of Fortune: The Bettie Brown Story

Death of a Legend: The Myth & Mystery Surrounding the Death of Davy Crockett

Etta Place: Her Life and Times with Butch Cassidy and the Sundance Kid

Exploring the Alamo Legends

Eyewitness to the Alamo

Lawmen of the Old West: The Good Guys

Letters Home: A Soldier's Legacy

Red River Women

Return of Assassin John Wilkes Booth

Return of the Outlaw Butch Cassidy

Spindletop Unwound

The Star Film Ranch: Texas' First Picture Show

Tales of the Guadalupe Mountains

Texas Tales Your Teacher Never Told You

Republic of Texas Press

History (cont.)

Texas Ranger Tales: Stories That Need Telling

Texas Ranger Tales II

The Alamo Story: From Early History to Current Conflicts

The King Ranch Story: Truth and Myth

The Last of the Old-Time Cowboys

The Return of the Outlaw Billy the Kid

The Last Great Days of Radio

Volunteers in the Texas Revolution: The New Orleans Greys

Cooking

Dirty Dining: A Cookbook, and More, for Lovers

Making it Easy: Cajun Cooking

The Ultimate Chili Cookbook

Top Texas Chefs Cook at Home: Favorite Recipes

Recreation/Field Guides

A Trail Rider's Guide To Texas

Critter Chronicles

The Texas Golf Guide

The Texas Golf Guide (2nd Ed.)

Horses and Horse Sense

They Don't Have to Die: Home and Classroom Care for Small Animals

Your Kitten's First Year

Your Puppy's First Year

Travel

Dallas Uncovered (2nd Ed.)

Exploring Branson: A Family Guide

Exploring Dallas with Children: A Guide for Family Activities

Exploring New Orleans: A Family Guide

Exploring San Antonio with Children: A Guide for Family Activities

Exploring Texas with Children

Los Angeles Uncovered

Seattle Uncovered

Salt Lake City Uncovered

San Francisco Uncovered

Tuscon Uncovered

Twin Cities Uncovered

Top sellers from Republic of Texas Press

1-55622-648-9 • $15.95

1-55622-537-7 • $16.95

1-55622-569-5 • $18.95

1-55622-613-6 • $16.95

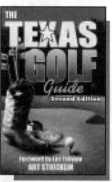

1-55622-575-X • $14.95

1-55622-624-1 • $18.95

1-55622-536-9 • $16.95

1-55622-377-3 • $16.95

1-55622-571-7 • $18.95